# The A to Z of the Orthodox Church

Michael Prokurat
Alexander Golitzin
Michael D. Peterson

*The A to Z Guide Series, No. 175*

THE SCARECROW PRESS, INC.
*Lanham • Toronto • Plymouth, UK*
2010

Published by Scarecrow Press, Inc.
A wholly owned subsidiary of
The Rowman & Littlefield Publishing Group, Inc.
4501 Forbes Boulevard, Suite 200, Lanham, Maryland 20706
http://www.scarecrowpress.com

Estover Road, Plymouth PL6 7PY, United Kingdom

Copyright © 1996 by Michael Prokurat, Alexander Golitzin, and Michael D. Peterson

*All rights reserved.* No part of this book may be reproduced in any form or by any electronic or mechanical means, including information storage and retrieval systems, without written permission from the publisher, except by a reviewer who may quote passages in a review.

British Library Cataloguing in Publication Information Available

**Library of Congress Cataloging-in-Publication Data**

The hardback version of this book was cataloged by the Library of Congress as follows:

Prokurat, Michael, 1950–
  Historical dictionary of the Orthodox church / by Michael Prokurat, Alexander Golitzin, and Michael D. Peterson
    p. cm. — (Religion, philosophies, and movements, no. 9)
  Includes bibliographical references.
  1. Orthodox Eastern Church—History—Dictionaries. 2. Orthodox Eastern Church—Dictionaries. I. Golitzin, Alexander, 1948–. II. Peterson, Michael D., 1945–. III. Title. IV. Series.
BX230.P76 1996
281.9'09—dc20                                                  95-37165
                                                                  CIP

ISBN 978-0-8108-7602-6 (pbk. : alk. paper)

♾™ The paper used in this publication meets the minimum requirements of American National Standard for Information Sciences—Permanence of Paper for Printed Library Materials, ANSI/NISO Z39.48-1992.
Printed in the United States of America

# OTHER A TO Z GUIDES FROM THE SCARECROW PRESS, INC.

1. *The A to Z of Buddhism* by Charles S. Prebish, 2001. *Out of Print. See No. 124.*
2. *The A to Z of Catholicism* by William J. Collinge, 2001.
3. *The A to Z of Hinduism* by Bruce M. Sullivan, 2001.
4. *The A to Z of Islam* by Ludwig W. Adamec, 2002. *Out of Print. See No. 123.*
5. *The A to Z of Slavery and Abolition* by Martin A. Klein, 2002.
6. *Terrorism: Assassins to Zealots* by Sean Kendall Anderson and Stephen Sloan, 2003.
7. *The A to Z of the Korean War* by Paul M. Edwards, 2005.
8. *The A to Z of the Cold War* by Joseph Smith and Simon Davis, 2005.
9. *The A to Z of the Vietnam War* by Edwin E. Moise, 2005.
10. *The A to Z of Science Fiction Literature* by Brian Stableford, 2005.
11. *The A to Z of the Holocaust* by Jack R. Fischel, 2005.
12. *The A to Z of Washington, D.C.* by Robert Benedetto, Jane Donovan, and Kathleen DuVall, 2005.
13. *The A to Z of Taoism* by Julian F. Pas, 2006.
14. *The A to Z of the Renaissance* by Charles G. Nauert, 2006.
15. *The A to Z of Shinto* by Stuart D. B. Picken, 2006.
16. *The A to Z of Byzantium* by John H. Rosser, 2006.
17. *The A to Z of the Civil War* by Terry L. Jones, 2006.
18. *The A to Z of the Friends (Quakers)* by Margery Post Abbott, Mary Ellen Chijioke, Pink Dandelion, and John William Oliver Jr., 2006.
19. *The A to Z of Feminism* by Janet K. Boles and Diane Long Hoeveler, 2006.
20. *The A to Z of New Religious Movements* by George D. Chryssides, 2006.
21. *The A to Z of Multinational Peacekeeping* by Terry M. Mays, 2006.
22. *The A to Z of Lutheranism* by Günther Gassmann with Duane H. Larson and Mark W. Oldenburg, 2007.
23. *The A to Z of the French Revolution* by Paul R. Hanson, 2007.
24. *The A to Z of the Persian Gulf War 1990–1991* by Clayton R. Newell, 2007.
25. *The A to Z of Revolutionary America* by Terry M. Mays, 2007.
26. *The A to Z of the Olympic Movement* by Bill Mallon with Ian Buchanan, 2007.
27. *The A to Z of the Discovery and Exploration of Australia* by Alan Day, 2009.
28. *The A to Z of the United Nations* by Jacques Fomerand, 2009.
29. *The A to Z of the "Dirty Wars"* by David Kohut, Olga Vilella, and Beatrice Julian, 2009.
30. *The A to Z of the Vikings* by Katherine Holman, 2009.
31. *The A to Z from the Great War to the Great Depression* by Neil A. Wynn, 2009.
32. *The A to Z of the Crusades* by Corliss K. Slack, 2009.
33. *The A to Z of New Age Movements* by Michael York, 2009.
34. *The A to Z of Unitarian Universalism* by Mark W. Harris, 2009.
35. *The A to Z of the Kurds* by Michael M. Gunter, 2009.
36. *The A to Z of Utopianism* by James M. Morris and Andrea L. Kross, 2009.
37. *The A to Z of the Civil War and Reconstruction* by William L. Richter, 2009.
38. *The A to Z of Jainism* by Kristi L. Wiley, 2009.
39. *The A to Z of the Inuit* by Pamela K. Stern, 2009.
40. *The A to Z of Early North America* by Cameron B. Wesson, 2009.

41. *The A to Z of the Enlightenment* by Harvey Chisick, 2009.
42. *The A to Z Methodism* by Charles Yrigoyen Jr. and Susan E. Warrick, 2009.
43. *The A to Z of the Seventh-day Adventists* by Gary Land, 2009.
44. *The A to Z of Sufism* by John Renard, 2009.
45. *The A to Z of Sikhism* by William Hewat McLeod, 2009.
46. *The A to Z Fantasy Literature* by Brian Stableford, 2009.
47. *The A to Z of the Discovery and Exploration of the Pacific Islands* by Max Quanchi and John Robson, 2009.
48. *The A to Z of Australian and New Zealand Cinema* by Albert Moran and Errol Vieth, 2009.
49. *The A to Z of African-American Television* by Kathleen Fearn-Banks, 2009.
50. *The A to Z of American Radio Soap Operas* by Jim Cox, 2009.
51. *The A to Z of the Old South* by William L. Richter, 2009.
52. *The A to Z of the Discovery and Exploration of the Northwest Passage* by Alan Day, 2009.
53. *The A to Z of the Druzes* by Samy S. Swayd, 2009.
54. *The A to Z of the Welfare State* by Bent Greve, 2009.
55. *The A to Z of the War of 1812* by Robert Malcomson, 2009.
56. *The A to Z of Feminist Philosophy* by Catherine Villanueva Gardner, 2009.
57. *The A to Z of the Early American Republic* by Richard Buel Jr., 2009.
58. *The A to Z of the Russo-Japanese War* by Rotem Kowner, 2009.
59. *The A to Z of Anglicanism* by Colin Buchanan, 2009.
60. *The A to Z of Scandinavian Literature and Theater* by Jan Sjåvik, 2009.
61. *The A to Z of the Peoples of the Southeast Asian Massif* by Jean Michaud, 2009.
62. *The A to Z of Judaism* by Norman Solomon, 2009.
63. *The A to Z of the Berbers (Imazighen)* by Hsain Ilahiane, 2009.
64. *The A to Z of British Radio* by Seán Street, 2009.
65. *The A to Z of The Salvation Army* by Major John G. Merritt, 2009.
66. *The A to Z of the Arab-Israeli Conflict* by P. R. Kumaraswamy, 2009.
67. *The A to Z of the Jacksonian Era and Manifest Destiny* by Terry Corps, 2009.
68. *The A to Z of Socialism* by Peter Lamb and James C. Docherty, 2009.
69. *The A to Z of Marxism* by David Walker and Daniel Gray, 2009.
70. *The A to Z of the Bahá'í Faith* by Hugh C. Adamson, 2009.
71. *The A to Z of Postmodernist Literature and Theater* by Fran Mason, 2009.
72. *The A to Z of Australian Radio and Television* by Albert Moran and Chris Keating, 2009.
73. *The A to Z of the Lesbian Liberation Movement: Still the Rage* by JoAnne Myers, 2009.
74. *The A to Z of the United States–Mexican War* by Edward R. Moseley and Paul C. Clark, 2009.
75. *The A to Z of World War I* by Ian V. Hogg, 2009.
76. *The A to Z of World War II: The War Against Japan* by Ann Sharp Wells, 2009.
77. *The A to Z of Witchcraft* by Michael D. Bailey, 2009.
78. *The A to Z of British Intelligence* by Nigel West, 2009.
79. *The A to Z of United States Intelligence* by Michael A. Turner, 2009.
80. *The A to Z of the League of Nations* by Anique H. M. van Ginneken, 2009.
81. *The A to Z of Israeli Intelligence* by Ephraim Kahana, 2009.
82. *The A to Z of the European Union* by Joaquín Roy and Aimee Kanner, 2009.

83. *The A to Z of the Chinese Cultural Revolution* by Guo Jian, Yongyi Song, and Yuan Zhou, 2009.
84. *The A to Z of African American Cinema* by S. Torriano Berry and Venise T. Berry, 2009.
85. *The A to Z of Japanese Business* by Stuart D. B. Picken, 2009.
86. *The A to Z of the Reagan–Bush Era* by Richard S. Conley, 2009.
87. *The A to Z of Human Rights and Humanitarian Organizations* by Robert F. Gorman and Edward S. Mihalkanin, 2009.
88. *The A to Z of French Cinema* by Dayna Oscherwitz and MaryEllen Higgins, 2009.
89. *The A to Z of the Puritans* by Charles Pastoor and Galen K. Johnson, 2009.
90. *The A to Z of Nuclear, Biological and Chemical Warfare* by Benjamin C. Garrett and John Hart, 2009.
91. *The A to Z of the Green Movement* by Miranda Schreurs and Elim Papadakis, 2009.
92. *The A to Z of the Kennedy–Johnson Era* by Richard Dean Burns and Joseph M. Siracusa, 2009.
93. *The A to Z of Renaissance Art* by Lilian H. Zirpolo, 2009.
94. *The A to Z of the Broadway Musical* by William A. Everett and Paul R. Laird, 2009.
95. *The A to Z of the Northern Ireland Conflict* by Gordon Gillespie, 2009.
96. *The A to Z of the Fashion Industry* by Francesca Sterlacci and Joanne Arbuckle, 2009.
97. *The A to Z of American Theater: Modernism* by James Fisher and Felicia Hardison Londré, 2009.
98. *The A to Z of Civil Wars in Africa* by Guy Arnold, 2009.
99. *The A to Z of the Nixon–Ford Era* by Mitchell K. Hall, 2009.
100. *The A to Z of Horror Cinema* by Peter Hutchings, 2009.
101. *The A to Z of Westerns in Cinema* by Paul Varner, 2009.
102. *The A to Z of Zionism* by Rafael Medoff and Chaim I. Waxman, 2009.
103. *The A to Z of the Roosevelt–Truman Era* by Neil A. Wynn, 2009.
104. *The A to Z of Jehovah's Witnesses* by George D. Chryssides, 2009.
105. *The A to Z of Native American Movements* by Todd Leahy and Raymond Wilson, 2009.
106. *The A to Z of the Shakers* by Stephen J. Paterwic, 2009.
107. *The A to Z of the Coptic Church* by Gawdat Gabra, 2009.
108. *The A to Z of Architecture* by Allison Lee Palmer, 2009.
109. *The A to Z of Italian Cinema* by Gino Moliterno, 2009.
110. *The A to Z of Mormonism* by Davis Bitton and Thomas G. Alexander, 2009.
111. *The A to Z of African American Theater* by Anthony D. Hill with Douglas Q. Barnett, 2009.
112. *The A to Z of NATO and Other International Security Organizations* by Marco Rimanelli, 2009.
113. *The A to Z of the Eisenhower Era* by Burton I. Kaufman and Diane Kaufman, 2009.
114. *The A to Z of Sexspionage* by Nigel West, 2009.
115. *The A to Z of Environmentalism* by Peter Dauvergne, 2009.
116. *The A to Z of the Petroleum Industry* by M. S. Vassiliou, 2009.
117. *The A to Z of Journalism* by Ross Eaman, 2009.
118. *The A to Z of the Gilded Age* by T. Adams Upchurch, 2009.
119. *The A to Z of the Progressive Era* by Catherine Cocks, Peter C. Holloran, and Alan Lessoff, 2009.

120. *The A to Z of Middle Eastern Intelligence* by Ephraim Kahana and Muhammad Suwaed, 2009.
121. *The A to Z of the Baptists* William H. Brackney, 2009.
122. *The A to Z of Homosexuality* by Brent L. Pickett, 2009.
123. *The A to Z of Islam, Second Edition* by Ludwig W. Adamec, 2009.
124. *The A to Z of Buddhism* by Carl Olson, 2009.
125. *The A to Z of United States–Russian/Soviet Relations* by Norman E. Saul, 2010.
126. *The A to Z of United States–Africa Relations* by Robert Anthony Waters Jr., 2010.
127. *The A to Z of United States–China Relations* by Robert Sutter, 2010.
128. *The A to Z of U.S. Diplomacy since the Cold War* by Tom Lansford, 2010.
129. *The A to Z of United States–Japan Relations* by John Van Sant, Peter Mauch, and Yoneyuki Sugita, 2010.
130. *The A to Z of United States–Latin American Relations* by Joseph Smith, 2010.
131. *The A to Z of United States–Middle East Relations* by Peter L. Hahn, 2010.
132. *The A to Z of United States–Southeast Asia Relations* by Donald E. Weatherbee, 2010.
133. *The A to Z of U.S. Diplomacy from the Civil War to World War I* by Kenneth J. Blume, 2010.
134. *The A to Z of International Law* by Boleslaw A. Boczek, 2010.
135. *The A to Z of the Gypsies (Romanies)* by Donald Kenrick, 2010.
136. *The A to Z of the Tamils* by Vijaya Ramaswamy, 2010.
137. *The A to Z of Women in Sub-Saharan Africa* by Kathleen Sheldon, 2010.
138. *The A to Z of Ancient and Medieval Nubia* by Richard A. Lobban Jr., 2010.
139. *The A to Z of Ancient Israel* by Niels Peter Lemche, 2010.
140. *The A to Z of Ancient Mesoamerica* by Joel W. Palka, 2010.
141. *The A to Z of Ancient Southeast Asia* by John N. Miksic, 2010.
142. *The A to Z of the Hittites* by Charles Burney, 2010.
143. *The A to Z of Medieval Russia* by Lawrence N. Langer, 2010.
144. *The A to Z of the Napoleonic Era* by George F. Nafziger, 2010.
145. *The A to Z of Ancient Egypt* by Morris L. Bierbrier, 2010.
146. *The A to Z of Ancient India* by Kumkum Roy, 2010.
147. *The A to Z of Ancient South America* by Martin Giesso, 2010.
148. *The A to Z of Medieval China* by Victor Cunrui Xiong, 2010.
149. *The A to Z of Medieval India* by Iqtidar Alam Khan, 2010.
150. *The A to Z of Mesopotamia* by Gwendolyn Leick, 2010.
151. *The A to Z of the Mongol World Empire* by Paul D. Buell, 2010.
152. *The A to Z of the Ottoman Empire* by Selcuk Aksin Somel, 2010.
153. *The A to Z of Pre-Colonial Africa* by Robert O. Collins, 2010.
154. *The A to Z of Aesthetics* by Dabney Townsend, 2010.
155. *The A to Z of Descartes and Cartesian Philosophy* by Roger Ariew, Dennis Des Chene, Douglas M. Jesseph, Tad M. Schmaltz, and Theo Verbeek, 2010.
156. *The A to Z of Heidegger's Philosophy* by Alfred Denker, 2010.
157. *The A to Z of Kierkegaard's Philosophy* by Julia Watkin, 2010.
158. *The A to Z of Ancient Greek Philosophy* by Anthony Preus, 2010.
159. *The A to Z of Bertrand Russell's Philosophy* by Rosalind Carey and John Ongley, 2010.
160. *The A to Z of Epistemology* by Ralph Baergen, 2010.
161. *The A to Z of Ethics* by Harry J. Gensler and Earl W. Spurgin, 2010.

162. *The A to Z of Existentialism* by Stephen Michelman, 2010.
163. *The A to Z of Hegelian Philosophy* by John W. Burbidge, 2010.
164. *The A to Z of the Holiness Movement* by William Kostlevy, 2010.
165. *The A to Z of Hume's Philosophy* by Kenneth R. Merrill, 2010.
166. *The A to Z of Husserl's Philosophy* by John J. Drummond, 2010.
167. *The A to Z of Kant and Kantianism* by Helmut Holzhey and Vilem Mudroch, 2010.
168. *The A to Z of Leibniz's Philosophy* by Stuart Brown and N. J. Fox, 2010.
169. *The A to Z of Logic* by Harry J. Gensler, 2010.
170. *The A to Z of Medieval Philosophy and Theology* by Stephen F. Brown and Juan Carlos Flores, 2010.
171. *The A to Z of Nietzscheanism* by Carol Diethe, 2010.
172. *The A to Z of the Non-Aligned Movement and Third World* by Guy Arnold, 2010.
173. *The A to Z of Shamanism* by Graham Harvey and Robert J. Wallis, 2010.
174. *The A to Z of Organized Labor* by James C. Docherty, 2010.
175. *The A to Z of the Orthodox Church* by Michael Prokurat, Michael D. Peterson, and Alexander Golitzin, 2010.
176. *The A to Z of Prophets in Islam and Judaism* by Scott B. Noegel and Brannon M. Wheeler, 2010.
177. *The A to Z of Schopenhauer's Philosophy* by David E. Cartwright, 2010.
178. *The A to Z of Wittgenstein's Philosophy* by Duncan Richter, 2010.
179. *The A to Z of Hong Kong Cinema* by Lisa Odham Stokes, 2010.
180. *The A to Z of Japanese Traditional Theatre* by Samuel L. Leiter, 2010.
181. *The A to Z of Lesbian Literature* by Meredith Miller, 2010.
182. *The A to Z of Chinese Theater* by Tan Ye, 2010.
183. *The A to Z of German Cinema* by Robert C. Reimer and Carol J. Reimer, 2010.
184. *The A to Z of German Theater* by William Grange, 2010.
185. *The A to Z of Irish Cinema* by Roderick Flynn and Patrick Brereton, 2010.
186. *The A to Z of Modern Chinese Literature* by Li-hua Ying, 2010.
187. *The A to Z of Modern Japanese Literature and Theater* by J. Scott Miller, 2010.
188. *The A to Z of Old-Time Radio* by Robert C. Reinehr and Jon D. Swartz, 2010.
189. *The A to Z of Polish Cinema* by Marek Haltof, 2010.
190. *The A to Z of Postwar German Literature* by William Grange, 2010.
191. *The A to Z of Russian and Soviet Cinema* by Peter Rollberg, 2010.
192. *The A to Z of Russian Theater* by Laurence Senelick, 2010.
193. *The A to Z of Sacred Music* by Joseph P. Swain, 2010.
194. *The A to Z of Animation and Cartoons* by Nichola Dobson, 2010.
195. *The A to Z of Afghan Wars, Revolutions, and Insurgencies* by Ludwig W. Adamec, 2010.
196. *The A to Z of Ancient Egyptian Warfare* by Robert G. Morkot, 2010.
197. *The A to Z of the British and Irish Civil Wars 1637–1660* by Martyn Bennett, 2010.
198. *The A to Z of the Chinese Civil War* by Edwin Pak-wah Leung, 2010.
199. *The A to Z of Ancient Greek Warfare* by Iain Spence, 2010.
200. *The A to Z of the Anglo–Boer War* by Fransjohan Pretorius, 2010.
201. *The A to Z of the Crimean War* by Guy Arnold, 2010.
202. *The A to Z of the Zulu Wars* by John Laband, 2010.
203. *The A to Z of the Wars of the French Revolution* by Steven T. Ross, 2010.
204. *The A to Z of the Hong Kong SAR and the Macao SAR* by Ming K. Chan and Shiu-hing Lo, 2010.

205. *The A to Z of Australia* by James C. Docherty, 2010.
206. *The A to Z of Burma (Myanmar)* by Donald M. Seekins, 2010.
207. *The A to Z of the Gulf Arab States* by Malcolm C. Peck, 2010.
208. *The A to Z of India* by Surjit Mansingh, 2010.
209. *The A to Z of Iran* by John H. Lorentz, 2010.
210. *The A to Z of Israel* by Bernard Reich and David H. Goldberg, 2010.
211. *The A to Z of Laos* by Martin Stuart-Fox, 2010.
212. *The A to Z of Malaysia* by Ooi Keat Gin, 2010.
213. *The A to Z of Modern China (1800–1949)* by James Z. Gao, 2010.
214. *The A to Z of the Philippines* by Artemio R. Guillermo and May Kyi Win, 2010.
215. *The A to Z of Taiwan (Republic of China)* by John F. Copper, 2010.
216. *The A to Z of the People's Republic of China* by Lawrence R. Sullivan, 2010.
217. *The A to Z of Vietnam* by Bruce M. Lockhart and William J. Duiker, 2010.
218. *The A to Z of Bosnia and Herzegovina* by Ante Cuvalo, 2010.
219. *The A to Z of Modern Greece* by Dimitris Keridis, 2010.
220. *The A to Z of Austria* by Paula Sutter Fichtner, 2010.
221. *The A to Z of Belarus* by Vitali Silitski and Jan Zaprudnik, 2010.
222. *The A to Z of Belgium* by Robert Stallaerts, 2010.
223. *The A to Z of Bulgaria* by Raymond Detrez, 2010.
224. *The A to Z of Contemporary Germany* by Derek Lewis with Ulrike Zitzlsperger, 2010.
225. *The A to Z of the Contemporary United Kingdom* by Kenneth J. Panton and Keith A. Cowlard, 2010.
226. *The A to Z of Denmark* by Alastair H. Thomas, 2010.
227. *The A to Z of France* by Gino Raymond, 2010.
228. *The A to Z of Georgia* by Alexander Mikaberidze, 2010.
229. *The A to Z of Iceland* by Gudmundur Halfdanarson, 2010.
230. *The A to Z of Latvia* by Andrejs Plakans, 2010.
231. *The A to Z of Modern Italy* by Mark F. Gilbert and K. Robert Nilsson, 2010.
232. *The A to Z of Moldova* by Andrei Brezianu and Vlad Spânu, 2010.
233. *The A to Z of the Netherlands* by Joop W. Koopmans and Arend H. Huussen Jr., 2010.
234. *The A to Z of Norway* by Jan Sjåvik, 2010.
235. *The A to Z of the Republic of Macedonia* by Dimitar Bechev, 2010.
236. *The A to Z of Slovakia* by Stanislav J. Kirschbaum, 2010.
237. *The A to Z of Slovenia* by Leopoldina Plut-Pregelj and Carole Rogel, 2010.
238. *The A to Z of Spain* by Angel Smith, 2010.
239. *The A to Z of Sweden* by Irene Scobbie, 2010.
240. *The A to Z of Turkey* by Metin Heper and Nur Bilge Criss, 2010.
241. *The A to Z of Ukraine* by Zenon E. Kohut, Bohdan Y. Nebesio, and Myroslav Yurkevich, 2010.
242. *The A to Z of Mexico* by Marvin Alisky, 2010.
243. *The A to Z of U.S. Diplomacy from World War I through World War II* by Martin Folly and Niall Palmer, 2010.
244. *The A to Z of Spanish Cinema* by Alberto Mira, 2010.
245. *The A to Z of the Reformation and Counter-Reformation* by Michael Mullett, 2010.

Dedicated to the Celebration of the
Bicentennial of Orthodox Christianity in North America
1794–1994

# Contents

| | |
|---|---|
| Editor's Foreword | ix |
| Preface | xi |
| Acronyms and Abbreviations | xv |
| Introduction | 1 |
| Chronology | 11 |
| Map | 19 |
| The Dictionary | 21 |
| Appendix | 347 |
| Bibliography | 349 |
| About the Authors | 439 |

# Editor's Foreword

Of the three major branches of Christianity, Orthodoxy is certainly less well known—and more often misunderstood—than Roman Catholicism and Protestantism. But it is a no less sturdy branch that has managed to grow and frequently flourish even within extremely hostile environments. The Orthodox Church miraculously withstood centuries of Turkish domination and Islamic influence in the Middle East and parts of Eastern Europe and then a shorter but even more constraining period of communism. Now, freed of many constraints, it enters a period of exceptional promise in countries with a long Orthodox tradition.

So this is a particularly good time to learn more—and overcome some misunderstandings—about the Orthodox Church and its various constituent churches. This applies not only to ecclesiology, theology, and philosophy but also to art and architecture, all of which are covered in this book. It applies equally to the many great men and women who have played significant roles as church officials, theologians, teachers, monks, and saints. There are also numerous entries on them. The chronology makes it easier to follow some two thousand years of history. And the bibliography helps readers find more information on subjects of special interest to them.

This *Historical Dictionary of the Orthodox Church* is the result of a joint effort by several eminent authorities. The body was written by Michael Prokurat and Alexander Golitzin. Dr. Prokurat is Assistant Professor at the School of Theology of the University of St. Thomas at St. Mary's Seminary, Houston, and Dr. Golitzin is Assistant Professor at the Department of Theology of Marquette University, Milwaukee. Both have published significant works and taught or lectured at other institutions. The bibliography was compiled by Michael Davis Peterson, who is the Branch Librarian at the San Anselmo collection of the Graduate Theological Union Library, Berkeley. And the map and illustrations were drawn by Melanie Gogol-Prokurat. They have produced a very useful book that can serve as an introduction for newcomers while still enlightening the more advanced.

Jon Woronoff
Series Editor

# Preface

The historical scope of this work focuses on the last 150 years, although major topics from the second century A.D. to the present are also treated. Some of the entries from earlier periods have been discovered only in the last century and are vital to the way the reading of Christian history has changed in the twentieth century. Unfortunately, length is a primary factor in a one-volume reference work and so too in the process of selection of topics, and for this reason many items had to be excluded—not least of which were general Scripture entries and the sweep of history from Moses to Jesus from the perspective of the Eastern Church. Since these subjects are the most ancient, and a considerable library of dictionaries and encyclopedias exists on them in English, it seemed a justifiable decision to limit our entries to those roughly after the New Testament period and corpus.

Our goal in writing a dictionary was specifically to meet a need for Orthodox and non-Orthodox alike; and it led us to a result that is different from other extant reference works on Orthodoxy. The excellent books *The Oxford Dictionary of the Christian Church* (edited by F.L. Cross and E.A. Livingston, Oxford University Press, 1978) and *The Orthodox Church* (by Timothy Ware [Bishop Kallistos of Diokleia], Penguin Books, 1993) served as approximate examples for us, but we tried to broaden the number of subjects by reviewing extant histories, dictionaries, and encyclopedias on Orthodoxy, Christianity, Byzantium, Russia, and so on. We found *Orthodox America 1794–1976* (edited by Constance J. Tarasar, Orthodox Church in America Department of History and Archives, 1975) to be a good one-volume resource for American Orthodox church history, but the indexing and cross-listing is difficult for quick reference. Our goal in writing may be described as a dictionary insofar as that format might include a one-volume desk encyclopedia or a reference work sometimes called a handbook.

The need for a dictionary of the Orthodox Church in the narrow sense of a list of words with definitions has been provisionally met by *Webster's Third New International Dictionary*. Many, if not most, of the technical Greek and Russian theological words and terms that would otherwise be underlined and treated as foreign—up until *Webster's Third*—are now listed as "American" words. (We call them "American" words rather than "English" because they cannot be found in the *Oxford English Dictionary*, and scholars who identify solely with the *OED* English-language tradition will doubtless continue to treat the words listed in *Webster's Third* as foreign.) The fact that these terms exist in a large American dictionary should be credited to Fr. Georges Florovsky's serving as an editor for *Webster's Third* and to the inimitable American characteristic of positively accepting as its own the culture and language of large segments of its population. We recommend *Webster's Third* to those looking for word definitions, and we have occasionally supplemented or changed those of their definitions that seem to us inadequate.

Since there were three of us writing, a certain division of labor was tentatively in force during the composition process. The initial plan, the long list of individual entries and the category divisions in the bibliography, were selected by Michael Prokurat. The selection was based on the pragmatic criterion of the availability of resources rather than on any preconceived theological or historical outline. From the long list, Alexander Golitzin and Michael Prokurat chose specific topics for research — Golitzin usually chose the Byzantine and Prokurat the Russian, although not exclusively — and both edited the final product. Michael Peterson, as Branch Librarian at the San Anselmo collection of the Graduate Theological Union, was the best equipped to compile the bibliography, which concentrates on books published in English during the last fifteen years. After Peterson prepared drafts of the bibliography, the other two writers reviewed and supplemented them with older classics and specific books used in the field, especially foreign language selections. Peterson also prepared some biographical information on living persons. Melanie Gogol-Prokurat drew the map and provided several drawings for entries better understood by illustration than by text.

At the outset we decided against presenting just the bare facts. We have included controversial items and opinions (theologoumena) in order to illustrate living traditions and to give what we think is an intelligent position or choice in formulating questions or in resolving some current debates. Similarly, in matters of biography, when theologians and hierarchs were or are known to us personally, we did not avoid a special note in addition to the *Curriculum Vitae* information.

Although various English translations of the Bible may be found in use in the Orthodox Church — especially the Revised Standard Version, the New American Bible, and the King James Version — abbreviations for the books of the Bible and biblical quotations cited herein follow the New Revised Standard Version unless otherwise indicated. (For example, occasional adjustments are made for a translation from Greek rather than Hebrew, liturgical language, or theological differences.) Some of the best Orthodox biblical scholars worked on both the Revised Standard Version and the New Revised Standard Version, and with the maps, articles, and annotations of the Oxford Annotated edition, it is arguably the best "ecumenical Bible" in use in the English-speaking world today. Transliterations herein follow the Library of Congress system unless superceded by convention; and foreign language names have been translated into their English-language equivalents whenever possible, unless the translation would make the reference unrecognizable. A listing of acronyms and abbreviations can be found before the introduction.

Special thanks goes to Fr. Thomas Hopko, Dean of St. Vladimir's Orthodox Theological Seminary, Crestwood, New York, for recommending us to Scarecrow Press. We express our appreciation to our colleagues who encouraged us in this endeavor, as well as to the library staffs of the Graduate Theological Union, Marquette University, the Patriarch Athenagoras Orthodox Institute, St. Vladimir's Seminary, St. Mary's Seminary, Houston, and the University of California—Berkeley, for their expert knowledge and kind assistance. Finally, our gratitude goes to Margaret Prokurat for typing the final drafts of the manuscript.

Michael Prokurat<br>
School of Theology<br>
University of St. Thomas<br>
Houston, Texas<br>
21 November 1995<br>
Entry of the Theotokos

# Acronyms and Abbreviations

| | |
|---|---|
| 1 Chr | 1 Chronicles |
| 1 Cor | 1 Corinthians |
| 1 Esd | 1 Esdras |
| 1 Jn | 1 John |
| 1 Kgs | 1 Kings |
| 1 Macc | 1 Maccabees |
| 1 Pet | 1 Peter |
| 1 Sam | 1 Samuel |
| 1 Thess | 1 Thessalonians |
| 1 Tim | 1 Timothy |
| 2 Chr | 2 Chronicles |
| 2 Cor | 2 Corinthians |
| 2 Esd | 2 Esdras |
| 2 Jn | 2 John |
| 2 Macc | 2 Maccabees |
| 2 Pet | 2 Peter |
| 2 Sam | 2 Samuel |
| 2 Thess | 2 Thessalonians |
| 2 Tim | 2 Timothy |
| 3 Jn | 3 John |
| 3 Macc | 3 Maccabees |
| 4 Macc | 4 Maccabees |
| AACC | All African Conference of Churches |
| Add Esth | The Additions to Esther |
| Bar | Baruch |
| Bel | Bel and the Dragon |
| c. | century |
| Cmte. | Committee |
| Col | Colossians |
| Dan | Daniel |
| Deut | Deuteronomy |
| Eccl | Ecclesiastes |
| Eph | Ephesians |
| Esth | Esther |
| Ex | Exodus |

| | |
|---|---|
| Ezek | Ezekiel |
| Fr. | Father |
| Gal | Galatians |
| Gen | Genesis |
| GOYO | Greek Orthodox Youth Organization |
| GTU | Graduate Theological Union |
| Hab | Habakkuk |
| Hag | Haggai |
| Heb | Hebrews |
| Is | Isaiah |
| Jas | James |
| Jdg | Judges |
| Jdt | Judith |
| Jer | Jeremiah |
| Jn | John |
| Jon | Jonah |
| Josh | Joshua |
| Lam | Lamentations |
| Let Jer | The Letter of Jeremiah |
| Lev | Leviticus |
| Lk | Luke |
| LXX | Septuagint |
| Mal | Malachi |
| Mk | Mark |
| Mt | Matthew |
| NCC | National Council of Churches |
| Neh | Nehemiah |
| NRSV | New Revised Standard Version |
| Num | Numbers |
| Ob | Obadiah |
| OCA | Orthodox Church in America |
| OED | Oxford English Dictionary |
| O.S. | Old Style, Julian Calendar |
| PAOI | Patriarch Athenagoras Orthodox Institute |
| Patr. | Patriarch |
| Philm | Philemon |
| Philp | Philippians |
| Pr Man | Prayer of Manasseh |
| Prov | Proverbs |
| Ps | Psalms |
| q.v. | *quod vide*, which see (single occurrence) |
| qq.v. | which see (multiple occurrences) |
| RCC | Roman Catholic Church |
| Rev | Revelation |

| | |
|---|---|
| Rom | Romans |
| RSV | Revised Standard Version |
| SCOBA | Standing Conference of Orthodox Bishops in America |
| Sir | Ben Sirach |
| Song of Thr | The Song of the Three Children |
| St. | Saint |
| Sus | Susannah |
| Tob | Tobit |
| UCB | University of California—Berkeley |
| UOC | Ukrainian Orthodox Church |
| UOC-KP | Ukrainian Orthodox Church-Kievan Patriarchate |
| WCC | World Council of Churches |
| Wis | Wisdom of Solomon |
| Zech | Zechariah |
| Zeph | Zephaniah |

# Introduction

The Orthodox Church may simply be described as God's embassy to creation, wherein God reveals his will, humanity finds its rightful citizenship, and the cosmos is redeemed. An embassy fully and adequately represents its home country: Even its soil is considered to be that of its sovereign nation. Still, by definition it exists in a foreign land, does not fully encompass the homeland, and equips its citizens to live in a strange place, while providing them safe haven, a refuge. Embassies exist in many different nations, speaking their languages and functioning within their cultures, while always representing the interests of the one sovereign or president. Ambassadors and liaisons do their work in various ways in each foreign land, but the citizenship and interests they maintain are solely those of their mother country. In all these particulars it is so too with the Church.

Just as with the embassy, knowledge of the sovereignty represented may be approached through reading, visits, or tourism; but true knowledge is attained only by experience. It is not gotten by a map, shopping, or an adventure. Experience involves knowing the sovereign and his will, taking the responsibilities of full citizenship, and making that kingdom one's home—including all the joys and sorrows of celebration and sacrifice, rewards and taxes, freedom and military service. Citizenship is open to all. Nevertheless, such a comparison between state and Church, sojourner and Christian, does not do justice to the simplicity, or the complexity, of God's plan.

## Belief

The classical statement of faith or belief within the Orthodox Church is the Nicene-Constantinopolitan Creed. The articles were written on the Father and the Son at the First Ecumenical Council in Nicaea (A.D. 325) based upon a credo thought to be already in use. The articles on the Holy Spirit and the Church were added at the Second Ecumenical Council in Constantinople (A.D. 381), largely under the influence of St. Basil the Great and St. Gregory of Nazianzus. It has remained unchanged within the Orthodox Church since the Second Ecumenical Council.

The Orthodox understanding of the Nicene-Constantinopolitan Creed is that it does not define (or redefine) the faith, but rather that it expresses the basic catholic belief—universal in time and place—of the entire Christian Church. Further, the content of the Creed may be altered only by an Ecumenical Council in the same way that it came into being. That is to say, any later interpolation into the Creed as occurred in the West (i.e., the *filioque*) is not acceptable to the Orthodox—regardless of whether the interpolation might be theologically correct—unless it is approved by an Ecumenical Council. That the Creed serves as the normative statement of faith is witnessed by the fact that it is read at every Baptism and Confession service, as well as at each Divine Liturgy.

The English text of the Creed reproduced below is the final distribution draft (1994) of the Liturgical Translation Committee of the Standing Conference of Orthodox Bishops in America. (Those phrases or words most often mistranslated into English are printed in boldface, with the most usual mistranslations footnoted with brief explanation.) The arrangement of the Creed varies from book to book, sometimes printed with continuous text, at other times separated into twelve "articles," etc. The arrangement of the text below is based on the translators' understanding of how to best render Greek syntax into contemporary American English.

The Nicene-Constantinopolitan Creed

I believe in one God, the Father, the Almighty, Creator of heaven and earth, and of all things visible and invisible.

And in one Lord, Jesus Christ, the only-begotten Son of God, begotten of the Father before all ages, Light of Light, true God of true God, begotten, not created, of one essence with the Father, through whom all things were made; who for us and for our salvation came down from heaven and was incarnate of the Holy Spirit and the Virgin Mary and became **human**[1]; who was crucified for us under Pontius Pilate, and suffered and was buried; who rose on the third day, according to the Scriptures, and ascended into heaven and is seated at the right hand of the Father; and **who is coming**[2] again with glory to judge the living and the dead; and his kingdom will have no end.

---

[1]**Human:** Although this word in Greek could be translated "Man," with a capital, the point of the phrase is that Jesus Christ became one of us, a human being, and not that he became a male person—which is what is connoted in modern American English if the word "man" is used.

[2]**Who is coming:** Either "comes" or "is coming" is the only possible translation, although "will come" is a translational mistake that has been in the English-speaking world for centuries, and can be found in almost all, if not all, churches of any denomination which use English and this Creed. When this mistake is coupled with that found in Footnote #3, the result is that it looks as if the Messiah will come at a different time and in a different place, both of which are in the future: "pie in the sky, by and by." This was not intended by the original Greek Church Fathers, and the theological implications of the incorrect translation are potentially devastating—and make the Eucharist somewhat incomprehensible.

And in the Holy Spirit, the Lord, the Giver of Life, who proceeds from the Father, who together with the Father and the Son is worshiped and glorified, who spoke through the prophets.
In one, holy, catholic, and apostolic Church.
I acknowledge one baptism for the forgiveness of sins.
I look for the resurrection of the dead, and the life of the **age**[3] to come. Amen.

## History

The usual historical identification of Orthodoxy as the church of the Seven Ecumenical Councils (used as a theological locus) is somewhat deceptive in that the Orthodox Church openly claims a broader, more pervasive ecumenical and catholic character. Although the "Seven-Council" designation might be provisionally helpful in comparing the Church of the East with that of the West, as a full definition it is lacking in various ways. The Orthodox have a history and origin that long precede and follow the Seven Councils.

As the chronology after this Introduction indicates, the Orthodox—with the Jews, Muslims, and other traditional Christians—trace their beginnings back to the Patriarchs, Abraham, Isaac, and Jacob, and then to Moses—if not before the Patriarchs to humankind's prototypical parents, Adam and Eve. These stories are so well-known that they hardly bear repeating here. But it is worthwhile to point out that the Orthodox understand this "history" (not always history in the modern sense) as a chronicle of God's revelations, not only to particular human beings, but to humankind in general. The revelations are infrequently, if ever, individual in the restrictive sense of the word, but are meant to guide all of humanity by ultimately forming a people (the People of God) that lives its community life in communion with the one self-revealing God.

Further, for the Orthodox this revelation continued personally in Jesus Christ, the unique and preexistent Son of God and Lord, and personally as well in the revelation of the Holy Spirit. The Spirit and revelation are ongoing in the life of the Church—one God in three Persons. Indeed, the Orthodox faith described as the Church of the Resurrection of Jesus Christ and the life of the Holy Spirit is arguably more apropos than that of the Ecumenical Councils, since religious faith and experience are more meaningful and readily accessible to the average American than the difficult historical and theological questions of the conciliar period. Orthodox history, most simply put, is a retrospective view and present appreciation of the life of God's Spirit embracing humanity.

---

[3]**Age:** "The age to come" is a known biblical phrase from both the Hebrew of the Old Testament and the Greek of the New. See Footnote #2 above.

Probably the most striking historical witness of the Orthodox Church for modern Christians is its uninterrupted presence at the holy places described in the life of Jesus of Nazareth, the Apostle Paul, or the Bible generally. Further, the Orthodox may also be found speaking the descendant language(s) in which the words of the Bible were originally spoken and written—appreciating these words from *within* their own languages rather than from without. When Western Christians make pilgrimage to the Holy Land or look at the Church's roots, they invariably meet the Orthodox firmly and permanently entrenched on these foundations—whether in the Church of the Resurrection (Holy Sepulcher), on the Ascension Mount, or in the ancient churches of Thessalonika or Athens. This history is intrinsically connected with classical Western history from Rome to Charlemagne, on to the Crusades, Renaissance, Reformation, and up to the present.

## Hierarchy and Administration

The hierarchy and administration of the Orthodox Church, an aspect of what is technically termed ecclesiology, is based upon the ancient orders of bishop, priest, and deacon. Every diocese, or bishop's territorial see, has integrity as the full expression of the Church, while maintaining a common faith and communion (including Eucharistic Communion) with every other diocese. Dioceses are generally joined together nationally and/or territorially under the local jurisdiction of an archbishop, metropolitan, or patriarch; and this presiding bishop functions as a first among equals with his other bishops in order to address topics of common need and interest, e.g., external affairs (comparable to foreign affairs in secular government), national policies, support of seminaries, etc.

The description above, regarding the integrity and autonomy of the diocese, may be claimed to a large degree for the local parish as well. The parish is generally the first institutional encounter and witness of the fullness of the Church—and for many the parish might well be the first and last experience of the Church. This is not theologically interpreted as congregationalism, since each congregation knows that the Church is greater than a single parish, but it is a matter of the fullness of the Eucharistic expression of the faith in each and every place at all times, and a matter of simple utility.

What this has meant at the parish level from the earliest times is that there is a certain fluidity between the role of bishop and priest, with the exception of the prerogative of ordination. However the number of bishops might be determined for a given area—and this reckoning differs from place to place and time to time—the equation of one priest per parish has remained relatively constant. The priest, for all practical purposes, functions with all the rights and privileges of a bishop, excepting ordination, making the parish the primary Christian witness to the local community and to the world.

The politics of the hierarchy of the Orthodox Church on the international level is too complex and nuanced to be adequately described briefly. The following dynamics are generally acknowledged as true: Older patriarchates are seen as having certain prerogatives supported by ancient custom. Among these, Rome and Constantinople historically have enjoyed special recognition and privilege based on their adherence to orthodoxy, access to political power, and size. Since the schism between East and West, the fall of Constantinople, and the advent of stronger theological and political papal claims, all of the supposed criteria—orthodoxy, political power, and size—do not definitely lead in any one direction. An argument can be made from the criteria of "orthodoxy" and "size" that the Patriarch of Moscow is in fact the leading spokesman of the Orthodox Church in the world today. Nevertheless, deference is made to the Patriarch of Constantinople on traditional grounds. Still, most Orthodox imagine that the Pope of Rome would preside as first among equals if the East and West were reunited, a possibility encouraged by ecumenical dialogue, but made more remote by the creation of Western dioceses within the traditional territories of the Eastern Church.

## Orders of Clergy

As we have seen, the primary responsibilities of bishops and priests are in presiding at the Eucharistic assembly and in administering the diocese and parish, respectively. Archbishops and metropolitans are usually bishops of larger, metropolitan areas and work with many episcopal colleagues. They may also be the heads of autocephalous (self-governing) churches, but wherever the local church has been continuously autocephalous for a long period of time, the title patriarch is usually bestowed upon the presiding archbishop.

In addition to the episcopacy (bishop) and presbytery (priest), the diaconate (deacon) is the next major order whose function is classicaly defined as "serving table," usually interpreted as both serving at the Lord's table (Eucharist) and in the distribution of foodstuffs to the needy. The diaconate is a permanent office in the Eastern Church and not just a step to the priesthood, though it can be; and it is common in the Russian Church for every parish to have a deacon. Whether the deacon serves only a liturgical function, or as a full- or part-time minister within a diocese or parish, is largely a matter of need and training. Other types of deacon are protodeacon and archdeacon, both of which are classically supervisory roles over other deacons, but in practice indicate a bishop's deacon or an honorary title. These offices are similar to those of archpriest, protopresbyter, archbishop, etc., wherein the classical definition has to do with leadership over others of the same rank, but practically speaking nowadays the title is frequently an honorific. Primary reasons for titles as honorifics stem from (1) the practice of the Russian Church, wherein Peter the Great made ecclesiastical rankings correspond exactly to civil service seniority rankings (disregarding their functional, ecclesial aspect) and (2) the desire to give titular honors. Although most agree that this "system of awards" needs to be reformed, the discipline to do so is not overabundant.

Other "lower orders" of clergy include subdeacons and readers. Subdeacons are altar servers who are trained to assist at the pontifical (bishop's) services. Readers or cantors chant and read the epistle and people's parts of the services. All deacons, subdeacons, and readers are technically ranked among the laity, while bishops and priests are considered clergy.

Before listing the ranks of monastic clergy, two items should be pointed out. First, unlike the Roman Catholic Church (after the Cluny Reform), the parochial clergy of the Orthodox Church are not usually celibate or monastic, but are married or "white" clergy. Orthodox bishops (after the Seventh Ecumenical Council) must be elected from among the monastic or "black" clergy. The matter of marriage or celibacy of clergy is thus disciplinary and not doctrinal. Second, monastic men and women who are not ordained are reckoned among the laity and not among the clergy. Ordained monastics have special titles: a hierodeacon is a monk-deacon; a hieromonk is a monk-priest; a hegumen is an abbot of a smaller religious community; while an archimandrite is abbot of a larger monastery. An elder, a spiritual father, or a spiritual mother need not be of special monastic rank.

**Content: World Perceptions**

What makes Orthodoxy what it is, and different from other religions, is an area of debate, sparked in part by Eurocentrist concerns and ecumenism. From the *inside,* many Orthodox are happy to focus on the differences between the Christian East and West, since that is what Westerners—and Orthodox who are content with uniqueness—are interested in examining: Orthodoxy as another "denomination" among Christian denominations. This type of denominationalism gives rise to a practical theological problem, albeit a longstanding one, which is foreign to the catholic tradition of the Church. Further, psychological difficulties of balance between triumphalism and sectarianism, both of which create an isolationist atmosphere, plague almost every Orthodox ethos, and might well be a result of modern nationalist tendencies. Still, no attitude of exclusion—other than on the basis of sin—does justice to the historical claims of the Church as one, holy, catholic, and apostolic.

From the *outside,* Orthodox cultures seem to be given an anomalous "Third-World" status by contemporary Western historians and the media, even though they constitute a sizable portion of Europe. Noteworthy to the Orthodox themselves is that almost every nation with a significant Orthodox population has been invaded at least once in the twentieth century by countries identifying themselves as Western Christian. The Russian Orthodox are sensitive to the fact that the national genocide which occurred under the Bolsheviks, and more particularly under Stalin, murders that numbered in the tens of millions, elicited a marginal response from the West, and even today is not well-known. Similar sensibilities may be found among Armenian, Serbian, Arab, and other Christians—all cases in which twentieth century genocide has been denied, let alone acknowledged with sympathy or addressed as criminal. This is not to say that totalitarianism or uncontrolled tragedies do not occur, but the fact that the occurrences are not well reported or responded to in the West is remarkable.

In such a context, is it strange that the Orthodox are not always trusting when in dialogue with Western Christians? Or is it the fault of the Orthodox themselves, who still speak about long-past atrocities of the "glorious Crusades," when they should abandon diplomatic subtlety and speak directly about what they really mean—recent aggressive tendencies from the West.

### Present Geographic Spread and Populations of Believers

Although the map following this Introduction gives some idea of the territorial divisions of the Orthodox Church in the Old World, a brief look at populations of believers on all continents is also in order. Before embarking on this discussion, a few caveats should be noted. To begin, it seems that counting the People of God has been problematical since the census of King David, when the Lord incited David against the people to take a census (2 Sam 24:1), or rather Satan enticed David to count (1 Chr 21:1). Willingness to be counted, or lack of it, and responsibilities laid on people counted, make the process tenuous. In American polls (e.g., Harris's) the very recent trend has been to ask people how many times they have attended church or synagogue in recent months, and to gauge membership on these figures rather than on other indicators such as number of people in an ethnic group, number of baptisms, number of dues-paying members, etc. After decades of exposure to the difficulties of census figures in Orthodox churches, we opine that the Harris polls' criteria are the most realistic for ascertaining who is a member of the Orthodox Church—that is, those you regularly see in an Orthodox church.

Unfortunately, the census numbers here presented do not originate with the consistent application of any criteria, since they come from many different countries and cultures. It is reasonable to assume that the figures represent the numbers of people baptized and (nominally) now of the Orthodox faith. The following list ranges from largest to smallest. In a few cases there might be some double counting, since most Orthodox in North America, Great Britain, and France belong to exarchates (especially the Patriarchate of Constantinople), that is, mother churches with "jurisdictions" in these countries.

| | |
|---|---|
| Russia, Ukraine, Belarus | 100,000,000–150,000,000 |
| Non-Chalcedonian Churches (Assyrian, Syrian, Coptic, Armenian, Ethopian, etc.) | 27,000,000 |
| Romania | 20,000,000 |
| Greece | 9,025,000 |
| Bulgaria | 8,000,000 |
| Serbia | 8,000,000 |
| Constantinopolitan Patriarchate | 4,500,000 |
| Georgia | 3,000,000 |
| United States, Canada | 4,000,000 |
| Antiochene Patriarchate | 750,000 |
| Poland | 570,000 |
| Cyprus | 442,000 |
| Alexandrian Patriarchate | 350,000 |
| Albania | 160,000 |
| Jerusalem Patriarchate | 60,000 |
| Finland | 56,000 |
| Czech and Slovakia | 55,000 |
| Japan | 25,000 |
| China | 20,000 |
| Sinai | 900 |

(Current census figures are not available for South America, and Australia.)

A quick glance at this list of countries and their church memberships is quite revealing. First, the estimate of a worldwide Orthodox population including the Non-Chalcedonian Churches ranges from approximately 200 to 250 million. Second, of this population about one-half to two-thirds is ethnically Slavic and has spent the greater part of the twentieth century behind the Iron Curtain. Third, none of the European and Asian regions is identified with the roots of mainstream America and, if examined seriously, these territories and peoples fall primarily under the heading of "Ethnic Studies" in the United States.

## Present Accomplishments

The twentieth-century accomplishments of Orthodoxy are difficult to describe because of their profundity. The single greatest witness of the Church may best be evaluated in terms of human sacrifice or martyrdom. It is beyond imagination that twentieth-century communist totalitarianism in Slavic countries produced more martyrs to the faith than all the Christian martyrdoms of the preceding centuries combined. The only comparable historical phenomenon is the tragic extermination of tens of millions of

Chinese in this century by their own totalitarian regime. The parallels are stupifying: More people seem to have died in peacetime under these two regimes than all the casualties of all the wars of the last two centuries—and in each case the West was relatively silent about the fates of these peoples, though less so in later evaluating the dangers of communism as it encroached on Western interests. Thus, the great gift of the Orthodox Church to this century is its continued survival and life, through sacrifice and death.

A comparatively lesser, but nonetheless important, achievement of Orthodoxy today is its continued, consistent presence in ecumenical dialogue with other Christians, attesting to the credal dictum that the Church is one, holy, catholic, and apostolic. Coming from a nineteenth-century context wherein lack of communication and distance made East and West mutually foreign, the twentieth century has been one of not only formal introduction, but of serious exchange and dialogue. This ecumenical spirit has promoted mutual understanding and given theological definition to areas where only suppositions and suspicions once reigned free. As a practical result, the dialogue has increased interdenominational charity and helped end profligate missionizing of Christians by Christians. Both the present Patriarch of Constantinople and the Patriarch of Moscow have made it a point to encourage ecumenical dialogue officially in recent archpastoral addresses to the Church at large.

## Future Challenges

Challenges facing the Orthodox in the coming century—or millennium—are manifold; and the problematic situation in North America is very much a microcosm of worldwide questions. Before describing these particulars, it is important to reiterate the classic goals of the Church with which it began: to preach the Gospel and serve the Sacraments, in short to provide salvation as the embassy of the Kingdom of God. All other goals are subservient to the primary task of the Church qua Church.

In North America the Orthodox Church is historically an émigré phenomenon with ethnocentric associations, long before the word "ethnocentric" became a politically correct part of the American vocabulary. The difficulties experienced by American society at large with ethnocentricity—philosophically speaking the question of "the one and the many"—are the same as those experienced for centuries by the Orthodox Church under the rubric of phyletism: What is the essence of the one society as it is represented now in the western hemisphere by the many ethnic groups? Or the one Orthodox Church represented by the ethnic Orthodox?

The question is first and foremost one of the communication of the Church's evangelical witness. But the question of "ethnic" form and "faith" content is compounded by a phenomenon unfamiliar to Americans, a phenomenon relatively common in wealthier Greek and Russian international circles—cultural colonization. Simply put, this entails living comfortably in a foreign country, while completely maintaining one's own high culture and ethnic identity as a sort of resident alien. For such resident alien communities, for Greek émigrés suppressed at home by Turks or Slavs suppressed by communists, assimilation to the host language and culture may be tantamount to a betrayal of one's family and civilization, or at best an acquiescence to a less venerable cultural tradition. The question of ethnic identity is less pressing for the emigrant peasant or the forced refugee. But surprisingly, they too might accept the stricter interpretation of cultural loyalty given by resident alien captains of industry or expatriates from the intellectual elite of the mother country. In such a complex debate, the evangelical witness of the Orthodox Church in a "new" society is frequently the victim of Old World cultural imperialism, an attitude ironically defended by "loyalty to tradition"— unfortunately, not the Church's Tradition.

Another challenge facing the Orthodox Church in the years to come is in identifying an effective witness or voice for Orthodoxy throughout the world. Although decentralized local churches (internationally speaking) serve well in their autonomy and allow tremendous flexibility in addressing regional situations, a united witness of Orthodoxy on the international scene has been lacking. With communication networks around the globe providing immediate access to news and information, authoritative and timely responses of an Orthodox Christian witness to events and social issues are desirable—and even necessary. One solution to this circumstance might be tied to the question of international hierarchical leadership, i.e., a particular patriarchate, although it need not be so. Other solutions might present themselves as more viable—conciliar discussions, World Council of Churches deliberations, theological think tanks, news services, etc. Any movement toward the resolution of this situation would not only provide more communication among the Orthodox themselves, but would be a positive statement of the Orthodox faith to the world—and at the very least begin a dialogue on difficult issues.

For a longer introduction to the Orthodox Church, which introductions usually follow one of two classic formats described below, one may read either of two series of dictionary entries. First, the traditional theological triad, God, Humanity, Cosmos, may be approached by reading the longer entries relating to God (God, Theology, Trinity, Christology, Holy Spirit), Humanity (Anthropology), and the Cosmos (Cosmology). Second, the standard approach related to Holy Tradition may be investigated by reading the entries on topics constitutive of Holy Tradition itself: Scripture, Liturgy, Church Fathers, Ascesis, Saints, and Canon Law. Either of these methods, reflected in two series of entries, provide the interested reader with information along lines used by theologians and laity, Orthodox and non-Orthodox alike.

# Chronology

| B.C. | |
|---|---|
| 2000 | Origins (described in Gen 1–11) |
| 1900 | |
| 1800 | |
| 1700 | Patriarchs: Abraham, Isaac, Jacob, and Joseph in Egypt (dates unknown; described in Gen 12–50) |
| 1600 | |
| 1500 | |
| 1400 | |
| 1300 | Moses, the Exodus, the Law at Sinai (ca. 1240 f.; described in Ex, Lev, Num) |
| | Tentative possession of Canaan (ca. 1210; described in Josh) |
| 1200 | Judges (ca.1200–1025) |
| | Deborah (ca. 1125) |
| 1100 | Philistine victory at Aphek (ca. 1050) |
| | Samuel and Saul (described in 1 Sam) |
| 1000 | David (ca. 1010–970; described in 2 Sam) |
| | Solomon (970–931) and the monarchy to ca. 850 (described in 1 Kings) |
| | 1st Temple built (4th yr. of Solomon) |
| 900 | Ahab (+853; year of Battle at Qarqar) |
| | Elijah-Elisha and the monarchies through to their destructions (described in 1 & 2 Kings) |
| 800 | Amos and Hosea (ca. 750) |
| | Fall of Samaria (721) |
| | Is 1–39 and Micah |
| 700 | Hezekiah |
| | Byzantium founded (660) |
| | Josiah (640–609) and Reform |
| | Deut |
| | Zeph, Nahum, Hab |
| | Jeremiah |
| 600 | Ezekiel |
| | Fall of Jerusalem and Exile (587) |

|       | |
|-------|---|
|       | Exilic codification of Scripture |
|       | Deuteronomistic Historian, Is 40–55, Lam, Ob, Job |
|       | Cyrus establishes Persian Empire (539–333) |
|       | Return (538 f.) |
|       | Hag, Zech 1–8 |
|       | 2nd Temple built (519–515) |
|       | Is 55–66 |
| 500   | Zech 9–14, Mal |
|       | Ezra and the Torah (458) |
|       | Neh (445/444) |
|       | 1, 2 Chr, Ruth |
| 400   | Joel, Jon |
|       | Plato (+347) |
|       | Greek Period (333–63 B.C.) |
|       | Alexander conquers Palestine (333–330) |
|       | Let Jer (317?) |
| 300   | Eccl |
|       | LXX Translation begins |
|       | Tob (225–175) |
| 200   | Bar (200–60?) |
|       | Sir (before 180) |
|       | I Enoch (date unknown) |
|       | Dan (167–164) |
|       | 1 Esd, Esth (after 164) |
|       | Jdt (135–105) |
|       | Qumran founded |
|       | Additions to Dan: Song of Thr, Sus, Bel (2nd c) |
|       | Add Esth (114 f.) |
|       | 1 Macc (104) |
|       | 2 Macc (104–63) |
| 100   | Letter of Aristeas, 3 Macc (ca. 100) |
|       | Wis, Pr Man (late 1st c.) |
|       | Roman Period (63–A.D. 135) |
| 0     | Birth of Jesus (6 B.C.?) |
| A.D.  |          Judaizers |
|       |          Docetists |
|       |          Dualists |
|       | Jesus' ministry (ca. 30) |
|       | Paul's Letters: 1 Thess, Gal, 1 & 2 Cor, Philp, Rom, Philm |
|       | Martyrdom of Peter and Paul (+64) |
|       | Jewish Revolt and Destruction of Jerusalem (66–70), Mk |

100

200

300

Mt
Completion of Pauline corpus: 2 Thess, Col, Eph
Lk–Acts
Jn, 1–3 Jn
2 Esd, 4 Macc (dates uncertain)
Heb
Rev (ca. 95)
1 Clement (95/96)
    Gnostics
    Montanists
    Modalists
    Advent of Rabbinic Pharisaism
    Roman persecutions
Epistle to Barnabas, Didache (ca. 100)
Jas, 1 Pet, Jude
Ignatius of Antioch (+115)
Pastoral Letters; 1 Tim, 2 Tim, Titus
Bar Cochba Revolt (132–135); Aelia Capitolina f.
2 Pet (ca. 140)
Shepherd of Hermas (ca. 148)
Protoevangelium of James (ca. 150)
2 Clement (date unknown, possibly ca. 150)
Polycarp of Smyrna (+156)
Apologists: Justin Martyr (+165) et al.
    Cont. above plus
    Adoptionists
    Novationists (mid c.)
    Manichaeans
    Encratites
    Subordinationists
    Plotinus (+270)
Irenaeus of Lyons (+ca. 200)
Clement of Alexandria (+215)
Hippolytus of Rome (+236)
Origen (+254)
Cyprian of Carthage (+258)
Didaskalia (late 3rd c.)
    Donatists
    Arians
    Eunomians
    Messalians (?)
    Apollinarians
LXX Versions: Lucian's-Constantinople, Hesychius's-Alexandria, Origen's-Palestine

Church of Armenia (315), Gregory Illuminator
1st Ecumenical Council in Nicaea (325)
Patriarchate of the Church of Alexandria (325)
Patriarchate of the Church of Antioch (325)
Church of Georgia (330)
Constantinople founded by Constantine (330)
Eusebius of Caesarea (+340)
Church of Ethiopia (Abyssinia, mid c.)
Desert Fathers: Pachomius (+347), Antony (+356), Macarius of Egypt (+390)
Ephrem the Syrian (+373)
Athanasius of Alexandria (+373)
2nd Ecumenical Council in Constantinople (381)
Cyril of Jerusalem (+386)
Cappadocians: Basil (+379), Gregory Nazianzus (+389), Gregory of Nyssa (+394), John Chrysostom (+407)
Ambrose of Milan (+397)
Evagrius of Pontus (+399)
Makarian (Ps.) Homilies (date unknown)

400      Nestorians
     Pelagians
     Eutychians
     Monophysites

John Chrysostom (+407)
Autocephaly of the Church of Cyprus (413)
Jerome (+419)
Lausiac History (419)
Theodore of Mopsuestia (+428)
Augustine of Hippo (+430)
3rd Ecumenical Council in Ephesus (431)
Cyril of Alexandria (+444)
Tome of Leo (449)
4th Ecumenical Council in Chalcedon (451)
Ecumenical Patriarchate of the Church of Constantinople (451)
Patriarchate of the Church of Jerusalem (451)
Theodoret of Cyrrhus (+466)
Fall of Rome, 3rd barbarian invasion (476)
Acacian Schism (482–519)

500      Origenists

Dionysius (Ps., dates unknown)
Code of Justinian (529)
Hagia Sophia rebuilt (537)
Leontius of Byzantium (+543)

Chronology • 15

|      |                                                           |
|------|-----------------------------------------------------------|
|      | 5th Ecumenical Council in Constantinople (553)            |
|      | Romanos the Melodist (+555)                               |
|      | Jacob Baradeus (+578)                                     |
| 600  | Advent of Islam                                           |
|      | Monothelites                                              |
|      | Paulicians                                                |
|      | John Climacus (+649)                                      |
|      | Pope Martin (+655)                                        |
|      | Maximus Confessor (+662)                                  |
|      | 6th Ecumenical Council in Constantinople (680–681)        |
| 700  | Iconoclasts                                               |
|      | Andrew of Crete (+740)                                    |
|      | John of Damascus (+749)                                   |
|      | 7th Ecumenical Council in Nicaea (787)                    |
|      | Donation of Constantine (date unknown)                    |
| 800  | Iconoclasts                                               |
|      | Filioquists                                               |
|      | Charlemagne/Carolingians (800 f.)                         |
|      | Theodore of Studion (+826)                                |
|      | Triumph and Synodicon of Orthodoxy (842–843)              |
|      | Constantine-Cyril and Methodius (mid c.)                  |
|      | Encyclical Letter of Photius (867)                        |
| 900  | Bogomils (10th–14th c.)                                   |
|      | Naum of Ochrid (+910)                                     |
|      | Clement of Ochrid (+916)                                  |
|      | Patriarchate of Bulgaria (917)                            |
|      | Baptism of Kievan Rus' (988)                              |
| 1000 | Azymites                                                  |
|      | Platonists                                                |
|      | Crusaders (1095–1291)                                     |
|      | Athanasius of Athos (+1003)                               |
|      | Symeon the New Theologian (+1022)                         |
|      | Mutual excommunications, West and East (1054)             |
|      | First Letter of Michael Cerularius to Peter of Antioch (1054) |
|      | Autocephaly of the Church of Georgia (1089)               |
|      | Primary Chronicle of Rus'                                 |
| 1100 | Novgorodian Tradition (1156–1471)                         |
|      | Novgorodian "Questions of Kirik" (mid c.)                 |
|      | Zonaras, Balsamon, Canon Lawyers (mid c.)                 |
|      | Finnish Orthodox Church                                   |
| 1200 | Crusaders occupy Constantinople (1204–1261)               |

## 1300

Autonomy of the Church of Serbia (1219)
Tartar invasions of Rus' (1237)
Alexander Nevskii (+1263)
Barlaamites
Advent of Ottoman Empire
Patriarchate of the Church of Serbia (Pec, 1346)
Councils of Constantinople on Hesychasm (1341, 1351)
Gregory Palamas (+1359)
Battle of Kossovo (1389)
Sergius of Radonezh (+1392)
Zyryan Mission, Stephen of Perm

## 1400

Latinophones
Judaizing Heresy
Encyclical Letter of Mark of Ephesus (1440–1441)
Autocephaly of the Church of Russia (1448)
Fall of Constantinople (1453)
Confession of Faith by Gennadius of Constantinople (1455–1456)
Novgorodian Gennadievskii Church Slavic Bible (1499 f.)

## 1500

Protestants
Joseph of Volokolamsk (+1515)
Muscovite Council of 100 Chapters
Replies of Jeremias II to the Lutherans (1573–1581)
Ostrog Church Slavic Bible (1580–81)
1st Patriarchate of the Church of Russia (1589–1700)

## 1600

Uniates
Old Believers
Calvinists
Confession of Faith by Metrophanes Kritopoulos (1625)
Cyril Lukaris, Patriarch of Constantinople (+1638)
Confession of Peter Moghila (1642, Council of Jassy)
Kievan metropolitanate joins Moscow (1654)
Confession of Dositheus (1672, Synod of Bethlehem)

## 1700

Freemasons
Spiritual Regulation of Peter (25 January 1721)

Answers to the Non-Jurors of the Orthodox Patriarchs (1718, 1723)
Philokalia (1782, 1793)
Alaskan Mission, Herman of Alaska (1794)
Makrakians
Tolstoyans
Radstockists
Platon Levshin, Metropolitan of Moscow (+1812)
Seraphim of Sarov (+1833)
Slavophile Movement (1840–1850)
Reply to Pope Pius IX of the Orthodox Patriarchs (1848)
Autocephaly of the Church of Greece (1850)
Autocephaly of the Church of Romania (1859, 1885)
Japanese Orthodox Church (1873)
Russian Bible completed (1875)
Innocent, Metropolitan of Moscow (+1879)
Reply to Pope Leo XIII of the Synod of Constantinople (1895)
Pashkovists
Imyabozhniki
Old Calendarists
Living Churchmen
Advent of Communism
Reforms of the Russian Church (1905–1918)
Autocephalous-Catholicate of the Church of Georgia (1917)
2nd Patriarchate of the Church of Russia, Tikhon Belavin (1918)
2nd Patriarchate of the Church of Serbia (1920)
African (Ugandan) Orthodox Church (1920)
Encyclical Letters of the Patriarchate of Constantinople on the unity of Christians and the "Ecumenical Movement" (1920, 1952)
Autonomy of the Church of Czechoslovakia (1923)
Autonomy of the Church of Finland (1923)
Autocephaly of the Church of Poland (1924)
Patriarchate of Romania (1925)
Autocephaly of the Church of Albania (1937)
Autocephaly of the Church of Czech and Slovakia (1951)

Standing Conference of Orthodox Bps. in America (1960)
3rd Patriarchate of the Church of Bulgaria (1961)
Autocephaly of the Orthodox Church in America (1970)
Autonomy of the Ukrainian Orthodox Church (1993)

# The Dictionary

## -A-

**ACATHISTUS HYMN** *see* Mariology.

**AESTHETICS.** The philosophy of dealing with beauty and matters of taste, which may also describe the science of the arts and the wondrous experience of the worshiper. Although secular aesthetics may take the science of sensual knowledge as its point of departure, in the Christian experience aesthetics would not be strictly limited to the sensual. Generally speaking, there is an assumption that the true beauty of Orthodox worship comes from its co-participation in angelic worship and its manifestation of holiness. This does not mean that proportion, balance, and detail are neglected in music, architecture, iconography (qq.v.), etc., but rather the opposite is true. The aesthetics of the arts of the church are not valued for their own quiddity, but by how—in their ultimate expression—they are "transparent" to the Kingdom of God.

**AFANASIEV, NIKOLAI N.,** priest, theologian (4 September 1893 [O.S.]–4 December 1966). Born in Odessa, the son of a lawyer, he studied at the University of Novorossiisk, with a university level in mathematics and medicine. In 1920 he evacuated to Serbia, where he enrolled in the theological faculty of Belgrade University in the spring of 1921. There in 1927 he produced the thesis, in Serbian, "The Power of the State in the Ecumenical Councils." In Prague, 1925, he married Mariamna N. Andruskova, a niece of Heinrich Schliemann, after which he taught religion in a secondary school in Macedonia. In 1930 he moved to Paris to receive a stipendiary lectureship to teach at St. Sergius Orthodox Theological Institute (q.v.). He taught patristic history, then received the chair in Canon Law in 1932. He was made a deacon on 7 January 1940 and a priest the following day. In July 1941, he left France for Tunis to serve the Orthodox community there. He returned to Paris at the end of the war, continuing to teach at St. Sergius until his death. He was a founder of the Russian-language journal *Put*. His concept of "Eucharistic ecclesiology" has influenced a number of Orthodox thinkers, including Fr. Alexander Schmemann (q.v.).

**AFRICAN ORTHODOX CHURCH** *see* Ugandan Orthodox Church.

**AGRAPHA.** The term means literally "things not written." In Scripture (q.v.) studies it has the technical sense of sayings ascribed to Jesus, but not recorded in the canonical Gospels. These include sayings in other New Testament writings (e.g., Acts 20:35), various New Testament manuscripts, apocryphal gospels, early liturgies, rabbinical writings, and notably writings of the Church Fathers (q.v.). The first systematic study of agrapha was done by A. Resch in 1889, and had as its purpose the same goal as subsequent scholarship on the topic—to compile all agrapha and evaluate their authenticity. Among the Church Fathers, e.g., in Basil the Great's (q.v.) treatise *On the Holy Spirit* and in succeeding writers, the term connotes the liturgical practice of the Church, especially as a source of authority, together with the Scriptures (*he graphe*), for the articulation of Christian doctrine.

**ALASKA.** First missionized in 1794 by a group of about a dozen Russian monastic clergy from the Lake Ladoga region of Russia, Alaska hosted an Orthodox presence among the indigenous population that continues to the present. The clergy who first went there followed the Russian fur trade and began ministering to fellow Russians. These clergy had received a tacit, if not explicit, education in the evangelization of peoples with animistic beliefs in their travels across Russia and Siberia on their way to Alaska. As a result, they soon evangelized natives and expended considerable effort protecting them from their Russian overseers, who conscripted them into hunting for profit. During the time of the fur trade—which took the Russians as far south as Fort Ross (q.v.), California, just north of San Francisco—the native population was educated and served by such noteworthy people as the Elder Herman and Bishop Innocent (Veniaminov) (qq.v.). Historians have identified this era as the earlier history of "Russian America" (q.v.).

From 1867 to 1900, after Russia's sale of Alaska to the United States, the Russian Church spent more money on the education of Alaskan natives than did the U.S. government. The latter dealt with the natives by suppressing their languages and cultures, separating children from their families, and reeducating them, policies directly opposed to those of the Russian Church. These policies continued well into the 20th c. under the advocacy of the Bureau of Indian Affairs. By this time a number of natives had assumed clergy leadership roles in the vacuum created by the Russian Mission relocating to the "lower forty-eight." The Orthodox Church is widely recognized by modern scholars and historians as a principal cultural legacy of the history of Alaska.

As the largest Christian "denomination" in Alaska today, much of the indigenous population largely identifies its religion as Russian or native Orthodox. They are served and led by native clergy educated at the St. Herman's Seminary in Sitka. The last twenty years has seen an explosive revival in Alaska. In 1972 there were nine clergy and eighty communities, while in 1990 there were thirty-seven clergy, half of whom were native, and thirty-three new churches. The Orthodox Church was the only place native languages could be used to the present. The State of Alaska values the churches and traditions as a cultural treasure.

**ALBANIA.** The origin of the Albanians is a matter of conjecture and debate. Some hold that they stem from the inhabitants of Roman Illyria (q.v.) before the Slavic invasions of the 6th c., but this does not enjoy universal acceptance. They were subjected to the Byzantines and Orthodoxy (840) and later to the Slavs. From the 14th c. to the 16th c., Albania resisted the Turks and divided its Christian allegiance between Orthodoxy and Rome (qq.v.). Through persecution and favoritism, the Turks encouraged the population to accept Islam (q.v.). The country became independent in 1913 and its Orthodox Church became autocephalous (q.v.) in 1922. At present, approximately 20 percent of the population is Orthodox Christian—or at least of Orthodox background. The Church in Albania was under the jurisdiction of the Ecumenical Patriarch (q.v.) until achieving administrative independence in 1937, but the depredations of the regime of Enver Hoxa and his successors, in power from the end of World War II until the beginning of the 1990s, effected the official and total rejection of all forms of religious belief. The post-Hoxa era has seen the reestablishment of the church under Archbishop Anasatasios (Yannoulatos) (q.v.) with the assistance of the Ecumenical Patriarch.

**ALEXANDER NEVSKII,** prince, St. (ca. 1220–1263). He became Prince of Novgorod in his youth and led the city to a series of striking victories over the crusading order of Teutonic Knights, marking thereby the eastern limits of German expansion. His defeat of the Knights on the frozen waters of Lake Peipus in 1242 won him great renown, and his victory over the Swedes invading from the north on the banks of the frozen river Neva earned him the surname Nevskii.

Alexander is remembered in the Russian Church as a saint (canonized 1380), less for his exploits as a military hero, however, than as an intercessor for the Russian lands at the court of the Mongol Khans. In 1250 Alexander was appointed Grand Prince of Russia by the Khan, a title that entailed the supervision of taxation and the suppression of revolt. His nobility and true heroism lay in his patient endurance of continual humiliation, inflicted on him by resentful countrymen and overbearing masters. This he suffered for the sake of Russia's eventual liberation and the safeguarding of her Christian faith, the first of which he saw could not be achieved in his own lifetime. Exhausted by no less than three extended trips to the Khan's court in Mongolia seeking clemency for rebellious Russians, he died so journeying in 1263. The same year saw the establishment of one of his sons, Daniel (q.v.), as prince of the small city of Moscow, the beginning of the royal line that would accomplish Russia's freedom.

**ALEXANDRIA.** The city was founded by Alexander the Great just to the west of the Nile Delta in 331 B.C. Under the Ptolemies, Alexandria rose to prominence as capital of Egypt (q.v.) and one of the great cities of the Hellenistic world, indeed as that world's intellectual center. The Greek translation of the Hebrew Scriptures (q.v.), dating approximately to the 3rd c. and 2nd c. B.C., and the other Scriptures originally written in Greek, are associated most closely with the Jewish populations of Alexandria and Cyrene. The acceptance of this Septuagint (q.v.) translation by the Greek-speaking Jewish population of Egypt not only constituted a remarkable event in the history of religions, but made possible the later translations of the Jewish and Christian Scriptures into other languages.

Incorporated into the Roman Empire (q.v.), the city remained the intellectual capital of the larger Greco-Roman universe until its conquest by the armies of Islam (q.v.) in 642. Hence, the earlier period of the Christian Church, in particular of Greek-speaking Christianity, from the end of the 2nd c. until the Ecumenical Council (q.v.) of Chalcedon (451) was under the sway of Alexandria. Its great archbishops, Dionysius (q.v.), Athanasius (q.v.), Theophilus, Cyril (q.v.), and Dioscurus succeeded—with the exception of the last—in imposing their theological vision on the Christian *oikoumene* (q.v.), and were unquestionably the most powerful and influential churchmen outside of Rome (q.v.) itself.

One reason for dominance, outside of the demographic significance of this second largest city of the Empire, lay in the establishment of the Alexandrian School (of exegesis) in the late 2nd c. By no coincidence, in the preceding century Philo of Alexandria laid the foundation for this school with his extensive use of allegory (q.v.), which he employed to explain Jewish religion and Scripture to a Hellenistic world. A succession of remarkable Christian teachers and thinkers, including Clement in the 2nd c., Origen (qq.v.) in the 3rd c., and Didymus the Blind in the 4th c., sought to apply the insights of Greek philosophy and the techniques of Greek rhetoric systematically to the elaboration and explication of the Christian Gospel. Significantly, it resulted in the beginnings of Christian Hellenism (q.v.) and opened up the way to the great Church Fathers (q.v.) of later centuries and to the culture of Christian Byzantium (q.v.). This work, particularly in the hands of a series of bishops who were able thinkers in their own right, did much to inform and determine the great debates over the Trinity and Christology (qq.v.) in the 4th c. through 7th c.

Alexandria is still the offical title of a patriarchate (q.v.)—in fact, two of them. Both the Greek and the Coptic church (qq.v.) leaders take their name from this city, though both have been resident in Cairo for many centuries.

**ALEXIS II (RIDIGER),** Patr. of Moscow *see* Ridiger, Alexis.

**ALIVISATOS, HAMILKAR S.** (17 May 1887–14 August 1969). A Greek Orthodox lay theologian who obtained his doctorate in Athens (1908) for his thesis on John Chrysostom (q.v.), then studied church history at Berlin and Leipzig. He became professor of Canon Law and pastoral theology at Athens in 1918. In 1927 he took part in the Universal Christian Conference on Life and Work, Stockholm, and again at the World Conference on Faith and Order, Lausanne, 1927. In 1936 he organized and presided over the first International Congress of Orthodox Theology at Athens. He was a member of the World Council of Churches' Central Committee from 1948 to 1969, and served on the Faith and Order Commission and the Committee on Intercommunion. He was always a vocal proponent of Orthodox involvement in the ecumenical movement (q.v.). He was also actively involved in the Greek Ministry of Education and was a state representative to the Holy Synod.

**ALLEGORY.** The Greek root means literally "to say something else." In modern terms it refers to a veiled or figurative presentation, wherein the elements of the presentation are symbolic of substituted values. In the Hellenistic world, it signified the bringing out of hidden meanings from a sacred text, and was elaborated as a technique for the literary and philosophical exegesis of texts (e.g., Homer, Hesiod), which a cultivated society found embarrassing as sacred scripture. The term "allegory" is used in one place in the New Testament (Gal 4:24), though the technique is employed without the use of the term elsewhere (e.g., Is 5:1–6; Mt 13:19 f.); but it was a 1st c. Alexandrian Jew, Philo, who first applied the method in a thoroughgoing way to the Old Testament in order to explicate the sublime and lofty character of the Jewish faith. Christian writers of Alexandria (q.v.), perhaps as early as the *Epistle of Barnabas* (q.v.) in about 150, and definitively with

Clement and Origen (qq.v.) later, took Philo's lead and used the technique to demonstrate the rationality, moral quality, and mystical calling of Christianity. Gregory of Nyssa (q.v.) was the 4th c.'s most able practitioner of this art of exegesis, carrying on the torch of the great Alexandrians and contributing significantly to the development of Christian Greek thought—in particular with his *Life of Moses*. Allegory thus contributed to the Christian acquisition of the philosophical patrimony and to the "interiorization" of the Scriptures (q.v.) in the long Holy Tradition of Orthodox spiritual literature (q.v.).

**ALLELUIA.** This Hebrew transliteration into many languages means "praise the Lord" (Yah being short for Yahweh or the Lord). As in the Roman mass, the alleluia sung with interspersed psalm verses precedes the Gospel reading in the liturgies (q.v.) of St. John Chrysostom and St. Basil (q.v.). The singing of alleluia also precedes the troparia of matins during Holy Week. The recitation of alleluia during prayers occurs frequently, especially after psalm readings (kathismata) in the daily cycle of services (e.g., vespers, matins, hours). The definition in *Webster's Third International Dictionary,* which includes the statement, "an expression of humble mourning in the Eastern Orthodox Church," can only be taken as a misunderstanding, probably a result of the liturgical setting of alleluia funerary tones. If the context of any liturgical occurrence is closely examined, one finds that alleluia can never be a lament, but can only mean "praise the Lord," and is commensurately understood as such by the Orthodox.

Historically, in the singing of alleluia the movement of the music (q.v.) focuses on the last, most important syllable, which is as it should be, since this syllable is an abbreviated form of the divine name. In the Russian tradition another syllable (ee) has been added before "Yah," since the Greek transliteration of the Hebrew (ia = yah) was not understood to be a diphthong by the Church Slavic translators of the 9th and 10th centuries. The mistake is occasionally repeated in modern translations from Church Slavic (or Russian) into English.

**ALMSGIVING** *see* Ascesis.

**AMBROSE OF MILAN,** St. (ca. 339–397). This Latin Church Father (q.v.), considered one of the four traditional Doctors of the West, was a Roman magistrate, not yet baptized, when elected to the see of Milan in 374. He proved a wise choice as a powerful teacher, exegete, and defender of the moral authority of the Church, and interacted with several rulers of the Western Empire. His most noted exploit was doubtless forcing Emperor Theodosius I to do public penance in 390 for the latter's (not unprovoked) slaughter of Thessalonian rioters. He was perhaps more influential on subsequent Christian thought and culture through his deep acquaintance with Greek theology—in particular with Origen (q.v.)—and his transmission of some of this knowledge, however indirectly, to his great admirer, Augustine of Hippo (q.v.). In addition to composing hymns and writing letters, he is best known for his homiletical and written instruction on ethics and the sacraments, especially *De Sacramentis* and *De Officiis Ministrorum*.

**AMERICAN ORTHODOXY** *see* Orthodox Church in America.

**ANABAPTISTS** *see* Evangelical Brethren.

**ANASTASIOS (YANNOULATOS),** Archbishop of Albania *see* Yannoulatos, Anastasios.

**ANCYRA.** Now Ankara, a city of central Asia Minor (q.v.), the capital of the Roman province of Galatia and early the site of a Christian church, it rose to prominence and occasional notoriety as a theological center. Two important councils held there dealt with issues such as the reconciliation to the Church of those who lapsed during persecution and the penitential system (A.D. 314), and the Semi-Arian issue of Christology (q.v.) and the *"homoousios"* (358)—which term Bishop Basil of Ancyra rejected along with Arianism (q.v.). One of its best-known bishops, Marcellus (d. ca. 375), was roundly condemned by most of his eastern peers as a Trinitarian Modalist, but supported by Rome, Athanasius (qq.v.), and the West in general. The see was raised to the dignity of a metropolitanate in the 4th c. and continued to be one of the most important church centers in the region for the remainder of the first millennium. In the 20th c. Ankara became the capital of the Turkish Republic under Kemal Ataturk, marking the conclusion of the Ottoman Empire (q.v.).

**ANDERSON, PAUL B.,** churchman, international YMCA church projects facilitator (27 December 1894–26 June 1985). From 1913 to 1917 he served the YMCA in Shanghai, China, and from 1917 to 1918, directed aid for Russian and Siberian prisoners of war. He received a B.A. from the University of Iowa in 1920 and did graduate work at Oxford University. From the early 1920s on, he worked for the YMCA to aid Russian émigrés in Europe, particularly in Paris. Along with other YMCA officials, especially Gustave G. Kullmann and Ralph Hollinger, he was able to change the YMCA policy of organizing generic events in YMCA centers to the policy of giving aid to projects that were specifically meaningful to Russians and implemented within Russian organizations. Of special note, he was instrumental in founding (1924) and giving continuing support to St. Sergius Orthodox Theological Institute (q.v.), a branch of the Russian Student Christian Movement, and the YMCA Russian-language press in Paris, which he served as director and editor. Also, from September 1935 to November 1942 he played an important role in channeling American YMCA funds to support Orthodox Action, the Russian émigré Christian social action organization, working closely with Metropolitan Evlogii (q.v.) in all of these projects. He was honorarily awarded a Th.D. from St. Sergius Institute for his services. He was the editor of the journal *Living Church* and he is the author of *People, Church and State in Modern Russia* (1944). His reminiscences were published as *No East or West* (1985).

**ANDREW OF CRETE,** bishop, St. (ca. 660–740). Tonsured monk at the Church of the Resurrection (Holy Sepulcher) in Jerusalem in his youth and consecrated bishop in Crete ca. 700, Andrew is best known for his penitential "Great Canon," a long meditation on the Scriptures (q.v.) in poetic form, which is still read in Orthodox churches during Great Lent (q.v.). This work set the standard for a new and eventually dominant style of liturgical composition, the canon, to be further developed by John of Damascus (q.v.), a younger contemporary of Andrew's from his native city. Cosmas the Hymnographer, Theodore of Studion (qq.v.), Joseph of Studion, and Kassia the nun also contributed to the musical genre canon. (*See* Music.)

**ANNUNCIATION** *see* Feasts, Twelve Great.

**ANOINTING OF THE SICK** *see* Healing.

**ANTHONY (BLOOM),** Metropolitan of Sourozh *see* Bloom, Anthony.

**ANTHONY,** St. *see* Antony.

**ANTHROPOLOGY.** The word means the study, in our case theology, of the human being. It is important to stress two things about Orthodox anthropology: first, Orthodoxy's emphasis on the mystery of the human being and, second, that a proper appreciation of this mystery is necessary for the correct understanding of sin (q.v.), of salvation, of the person and work of Christ, and indeed of all theology (q.v.). The mystery of human existence is rooted in Gen, particularly Gen 1:26, and the creation of "Man" or humankind—i.e., both male and female—as "in the image and according to the likeness" of God. The "image of God" in the Church Fathers (q.v.) is understood in both an individual and a collective sense, as it is in Gen 1:27. "Adam" is at once the first human and all of humanity, *anthropos* in general. From the moment of creation, the first human is intended to sum up all of creation in "himself" and offer it to the Creator. In its original potential, human existence is therefore a microcosm, a little world, and is called to mediate between God in Trinity (q.v.) and the universe. Individually each human has the vocation to mirror the divine energies; and collectively all humanity finds its ultimate vocation in the call to image forth the uncreated Trinity as a union of persons bound together in a single life and love.

This is the vocation that Adam and Eve failed to accomplish and that Christ accomplished once and for all, *ephapax* (Heb 7:27). The Fall was a failure of the will, a deliberate rejection of the vocation to act as universal priest, and a turning instead, inwardly, to the glorification of self and, outwardly, to the worship of creation in place of the Creator. This is the original apostasy that, together with its consequences, Orthodoxy sums up under the phrase, "the ancestral sin" (*to propaterikon hamartema*). Here we may note significant differences with the thought of Augustine of Hippo (q.v.). The latter saw the inheritance of the Fall as that "original sin" from which every human being inherits both guilt and condemnation. It is a disaster so great that the image of God has been, if not obliterated, then at least rendered powerless. The will is frozen in evil. For Augustine this condemnation is transmitted from one generation to the next through sexual procreation, hence the extraordinarily great importance he attaches to sexual appetite, concupiscence (q.v.). The Greek Fathers, on the whole, differ from him. The ancestral sin does not destroy the will, but it does weaken it. The mystery of the divine image remains. Those consequences that the first sin unleashed, however, alter the conditions of existence in such a way as to render sin virtually inevitable. The powers of sin and death, as Orthodoxy reads Paul (e.g., Rom 5:12), have a personal, hypostatic existence. They are alien and inimical forces, the devil ("he who has the power of death," Heb 2:14) or "prince of this world" (e.g., Jn 14:30), who have invaded God's creation through the sin of the first humans. Instead of integration, the fallen world is thus locked in a process of disintegration and corruption that leads toward ultimate nonbeing, a relapse into the nil from which creation was originally called.

This process applies first and foremost to the human microcosm. Created as soul and body and meant to bring together spiritual and physical reality, and so finally to bridge the chasm between Creator and creation in such a way as to bring the community of the latter into the likeness of the divine community of the Trinity, the fallen human composite is the first to come apart. Soul and body are at war with each other, each part feeding on its inferior. The intellect (*nous*) looks to the emotions for satisfaction. The emotive capacity of the soul turns to the body and its natural appetites, while the body takes its sustenance from lifeless matter. All is therefore reversed. Everything becomes a matter of appetite fueled in the last analysis by the demands of a demonic pride.

Into this cycle of consuming and dying Christ, the "Second Adam," came to restore humanity to its original calling by accomplishing that vocation, once and for all, in himself. Through his birth, death, and resurrection, he restored the lost integration of humanity and established the "new creation." It is up to the individual Christian, however, to discover in him- or herself the realization of Christ's accomplishment and presence, i.e., to arrive through him in the Holy Spirit (q.v.) at the manifestation of his likeness. All potential has been restored in Christ. The powers of sin and death have been overcome and "life reigns from the tomb," to quote the Easter oration of John Chrysostom (q.v.). Heaven and earth have been united forevermore.

Nonetheless, in Orthodoxy the mystery of the image of God in every human being demands the possibility of both assent and refusal. The grace (q.v.) of Christ cannot be "irresistible." Although the ontological condition of nature has been altered—or better, restored—in Christ, each person is required to bring his or her own will into conformity with the salvation that he, uniquely, has accomplished. This is the place for what Orthodox asceticism (q.v.) calls the "ordeal" (*agon*), the reeducation of the will. Nature has been healed, but the person—*hypostasis,* or irreducible individuality—of every human being is called, with the assistance of grace, to realize in itself what has already occurred through the union of human nature with the Second Person of the Trinity (the "hypostatic union"). Orthodoxy requires, in short, that every human person choose what he or she has already become in Christ Jesus. Hence, God permits his creature to be "tempted," i.e., put to the test. This life is thus the "arena," the place of combat—or better, the sphere of that choice required by the Creator out of respect for the mystery of his creature's freedom (q.v.).

In turning to the modern debate over human nature, particularly the issues of gender raised by contemporary feminism, "gay rights," and "alternative lifestyles," Orthodoxy displays at once a certain intransigence and a replay of debates from its own past in the patristic tradition. Intransigence because the nature of sexual relations—and sexual politics—must be read in the light of a revelation not easily dismissed in order to be in accord with contemporary fashions. Given the revelation, for example, it is difficult to see how an argument defending the possiblity of sexual intercourse between people of the same gender could be constructed. Holy Tradition (q.v.) is consistently unambiguous on that score.

The matter of gender, however, is much more complex. Here we might suggest that a key lies in the particular scriptural account of creation to which one gives precedence. Gen 1 presents male and female as simultaneously and (presumably) equally made "in the image." Gen 2, on the other hand, seems to have the male created first and the woman second as "an help meet for him" (KJV). A very ancient line of patristic exegesis, running from at least Origen to Gregory of Nyssa (qq.v.), sees the first account as eternally valid and the second as a divine provision for the Fall. According to this reading, probably influenced by gnosticism (q.v.), gender is a feature of fallen humanity. This approach, however, raised very serious problems for Christian Orthodoxy concerning the permanent value of the body. It led in practice to a kind of spiritualism that was also inimical, in the long run, to the cosmic significance of Christ. On the other hand, priority accorded to the second account, for example, the path of Symeon the New Theologian (q.v.), raises grave and perhaps justified contemporary difficulties regarding justice and equality. The issue is therefore open and the debate in the Orthodox world has only just begun.

**ANTIOCH.** This capital of the Seleucid Empire was founded in 300 B.C., and was the center of Hellenistic culture on the east Mediterranean seaboard from Palestine to Asia Minor (q.v.) and inland to Mesopotamia. Its incorporation into the Roman Empire (q.v.) in the 1st c. B.C. gave it a place as the third city of the realm and capital of the "East." Site of a Christian church from the beginnings of the faith and the place where the followers of Christ were first called Christians (e.g., Acts 11:19 ff.), traditionally its first bishop was identified as the Apostle Peter. We know from the Pauline corpus that the church there supported Paul's anti-Judaizing policy, and at least one of the Gospels was written there. The seven letter corpus of Ignatius (q.v.) is also associated with Antioch. Its bishop was ranked as third in importance, after Rome and Alexandria (qq.v.), and recognized as such by the First Ecumenical Council (q.v.) at Nicaea (325).

Just as with Alexandria, Antioch had its own distinctive tradition of scriptural exegesis and theological approach, although unlike Alexandrians the Antiochenes tended to eschew allegory (q.v.) and favor a more literal, historical approach to the sacred texts. This had its consequences in Christology (q.v.). Antiochene writers and scholars preferred a greater emphasis on the humanity of Jesus than was generally characteristic of the Alexandrians, so much so that it sometimes appeared the unity of God and man in Christ was imperiled. Of the most notable Antiochene exegetes—Diodore of Tarsus, Theodore of Mopsuestia, Theodoret of Cyrrhus (qq.v.), for example—only the last narrowly escaped posthumous condemnation. Antiochene theology held great sway in Constantinople, and resultingly in the entire Empire, through the Cappadocian Fathers and the Antiochene bishop transferred there, John Chrysostom (qq.v.).

The Christological controversies in the aftermath of the Ecumenical Council of Chalcedon (451) resulted in the loss of Antioch's power. The Church was divided into three warring powers: Nestorians, monophysites (qq.v.), and the Orthodox—the latter known as "Melchites" (q.v.), i.e., observers of the faith of the emperors. The rise of Islam (q.v.) two hundred years later completed the sad picture and ended in the conversion of that region away from Christianity. The school of Antioch did continue, indeed, but safely beyond the borders of the Empire among the east Syrian scholars of the Nestorian church (*see* Assyrian Church) where Theodore of Mopsuestia was revered as the master of exegetes. Today the Orthodox Church of Antioch presides over a community of half a million souls in Syria and Lebanon, primarily, but includes adherents in southeast Turkey (q.v.), Iraq, and the Americas. Altogether Arab-speaking in its homelands, it has been trying to adapt itself to its surroundings for the past century. Given the huge majorities of Muslims there today and the rising temperature of "fundamentalistic" Muslim feelings, its future appears such as will require great heroism.

**ANTIOCHIAN ORTHODOX CHRISTIAN ARCHDIOCESE OF NEW YORK AND ALL NORTH AMERICA.** Under the jurisdiction of the Patriarch of Antioch (q.v.), and historically the Syrian Antiochian Orthodox Archdiocese of New York and All North America, this group of approximately two hundred parishes in the United States and Canada is ruled by Archbishop Philip Saliba (q.v.) and four suffragans. Its formal origins date from the early 1930s when Antony Bashir (q.v.) was consecrated archbishop for America by the Antiochene patriarchate in order to care for the communities of Arabic-speaking Orthodox from Lebanon, Syria, and Palestine. Before this, these peoples were served by the Russian-trained Arab, Bishop Raphael Hawaweeny (q.v.), of the Russian Orthodox Missionary Diocese and Archbishop Victor Abu-Assaly.

The Archdiocese has been a leader in encouraging the translation of liturgical services into English and in the promotion of Western-rite Orthodox communities. Archbishop Philip is an important member of the Standing Conference of Orthodox Bishops in America (q.v.), of which his predecessor was a key founder, as well as a persistent advocate of the canonical normalization of the chaotic diaspora.

**ANTONY,** monk, ascetic, St. (ca. 250–356). An Egyptian ascetic called with some justice the father of monasticism (q.v.), his *Life,* traditionally the composition of Athanasius of Alexandria (q.v.), was composed shortly after his death. It played nothing less than a revolutionary role in the Empire of late antiquity through its portrayal of the "man of God." Although the *Life* has clear connections with the stories of "divine men" popular in pagan literature of the time and was the Christian "best-seller" of the 4th c., its fundamental thrust is the presentation of a figure akin to the great prophets and saints of the Old and New Testaments: Antony is one in whom the power of the Spirit, the gift of the risen Christ, lives and acts. He was, says Athanasius, the "physician of all Egypt" and beyond. The *Life* records the arrival of pilgrims to the hut of the holy man (q.v.) coming to him from throughout the Empire. Even the emperor is said to have corresponded with him. While doubtless shaped by the rhetorical conventions of the day, it is hard to deny that this account, coming so soon after the saint's death, had a basis in actual experience. Whatever the case, it is incontestable that the story of Antony the hermit and saint influenced—and continues to influence—the life of countless Orthodox Christians. The portrait it presents became the paradigm of the ascetic and charismatic elders (*gerontes, startzi*). They serve in every generation as an example for other monks and confessors of the faithful—an assurance for all that the Kingdom of God is not "pie in the sky" but an immanent reality and a genuine possiblity.

**ANTONY (KHRAPOVITZKY),** Metropolitan *see* Khrapovitzky, Antonii.

**APHTHARTODOCETISM** *see* Julian of Halicarnassus.

**APOCATASTASIS.** Fully, *apocatastasis panton* is "the restoration of all things." The source of this phrase, i.e., that all things and beings (angels and demons included) will ultimately be restored to unity with God, is 1 Cor 15, when God will be "all in all." Its best-known advocate was Origen of Alexandria, though Gregory of Nyssa (qq.v.) a century later echoed the latter's views on this issue. The proposal that hell cannot be eternal is surely to be ascribed to a certain optimism, with origins in Platonism, that evil cannot reasonably have the last word for any rational creature. Although this doctrine was condemned by the Council of Constantinople (553), it took the work of Maximus the Confessor (q.v.) a century later to demonstrate that true respect for the depths of human freedom (q.v.) requires the possibility of an everlasting perdition. Fear of a revival of the doctrine also lay behind the initial Greek reaction to the Latin Church's doctrine of purgatory, worked out in the 13th c. The latter's "purifying fire" smacked all too much for the Greek bishops at the Reunion Council of Ferrara-Florence (q.v.) of

Origen's view that hell was temporary. While it is possible to give an Orthodox reading of the Latin teaching, it is also the case that the latter, based as it was (is?) on ideas of penalty and satisfaction, would itself have to undergo a certain evolution in order to satisfy Orthodox concerns.

**APOCRYPHA** *see* Scripture.

**APOLOGETICS AND APOLOGISTS.** The genre, apologetics, is concerned with the defense and explanation of the faith to those who do not share it, and by extension, to those who dissent from it. This type of writing began with the Christian Apologists of the 2nd c. who sought to defend the reasonableness of Christianity to the Roman emperors and the public. Theirs were the first conscious attempts to reach out, therefore, to the larger world of Greco-Roman educated opinion, i.e., to the philosophical and pagan patrimony of antiquity, as well as to specifically Jewish objections. Writing in Greek during this period were Quadratus (fl.130s), Aristides (140s), Justin Martyr (d.163 [q.v.]), Tatian (170s), and Theophilus of Antioch (180s). Tertullian (q.v.) and Minucius Felix wrote important works in Latin around 200. The genre would continue into the 3rd and 4th c. with both Origen and Eusebius of Caesarea (qq.v.) providing powerful replies to pagan criticisms of Christianity.

**APOLOGISTS** *see* Apologetics.

**APOPHATIC THEOLOGY.** From *apophasis* (*apo phemi*, literally "to say away," or as a noun, "negation"), it is the opposite of *kataphasis* (affirmation). Applied to God (q.v.), the term means to say what God is not. Evidence of apophatic sensibilities expressed in Scripture (q.v.) may be found in the revelation of the name of God in Ex, the ascent of Moses on the mountain, Paul's description of his ecstatic spiritual experience, et al. Later in Platonism, and especially the late Platonism of the Church Fathers (qq.v.), it was commonplace to refuse to ascribe to God (or the One) any predicate derived from the phenomenal world. The One precisely as "One," unity, precludes any intellectual construct: all constructions and all ideas belong to the multiple. Taken up by Christian writers as early as Irenaeus (q.v.), and achieving its definitive expression in Dionysius the Areopagite (q.v.), apophatic theology became a given of Orthodox thought. At the hands of these Fathers, however, it referred to God's transcendence as Creator and hence to the infinite chasm between the Maker and all that is made. Thus, the *ousia*, or essence of God, is everlastingly unknowable and unattainable.

**APOSTASY.** From the Greek "defection" (or literally "standing off") and beginning with a political association ("rebel"), it came to mean an abandonment or renunciation of God and religion in the Septuagint (q.v.) (Josh 22:22; 2 Chr 29:19). Paul is accused of apostasy in Acts 21:21 when he did not require Christian Jews to keep the Law of Moses. Another different reference to general apostasy is recorded in 2 Th 2:3–4, which reflects Jewish apocalyptic expectations (cf. Dan 11:36–37) of the end time. Apostasy from Christianity is considered an unpardonable sin in Heb 6:1–8. Theological justification for strictness in dealing with apostasy is given in 2 Clement 8: Since there is no repentance after death, it is important to keep the flesh pure and the seal of baptism undefiled (see also chs. 9, 17). Whether these references were a localized interpretation, tautological (i.e., one who is defecting cannot be simultaneously repenting), or the universal teaching in the 1st c. A.D., denunciations of apostates soon changed somewhat and appeared in a modified form. In the earliest Christian interpretation, apostasy—as murder or fornication—was accounted unpardonable sin (q.v.).

In the *Shepherd of Hermas* (q.v.), dated to about the same time as 2 Clement (mid–2nd c.), there are numerous references to the possibility of repentance after apostasy, although apostates are in the last instance labeled worse than unbelievers (Similitude 9.XVIII.1–4). Mandate 4.III speaks of repentance for sin after Baptism (q.v.), and the next section goes on to talk about second marriages. Sim. 8.VI explains the possibility of repentance with many examples illustrating that almost every, if not every, apostasy or sin may be absolved. Similarly, Sim. 9.XIII.6 f. describes the "rejected stones" who were apostate after fleshly things, and that they also have the possibility of repentance (9.XIV.1–3). The Church continued to utilize the antithetical tension between Hebrews and Hermas, frequently requiring public penance of baptized persons guilty of apostasy. (*See* Confession.)

**APOSTLE.** 1) From Greek meaning a "messenger" or "one sent," it is most probably Biblically related to the Hebrew *shaliach,* which is used of Moses, Elijah, Elisha, and Ezekiel, who function as God's ambassadors. Thus, Jesus identified himself as being "sent" by the Father and his followers became apostles when they were "sent out" by him to proclaim the Gospel and continue his ministry, previous to which they were only disciples. Noted apostles include the Twelve, Matthias who replaced Judas, and Paul and Barnabas as apostles to the Gentiles. Still, the Orthodox Church continues the list to include the Seventy (Lk 10), if not the 500 (1 Cor 15), then all who subsequently function as apostles to other peoples, e.g., Mary Magdalene, Nina of Georgia, Constantine-Cyril and Methodius, Innocent Veniaminov (qq.v.), et al.

The significant difference between this reckoning and the Western definition is that many women are included in the Eastern list, possessing the same "authority" as apostle as their male counterparts. Also, the list of apostles is clearly distinguishable from the list of bishops, since the ministries function differently. Apostleship is clearly a ministry open to women in the Eastern Church. Further, the honorific "equal-to-the-apostles" is applied to temporal rulers responsible for establishing Christianity in their domains. Thus, the pairs Constantine and Helen, and Vladimir and Olga, are accorded the titles equal-to-the-apostles for making Christianity the state religion of the Roman-Byzantine and Rus'-Russian Empires, respectively. It is well known in the Orthodox ethos that the Christian commitment of the older matriarch in each of these two pairs preceded that of the male; and the conversions of two of the largest empires was initiated by and is dependent upon these women. 2) The name of the epistle reading during the Divine Liturgy, always taken from Acts or one of the epistles; similarly, it is the name of the liturgical book (q.v.) containing Acts and all the epistles.

**APOSTOLIC CONSTITUTIONS.** A Syrian work of the late 4th c. incorporating earlier elements, e.g., the *Didaskalia Apostolorum* (q.v.), this is an early church order detailing the roles of bishops and other clergy, the celebrations of the sacraments (Baptism and Eucharist [qq.v.]), and especially the discipline of penitents. It is presented as a series of instructions or "injunctions" delivered by the Apostles (q.v.) to their successors. Its compiler may have been a bishop of Arian persuasion (in the broad sense of "Arian"), named Julian of Neapolis, obliged to express his ideas via the medium of an "apostolic" discourse, due to the prior approval of the Nicene Creed (q.v.) and the Council of Constantinople in 381. The work was condemned as a heretical forgery by the Council in Trullo (691), but did manage to remain in manuscript circulation. It is an invaluable witness to 4th c. liturgy (q.v.); and the compiler's particular theological opinions only occasionally obtrude.

**APOSTOLIC SUCCESSION.** The phrase refers in sum to the continuity of the authority of the twelve Apostles (q.v.), in particular via the Church's episcopate. The underlying idea is that the Church of today is fundamentally one with that of the Apostles and of Christ, with the bishops the primary guarantors of this continuity. The phrase, or at least the idea, surfaces earliest in Clement of Rome and, in particular, in Irenaeus of Lyons's arguments against gnosticism (qq.v.).

Christian gnosticism claimed to be representing the true faith of Christ's disciples, or at least of the select few whom the Savior led into an alleged secret tradition. Irenaeus replied that the faith of the chosen was never hidden, but indeed is proclaimed openly in the "apostolic" sees. The communion among these sees and with all "catholic" (q.v.) communities demonstrates that the teaching succession of the Apostles is not the property of a select few. It is one and the same with the teaching proclaimed by all the bishops throughout the world who remain in communion with one another. The idea of the succession will later acquire its association with the physical laying on of hands in the service of the consecration of bishops.

**APOSTOLIC TRADITION.** Although appearing in the manuscript tradition without either title or author and called the "Egyptian Church Order" in the 19th c., this document appears to have been the work of Hippolytus (q.v.) of Rome (fl. early 3rd c.). As such, it constitutes the earliest church order extant and is thus a priceless witness to the liturgy (q.v.) of the first Christian centuries. The outline and prayers of the Eucharist (q.v.), of episcopal, presbyterial, and diaconal ordination, are all given, as are a brief account of the requirements of the catechumenate (q.v.) and the text of the baptismal service. It is highly likely that the services described are those of the Roman Church.

**ARABIC CHURCH.** Christian penetration of Arabic-speaking territories, at least in their northernmost regions, certainly dates to the earliest years of the Church. Documentary evidence, other than Paul's reference to a stay in Arabia in Gal 2 (probably the Nabateaan kingdom in present-day south Jordan), is limited to the mid–3rd c. The *Dialogue with Heraclides* comprises minutes of an Arabian synod starring no less than the great Alexandrian theologian, Origen (q.v.), who was imported by the local bishops to settle theological questions with one of their number. Beyond the Roman province of Arabia, though, evidence is scarce until later centuries. Certainly by the 6th c., Christian communities existed in the Persian Gulf territories (Isaac of Nineveh [q.v.] was a native of Qatar), the Yemen, and Oman. The translation of the Scripture (q.v.) into Arabic seems to have occurred coterminously with the rise of Islam (q.v.), although the version now in use dates to much more recent times. The contemporary Orthodox churches of Antioch (Damascus), Alexandria, and Jerusalem (qq.v.) — in particular the first and third — are comprised primarily of Arabic speakers who have been worshiping in their own language for several hundred years.

**ARCHITECTURE, CHURCH.** The house-church at Dura-Europas (ca. 200–250) is the oldest one yet discovered. The earliest Christians worshiped secretly in both houses and catacombs, and no distinctive architecture seems to have been developed until Christianity became the official religion of the Empire. Even then, the early (Christian) basilica design (drawings #1, #2) employed in the construction of the Constantinian churches was largely adoptive and is called the "long design." Simultaneously, the adoptive round or polygonal domed church (drawings #3, #4), technically termed the "central-plan design," was constructed by Constantinian imperial patrons. The focuses of the two designs are radically different. Apparent from the drawings, one can see that the basilica design draws attention to the transept and apse at one end, while the round domed design focuses toward the center.

New and original designs appeared in the next few centuries with cruciform exterior shapes (drawing #7), and notably with a dome sprung off four reinforced columns (drawings #5, #6) in a transformed basilica-type construction. This evolved into a domed cruciform design, whether the cross was the shape of the exterior walls or only inscribed within rectangular basilica walls. Russian churches (drawing #8) largely followed Byzantine floor plans, but with the significant addition of cupolas of varying types. Although the drums and "onion domes" are primarily an exterior aesthetic feature that beautifully blossom in flat terrain and expansive sky, they are also well-suited to handle the heavy snow loads of the northern climes.

Identifying the function of interior areas of ancient and modern churches is relatively easy, if one keeps in mind the fact that the architectural structures follow liturgical function and not vice versa. Classically churches, East and West, are internally divided into three parts, the narthex or vestibule, the nave or main body, and the altar area at the east end, apsed at the high place or easternmost niche. A baptistry, permanent or portable, is frequently found in the narthex or forecourt (atrium), since these areas are associated with teaching, penance, and Baptism (qq.v.). The nave is not only the place "where the believers stand," but the central place of liturgy (q.v.) other than the altar. In the pontifical Divine Liturgy the bishop begins the service in the nave, and during daily services frequently stands or sits on his throne in the southeast corner of the nave, the altar being used only minimally. The wall separating the nave from the altar area is the iconostasis (q.v.), which may range from an ornate railing to a full wall, ceiling to floor, covered with icons (q.v.).

The altar area is partitioned into three parts. The bema or central part is the altar proper, with the ambo in front and the apse and high place behind the square table. The prothesis (preparation of the bread and wine) is the name of the room north of the bema, and the procession of the Holy Gifts in the Great Entrance proceeds from this room to the bema; but frequently the prothesis table is moved into the bema proper and the procession is correspondingly adjusted. The north altar room may also be used to collect food for the poor, as a reliquary, etc. The south altar

Architecture, Church • 39

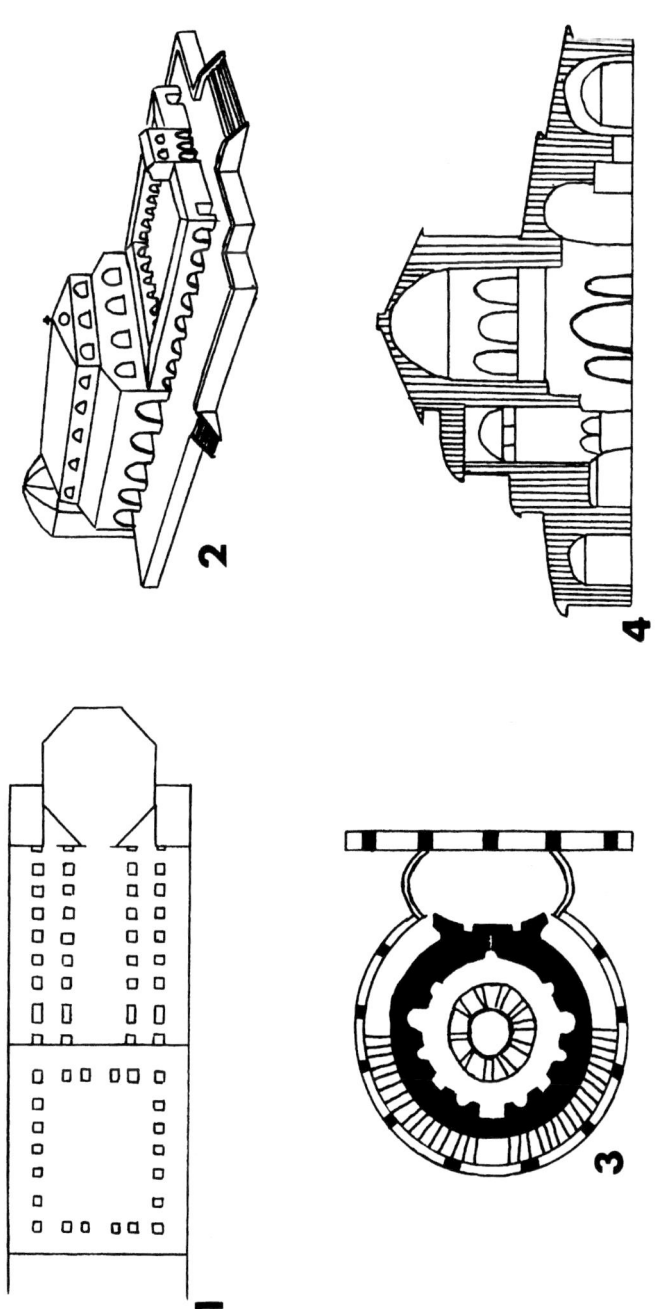

Architecture Drawing #1

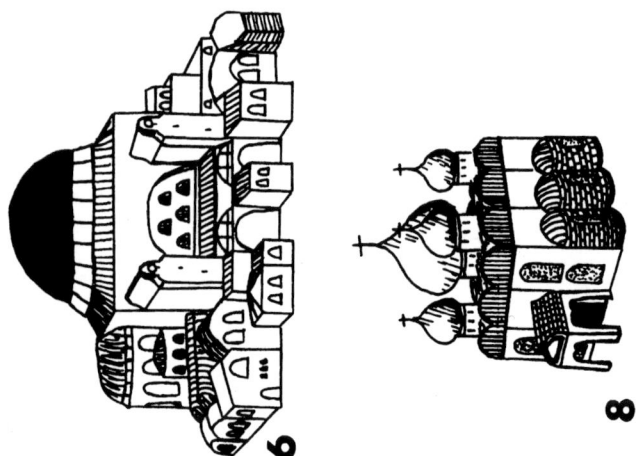
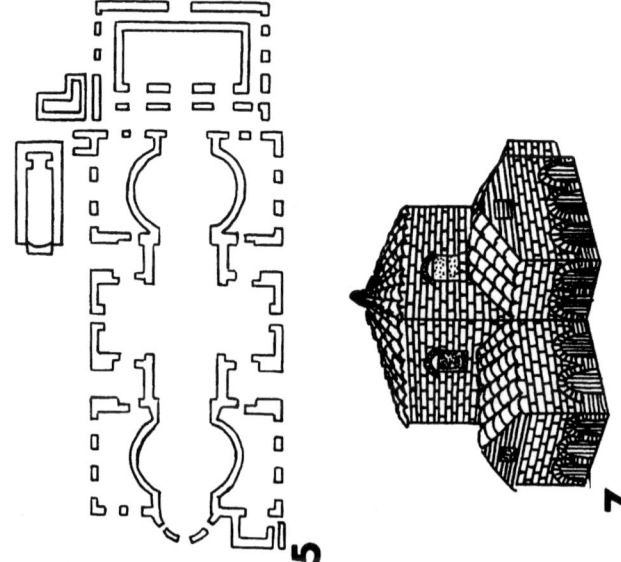

Architecture Drawing #2

room is the diaconicon, a sacristy for the servers, vestments, and liturgical utensils (qq.v.). (*See* Icon; Iconostasis; Liturgical Utensils.) DRAWINGS: 1. Interior of the Constantinian basilica (i.e., long church), Church of the Nativity, Bethlehem, A.D. 326. 2. Conjectural elevation of Constantinian basilica, Old St. Peter's, Rome, ca. A.D. 333. 3. Central plan church, Santa Costanza, Rome, ca. A.D. 350. 4. Cross section of Santa Costanza. 5. Byzantine foundations indicating floor plan of Hagia Sophia (q.v.), 532–537, Architects Anthemius of Tralles and Isidorus of Miletus. 6. Domed basilica, Hagia Sophia, combining long and central plan; the dome is sprung from pendentives (i.e., dome-on-dome construction). 7. Central plan dome with cruciform basilica influence, Mausoleum of Galla Placidia, Ravenna, A.D. 425–450; first successful example of combining the long and central plan. 8. Square plan Russian church enclosing a Greek cross with a large dome at the cross's center; cupolas (onion domes) adorn the roof like great candle flames, helping to bear the snow load.

**ARCHONDONIS, BARTHOLOMEW,** Archbishop of Constantinople, New Rome and Ecumenical Patriarch (12 March 1940– ). Born on the Turkish island of Imvros, he graduated from the Halki Theological Academy in 1961, and served two years in the Turkish army. He was ordained to the diaconate and, in 1963, commenced doctoral studies at the Pontifical Oriental Institute, Rome, where he received a doctorate for a dissertation on the codification of the canons. His dissertation was published in Greek at Thessalonica (q.v.) in 1970 as part of the series Analecta Vlatadon. He also studied at the Ecumenical Institute, Bossey, Switzerland, and the University of Munich. In 1968 he was appointed vice-rector of the Halki Theological Academy and was ordained priest in 1969 and, soon after, archimandrite. When the Turkish authorities closed the Halki Academy in 1971, he became personal secretary to his predecessor, Patriarch Dimitrios. Consecrated Metropolitan of Philadelphia in late 1973 and made a member of the Holy Synod in 1974, he continued as personal secretary to the patriarch until January 1990, when he became Metropolitan of Chalcedon and Dean of the Holy Synod. He was unanimously elected patriarch on 22 October 1991, and was enthroned on 2 November. His tenure as patriarch has been characterized thus far by interorthodox cooperation and diplomatic trips to other Orthodox countries seldom previously visited.

**ARIANISM** *see* Arius.

**ARISTOTLE** *see* Philosophy; Plato.

**ARIUS** (ca. 250–336). A presbyter of the Church of Alexandria, early in the 4th c. he questioned the contemporary Logos Christology (qq.v.) of his bishop, Alexander, in such a way as to trigger the controversy, around 318, over the Trinity (q.v.), which would preoccupy virtually the whole of the century. Arius's thesis was that the Word of God (q.v.), Christ, was not itself divine, but a being created by the Father to serve as the latter's instrument in creation and redemption. His great opponent was Alexander's deacon and eventual successor, Athanasius (q.v.). While Athanasius painted with far too broad a brush in declaring all of his adversaries "Arians," there is no doubt that Arius must be accorded due credit for his role as instigator of the crisis. Very little remains of what Arius might have written, aside from fragments of popular songs. What we do know of him is from Athanasius, Epiphanius, and the church historians (qq.v.).

**ARMENIAN ORTHODOX CHURCH.** An ancient nation and people in the region of the Caucasus Mountains and northeast Asia Minor (q.v.) and very much alive today, the Armenians boast of having been the first nation to convert to the Christian faith. King Trdat III (d. 330) thus anticipated the Emperor Constantine by perhaps a decade. His instructor in the new religion and later the patron saint of Armenia was Gregory the Illuminator (q.v.). He carried Christianity to his adopted people from Caesarea in Cappadocia (qq.v.), the ecclesiastical region to which the local church was subject until the beginning of the 6th c. The Armenian alphabet and early translation of the Scriptures (q.v.) into Armenian is credited to Mesrop Mastoc (q.v.). Armenian eccesiastical independence dates to their church's refusal of the Council of Chalcedon (q.v.) at the local councils of Vagharshapat (491) and Dvin (527). Even so, contacts with Byzantium (q.v.) were never entirely broken. Throughout the Empire's life Armenians made significant contributions as soldiers, even providing occasional emperors. They also shared Byzantium's ultimate fall to the Ottoman Turks, though, as with the Greeks, their church continued to sustain the nation's life and identity. In an effort to suppress the latter toward the end of the 19th c. the Ottoman Empire, already smarting from the loss of the Balkans (qq.v.), reacted with extraordinary ferocity. A series of state-inspired outrages and massacres occurred in the 1890s and again during World War I with a savagery not equaled until Hitler's holocaust of the Jews.

**ART** *see* Aesthetics; Icon; Sculpture.

**ASCENSION** *see* Feasts, Twelve Great.

**ASCESIS.** A Greek word meaning "exercise," in the Orthodox context the exercise in question signifies the "working out" of the believer's salvation, especially through *prayer* (q.v.), *fasting,* and *almsgiving.*

*Prayer:* Taking seriously Paul's admonition to "pray without ceasing" (1 Th 5:17), together with Christ's warnings to stay awake and keep watch in prayer (e.g., Lk 21:36), the early Church, as evidenced in Hippolytus's *Apostolic Tradition* (qq.v.), encouraged vigils and prayer from the earliest times. With the rise of monasticism (q.v.), prayer received the greatest attention as comprehending the whole effort of the monk to penetrate his or her own heart and to arrive at the conscious perception of the risen Christ. Thus, there is present in early monasticism the regular invocation of Christ's name, Jesus, coupled with a petition for mercy.

The "Jesus prayer," as it emerges in the 14th c. controversy over hesychasm (q.v.), is certainly the manifestation of an ancient tradition based upon the exaltation of the divine Name (Ex 3:14, Philp 2:9–11) coupled with faith in the indwelling presence of the Spirit of Christ (cf. 1 Cor 6:19, Rom 8). *Hesychia* means "quiet" or "retreat," and hesychast denoted simply and from earliest monasticism one who practices prayer in silence. The hesychasts of Mt. Athos—whom Gregory Palamas (qq.v.) defended and whose claims of a mysticism featuring direct encounter with Christ in his uncreated glory he sought to justify with his celebrated distinction between God's essence and energies—were the continuation of a tradition with roots in early Christianity and the Hebrew Scriptures (q.v.). For the latter, as for the New Testament texts, the heart is the center of the human being. It is there that the discovery of the divine presence takes place. In order to clear a path for this meeting with Christ, who is already given in Baptism (q.v.), the Christian is, however, obliged to confront the obstacles within his or her being that block the encounter. Hence the exercise of:

*Fasting:* This term embraces the struggle of the monk, and of the believer generally, against the "passions," i.e., those forces and habits of body and mind that result from, first, the conditions of fallen existence and, second, one's own willing acquiescence to the same—in short, sin (q.v.). Through bodily exercises such as fasting, limitation of sleep, and sexual continence, the Christian ascetic strives to reach and influence the more subtle and deep-rooted diseases of mind and heart. Through the aid of divine grace (q.v.), both mind and body are brought into conformity with prayer—indeed, making one's intellectual, emotional, and physical life one single act of the remembrance of Christ. In consonance with this integral devotion to the love of God, the ascetic is led to the imitation of—or better, participation in—the love that God has shown humanity in Christ. Hence:

*Almsgiving:* The expression of this third component of Orthodox asceticism includes, generally, love of one's neighbor and, more specifically, practices that involve the ascetic's physical and spiritual being. Of the former, "nonpossession" (*aktemosyne*), the principle that one is not to be an "owner," is perhaps the most important and striking. In common-life monasticism, possessions are thus required to be divided up among the community according to need and made available to the larger society, one's brothers and sisters in the "world," upon request and at need. More subtly, all pretense of power and authority over one's neighbor must be carefully eschewed. Classical Orthodox monasticism, for example, has for this reason always been cautious about ordination (q.v.) to the priesthood. Finally, the state of nonpossession, together with the virtues of humility and meekness to which it is intended to give rise, is believed to lead to a complete openness to others. This entails a readiness to respond with the freedom gained by deliverance from passionate attachment to one's "property," the latter term including both physical possessions and less tangible goods, such as reputation, status, dignity, etc.

**ASCETICISM** *see* Ascesis.

**ASIA MINOR.** The region approximately embracing the modern state of Turkey (q.v.), less the latter's territories in Europe, it has been playing a role in recorded history beginning with the Hittite Kingdom of the second millennium B.C. through to the Persians, the Greeks (settled on its coast from the 6th c. B.C.), and on to the present. It was the site of the ancient cities and later Christian centers of Ephesus (q.v.), Smyrna, Chalcedon (q.v.), Nicaea, Ancyra (q.v.), Caesarea (q.v.) in Cappadocia (q.v.), Trebizond and Sinope—to name a few. During the Byzantine era it formed the bulk of Constantinople's territories, following the loss of Egypt and Syria (qq.v.) in the 7th c., until the disastrous battle of Mantzikert in 1071. This marked the beginning of the Empire's terminal decline and the inauguration of Turkish Muslim rule, beginning with the Seljuk Sultanate of Icononium (modern Konya) and followed in turn by the Ottoman Empire (q.v.), and finally the Republic of Turkey. The process of Islamicization also began with Mantzikert and would eventually see the disappearance of Orthodox Christianity, a loss capped by the Armenian slaughters and by the expulsion of the ancient Greek community in the population exchanges of 1924.

**ASSUMPTION** *see* Feasts, Twelve Great (Dormition).

**ASSYRIAN CHURCH** *see* Iran; Mesopotamia; Syriac Church; Syro-Chaldean Patriarchate.

**ATHANASIUS OF ALEXANDRIA,** Archbishop of Alexandria, St. (c. 296–373). Educated in the Alexandrian catechetical school, he attended the First Ecumenical Council (q.v.) in Nicaea as a deacon. This hierarch (328–373) of Alexandria won a lifelong theological battle against Arianism (q.v.), the struggle for the Orthodox doctrine of the Trinity and for a Christology (qq.v.) which emphasized as its central thesis the statement: "God became man that we may be made divine" (*On the Incarnation*, 54). Orthodoxy holds that he was saying nothing fundamentally new, but rather defending the essential meaning of Christ's death and resurrection.

Clinging to this truth and seeing it through to its triumph, however, required all the force and endurance of an exceptionally powerful personality. Exiled by emperors hostile to his theology no less than five times (in 335, 339, 356, 362, and 365), often for years at a time, Athanasius found allies in the monks of the Egyptian desert (e.g., Pachomius [q.v.], Serapion, and Antony [q.v.]) and in the courts of the popes of Rome. Ultimately he would recognize in the great Cappadocian Church Father, Basil of Caesarea (qq.v.), an ally and like-minded theologian, and it would be Basil (also posthumously) and the other Cappadocians' task to crown his triumph at the Second Ecumenical Council (381). In spite of many difficult circumstances Athanasius produced an impressive body of written works, in particular his theological treatises *On the Incarnation* and *Against the Arians* (in three books), his pastoral letters—especially a paschal encyclical that is the first historical document to list our present canon of the New Testament—and, traditionally, the enormously influential *Life of Antony*. If the latter was not by him, as some argue today, it in any case reflects his own deepest concerns in its picture of a deified human being, i.e., one in whom the grace (q.v.) and power of Christ are fully present.

**ATHANASIUS OF ATHOS,** monk, St. (ca. 920–1003). A monk of Bithynia who moved to Mt. Athos (q.v.) and established its first monastery, the Lavra (961). Supported by the emperors, he was made head of all the communities there, which numbered fifty-eight by the time of his death.

**ATHENAGORAS.** 1) The Apologist (q.v.) Athenagoras (fl. 170s). 2) Athenagoras Spyrou, Ecumenical Patr. *see* Spyrou, Athenagoras.

**ATHOS, Mount.** Known as the Holy Mountain, Athos is a peninsula in northeastern Greece out into the Aegean Sea approximately one hundred miles southeast of Thessalonica (q.v.). Established by the Emperor Nicephorus Phocas in 963 under the leadership of St. Athanasius (q.v.) as the exclusive property of the monks, the world's only "monastic republic" has endured the vicissitudes of Byzantium's fall, the depredations of the Crusades (qq.v.), the relatively benign neglect of the Turkish Sultans, and since 1912 the perhaps more dangerous designs of the modern state of Greece. It has been the largest concentration of Orthodox monks virtually since its inception. Its twenty monasteries are: the Great Lavra of Athanasios of Athos (963), Vatopedi (10th c.), Agiou Paulou (10th c.), Iveron (10th c., orginally Georgian), Xeropotamou (10th c.), Ephigmenou (11th c.), Panteleimon (11th c., Russian), Docheiariou (11th c.), Xenophontos (11th c.), Constamonitou (11th c.), Caracallou (11th c.), Philotheou (12th c.), Hilandar (12th c., Serbian), Koutloumousiou (12th c.), Pantokrator (12th c.), Simonos Petras (13th c.), Dionysiou (13th c.), Gregoriou (13th c.), Zographou (13th c., Bulgarian), and Stavronikita (16th c.). Over the past millennium of its existence, Athos has been of incalculable importance for the Orthodox *oikoumene* (q.v.), marked by two great revivals: the first in the 14th c. and 15th c., characterized by the writings of Gregory Palamas and the Orthodox-wide movement of hesychasm (qq.v.), and second during the 18th c. and 19th c., which saw the publication of the *Philokalia* by Nicodemus the Athonite in Greek and Paisii Velichkovsky (qq.v.) in Slavic and Romanian. These two periods have indelibly imprinted the life and thought of the Orthodox Church. The present modest revival of monastic life, very much in the spirit of its predecessors, began in 1968 and may well bring the same kind of benefits to the whole Church.

The benefits Athos gives the Church are not easily summarized. It produced no universities, no enduring institutions, nor, while contributing a number of bishops and the occasional patriarch over the centuries, has it established any succession of reforming hierarchs akin to the progeny of the early medieval monastery of Cluny, which changed the face of the Western Church and of Europe in general. The Holy Mountain's gifts to Orthodoxy are altogether of the intangible variety, perhaps best summed up by an epithet for it popular among some of the monks: "the Mountain of silence." The silence in question is that of theophany (q.v.), of the divine presence, and the saints who have come out of that presence in an unfailing stream are the sum and entirety of Athos's gift to the Church. Rightly, the latter has always prized this contribution beyond any other. The glory of God, to paraphrase St. Irenaeus (q.v.), is the human person radiant in the Spirit. Athos has, over its thousand years, provided time and again the proof of the Spirit's presence in a sorry world; and that, at least for Orthodox Christians of the past fifty generations, is enough and more. (*See* Ascesis; Monasteries; Monasticism.)

**ATONEMENT.** Classically defined as the reconciliation of human beings with God through the sacrificial death of Jesus Christ, the doctrine has received much less attention in the East than in the West, especially since the Middle Ages (with the possible exception of post-Petrine Russia). Atonement may be rooted in many Old Testament concepts, whether it be the sacrificial system, the sacrifice associated with the establishment of a covenant, or the Isaianic expectation of a "suffering servant." These themes all reverberate in the New Testament, not only in Heb, but in relation to the sacrificial system (Mk 10:45: "to give his life a ransom for many"; Rom 3:25; I P 1:18–19), the establishment of a new covenant (Eucharistic words of institution, and the Johannine parallels between the Lamb of God and the Paschal lamb), and the "suffering servant" as Jesus' self-identification (Lk 22:37), and his identification by the emerging church (I Cor 15:3; Acts 8:32–35).

Later, Origen, probably under the influence of gnosticism (qq.v.), developed the doctrine to include Satan: Satan had rights over humanity because of the Fall, and Christ's death was a necessary ransom payment. Remarkably, Origen's view of atonement was not accepted by the Cappadocians in the East, probably due to the influence of Athanasius's (qq.v.) theology of the incarnation: God became human so that we could become divine. Origen's view was accepted in the West, i.e., by Hilary of Poitier, Augustine (q.v.), and Leo, but with a sensitivity toward the defeat of Satan in the victory of Christ's Resurrection (q.v.). The addition of Satan to the equation notwithstanding, the Eastern Fathers and Orthodox theologians today would prefer the balance struck between the Cross and the Resurrection—to which they quickly append the Transfiguration.

Since the East holds a different theology of "original sin" (q.v.) from the West, the atonement most likely did not take on the same immediacy as in the West, which typically separated it from the Resurrection and the Transfiguration. When Augustinian original sin dictated the "necessity" of the Incarnation to satisfy conditions of redemption—someone without "original sin" must be born to satisfy the equation—the atonement fit into this "negative" description without reference to the corresponding "positive" theologies of the resurrection and the transformation of life.

Contrary to this, the entire patristic (q.v.) tradition on the atonement sees Christ as representative of humanity rather than as a substitutute for it. The representative does those things that are paradigmatic for every person—Transfiguration, Cross, and Resurrection. The actions of Jesus are considered "normative" for Christian life, and not merely a "miraculous" intervention that has nothing to do with subsequent Christian behavior. It should be pointed out that this position is not merely an Eastern interpretation, but the synoptic Gospel tradition: After Peter's confession of faith, the Cross, the Resurrection, and the Transfiguration occur together as the centerpiece of Mk, Mt, and Lk. Some theologians of the Eastern Church would go beyond this to say that the Incarnation would have occurred even without the Fall, because God (q.v.) is self-revealing and desirous to bring humankind to himself. This understanding evaluates theologies that focus exclusively on original sin and the atonement as null and void.

**AUGUSTINE OF HIPPO,** bishop, theologian, St. (354–430). Greatest of the Latin Church Fathers (q.v.), Bishop of Hippo Regius in North Africa near Carthage from 395–430, his influence has been enormous on subsequent Western Christian thought, determining the main lines of its theological development from his immediate successors to the leaders of the Reformation. Augustine was for centuries after him the Church Father par excellence. It was a reputation justly won through the production of a vast library of theological works, virtually any one of which would have sufficed to secure the reputation of a lesser thinker.

In one field of theological inquiry after another, especially in responding to three threatening heresies (q.v.), Augustine set the standard for Latin Christian thought. His great work *On the Trinity* established Western triadology along lines it has never abandoned, nor seriously criticized. Prominent within it is a portrayal of the central Christian mystery on the psychological model, i.e., the human soul as the created analogue of the Trinity (q.v.). His *City of God* provided a theology of history that is still powerfully influential and, moreover, had no equivalent in the Christian East. The many treatises on the Donatist Schism established fundamental guidelines for later thought on the nature of the Church and the sacraments (qq.v.). Augustine's spiritual autobiography, the *Confessions,* pioneered a new approach to the mysteries of the interior life, which would afterward have imitators to the present day. No ancient writer before or after him had ever revealed himself in such detail or sought to expose the workings of divine grace (q.v.) with such personal insight or such moving prose. His commentaries on the Scriptures (q.v.) fill yet more volumes, the fruit of his daily preaching in the cathedral of Hippo in the exercise of his pastorate. Yet, of all these, he is perhaps best known for the writings of his old age against Pelagius, the British monk who claimed (so Augustine said, in turn) that the believer could achieve salvation by self-efforts. For one so acutely conscious of the insidious and subtle corrosion of sin as this writer, Pelagius's position was utter anathema. In responding to this threat to the sovereignty of divine grace, as Augustine saw it, he elaborated a strikingly pessimistic view of human nature that viewed humanity after the Fall as thoroughly corrupted and, in addition, as laboring under the condemnation of God originally pronounced upon Adam.

A number of things, all very influential in subsequent Western Christian anthropology (q.v.), followed from this. First, Augustine maintained that everyone descended from Adam inherited the *personal* judgment decreed for that forefather. Everyone is born guilty of the original sin (q.v.). Second, so corrupted is the "damned mass" of the human race that its members no longer have the power to avoid sin (*posse non pecare*). Thus, without true freedom (q.v.) to act, third, all are utterly dependent on the free gift of divine mercy. Fourth, that mercy, completely gratuitous as it consequently must be, is not obliged to save all or any. Those whom God does choose to save are completely his to choose, and that choice has been established in the divine counsel before the world. Thus, fifth, those whom he has chosen and those whom he has not are so designated from before their birth, predestined. The doctrine of predestination has been a kind of leitmotiv, or at least a counterpoint, throughout the following centuries of Western Christian theology. (Thomas Aquinas has it, so does Luther, and so, of course, does its best-known exponent, John Calvin.)

Perhaps most important for the Orthodox Holy Tradition, Augustine was not translated into Greek until the 14th c., nor did he have any influence on the chief lines of Orthodox thought until 17th c. Ukraine and 18th c. Russia (qq.v.). For anyone approaching Eastern Christianity from the West this capital fact must continually be kept in mind, for it affects every aspect of what is, in general, a common faith.

**AUTHORITY.** The question of authority, and with it "infallibility," in the Orthodox Church is primarily dependent on the Holy Spirit (q.v.) or pneumatology, and not upon human agency. Thus, the way the question is handled in the East is different from its treatment in the West. When the Holy Spirit is recognized as the ultimate source of authority, claims to inerrant authority for the hierarchy (e.g., "papal infallibility") or for Scripture (e.g., *sola Scriptura*) can be relegated to high-level political posturing; for the claims are actually for *a particular hierarch's* interpretation of the matter, and not all hierarchs' (universal) understanding, and *a particular group's interpretation of Scripture* (q.v.), and not how Scripture has been understood by the Church throughout the ages. The Orthodox generally consider the question as posed in the West in the last half millennium, with due respect to Roman Catholic and Protestant theologians, to be a wrong question predicated on unfortunate political developments, both before and after the Reformation.

Having said this, it should be pointed out that in the East the same questions of ecclesiastical and civil authority have been as acutely felt as in the West, but with differing appeals:

I. The appeal to the Council of Jerusalem (Acts 15) as paradigmatic for church decision-making procedure is frequently made by those emphasizing the importance of the hierarchy in the process of defining the faith: "The apostles and the elders met together to consider this matter" (v. 6). This citation has as its strength the witness of Scripture and the successful resolution of a difficult problem in the nascent Gentile mission, seemingly a perfect example. On closer examination, the example is problematical. Did the hierarchy really make the decision? First, Peter makes a speech and in it takes responsibility for the Gentile mission; but then James, the brother of the Lord, speaks and states, "I have reached a decision. . . . " Next, we find that "the apostles and the elders with the consent of the whole church decided . . . " (v.22); and again, when we read Paul's account of what is ostensibly the same Council (Gal 2:1–10), he states that he is the leader of the Gentile mission and the meeting in Jerusalem added nothing to his message or method. Finally, the Council was not really about orthodoxy at all, but about orthopraxy: The decision did not involve theology (q.v.) or the content of the faith, but only whether circumcision and certain types of abstinence would be practiced. Excepting these controversial items, the Orthodox have preserved the formula, "For it has seemed good to the Holy Spirit and to us" (Acts 15:28), in concluding their conciliar deliberations.

II. The appeal to ecumenical conciliarity (*sobornost,* in Russian) and the emperor are frequently taken as normative for the Eastern Church's self-expression. Certainly the Seven Ecumenical Councils (q.v.) have unique authority in the East, and the emperor was looked upon as blessed by God to enforce secular, if not religious, justice. The problem with the councils and the emperor, briefly put, is that terrible difficulties in the conciliar period began immediately with Constantine the Great (q.v.). Councils were convened that attributed "ecumenical authority" to themselves, but which were subsequently judiciously overturned. Similarly, the emperor soon showed himself capable of being as much a hindrance to the faith as a help. Heretical laws were passed and enforced. The state interfered in the Church and itself created new martyrs (q.v.) — most recently with Soviet sovereignty. One of the worst conciliar debacles occurred with the Council of Ferrara-Florence (1438–1439) wherein all the sitting hierarchs except Mark of Ephesus (q.v.) capitulated to Rome; and on returning to their dioceses they met an angry reception — and most swiftly recanted in order to hold their sees. Nonetheless, the conciliar model retains most of its integrity and remains an ideal in Orthodoxy. Without a Christian emperor and a clear enunciation of which and how clergy and laity interact in council, the inspiration for convening such councils is at times lacking.

III. The appeal to Holy Tradition (q.v.) (including Scripture and/or the Councils [qq.v.]) is recognized as of ultimate authority, since it is tantamount to an appeal to the entire experience of the

Church. Holy Tradition is seen as consisting of many elements, including Scripture, liturgy, Canon Law, patristics (qq.v.), etc. The primary hurdle in appealing to Holy Tradition as an authority lies in the selection of appropriate sources, applicable to a given situation. Similarly, precedent is difficult to establish quickly, since the selection of sources itself is a matter of interpretation, and the question raised might not have been asked previously (e.g., in the question of women's ordination [q.v.] to the priesthood). Everyone agrees that Holy Tradition is authoritative, but which beliefs and practices truly manifest Holy Tradition is open to a variety of interpretation.

IV. Various appeals to the authority of ancient patriarchates, especially Rome and Constantinople (qq.v.), have been made throughout history. Given the relative size and resources available to large episcopal sees, one would expect more cumulative experience and a more precise articulation of the faith from the leading cities of the Mediterranean than from the smaller "suburbs." These centers had political exposure, and at times access to the emperor, which increased their abilities and standing. During the later Ecumenical Councils (q.v.) the Roman Church had a remarkable record of protecting orthodoxy from heresy (q.v.), less so Constantinople. Unfortunately, dominant heresies occurred in each of these centers; so, one finds Hippolytus's papal adversaries and Honorius I in Rome, and Theodore of Mopsuestia and Cyril Lukaris (qq.v.) in Constantinople, as notable, fallible examples. In spite of the heresies, it became part of tradition to accord the position of *primi inter pares* or "first among equals" to the bishops of these sees, and appeals to the patriarchs and popes are considered valid.

V. Following the Enlightenment there has been an increased appeal to the authority of democracy and/or egalitarianism within the Eastern Church, especially in response to centralization or "hierarchicalism" discussed above. The strengths of this appeal lie in a recognition of every Christian's responsibility for the whole of the faith, whether clergy or laity, and in involving everyone in the ecclesiastical decision-making process. The shortcomings of this appeal are usually in its inability to recognize the value of legitimate ministries (the "hierarchical principle"), and in acknowledging that the will of God is not produced by majority vote. In the Encyclical Letter of the Eastern Patriarchs to the Roman Pope (1848), we have an affirmation of this principle in the statement "neither the hierarchy nor councils could ever introduce novelty, since with us the guardian of piety and faith is the very Body of the Church, i.e., the people themselves."

**AUTOCEPHALOUS.** Literally, the term in Greek means "having one's own head." Churches that are autocephalous are self-governing and not under the jurisdiction of another church. They elect their own presiding bishop, frequently with the rank of patriarch, without outside permission or sanction. Defining autocephaly as "independence" is misleading, since all canonical churches are in communion with one another and provisionally responsible to one another in matters of faith, though not of administration. As a historical phenomenon, from a theological viewpoint, autocephaly is seen as an organic development of principles of church government laid down in the first of the Ecumenical Councils (q.v.). For example, during the reign of the Byzantine Emperor Justinian (527–565) (qq.v.) the Church was considered a Pentarchy, consisting of Rome, Constantinople, Alexandria, Antioch, and Jerusalem, five autocephalous patriarchates (qq.v.). In more recent times autocephaly is drawn along the lines of "national churches." As a political development autocephaly is more tenuous, being granted and withdrawn by "mother churches" (q.v.) for various reasons. It is safe to say that lasting autocephaly of a particular established, regional church usually functions de facto for a time and is later recognized de jure. A current list of autocephalous and autonomous churches and their hierarchs may be found in the Appendix.

**AZIZ, SAMUEL,** bishop (1920–1981). Born Sa'd 'Aziz in Cairo, Egypt, he was assassinated alongside Egyptian President Anwar al-Sadat in 1981. From youth he was associated with the Sunday School Movement. He graduated in law from Cairo University in 1942, and in 1944 earned a diploma in divinity from the Clerical College, while simultaneously working toward a B.D. from the American University, Cairo. In 1944 he was lecturer at Addis Ababa (Ethiopia) Theological Seminary, while volunteering at the Teacher's College and helping to establish a chapter of the Sunday School Movement. He returned to Egypt in 1946 and was ordained in the Coptic Orthodox Church (q.v.) in 1948. During this time, he took monastic vows under the name Makari (al-Surani), lived in several monastic communities, and lectured at the Coptic Orthodox Theological School, Cairo, from 1952 to 1954. In 1954 he was a member of the Coptic Orthodox delegation to the second World Council of Churches Assembly, Evanston, and taught social studies at the Higher Institute of Coptic Studies. In 1955 he obtained a Master's in Religious Education degree from Princeton Theological Seminary, and from 1955 to 1962 he taught pastoral theology at the Cairo Clerical College. He was later elevated to become bishop of public, social, and ecumenical services. Among his ecumenical activities are numbered permanent membership in the WCC Central Committee and vice-president of the All Africa Conference of Churches, which he cofounded.

## -B-

**BALKANS.** The word is Turkish in origin, signifying "thick woods," and particularly the great peninsula of southeastern Europe, which in biblical and Roman times embraced the ancient provinces of Illyria, Dacia, Thrace (Skudra), Macedonia (q.v.), and Achaia (Athens and the Peloponnesus). Invaded by the Slavs in the late 6th c. A.D., this territory eventually became home to the modern Orthodox churches of Serbia, Bulgaria, Romania, Greece, and Albania (qq.v.). Outside the territories of the former Soviet Union, it is the largest concentration of Orthodox Christians in the world. Under the rule of the Ottoman Empire (q.v.) from the late 14th c. to the waning years of the 19th c.—Bulgaria being the last to gain independence in 1879—the entire area bears the marks of this long occupation. Territorial and concomitant ecclesiastical disputes resulting from the breakup of the Turkish Empire, for example the "Bulgarian Schism" (1870–1945) and the Balkan Wars of 1909 to 1912, have troubled the Orthodox communities from the end of the last century to the present.

**BALSAMON, THEODORE,** canonist (ca. 1130–ca. 1195). Briefly Patriarch of Antioch, though in exile due to the Latin Patriarchates established by the Crusades, he was perhaps the most important commentator on Canon Law during the Byzantine era (qq.v.). He was the successor to a series of canonists during a period in the Empire when legal reform was receiving much attention and, perhaps not coincidentally, when Western Europe and the Western Church were rediscovering the Code of Justinian (q.v.) and preoccupied with the great drama of the Middle Ages, the contest between the German emperors and the papacy (q.v.). Gratian, compiler of the *Corpus Juris Canonici,* had worked earlier in the same century. Just as the latter, Balsamon was greatly influential. His *Exegesis on the Nomocanon in Fourteen Titles* is still consulted today.

Similar to his Latin counterpart, Gratian, the Byzantine churchman was a firm believer in the hierarchical ordering of the Church. His rulings on certain questions, such as those bearing on Confession, are in interesting and pointed contrast to the attitude, vigorously expressed, of Symeon the New Theologian (q.v.) on the same issues. Unlike Gratian, however, and in opposition to his predecessor, Zonaras (q.v.), Balsamon also upheld a very high view of the emperor's role in the balance of relations between Church and state (q.v.).

**BANQUET.** The image of the messianic banquet was popular in Ugaritic and biblical literature till the 1st c., and was used by Jesus in parables and miracles to refer to the Kingdom of God. In Christian times it was incorporated into the literature of Kievan Rus' (q.v.) through the portrait of the idealized Christian prince who provided food in abundance to his subjects. Notable among these were the feasts of Prince Vladimir (q.v.), who sent carts of food through Kiev for those physically prevented from attending. Entertainment provided by the prince was also included in the proceedings of the banquets, provision of which was elevated to the status of a Christian virtue in Slavic countries.

**BAPTISM.** Baptism, Chrismation, and the Eucharist (q.v.) are all administered together as Holy Mysteries (sacraments) that admit one into the membership of the Church, i.e., are rites of Christian initiation. Baptism is preceded by repentance and catechesis (qq.v.) in the case of adults, and assumes a continuous membership in a Christian community. Baptism of children occurs only in cases wherein the children are reared and taught in a Christian home and community, whether by parents or others. Baptism is not construed so much as a cleansing from "original sin" (q.v.), though it is for cleansing of sins as Paul teaches, but more especially as baptism into the death and resurrection of Christ. When the repentant sinner is immersed in the baptismal waters, he or she descends to death with Christ. When coming up out of the waters, the newborn Christian is resurrected with Christ, all in the name of the Holy Trinity (q.v.) (Mt 28:19). Rudimentary instructions on the administration of Baptism are found in the *Didache* VII (q.v.). With regard to the Baptism of adults in the Church today, the following items are normative from Holy Tradition (q.v.):

1) After evangelism, reception into the catechumenate and the assigning of sponsors occurs and is followed by catechesis;
2) The inscription of names or naming service begins a series of exorcisms (q.v.) and a forty-day lenten preparation; and
3) The liturgical rites of Baptism, Chrismation (the Kiss of Peace), and the Eucharist (qq.v.) proceed to a postbaptismal catechesis and a deepened experience of life in the Church. In the case of the Baptism of children, all of the elements above are to be included in the rearing and education of the child by the family.

**BAPTISM, FEAST OF JESUS'** *see* Feasts, Twelve Great.

**BARLAAM OF CALABRIA** (ca. 1290–1348). Barlaam was an Italo-Greek from Calabria, the instep of the Italian boot, and became something of a theological celebrity and an important church figure—he had been a tonsured monk—on his arrival in Constantinople (q.v.) in 1330. Welcomed at first and accorded both honors and serious ecclesiastico-political responsibilities, his criticism of the monks of Mt.

Athos (q.v.) later in the same decade, especially of their claims to the vision of the "uncreated light" of Mt. Tabor (site of the Transfiguration), sparked the last great theological debate in Byzantine Church history, the Hesychast (q.v.) Controversy. Barlaam's opponent in the fray was Gregory Palamas (q.v.), at the time a monk on Athos and later Archbishop of Thessalonica. Since Gregory proved the winner in the exchange, no further honors awaited Barlaam, at least not in Byzantium (q.v.). Gregory's *Triads in Defense of the Holy Hesychasts* was his greatest work. Its central thesis, the distinction in God between essence and energies, was recognized as Orthodox doctrine in the local councils of 1341, 1347, and 1351. Barlaam had left the city, the Empire, and the Orthodox Church by the time the first council had met. He ended his life back in Italy, a bishop in the Roman Catholic Church (q.v.), vainly endeavoring to teach Petrarch Greek.

**BARNABAS, EPISTLE OF.** Considered part of the New Testament by Clement of Alexandria, Origen (qq.v.), and the compiler of D\Codex Sinaiticus, it is now usually numbered among the "Apostolic Fathers" and was probably written at the end of the 1st c. or the beginning of the 2nd c. A.D. Although claiming authority by association with Barnabas the apostle, the companion of Paul, the writing proper does not contain his name and is actually an anonymous epistle (not a personal letter) addressed to the newly baptized, reflecting Alexandrian ideas in tract or treatise form. The main point of view originating within it is a warning to Christians against a literal, "Judaistic" interpretation of the Old Testament—all to be replaced by a "spiritual" or allegorical (q.v.) understanding. Main sections of the work are concerned with a Christian apology against Judaism (chs. 2–17) and the two ways (q.v.) (chs. 18–20).

**BARROIS, GEORGES A.,** priest, archaeologist, Old Testament scholar, cartographer, medievalist (17 February 1898–27 August 1987). A profound intellect and ever a faithful churchman, Professor Barrois is probably best known in the English-speaking world for the maps and brief article contributed to the Oxford annotated editions of the *New Revised Standard Version* and the *Revised Standard Version* of the Bible. Born into a traditional French Roman Catholic family (with Swabian roots) in Les Hautes Rivières near the Belgian border, Georges entered the Dominicans as a seminarian with the name Augustine and studied philosophy and theology in Tournai, Belgium. Seminary studies were interrupted while he completed his French military service, serving in Syria for two years under the League of Nations mandate. He returned to Tournai and was ordained priest (1923), received a Doctorate in Theology (1924), and proceeded to the French

Dominican Biblical School in Jerusalem. He obtained the *Prolyta in Sacra Scriptura* (1932) at the Vatican, and became one of the leading specialists in biblical archaeology at the Ecole Biblique. Barrois became professor of Old Testament at the Dominican Studium Generale (1935) at Etiolles near Paris after writing *Précis d'Archéologie Biblique* (1935), and here befriended other eminent French Roman Catholic theologians, e.g., Congar and Chenu. Prior to World War II there was an "antimodernist" witch-hunt among biblical scholars at the Ecole Biblique to which Barrois fell victim—his name would not be spoken there for some thirty years, until a fortuitous reconciliation with Pere Benoit in the mid–1970s. In any case, Barrois was in the good company of his colleagues Lagrange and Dhorme in the difficulties he experienced during these years. He departed for America and taught at Catholic University in Washington, D.C., as visiting professor, but was so shaken by personal and international events that he left the Roman Church completely. Although not a popular topic of research at the time, Barrois had developed an interest in Bernard of Clairvaux. (Among other things, Bernard was known for denouncing the persecution of the Jews.)

Barrois married, was accepted into the Presbyterian ministry (1942), and became professor of history and theology of the medieval Church at Princeton Theological Seminary (1945–68). Early in this period of his life he completed his magnum opus, *Manuel d'Archeologie Biblique* (2 vols., 1939, 1953), which was foundational to its English counterpart, Roland de Vaux's two-volume *Ancient Israel*, on social and religious institutions. Later in this period he wrote *Sermons de Jean Calvin sur le Livre d'Esaie, Chs. 13–29* (1961), as well as many scholarly articles for periodicals and reference works such as *The Interpreter's Bible* and *The Interpreter's Dictionary of the Bible*. He was a contributor to, and intimately acquainted with, both *La Bible de Jérusalem* and its English-language counterpart, *The Jerusalem Bible*.

At Princeton Professor Barrois met the retired Fr. Georges Florovsky (q.v.) and began attending Fr. John Turkevich's liturgy at the Princeton University Chapel. He was received into the Orthodox Church as a layman 15 December 1968 by Fr. Florovsky. (In private conversations, Barrois claimed he had been "orthodox" all his life.) Fr. John Meyendorff (q.v.) aptly described this pilgrim and his pilgrimage as "a significant witness to the inner agonies, the paradoxes and the antimonies of 20th-c. Christianity." Barrois continued teaching Old Testament at St. Vladimir's Orthodox Theological Seminary (q.v.) in Crestwood as a commuter from Princeton; and during this last period of his life he authored four enjoyable books: *The Face of Christ in the Old Testament* (1974), *Scripture Readings in Orthodox Worship*

(1977), *Jesus Christ and the Temple* (1980), and *The Fathers Speak* (1986). He is remembered by his students with warmth and respect — and by his Arab students from ancient cities and villages for his uncanny ability to describe the archaeological features of their hometowns on a house by house basis.

**BARTHOLOMEW (ARCHONDONIS),** Archbishop of Constantinople, New Rome and Ecumenical Patriarch *see* Archondonis, Bartholomew.

**BASHIR, ANTONY,** Metropolitan of the Antiochian Archdiocese of North America (15 March 1898–15 February 1966). Born in Lebanon, he studied at the Balamand Theological School and was ordained deacon (1916). He continued his education at the Law School of Baabda and the American University of Beirut, where he taught Arabic literature. The Patriarch of Antioch sent him to America (1922) at which time he was elevated to archimandrite (1923) and where he traveled for thirteen years building and serving parishes and continued his writing. In 1936 he was consecrated Archbishop of the Antiochian Archdiocese (q.v.) of North America, succeeding Archbishop Victor Abu-Assaly, and proceeded to unify the Archdiocese and set it on a sound financial base. Most important among his accomplishments was his vision to promote an American expression of Orthodoxy, both in worship and administratively. He encouraged the use of English in worship, translating and publishing more than thirty books on the faith. This was in addition to accepting converts, ordaining them to the priesthood, and supporting English-language church school education. Administratively, he helped organize the Federation of the Primary Jurisdictions of the Orthodox Greek Catholic Churches in America in 1942, and later the Standing Conference of Orthodox Bishops in America (q.v.) in 1960, of which he was vice-chairman.

**BASIL (KRIVOCHEINE),** Archbishop of Brussels *see* Krivocheine, Basil.

**BASIL THE GREAT,** bishop, theologian, monk, St. (ca. 330–379). Born of an aristocratic family in central Asia Minor, eldest of the Cappadocian Fathers, the older brother of Gregory of Nyssa and childhood friend of Gregory of Nazianzus (qq.v.), Basil and the latter Gregory received the best education available in the ancient world, having been trained both in rhetoric and, at the then "university town" of Athens, in philosophy. Raised as a Christian and from youth enamored with the great Christian thinker of the previous century, Origen (q.v.), Basil's intellectual and spiritual life represented a continuation of the latter's great task, the integration of Christian life and experience with the best of ancient Greek thought. He and Gregory of Nazianzus compiled a selection of quotes from Origen, bearing on prayer and the spiritual life, called the *Philokalia.* He was also significantly influenced by the nascent monasticism (q.v.), visiting Egypt as a young man and even attempting a not-altogether-successful experiment at the monastic life with his friend, Gregory. His life of active contribution to the Church began with his appointment as bishop to the metropolitan see of Cappadocia (q.v.), Caesarea, in 370. The nine years of life remaining to him he exhausted in a ministry of extraordinary effort and remarkable accomplishments.

Basil continued his lifelong interest in monasticism as a bishop, and the responses he wrote in reply to questions on the monastic life (the *Longer* and *Shorter Rules*), with their emphasis on communal life and social service, have exercised great influence in the history of cenobitic monasticism. His treatises *On the Holy Spirit* and the three *Against Eunomius,* written in reply to the attack on the teaching of the Trinity (q.v.)—the great ecclesiastical and imperial crisis of the era—laid down the main lines of Greek triadology. This work and his efforts to reconcile "Semiarians" to Orthodoxy would be confirmed at the Ecumenical Council of Constantinople (qq.v.) in 381, and expanded on by his brother and his friend, the two Gregories. His voluminous correspondence testifies to his skills and energy as pastor, ecumenical diplomat, and theologian. We have little from his commentaries on Scripture (q.v.) save his sermons on the opening chapter of *Genesis,* the *Hexaemeron* ("the six days"), but the latter bears eloquent testimony to his background in Greek philosophy and Christian theology, as well as to the sobriety and "Antiochene" sense for the value of the literal text, which characterize his use of Scripture in his other works. Finally, his sensitivity and deep biblical rooting are still remembered in the canon of the Eucharist, the *anaphora,* contained today in the liturgy (qq.v.). One liturgy bears his name and is celebrated ten times a year in the Orthodox Church. These great prayers display the marks of his thought and style, though the liturgy itself is now of a composite nature.

**BEBIS, GEORGE S.,** theologian. Born in Greece on the island of Crete, Bebis holds degrees in theology, B.A. and B.D., from the Holy Cross Greek Orthodox School of Theology (q.v.), an S.T.M. from Harvard University, and Lic. Theol. and a doctorate from the University of Athens. He also studied at the Center of Ecumenical Studies in Bossey, Switzerland.

He has taught at the Ecumenical Seminar at the Episcopal Theological Seminary (Cambridge, Massachusetts), and at the Pope John XXIII Center at Fordham University in New York. He has lectured in colleges, seminaries, and churches in this country as well as in Greece and in England. He holds the Chair of Patristics at Holy Cross Greek Orthodox School of Theology, and in 1989 he received the Archbishop Iakovos Faculty Award for his distinguished service as a professor and scholar.

Dr. Bebis is a member of many learned societies and the Liturgical Commission of the Greek Orthodox Archdiocese of North and South America, and has also been a member of the Orthodox-Roman Catholic Consultation for ten years. Currently, he is a member of the Anglican-Orthodox Consultation. In August 1991 he was elected president of the Orthodox Theological Society in America. In January 1990 Dr. Bebis represented the Patriarchate in the International Conference in Baar, Switzerland, sponsored by the World Council of Churches, which discussed "Theological Perspectives and Affirmations on the Contemporary Religious Plurality." He participated in the 7th Assembly of the World Council of Churches in Canberra, Australia, as a delegate and actively worked in the committee that discussed the topic, "Spirit of Truth, Come and Liberate Us."

His book on Nestorius was published in Greek and an English translation is forthcoming. He published numerous articles and book reviews in learned periodicals in this country and abroad. Dr. Bebis was a major contributor to the new book, *Nicodemos of the Holy Mountain,* published by Paulist Press (1989).

**BEHR-SIGEL, ELISABETH,** theologian (1907– ). This French Orthodox theologian lectures at the St. Sergius Orthodox Theological Institute (q.v.) and at the Catholic Institute, both in Paris. Baptized in the Lutheran tradition, she later became Orthodox. She has been active in ecumenical (q.v.) encounter, particularly from the late 1970s to the early 1980s in the World Council of Church's study of the Community of Men and Women in the Church. She has published *The Ministry of Women in the Church* (Eng. trans. 1991).

**BEKISH, IRENEY,** metropolitan (2 October 1892–18 March 1981). In 1914 he graduated from the Kholm Theological Seminary, was ordained priest in 1916, and served as assistant rector in the Cathedral of Lublin, Poland, from 1916 to 1919. From 1935 to 1947 he was a member of the Polish consistory Diocese of Pinsk, as well as chairman of the missionary commission. From 1938 to 1944 he was dean of the Counties of Sarna, Kamen-Kashursk, and Pinsk, but during World War II was a displaced person in Germany. From 1947 to 1952 he was rector of the Russian Orthodox Church in Charleroi, Belgium, then rector of Holy Trinity Church in McAdoo, Pennsylvania, from 1952 to 1953. From 1953 to 1960 he was the Bishop of Tokyo and Japan, from 1960 to 1965 the Archbishop of Boston and New England, and from 1965 until his death the Archbishop of New York and Metropolitan of all America and Canada of the "Metropolia," historically the Russian Orthodox Greek Catholic Missionary Diocese of North America. Following the autocephaly of the "Metropolia" as the Orthodox Church in America (q.v.), he became the first primate, serving from 1970 to 1977.

**BELAVIN, TIKHON,** Patriarch of Moscow and All Russia, American missionary, martyr, St. (19 January 1865–7 April 1925). Baptized Basil, he graduated from the St. Petersburg Theological Academy in 1888 and was appointed to the faculty of the Pskov Theological Seminary. Tonsured a monk and ordained priest in 1891, he became rector of the Kazan and Kholm Theological Seminaries, and in 1897 was made archimandrite and consecrated Bishop of Lublin.

In 1898 he was appointed Bishop of the Aleutian Islands and Alaska with the bishop's seat in San Francisco. Arriving at age thirty-three as one of the youngest hierarchs of the Russian Church, he entered his cathedral church in San Francisco on 23 December. In evaluating his archpastoral assignment, three difficult circumstances stand out: 1) The Missionary Diocese included Alaska, Canada, and the U.S., and was too big to successfully administrate; 2) this diocese of the Russian Church included all ethnic Orthodox from throughout the world, a huge diversity of languages and cultures; and 3) neither New York, Chicago, nor San Francisco had proper church buildings. In response to this circumstance, in 1902 two cathedrals were completed in New York, one Russian, one Syrian. In 1903 Holy Trinity Cathedral in Chicago was completed, as designed by Louis Sullivan. (This is the only Sullivan church in the world—built under the supervision of Fr. John Kochurov [q.v.].)

In 1903 to 1904 Tikhon successfully established an auxiliary bishopric in Alaska with its cathedral at Sitka and an auxiliary bishopric of Brooklyn for the Syro-Arabic Mission for which Archimandrite Raphael Hawaweeny (q.v.) was consecrated; at the same time, the Greek Holy Trinity parish in New York became the private property of three Greek laymen. In 1905 the episcopal see was transferred from San Francisco to New York and Tikhon was made archbishop. In 1906, after the San Francisco earthquake, Tikhon acquired the present site of Holy Trinity Cathedral, San Francisco (completed in 1909), one of the oldest Orthodox parishes in the western hemisphere.

In 1905 he assisted in the founding of the first Orthodox seminary in the continental United States, located in Minneapolis. The next year he published his project for a multinational and autocephalous Orthodox Church for America and commissioned and published *The Ser-*

*vice Book of the Holy Orthodox Catholic Church* translated by Isabel F. Hapgood, long the only comprehensive church service book in English. In 1907 he convened the first All-American Council in Mayfield, Pennsylvania, after which he left for Russia. That year, he was appointed to the see of Iaroslavl', Russia, and in 1914 to the see of Vilno. On 23 June 1917 he was elected to the see of Moscow by the diocesan assembly and granted the title of metropolitan. In 1917 to 1918 the Church Council elected Tikhon presiding bishop of the first general Council of the Russian Church since the time of Peter the Great; and he was elected Patriarch of Moscow and All-Russia on 18 November, the former patriarch ruling in the 17th c. From this time through 1925, he defended the Church and its people from the Bolsheviks, terror, and political abuse, himself being imprisoned. He did appeal for obedience to legitimate decrees of the Soviet state. The evening he died, his prophetic last words were, "Now I will sleep . . . for the night will be long." He was canonized in Russia only after the collapse of Soviet communism.

**BELGRADE.** In Serbian "Beograd" means "white city." At the confluence of the Danube and Sava, this city is built on the site of the ancient city of Singudunum in the onetime Roman province of Illyria (q.v.). Today it is the capital of Serbia and the primatial see of the Serbian Orthodox Church (qq.v.). Its Archbishop, Pavle, bears the title patriarch. He presides over a local church of some eight million living throughout the territories of the former Yugoslavia (q.v.).

**BERDIAEV, NICHOLAS,** philosopher-theologian (6 March 1874–24 March 1948). After studying science at the University of Kiev and philosophy at the University of Heidelberg, he was for a time a Marxist, but returned to the Russian Orthodox Church after the 1905 Revolution. He opposed the second Revolution, after which he taught philosophy at Moscow University. He supported himself throughout his life as a writer and journalist. Exiled from the Soviet Union in 1922, he moved to Berlin and then Paris where he taught free courses in philosophy and religion, editing the journal *Put* from 1926 to 1939, and concentrating mainly on his prolific writing career. Among his works relating to Christianity are *The New Religious Consciousness and Society* (1907), *The Meaning of History* (1923), *The Destiny of Man* (1931), *Christianity and Class War* (1933), *The Fate of Man in the Modern World* (1935), *Freedom and the Spirit* (1935), and *Spirit and Reality* (1937). Although his understanding of Christianity was nontraditional in part, especially regarding creation and will, he has contributed greatly to our understanding of 20th c. Christian ethics, symbol, social theory, and personality and spiritual freedom (q.v.).

**BIBLE** *see* Scripture.

**BIRTH** ... *see* Feasts, Twelve Great. ...

**BLACHERNAE.** The site in northwest Constantinople of a series of churches dedicated to the Virgin Mary (qq.v.), the oldest of which was founded ca. 450. Around 500 an imperial palace was built nearby and, six hundred years later under the Comnene dynasty, it became the official residence of the emperors.

**BLESSING.** The verb "to bless" and the noun "blessing/s" are used extensively in Orthodox cultures with a wide range of meanings not found in everyday English, but these uses are rooted in cultures and parlance reflecting sensitivities to the Bible. Thus, not only are types and degrees of blessing distinguished, but the subject and object of the blessing change—frequently not God (q.v.) but a human being. We shall follow *Webster's* definitions and expand wherever necessary.

1) "To consecrate or hallow by religious rite or words: make or pronounce holy (and God blessed the seventh day, and sanctified it)." We may fairly distinguish at least five important nuances under this definition used by Orthodox: a) when God initiates and blesses something without reference to human volition, as in the first creation account in Genesis, b) when God initiates and blesses with reference to human volition, as in the blessings of the patriarchs, c) when human beings pray for the indwelling of the Holy Spirit (q.v.) in a person or sanctified object used for sacramental purposes, d) when human beings pray for simpler, utilitarian blessings in which an object is used for its rightful purpose and for salvation, as in the blessing of a vehicle of travel, e) the separation or setting aside of a person or object for exclusive use in service to God, as in a Nazirite vow or the consecration of a chalice. Generally, the word "consecration" or "sanctification" is used in reference to the "strongest types" of blessings in the group.

2) "To make the sign of the cross upon or over—often used reflexively." In addition to devoting oneself in prayer and guarding from evil, the sign of the cross is used liturgically to communicate the "peace of God" and to lay claim to someone on behalf of the Kingdom of God, as at the service of enlistment before Baptism (q.v.). In Orthodox practice the blessing of the sign of the cross is not restricted to the clergy, but is made by the laity as well, e.g., a mother over a child, spouses over one another before sleep, etc.

3) "To invoke divine care for: Pray for." To this definition we would add "to obtain permission or approval, especially in cases where obedience or spiritual authority are involved," e.g., when a monastic seeks a blessing from the head of the monastery to travel.

4) "a) Praise, glorify: to extol for excellences . . . b) to regard with great favor: approve highly." The two halves of this definition should preferably be separated into two distinct definitions, insofar as the first refers exclusively to God, whereas the second might refer more properly to men and women. The first corresponds to the Hebrew *brk* and the Greek *eulogitos*, while the second corresponds to the Hebrew *ashr* and the Greek *makarios*. Sometimes the second pair of words is translated by "happy, fortunate," when it refers to material prosperity, but much depends upon the context for an accurate understanding—and "blessed" may be more desirable in many circumstances. In addition to these expansions, it should be noted that blessings, along with curses, were used formulaically in support of covenants, as in the blessings in Deut 28. Also, the Beatitudes of Jesus (Mt 5) are referred to as blessings and may be associated with the new covenant in Christ.

**BLOOM, ANTHONY,** Metropolitan of Sourozh (19 June 1914– ). Born in Lausanne, Switzerland, to Andre B. Bloom, a diplomat in the Russian Imperial Service, and Xenia N. Scriabin, sister of the Russian composer, he was educated in Paris at the Lycée Condorcet and the Sorbonne. Stateless until 1937, he became a French citizen and received a Doctor of Medicine from the Sorbonne in 1943. He served in the French medical corps and the Resistance, 1939–1945, and was a general practitioner in France, 1945–1949. He took monastic vows in 1943 and became a priest of the Russian Orthodox Church (Moscow Patriarchate) in 1948. Chaplain to the Fellowship of St. Alban and St. Sergius (q.v.), London, 1949–1950, he was the vicar attached to the parish of St. Philip, London (Russian Orthodox Church), in 1950. Made hegumen in 1953 and archimandrite in 1956, he became Suffragan Bishop of Sergievo, Moscow Exarchate of Western Europe, in 1957. Made Archbishop of Sourozh in 1960 and Acting Exarch from 1962 to 1965, he was appointed Metropolitan of Sourozh and Exarch of the Patriarch of Moscow and All Russia in Western Europe in 1965. He is the author of *Living Prayer* (1965), *School for Prayer* (1970), *God and Man* (1971), and *Courage to Pray* (1973). His office also publishes the journal *Sourozh*, and he possibly enjoys the most highly regarded reputation of any living Russian cleric, both as "elder statesman" and spiritual guide.

**BOBRINSKOY, BORIS,** priest, theologian (1925– ). Born in Paris, a married priest with three children, he has been professor of dogmatic theology at the St. Sergius Orthodox Theological Institute (q.v.) since 1953. He has taught at the Institut Supérieur des Etudes Oecuméniques since 1968. Rector of the French Orthodox parish of the Holy Trinity, Paris, 1968–1979, and rector of the Russian Orthodox cathedral in Paris since 1979, he has also been a member of the World Council of Churches Faith and Order Commission. His articles and books are mainly in French and tend to focus on the Trinity, the Eucharist, and the ecumenical movement.

**BOGOMIL.** A dualist movement in Byzantium, particularly the Slavic territories in the Balkans (qq.v.), from the 10th–14th c., it was first preached by the Bulgarian priest, Bogomil. He rejected the sacraments (q.v.) and hierarchy of the Orthodox Church in favor of a spiritualized Christianity that saw matter and the world as intrinsically evil and reserved salvation for those who rejected this creation. Perhaps related to the Paulician heresy (q.v.) originating in Syria and Armenia in about the 7th c. or before, and with roots extending into ancient Manichaeism and gnosticism (q.v.), the movement is usually held to have played an important role in medieval Bosnia (q.v.) and to have taken on a second life in the Cathari or Albegensians of southern France during the 12th–13th c.—just when the Paulicians disappeared.

**BOROVOY, VITALI** (18 January 1916– ). Born in Belarus, he studied at Vilna Theological Seminary and Warsaw University. Ordained priest in 1944 to become vice-dean of the Minsk Theological Seminary, 1944–1954, then professor of ancient church history at the Leningrad Theological Academy, 1954–1962, from 1973 to 1978 he was dean of the Moscow Patriarchal Cathedral and professor of Byzantine church history at the Moscow Theological Academy. He has been deputy chairman of the department of external affairs of the Moscow Patriarchate and professor of history of the Western Church at the Moscow Theological Academy since 1985. He has represented the Russian Orthodox Church at the World Council of Churches from 1962 to 1966 and from 1978 to 1985. From 1966 to 1972 he was a member and assistant director of the Secretariat for Faith and Order, and is a member of the Central Committee and the Faith and Order Standing Committee. From 1962 to 1965 he served as an Orthodox observer at Vatican II, following up as a member of the WCC-RCC Joint Working Group, 1965–72, and, throughout, attending Christian World Communions annual meetings, 1962–85. He was a member of the WCC Baptism, Eucharist, and Ministry (BEM) steering group. His writings focus on ecumenical issues.

**BOSNIA.** The region in the north central area of the former Yugoslavia (q.v.) and, until recently, characterized by a mixed population of Orthodox Serbs, Catholic Croats, and Muslim Slavs, with the latter holding the plurality. The medieval state of Bosnia, more or less contiguous with the boundaries of the former Yugoslav republic, flourished in the 12th–14th c. Poised between the Roman Catholic world, represented chiefly by Hungary, and the Orthodox in Serbia (q.v.), its rulers have been accused of opting for a religion which sided with neither. Rather, they espoused the medieval dualism of the Bogomils (q.v.), though this is perhaps less certain than has often been maintained. With the Turkish conquest of all the Balkans in the 14th and 15th c., the formerly Christian (or Bogomil) population seems to have converted more or less en masse to Islam (q.v.). Their descendants thus constitute the largest group of Muslims among present-day Slavs (q.v.).

**BRECK, JOHN R.,** priest, New Testament scholar, theologian (1939– ). One of the few Orthodox Scripture scholars in America, John Breck earned a B.A. from Brown University (1960), an M. Div. from Yale Divinity School (1965), and a Dr. Theol. from Ruprecht-Karl University in Heidelberg (1972), as well as doing post-doctoral studies at St. Sergius Orthodox Institute (q.v.) in Paris. He has served as a director of continuing education for pastors of the Swiss Reformed Church in Switzerland (1972–75), professor of New Testament and patristics at St. Herman's Orthodox Seminary in Kodiak, Alaska (1975–78), professor of New Testament and director of studies at St. Sergius Orthodox Institute (1978–84), and since then has served as professor of New Testament and ethics at St. Vladimir's Orthodox Theological Seminary (q.v.) in New York.

In addition to belonging to several professional organizations and writing numerous articles on the New Testament and on medical ethics for scholarly journals, Breck has edited the periodical *Orthodox Alaska* and is currently editor of *St. Vladimir's Theological Quarterly*. His best-known short works are the introductions and annotations to 3–4 Macc in *The New Oxford Annotated Bible with Apocrypha* (1991). Majors works include *The Power of the Word* (1986), *The Spirit of Truth: The Origins of Johannine Pneumatology* (1991), and *The Shape of Biblical Language: Chiasmus in the Scriptures and Beyond* (1994).

**BUDDHISM, LAMAISM, IN TSARIST RUSSIA.** Westerners generally assume that the tsarist government in Russia always supported Orthodox Christianity to the exclusion of other faiths during the time of the Russian Empire. The historical record does not confirm this supposition. The winds of government, and we may include the opinions of the intelligentsia as well, blew in many directions in tsarist Russia.

During the 18th and 19th c. the lamas competed with Russian Orthodox missionaries among the peoples of eastern Siberia. The lamas taught Buddhism among these peoples in its Tibetan-Mongolian form, so-called lamaism. They easily adapted to prevailing social conditions by including in their pantheon the local gods and enlarging their cult with the local rites. By the first half of the 18th c. they obtained recognition of independent Siberian lamaism from the tsarist government, advancing as the chief agent of tsarism in Buryat-Mongolia. This accounted for the sympathy shown lamaism by the central, as well as the provincial, governments and the competition that they provided with Orthodox missionaries.

**BULGAKOV, MAKARII,** Metropolitan of Moscow, historian, dogmatician (1816–1882). Mikhail Bulgakov studied at the Belgorod Seminary and the Kiev Theological Academy where he received his master's degree for the book, *The History of the Kiev Theological Academy* (1843), during which time he was tonsured Makarii and accepted the chair in Russian and Church history. He was made professor at the Petersburg Theological Academy and received his doctorate of theology for his published lectures, *Introduction to Orthodox Theology* (1847), soon followed by a five-volume *Dogmatic Theology* (1851–53). A member of the Academy of Sciences (1854), he was consecrated Bishop of Tambov (1857), transferred to Kharkov (1859), to Vilna and Lithuania (1868), and finally to the metropolitanate of Moscow (1879). He wrote a condemnatory *History of the Russian Schism of Old Belief* (*see* Old Believers) in 1854, but changed his opinion of the controversy in volume six of his monumental history. That work, *The History of the Russian Church* (1857–82), was left unfinished in the thirteenth volume, and covered the period from 992 to 1667 as the first major history of the Russian Church. The appendixes to the volumes reveal important historical documents discovered by the Metropolitan in his research. Makarii is a good representative of 19th-c. Russian theologians, relying on Scripture and Holy Tradition (q.v.), but his history has been criticized for reflecting the official government position of Ober-Procurator Protasov (*see* Russian Orthodox Church).

**BULGAKOV, SERGIUS,** priest, theologian, educator, ecumenist (16 June 1871–12 July 1944). S. Bulgakov was professor of national economy in the Polytechnical Institute of Kiev in 1901, then lecturer at the University of Moscow, 1906, from which post he resigned in 1911 in protest of government policies in the university. He was also a member of the Duma in 1906.

Although he began as a Marxist, he eventually returned to his roots in the Orthodox Church and produced a stinging indictment of Marxism and "scientific" atheistic socialism (*From Marxism to Idealism,*

1904, et al.). At the same time, he sponsored journalistic endeavors (*Novy Put, Voprosy Zhizni*) with Nicholas Berdiaev (q.v.). In 1917 he was an active member of the All-Russian Church Council, serving on its Supreme Church Board, and wrote his primary religio-philosophical work, *The Unfading Light*. He took holy orders in 1918 and left Moscow for Sympheropol, where he taught at the university. The Soviet government banished him in 1922 with other writers and politicians, and he relocated to Prague to teach political economy at the Russian Graduate School of Law.

In 1925 he moved to Paris to teach dogmatic theology at the St. Sergius Orthodox Theological Institute (q.v.), later to become its dean. While in Paris he became instrumental in facilitating ecumenical dialogue, especially with the Anglicans. His philosophy of language, sympathetic to *imiaslavie* ("glorification of the Name"), is contained in *The Philosophy of Words* (1924/1930). While at St. Sergius he became involved in controversy over his attempt to interpret all Christian doctrine through the perspective of Sophia or Holy Wisdom, similar to Vladimir Soloviev (q.v.). The political climate with Moscow and with other émigrés, e.g., the Synod in Exile (q.v.), made open theological discussion unlikely, and complex theological speculation about metaphysics impossible. His most important books in English include *The Wisdom of God, A Brief Summary of Sophiology* (1927) and *The Orthodox Church* (1935). He is remembered as one of the outstanding speculative Russian theologians of the 20th c.

**BULGARIAN ORTHODOX CHURCH.** The modern state of Bulgaria is located north of Greece, east of Yugoslavian Macedonia, and south of Romania. Its capital is Sofia, the primatial see of the church, and its population of seven to eight million is more than 80 percent nominally Orthodox. The medieval kingdoms of Bulgaria were, from the original Bulgar invasion in 681 until the country's temporary absorption into Byzantium (q.v.) in 1018, and again from 1188 to 1373, the major rival to the Byzantine Empire (q.v.) for dominance of the latter's European territories. Originally of Turkic stock and language, the invaders had been largely absorbed into the local Slavs by the time of the country's conversion to Orthodox Christianity under Tsar Boris in 864. During the reign of Tsar Simeon (893–927) the Bulgarian Church became autocephalous (q.v.) with its patriarchal see at Preslav and then Ochrid (971). Medieval Bulgaria subsequently became a major center of translation work from Greek into Church Slavic through the work of Constantine-Cyril, Methodius, Clement of Ochrid, and Naum (qq.v.). Its missionaries and translations were thus poised to play a significant role in the conversion of Russia in the late 10th c. and following.

Although the patriarchate was suppressed by the Byzantines in 1018, it was restored from 1235 to 1393 at Trnovo. During its Turkish period the church was dominated by Constantinople (q.v.) and eventually lost its independence in 1767. After gaining political freedom it reasserted itself in 1870, and in 1953 the Metropolitan of Sofia again took the title of patriarch and is recognized as such throughout the Orthodox world.

**BURIAL PRACTICES.** Recently, it has been argued that the burial practices of the people of God since the Iron Age have been quite modest. The de-emphasis of material goods in tombs is thought to point to a recognition of an afterlife beyond the realm of earthly riches in the bosom of Abraham, Isaac, and Jacob. This attitude contrasts sharply with the elaborate and expensive funeral rites one may find in Egyptian, Greek, or Roman non-Christian cultures of the same period—and to a certain degree with the modern funeral industry of North America.

Whether this argument holds from the Iron Age to the early Roman period, it does seem to be supported by the archaeological evidence and literature we have from the early and imperial church, that is, the late Roman and Byzantine periods. For example, the early Christian attitude toward the body and the Byzantine canons related to burial both show a sensitivity toward the witness of a transformed flesh, so to speak, and a proscription against the elaborate and expensive rites of cremation. The deceased was—and still is—buried facing the east so that he may arise facing Christ on the day of the general resurrection (q.v.). The resurrection of the body, rather than cultural rites and votive offerings of a material nature, became the focus of the Christian burial rite.

The present-day liturgical rites of burial are thematic and include special times of prayer (q.v.). The liturgical themes, even when sung within funerary tones, speak primarily of salvation, the deliverance God provides his people, and resurrection. The liturgical colors are specified as bright.

The Western Christian practices of meditating on the Cross and death and wearing dark liturgical colors for funerals, probably originating around the 8th c., are not indigenous to the Orthodox Church. These may even be considered inappropriate because the Cross and death are primarily baptismal themes, i.e., in Baptism (q.v.) the new Christian dies with Christ and takes on a new life through the Cross. On the pastoral and human level, the clergy of the Orthodox Church consider it inhumane to the surviving family and friends of the deceased to focus on the Cross and death, since they have experienced enough of this tragedy in their loss: The message they need is that of salvation, deliverance, resurrection, and hope.

The special liturgical times of prayer at death—before death: penance, an anointing, and Holy Communion are appropriate—include prayers at the departure of the soul from the body, and again on the third, ninth, and fortieth days. The funeral service, patterned after the matins and including the interment, is usually served within three days when possible. The significance of the prayers at the departure of the soul is obvious; that of the third day is patterned after the three-day resurrection of Christ (counting Friday as the first day and beginning the third day in the evening, according to the Jewish and Christian liturgical reckoning); that of the ninth and fortieth days is after the vision of Macarius of Alexandria who saw these particular days as times of personal judgment. (*See* Cremation.) Celebrating the Divine Liturgy is not required for the funeral service, and the Orthodox have no Eucharistic celebration that is distinguished as a "Funeral Mass" per se. The funerals of priests and bishops are distinguished liturgically from those of the laity.

Although local burial practices are influenced by their respective cultures, of note are the current burial practices in monasteries on Mt. Athos (q.v.). The body of the deceased is interred on the day of death after only a brief (one-half hour) funeral service. After a sufficient period of time for the decomposition of the flesh, usually a year, the bones are placed in a general monastery ossuary and the skull is placed on a shelf in the ossuary vault with other skulls. A favorite epitaph on the skull shelf reflects the spiritual discipline of meditating on death: "Take heed, those of you who look in here, for you will soon be looking out." There are striking similarities between this burial practice and that mentioned above for the period from the Iron Age to the early Roman period. Among other burial practices in monasteries in Slavic countries, notably the Pechersk Lavra of the Kievan Caves, saintly relics are preserved through mummification.

**BYZANTINE ERA.** 1) The period of the Byzantine Empire extending from Constantine's founding of the New Rome, Constantinople (qq.v.), in 330 to Sultan Mohammed II's conquest of the latter on 29 May 1453. Quite the longest and most influential period in the history of the Orthodox Church, it left its impress on the latter's worship, theology, spirituality, and liturgy (qq.v.). The Byzantine era, moreover, enjoyed a kind of half-life—"Byzance après Byzance"—in the centuries of the Ottoman Empire when the Ecumenical Patriarch (qq.v.) acted similar to a surrogate emperor for the Ottomans' Christian population. In a sense, the Byzantine era in the Balkans and Middle East (qq.v.) does not truly end until the rise of nationalism and the emergence of the state churches in the 19th c.

2) A second, more technical sense of this phrase is that of a system of calendrical computation worked out in the 630s by the monk

George, which became the standard method of dating by the 10th c. Papers, including the decrees of emperors and patriarchs, were dated from the creation of the world, reckoned to have occurred in the year 5508 B.C. In Russia this system of dating, inherited from the Byzantines, was changed under Peter the Great in 1700. The system can still be seen in use among those Orthodox with archaizing tendencies.

**BYZANTINE LAW.** Up until the last two centuries of its existence, the law of Byzantium was Roman law as codified under Justinian (qq.v.) and as supplemented by the later additions of several emperors, as in Leo VI's *Ecloga* and *Novels* dealing with marriage and criminal law, or the summary, the *Epanagoge* (q.v.) prepared during the reign of the same emperor. This web of legislation, already venerable at the beginning of the Byzantine era (q.v.), contributed significantly to Byzantium's remarkable stability and placed effective, if not theoretical, limits on the powers of the emperor. Perhaps more importantly, it was also the matrix within which the Orthodox Church enacted its Canon Law (q.v.), the emperor being the latter's enforcer. Together with the scriptural, liturgical, and patristic sources provided to the Slavic churches in translation, a substantial selection of this legal tradition was also transmitted, for example in such collections as the Slavic *Kormchaya Kniga*. These collections included, as was the case in Byzantine law, both civil and ecclesiastical legislation.

**BYZANTINE RITE.** According to the use beginning in the Roman Catholic Church (q.v.), "rite" signifies both a form of Christian worship and the accompanying matrix of theology and spirituality (qq.v.) that the worship expresses and out of which it has grown. Thus "Byzantine rite" means the liturgy of Byzantium, more specifically as celebrated at the "Great Church" of Constantinople (qq.v.), and includes other elements, as the liturgist Fr. Robert Taft has rightly observed, such as architecture, iconography (qq.v.), etc. The Constantinopolitan liturgy was itself a fusion of different worship traditions in the ancient church, in particular those of Antioch, Jerusalem, and Cappadocia (qq.v.).

In place by the 9th c. and in virtually its present form by 1400, the liturgy of the Great Church had also become by this time the one and unique mode of worship in the Orthodox Church. Although local use may differ in minor degrees from country to country, region to region, or even from village to village, it is fundamentally the same texts, the same exterior and interior arrangement of the church building, and the same piety (q.v.), which reigns in Orthodoxy from the Adriatic coast to the Aleutian islands. It is accurate to say that the primary difference between "national" Orthodox churches today is merely the language of worship, and not its form or content. The Byzantine rite has thus served as the single greatest factor ensuring the unity of the Orthodox Church, in a way perhaps analogous to what used to prevail in the Anglican communion with respect to the old *Book of Common Prayer*. While generally characterized as sumptuous in its use of art, incense, and poetry, the frequent perception that this is the most static of the great Christian "rites" is a misconception—in fact, the opposite is nearer the truth. Of all ancient liturgies, the Byzantine has perhaps been the most fluid, in a state of continuous change since its beginnings in Constantinople and marked by at least two great shifts—in the 9th c. and 14th c.—during its growth in the Byzantine era (q.v.) alone.

**BYZANTIUM.** Founded in 660 B.C., this ancient Greek city on the Bosphorus was chosen by Constantine the Great as the site of his new imperial capital, Constantinople (qq.v.). The ancient name of the city was extended by Western European scholars in the 16th c. to include the empire that the city headed, hence the "Byzantine Empire." It should be remembered that the citizens of the Empire never referred to themselves as "Byzantines," unless they were inhabitants of the capital itself, or to their state as "Byzantine." They were, in their own eyes and down to practically the present day in the old territories of the Empire, instead "Romans" (*Rhomaioi* in Greek, *Rum* in Arabic), and their king was the "Roman Emperor" (*Basileus ton rhomaion*). As such, the emperor was the continuation of the sovereign rule begun in Augustus Caesar and, for Christianity, the visible head of the universal Christian commonwealth. The fundamental perspective of the "Byzantines" was that their empire was, in theory if certainly not in fact, "ecumenical," i.e., worldwide, and so the civil expression of the one, holy, catholic (q.v.), and apostolic Church. This universalist vision would live on in the office of the Ecumenical Patriarch in the years of the Ottoman Empire (qq.v.). It found a rival beginnning in the 16th c. in the constellation of popular Russian beliefs around the tsar and his capital, Moscow, as the "Third Rome," and thus as rightful head of the Orthodox *oikoumene* (q.v.). The rise of the nation states in the Balkans (q.v.) during the last century has further diluted the sense of a single center of the Orthodox Church, although the Ecumenical Patriarch retains his primacy of honor.

## -C-

**CABASILAS, NICHOLAS,** St. (ca. 1322–ca. 1390). Canonized by the Church of Greece in the 1980s, Cabasilas was a layman (perhaps a monk at the end of his life) active in the politics and social debate of Byzantium (q.v.), in particular of the city of Thessalonica (q.v.). His fierce social conscience, expressed in treatises such as his *On Usury*, led him to involvement in the crises affecting the failing Empire. He was at the same time an accomplished theologian, steeped in the spiritual and liturgical tradition (q.v.) of the Church. His *Commentary on the Divine Liturgy* and *On the Life in Christ* are masterpieces of Orthodox theology (q.v.) that continue to exercise a positive effect on contemporary Orthodox thought and piety (q.v.). Cabasilas was certainly acquainted and in sympathy with Gregory Palamas and Byzantine hesychasm (qq.v.), and his works reflect an attempt to bring Palamas's insights to bear on lay Christian life. Previously, the audience had been almost exclusively monastic.

**CAESAREA.** The name of several important cities, two of which were episcopal sees in the ancient church: Caesarea Maritima in Palestine and Caesarea in Cappadocia (q.v.). Both were regional centers, i.e., capitals of their respective provinces, and thus the home of archbishops or metropolitans. Caesarea in Palestine, formerly "Straton's Tower" and rebuilt by Herod the Great as his chief port with a remarkable harbor, was visited by the apostles (q.v.) Peter, Paul, and Philip, and was later the residence of Origen, Bishop Eusebius (qq.v.), and Jerome. It was captured by the Crusaders (q.v.) in 1101 and demolished by them in 1265. Basil the Great (q.v.) made the other Caesarea, his see in Cappadocia, famous in the latter half of the 4th c. and it remained a locus of ecclesiastical activity until the 11th c.

**CAESAROPAPISM.** This term denotes an ecclesiastical or political system wherein the head of state acts also as head of the church, including a predominant role in the formulation of doctrine. Caesar, in other words, acts also as pope. As such, the word has been frequently applied to Byzantium as well as to the authoritarian relationship between Church and state (qq.v.) in other and subsequent local Orthodox Churches, e.g., the Russian Church (q.v.) under the tsars (and the Communist state). This use, however, and the term itself are misleading—and indeed abusive. "Caesaropapism" is, at best, an anachronism, a reading of Church and state in Byzantium through the spectacles of the Western Middle Ages and Renaissance/Reformation. Relations between Church and emperor were far more complex and subtle than "caesaropapism" implies. Moreover, those relations were in continual evolution. Either Justinian in Constantinople or Peter the Great in Russia (qq.v.) came as close as anyone to fulfilling what the term implies, but even they fell short of it. Peter, for example, while seeking to reduce the Russian Church to a department of state, never claimed the right to define the Church's faith. His reforms, the Spiritual Regulation (q.v.), were of an administrative and disciplinary character, but were not doctrinal. Even Justinian felt compelled to acquire the blessing of the Church's leaders—though often, admittedly, via coercion. Happily, historians in more recent times, with the exception of those grinding away at obvious axes, have largely abandoned the word and its implications. (*See* Authority; Church and State.)

**CALIVAS, ALKIVIADIS,** priest, theologian (1932- ). Born in northern Epirus, Calivas grew up in New York City and completed his studies at Holy Cross Greek Orthodox School of Theology (q.v.), earning a B.A. (1956). He received his S.T.B. (1960) from General Theological Seminary, New York, the Th.M. (1970) from St. Vladimir's Orthodox Theological Seminary (q.v.), and the Th.D. (1982) in Liturgics from the University of Thessaloniki School of Theology. In 1956 he was ordained a priest of the Greek Orthodox Archdiocese (q.v.).

Fr. Calivas is professor of liturgics at Holy Cross Greek Orthodox School of Theology. He has been teaching at Holy Cross since 1978, and was dean from 1980 to 1993. Active in ecumenical, interfaith, and pan-Orthodox consultations and conferences, he has served on several Archdiocesan commissions and boards, and as president of the National Council of Presbyters. He has written several articles and books, including *The Divine Liturgy: The Time of Its Celebration, Come Before God,* and more recently, *Great Week and Pascha in the Greek Orthodox Church.*

**CANON LAW.** The term "canon" is a Greek word that comes from Hebrew and means a "reed or straight rod" used for measuring, i.e., a "yardstick" (which has the same bivalent senses in English). In early Christianity it was used to connote a rule or norm of behavior, truth, or faith (Gal 6:16). Canons are distinguished from dogmas (q.v.) in that canons are generally disciplinary rules for the organization and administration of the Church, whereas dogmas are immutable doctrines and basic principles of faith. For example, canons may be changed by human agency but dogmas may not. The canons of the Seven Ecumenical Councils (q.v.) are given certain precedence in the Eastern Church over laws of local churches.

Canons differ also from state laws on Church matters, an important point since Orthodoxy has a long history of relations between Church and state (q.v.). Every state defines the relationship between itself and Church bodies, but this is not Canon Law. Canon Law differs both in origin and discipline from state law, e.g., Byzantine law (q.v.). Canon Law is made by the Church, while state law is issued by secular powers—two different institutions of society. Further, the principle of Church discipline is voluntary obedience and not forced constraints, as it is with the state. It is true that the Church may impose disciplinary punishment for violation of Canon Law, but these disciplinary measures are to be voluntarily accepted and followed: they are not forced. The most severe ecclesiastical discipline is excommunication, which in itself might not even physically separate the individual from the community. In summary, Canon Law is passed by the Church itself and established by its own legislative bodies. Church law does not lose its specific character if, as sometimes happens, the state assumes responsibility for it and approves it. Ultimately the Church is responsible for the formulation and application or "economy" (q.v.) of its own laws.

Eastern Orthodox Canon Law comes from three sources: Holy Scripture, Church legislation, and Church custom. Although the Scriptures (q.v.) are the basic source of Canon Law, one would search in vain there for a detailed system of Church organization. The significance of Scripture as it relates to Canon Law is that it embodies principles of Christian doctrine from which rules may be extrapolated for solving disciplinary problems within the Church—but only the Church itself may do that. The second source, Church legislation, originated not only as written rules, but also as oral tradition. The legislation is comprised of the local church councils preceding the Ecumenical Councils, the Ecumenical Councils themselves, and the local church councils afterward. Church custom or usage is different from Holy Tradition (q.v.) in that Holy Tradition is looked to for dogma, while custom is a source for ecclesiastical discipline. For example, Basil of Caesarea (q.v.) emphasized repeatedly that some disciplinary rules were accepted "not on the ground of any canon but only on the ground of usage followed by those who have preceded us" (Canon 4, 87). Still, not every custom may be a basis of Canon Law. In order to be so, the custom must have been observed for a long time, it must have been freely subscribed to, and it must be in conformity with principles of faith and order.

The body of Canon Law of the early Church included the Apostolic Canons, the Canons of the Ecumenical Councils, the Canons of the Local Councils, and the Canons of the Holy Fathers. Later collections that were popularly used are those of Dionysius Exiguus, John Scholasticus, *Syntagma Canonicon, The Nomocanons,* and the 12th c. *Canonical Editions* of Aristenus, Zonaras, and Balsamon (qq.v.). The most extensive, comprehensive collections in modern times were made by Russian, Greek, Serbian, and Bulgarian scholars of the 19th c. The best available English edition of the canons of the undivided Church is H. R. Percival's volume XIV of the *Library of Nicene and Post-Nicene Fathers.*

**CAPPADOCIA.** This semiarid region is in the east central area of Asia Minor with Caesarea (qq.v.) its principal city. The site of a minor kingdom in the Hellenistic era, it became a Roman province in A.D. 17, but remained a backwater until brought to prominence by the Cappadocian Fathers (q.v.) of the late 4th c. For many centuries it served as the primary military reserve of Byzantium (q.v.) until the disastrous battle of Mantzikert in 1071, which resulted in the permanent loss of eastern and central Asia Minor first to the Seljuk Turks and then to the Ottomans. While the population of Cappadocia was largely converted to Islam (q.v.), it seems that within a matter of decades, pockets of Christian Greeks and Armenians survived in the area until the latter's massacre during World War I and the forced population exchange involving the former in 1924.

**CAPPADOCIAN FATHERS.** While in theory this phrase could include other Church Fathers (q.v.) such as Gregory the Wonderworker (late 3rd c.) or Amphilocius of Iconium (late 4th c.), it is normally reserved for three of the most important ecclesiastical figures of the 4th c.: Basil the Great, Gregory of Nazianzus, and Gregory of Nyssa (qq.v.). It is difficult to exaggerate the significance of the contribution these three made to the following areas of Orthodox thought: the theology of the Trinity, Christology, anthropology (qq.v.), creation, soteriology, liturgy (q.v.), asceticism/monasticism (qq.v.), and mysticism. Theirs was the leadership, both intellectual and ecclesiastico-political, that enabled the final defeat of the challenge to all of the above categories—especially the Trinity—mounted by 4th-c. thinkers such as Arius and Eunomius (qq.v.). Their thought provided the foundations for the correction of Origen, the synthesis of Maximus the Confessor (perhaps the principal theologian of later Byzantium), and of Gregory Palamas (qq.v.).

**CAROLINGIANS.** This name refers to the court of Charlemagne (q.v.), and in particular to the theologians and church leaders whom that king and his successors sponsored in the late 8th and early 9th c. The importance of the Frankish Kingdom (present-day northern France and West Germany) begins in fact with Charlemagne's father and founder of the dynasty, Pippin I, and the latter's alliance with Pope Stephen II and the papacy (q.v.) in 754. The alliance promised the popes freedom from the manipulations of princes (including the emperors at Byzantium [q.v.]) in return for recognition of the dynasty's legitimacy. It marked thus an epochal shift in the ancient axis of the Christian *oikoumene* (q.v.), from a line running east-west along the Mediterranean Sea to a north-south extension from Rome (q.v.) to the mouths of the Rhine. In this shift the Western Church turned in on itself and, more importantly, away from Constantinople (q.v.) as the throne of the sole Christian emperor. (One should note that the East under the Isaurian

Dynasty [q.v.] was going through a similar process.) The shift is marked at once by a political schism, the crowning of Charlemagne by Pope Leo III in 800 as "Roman Emperor," and by the efforts of the new emperor's court theologians to isolate the "Greeks," in support of their sovereign's universal claims, by branding the Church of Constantinople and the Empire it served as heretical. They drew strength from the establishment and stimulation of new schools and a program in Latin, all of which took place in the context of the Church.

The Carolingian theological program saw, among other things, the addition of the *filioque* to the Nicene-Constantinopolitan Creed (qq.v.), together with an insistence on the addition as a necessary article of the Christian faith. Particular stress was also laid on the papal office, an emphasis that was marked in turn by the creation of documents, such as the *Donation of Constantine* (q.v.), purporting to be ancient testimonies to the pope's role both as governor of the universal Church and as source of all Christian political legitimacy. In effect a kind of revolution, the Carolingian reform paved the way for modern Europe and, more proximate to its own time, for the Gregorian reforms of the 11th c., the ensuing final rupture between the East and West, and the great papal theocracy of the High Middle Ages.

**CASSIAN, JOHN**, St. (ca. 360–ca. 432). Born in Marseilles, he was a trusted adviser to Pope Leo the Great (q.v.). Though a Latin, it is in the Orthodox Church that John is included in the calendar of saints. Familiar with Egyptian monasticism (q.v.) and especially with Evagrius of Pontus (q.v.) by virtue of a long stay in the monastic center of Scete, locale par excellence of the Desert Fathers (q.v.), John became the vehicle through whom the spirituality and insights of the desert were transferred to the Western Church. He accomplished this both by establishing monasteries, notably his foundation at Lerins in southern Gaul, and through his writings, especially his *Institutes* and *Conferences*. His hesitations concerning—or outright rejection of—certain tenets of Augustine of Hippo (q.v.), especially the latter's doctrines of "original guilt" and predestination, would make him suspect in the eyes of later Western theologians who labeled him "Semi-Pelagian" (which charges Eastern theologians consider false), though no such accusations affected him or his reputation greatly during his own lifetime. His career as a theologian is marked by its influence on Pope Leo, who held him in high esteem, especially for his seven volumes entitled *De Incarnatione Domini,* and whose opposition to Nestorius (q.v.) bears the marks of Cassian's thought. The latter owes much both to the Cappadocian Fathers and to John Chrysostom (qq.v.), who had ordained Cassian deacon at the turn of the 5th c. In the Orthodox East, John is remembered as "St. Cassian the Roman," on 29 February, and

Nicodemus of the Holy Mountain, while compiling the *Philokalia* (qq.v.), included a selection from his writings under that heading.

**CATECHESIS.** In the first four centuries of the Church's history, the teaching of ethics and basic doctrine—followed by Baptism (q.v.), Chrismation, and the reception of the Eucharist (q.v.)—took place during a catechumenate that lasted from one to three years. This situation changed drastically in the 5th c. when the Christianization of the Byzantine Empire meant that infant Baptism became the prevalent way to receive people into the Church.

In the early Church (and in some places today) the instruction of catechumens was not usually given by bishops and priests until the final baptismal phase. (*See* Cyril of Jerusalem.) Although many people came from pagan backgrounds, this fact alone did not account entirely for the length of instruction in comparison with later practice. Much more information was thoroughly taught in the early centuries. For example, it was common for catechumens to attend a daily matins service. Over the course of the instruction, the entirety of the Scriptures (q.v.) would be read to them and explained by specially appointed teachers. It was expected that the length of the catechumenate would be sufficient to test the ethics of the individual. "Exorcism" (q.v.) as a class in moral behavior followed by a prayer of deliverance from a particular evil—a kind of preparation for confession of sins in the modern practice—was also administered by the laity. The catechumenate was also long enough to secure the person's full participation in, and assimilation into, the Christian community. Only at the end of this process was the Nicene-Constantinopolitan Creed (q.v.) and the Lord's Prayer taught to the catechumen.

The Church has historically differentiated between those people who have already participated in Baptism and the Eucharist and those who have not. The lack of differentiation between these two groups seeking to enter the Orthodox Church has clouded the issue of why catechumens were dismissed from the Divine Liturgy in the past: People without experience of Baptism and the Eucharist are not able to understand what happens during the liturgy (q.v.) of the faithful. Further, the catechumens were most likely not "sent away" in their dismissal, but were *sent to* continued instruction, which did not preclude fellowship with the community.

Today as the Divine Liturgy is celebrated, the trisagion hymn is periodically replaced by the hymn, "As many as have been baptized into Christ have put on Christ, Alleluia." This biblical hymn marks customary days of Baptism within the Church, and occurs on Christmas (25 December), Theophany (6 January), Holy Saturday (Easter) and the whole of Bright Week (i.e., the eight days or octave of the feast),

## TABLE 1
### FORMAT FOR ADULT CATECHESIS

| | Evangelism: First Period | First Liturgical Action | Catechesis: First Stage | Second Liturgical Action | *Catechesis Second Stage | Third Liturgical Action | Catechesis: Third Stage |
|---|---|---|---|---|---|---|---|
| NATURE | Time of evangelization or pre-catechumenate; spiritual awakening of faith. | Reception into the catechumenate; assigning of sponsors | Time of catechumenate (education in faith) | Rite of election or inscription of names; names included in prayer for catechumen and in Great Entrance. Exorcisms. | Time of baptismal retreat; time of purification and enlightenment (consecration of faith) | Entrance into the Church: Baptism; Chrismation; Kiss of Peace; Eucharist. | Time of post-baptismal catechesis or mystagogia (full maturation in faith) |
| TEACHING | Need for repentance; Two Ways; Kingdom of God | The Way of the Lord The Covenants The Gospels | | The Trinity The Creed The Lord's Prayer | | Baptism, Chrismation, Eucharist, and other sacraments, ethics from the new spiritual viewpoint | |
| SIGNIFICANCE | First proclamation of the Kingdom of God and Jesus Christ | The individual is "claimed" for the Kingdom of God; first welcome into the Church | Experience of the Kingdom of God and the Christian life: Vespers; Matins; Liturgy of the Word | Formal admission to the list of those to be baptized | Intensive preparation and fasting for the reception into the Church | Rebirth from death; resurrection with & lifting liturgical experience and life in the Church putting on Christ | |
| Gift Received | None suggested | Holy Scriptures | | Prayer Book and Icon | | Cross (Baptismal Garment) | |
| Length** | Unlimited | From one to three years | | Begins Lent | 40 days | weeks following feast: 1 to several | |
| Name of Subject | Inquirers | | Catechumens | | The Elect (Baptizands or Fotizomenoi) | | Neophytes |

*Those persons who are baptized, but not chrismated and in full communion with the Orthodox Church, fall into this second area.

**These time spans are normative and pastorally adaptable.

and on Pentecost. These traditional days of Baptism occur at the end of three catechetical seasons in which catechumens are prepared for reception into the Church. Each season is ended by a day on which is read a text directly relating to Baptism, as listed below.

**BAPTISMAL DAYS**
1. Holy Saturday Paschal Service
Mt 28:1–20 ("Go therefore and make disciples of all nations baptizing them. . . . ")
2. Pentecost
Jn 7:37–52, 8:12 ("If anyone thirst, let him come to me and drink. . . . ")
3. Theophany
Mt 3:13–17 (The baptism of Jesus)

**CATECHETICAL SEASONS**
1. Forty days of Great Lent
2. Forty days from Thomas Sunday to Pentecost
3. Forty days of the pre-Nativity fast

Table #1 has been used recently to describe the renewal of adult catechesis in the Orthodox Church.

**CATECHUMEN-CATECHISM** *see* Catechesis.

**CATHOLIC.** This adjective derives from a compound of the Greek *kata* (according to) and *holon* (the whole). Its precise meaning is debated, though it probably has the original sense of "complete" or "full." Later on, it acquires the meaning of "universal," i.e., as in extent or territory. Ignatius of Antioch (q.v.) in the *Epistle to the Smyrneans* first used it to describe the church, *he katholike ekklesia,* and then Irenaeus of Lyons (q.v.) used it to signify the true Church of Christ in contrast to the sects and conventicles of, in particular, gnosticism (q.v.). Following Irenaeus's use, the word became standard among Christian writers, hence its deployment in the article on the Church in the Nicene-Constantinopolitan Creed (q.v.). The later Church Slavic translation of the Greek word as *sobornaya,* from the verb *sobirat'* (to gather), together with the substantive *sobornost* derived therefrom, has influenced a particular strain of Russian ecclesiology since Alexis Khomiakov (qq.v.) in the 19th c. Khomiakov, and the many who followed his lead, saw this term as expressing the conciliar and communal nature of the Orthodox Church, in particular with regard to the question of authority (q.v.) and in contradistinction to both papal centralization and Protestant divisiveness (denominationalism).

**CATHOLICITY.** From "catholic" (q.v.), hence the quality of completeness or wholeness possessed by the catholic Church. The term acquires later in church history the sense of "universality," first of all meaning "inclusiveness," i.e., the Church as the proper home of all humankind, and secondly and still later of "extension," i.e., the Church as including all of its local manifestations. Hence the phrase, "catholic Church," comes to mean something distinct from and greater than the local church in much the same way that people today distinguish an entire corporation from its local, or branch, office. Orthodox theologians tend at present to believe the last meaning to be at best misleading and, at worst, a serious distortion of catholicity's original meaning. (*See* Ecclesiology.) If an extension of the definition is to be made on a geographic basis, then many Orthodox theologians would insist that it be extended on a temporal basis as well.

**CERULARIUS, MICHAEL,** Patriarch of Constantinople (ca. 1005–1059). Cerularius was the subject of the excommunication laid down by Cardinal Humbert da Silva, papal legate, on 16 July 1054, the date customarily given as marking the schism between Rome and the East. It is a peculiar irony that Patriarch Michael, an arrogant and ambitious man who had raised the claims of Church (the patriarch) over the state (the emperor) to their highest pitch ever in the history of Byzantium (q.v.), should have quarreled with Humbert, an equally ambitious and choleric individual who was also a mainstay of the great papal reforms with their claims advancing the papacy (q.v.) as supreme in the spheres of both Church and state. While it is the case that the Crusades (q.v.) were unquestionably more important in creating and sustaining the schism, it is also true that the rupture that took place because of Cerularius and Humbert was never subsequently healed. This Patriarch himself did grow extremely powerful. Particularly after the incident in 1054, he ran the government until suffering exile at the hands of Emperor Isaac I, whom he had helped place on the throne.

**CHALCEDON, COUNCIL OF.** Fourth of the Ecumenical Councils (q.v.), the synod at Chalcedon—an ancient city that had become and remains a suburb of Constantinople—was convoked by the Emperor Marcion in 451 to deal with the heresy (q.v.) of Eutychius and the machinations of the Patriarch Dioscurus of Alexandria. The definition of the union between God (q.v.) and man in Christ promulgated by the council led to the permanent rupture in communion between the Churches of Rome and Constantinople (qq.v.), on the one hand, and the local Churches of Alexandria, Armenia, Ethiopia, and much of Antioch (qq.v.), on the other. Debate centered over a single phrase in Christology (q.v.): Christ is one person (*hypostasis*) *in* two natures (*en* *dyo physesin*). The difficulty lay in the "in." To the dissidents, this preposition sounded like the affirmation of two Christs, one God and the other man. They held instead to the formula dear to Cyril of Alexandria (q.v.), "one nature of God the Word incarnate," i.e., Christ, though human and divine, is yet one, truly God become human. This formula led to the epithet "monophysite" (*mia physis*, one nature), not of their choosing, by which they have usually been known.

The troublesome phrase had been received by the council fathers in a letter from Pope Leo I (q.v.), and the latter had been strikingly preemptory in his insistence on its adoption. The Church of Rome would afterward be consistent in its sensitivity to any possible threat to the council with which it saw its prestige identified. This double dilemma, Roman intransigence on the one side and stubborn loyalty to the older formula of Cyril on the other, explains much about the 230-year debate that followed this council, punctuated by the Fifth Ecumenical Council at Constantinople in 553, and concluding with the Sixth, again at the capital, in 681. The emperors, in particular Justinian (q.v.) and Heraclius, sought consistently to bring the dissidents back into communion with the Church of Constantinople, and thus with the Empire, while at the same time trying to keep the nervous authorities in Rome content, keeping open the possibility of reconquest in the West. The task proved impossible and, with the rise of Islam (q.v.) and the ensuing loss of the Roman Near East, the efforts came to an end. The schism in the East, however, remains to the present day, although talks between the Chalcedonian and Oriental Orthodox (q.v.) over the past thirty years lend some substance to the hope that it might come to an end in the foreseeable future.

**CHARLEMAGNE,** Emperor (742–814). The son of Pippin I, King of the Franks, Charlemagne (the name means "Charles the Great") succeeded his father in 771 and was crowned Roman Emperor by Pope Leo III at Rome on Christmas Day, 800. In some respects the founder of modern Western Europe, Charlemagne was a remarkably able military leader, at his death leaving an Empire stretching from the Pyrenees to the borders of modern Poland, and from northern Italy to the mouths of the Rhine. His legislation laid the foundations for the later rise of the European universities, the dominance of the Benedictine order of monks, and provided for a widespread revival of Latin learning that, though short-lived, still provided a memory that would begin to flower two centuries later.

Western Europe itself lives, in a sense, on his memory. It was Charlemagne, both in his policies and his actual coronation, who marked the decisive move on the part of the newly baptized nations of the West to break away from the suzerainty of Byzantium (q.v.)—titular in fact, if not in theory. The political and cultural schism fostered by the Carolingians (q.v.) foreshadowed the ecclesiastical rupture that would come two and a half centuries later. While the last political echo of Charlemagne's Empire died with the dissolution of the Austro-Hungarian Empire in 1919, his legacy endures. It is surely no accident, though probably not deliberate, that the founding members of the early European Economic Community corresponded essentially (less southern Italy) with the territories of his 9th-c. kingdom.

**CHILIASM** *see* Millennialism.

**CHITTY, DERWAS J.**, priest, educator (1901–1971). Educated at Winchester School, in 1920 he attended New College, Oxford, completing his Theology Finals in 1925. He lived in Jerusalem and Egypt off and on between 1925 and 1931. In Jerusalem he came in contact with his lifelong passion, the Orthodox Church. In 1927 he returned to England to begin training for the Anglican ministry at Cuddeston Theological College; and he attended the founding of the Fellowship of St. Alban and St. Sergius, making the lasting acquaintance of Vladimir Lossky (q.v.) and other important Orthodox thinkers. He was ordained deacon in the Anglican Church in 1928 and priest in 1929. While in Jerusalem from 1929 to 1931, he came very close to joining the Orthodox Church—partly because of the influence of Archbishop Anastasii of the Russian Mission. He served the parish of Upton, Berkshire, from 1931 to 1940 and 1946 to 1968, and retired from the Anglican ministry. His book on monasticism (q.v.), *The Desert a City,* from the Birkbeck Lectures delivered at Cambridge in 1958 to 1959, has been influential among Orthodox and non-Orthodox alike.

**CHRISTMAS** *see* Feasts, Twelve Great.

**CHRISTOLOGY.** Literally, this term means the doctrine of the Messiah, Jesus of Nazareth. The question that Jesus directed to his disciples in all three of the Synoptic Gospels, "Who do you say I am?" drew the response from Peter, "You are the Messiah, the Son of God." The full implications of Peter's reply remained to be worked out. "Messiah," "Son of God," and so on, were all different appellations that could mean much less than a divine and preexistent being. Other New Testament texts, however, the earliest being Philp 2:5–11 and a later one the prologue from Jn (1:1–18), taught the preexistence of the divine Son. Just how, though, humanity and divinity coexist in Christ, and the meaning of each in relation both to the Father and to the rest of humankind, were the subjects of fierce debate throughout most of the first Christian millennium. Orthodox Christology, as it emerges in John of Damascus (q.v.) in the 8th c., is the product of that long debate. The key refrain or leitmotiv throughout the centuries of argument in Eastern Christendom is the notion of deification, *theosis* (q.v.). Christology is always linked to and expressive of an understanding of salvation that is articulated as early as 2 Pet 1:4, that in Christ human beings become "partakers of the divine nature"—which the Orthodox see as at least implicit in other New Testament documents. (For example, the "glory" shared by the Son and the Father is from eternity, and is given by Christ to his followers, Jn 17:5, 22–24.) With this reading of the Christian Scriptures (q.v.), the struggle over Christology may be viewed as an attempt to keep in balance Christ's humanity and divinity in such a way as to preserve both the paradox of their union in his person (so toward the "hypostatic union" of Chalcedon [q.v.]) and the possibility of human communion in the divine life.

The battle had obviously been joined by the time of the earliest Christian writings: Paul struggles in his letters to the Corinthians against what appears to be a nascent Christian gnosticism (q.v.). The Johannine works are clearly directed in part against a popular docetism, i.e., the notion that Christ's flesh or humanity was a mere seeming or phantom. In the 2nd c. dualism was very prevalent in the ancient world, whether in the sophisticated version of Plato's (q.v.) divide between sensible and intelligible worlds or in the popular equation of matter with evil and the immaterial with good (which would show up with especial force in 3rd-c. Manichaeism). Dualism took shape in the gnostic movement. The dualistic portrait of Christ as the manifestation, in the appearance of flesh, of the realm of pure spirit found vigorous opponents in, among others, Irenaeus of Lyons and Tertullian of Carthage (qq.v.). Irenaeus insisted upon the full reality of the Word's coming in the flesh, his incarnation, and thus that Jesus, as the second Adam and model—as divine Son—of the first, accomplished the recapitulation of all creation and its redemption from the powers of sin (q.v.) and death. This triumph, he continued, would become manifest at the Second Coming or Parousia. (*See* Millennialism.)

The 3rd c. saw the Church Fathers (q.v.) struggling with adoptionism, a doctrine associated particularly with Bishop Paul of Samosata, and modalism, linked especially with the Roman presbyters, Praxeas and Sabellius. Adoptionists argued that the man, Jesus, had been adopted by God (q.v.) the Father at the moment of the former's baptism (cf. Mk 1:9–12). Modalists saw the three persons of the Trinity (q.v.) as three moments in the revelation of the one divine person. On occasion both adoptionism and modalism were combined, as in the case of Paul of Samosata. Tertullian wrote extensively, particularly in his *Against Praxeas,* in answer to the modalists, while Dionysius of Alexandria chaired a local synod at Antioch (qq.v.) in 261 that deposed Paul of Samosata. Of note for the future was the latter council's explicit condemnation of the term "*homoousios*" (of the same substance), which Paul had used in order to explain that the Word of God, as a mere aspect or power of the Father and not as a separate person in his own right, had been bestowed upon Jesus of Nazareth at his messianic anointing.

This early condemnation of *homoousios* would play a significant role in the controversy of the 4th c. regarding the Alexandrian presbyter, Arius, and the struggle over the Nicene Creed (qq.v.). Arius had proposed that the Word of God incarnate in Christ was less than divine, a creature of the one God and Father. His understanding of salvation seems in consequence to have been based upon a "heroic" model of Christ as trailblazer and exemplar. Against this view, first Alexander and then Athanasius of Alexandria (q.v.) championed the teaching of Irenaeus: that God himself had taken on humanity in order to make his creatures participants in his divinity. The First Ecumenical Council (q.v.) at Nicaea in 325 endorsed a creed that incorporated the word *homoousios* in order to underline the Word's co-divinity or consubstantiality with the Father and so retain the traditional doctrine of *theosis.* Due to the term's prior association with modalism, however, it was not accepted readily by the Eastern bishops.

Athanasius was quite wrong to brand all of his opponents with the label, "Arians." Most of the educated, Greek-speaking episcopacy were theological followers of Origen (q.v.) and embraced the latter's use of *hypostasis* (usually translated now as "person," but more literally meaning something closer to "substance") for the three persons of the Trinity. In consequence, though, they were obliged to assume Origen's subordinationism as well, that is, the notion that Son and Spirit stand in a lesser, subordinate relationship to God the Father. It was this tendency in Origen's thought that contributed substantially to Arius's initial success in persuading some — scarcely all — of the Eastern bishops to approve his program. Most disliked both him and Athanasius, and with some justice. It required the singular genius of the Cappadocian Fathers (q.v.) to find a solution incorporating both Athanasius's insistence on the full divinity of the Son and Origen's terminology, an accomplishment sealed by the endorsement of the expanded Nicene Creed at the Second Ecumenical Council at Constantinople (q.v.) in 381. Counter-Arian arguments continued to play an important role in the Christian West; and following the fall of the Western Empire its Gothic and Visigothic masters were Arians. It is against this background, the need to insist on Christ's divinity, that we are to understand the introduction of the *filioque* (q.v.) clause into the Nicene-Constantinopolitan Creed at the Council of Toledo in 589.

Debate in the 5th c. took its start from the arguments that Apollinaris of Laodicea had advanced during the counter-Arian debates of the 4th c. Apollinaris argued that the divine Word had become incarnate not in a complete humanity, but merely in a physical body. Gregory of Nazianzus (q.v.) had responded with the formula, "What is not assumed is not saved." Christ had to have been a complete human being for *theosis* to be a reality. Continuing this line of thought, notable representatives of the Antiochene school such as Theodore of Mopsuestia (q.v.) and Diodore of Tarsus so emphasized the completeness of Christ's humanity as to throw the union between the "assumed man" (Jesus) and the divine Son into some doubt. Christ, at least to the critics of this school, took on the aspect of a committee of two. A pupil of Theodore's, Nestorius of Constantinople, was led in 428 to deny that Mary the Virgin (q.v.) could rightly be called *Theotokos* ("Birthgiver of God"), but could only be considered as the bearer of Christ, *Christokos*. This drew the formidable opposition of Cyril of Alexandria (q.v.), who saw Nestorius's distinction as threatening the unity of the God-man and, in consequence, the believer's hope of deification. Cyril won his case at the Third Ecumenical Council at Ephesus in 431. His often unscrupulous and violent methods, however, together with some real ambiguities in his theology, led to the secession of the whole east, Syriac-speaking Church of Persia from communion with the Church of the Byzantine Empire (qq.v.). This community, wrongly identified too strictly as adherents of "Nestorianism," persists to the present day.

Cyril's imprecise terminology, together with his stature as *the* interpreter of the incarnation, led to further difficulties following his death in 444. Later in the same decade, a Constantinopolitan archimandrite named Eutyches advocated a union of God and man in Christ, which was, in effect, a blending of the two wherein Jesus' humanity was seen as entirely swallowed up by the glory of his godhead. The *Tome* of Pope Leo the Great (q.v.) was written in response to Eutyches and served as the basis for the doctrinal definition at the Fourth Ecumenical Council at Chalcedon in 451. Leo's balanced thought and phrasing stressed the completeness of Christ's two "natures" (q.v.), human and divine, and their union in the one person or *hypostasis* of the Word. Unfortunately, the pope's insistence on the phrase, "in two natures," led to great resistance on the part of the entire Church of Egypt and much of that of Syria (qq.v.). The latter's standard of orthodoxy was the phrase, "one nature of the incarnate Word," which Cyril (q.v.) had often used in the (mistaken) belief that it came from Athanasius—it was actually Apollinaris's invention. To the "monophysites," Leo's phrase smacked of Nestorius. The so-called "monophysite heresy" was thus not so much a heresy as a schism (qq.v.). Monophysitism (q.v.) in fact, less the unhappy Eutyches, was nothing more or less than a dogged clinging to the thought and language of Cyril. The schism did, however, take the local churches of Egypt, Ethiopia, Armenia, and substantial portions of Syria (qq.v.) out of communion with the imperial church. It thus constituted an internal crisis of the Eastern Empire that the latter's emperors sought over the following two centuries to address and repair. The Emperor Justinian (q.v.) looked to assuage "monophysite" objections to Chalcedon by convoking the Fifth Ecumenical Council (Constantinople II, A.D. 553) in order to affirm the theopaschism of Cyril's "Twelve Anathemas" of Nestorius, and thus to affirm that it is indeed the Word of God who is the subject of all attribution in the incarnate Christ. His initiative failed to solve the schism.

A later effort, sponsored by the Emperor Heraclius (610–645), and articulated by the Patriarch Sergius of Constantinople, put forward a compromise formula which, while stressing Chalcedon's "two natures," argued that in Christ there is only one activity and will, the divine. This, the true heresy of monotheletism (*mono,* same, and *thelema,* will), was resisted by Pope Martin I and, in particular, Maximus the Confessor (qq.v.). Maximus asserted that the compromise betrayed a defective anthropology (q.v.), leaving no room for the necessary human response to the divine initiative accomplished in Christ. Deification, in short, is not an absolutely one-sided process. The Son of God took on a complete humanity and restored the "old Adam" entirely, but this meant first of all that the human will had to have been redeemed and, secondly, that each believer is called upon to discover and exercise his or her personal will in acceptance of the salvation accomplished once and for all in Jesus. Maximus's argument was ratified, by the Sixth Ecumenical Council (Constantinople III, 681) some nineteen years after his death in exile.

The 8th and 9th c. debate over the holy icons (q.v.) and iconoclasm might be taken as the conclusion to Christological debate in the East. The arguments in particular of John of Damascus and Theodore of Studion (qq.v.) react against the iconoclasts' implicit denigration of matter as adequate to theophany. Precisely because human and divine have been made one in Christ, icons—and by extension, of course, all the sacraments (q.v.)—are rendered not only possible, but necessary. The perfect confession of the incarnation requires them. The "energies" of God shine forth from the transfigured flesh of Christ and in that flesh, that humanity or "second Adam," embraces the whole created universe of souls and bodies, of spirit and matter. This, the presence of the eschaton in some sense already at work among us, is made known in the Church's sacraments and in the images she has sanctioned for veneration. Here, too, in this Christological understanding of the holy icons, we may find the seeds of the later work of Gregory Palamas in defense of the holy hesychasts of Athos (qq.v.) that concluded the theological contributions of the Byzantine era—and that continues to live at the center of Orthodox thought and piety today.

**CHRYSOSTOM, JOHN** *see* John Chrysostom.

**CHRYSOSTOM (KYKKATIS),** Archbishop of New Justiniana and All Cyprus *see* Kykkatis, Chrysostom.

**CHURCH AND STATE.** Until the 19th-c. rise of nationalism and the consequent appearance of state churches, and with the notable exception of Russia and certain earlier local churches (e.g., Armenia, Georgia [qq.v.], etc.), the understanding of the state in the Orthodox Church had been governed by the latter's relationship to the two great Empires, Roman and Ottoman (qq.v.), which dominated the eastern Mediterranean basin for two millennia. Early Christian attitudes to the Roman Empire oscillated, depending on persecutions, between seeing the emperor and his imperium as the providential guardians of law and order (e.g., Rom 12), or else as the agents of the devil and the antichrist (e.g., Rev). The imperial cult of the emperor's spirit or *genius* was, of course, consistently resisted.

Radical change came with the accession to power of Constantine the Great (q.v.). Eusebius of Caesarea (q.v.), in numerous writings including his *Church History* and especially his oration *In Praise of Constantine,* sketched the outlines which would become the official, political theology of Byzantium (q.v.). This held that the Empire was a providential gift, intended by God to stretch across the *oikoumene* (q.v.; or "inhabited earth") and to parallel the universal Church of Christ, to become in short the secular arm or reflection of the Church. The emperor, while no longer divine, was presented as the "image of Christ," i.e., in Christ's capacity as governor and ordering power of the universe (*pantacrator*). In a famous phrase, Constantine therefore called himself the "bishop" or overseer of the Church's outer life—in effect, its chief executive officer—though he never claimed the right to define its faith. (*See* Caesaropapism.)

Some two centuries later, Justinian (q.v.) articulated the doctrine of "symphony": *imperium* and *sacerdotium* coexist as the mutually complementary and supporting aspects of a single Christian polity, with the emperor seeing to its good order and defending its orthodoxy and the bishops retaining full authority (q.v.) for Christian teaching and discipline, and in particular the exclusive right to pronounce on the truth or falsity of doctrine. It was thus the emperor's general duty to enforce the standards of the Church and, in times of doctrinal debate and imperial crisis, to convoke a universal synod of the episcopate, the Ecumenical Council (q.v.), for a decision on the disputed issues. While this was the theory, the practice depended on the relative strengths of the different emperors, patriarchs, and bishops, and, not least of all, the influence of the monks as a third and often very powerful element.

Imperial attempts to dominate the Church were formidable throughout the 4th c., in the late 5th c. under Zeno, in the reign of Justinian in the 6th c., and especially in the 8th–9th c. dynasty of the Isaurians (q.v.). The latter in particular laid claims precisely to a sacerdotal authority and came closest to realizing a genuine Byzantine caesaropapism (q.v.). Their defeat at the Seventh Ecumenical Council marked the end of any offical claims on the part of the state to the adjudication of doctrine, although later emperors such as Michael VIII (13th c.) and John VIII (15th c.) exercised considerable pressure on the episcopate to accede to the decisions of the Reunion Councils held with the papacy (qq.v.), though it proved in vain.

Post-Byzantine developments until the 19th c. were dominated, on the one hand, by the Ottoman Empire and, on the other, by the Russian monarchy. The Turkish sultans governed their subjects by treating each religious group as a distinct nation (*millet*), with the *rum millet* ("Roman," i.e., Orthodox nation) subject in all but capital cases to the rule of the Ecumenical Patriarch (q.v.) as *millet-bashi* (*see* Ethnarch) and therefore as the religious and civil head of the Orthodox peoples under Ottoman rule. The Church, in short, was gifted with the powers of the state and the patriarch, in effect, with the ancient role of the emperor—although, obviously, he was to be emperor of a "second-class" people. The contemporary wardrobe of Orthodox bishops reflects this development, in particular the vestments (q.v.) of the *sakkos* and *mitra,* the imperial robes, first affected by the patriarchs during the Ottoman years and later copied by the rest of the episcopate. One could also, up until the death of the late Archbishop Macarius in the 20th c., see a survival of the Ottoman system still at work on the island of Cyprus.

In Russia the tsars succeeded to the role of the Byzantine emperors as the civil guardians and patrons of the Church. Their role, indeed, was seen by many as extending beyond the borders of Russia itself to include the entire Orthodox *oikoumene.* Hence the popular notion grew, sponsored by clerical and monastic circles and favored (though never officially adopted) by the crown, of Moscow as the "Third Rome," i.e., the providential successor of the "Second Rome," Constantinople, which had fallen to the infidel. In Muscovite Russia (q.v.), however, and in the later Petersburg Empire, relations between tsars and the Church were markedly less nuanced than in Byzantium. In the latter the emperors had always been limited by a web of convention and the force of public opinion as represented, in particular, by the monks. Russia was much less sophisticated a nation. Its government, from the reign of Ivan III in the mid–15th c., was influenced from quite early on by the impress of "statist" political philosophy coming to it from Renaissance Italy—a philosophy that was itself the product of reaction to the papal theocracy of the High Middle Ages.

Russian stress on the powers of the ruler reached an early high point under Ivan IV, but especially so during the reign of Peter I (d. 1723) whose regime obtained to the end of the tsardom in 1917. Peter's Spiritual Regulation (q.v.), issued in 1721, was influenced by the example of the Prussian *Staatskirche* and sought to make the Russian Church a "department of state." While it is fair to say this project did not completely reduce the Orthodox Church to a bureaucracy, it is also the case that it came very close to doing so, in particular under the ober-procurators of the Holy Synod (*see* Russian Orthodox Church) who ruled on behalf of the tsar. Moreover, this regime was not welcomed by the clergy, as the replies of the sixty-five diocesan bishops to the ober-procurator's questionnaire in 1905 make evident. All but three of the bishops condemned the state's role in the Church.

Nonetheless, the nationalist revival in the Balkans (q.v.) saw in the Russian Church a model to imitate. Peter I's subordination of Church to state provided a template for the organization of the autocephalous church of Greece in 1831, and the newly independent states of Serbia, Bulgaria, Romania, and finally Albania (qq.v.) would follow suit. This is, indeed, the situation which obtains to the present day, less of course the seventy-year violent interruption of Marxist-Leninist governments wholly bent on the eradication of religious belief and institutions. Now that that episode has concluded, however, the Orthodox Church confronts a world where the old verities of empire no longer apply and the newer arrangements to accommodate nationalism appear increasingly problematical.

**CHURCH ARCHITECTURE** *see* Architecture, Church.

**CHURCH FATHERS.** An important identification for Orthodox theology and life, the fathers and mothers of the Church are related to Holy Tradition, that is, the transmission of the Holy Spirit (qq.v.) from one generation to another. In classical Western Christian historiography, the "Age of the Fathers" signifies the early centuries of the Church, from about A.D. 100 to the close of antiquity, that is, the 7th c. in the West and the 8th c. (John of Damascus [q.v.]) in the East. While the centuries that saw the Ecumenical Councils (q.v.) in the Orthodox Church are singularly important, every generation is felt in some sense to "father" the Church for the generation succeeding it. Thus, a Gregory Palamas in the 14th c. is as much a Church Father as a John Chrysostom in the 4th c. or a Maximus the Confessor (qq.v.) in the 7th c. The life in Christ, in the words of Symeon the New Theologian (q.v.), is a single continuum, "a flame," handed down through the generations from one illumined soul to those who come after. There are, to be sure, those who stand out particularly in this chain of saints, the "fathers" par excellence, in particular those who contributed significantly to the Church's central doctrinal affirmations. For example, those cited above are frequently listed as "the Fathers" with Irenaeus, Athanasius, the Cappadocians, etc. (qq.v.); but it will not be only and always the ancients whom contemporary believers have in mind. To limit the fathers to one era alone would be tantamount to limiting the Holy Spirit—to denying the living and creative Spirit who is the Church's very life.

**CLEMENT OF ALEXANDRIA,** theologian, St. (ca. 150–ca. 215). The second head of the catechetical school of Alexandria (q.v.) who taught there from ca. 190 to 202. Clement left three major works, *The Exhortation, The Pedagogue,* and the *Miscellanies* (*Stromateis*), together with fragments of another known as the *Excerpts from Theodotus.* The influence of these works was great, indeed. To Clement has been attributed "the beginnings of Christian Hellenism." Characterized by a remarkable openness, he embraced the late Platonist philosophy of his day, seeing in Plato (q.v.) the "Moses of the Greeks," i.e., a providential preparation for the Christian Gospel. Similarly, he considered all religions to be divinely inspired and a preparation of different peoples for Christianity, which he spoke of as the true religion. This attitude toward non-Christian religions as positive phenomena continues in Orthodox theology to the present. (*See* Dual-Faith.)

Clement prepared the way for the Christian appropriation of Greek philosophy that characterized centuries of debate on the great themes of Christ and Trinity (q.v.). Of particular value for later theology was his emphasis on God's simultaneous unknowability (apophatic theology) and gift of himself through his "powers" or "energies." His handling of Old Testament texts, particularly in the face of the polemic against them launched by gnosticism, set the stage for Origen's (qq.v.) vast efforts. Finally, Clement's readiness to accept positive elements from gnosticism led to his elaboration of the portrait of the "Christian gnostic" in Book VII of the *Stromateis*. In this one essay he foreshadowed the figures of the ascetic holy men and women who would—and do—play an extraordinarily important role in the history and piety of the Orthodox

Church. Again, his is much of the original vocabulary that later characterized Christian mystical literature in both East and West.

**CLEMENT OF OCHRID,** bishop, translator, St. (?–916). One of the premier saints commemorated in modern Bulgaria, Clement was a disciple of Methodius and colleague of Naum (qq.v.) in the Ochrid school, which translated Scripture and liturgical texts into Glagolitic and Church Slavic. When Methodius died in 885 in Moravia, Clement and Naum were imprisoned and then exiled from the country—Constantine-Cyril and Methodius's lifework ostensibly in ruins. He and Naum dealt directly with Boris of Bulgaria, and their work was supported by Constantinople (q.v.). In 886 Clement went to Macedonia to the region near Ochrid in order to baptize, serve the liturgy (q.v.) in Slavic, translate Church books, and train indigenous clergy, being appointed bishop in 893 when he was joined by Naum. In this year the Bulgarians also adopted the "Cyrillic" script, possibly following Naum's initiative. After Clement's thirty years spent in Christian ministry and teaching (almost 3,500 disciples) in the environs of Ochrid, it became a leading city of Slavic Christian culture in Europe. Clement is remembered as a founder of Slavic literary culture, an enemy of paganism, and a member of a school that anticipated later high institutions of learning. His *Vita* was written by Theophylact, Archbishop of Ochrid (ca. 1090–1109), based in part on an earlier Slavic version.

**CLEMENT, OLIVIER,** lay theologian, author (17 November 1921- ). Born in the city of Aniane in Languedoc, a region with a tragic religious history involving the Cathari and Camisards, Clement received neither baptism nor religious education as a child. He graduated from the University of Paris, writing a thesis on Peter the Venerable, Abbé of Cluny. There he was a student of Alphonse Dupront, a founder of "religious anthropology," and with whom he collaborated in the Resistance during the later years of World War II. Following the war he taught in Paris at the Lycée Louis le Grand.

After his conversion to Christianity in 1951 Clement participated in theological study organized by the Patriarchate of Moscow in which V. Lossky, L. Ouspensky, and S. Sakharov (qq.v.) were teaching. Due to the premature death of V. Lossky in 1958, Clement edited several of Lossky's manuscripts which were subsequently published. At St. Sergius Orthodox Theological Institute (q.v.) Clement replaced Lev Zander as professor of comparative theology and Paul Evdokimov (q.v.) as professor of moral theology. He also has taught the history of the Ecumenical Councils (q.v.) and Byzantine theology, and continues at the Higher Institute of Ecumenical Studies, Paris. During the 1960s he formed a committee to help shed light on the condition of

Christians in the USSR, and he protested with Pierre-Emmanuel in favor of Russian Christians. From 1976 to 1994 he was also president of the association of "Believer-Writers," a group of Christian (all denominations), Jewish, and Moslem writers. Clement has edited *Desclée de Brouwer,* the collection *Théophanie,* and the journal *Contacts,* a French-language Orthodox journal. He is author of *The Spirit of Solzhenitsyn* (trans. 1976), but his most influential book, recently translated into English, is a two-volume catechesis entitled *The Living God.* He has written *Notes sur le temps à la lumière de la tradition orthodoxe* (1959), *Byzance et le christianisme* (1964), *Dialogues avec le patriarche Athénagoras* (1969, 1976), *Le Christ terre des vivants* (1977), *Le visage intérieur* (1978), *Le chant des larmes, essai sur le repentir* (1983), *Sources, les mystiques chrétiens des origines* (1983, 1989, 1992), *Deux témoins: Vladimir Lossky et Paul Evdokimov* (1985), *Berdiaev, un philosophe russe en France* (1991), *Trois Prières* (1993), and *Corps de mort et de gloire* (1995). In addition, he has authored books on Western Christianity, modernity, and non-Christian religions, and has received honorary doctorates from the Institute of Theology of Bucharest and the Catholic University of Louvain.

**CODE OF JUSTINIAN** *see* Justinian, Code of.

**COMMENTARIES, LITURGICAL.** These are commentaries on the public worship of the Church, particularly the sacraments and, of the latter, especially the Divine Liturgy or Eucharist (qq.v.). An important genre of theological writing during the Byzantine era (q.v.) and even subsequently, these commentaries properly begin with the catechetical homilies, explanatory sermons delivered to the newly baptized just prior to and following their initiation, given in the 4th and 5th c. by Cyril of Jerusalem, Ambrose of Milan, John Chrysostom, and Theodore of Mopsuestia (qq.v.) — to name those whose homilies are still extant. Thus, they appear prominently after the Christianization of the Byzantine Empire.

Later, with Dionysius the Areopagite's (q.v.) *Ecclesiastical Hierarchy,* we find a simultaneously theological and metaphysical meditation on the sacraments employing significant themes taken from Neoplatonism (q.v.). Maximus the Confessor (q.v.) carries on Dionysius's metaphysical strain in his *Mystagogy* (7th c.), while Germanos of Constantinople (8th–9th c.) seeks to combine the Dionysian elements with the motif of the liturgy as meditation on Christ's life found earlier in Theodore of Mopsuestia. Nicholas Cabasilas (14th c.) and Symeon of Thessalonica (15th c.) round out the important commentaries of the Byzantine period (qq.v.). Popular commentaries of this type, however, such as Nikolai Gogol's (q.v.) *Meditation* in the 19th c., have continued to appear to the present.

**COMMUNION** *see* Eucharist; Theosis.

**CONFESSION.** The complex topic of confession is complicated by terminological difficulties, for example, its relationship to apostasy, repentance, and sin (qq.v.), and its history as a sacrament (q.v.) within the Church. Although it may be convenient to divide the subject into three subtopics, confession of sins, confession of faith, and confession in relation to spiritual guidance, the three items are probably all aspects of one topic.

The case for a negative confession of sins, which must necessarily be complemented by a positive confession of faith, is the understanding of a particular biblical worldview. In both Hebrew and Greek "to sin" means "to miss the mark," that "mark" being God. "Confess" in Hebrew is a form of the verb "to shoot," thus "to hit the mark, i.e., God." "To confess" in Greek is "to speak out, publish, divulge." Although one can find instances of confession of sins by itself in the Old Testament (Ps 32:5; 38:18), the case for confession of sins with an accompanying positive confession of faith is also found. For example, a confession of sins is a necessary precedent for sacrifice (Lev 5:5; Ps. 51); and the "Great Confession" accompanies the reading of the Law and the covenant to support God's house (Neh 9). Similarly, in the New Testament one may find simple confession for repentance (Mk 1:4f; 1 Jn 1:8f.) or the (negative) confession of sins (Mt 3:4), which is followed by the (positive) reception of the Holy Spirit (Mt 4:11) or of healing (Jas 5:16).

The most familiar New Testament citation of confession is the solely positive one, the confession of Jesus as Lord, the Christ, and so on. Represented par excellence by Peter's words at Caesarea Philippi, this helps form the centerpiece of the three Synoptic Gospels (confession, Cross-Resurrection, Transfiguration), as well as a major theme forced back onto the reader by the Gospel of John: Who is Jesus? In the apostolic Church it describes the profession of faith made by a martyr (2 Cor 9:13; 1 Tim 6:13). Although it might go unnoticed, the theme of Peter's confession in the Gospels is later offset by his three denials of Jesus during his trial. Peter is nonetheless a principal witness of the resurrected Lord; and John's Gospel balances Peter's three sinful denials with three affirmations of his love (21:15f.). The denials of Peter naturally lead to an investigation of apostasy (q.v.), which is the opposite of a positive confession of faith, and should be consulted before proceeding to sacramental confession.

Historical developments in the early Church considered to be formative to the sacrament of confession are many. Both the question of the Lapsi (Latin: "the fallen") in the mid–3rd c. and the Donatist Schism (q.v.) in North Africa in the early 4th c. were important events that focused on the appropriate confession of faith for those who had denied Christ under persecution. Many local councils, often comprised of Christians who had been crippled or lost friends and family during imperial persecutions, legislated on the equity of accepting back into the Church members who had fallen away during persecution. The legislation of local councils continued on into the seven Ecumenical Councils (q.v.), and became associated with the Eucharist (q.v.) when the penitential ranks were institutionalized and assigned a place approaching, but not participating in, the Holy Mysteries (sacraments).

During this same period asceticism and monasticism (q.v.) flourished publicly, and with it came selfless obedience and spiritual direction. As early as Antony (q.v.) and the ascetics of the desert, we witness a profound sensitivity toward obeying a spiritual guide who is capable of identifying the signposts of the way (q.v.) of the Lord, the spiritual journey of the wayfarer, the pilgrim. Over the centuries the parish tradition of liturgical confession in preparation for the Eucharist and the monastic tradition of spiritual direction were combined. In Greek such a confessor/director is called a *geron* and in Russian, a *starets*. Although the two functions of liturgical confessor and spiritual director are entirely separable, a combination of the two is considered a great gift. A well-known Russian spiritual father of the 19th c. was Fr. John of Kronstadt, and of the 20th c. Fr. Alexander Elchaninov (qq.v.).

The liturgical service of sacramental confession in the Orthodox Church, though popularly associated with the confession of sins, still has as its focus the confession of faith—namely the Nicene-Constantinopolitan Creed (q.v.). It is notably devoid of the classical *ego absolvo* ("I absolve thee") found in corresponding Western liturgy (q.v.) (except in a version of the Russian service); and is taken in form to be a public, rather than private, service. When administered privately, which is usually the case, the service is performed en face with the priest and penitent both standing before the Gospel and Cross, the priest standing as a witness for the whole Church.

**CONSTANTINE THE GREAT,** emperor, St. (273–337). Son of Constantius Chlorus and the latter's concubine, Helen, Constantine was born in the present-day city of Nish, Serbia (q.v.). On his father's death in 306 he began his quest for the throne of the Roman Empire in York, Britain. He made good on his claim for the Empire's western half in 312 at the battle of the Milvian Bridge, and for the east in 323. In the process his advocacy of Christianity became clear, first in the so-called Edict of Milan (313), which ended official persecution of

Christianity and restored church properties lost to state confiscation. In a series of decisions and decrees in following years, he steadily expanded the Church's privileges, in particular those of its clergy. His ambitious building program included the construction of church buildings throughout his domains, including the Church of the Resurrection (Holy Sepulcher) in Jerusalem (since much altered, but still standing) and Old St. Peter's in Rome. Constantine convoked the first of the Ecumenical Councils (q.v.) at Nicaea in 325. Five years later he dedicated his new capital, Constantinople, intended to serve as the center of a Christian Roman Empire (qq.v.). He is thus the man primarily responsible for the inauguration of Christendom in both Western and Eastern Europe, i.e., the idea and fact of a Christian society. Ten later emperors in Constantinople were to carry his name, including the last, Constantine XI Paleologus. The forebear's own Empire lasted well over a millennium.

**CONSTANTINE-CYRIL,** "The Philosopher," Apostle to the Slavs, linguist, St. (ca. 820/7–869). Brother of Methodius (q.v.), the two were sons of a Byzantine official in Macedonia (q.v.). Constantine was a scholar and linguist, a protégé of the immensely learned Patriarch Photius (qq.v.), and was trusted at different points in his life with the chair of philosophy at the imperial university, sensitive diplomatic missions to the Arabs and Khazars, and the care and keeping of the patriarchal chancery. He and his brother were therefore singled out in 863 to head the mission to the Slavic kingdom of Moravia requested by its prince, Rastislav. Constantine met the challenge of his final assignment by preparing an alphabet for the Slavs (the script that survives under the name Glagolitic) and by beginning the task of translating the Scriptures and liturgical texts. Finding resistance in Moravia to his mission—German clergy were already in the field and resented the newcomers working on quite different missionary principles—he and Methodius traveled to Rome (q.v.) to seek the support of Pope Hadrian. It was granted willingly (though withdrawn by Hadrian's successor), but Constantine-Cyril's life came to an end while in the city. He received monastic tonsure on his deathbed under the name of Cyril, by which he continues to be commemorated in the Orthodox world. He died in May 869.

While Methodius did try to continue the mission, the work of the two brothers was not to succeed in Moravia. On the other hand, their disciples Naum and Clement of Ochrid (qq.v.) found more fertile ground for their labors. They (probably Naum) originated important work with the Cyrillic alphabet, while continuing to work in Glagolitic (i.e., Clement) as well. The nations of Bulgaria, Serbia, Russia, and Ukraine (qq.v.) all owe their Christianity, and in important ways their language and literature, to the brothers' efforts.

**CONSTANTINOPLE.** Literally, the city of Constantine (q.v.), it was built on the foundations of an ancient Greek city on the Bosporus, the straits leading from the Black Sea to the Sea of Marmara and, eventually, to the Mediterranean. The new capital was ideally placed to serve as a center of commerce and communication. Massively fortified by Constantine and, a century later, by Theodosius II, its walls on land and sea successfully resisted all attempts at capture until the Fourth Crusade (q.v.) in 1204. During the Byzantine era (q.v.), the city's population numbered between a half million and a million souls—overwhelmingly the largest urban concentration in the medieval Christian world. From the 7th c. on, following the loss of Alexandria and Antioch to Islam (qq.v.), it was incontestably **the** city of the Byzantine Empire, the latter's center of culture and thought as well as of administration, military force, and wealth. From 381 its bishop, the Ecumenical Patriarch (q.v.), held the first place among the local churches of the East. Constantinople's contribution to the Orthodox Church is quite incalculable: liturgy, theology, spirituality (qq.v.) all owe most of their current shape to the generations-long influence of the imperial city.

**CONSTANTINOPLE, PATRIARCHATE OF.** At the opening of the 4th c. the three leading sees of the Christian world were, in order, Rome, Alexandria, and Antioch (q.v.)—not coincidentally, the largest cities of the Roman Empire. With the establishment of Constantinople (qq.v.) as the new capital, the latter's size and importance came quickly to rival its three older sisters. Accordingly, the importance of its bishops also grew, particularly as they were in immediate proximity and had access to the emperor and his court. Recognizing this fact, the Second and Fourth Ecumenical Councils (q.v.), in 381 and 451, elevated Constantinople's bishop to the rank second only to Rome's, according him in the process jurisdiction over broad areas of the East.

The popes of Rome, notably Damasus and Leo the Great (q.v.), reacting to the councils in 381 and 451, respectively, protested what they saw as a concession to worldly criteria of importance, i.e., what is usually referred to as eastern "accommodationism." The popes began to oppose the latter with their own idea of "apostolicity," meaning that only a church founded by an apostle—more specifically, by Peter—could lay claim to the first rank among Christian communities. This difference of opinion over the origins of authority (q.v.), although long overlooked by both halves of Christendom in the interests of maintaining Church unity, ran on for centuries beneath the niceties of ecclesiastical and imperial diplomacy. It would flare up on occasion, for example during the "Photian schism" of 867 (*see* Photius) or the "Acacian schism" from 482 to 519, only to subside again until the final rupture conventionally dated at 1054.

**CONTOS, LEONIDAS C.**, priest, theologian (1920–1995) Graduated from Holy Cross Theological School, Brookline, Massachusetts (1943), he served as pastor of the Church of the Archangels, Stamford, Connecticut, from 1944 to 1951. In 1950 he received a B.A. from the University of Bridgeport. From 1951 to 1965 he served as dean of Saint Sophia Cathedral in Los Angeles, during which period he received a D.Phil. from Oxford University (1963). From 1965 to 1966 he served as director of communications and ecumenical relations for the Greek Orthodox Archdiocese of North and South America (q.v.), headquartered in New York City. From 1966 to 1972 he was president of Hellenic College and Holy Cross Theological School. From 1972 to 1973 he was Senior Editor for the *Saturday Review*. From 1979 to 1988 he served as pastor of the Church of the Holy Cross, Belmont, California, then Vicar General of the Diocese of San Francisco, 1989–92. He was a cofounder and president of the Patriarch Athenogoras Orthodox Institute (q.v.) at the Graduate Theological Union, Berkeley, California, and Alexander G. Spanos Professor of Orthodox Studies. He has written on Gregory Palamas (q.v.) and ecumenical relations. Most recently he completed a private publishing project of liturgical translations, the first of which is the Septuagint *Psalter* (1994), as well as *The Holy Week Services* (1994). Fr. Contos displayed good skills for simultaneous translation from Greek to English, and was liked especially for his congeniality and eloquence.

**COPTIC CHURCH.** The indigenous Church of Egypt (q.v.), its name, the ethnic name of its adherents ("Copts"), derives from the local pronunciation of the Greek word, *Aegyptos*. While certainly dating from apostolic times (local tradition ascribes the missionary work to St. Mark), little is known about the Egyptian Church before the writings of Clement of Alexandria (qq.v.), and the latter says little or nothing about the non-Greek, native Christians. Coptic Christianity properly emerges with the rise of monasticism (q.v.) in the 4th c. Its founders, Antony, Macarius, and Pachomius (qq.v.), were all Copts. The leadership of the Egyptian church, however, was concentrated in Alexandria (q.v.), which was Greek. Some scholars have therefore read the schism following the Ecumenical Council of Chalcedon (qq.v.) as a movement toward native Egyptian independence. While this is not entirely convincing, there is doubtless some truth to it. Within a few generations following Chalcedon, the Egyptian countryside was solidly "monophysite." The rise of Islam (q.v.) and the Arab conquest of Egypt in the 640s contributed to the permanence of the breach in communion. Today the Copts are a minority in their own land, though this is somewhat offset by their being the educated class. They number between 5 and 10 percent of the Egyptian population, but are victimized by Islamic "fundamentalists" who oppose government toleration of other religions. Their patriarch is based in Cairo, though still bearing the title of Alexandria. While Coptic, the last expression of the language of the pharaohs, is still used in this Church's liturgy, it is increasingly giving way to Arabic. The past thirty years have also seen a renaissance in the Coptic Church and increased contact with both the other "Oriental Orthodox" (q.v.) and the Eastern Churches adhering to Chalcedon.

**COSMAS AND DAMIAN,** Saints (third century). Cosmas and Damian were brothers and are commemorated in the Church catholic as "unmercenary physicians," that is, doctors who practiced medicine without demanding money. They are remembered as healers of humans and animals from a time late in the 3rd c. Although immensely popular among the Byzantines and mentioned in both the Western and Eastern liturgies, their lives for the most part defy research—to such a degree that one has a choice among three pairs of twin brothers by the same names who were unmercenary physicians at the same time from vastly different parts of the ancient world. Tradition holds that the first pair came from Asia Minor (q.v.), the second from Rome (q.v.), and the third from Arabia. As unmercenary physicians, the *anargyroi,* they are commemorated at each Divine Liturgy together with the prophets, apostles, evangelists, martyrs, confessors, illuminators, and righteous (i.e., monastics). As physicians who healed without payment, they are seen as assimilated to the likeness of Christ, "the physician and healer of souls and bodies."

**COSMAS THE HYMNOGRAPHER** (MELODUS), Bishop of Maiouma, St. (ca. 675–752). By tradition Cosmas was the adopted brother of John of Damascus (q.v.). He became a monk together with his sibling at the Monastery of Mar Sabba in Palestine. He was later elevated to the see of Maiouma near Gaza. His liturgical poems, composed in particular for the great feasts (q.v.) commemorating the events of Christ's life, continue to be sung in the Church. Their artistry and theological sophistication compare favorably with the Damascene's. Together they permanently influenced the style and shape of Orthodox liturgy and music (qq.v.).

**COSMOLOGY.** Literally, this word means the study or rationale of the universe and, in Christian thought, the theology or meaning of the universe as created by God (q.v.). The distinctions implied in the halves of the preceding sentence provide the key to much debate in the early Church. Neoplatonism, the dominant philosophy of the era of the Church Fathers (qq.v.), did see the universe as a kind of theophany (q.v.), but a theophany tied to divinity by impersonal chains of causal necessity. Gnosticism (q.v.), on the other hand, argued that the physical world was entirely unrelated to the good and true God and instead the product of evil forces. Clement and Origen of Alexandria (qq.v.) were among the earliest writers to attempt to find a Christian expression for the world as, on the one hand, the product of a personal Creator, and on the other, consistent with the best insight of the pagan philosophers. Their attempts to accomplish this double task were flawed in ways that contributed to the controversies of the 4th c. and following, over the divinity of Christ and the Trinity (q.v.). The later work of Gregory of Nyssa and Maximus the Confessor (qq.v.) built on the foundations laid by the two Alexandrians. The corrections that Gregory and Maximus applied lay chiefly in their reevaluation of change (*kinesis*), and in their rooting of universal meaning in the Incarnate Word. The universe, in short, finds the fulfillment of its being and movement in Christ. The latter is the end or goal (*telos*) for which God made the invisible (angelic) and visible worlds. This adjustment of Origen's position, which considered material existence a temporary expedient provided for fallen spirits by God's mercy (*see* Apocatastasis), owed much to Irenaeus's (q.v.) idea of "recapitulation," i.e., the re-creation or renewing of humanity and the world in Christ. The cosmology of the Orthodox Church, evident in both its liturgy and its formal theology (q.v.), is the result of this reworking.

**COUCOUZIS, IAKOVOS,** Archbishop of the Greek Archdiocese of North and South America, Exarch of the Ecumenical Patriarchate, (29 July 1911- ). In 1934 he graduated from the Theological School of Halki, was ordained to the diaconate, and served as archdeacon from 1934 to 1939. In 1940 he was ordained to the priesthood, serving several U.S. parishes until 1954 when he became dean of Holy Cross Theological School, Brookline, Massachusetts. He received an S.T.M. from Harvard in 1945, was elevated to the episcopate in 1954, became metropolitan in 1956, and archbishop in 1969. Always active in ecumenical affairs, he represented the Ecumenical Patriarchate (q.v.) at the World Council of Churches, Geneva, between 1955 and 1968. His ministry as exarch (q.v.) to the Ecumenical Patriarchate has been characterized by the involvement of the Greek Orthodox Archdiocese of North and South America (q.v.) in American culture.

**COUNCILS.** In contemporary Orthodox use *synodos*, a synod or council, might indicate either the regular assembly of the bishops of a local church, for example, the "Holy Synod" of Greece or Serbia, as that community's highest governing authority, or it might signify those extraordinary gatherings of bishops that, from time to time in the

Church's history, have been convoked to reply to theological questions. The pattern of the council, in both forms, as the highest authority (q.v.) is typically seen as having been established in Acts 15. James, who presides over the assembly of the Church in St. Luke's account, pronounces the verdict of the whole with the formula: "It has seemed good to the Holy Spirit (q.v.) and to us...." In this phrase the Orthodox Church sees an affirmation and a denial. On the one hand, the guidance of the Spirit will never leave the Church; and, on the other hand, no one person or office can without fail faithfully represent the Church's mind. This mind is instead preserved and maintained by the whole body of the Church, of which the council is normally—though not inevitably—the highest expression.

Orthodox ecclesiology (q.v.) has in recent years held that this conciliar idea is rooted in the notion of "catholicity" (q.v.) itself and, more particularly, that the conciliar idea and catholicity discover their meaning and justification in the Eucharist (q.v.). As the Eucharist, through the Holy Spirit, makes present the body of Christ in whom all division is overcome and broken humanity remade, so it too provides the model for the council as the assembly of Christians gathered in one mind for a common purpose. One finds in consequence that councils have punctuated the Church's history from the earliest times. Eusebius (q.v.) tells of several councils in the 2nd c., and there is direct evidence of various African councils held at Carthage and Antioch (q.v.) in the 3rd c. One must add to these the Seven Ecumenical Councils, the Reunion Councils, the three councils held at Constantinople to decide on the teaching of Gregory Palamas (qq.v.), and the Council of Jassy in the 17th c.—which condemned the teachings of Cyril Lukaris and published a confession of faith. All, save the Reunion Councils, were accorded an authority seen as applying to the universal Church.

**COUNCILS, ECUMENICAL** *see* Ecumenical Councils.

**COUNCILS, REUNION** *see* Reunion Councils.

**CREED** *see* Nicene-Constantinopolitan Creed.

**CREMATION.** Cremation is proscribed for Orthodox Christians by Byzantine Canon Law (qq.v.). The original ban was made due to the associations of cremation with paganism and possibly also gnosticism (q.v.). Cremation in Roman pagan religion (and in Russia) was an expensive rite, easily the most lavish of ancient burial practices (q.v.). For pagans or gnostics who denied the value of the body and creation's goodness, cremation represented an affirmation of the valuelessness of the body—as it also affirmed the victory of an intangible spirit, that is a spirit disassociated from the body. Such an attitude may be contrasted with Jewish and Christian attitudes expressed toward Jesus' body by Joseph of Arimathea in the Gospels (a Jewish attitude which fulfills the Law) or that of the early Christians toward Polycarp's (q.v.) body in the early 2nd c. in the *Martyrdom of Polycarp,* an early attestation to the Christian practice of venerating relics.

Recently a debate has been generated in the United States and Japan where cremation is the most modest burial in urban areas. The argument has been advanced that since cremation is no longer considered a pagan rite, but is frequently the only burial that can be afforded by the poor, it should once again be permitted (and has been on a limited basis by some clergy). On the opposite side are those who say that cremation still implicitly denies the value of the body, and therefore people who consider their bodies worthless or vile will be attracted to cremation. Last, cremation might also prevent the preservation of relics.

**CRETE.** The largest island and southernmost territory of modern Greece (q.v.), and also one of the latest to be added to that country's sovereignty (1912). Site of an ancient church claiming apostolic foundation in the Pauline epistle to Titus, at present the Church of Crete is an autonomous jurisdiction, dependent on the Ecumenical Patriarch (q.v.) for recognition of its primate. Its eight dioceses otherwise function quite independently. The survival of this local church is remarkable in view of the long occupations by foreign powers—the Arabs from 824 to 961, Venice from 1204 to the 16th c., and the Ottoman Empire (q.v.) down to the 20th c.

**CROATIA.** Newly independent in the north of the former Yugoslavia (q.v.), with its capital at Zagreb, it was dominated from the 14th c. first by Hungary and then by Austria-Hungary. Croatians joined the Kingdom of the Serbs, Croats, and Slovenes under the Serbian crown in 1919. Restive under Serbian domination and divided from the latter by its profession of Roman Catholicism, Croatia broke from Serbia during World War II and under German patronage. During this brief "independence," the country was ruled by a party of homegrown fascists, the *Ustasha.* They sought to rid Croatia of its large Serbian minority by, in the words of one of the party's spokesmen, "converting one third [to Catholicism], forcing one third to emigrate, and killing the rest." Mass killings did ensue and included Serbs, Jews, and Gypsies as their targets. Estimates vary, but to say that more than half a million Serbs alone were systematically put to death would probably not be far off the mark. The recent revival of Croatian independence after the Tito years, together with that country's use of symbols and rhetoric from the period of the *Ustasha,* go far toward explaining the violent Serbian reaction in both Croatia, beginning in 1991, and in Bosnia (q.v.), beginning in 1992.

**CRUSADES.** A Western Christian military and religious movement lasting two hundred years, from 1095 in Clermont, France, to the fall of Acre in Palestine in 1291. Ironically, originally called for by Pope Urban I in the hope of aiding Byzantium (q.v.) and thus bringing the latter into union with the Roman Church (q.v.), the mass movement that resulted ended by having the opposite effect.

The Crusades did much for Western Europe. They fostered trade and stimulated intellectual life, immensely broadening the horizons of the formerly provincial cultures of the north. Ideas, manuscripts, scholars, tradesmen, and soldiers all traveled as a result. Religiously, however, the Crusades marked and sealed the schism (q.v.) between Christian West and East, and also left a legacy of hatred and resentment in the Muslim world from which it was primarily the Eastern Christians who were to suffer.

The First Crusade (1095–99) established an independent kingdom at Jerusalem, and duchies and counties in the rest of the Levant, including Antioch and Edessa (qq.v.). In Jerusalem and Antioch particularly, Latin hierarchs were appointed in place of the former Greek incumbents. The parallel hierarchy was the first clear sign of the schism's reality. Gathering mistrust and mutual hatred between the Western soldiers and the Byzantines culminated in the Fourth Crusade, 1204, which took and sacked the imperial capital, Constantinople (q.v.), and set up an "empire" that disregarded the indigenous culture and ruled in the imperial city from 1204 to 1261, and that further survived in pockets of Western (especially Venetian) rule until the 16th c. Even today one can see Byzantine ecclesiastical art treasures in the St. Mark's collection of Venice—as reshaped collages that ignore their original form and function.

So great was popular hatred of the West as a result of this forced occupation that the later attempts of the Reunion Councils (q.v.) were doomed from the start. The choice between Ottoman Turks and Western Europe was clear by the end of Byzantium (q.v.), and the Greeks chose the Turks as less threatening to their inheritance. A very similar phenomenon and choice, between the Teutonic Knights (a crusading order) and the Tartars, was exercised by Russia (q.v.) during the 13th c. (*See* Alexander Nevskii; Novgorodian Tradition.)

**CUSTOM** *see* Canon Law; Tradition, Holy.

**CYPRIAN OF CARTHAGE,** Bishop, St. (?–258). A rhetorician converted from paganism in the 240s, Cyprian was elected Bishop of

Carthage in North Africa in 249 and presided over the African Church until his death by martyrdom. His writings deal chiefly with the Church, sacraments (q.v.), and hierarchy; and appear to have been translated early into Greek and to have exercised no little influence on Orthodox ecclesiology (q.v.).

Two issues in particular drew Cyprian's attention, the confession of penitents who had fallen into apostasy (q.v.) during the persecution of the Emperor Decius (250–51), and the recognition of the sacraments (q.v.) of schismatic or heretical Christian communities. His replies have the virtue of clear thinking and a rigorously consistent and rhetorically effective presentation. In response to the first issue, Cyprian maintained that it was wholly the province of the Church's bishops to pronounce the forgiveness of sin and to assign penances. This was over and against the claims being advanced by those who had suffered during the persecutions (the "confessors") who argued that they alone had the moral right to pronounce on this issue. Regarding the second issue, he held that any who had left or were born outside the visible communion of the Church catholic, that is, belonged to communities not part of the united episcopate, were not to be reckoned as within the Church in any sense: "outside the Church there is no salvation." The sacraments of dissidents therefore had no authenticity whatsoever.

Cyprian found an ally for this opinion in Firmilian of Cappadocia and an adversary in Bishop Stephen of Rome. The latter appears to have been the first to have appealed to his own authority (q.v.) as the unique successor of the apostle Peter. Cyprian, to the contrary, held that all bishops share equally in the "chair of Peter." The controversy between the two thus appears as the first instance of that tension in the ecclesiology (q.v.) of the Church between a "papal" and an "episcopal and conciliar" vision that finds its ultimate expression in the division between Roman Catholicism and Orthodoxy (qq.v.).

**CYPRIOT ORTHODOX CHURCH.** The largest island in the east Mediterranean, situated to the south and west of the Turkish and Syrian coasts, is divided today by a population 80 percent Greek and 20 percent Turkish, each maintaining separate governments since 1974. It is also the site of an ancient and fully autocephalous (q.v.) church that dates back to Paul and Barnabas (Acts 13) and was home to many early Christians, attested in the Byzantine lives of the saints. Taken over by the Arabs and then freed in the 10th c., the island—more especially the Church—spent four centuries under the Crusaders (q.v.) until being rid of the Latins by the Turks in 1571. The Turks allowed the Church to be reconstituted in four dioceses.

At present, Cyprus's five dioceses are presided over by Archbishop Chrysostom Kykkatis (q.v.). Its active monasteries, particularly Kykko in the Paphos range and Stavrovounion, continue to be important centers of devotion and inspiration. Since the regime of the late Archbishop Macarius (*see* Mouskos, Makarios III), the Cypriot Church has also been active in the mission to Africa. Cypriot donations built the seminary for East Africa at Nairobi, and the current Bishop of Kenya is himself a Cypriot, Macarius Tellyrides.

**CYRIL** *see* Constantine-Cyril, St. (ninth century).

**CYRIL OF ALEXANDRIA,** patriarch, theologian, St. (?–444). Patriarch from 412 to 444, Cyril was the extraordinarily energetic and capable—not to say ruthless—theological and political opponent of Nestorius of Constantinople (qq.v.). The theological question turned around the unity of Christ's person. The political issue was the new prominence of Constantinople at the expense of Alexandria (q.v.).

Cyril objected vehemently to Nestorius's denial that Mary the Virgin (q.v.) be called *Theotokos,* literally, "she who gives birth to God." The Constantinopolitan patriarch argued for the title, *Christotokos,* on the seemingly reasonable ground that God could not be said to have been born of a woman, but that the man, Jesus, could. Cyril replied that to make such a distinction was effectively to divide Christ into a committee of two, God the Word and Jesus of Nazareth. His arguments drew particularly on his great predecessor on the throne of Alexandria, Athanasius, and focused especially on the question of *theosis* (qq.v.). If, Cyril said, Christ was not truly God become man— "one nature of the Incarnate Word," to quote his favorite formula— then human beings could hope for no true communion with God (q.v.).

The argument was powerful, and one must note that it was delivered from the depths of Cyril's own personal conviction, as is evidenced in the eloquence and power of his voluminous and non-polemical commentaries on the Scriptures (q.v.). Thus it was Cyril who prevailed at the Third Ecumenical Council (q.v.) at Ephesus in 431. The violence with which he accomplished his victory, however, together with the lack of flexibility many of his followers had with regard to theological formulas, were at the root of the schisms of the Persian ("Nestorian") Church and, after the Council of Chalcedon (q.v.) twenty years later, of the "monophysite" churches as well.

**CYRIL OF JERUSALEM,** St. (ca. 313–ca. 386). Archbishop of Jerusalem (q.v.) during the 360s, Cyril was a successful pastor and an innovating liturgist. He coped admirably with an exceedingly difficult period in the history of the Eastern Church, the Arian crisis—which troubled the orthodox almost the entire century (*see* Arius). While not siding openly with the formula of the Council of Nicaea, his resistance to extreme Arian pressures earned him exile on at least two occasions. His *Catechetical Homilies*, delivered as a final catechesis for those preparing for Baptism (qq.v.), together with his five short *Mystagogical Homilies* on the sacraments (q.v.) of Baptism, Anointing, and Eucharist (q.v.), are still preserved, and the latter constitutes one of the earliest commentaries on Christian worship extant.

Responding to the new establishment of the Church inaugurated earlier in the century by Constantine (q.v.), and to the new prominence given as a result to the Holy City, he appears to have been among the first, if not the first, to begin an elaborate cycle of daily and festal services. The latter were clearly tied to the unique privilege of Palestine, i.e., that it was the site of the events recorded in the Scriptures (q.v.), and certainly must have been encouraged by the pilgrims who had begun to arrive in great numbers, for example, Egeria (q.v.). The liturgical practices begun by Cyril in Jerusalem eventually found their way, in whole or in part, to the Great Church in Constantinople (qq.v.), and exercised an influence on the whole Christian world as well.

**CYRIL LUKARIS** *see* Lukaris, Cyril.

**CZECH AND SLOVAK ORTHODOX CHURCH.** Granted autocephaly (q.v.) by Moscow in 1951, until recently the Orthodox Church of Czech and Slovakia has suffered the systematic persecutions and destructive policies of its zealously antireligious Communist government along with the rest of the Christian population. Since 1946, it has been associated with its mother church (q.v.), the Moscow Patriarchate. Still, its most notable 20th c. legacy is its sainted martyr, Bishop Gorazd, who was killed by the Germans in World War II and canonized in 1987. The forced reunion of 200,000 Uniates (q.v.) with Czech Orthodoxy in 1950 was short-lived (till 1968) and caused many bitter resentments. After the fall of Communism, Czech Orthodox churches were returned to Roman Catholics by the government, and the Czech Orthodox are hard-pressed to rebuild. Its Metropolitan Dorotheus currently holds the title of Archbishop of Prague, Metropolitan of the Czech and Slovakia Republics.

**CZERNAGORA.** The Slavic place-name translated as "Montenegro" (black mountain) designates a small republic of the former Yugoslavia located south of Bosnia and west of Serbia (qq.v.). Its population is overwhelmingly Serbian-speaking and, at least by cultural designation, Orthodox. The region, exceptionally rugged and mountainous, does have the distinction of never having been conquered by the Ottoman Empire (q.v.). For centuries the resistance was led by a succession of prince-bishops, a development unique in Orthodox history.

**DAMASCUS.** One of the oldest cities in the world, referred to by Pharaoh Thutmoses III, and prominently mentioned in both the Old and New Testaments (e.g., Acts 9), the city has been continuously home to Christians since the Apostles (q.v.). Damascus again became the capital of Syria (q.v.) in the 1920s, after having been eclipsed by Antioch (q.v.) from the Seleucid period, and has been the residence of the patriarchs of Antioch for several hundred years. As the patriarch's see, it exercises primacy over the Orthdox communities in Lebanon, Iraq, and southeast Turkey (qq.v.). Since the 1890s, its leaders have all been Arabic-speaking, following centuries of leadership exercised by the Greek community in Constantinople, a situation that contributed to the schism of the Melchites (qq.v.).

**DANIEL,** St. 1) the Stylite (ca. 409–493). Taking his name from the prophet and book of the Old Testament—which in turn was taken from the character Dan 'El of Semitic folklore—Daniel was a stylite, an ascetic who followed the unusual discipline of spending his life on a platform atop a column (*stylos*). As a disciple of a more famous stylite, Symeon (q.v.), Daniel's *Life* holds that he was blessed by his master to be the latter's "Elisha." Making his home on a pillar for thirty-three years just outside the imperial capital, Constantinople (q.v.), he was indeed accorded great respect by both the ecclesiastical and civil authorities, doubtless in great part as the result of his immense popular following. He is said to have left his pillar only once (ca. 476) to rebuke Emperor Basilicus's monophysitism (q.v.).

2) Prince of Moscow (1261–1303). Youngest son of Alexander Nevskii (q.v.), Daniel became ruler of Moscow and inaugurated its rise to power within his family, devoting himself to a peaceful Tartar appanage and expanding its borders. On the bank of the Moscow River a church with a cloister was founded in his honor, in which he took monastic vows before his death. On 30 August 1652, his relics were transferred to the famous St. Daniel's (Danilov) Monastery in Moscow. The site has a particular contemporary importance: it was very recently renovated while the Soviets were still in power, being one of the first large-scale (trial run) ecclesiastical renovations in Russia. It houses the important Russian patriarchal Department of External Affairs (comparable to a foreign office or secretary of state).

**DAPHNI.** The name of the ancient Greek shrine to Apollo on Mt. Parnassus to the north of Athens and site of an oracle famous throughout classical Greece and, later, the early Roman Empire (q.v.). With a slight change in spelling, Daphne is the site of a Byzantine monastery church still standing six miles to the west and south of Athens. The church, together with its interior iconography, is considered one of the finest examples of Byzantine art and architecture (qq.v.) extant in Greece.

**DEIFICATION** *see Theosis.*

**DEMETRIUS, martyr, St.** (?–306). Later tradition holds that he was a soldier of the Roman army slain during the persecution of Galerius (A.D. 303–308), though he was originally portrayed as an urban aristocrat. Although his cult began in the ancient city of Sirmium, near modern Belgrade (q.v.), by the 6th c. he was indissolubly connected with Thessalonica (q.v.) to the south. His basilica in the latter city has been a pilgrimage center ever since, and the Slavs have a particular devotion to his cult. His feast day on 26 October is an occasion to remember departed Christian soldiers. Some twenty other saints on the Orthodox calendar are listed under this name, in part a singular attestation to his popularity.

**DESERT FATHERS.** The expression is used to signify the original Egyptian fathers of monasticism (q.v.) who flourished from the late 3rd c. to the early 5th c., in particular those gathered around SS. Antony and Macarius in Egypt (qq.v.). Macarius's settlements at Nitria and later at Scete provided most of the stories and sayings recorded in one of the original source books of monastic spirituality, the *Sayings of the Fathers* (*Apophthegmata Pateron* or *Gerontikon*). The Desert Fathers have remained the standard for later Orthodox monks, their words and gestures functioning as paradigmatic. Another of their communities also included a number of women, such as Synkletiki and Sara.

**DIDACHE.** "The Lord's Teaching according to the Twelve Apostles," not to be confused with the *Didaskalia Apostlorum* (q.v.), is generally considered the earliest manual of Christian instruction on morals and worship. Chs. 1–6 are a prebaptismal catechesis on the Way (qq.v.) or alternatively the Two Ways. Chs. 7–15 are a series of instructions on worship, including Baptism, fasting, the Eucharist (qq.v.), treatment of "clerical orders"—prophets, apostles, bishops, and deacons—and Sunday prayer. The final ch. 16 is on the Antichrist and eschatology. Discovered in 1875 by P. Bryennios in Constantinople, and known previously only by title and hypothetical reconstruction, the dating and provenance of the document are difficult, since it is a composite and went through recensions, such as the later *Apostolic Constitutions* (q.v.). In any case, the disputed time frame is between the 1st c. and

2nd c., and there appear to be literary connections between it and Barnabas and the Shepherd of Hermas (qq.v.). Some scholars tentatively identify its origins with Syria. Two copies of a Latin version have subsequently been discovered.

**DIDASKALIA.** The Greek word means, literally, "teaching." The influential book, the *Teaching of the Apostles* (*Didaskalia Apostolorum*), was originally written in Greek ca. the late 3rd c. It is a church order, later incorporated into the *Apostolic Constitutions* (q.v.), that survives only in a 4th-c. Syriac and later Arabic, Ethiopic, and Latin translations. Its present shape is that of a rather mixed and even confused amalgam, but its original core appears to have been built around an essay on the duties of the three major orders, bishops, priests, and deacons. (*See* Apostolic Constitutions.)

**DIODORUS,** Patriarch of Jerusalem (Damianos Karivalis) *see* Karivalis, Diodorus (Damianos).

**DIONYSIUS THE AREOPAGITE.** 1) According to Acts 17 he is one of the few converts won by Paul's preaching at the Areopagus before the altar of the Unknown God, and by tradition the patron saint of the city of Athens.

2) An anonymous Syrian (of whom we know nothing certain) who sometime around A.D. 500 used this name as a pseudonym for the writing of a corpus consisting of four extant treatises, the *Mystical Theology,* the *Divine Names,* the *Celestial Hierarchy,* and the *Ecclesiastical Hierarchy,* together with ten "Epistles," a body of work that would enjoy an immensely important role in both the Greek and Latin Middle Ages. The works of Dionysius (or "Pseudo"-Dionysius) are marked by the deep impress of 5th-c. Neoplatonism (q.v.), although they are equally influenced by the Cappadocians, the liturgical commentaries of the 4th and 5th c., Clement and Origen of Alexandria, and perhaps Evagrius of Pontus (qq.v.).

Accepted as much for their profundity as for their subapostolic pseudonym, the Dionysian works left a deep impression on such subsequent writers as Maximus the Confessor, John of Damascus, Symeon the New Theologian, Gregory Palamas, and Nicholas Cabasilas (qq.v.). Dionysius was particularly valued for the primacy he accorded apophatic theology, though his works on the hierarchies—a term he appears to have invented—are probably at least as influential, as much for their effect on church architecture and liturgical piety as on theology (qq.v.) per se. Work on his possible relation to the tradition of the Syriac Church (q.v.) has been slower to develop, although significant discoveries may await researchers in that area.

**DMITRI OF ROSTOV**, St. *see* Hagiography.

**DOGMA.** Originally signifying "that which seems good" in a philosophical school or in a public decree, the word is used in the latter sense in both the Septuagint (q.v.) and New Testament. Following the first definition regarding philosophical good and truth, it has come to mean a necessary truth of Orthodox faith and experience, inaugurated by divine revelation and solemnly defined by the Church. The definitions occur not only in Scripture, but in the Seven Ecumenical Councils (qq.v.), or in a local council subsequently accepted as having ecumenical significance, e.g., the local councils held at Constantinople (q.v.) in 1341, 1347, and 1351, which declared that the teaching of Gregory Palamas (q.v.) on the distinction between the essence and energies of God was the faith of the Church.

**DONATION OF CONSTANTINE.** This document dates from the late eighth century. It was probably composed at either the papal chancery or, perhaps, the abbey of St. Denis near Paris; and purports to be a letter of the Emperor Constantine to Pope Silvester acknowledging the papacy's (q.v.) universal ecclesiastical primacy, granting the pope and his successors temporal authority over the west half of the Roman Empire (q.v.). Likely the result, and retroactive justification, of Pope Stephen II's alliance with the Frankish kingdom of Pippin I in 754, the *Donation* also served to justify what medieval canonists would later call the translation of empire (*translatio imperii*) from Byzantium to Charlemagne (qq.v.) in the year 800. It was referenced first in 1054 to legitimize papal claims in a letter from Pope Leo IX to Patriarch Michael Cerularius. The document was thus important in providing a legal rationale for the great papal theocracy of the High Middle Ages, e.g., the pontificate of Innocent III (1198–1215). Finally, it also appears to have entered the ecclesiastico-political bloodstream of Russia at just about the time when it had been discredited in Western Europe (ca. 1490) via the "Tale of the White Cowl" and the city of Novgorod, at that time one of the few Russian cities with extensive contacts with the West. The "Tale," a variant of the *Donation,* contributed significantly to the later mythos of Moscow as the "Third Rome."

**DORMITION OF THE THEOTOKOS** *see* Feasts, Twelve Great.

**DOSITHEUS**, patriarch, scholar (1641–1707). Patriarch of Jerusalem from 1669 to 1707, Dositheus was arguably the most important Orthodox church leader of the seventeenth century. Active in church life at a very young age due to the death of his father and placement in a monastery in 1649, he became Archdeacon of Jerusalem in 1661 and

Archbishop of Caesarea five years later. An indefatigable scholar, writer, and polemicist, he spent perhaps the greatest part of his pontificate in Romanian Moldavia (q.v.) where, in the city of Jassy and at some distance from the Turkish authorities in Constantinople, he was free to set up the first printing press in the Ottoman Empire (q.v.). Jassy is where the Synod of 1642 condemned the "Confession" of Cyril Lukaris (q.v.) and published, in slightly edited form, the highly "Latinized" reply, the "Confession" of Peter Mogila (q.v.). Dositheus won general, pan-Orthodox approval for his own "Confession" at the Synod of Bethlehem in 1672, a more balanced and traditionally Orthodox document than Mogila's, the Kievan metropolitan. He also published much valuable patristic material, including the *Tomos of Joy* with the minutes of the Council of Constantinople in 879 and writings of Gregory Palamas (q.v.), as well as timely polemical works and a thirteen-volume history of the Patriarchate of Jerusalem (q.v.).

**DOSTOEVSKY, FEODOR MIXAILOVICH** (1821–1881). Ranked as one of the greatest—if not *the* greatest Russian novelist of the 19th c., the journalist and diarist Dostoevsky mastered the dominant artistic literary genre of his time, the long novel. He brought to it an intellect steeped in Orthodox tradition and the aspirations of the radical intelligentsia, as well as an uncanny ability to prophesy the future tumultuous decades of Russia in his characters' personalities. Among his most compelling themes are personal freedom through love versus self-will, the myth of social utopianism, the religious problematics of human life, and the continuously impending apocalyptic collapse of individuals and society. Although during his lifetime he was known for journal and newspaper literature, subsequently his novels were better known, including *(Notes from) The House of the Dead* (1862), *Notes from the Underground* (1864), *Crime and Punishment* (1866), *The Idiot* (1869), *The Possessed* (1872), and *The Brothers Karamazov* (1880). It has been postulated that the dominant themes of Orthodox theology and 20th-c. philosophical questions can all be found in his works.

**DOUKHOBORS AND OLD BELIEVER SECTS.** The priestless Old Believers (q.v.) gave rise to many sects in imperial Russia over the intervening centuries since their beginnings in the third quarter of the seventeenth century. In general these priestless sects (*bezpopovtsy*) were like the ancient Montanists and Messalians. They had a negative worldview and believed their rites brought them into direct contact with the Holy Spirit (q.v.), so that Christ could be reincarnated in various persons generation after generation.

Beginning in chronological order, the Khlysts were a 17th c. dualistic Old Believer Russian sect, whose founder claimed to be God; and in succeeding generations one male disciple was Christ while a female disciple was the Mother of God. In 1740 more than 400 people were prosecuted in Moscow for this heresy, which later flourished underground so that there were 60,000 adherents by 1900. In doctrine they denied the Holy Trinity (q.v.): God inhabited the man Jesus who died, as he would inhabit other members of the Khlysts. When God is incarnate in the Khlyst, the spirit directs everything, making all books (including the Bible) and authority (q.v.) meaningless. Members were outwardly pious Orthodox parishioners (e.g., Rasputin) since liturgy (q.v.) was a symbol of their own mysteries, while privately their communities were each led by a "Christ" and "Mother of God", and their ritual was frenzied dance after which ecstatic prophesies were made. Their belief was dualistic, since they believed that the body is the prison of the spirit, marriage is condemned, and children are "incarnations of sin." In this way they are similar to previous gnostic (q.v.) groups.

One branch of the Khlysts from the late 18th c., the Skopts, practiced castration in order to prevent all sexual relations, naming it a "baptism of fire." Their leader was Conrad Selivanov, who was exiled under Tsarina Catherine II, but was personally known to both Tsars Paul and Alexander I and flourished under them. Tsar Nicholas I persecuted the group, and they were forced underground, and there continued in great numbers.

The Doukhobors (Spirit-Wrestlers) began as an 18th c. Ukrainian sect that combined Socinian doctrine (16th-c. unitarianism of the Italian Faustus Socinius), Freemasonry (q.v.), and Khlyst teachings. They believe in one God manifest in the soul as memory (Father), reason (Son), and will (Holy Spirit), while Jesus was not God but possessed the ultimate divine reason. (For the triad memory, reason, will, *see* Augustine; Trinity.) Scripture and dogma (qq.v.) are to be interpreted allegorically (q.v.), and the eternal human soul undergoes transmigration or metempsychosis. They were and are organized in strict pacifist communes, which prosper through hard work and sober living. The sect made contacts with famous people including Grigorii Skovoroda and Lev Tolstoy. Tolstoy and the Quakers provided funds in 1899 for a large group to emigrate to Cyprus and Western Canada where they live, but refuse to own land or register vital statistics.

An early moderate offshoot of the Doukhobors were the Molokans ("Milk-Drinkers"), who altered their doctrine to resemble Protestant evangelical sectarians (i.e., the Bible as the sole authority for faith), and reject the cult, icons, and fasting (qq.v.)—and drink milk on fast days. They evolved further in the early 19th c. under the influence of the Russian Bible (q.v.) Society, holding that the Bible alone was the means of salvation, giving up sacraments and patristic writings. A sizable group of Molokans emigrated to San Francisco in the 19th c. and continue their community there today on Potrero Hill.

The sect of the *Stranniki* ("Wanderers") was founded by a man named Evfimii in the 18th c. They regarded the other Old Believer groups (*soglasie*) as worshipers of the golden calf and prisoners of Antichrist. Taking vows as pilgrims, they wandered the highways and byways, avoiding any officials of the Russian government, regarding them as agents of the Antichrist. Another fanatical sect, the *Zaposhchevantsy*, was characterized by extreme asceticism and ritual suicide.

The Stundists also developed similarly to the Molokans in the second half of the 19th c. They espoused a Western Protestant type of sectarianism among Russian and Ukrainian peasants, emphasizing personal meditation on Scripture, the singing of hymns in common, and promptings of the Spirit. Originally influenced by German Mennonites, by the end of the century they were under the sway of Baptist preachers. This led to activities which were socially and politically inflammatory, so that Stundism was forbidden by the government (1894) and missionized against by the Russian Church (1895). In general the forced Russification policies of Ober-Procurator C. Pobedonostev toward these groups under the last two tsars, Alexander III and Nicholas II, were reactionary policies that created grave difficulties for all non-Orthodox religions in Russia, and especially the sects. Pobedonostev also limited religious freedom in the Russian Orthodox Church as well, and ended up as the last of the despotic Ober-Procurators.

**DROZDOV, PHILARET,** Metropolitan of Moscow, *see* Russian Bible; Russian Orthodox Church.

**DUAL-FAITH.** In Russian *dvoyoveriya,* the term "dual-faith" or "two beliefs," is familiar due to its use in describing the popular religion of old Kievan Rus' (q.v.) after the baptism of Prince Vladimir, when Christianity and paganism existed side by side—and joined together—among the common folk. It has been used subsequently to describe syncretism between any two faiths.

-E-

**ECCLESIOLOGY.** The word means the study or rationale of the Church. Never rigorously discussed in its own right in the earlier centuries, the Church emerged a theological subject of first importance only in the 20th c. and as a result of the ecumenical movement (q.v.). Orthodox theologians in this century, following and attempting to articulate the hints present in the New Testament and Church Fathers (q.v.), have sought to define the Church fundamentally as sacrament, i.e., as the presence in this world and communication of the Kingdom of God, the body of the risen Christ animated by the Holy Spirit (q.v.). In particular Russian theologians such as Nikolai Afanasiev, Georges Florovsky, John Meyendorff, and Alexander Schmemann, together with Greeks such as John Zizioulas and the Romanian Dumitru Staniloae (qq.v.), have advanced an ecclesiology based on the Eucharist (q.v.) as central—to the other sacraments (q.v.) and the Church's historical self-understanding, e.g., the evolution of the three sacred orders (sacramental ministers).

The contribution of these men has been admired by and influenced other Christians, notably Roman Catholics; but they have raised the legitimate question that Eucharistic ecclesiology does not address the political reality of the universal Church, i.e., the Christian Church is a worldwide society whose unity requires an officer charged with the responsibility for the whole. They see this office in the "petrine ministry" exercised by the papacy (q.v.). The question of primacy is perhaps the burning issue facing the Orthodox Church as it approaches the 21st c. The old relations between Church and state (q.v.) that obtained in the Christian East up until the opening of the 20th c., wherein the Church's unity was in great part the responsibility of the Christian state, now no longer apply. Recent initiatives on the part of the Ecumenical Patriarch (q.v.) allow some hope that contemporary Orthodoxy is moving toward a possible resolution of the question.

**ECKARTSHAUSEN, KARL VON** (1752–1803). Exceptionally popular in nineteenth-century Russia and unknown elsewhere, Karl von Eckartshausen began his career in Bavaria as a jurist, and then turned to mysticism and alchemy. The popularity of his numerous writings, all of which had to be translated into Russian, may be credited to two circumstances: the first was preoccupation with mysticism among the elite dilettantes of the early 19th c., e.g., Tsar Alexander I, A. Golitsyn, R. Koshelev; the second was his personal acquaintance with I. V. Lopukhin, who translated his writings and devoted himself to publishing mystics and Freemasons at Moscow University.

**ECONOMY.** This Greek word *oikonomia* means, classically, the management of a household (*oikos*/house, *nomos*/law or rule). In theology the term refers first of all to God's (q.v.) providence as the divinity extends itself beyond the inner life of the Trinity (q.v.): all that pertains to the created worlds and to the divine actions taken on their behalf and for their salvation. The supreme example of the divine economy is therefore the Incarnation, i.e., the birth, life, death, and resurrection of Jesus Christ. From the risen Christ comes the gift of the Holy Spirit (q.v.), and in the latter the presence in the fallen world of the Kingdom of God, i.e., the Church. As the Church exists in a fallen world, its fundamental concern must be the salvation of the souls whom it embraces. Thus the second and directly related meaning of economy: actions taken by the Church in the person of its officers (bishops, and by extension priests) for the redemption of individual believers in the sphere of Canon Law (q.v.). While representing the Church's governing of souls and communication of grace, the canons are never in themselves absolute. They may be enforced literally, *kat'akribeian,* or with discretion, *kat'oikonomian,* depending on the discernment of the needs of the particular soul. "Economy" of canonical application can therefore mean *either* a loosening of the canonical prescriptions (akin to Roman Catholicism's "dispensation"), *or* the imposition of a discipline stricter than that which the canons provide.

**ECUMENICAL COUNCILS.** Councils comprised primarily of the Church's bishops which have been reckoned as having embraced the Christian *oikoumene* and therefore as possessing universal authority (qq.v.). In practice during the first Christian millennium, the *oikoumene* meant effectively the territories of the Christian Roman Empire (q.v.). So far as their geopolitical reality is concerned, the Ecumenical Councils were more accurately *imperial* councils, convoked by the emperor of Constantinople (q.v.) and subsequently enforced by him as imperial law. The Orthodox Church recognizes the decrees of seven of these assemblies as binding on all believers: Nicea I (325), Constantinople I (381), Ephesus (431), Chalcedon (451), Constantinople II (553) and III (681), and Nicea II (787). The first two dealt with the theological crisis prompted by Arius and resulted in the agreement on the Nicene-Constantinopolitan Creed (qq.v.) as the standard of the Christian faith. The Third Council condemned Nestorius and upheld the Christology of Cyril of Alexandria (qq.v.). The Fourth, dominated by Pope Leo the Great (q.v.), affirmed against monophysitism (q.v.) the completeness of Christ's divinity and humanity. The Fifth and Sixth sought to address the problems and confusions deriving from the Fourth, in particular the schism of the Coptic, Armenian, and Jacobite (qq.v.) communities. The Emperor Justinian (q.v.) thus convoked Constantinople II to condemn the Nestorianizing Christology of the "Three Chapters" and affirm the unity of Christ's person. The Sixth Council condemned another imperial initiative in the 7th c., the proposal that Christ had but one will, monotheletism (q.v.). The Seventh Council met to condemn the iconoclasm of the Isaurian Dynasty (q.v.), and thus to affirm the veneration of images. By an agreement that appears to be in place in the Orthodox world, possibly the council held in 879 to vindicate the Patriarch Photius (q.v.) will at some future date be recognized as the eighth council.

**ECUMENICAL MOVEMENT.** This phrase signifies the general impetus toward Christian unity that took form as a movement, beginning with the larger Protestant communities, at the beginning of this century and that resulted, in 1948, in the formation of the World Council of Churches (WCC) and various national bodies such as, in the United States, the National Council of Churches (NCC). Orthodox participation, led in particular by the Ecumenical Patriarch (q.v.) since the 1920s, has been consistent, though not without controversy. Notable Orthodox theologians, e.g., Georges Florovsky and John Meyendorff (qq.v.), have played important roles in the Faith and Order commission of the WCC. They have also taken care not to compromise the catholic (q.v.) claims of Orthodoxy. Not all Orthodox participants over the years have been so careful. As a result, sharp criticisms have been leveled against any involvement in ecumenism by the more conservative elements in the Orthodox world, in particular the monasteries of Mt. Athos (q.v.). The issue remains a source of contention to the present.

**ECUMENICAL PATRIARCHATE.** This title, dating from the sixth century, belongs to the bishop (patriarch) of Constantinople (q.v.). Elevated by the Second and Fourth Ecumenical Councils (q.v.) to second place in the hierarchy of the ancient sees after Rome (q.v.), this see has, by default, held the first place in the Orthodox Church since the schism (q.v.) with the West. The exact scope of that primacy, however, is considerably debated. The problem is compounded by the fact that, since the anti-Greek riots in Istanbul in 1955, the patriarchate has been substantially without a flock in its home territories. Severely hampered by this and by the continuing obstructionism of the Turkish government, it has had a difficult time impressing other local Orthodox churches with the legitimacy of its function as center of the Church's unity. In addition, the unhappy legacy of Phanariot (q.v.) manipulation of the Slavic and Romanian populations in the service of Greek nationalism during the 18th c. and 19th c. within the Ottoman Empire (q.v.), together with a continuing rivalry with the Russian Orthodox Church (q.v.), have left a fund of difficult historical memories. The patriarch does exercise authority over the Greek Orthodox in "diaspora," as well as over certain other communities living outside the traditionally Orthodox lands; but this has tended to reinforce the impression that the patriarch functions primarily as a Greek ethnarch (q.v.). This impression—and, to a degree, reality—will have to be transcended if the patriarchate is ever to exercise a ministry of unity in an effective way. (*See* Archondonis, Bartholomew; Spyrou, Athenagoras.)

**EDESSA.** Founded by Seleucus in 304 B.C., now the Turkish city of Urfa, Edessa was the early "capital" of Syriac-speaking Christianity in Syria and Mesopotamia (q.v.). According to a popular tradition, its Nabataean king, Abgar, was converted on receiving a miraculous image impressed upon a towel from the still living Jesus of Nazareth. It is certain that Christians were present in the city from very early times. Bardesanes, a gnostic, was the first of its famous Christian writers in the late 2nd c. The church building there, destroyed in A.D. 201, is the oldest known Christian structure. Edessene Christianity appears to have been marked in its earliest stages by a great variety of different and mutually antagonistic groups. By the late 3rd c. its catholic bishop had been attached to the oversight of Antioch (q.v.). St. Ephrem (q.v.) lent his presence to the city from 363 to 373, and apparently assisted in the formation of a school of exegesis that would exercise great influence for about seventy years. The city also hosted a Nestorian "Persian School" until 489 and was a center for "monophysitism" (q.v.) down through the Arab and Byzantine occupations until the present century.

**EDICT OF MILAN.** A decree issued in 313 by Constantine (q.v.) and his co-emperor, Licinius, which legalized Christianity for the first time in the history of the Roman Empire (q.v.), restored church property formerly confiscated or destroyed, and accorded Christianity equal privileges (soon to be expanded) with the other religions of the Empire. The Edict was one of toleration, and did not establish Christianity in the position it would later enjoy as **the** religion of the Empire. Its historicity has recently been called into question so far as its revolutionary character is concerned.

**EGERIA** *see* Pilgrimages.

**EGYPT.** The Roman province of Egypt included the Nile valley to the First Cataract, the present-day Aswan Dam, and the territory of Cyrenica, the coastlands of modern Libya. An intensely conservative peasantry and pagan priesthood were politically and culturally dominated by the Greek-speaking capital, Alexandria (q.v.). While most of the Christian literature coming from Egypt through the 4th c. and 5th c. was in Greek, the conversion of the peasantry by the latter century gave birth to monasticism (q.v.) and to the earliest Coptic literature. Following the Council of Chalcedon (451), the Egyptian or Coptic Church (q.v.)—i.e., the vast majority of indigenous Christians—broke communion with the sees of Rome and Constantinople (qq.v.). Much reduced by the presence of Islam (q.v.) over the past thirteen centuries, this community today numbers perhaps five to six million, about 5 to 10 percent of the population of modern Egypt, but enjoys a leadership role in the modern nation disproportionate to its size.

**EIGHTH DAY.** Referring to Sunday as the "Eighth Day," as well as the first day of the week, is an early Christian adaptation of Jewish apocalypticism and messianism. The Jewish context for the reference can be found in the Book of Enoch. In this eschatological way of thinking, the Eighth Day was the first day of the new aeon, something that went beyond the seventh-day Sabbath, as a new "first and last" day, and ushered in the time of the messiah—or rather stood outside time itself! With belief in the Resurrection of Jesus on Sunday, after his Sabbath's rest, the theology of the Eighth Day was co-opted by Christians in order to identify Jesus with the awaited messiah and to see this event as the advent of the new creation, the new aeon. As Jean Danielou and Alexander Schmemann have shown, the Eighth Day is not only the day of resurrection but also the day of the Christian Eucharist (q.v.). Thus, references to the celebration of the Eucharist from the beginning are associated with a fixed day (*statu die*), not a day of rest—which came only later with the Christianization of the Roman Empire—but a day that went beyond time to an eschatological point of completion, and the time of a new creation. As a result, scriptural and early Church documents refer to the celebration of the Eucharist on the Eighth Day. The Church Fathers (q.v.) of late antiquity were also well aware of the theology of the Eighth Day, which after a hiatus has again come to the fore in some 20th-c. Christian circles.

**ELCHANINOV, ALEXANDER,** priest, spiritual director (1881–1934). One of the most gifted priests in the Russian emigration in Paris, Elchaninov is best known for his spiritual direction, which has been excerpted posthumously in *The Diary of a Russian Priest*. After graduating from the University of St. Petersburg with a degree in history and philology, Alexander gave up his scholarship and lived in Russia's religious-philosophical circles of the progressive and artisitic intelligentsia (1900–10), including people like Sergius Bulgakov, Nicholas Berdiaev, Pavel Florensky (qq.v.), S. Merezhkovsky, and others. During the first Russian revolution (1905–06) this group tried to enter politics as the "Christian Brotherhood of Struggle," an underground organization with anarchical tendencies. After experiencing the repressiveness of revolutionaries, every member in the group became conservative, endured the second revolution, and was expelled from Russia by the Communists, several becoming priests, including Elchaninov. After establishing himself in France, Fr. Elchaninov continued teaching adolescents as he had in Russia, and was spiritual director of the Russian Christian Student Movement in Exile. Known as a "serene and kind counselor" (Dimitri Obolensky), his gifts lay in his mastery of spiritual self-examination and in his ability to guide others in this discipline.

**EMPEROR** *see* Authority; Church and State.

**ENTRANCE OF THE LORD, THEOTOKOS** *see* Feasts, Twelve Great.

**EPANAGOGE.** The term means "return," more properly an *eisagoge* (introduction), thus the publication in 886 using this title by the Emperors Basil I and Leo VI, with the assistance of the Patriarch Photius (q.v.). The *Epanagoge in Forty Titles* was intended to serve as an introduction and guide to the whole of imperial legislation, including both civil and ecclesiastical law. It was and remains one of the most important sources for Orthodox Canon Law (q.v.).

**EPARCH.** Originally a Byzantine imperial title—e.g., the "Eparch of the City"—eparch today is used in the Russian and Uniate Slav churches to mean a diocesan bishop, the local "ordinary" in Roman Catholic terms. Similarly in these communities, a diocese is known as an "eparchy." During the period of the Ecumenical Councils (q.v.) the word eparchy was also used to refer to an ecclesiastical province, a metropolitanate, or an exarchate.

**EPHESUS.** One of the largest cities and great ports of the Roman Empire (q.v.), its ruins are located on the southern Aegean near the modern Turkish city, Selcuk. As the capital of the Proconsular Province of Asia Minor (q.v.) in the New Testament era, Ephesus was famous for one of the "Seven Wonders of the World," the great temple of Artemis (or Diana) built in 330 B.C. Ephesus was also one of the most important cities of the ancient church, linked for example to the Apostle John and the labors of Paul (Acts 18–19; Eph), and is one of the seven churches addressed in Rev (ch. 2). It was later the site of the Third Ecumenical Council (q.v.), which probably took place in the double church near the theater, the remains of which are still visible today. Its dominance over Asia Minor was, however, superceded by the rise to prominence of Constantinople (q.v.) at the close of the 4th c.

**EPHREM THE SYRIAN** (ca. 306–373). Perhaps the greatest Christian writer in Syria, and certainly the greatest poet of the Church Fathers (q.v.), Ephrem was born in Nisibis, moving to Edessa (q.v.) in

363. His dates make him a contemporary of the Cappadocian Fathers (q.v.), and his writings indicate that he shared in many of their theological concerns—theosis, for example, and the Trinity (qq.v.)—although he expressed himself in an entirely different idiom. That idiom was verse, always inspired by Scripture (q.v.), and included exegetical, dogmatical, and ascetical works. Enormously popular in the Syriac Church (q.v.) to the present day, many of his poems and hymns were translated into Greek during his lifetime and thereafter (together with a great many *spuria*). He found a ready and appreciative audience wherever his writings appeared, especially among monastics where his works continued to be read throughout the Byzantine era (q.v.) and following. His poetry (q.v.) had a lasting influence, via the hymns of Romanos the Melodist, on the Byzantine rite and music (qq.v.). Early translated into Slavic, he is also enduringly popular among the Russian Orthodox, both lay and clerical, to the present.

**EPIPHANIUS,** bishop, ascetic (ca. 315–403). Bishop of Salamis (modern Famagusta) in Cyprus from 365 to 403, Epiphanius was an ascetic, born in Palestine, where he established a monastery in Judaea (ca. 335), though he was brought up in Egypt. His compendium of heresies (q.v.), the *Panarion,* has provided scholars with useful, if highly partisan and not seldom inaccurate, descriptions of the different personalities and movements troubling the peace of the Church in the late 4th c. His theological sympathies, consistently allied with Rome and Alexandria (qq.v.), reveal his Egyptian training. His treatise "Ancoratus" contains the earliest known text of the Nicene-Constantinopolitan Creed (q.v.). He is reckoned a saint of the Orthodox Church, as much—if not more—because of his sincere efforts to pastor his flock as for his zeal in combatting heretics.

**EPIPHANY** *see* Feasts, Twelve Great.

**EPITIMION.** Part of the sacrament of confession (q.v.), or penance and reconciliation, the epitimion is the penance set by the confessor or elder for the penitent. In ancient practice, this could be quite severe—for example, up to seven years exclusion from the Eucharist (q.v.), accompanied by arduous ascetic exercises, for the gravest sins (q.v.). Even so, the epitimion was never conceived of in the East as a penalty or punishment, still less a "satisfaction," for the sins committed, but was always understood as medicinal, part of the cure for the disease of sin. The confessor stands thus in the role of physician, diagnosing the malady and prescribing the cure. Modern usage tends to assign lighter penances, when indeed such are assigned at all. Such amelioration begins with the

Desert Fathers (q.v.), who often resisted the over-exacting penances imposed by the ecclesiastical hierarchy. (*See* Economy.)

**ERICKSON, JOHN H.**, canonist, church historian, theologian, educator, musician (4 October 1943- ). One of a few American lay canonists, Erickson earned a B.A. from Harvard (1966), a M.Phil. from Yale (1970), a M.Th. from St. Vladimir's Orthodox Theological Seminary (q.v.) (1984), and has been a fellow at both Dumbarton Oaks Center for Byzantine Studies and the University of California School of Law in Berkeley. Actively involved in ecumenical and church affairs, he is a member of the North American Orthodox/Roman Catholic Bilateral Consultation, the North American Anglican/Orthodox Consultation, several commissions of the Orthodox Church in America (q.v.) and various professional organizations.

Professor Erickson has taught church history and Canon Law at St. Vladimir's Seminary since 1973 and currently holds the rank of associate professor. He additionally serves as associate dean of academic affairs, registrar, and faculty secretary. Besides articles and reviews in scholarly journals, he has edited several books, including *Orthodox America, 1794–1976* (1975) and the five-volume series *The Orthodox Church in History,* and has authored *The Challenge of Our Past: Essays in Orthodox Canon Law and Church History* (1991). During the 1980s he also cooperated in the arrangement and publication of five volumes of liturgical music. His current projects include a popular survey concerning "The Orthodox Church Yesterday and Today," and books on the Orthodox/Roman Catholic dialogue and on the Eastern canonical tradition of *oikonomia.* Erickson has distinguished himself as a sober theologian, and is well respected by his colleagues for his hard work and balanced presentations.

**ETHIOPIAN (ABYSSINIAN) CHURCH.** Although mentioned as early as the Acts of the Apostles (ch. 8), this Semitic people is not recognized as having its own local church until the fourth century. Its beginnings are credited to a Syrian monk, Frumentius, who received episcopal consecration from Athanasius of Alexandria (q.v.) and converted King Alzanas in mid-century. Long under the ecclesiastical domination of the Coptic Church (q.v.), Ethiopia thus shared in Egypt's break in communion with Rome and Constantinople following Chalcedon (qq.v.). Its isolated position, surrounded on its highland plateau by Muslim nations and tribes in the lowlands, further cut it off for centuries from extensive contacts with the rest of the Christian world. The result was and is a church marked by singular local characteristics, notably a distinctively Old Testamental and Semitic flavor, and a canon of Scripture of particular value for scholars in that it preserves in Ethiopic translations copies of texts from the Old and New Testament apocrypha, e.g., Enoch, the Ascension of Isaiah, Jubilees, and Eusebian works, of centuries before and after Christ. From the 16th c. to the 19th c. the country drew the attention of missionary efforts from various Roman Catholic orders, with marginal success outside of an Eritrean Uniat group. Under its own native bishops since the 1950s, the Ethiopian Church has been an active participant in the Oriental Orthodox-Orthodox Dialogue (q.v.) since the latter's inception in the 1960s.

**ETHNARCH.** Literally meaning "head or ruler of a nation," the origins of this word lie perhaps in the world of Hellenistic Judaism where it signified the local head of the Jewish community. As used by the Byzantine state, it seems to have meant the commander of a band of foreign mercenaries. Later, in the history of the Orthodox Church after Byzantium (q.v.), it serves to translate the Turkish phrase *millet-bashi*, used during the Ottoman Empire (q.v.). Since the Ottomans followed the practice of Islam (q.v.) and did not distinguish between Church and state, this title and its accompanying civil responsibilities were assigned to Orthodox ecclesiastics during the Turkish period, in particular to the bishops and preeminently the Ecumenical Patriarch (q.v.). The latter therefore enjoyed both civil and religious jurisdiction over his flock. This legal linkage between nation and church was reinforced by revivals of nationalism in the 19th c. Balkans (q.v.) with consequences that still afflict the Orthodox Church today.

**EUCHARIST.** From the Greek word meaning "thanksgiving," and variously called Holy Communion, the Lord's Supper, the Last Supper, and the Liturgy, this thanksgiving first involved Jesus (1 Cor 11:24), and subsequently everyone with the name Christian who is to "do this in remembrance of me," following the command of Christ for the messianic banquet. Both the institution and the periodicity, the "eighth day," of this sacrament (qq.v.) as the primary Christian worship can be demonstrated from the Gospels and other of the earliest documents. To deny the centrality and frequency of the Eucharist in the face of our current knowledge of the worship of the early Church, let alone Holy Tradition (q.v.), can only be labeled an intentional distortion. This datum, continuously shared by the Eastern and Western Church alike, should be taken very seriously by those who claim to be "Biblically Christian" and who teach differently in doctrine or in personal piety (q.v.).

In traditional liturgical texts used in the Church many Old Testament images and institutions are looked upon as prefiguring the Eucharist. For example, the table and cup described in Ps 23, the bread and wine presented by Melchizedek (Gen 14), the Levitical offerings of thanksgiving, the paschal lamb, the banquet of Wisdom (Prov 9), et al. are among those precursors and types. The New Testament references are almost all direct, including Paul (1 Cor 11) and the synoptic Gospels (Mt 26; Mk 14; Lk 22), with only a veiled reference in Jn 6. Acts gives further information about the Eucharist as it was celebrated by the Jerusalem community (ch. 2) and by Paul in Troas (ch. 20). Other of the earliest Christian sources cite occurrences of the Eucharist as central to Christian life, including the Didache (ch. 9), Ignatius ("Epistle to the Philippians," 4f.), and Justin Martyr ("First Apology," 1) in spite of the *disciplina arcani,* a reticence to speak of the sacred mysteries. After the Christianization of the Roman Empire, many of the Church Fathers, e.g., Cyril of Jerusalem, John Chrysostom, Augustine (qq.v.), made contributions to a popular understanding of the centrality of this sacrament—to the extent that all of Christian spiritual life would henceforth be explained classically in terms of either Baptism (q.v.) or the Eucharist.

For the Orthodox it is important to say that the Eucharist manifests the mystical communion of the individual believer with God, of believers with one another, and of the unity of the Church. (*See* Ecclesiology.) There is no church, no theology, no mysticism, no individual that may disregard the eucharistic assembly (cf. "The Life of St. Seraphim of Sarov"). Fortunately, the East was not doctrinally affected by the exhausting Western debates regarding transubstantiation, and maintained a holistic view of the process of the entire Divine Liturgy—probably due to the understanding of the Eucharist expressed within the liturgical prayers themselves. (A recognized spiritual discipline of the East demands that one not overintellectualize a mystical event, but humbly and silently experience that reality—rather than merely talk about it.)

Temptations to Orthodox communities in their communion practices have come and continue to come from other sources: a misguided understanding of sin and confession (qq.v.), and a "hyper-pious" attitude to sacraments (q.v.), which puts them beyond human reach. These temptations are being addressed through new translations of liturgical texts that make the "plain meaning" and liturgical action intelligible, and through the sound spiritual advice that Christians are judged not only in what they do, but also in what they refuse to do sacramentally.

**EUSEBIUS OF CAESAREA,** bishop, theologian, historian (ca. 265–ca. 340). One of the most important early fourth-century figures in the Eastern Church and the editor and writer of the preeminent *Ecclesiastical History,* Eusebius also framed the theology (q.v.) of the Christian Empire that would inform the relations between Church and state

throughout the Byzantine era (q.v.) and beyond. He became bishop in ca. 315, and after the enthronement of Constantine (q.v.) was active in not only the shaping of the theory of the Christian Empire, but its day-to-day affairs as well, writing both a *Chronicle* and a *Life of Constantine.*
His theology of the Trinity (q.v.), deeply influenced by Origen (q.v.), was the model for most of the Greek episcopate until the synthesis of the Cappadocian Fathers (q.v.). Not a follower of Arius (q.v.), he nonetheless found the *homoousios* formula of the Creed of Nicaea too radical a departure from what he deemed the norms of trinitarian theology, and thus landed in the camp opposing the great patriarch of Alexandria, Athanasius (q.v.). He is also noted for his important works on Christian apologetics (q.v.), especially the *Preparation for the Gospel* and the *Demonstration of the Gospel* (aimed in great part at rebutting the pagan philosopher Porphyry's *Against the Christians*), and for his scriptural commentary. Of special value for the Church are his *Martyrs of Palestine,* which events he personally witnessed, and the *Onomasticon,* which describes biblical topography.

**EVAGRIUS OF PONTUS,** monk, ascetic (346–399). Evagrius was a friend and protégé of Gregory of Nazianzus (q.v.) and was ordained deacon by the latter. Following a midlife crisis, he embraced the monastic life in place of a brilliant career as a secular churchman, and ended his days at the retreat of Nitria in Egypt, spending some time with Macarius (qq.v.). He was the most intellectually cultured and sophisticated of the Desert Fathers, and deeply shaped by both the Cappadocians and the master whom he shared with them, Origen (qq.v.). His writings, couched mostly in the form of aphorisms, though including a significant body of correspondence, contributed enormously to the development of Orthodox asceticism (q.v.) and, in particular, to the "art of prayer."
Due to the impress of certain of Origen's speculations, he remained a controversial figure for a century and a half after his death and was ultimately condemned posthumously at the Fifth Ecumenical Council (q.v.) for Origenism. His works survive partially in Greek, and then chiefly under different names. They were nearly all translated into Latin and Syriac, where, modified somewhat in the translation, they continued to be greatly esteemed. His *Praktikos* and *Chapters on Prayer* are important works available in English.

**EVANGELICAL BRETHREN** (in Russia). This group, including Herrnhutters, Mennonites, and Moravian Brethren, may be identified as Anabaptist—or have so subsequently identified themselves—and may be considered generally as German sectarians. The history of their spiritual legacy in Russia is not well known. They settled in Russia during the reign of Catherine II, largely due to conscription in their home countries and their pacifist political stance. The tsars for the most part respected their religious pacifism and pardoned them from governmental service, while establishing them as large communities in agricultural areas where they retained their own culture and language. They seem to have been tolerated by the Church as benign and understood as a type of primitive Christian community in dogmatics and social organization.

Theologically, they brought with them an orientation toward apocalypticism and some adventism, and were disposed toward allegory (q.v.) and "spiritual" interpretation of the Bible. Some left Russia in the 19th c. with the threat of conscription from unsympathetic tsars and because of the forced Russification under Ober-Procurator Pobedonostsev. Stalin is said to have eradicated five million Germans in his purges of the Volga River basin, most of whom would have been Lutheran and Evangelical Brethren.

**EVANGELISM.** The English is from the Greek *evangel,* the Gospel or good news of Jesus Christ. Throughout the New Testament period it is assumed that the primary mode of the growth of the Church is effective evangelism. The image of it given in the New Testament is the making of disciples, the story of the draught of fishes. Individuals who hear the Gospel are expected in turn to proclaim it.

Regarding evangelism within parishes, there are only three means whereby people become members of the Church—birth, transfer, and evangelism. Christian parenting is not expected to be the primary means of parish growth, nor is transfer membership, because transfer to a "new" parish entails an "old" parish losing a member. Evangelism is still the primary means of healthy parish growth. (*See* Catechesis.)

**EVDOKIMOV, PAUL N.,** Russian lay theologian (2 August 1901–16 September 1970). In 1907 his father, a military colonel of an aristocratic family, was assassinated. In 1917 the family moved to Kiev where Paul attended the Theological Academy, but his training was cut short when he was called into the army. In 1920 the family moved to Odessa, then went into exile at Constantinople, and from there to Paris in 1923. In 1923 he received a master's degree in philosophy from the Sorbonne, a master's degree in theology from the St. Sergius Orthodox Theological Institute (q.v.) in 1928, and a doctorate in philosophy from the Faculty of Letters of Aix-en-Provence in 1942 for a thesis on Dostoevsky (q.v.). From 1953 on he was professor of moral theology at St. Sergius. Always interested in ecumenism (q.v.), from 1967 he taught at the ecumenical school of the Catholic Institute,

Paris. The main trend of his theological thought is pneumatological, and his works are primarily available in French. He is the author of a pair of books on the subject of marriage and human sexuality, *The Sacrament of Love* (trans. 1985) and *Woman and the Salvation of the World* (trans. 1994).

**EVIL EYE.** Belief in the evil eye is common to many European cultures, and is usually associated with the glance or stare of a person who is thought to be capable of inflicting injury, wittingly or unwittingly, on another. In the Orthodox Church the understanding of the phenomenon, which may be ascertained by reading the prayer against the evil eye, is more spiritually substantive than superstitious: The evil eye is clearly identified with the covetous glance or the jealous stare. A prime example of the evil eye is the jealousy or covetousness aroused in a barren woman against another's newborn child, as in 1 Kings 3 wherein Solomon renders wise judgment between two women claiming the same child. Thus, according to such a definition one might provoke the evil eye through pride, ostentatious display, or braggery. Conversely, one might protect one's self from the evil eye through humility, modesty, and thankfulness.

**EVLOGII,** Metropolitan *see* Georgievskii, Evlogii.

**EXALTATION OF THE CROSS** *see* Feasts, Twelve Great.

**EXARCH.** A political term of the Byzantine (q.v.) state, an exarch was an official who had charge of a province at some distance from the capital and was endowed with military powers as well as civil authority. The term thus came to signify in Byzantine church use a bishop charged with the oversight of a flock that lay outside the Empire's effective boundaries, or else simply the ruling bishop or eparch (q.v.) of a primatial see. Today the former use still obtains in the Orthodox Church. Thus, for example, in the United States the archbishop of the Greek Archdiocese is also the exarch of the Ecumenical Patriarch for the Americas.

**EXORCISM.** We do not know as much as we would like about the content and expression of the daily exorcisms that accompanied instruction in the early catechumenate. The texts we have are the same or similar to those that begin the reception into the catechumenate; and these are known to be markedly different in scope and specificity from the daily exorcisms that were performed by the catechists. It would be safe to say that the exorcisms that we now have were the summary statements made by the clergy over the newly enlisted Christian, claiming that person for the Church and removing him from the power of evil. Similarly, the daily exorcisms most probably dealt with very specific sins (q.v.), which were to be overcome before Baptism (q.v.) could take place. It is pointless to propose for this daily practice any of the curious aspects of exorcism currently popular in the American media, when what was most likely at stake was good, sound spiritual direction against sin over a prolonged period of time. This spiritual approach gives us a principle related to the ethics of the way (q.v.) of the Lord, or two ways, providing practical advice for the daily spiritual life of the catechumen, and at the same time demanding accountability from him.

When the adult catechumenate is restored, the first three exorcism prayers of the baptismal service should be included at the beginning of catechesis (q.v.), or perhaps interspersed throughout it; and they should be explained as claiming that person for the Kingdom of God and the Church, and removing him or her from the power of evil. Throughout the catechetical period, the teaching of the Two Ways may serve as a guide to deal with specific sins, which are to be overcome before reception into the Church can take place. This is to provide continuing practical advice for the daily spiritual life of the catechumen. The process logically and naturally leads to the individual's later participation in the sacrament of Confession (qq.v.). Basically, catechesis, exorcism, and confession require good, sound spiritual direction against sin, and accountability to God (q.v.).

-F-

**FASTING** *see* Ascesis.

**FEASTS, TWELVE GREAT.** After Pascha (q.v.) or Easter and the Sunday resurrectional liturgy (q.v.), the Twelve Great Feasts commemorate the most important saving events connected with the life of Jesus Christ that the Church celebrates throughout the course of the year. Although a few of the feasts (Palm Sunday, Ascension, Pentecost) are movable because they are dependent on Pascha, all the rest are on fixed calendar days. The Christian ecclesiastical year, just as the Jewish year, begins in September, and so the feasts are thus arranged:
1) 8 September, Nativity of the Theotokos (q.v.)
Originating in Syria-Palestine in the 6th c. and celebrated in Rome in the 7th c., this feast commemorates Mary's (q.v.) birthday, not for its historical accuracy—because we do not know the exact date of her birth—but as the first feast of the new year, in a certain way making all other of the feasts possible. The words of the liturgical celebration express it well: "Your birth, O virgin mother of God, announces the joy of the whole world, for from you has come and shines the Sun of Justice, Christ our God."

2) 14 September, Exaltation of the Cross
This day commemorates three historical occasions that are separable, each of which involves the Cross on which Jesus was crucified: A. The first is the legend of the finding of the Cross by Helen, Constantine's (q.v.) mother, with his patronage. B. Second is the anniversary of the completion of the Constantinian basilica Church of the Resurrection (Holy Sepulcher) in Jerusalem, which also covers the site of the crucifixion. C. Last is the recovery of the Cross from the Persians in 629 by the Emperor Heraclius. We know from the pilgrim Egeria's (q.v.) diary that the first two feasts were already celebrated in the 4th c. in the East.

3) 21 November, Entrance of the Theotokos into the Temple
This first feast of the Christmas-Epiphany fast (beginning on 15 November) is based on the story of Mary's life in the Temple as a child, found in the Protoevangel of James (ca. 150), an "apocryphal" work. The feast, also called the presentation, anticipates the Christmas-Epiphany theophanic themes and shows Mary to be the holy fulfillment of the First Covenant. It also develops the comparison between the Temple of stone and the living temple, Mary, and, by extension, the temple of the Holy Spirit (q.v.) of every human being. It seems to have first been celebrated in Syria at the end of the 6th c.

4) 25 December, Nativity of our Lord, Jesus Christ
This later and lesser of the two winter theophany feasts (i.e., Epiphany and Christmas) was first popularized in the West in the 4th c. in order to compete with the pagan festivals of the winter solstice, *Natalis Solis Invicti* and *Saturnalia*. Soon popular in the East as well, possibly due to the heated Christological controversies of the 4th–6th c., the liturgical texts focus on the Incarnation and the birth accounts in the Gospels of Mt and Lk. The modern celebration curiously juxtaposes some of the most profound theological insights with popular druid, and now capitalist-commercial, festivities.

5) 6 January, Epiphany (or Theophany)
The greatest of the winter theophanic feasts, Epiphany remembers the Baptism (q.v.) of Jesus, prototypical for every Christian, and the revelation of the Trinity (q.v.). Marking the beginning of Jesus' ministry, this holy day is not only one of personal baptism, but of the blessing of all water, a source of human life, and through that water the blessing of the cosmos. This feast, like Pascha and Christmas, is celebrated in a three-day cycle followed by great feasting.

6) 2 February, Meeting of the Lord in the Temple
This feast, as old as the 4th c. in Jerusalem and spread throughout the Empire by Justinian (q.v.) in 542, commemorates the fulfillment of the Law of Moses (Lev 12; Num 18) forty days after Jesus' birth. Alternately called the Presentation in the West and greatly expanded contextually there, in the East the liturgical texts especially commemorate the Lucan

narrative of the meeting of the Lord by Simeon and Anna, and the recitation of the beautiful *Nunc Domitis*.

7) 25 March, Annunciation

As early as Hippolytus and Tertullian (qq.v.) in the 3rd c., there is mention of the crucifixion on 25 March, and with it in Hippolytus and other later writers, the Annunciation. But the earliest reference to a liturgical celebration is at the Council of Toledo in 656, though there is a church commemorating the Annunciation built in Nazareth before 400. The feast celebrates the visitation of the Archangel Gabriel to Mary in Lk 1, announcing to her the birth of Jesus, Son of the Most High. It focuses on its connection with the nativity of Jesus and the real role that Mary's sanctity and volition played in that event.

8) One week before Pascha, Entrance of the Lord into Jerusalem

Known popularly as Palm Sunday (although it falls on Monday in the Gospel of John), this feast inaugurates Holy Week—separate from Lent (q.v.) in the East—and is intrinsically linked with the raising of Lazarus and the causal events that led to Jesus' arrest and crucifixion. On this day the faithful hold palms, or branches of willows in the Russian Orthodox tradition, to identify themselves with the people who greeted Jesus as he entered Jerusalem, an entrance that was both a display of political and eschatological significance as the beginning of the last week.

9) Forty days after Pascha, Ascension

Celebrated by the whole Church from at least the 4th–5th c., this feast commemorates the end of the Resurrection appearances and the joyous "sitting down of Jesus Christ at the right hand of the Father." Although the Eastern Church liturgically follows the Lucan chronology (Lk 24; Acts 1), the only one that gives us a forty-day ascension, it is not unaware of the other alternatives that see the Resurrection-Ascension-Pentecost as a single event, since the Johannine readings are prescribed for the forty-day period. A Russian Orthodox monastery sits atop the Mount of Olives and marks the traditional identification of the site of the Ascension.

10) Fifty days after Pascha, Pentecost

The fiftieth day after Passover is the Feast of Weeks in Jewish practice, or Pentecost; and in the Lucan chronology (Acts 2) is identified as the day the Holy Spirit descended upon the apostles (q.v.). Pentecost marks the birth of the Church and falls near the end of the Paschal celebrations, although the whole of the time between Easter and Pentecost has occasionally been referred to as Pentecost, a fast-free time when the liturgical book (q.v.) the pentecostarion is used. On this day, in addition to the descent of the Holy Spirit, the Orthodox especially remember the confusion of tongues at the Tower of Babel as contrasted with the translation of the Good News into languages comprehensible to all.

11) 6 August, Transfiguration of the Lord

Celebrated in Asia, probably by Armenians, as early as the 4th c., it was in wide use in the East before 1000, but not in the West until it additionally commemorated the defeat of the Turks at Belgrade in 1456. The Gospel event is recorded in the synoptics (Mt 17; Mk 9; Lk 9), alluded to in 2 Pet 1, and marks the center of all the synoptic Gospels, along with the confession of Peter and the prediction of the Cross and Resurrection (q.v.). The understanding of transfiguration and *theosis* (q.v.) are quite different in the East from the West. Whereas the West might see the event on Mount Tabor primarily as a revelation of Jesus as God, the East understands it, not only as a revelation of the Trinity (q.v.), but as the visible manifestation of the transformed humanity of Jesus, a glory shared by Moses and Elijah.

12) 15 August, Dormition of the Theotokos

Known in the East also as the feast of the Falling Asleep of Mary, and in the West as the Assumption, the holy day was observed in Syria-Palestine from at least the 4th–5th c. Belief in the bodily assumption of Mary was a topic of the 6th c. among Gregory of Tours, Dionysius (Ps.) the Areopagite (q.v.), and later Germanus of Constantinople. The celebration not only draws attention to the sanctity and faithfulness of Mary's life, but to the recapitulation of the experience of the whole Church and the life of the believer in her: "The source of life is laid in the grave and her tomb becomes a ladder to heaven." This feast is an apt conclusion to the cycle of the liturgical year, which began with Mary's birth.

**FEDOTOV, GEORGE P.**, Russian church historian, educator (1886–1 September 1951). A Marxist student who emigrated to Germany in 1906 to study history, he returned in 1908 to graduate from the University of St. Petersburg in the historico-philological department. He taught the history of the Middle Ages as privat-docent at St. Petersburg and in Saratov. Disenchanted with the Left, he departed Russia in 1925 to settle in Paris, where in the same year he began teaching church history at St. Sergius Orthodox Theological Institute (q.v.). In 1931 he published *Saints of Ancient Russia, X-XVII* (in Russian), utilizing his extensive grasp of hagiography, in which he expressed particular veneration for Paisii Velichkovsky and Seraphim of Sarov (qq.v.). From 1930 to 1939 he was coeditor of the Russian language journal *Novii Grad (New City)*. On 27 September 1935 he was among the founding members—including Mother Maria (Skobtsova), Nicholas Berdiaev, Sergius Bulgakov (qq.v.)—of Orthodox Action, the Russian émigré Christian social-action organization. Arriving in the United States in 1941, he became professor of church history at St. Vladimir's Orthodox Theological Seminary (q.v.), New York. Metropolitan Theophilus requested that he and Professor Peter P. Zouboff compose a memorandum to reorganize the seminary as a graduate school for theological studies. This plan was formulated by them and adopted at the Seventh All-American Sobor in 1946. His collected works in English (latest publication, 1988) include *St. Filipp, Metropolitan of Moscow, A Treasury of Russian Spirituality, The Russian Religious Mind* (2 vols.), and *Peter Abelard.* His works are characterized by an intelligent selection of materials representative of the history of intellect and spirituality, and good, thorough scholarship.

**FELLOWSHIP OF ST. ALBAN AND ST. SERGIUS.** The Fellowship is an association, founded in 1928, for ecumenical (q.v.) exchange between the Anglican Communion and the Orthodox Church. Its main organ, the journal *Sobornost,* publishes articles of scholarly and ecumenical interest, often the published form of papers given at the Fellowship's annual conference in England. Theologians of the Russian emigration such as Sergius Bulgakov, Georges Florovsky, Vladimir Lossky, and Nicholas Zernov (qq.v.) were particularly active in the Fellowship's founding and early years.

**FERRARA-FLORENCE, COUNCIL** *see* Councils, Reunion.

*FILIOQUE.* This Latin phrase means "and (from) the Son," and refers to a late Western Latin interpolation into the third part of the Nicene-Constantinopolitan Creed (q.v.), specifically to the clause on the procession of the Holy Spirit (q.v.). The phrase was added to the text of the Creed by the Spanish Church at the Council of Toledo in 589, then two centuries later found its way to the imperial chapel of Charlemagne (q.v.) at Aachen, and thence to Rome (q.v.) at the beginning of the 11th c. Never accepted by the Orthodox Church, the *filioque*—together with the understanding of papal primacy—remains the most important, single theological issue dividing the Western and Eastern Churches. (*See* Carolingians; Holy Spirit; Trinity.)

**FINNISH ORTHODOX CHURCH.** Although overwhelmingly Lutheran by confession, modern Finland also counts a small Orthodox Church that, together with the Lutheran Church, enjoys official status as a state-supported institution. The origins of Christianity in Finland go back at least to the 12th c., and possibly earlier to the founding of the Valaam Monastery. Although the country became Lutheran in 1523, the eastern part remained Orthodox, even through a 17th-c. Swedish persecution. Orthodoxy grew when Finland came under Russian rule in 1809. The country gained independence in 1917 and autonomy was granted the Finnish Church by the Ecumenical Patriarch (q.v.) in 1923. Today it counts an archbishop, two metropolitans, and one vicar bishop attached to the archbishop's see (i.e., three dioceses). The theological faculty is affiliated with the university at Joensuu, and there are two monastic communities. The majority of Finnish Orthodox derive from Karelia, the eastern provinces lost to the Soviet Union in the Russo-Finnish wars of 1939 through 1944. The resettlement and scattering of Orthodox Finns throughout the rest of the country following that war continue to pose difficulties for this minority church, although in the most recent years the church has attracted converts and has begun to grow.

**FLORENCE, COUNCIL OF** see Councils, Reunion.

**FLORENSKY, PAVEL A.**, priest, theologian, scientist (1882–ca. 1946). Florensky, very popular in post-Soviet Russian Christian circles, is known primarily as a multidisciplined theoretician and metaphysician who maintained his identity as a Christian and priest in academe and society at large in the face of Soviet persecution. His primary theological works included a number of journal articles and the book *The Pillar and Foundation of Truth*. His contributions to the humanities and science remind one of Leonardo da Vinci: *Fictions in Geometry*, astronomical calculations of a geocentric conception of the universe, *The Doctrine of Dielectrics*, monographs on the history of art with a focus on wood carving, Moscow Soviet Arts School professor of perspectival painting, musician, inventor of 'dekanite' (non-coagulating machine oil), etc.

Just as with Vladimir Soloviev and Sergius Bulgakov (qq.v.), Florensky's metaphysics centers on sophiology—to the extent that he speaks of Sophia (Wisdom) as a fourth divine hypostasis (person), and it appears to function as a mediating principle between God (q.v.) and creation, among other things. For this position his entire theology has been called into question (Georges Florovsky [q.v.]) and described as unfounded in Eastern tradition and overly speculative.

Florensky was repeatedly imprisoned by the Soviets in the Solovki concentration camp, insisting that he renounce his priesthood. (When he occupied a chief post on the Commission for Electrification and attended the Supreme Soviet for National Economy, he always wore his cassock.) After his last ten-year term of imprisonment, he "disappeared" in the Soviet Union in 1946 and was unofficially reported dead to the European émigré community. It is assumed that he was one of the millions of silent martyrs (q.v.) who died under Stalin.

**FLOROVSKY, GEORGES V.**, priest, theologian, church historian, educator, ecumenist (28 August 1893–11 August 1979). Son of a priest and educator, as a theologian and church historian he was primarily an autodidact, since his studies at the University of Odessa were in philosophy and science. In 1919 to 1920 he was philosophy lecturer at that university, and from 1922 to 1926—after he and his family had fled from Russia to Sofia, Bulgaria, then to Czechoslovakia—he taught philosophy of law in the Russian Faculty of Law at Prague and in 1923 received a Phil. Mag. degree there.

From 1926 to 1948 he was a professor of patristics and systematic theology at St. Sergius Orthodox Theological Institute (q.v.). He opposed the sophiological (theological) orientations of both Frs. Bulgakov and Florensky (qq.v.), considering the position unjustifiable in terms of iconography and liturgical texts (qq.v.). In 1932 he was ordained a priest under the canonical jurisdiction of the Ecumenical Patriarchate of Constantinople (q.v.), and for the rest of his life remained affiliated with it. In 1948 he settled in the United States, becoming a naturalized citizen in 1954. From 1948 to 1955 he was a professor of divinity at St. Vladimir's Orthodox Theological Seminary (q.v.) and its dean from 1950 to 1955. Concurrent to his deanship he was adjunct professor of history and theology of Eastern Orthodoxy at Union Theological Seminary, New York, and adjunct professor of religion at Columbia University.

In 1955 he left St. Vladimir's to become associate professor of Orthodox church history and dogma at Holy Cross Greek Orthodox Theological School (qq.v.), Brookline, Massachusetts, where he remained until 1959, returning from 1963 to 1965 to be professor of patristic theology and the philosophy of religion. From 1956 to 1964 he was professor of Eastern church history at the Harvard Divinity School, and professor emeritus there from 1964 until his death. From 1964 to 1972 he was visiting professor of religion and Slavic studies at Princeton University, and a visiting lecturer at Princeton Theological Seminary from 1972 until his death. Profoundly committed to the concept of the Orthodox Church as the universal Church, he was very active in ecumenical (q.v.) encounter. A founding member of the World Council of Churches, serving on provisional committees until 1948, he was a member of the Central and Executive Committees from 1948 to 1961. He had a decisive influence on the pro-Orthodox outcome of the WCC Toronto Statement of 1950. From 1954 to 1957 he served as vice president of the National Council of Churches in the United States.

His writings are typified by their Christological and patristic (qq.v.) emphasis—he spent his adult life attempting to construct a neopatristic synthesis—while he tends to be more of an essayist in approach than a writer of monographs. Chief works are *Human and Divine Wisdom* (1922), *The Death on the Cross* (1930), and *The Eastern Tradition in Christianity* (1949). His collected works in English began appearing in 1974, currently numbering fourteen volumes. Of these, the most important are the four volumes on the Eastern and Byzantine fathers and the two volumes entitled *Ways of Russian Theology*.

**FOOLS IN CHRIST.** This phrase signifies at once a class of saints and a type of asceticism (q.v.). In Greek, these are the *saloi* and in Russian the *yurodeviye*. The first *salos* is generally taken to be Symeon of Emesa in the late 6th c. Although other examples followed in Byzantium (q.v.), e.g., Alexios, the "man of God," Russia was perhaps the true home of the holy fool. That Church, indeed, recently canonized the 18th c. *yurodeva*, Xenia of Petersburg. As a type, the holy fool seeks humility by feigning madness, thus exposing him- or herself to ridicule and, often, physical abuse. Even before its advent as a discernible category of asceticism, such behavior was not unknown among the early practitioners of monasticism (q.v.). Just as other great ascetics, the holy fools have often been perceived as gifted with extraordinary *charismata*, e.g., clairvoyance, the spirit of prophecy, healing (q.v.), etc.

On the one hand, their deliberate rejection of social status—similar to other notable ascetics (e.g., the stylites)—often accorded them a paradoxical access to and influence on the leaders of Church and state. On the other hand, this category of saint has been a controversial one over the centuries. At times the Church has questioned whether or not to recognize it. The basis of the controversy regarding holy fools may be summarized to say (possibly, too simply) that the saints could not easily be distinguished from the retarded, the demented, and others. Thus, the term "holy fool" frequently had, and still has, a slightly pejorative connotation. One may find similar phenomena in Western Europe through the medieval period, for example Francis of Assisi, or even, in a wholly secular context, the character of the fool in Shakespeare's *King Lear*.

**FORT ROSS** (1812–1841). Situated ninety miles north of San Francisco Bay on the Sonoma Coast and now a National Park, the fort was established along with Port Rumyantsev (Bodega Bay) and a hunting camp on the Farallon Islands off the Golden Gate in order to extend Russian land (especially, agriculture) and fur trade claims to its maximum southern limit in Alta California. The name itself is most probably an adaptation of "Rus'," the old name for "Russian" in that language. The colony, made up primarily of Native Americans, was the southernmost extension of Russian America from Alaska (qq.v.). The fort was built by Ivan Kuskov, deputy to Alexander Baranov, governor of the Alaskan Russian-American Company, after which it was inspected and relations established by Lt. G. Moraga representing the Spanish governor, J. J. Arrillaga.

Impetus for trade contact and the Alta California venture may be taken back to the visit of Count Nikolai Rezanov to Lt. L. Arguello in 1806. Extensive trade took place between the Russians and the

Hispanics in San Francisco, Mission San Rafael, and Mission Sonoma, largely on an unofficial basis; but one historian, D. S. Pritchard, aptly describes the Russian trade relationship with the Hispanics as that of "most favored nation status" ("Joint Tenants of the Frontier: Russian-Hispanic Relations in Alta California," *Russian America: The Forgotten Frontier,* pp. 81–94). By 1832 the secularization of the Spanish Missions and Yankee competition caused deprivation at Fort Ross. It was sold by the Russians to John Sutter, later of Gold Rush fame, in 1841 after the fur supply was largely exhausted and the Russians were unsuccessful at establishing agricultural operations extensive enough to support themselves or their Alaska holdings. Fort Ross was built with a chapel that was visited by Fr. Innocent Veniaminov (q.v.), and is still used for religious services by the Russian Orthodox today on Memorial Day and the Fourth of July.

**FORTY MARTYRS OF SEBASTEIA.** Commemorated on 9 March, the feast traditionally reckoned the end of winter by the monastic typicon of Mt. Athos (q.v.). These martyrs (q.v.) were forty Christian soldiers put to death, according to the "Life," at the order of the Emperor Licinius in the second decade of the 4th c. They were stripped and forced to stand in a freezing lake until death took them. The cult of the Forty Martyrs was encouraged by Gregory of Nyssa and Ephrem the Syrian (qq.v.), among others.

**FREEDOM** *see* Liberty-Freedom.

**FREEMASONRY.** 1) In eighteenth-century Russia: Origin of the Freemasons seems to go back to a twelfth-century English religious brotherhood formed to guard trade secrets. It has a varied history in different countries, sometimes professing an undoctrinal Christianity (England, Germany) and at other times being openly hostile to religion and the Church (France, Italy, Latin countries). In the 18th c. English Freemasonry embraced Deism, and from here (and other Western countries) it came to Russia during the reign of Tsarina Elizabeth, burgeoning under Catherine II. Members—the educated gentry in St. Petersburg, Moscow, and some provincial towns—numbered approximately twenty-five hundred.

At this time in Europe Voltairianism was a spiritual and moral disease among those converted to Western values due to its complete lack of spiritual concentration and the moral bankruptcy that accompanied it. Two trends in Freemasonry addressed deficiencies in this Enlightenment culture. One was mystical, focusing on meditation and self-perfection. The other was ethical/social, reaching out to the world in education and publishing. The latter was centered on the University of

Moscow and Nicholas Novikov, 1744–1818, Catherine's most active publicist. The Moscow Rosicrucian group became the most influential of the Russian centers, adding mystical and ascetical elements to disciplines of the lower forms of Freemasonry. The "occult sources" of Romanticism were derived from the higher levels of Freemasonry, and it shared with Romanticism a feeling of world harmony and anthropocentric self-awareness. Both trends, the mystical and ethical/social, are aspects of human nature that the Age of Reason could not adequately express.

As far as Russia was concerned, the newly educated converts to the Western European spirit became true Western bureaucrats, understanding their existence in terms of their utility to the state, where they were placed on Peter I's "Table of Ranks" (a fourteen-step government table of civil servants). This psychologically prepared and confirmed for them the many stepped ascent of the Masonic Orders. With the revolutionary character of the Enlightenment showing itself on the continent, Catherine the Great—clearly to safeguard the government and the wealthy—put an abrupt end to ideas and people that represented its ideals, among them the Masons. Nonetheless, a few scholars have seen the inspiration for and continuation of the movement in the later Slavophiles (q.v.).

2) In the United States today: In recent history the Orthodox experience of Freemasonry has largely been socioeconomic. Newly arrived immigrants consider that they have "made it" when they belong to a knife-and-fork business club, just like other successful Americans. The Church has not officially encouraged membership in Freemasonry due to the fact that at its higher levels, or degrees, it has a separate theology that is not in agreement with Orthodoxy (q.v.). Many clergy have spoken out against the Masons and reminded their people of the official condemnations issued by the Church from time to time in different countries—condemnations that were not de facto binding on the American Orthodox population. In some United States contexts even members of the clergy joined the Masons. If the socioeconomic theory is correct, the phenomenon in immigration will probably die its own silent death.

**-G-**

**GENNADIEVSKII BIBLE.** During the "Judaizing heresy" and the possessor/non-possessor (q.v.) controversy, the first complete Church Slavic Bible was compiled in Novgorod (q.v.). The translation effort included other texts besides the Bible, such as pieces focusing on messianism in Scripture (q.v.), polemics against Jews, and Church-state (q.v.) debates on property. Basically the entire effort responded to the above-mentioned movements and was authorized by Archbishop Gennadius of Novgorod—and became known in Russian as the Gennadievskii (Gennadius's) Bible (1499). Political and polemical considerations undermined the effort from the beginning. Neither Hebrew, Greek, nor extant Slavic translations were employed as primary texts from which to translate, but only the Vulgate. This phenomenon is indicative of a general orientation of Russia toward the Occident after the fall of Constantinople (q.v.). The Vulgate was supplied by a Dominican, Friar Benjamin (Veniamin), whose appearance in Novgorod might have been for this specific purpose. The section headings for Gennadius's Bible were co-opted from a recently published German edition. Russian evaluations of the translation through modern times have been negative, and focus on the "incursionary" presence of Roman Catholic (q.v.) politics on Russian soil.

**GENNADIUS OF CONSTANTINOPLE,** patriarch, theologian (ca. 1405–1472). The first to serve as Ecumenical Patriarch following the fall of Constantinople (qq.v.) in 1453, he was appointed and confirmed in office by Sultan Mohammed II, though he suffered (as was to become the pattern) periodic exiles as a result of the Sultan's displeasure. The Sultan established with him the concordat, which lasted until 1923, and which governed the relationship between the Orthodox Church in Constantinople and the Moslem ruler.

His name before monastic tonsure was George and his surname Scholarius (the scholar). He was one of the most noted intellectuals at the close of the Byzantine era (q.v.), and one of the few Greeks to learn Latin, evidenced by his translations of and admiring commentary on Thomas Aquinas. As such, Scholarius was invited to accompany the Byzantine delegation to the Reunion Council (q.v.) of Ferrara-Florence in 1438 to 1439, and was one of the signers of the Decree of Union. Afterward, converted to opposition to the Union by Mark of Ephesus (q.v.) and tonsured by the latter, he led the resistance following Mark's death. Doubtless, this opposition to union with the Roman Catholic West was one of the reasons for his appointment by the Sultan, although Gennadius was also the most qualified of available candidates for other reasons. He died in exile in the year of Constantinople's formal repudiation of the Florentine Union.

**GEORGIAN ORTHODOX CHURCH.** Ancient Iberia, Georgia is a trans-Caucasian nation bordering Russia and Armenia, and boasts of being one of the first kingdoms to convert to Christianity. The "Apostle to the Georgians" was an anonymous woman, later given the name Nina, who converted the king, Mirian, around 330. Early placed under the jurisdiction of Antioch, the Georgian Church achieved self-governing status around 506, in connection with its (temporary) repudiation of Chalcedon in alliance with the Church of Armenia (qq.v.). The breach with Byzantium (q.v.) was repaired the following century, but the local Church retained its independence. From the 6th c. the primate of Georgia has borne the title "Catholicos," and the Church first became autocephalous (q.v.) in the 8th c. Under constant pressure from Persia to the east, the Georgian Church and nation nonetheless achieved a peak of prosperity under the local branch of the Bagratid family (also ruling in Armenia), culminating in the "golden age" of Queen Tamara (d. 1212).

Georgian manuscripts from the period of the country's medieval zenith provide valuable materials for scholars in both Scripture and patristic (qq.v.) studies. This is largely the fruit of medieval Georgian monasticism (q.v.) from its origins in Peter the Iberian (ca. 413–491). It spread throughout the Byzantine Near East, as witnessed by the late medieval foundation on Mt. Athos (q.v.) of the monastery of Iviron.

Struggles with both Iran and the Ottoman Empire (q.v.) compelled its last king to plead for Russian protection. The Georgian Kingdom was absorbed into the tsar's Empire in 1811. Its local church became part of the Russian Church—perhaps the most notable case of Russian ecclesiastical imperialism. Autonomy was again secured, ecclesiastically if not politically, following the Bolshevik coup d'état in 1917. It remains in effect today as the Georgian Church is experiencing a modest revival under its Catholicos, Ilias II.

**GEORGIEVSKII, EVLOGII,** Metropolitan of Western Europe (1868-1946). Graduated from the Tula Theological Seminary in 1892 and the Moscow Theological Academy in 1894, he taught in Tula the next year and became a monastic. He was supervisor of Vladimir Seminary from 1895 to 1897, and from 1897 to 1903 rector of Chelm Seminary. In 1903 he became Bishop of Lublin and Vicar of the Warsaw-Chelm Diocese. As a member of the Moderate Rightists, he was a deputy to the Second Duma, and was one of two bishops represented in the conservative Third Duma. In October 1909 he became a member of the new Nationalist Party in the Duma, included in Stolypin's rightist bloc—always staunchly Russian nationalist. In June 1912 he was elevated to the rank of archbishop, and the Holy Synod disallowed his election to the Fourth Duma because he refused to organize a separate clerical party. In 1914 he became head of the Diocese of Volhynia, and in April 1915 he was sent to Galicia to administer Orthodox Church affairs in occupied territories.

He left Russia in January 1920 and his see was first in Berlin, then transferred to Paris in 1922. In 1923 he was made metropolitan of all Russian Orthodox churches in Western Europe by decree of Patriarch

Tikhon (q.v.), at the same time the patriarch dismissed the ecclesiastical administration of the Synod in Exile (q.v.) created by a council of emigrant bishops at Sremski Karlovci, Yugoslavia. In 1925 Evlogii established St. Sergius Orthodox Theological Institute (q.v.), Paris. Because of the confounding ecclesiastical situation, Evlogii's exarchate fell successively under two patriarchates (qq.v.), Moscow from 1921 to 1931 and 1945 to 1946, and Constantinople from 1931 to 1945. He submitted to the authority of the Moscow Patriarchate in 1945, but the decision in favor by the exarch diocese was not established until after his death. His primary written work is *My Life's Path: The Memoirs of Metropolitan Evlogii, Based on His Own Accounts by T. Manukhina* (in Russian). The first half of the book describes Russian church life at the turn of the century, and the second half is a detailed history of the Russian émigré church in Europe.

**GERMANOS (STRENOPOULOS)**, Metropolitan of Thyateira *see* Strenopoulos, Germanos.

**GHEORGHIU, CONSTANTIN V.**, bishop, novelist, diplomat (1916–22 June 1992). He fled Romania in 1944, settled in France, and published his best-selling novel *The Twenty-Fifth Hour* (1948). The novel is a denunciation of Nazism and Communism (English trans. 1950), and became a film. He has also published a biography of Ecumenical Patriarch Athenagoras (q.v.) in French (1969). Gheorghiu was ordained priest in 1963 and in 1971 became the bishop of the Romanian Orthodox Church in France.

**GIANNARAS, CHRESTOS** *see* Yannaras, Christos.

**GILLET, LEV,** "A Monk of the Eastern Church," monastic priest, theologian, ecumenist (1892/3–29 March 1980). Reared in a Roman Catholic family near Grenoble, he studied philosophy there and at Paris. In 1914 he served in the French army, was wounded and taken prisoner, and served two years in a German camp. Released in 1917, he settled in Geneva to pursue studies in mathematics and psychology. In 1920 he entered the French Benedictine Abbey of Farnborough, England, and came under the influence of the Uniate Metr. Andrew Szeptyckyi of Lvov. The community sent him to study at St. Anselmo, Rome, where he collaborated with Dom Lambert Beauduin on ways to bring about the unity of the Roman and Russian Churches.

Deeply influenced by the ecumenical outlook of Vladimir Soloviev (q.v.) and unsupported at Farnborough in his Orthodox interests, he went to Lvov in 1924 where Metropolitan Szeptyckyi ordained him deacon and priest following profession as monk. He served briefly as

Szeptyckyi's secretary. In 1927 he did relief work for the Russian emigrants in Nice, and on 25 May 1928 he concelebrated Divine Liturgy with Metropolitan Evlogii (q.v.). Archimandrite Lev was thus received into the Orthodox Church, and from 25 May until his death served only the Orthodox. From 1928 he did charity work for the Russian Student Christian Movement and was assigned by Evlogii to serve the chapel of Mother Maria Skobtsova's (q.v.) "hermitage," and was the rector of Paris's only French-speaking Orthodox parish. In Paris he became interested in the ideas of Sergius Bulgakov and was a close friend to Paul Evdokimov (qq.v.), and lived there until his departure for London in February 1938.

In the early 1940s he had a research fellowship to study Jewish-Christian relations at Selly Oak College, Birmingham. From 1948 until his death he served as Orthodox chaplain to the Fellowship of St. Alban and St. Sergius (q.v.), London. He is author of *Communion in the Messiah* (1942), *Orthodox Spirituality: An Outline of the Orthodox Ascetical and Mystical Tradition* (trans. 1945), *On the Invocation of the Name of Jesus* (trans. 1949), *Jesus, A Dialogue with the Saviour* (trans., 2nd ed. 1963), *In Thy Presence* (trans. 1977), *The Jesus Prayer* (trans., rev. 1987), and *Encounter at the Well: Retreat Addresses* (1988).

**GNOSTICISM.** Divided about its origins, many scholars hold that it was a first and second century movement deeply influenced by Persian dualism, mediated by heretical Jewish and Christian thought, elements of popular pagan religion, and a sort of middlebrow Platonism (q.v.). The result for Christianity (Christian gnosticism) was a pattern of religious thinking that, though it spawned a bewildering variety of systems, had certain common traits: 1) the assertion that the physical world is evil; therefore 2) that its creator is evil and not the God of Jesus Christ, who only appeared to be human; thus 3) that the Old Testament is the work of an evil Demiurge while the Gospel of Christ is the message of the Divine Being.

This dualism was further reflected in the division of human beings into two or three categories: the fleshly, i.e., those belonging wholly to this world and so immune to spiritual truth, and the spiritual, for whom Christ descended from the heavenly realm above this world of delusion. The spiritual are further divided into those who know the truth and those still unaware of who must receive the saving knowledge (q.v.), *gnosis* in Greek—hence the name of the movement. Gnosticism produced an immense literature, almost entirely lost until discovery of a 4th-c. cache of texts near the Egyptian village of Nag Hammadi in 1945 and 1946. The find included treatises, "gospels," apocalypses, epistles, etc., many of which purported to come from an apostle, Mary Magdalene, or Christ himself.

The response of the Great Church (q.v.) to gnosticism was twofold. While pointing out the pagan features of gnosticism and its emphasis on secrecy, Irenaeus of Lyons (q.v.) defended the public and continuous institutional integrity of the Church, its sacraments and Scriptures (q.v.), limited to the four Gospels, the epistles of Paul, and the Old Testament (Septuagint) Scripture. His defense included a vigorous apology for the created goodness of the world, the reality of the Incarnation, and the Eucharist (q.v.) as the central affirmation confirming all the above. The Alexandrians, Clement and Origen (qq.v.), sought to redeem the authentic interests of gnosticism in the subjective and experiential by exploring the human psyche and presenting an ideal and method of Christian spirituality. Hence Clement produced an outline of the Christian (orthodox) "gnostic" that foreshadowed the enlightened elders of later monasticism (q.v.), while Origen employed allegory (q.v.) to interpret Scripture, in particular the Old Testament, into a journal and guidebook of the soul's return to God. (For Russian gnosticism *see* Doukhobors.)

**GOD.** According to the theology (q.v.) of the Orthodox Church, as in for example Gregory of Nyssa and Dionysius the Areopagite (qq.v.), the word "God" denotes an activity of the transcendent and ineffable Creator. When it does not refer to the person of God the Father, it thus indicates the divine providence. "God" is how the divinity manifests itself to us and saves us. Divine providence has revealed itself most fully and finally in Jesus Christ, and thus in the persons of the Holy Trinity (q.v.). In confronting Orthodox thought, one must keep in mind its twin emphases on person and action. "God" is never abstract, never a mere concept. One does not, and cannot, approach the godhead as essence or being. The popular American phrase, "Supreme Being," would not, for example, have found ready acceptance among the Church Fathers (q.v.) because they would have read it as wrongly including the divinity within the hierarchy of beings that constitutes created existence. Being and essence are instead the gifts of "God," pointing to the divine activities ("energies") that create and sustain the universe. Knowledge of God therefore means the experience of his grace and the encounter, in the Holy Spirit (q.v.), with the person of the incarnate Son of the Father.

**GODPARENT** *see* Sponsor.

**GOGOL, NIKOLAI V.,** Russian author (1809–1852). Liked especially for his satire and humor, Gogol founded the Russian school of realism. His own religious temperament was fearful, though he might be described as a pietistic humanist who read the Bible for its prophecies and apocalypses. He spent a prolonged period of time in Rome and was fond of the *Imitation of Christ* and Thomas Aquinas, but read the Eastern Fathers as well. Although not known for his religious writing but for such works as the collection *Evenings on a Farm near Dikanka* or the play *The Inspector General,* nevertheless he authored a symbolic liturgical commentary entitled *Meditations on the Divine Liturgy* (1842–43), which was quite popular in Russia. The characters in *Taras Bulba* well illustrate the tension that prevailed between (Russian) Ukraine and the (Polish) West in religious affairs and otherwise. In *Selected Passages from Correspondence with Friends* one can get glimpses of the religious crisis of the 19th-c. Russian intelligentsia and Gogol's own desire for a socioreligious utopia, a theocratic tsardom. His greatest novel, *Dead Souls* (1842), had a sequel which he destroyed in a religious and moral frenzy that ended in his death.

**GOLITSYN, ALEXANDER N.,** ober-procurator (1773–1844). A favorite of Tsar Alexander I, this prince enjoyed a religious temperament characterized by extreme biblicism and mysticism. These traits, peculiarly juxtaposed, would have been of little consequence had Golitsyn not been appointed ober-procurator of the Holy Synod, chief of the department of foreign confessions, minister of public education, and elected president of the Russian Bible Society, as well as other offices. A philanthropist and aristocrat, Golitsyn's tenure in religious affairs has been described as dictatorial and ruthless. He advocated his understanding of the Bible and mysticism by advancing like-minded obscurantists to official posts; but he did help initiate a Russian Bible (q.v.) translation project with Metropolitan Philaret (Drozdov) that produced a new translation of the complete Bible into Russian rather than Church Slavic, a translation that is the basis of the current Russian Bible. His career in religious matters ended abruptly in 1824 due to charges of insufficient Orthodoxy, although he remained head of the postal department and on the Council of Ministers and State Council.

**GONDIKAKIS, VASILEIOS,** archimandrite, of Iviron (1936-  ). Abbot of Stavronikita Monastery, Mt. Athos, he is a leader in the movement reviving monasticism on Athos (qq.v.) and author of *Hymn of Entry: Liturgy and Life in the Orthodox Church* (trans. 1984).

**GORAZD,** bishop, St. *see* Czech and Slovak Orthodox Church.

**GRABAR, ANDRE,** art historian, archaeologist (26 July 1896–5 October 1990). He studied at the universities of Kiev and Petrograd under Professors N. P. Kondakov and D. V. Ainalov. Settling in Strasbourg in 1922, he studied under Professors Paul Perdrizet and Gabriel Millet. Professor of the history of art at Strasbourg University, 1928–37, he moved permanently to Paris to succeed Professor Millet as the director of studies (Christian and Byzantine Archaeology) at the Ecole Pratique des Hautes Etudes, 1937–66, and was professor of early Christian and Byzantine archaeology at the Collège de France, 1946–66. In 1955 he became a member of the French Academy. He is the author of *Christian Iconography: A Study of Its Origins* (trans. 1968) and numerous other works. He was awarded the title of doctor honoris causa of the Universities of Princeton, Uppsala, and Edinburgh.

**GRACE.** The Greek word, *charis,* means free gift, gratuity. Grace in Orthodox theology is thus the unmerited gift of God (q.v.). More specifically, it signifies the Father's gift of himself through Christ in the Holy Spirit (q.v.). The distinction, important for Latin Scholasticism (q.v.), between created and uncreated grace finds no equivalent in the Christian East. The two concepts of grace clashed in the debate over the holy hesychasts, won by Gregory Palamas (qq.v.). Gregory's clear insistence on grace as finally God himself in his uncreated energies was upheld by local councils held in Constantinople (q.v.) in 1341, 1347, and 1351. The particular, Western concern with the relationship between (or opposition of) nature and grace, seen especially in Augustine of Hippo's (q.v.) debate with Pelagius and resulting in the former's advocacy of predestination, continued to affect Western Christianity into the Reformation (e.g., Luther and Calvin) and beyond, but has no counterpart in the Orthodox East. The latter's theology and anthropology (qq.v.), while insisting on the divine initiative and on *theosis* (q.v.) as the content of salvation, simultaneously requires room for the free response of the human being. The whole sphere of Orthodox asceticism (q.v.) bears witness to this notion of *synergia*, cooperation, between divine grace and created nature (q.v.). The two are never read in opposition to one another or as mutually exclusive. This insistence is at least as old as Irenaeus of Lyons (q.v.), especially his vision of created nature, summed up in the human being, as presupposing grace in order to become truly itself. In other words, whatever is without grace is, for Irenaeus and the whole patristic tradition of the East, at the same time less than "natural," i.e., fallen.

***GRAMMATA.*** In Greek, literally meaning "letters," parallel to the English "letter of commendation," and used as a singular noun in Russian and English, a *grammata* usually takes the form of a certificate of commendation. It is presented by a bishop or group of hierarchs as a citation and award to an individual or group in recognition of an act of outstanding stewardship.

**GREAT CHURCH.** Applied to the early Church, this phrase customarily signifies the catholic (q.v.) Church of the early centuries, i.e., the Church as defended by such as Ignatius of Antioch, Irenaeus of Lyons, Cyprian of Carthage, and Origen of Alexandria (qq.v.), and characterized as possessing a single teaching and communion over and against the divisions of the sects, e.g., gnosticism, and the heresies (qq.v.). In the Byzantine era, the phrase comes to be associated with Hagia Sophia, the enormous cathedral (*see* Architecture) in Constantinople built by Justinian (qq.v.), with the idea that this church constituted the sum of Christian Orthodoxy and the standard to which the faith and liturgy of other communities within the *oikoumene* (qq.v.) were expected to conform.

**GREAT LENT** *see* Lent.

**GREECE** *see* Greek Orthodox Church, modern.

**GREEK.** As the language of the Septuagint (q.v.), New Testament, and the majority of the Church Fathers (q.v.), Greek enjoys a privileged place among the languages of the Orthodox *oikoumene* (q.v.). It is the linguistic medium shaped by the long struggle with pagan Hellenism (q.v.), both ancient and modern, and possesses a unique prestige and authority, along with a technically defined theological vocabulary. It was, however, never the unique language of the Church in the East, since Aramaic, Syriac, Armenian, Georgian, Coptic, Ethiopian, and Arabic were all languages in use by the 6th c. and earlier. In later centuries, Church Slavic, Romanian, Finnish, Hungarian, together with the languages of the Orient and the Americas would be added to the list. Greek has, therefore, a kind of "presidency" among the tongues of the Orthodox Church, a *primus inter pares* ("first among equals"). It provides the rule by which the translations of Scripture and patristic writings (qq.v.) are measured.

**GREEK CIVIL WAR.** Just as in neighboring Yugoslavia (q.v.), much of the resistance against Nazi occupation of Greece (q.v.) was carried on by members of the Greek Communist Party. The end of the war with Germany did not mean the end of combat in Greece as the Communists, supported by Stalin, made a vigorous attempt to seize power. Although aided by the West, and especially by the Truman administration, conflict was prolonged and often savage before the royalist forces prevailed by the early 1950s. Communist insurgency was particularly marked by atrocities against churches and clergy of the contested regions.

**GREEK ORTHODOX ARCHDIOCESE OF NORTH AND SOUTH AMERICA,** an exarchate of the Ecumenical Patriarchate (qq.v.). The founding of the Greek Orthodox Archdiocese was through the unilateral initiative of Meletios Metaxakis, an exceptional and controversial Orthodox prelate. Having been elected Archbishop of Athens (1918), he was forced out of Greece (1920) and came to America after the overthrow of Prime Minister Eleftherios Venizelos, his uncle. While some of the parishes with Greek parishioners in the United States, especially in the west and south, were in the jurisdiction of the Russian Church's Missionary Diocese, others had no affiliation. Clearly, the Greek parishes had no overall organization, though a Tomos of Ecumenical Patriarch Joachim III directed them to obtain their clergy from the Church of Greece.

Within months Archbishop Meletios provided leadership for all these dispersed groups and incorporated a "Greek Archdiocese of North and South America" under the jurisdiction of the Synod of Athens, of which he considered himself the primate. Thus, this was the first Orthodox ecclesiastical body to be organized in the western hemisphere on purely ethnic grounds and independent from the canonically established territorial diocese of the Russian Church (q.v.).

On 25 November 1921 Archbishop Meletios was elected Patriarch of Constantinople, which meant that his newly formed diocese in the United States would no longer be under his jurisdiction. At his investiture on 24 January 1922 he spoke of the ecclesiastical situation in America by which he "understood the measure in which the name of Orthodoxy would be exalted . . . if the two million Orthodox Christians of America were organized into one united ecclesiastical organization, as an *American Orthodox Church*" (text in B. Zoustis, *Hellenism in America,* in Greek, New York, 1954, p. 147).

If unity in America was the Patriarch's dream, he did not—or was not able to—facilitate that plan. Instead, he proceeded to transfer the newly formed Greek Archdiocese in America from the jurisdiction of Athens to dependence on the Patriarchate of Constantinople. In human terms this move was understandable, but unfortunately Metaxakis made no further attempts to unify all the Orthodox in America. As a result, the unilateral establishment of an ethnically "Greek" exarchate (q.v.) did more to divide the Orthodox in America than to unite them—because it became the paradigm for every patriarchate to establish an "ethnic" presence in America. Once a "cash flow" was established from an American "ethnic diocese" to a poor "mother church" (q.v.), the process flourished and became almost irreversible.

The original canonical structure of the Greek Archdiocese in America included three additional dioceses under the archbishop, and the bishops of these dioceses formed a synod and enjoyed an "autonomous" status. But the Archdiocese was soon confronted with a political rift between "Royalists" and "Venizelists," the "Royalists" proclaiming autocephaly (q.v.). Archbishop Athenagoras Spyrou (q.v.), 1931–1948, reunited the factions, but in doing so also did away with the organization's autonomy. There were no more separate dioceses and all bishops became vicars to the one archbishop, and membership was reserved to ethnic Greeks.

In spite of these limitations, Archbishop Athenagoras was also personally amenable to cooperation with other Orthodox. He established a theological seminary in Pomfret, Connecticut, which was later transferred to Brookline, Massachusetts, and became Holy Cross Greek Orthodox School of Theology (q.v.). He developed community life in America and the Clergy-Laity Congress.

When Athenagoras became the patriarch of Constantinople, he appointed the Metropolitan of Corinth, Michael, as the new archbishop in America in 1950. Archbishop Michael continued the direction set by his predecessor and further established the Greek Orthodox Youth Organization (GOYO), uniform parish bylaws, and became the first Greek clergyman to speak at a presidential inauguration in 1957. He was succeeded by Archbishop Iakovos Coucouzis (q.v.), who both strengthened the administration of the Archdiocese and actively engaged in public relations. This brought an awareness of the Orthodox Church to America. With the arrival of tens of thousands of Greek immigrants a year, the Greek Archdiocese became the largest Orthodox group in America—though retaining a strong Greek character and remaining administratively dependent on Istanbul. With twelve auxiliary bishops, Archbishop Iakovos is responsible for almost 500 large parishes. He is widely recognized as a major spokesman for Orthodoxy in the United States.

**GREEK ORTHODOX CHURCH,** modern. Greece is the oldest country in Europe, but it is a relatively new nation-state. Its independence from the Ottoman Empire (q.v.) dates only to the 1820s. The Greek Revolution of 1821 was significantly influenced, and the resulting state shaped, by men deeply impressed by the Western European movements of the Enlightenment and Romanticism. This proved to be a mixed blessing for the Orthodox Church and culture of the country: Church and state were ordered in ways more dependent on Western models and an already Westernized imperial Russia than on the Greek Christian past. The Byzantine era (q.v.) was held in contempt by the new establishment and contrasted to an uncritical and romantic portrait of classical Greece, a portrait again drawn largely from the European classicism of the Renaissance. The result was, and continues to be, a sort of national schizophrenia not unlike the debates between Westernizers and Slavophiles (q.v.), which divided 19th-c.

Russia and which have resurfaced in the post-Soviet era. (*See* Phanariot; Tikas, Seraphim).

**GREGORIUS, PAULOS MAR** *see* Verghese, Paul.

**GREGORY OF NAZIANZUS,** "The Theologian," monk, bishop, St. (329–389). One of the Cappadocian Fathers (q.v.), Gregory was the son of the bishop of Nazianzus and a lifelong friend of Basil the Great (q.v.), both of whom studied in Athens. Their friendship was severely strained by Basil's use of his friends in his campaigns against the "Neo-Arians." His tactics included filling up vacant episcopal sees with trusted acquaintances, and Gregory fell a reluctant and unhappy victim when snatched from his monastic refuge. Theologically, however, his loyalty to Basil was complete. His appointment in 379 as Bishop of Constantinople for the small party in the imperial city loyal to the Creed of Nicaea (qq.v.) provided the setting for a series of brilliant sermons, including the justly famed five *Theological Orations* on the Trinity (q.v.), which served to win the day for Trinitarian Orthodoxy at Constantinople and to win for Gregory himself the epithet, "the Theologian," by which he continues to be venerated. After being appointed Bishop of Constantinople and helping to convene the Second Ecumenical Council (q.v.), he was forced to resign by an episcopal cabal led by the Patriarch of Alexandria.

Gregory retired first to Nazianzus and then to his country estate in Cappadocia where he devoted his remaining years to asceticism (q.v.), correspondence, and the writing of theological poetry. While the last forms a considerable part of his remaining works, it is not usually as highly valued as his extraordinary sermons, which with his letters continue to be studied and greatly esteemed. His "Letters to Cledonius" on the Apollinarian controversy, in particular the phrase "what is not assumed is not saved," provided an important standard for the pronouncements of later Ecumenical Councils on Christology (q.v.).

**GREGORY OF NYSSA,** bishop, theologian, St. (ca. 340–ca. 394). Brother of Basil the Great (q.v.), Gregory was the youngest and perhaps most intellectually sophisticated of the Cappadocian Fathers (q.v.). He took little active part in the controversies of the late 4th c. during Basil's lifetime, though he did accept consecration to the episcopate at the latter's hands in 370. Following his brother's death in 379, however, he engaged himself thoroughly and quickly took the lead, remaining the single most important theologian in the East until his death.

Deeply read in Neoplatonism, as well as in prior Church Fathers, especially Origen (qq.v.), Gregory was more inclined toward speculative theology than either his brother or Gregory Nazianzus (q.v.). His concern with Origen and Neoplatonism, together with his loyalty to Basil's defense of Nicene Orthodoxy, led him to a profound reconsideration of anthropology and cosmology (qq.v.) in light of the Incarnation, and to an expanded defense of Trinitarian theology along the lines Basil had charted. Thus, he wrote his most extensive theological work, the *Contra Eunomium,* as well as the treatises *On the Making of Man* (elaborations of Basil's *Against Eunomius* and *Hexaemeron,* respectively), *On Not Three Gods,* and the opening of his masterful summary of Christian doctrine, *The Great Catechism.*

The most prolific of the Cappadocians, his works dwelt upon asceticism (q.v.) and mysticism in ways that at once supported his brother's concerns with monasticism (q.v.), and that provided the groundwork for the systematic incorporation of monastic experience into the dogmatic tradition (qq.v.) of the Church in the great debates of the following centuries. Here one should mention in particular Gregory's early treatise, *On Virginity,* the allegorical treatment of Moses' ascent of Sinai in *The Life of Moses,* the commentary *On the Song of Songs,* the treatise on *Christian Perfection,* and the life of his sister, St. Macrina. He was a defender of Mary as Theotokos (q.v.), but was influenced in his eschatology by Origen's apocatastasis (q.v.). The work begun by Gregory, i.e., the blending of the experiential with the revelation of God in Trinity and the background of late Platonism (qq.v.), reached a kind of culmination three centuries later in the thought of Maximus the Confessor (q.v.).

**GREGORY OF SINAI,** monk, ascetic, St. (ca. 1255/65–ca. 1337). Gregory is generally credited with the reinvigoration of Orthodox monasticism (q.v.) and general renewal associated with the hesychast (q.v.) movement of the fourteenth and fifteenth centuries. He promoted in particular the active practice of the "Jesus Prayer," i.e., the invocation of the divine name accompanied by a discipline of breathing. Coming from the monastery of St. Catherine on Sinai, where this discipline might have originated, he found a ready welcome at Mt. Athos (q.v.) and later at Paroria of Thrace on the Byzantine-Bulgarian border. The *Philokalia* of Nicodemus of the Holy Mountain includes a selection of his writings.

**GREGORY PALAMAS,** Archbishop of Thessalonica, theologian, monk, ascetic, St. (ca. 1296–1359). Palamas was born of Byzantine nobility and raised in the circle of the imperial court. In early life he broke off his schooling on completion of secondary education and embraced the life of monasticism on Mt. Athos, practicing the discipline of prayer brought there by Gregory of Sinai (qq.v.). His later fame arrived with his championship of the hesychasts (q.v.) and, with them, of the tradition of Eastern Christian asceticism against the charges of Barlaam of Calabria (q.v.). Gregory's greatest work, *The Triads in Defense of the Holy Hesychasts,* assembled the scriptural and patristic evidence for *theosis* (qq.v.), arguing that the claims to a direct experience of God (q.v.) by saints past and present were evidence of a distinction in God between the divine essence and activities, or energies. The *Triads*—following on the *Hagioritic Tome* Gregory had authored (1340/41) and the monks had signed—opened up an intense debate in the Orthodox Church that lasted for over a decade, and culminated in Gregory's official vindication at the local councils held at Constantinople (q.v.) in 1341, 1347, and 1351. The essence/energies distinction has subsequently been accepted as the official teaching of the Orthodox Church.

During his lifetime Gregory was convicted of heresy (q.v.) and excommunicated, and also captured and imprisoned by the Turks, but remained steadfast in his faith. Elected Archbishop of Thessalonica (q.v.) in 1347, he died in office. Some ten years after his death, ca. 1369, his lifelong disciple and admirer, the Patriarch Philotheos of Constantinople, saw to his canonization. He is commemorated in the Orthodox Church on the second Sunday of Great Lent (q.v.).

**GREGORY THE ILLUMINATOR,** missionary, Bishop of Armenia, St. (ca. 240–332). According to his *Life* by Agathangelos, Gregory was a native of Armenia, though not of Armenian background. He converted to Christianity at Caesarea in Cappadocia (qq.v.) and, on returning to his native land, survived the tortures inflicted on him by King Trdat (ca. 238–314) and won the king and his court to the faith around 314. He was consecrated bishop (or "catholicos," as it is called in the Armenian and Georgian Churches) and the office remained in his family for some generations. From Armenia he is also credited with beginning the mission to Georgia. No writings definitively ascribed to him have survived.

**GURII,** Archbishop of Kazan, St. (?–1595). Gurii was a member of the poor, noble Rugotin family. A monk of the Volokolamsk Monastery, Gurii was made archbishop of newly conquered Kazan by Tsar Ivan IV in 1555 in recognition of his work in prison while confined on a false accusation. For nine years in Kazan, he converted many thousands of pagans and Moslems to Christianity through preaching and the instruction of children. He taught the children to read and was such a zealous preacher that if sick, he would be carried to church on a stretcher to instruct his flock from there. During the last two years of his life he devoted himself to asceticism (q.v.), died in 1595, and was buried in the Transfiguration of the Savior Monastery. He is especially venerated in the Kazan region of Russia.

## -H-

**HAGIA SOPHIA.** The original church of the Holy Wisdom (*Hagia Sophia*) was a basilica built during the reign of Constantius II ca. 360, and then rebuilt in 415. After the second church had burned down during the Nika riots of 532, the Emperor Justinian (q.v.) engaged the architects Isidore of Miletos and Anthimos of Tralles to design and build a cathedral worthy of the imperial capital. The result was the present building completed in 537. Its splendor is said to have elicited from the emperor the cry: "Solomon, I have surpassed you!" The building features an enormous dome, 180 feet high, built over the plan of a cross. Its architecture (q.v.) provided the template for the classical Byzantine churches to come, although none would ever approach its scale. Converted into a mosque by Sultan Mohammed II after the conquest of Constantinople, Hagia Sophia was the Ottoman Empire's banner of victory over Christian Byzantium (qq.v.) and served again as a template, this time for the series of impressive mosques punctuating the skyline of Turkish Constantinople. With the regime of Kemal Ataturk in the 1920s, the building was declared a secular museum, an act that has permitted art restorers to recover some of the mosaics that had filled it prior to the Ottoman conquest.

**HAGIOGRAPHY.** According to the Greek roots, hagiography literally means the "writings on the holy ones," i.e., saints (q.v.), and includes writings on the lives and legends of the saints, generally without any modern critical claim to veracity or verification. The lives of the saints have constituted the popular reading of Byzantine, Russian, and other Orthodox believers down to the modern era. As all popular literature hagiography was, and is, highly stylized and employs a number of standard types and tropes.

Early hagiography before the 4th c. is generally limited to short entries on the time, place, and type of martyrdom of a particular saint(s), with a few notable exceptions such as the court record regarding the execution of Justin Martyr and his friends, the letters of Ignatius of Antioch (qq.v.) on the way to his death, etc. In the 4th c. Eusebius of Caesarea began to write much more than the single paragraph on martyrs (q.v.), and Athanasius of Alexandria wrote the famous *Vita Antonii,* the Life of Antony (qq.v.). Athanasius's artistic and purposeful life of Antony became the 4th c. equivalent to a modern best-seller, and with Eusebius's contributions, henceforth changed the form of hagiography for all time. Certain famous "Lives" served as paradigms for subsequent saints. Thus the *Martyrdom of Polycarp* (ca. 160) served as the model for martyrs, the *Life of Antony* (ca. 358) for monastic saints, Eusebius's *Life of Constantine* for devout rulers, etc.

Particular lives, in addition to the ones just mentioned, also demonstrated outstanding qualities, for example the *Life of St. Symeon the New Theologian* by Nicetas Stethatos, or Epiphanius the Wise's *Life of St. Sergius of Radonezh.*

For all the stereotyping, the Byzantine and later "Lives" convey a great wealth of both theological and historical material. They grant the historian a privileged glimpse into the daily lives and attitudes of the more ordinary folk customarily overlooked by court chroniclers. For believers, the saints' "Lives" provide a confirmation of faith in the transforming power of the Spirit, a person with whom one might identify.

Both in original composition and in translation, a great deal of ancient Slavic literature was devoted to hagiography. For example, the lives of Palestinian saints and the Syrian *Historia Religiosa* of Theodoret of Cyrrhus (q.v.) were two models of ascetic life for Kievan Christianity, and certainly must have been some of the earliest material translated from Greek. Within 100 years of the death of Boris and Gleb, sons of Prince Vladimir, in the early 11th c. three different hagiographies were written about them. Nestor the Chronicler (q.v.) wrote a "Life" of Theodosius of the Kievan Caves Monastery within twenty years of his death—even before he was canonized—as well as other lives he included in the Chronicle. The later style of Russian hagiography was established in the 15th c. by Epiphanius the Wise and Pachomius the Serb. From the 18th c. to the present the standard Russian collection of "Lives" consists of twelve thick volumes, one for each month, compiled by Dmitri of Rostov (d. 1709) during the last twenty years of his life.

Each local Orthodox Church compiles its *Synaxarion,* or collection of saints' lives. These normally run into several volumes. The *Great Synaxarion* of the Church of Greece, for example, includes fourteen volumes, and the more recent *Zhitie Svyatix* by the Serbian monk, Justin Popovich, twelve. Shorter compilations are also available, as the abbreviated *Synaxarion* in four volumes by Nicodemus of the Holy Mountain (q.v.) or the volume of abbreviated saints' lives in Bulgakov's *Nastolnaya Kniga.* None, however, are as yet available in English.

A note of caution is in order for the contemporary reader who might approach ancient hagiography with a modern literary viewpoint and thereby be disappointed. As literature (q.v.), hagiography served many different functions throughout history, from the mountaintops of spiritual edification on to the exalted heights of biographies of holiness (q.v.), and back to the familiar plateaus of entertaining legend and pious fiction. In this regard *Webster's* definition of hagiography as "biography of saints: saints' lives" is so brief as to be misleading, as seen in the short historical development outlined above. Not all hagiography is of the same quality and purpose.

Some Orthodox theologians, while respecting the Bollandists, look askance at modern efforts to critique ancient hagiography with hypercritical agendas they judge as inappropriate—e.g., proving or disproving the existence of someone/something, discrediting the miraculous, etc.—ultimately not allowing the genre to fulfill its original literary function. This is identified as the same modern critical tendency that led scholars of the last century to misidentify the Gospels as biographies of Jesus.

**HARAKAS, STANLEY S.**, priest, theologian, educator (13 January 1932- ). After receiving his diploma in theology from Holy Cross Greek Orthodox Theological School (q.v.), Brookline, Massachusetts, (1954), he was ordained priest (1956) and further received a B.A. (1957) and a B.D (1959). In 1965 he received a Th.D. from Boston University and was instructor at Holy Cross from 1966 to 1967, assistant professor, 1967–71, associate professor, 1971–72, and professor from 1972 to the present. Dean of the School of Theology, 1970–80, and dean of the affiliated Hellenic College, 1971–75, in 1986 he received the Archbishop Iakovos Chair of Orthodox Theology. Since 1961 he has been very active in ecumenical (q.v.) dialog. He has occasionally authored works under the pseudonym "Exetastes," and is the author of *Let Mercy Abound: A Chronicle of Greek Orthodox Social Concerns* (1983) and *Toward Transfigured Life: The Theoria of Eastern Orthodox Ethics* (1983) among other works.

**HAWAWEENY, RAPHAEL**, bishop, missionary (8 November 1860–27 February 1915). Born in Damascus, Syria, Raphael Hawaweeny was the first Orthodox bishop consecrated in America. After completing studies at the Ecumenical Patriarchate's Halki Theological School, he was ordained deacon and entered the Kiev Theological Academy. After graduation in 1894, he was appointed professor of Arabic language and literature at the Kazan Theological Academy by the Holy Synod.

At this time, the Arabic-speaking community in the United States was growing rapidly, and a Syrian Orthodox Benevolent Society was organized in New York City in 1895. The president, Dr. Ibrahim Arbeely, contacted Hawaweeny about the needs of the fledgling community, whereupon the latter was ordained to the priesthood in Russia and was elevated to the rank of archimandrite. This occurred so that he could serve Arab-Americans in the United States; and he proceeded there accompanied by two other "Syro-Arabs" who had been in Russia. Archimandrite Raphael was placed in charge of the whole of the Syrian Mission, and organized St. Nicholas Cathedral in Brooklyn. His extensive travels throughout the United States led to the establishment of many other parishes, and by 1898 he published a large Arabic liturgical book (q.v.).

In 1901 he was twice elected bishop by the Holy Synod of the Church of Antioch, if he would but return to Syria, but he deferred to his missionary work in the New World. After the approval of the Holy Synod of Russia Bishops, Tikhon Belavin (q.v.) and Innocent Pustynsky consecrated him Bishop of Brooklyn. Bishop Raphael's work was by no means limited to Arab-Americans, and he actively assisted Archbishop Tikhon. For example, he prepared the agenda for the historic first All-American Council at a clergy conference and also consecrated the new grounds of St. Tikhon's Monastery and Orphanage in Pennsylvania. He was the founder of the magazine, *Al-Kalemat*, in 1905—still published today by the Antiochian Orthodox Christian Archdiocese (q.v.) as *The Word*. He issued edicts to explain the complexities of the American religious scene to his people. At the time of his death thirty Syrian Orthodox parishes had been established in the United States with approximately 25,000 faithful. A proposal for Bishop Raphael's canonization was recently presented at the Patriarchate of Antioch.

**HEALING.** In reading the Psalms, the primary hymnbook of the Jewish and Christian church, one cannot but come away with the impression that sickness and death are humankind's most avaricious natural enemies, while wholeness and life are God's most precious blessings. In general, healing fits into this scheme, not as a supernatural action, but as the restoration of a human being to natural vitality. Healing overcomes the sickness and suffering of the fallen world and restores its pristine wholeness, and for this reason is both spiritual and physical.

Theology put forward in Duet asserts that in God's plan the good prosper and the wicked suffer. Popular interpreters of Duet, past and present, have drawn the further conclusion that if people suffer, with sickness for example, they must be wicked. Many societies since the time of Duet have engaged in the self-righteous and spurious occupation of postulating the wickedness of the sick, regardless of the actual contents of the book or the rules of logic. Such is the case with the first three friends of Job and with Jesus' disciples who, when they met a man born blind, asked Jesus whether this man or his parents sinned so that he was born blind. Jesus' response, that neither this man nor his parents sinned, denied the simple causality of sickness, sin (q.v.), and of inherited guilt.

Healing in the Church is looked upon as a sacrament (q.v.) that imitates the many healings of Jesus, is commanded by Scripture (Jas 5:13f.), and involves both soul and body. Historically, healers were not set apart by ordination but were recognized by their fruits. Special recognition is given by the Church to unmercenary healers, a class of saints (q.v.), who perform this sacred function without demanding money. In 20th-c. parochial use this sacrament has been suppressed for various reasons: a misunderstanding of the character of healing, confusion with "last rites," a misguided devotion to the full text of the sacrament (seven priests repeating seven sets of Gospel readings, prayers, etc.) without sensitivity to its function, etc. At present some theologians are working toward the reinstatement of healing to its rightful place in the life of the Church's sacraments.

**HEGESIPPUS** *see* Historians, Ecclesiastical.

**HELENA,** St. (ca. 250–ca. 330). The mother of Constantine the Great (q.v.), she was the daughter of an innkeeper in Roman Bithynia (whom legend made into a British king) who became the concubine of Constantius Chlorus, Constantine's father. She was faithful to both her man and her son, and appears to have influenced the latter's conversion to Christianity. Helena together with Olga of Rus' may be indirectly credited with the conversion of two great empires, the Byzantine and Russian. As a patroness of the Church advanced in years, she is associated with a pilgrimage to the Holy Land in 326 and Constantine's active program of basilica construction there (Mt. of Olives, Bethlehem), as well as with the discovery of the Cross of Christ. There may be some historical grounds for this identification since the tradition has 4th-c. roots. She is commemorated in the Orthodox Church on the same day, May 21, as her son. (*See* Feasts, Twelve Great — Exaltation of the Cross.)

**HELLENIC COLLEGE** *see* Holy Cross Greek Orthodox School of Theology.

**HELLENISM.** This term has two active senses within the present-day Orthodox Church. The first, and broader, refers to the patrimony of classical Greek and later Greco-Roman thought, the inheritance in particular of the great philosophers from Plato to Plotinus, together with the institutions of the later Roman Empire, especially the idea of Rome (q.v.) itself as a universal state. All of this constitutes that "Hellenism" that the Church Fathers (q.v.) breathed as their native air, and with which they struggled at every turn. Intellectually, this meant the great effort of Greek Christian—i.e., Byzantine—theology to recast the language and vocabulary of pagan thought into a vessel capable of bearing the Christian mystery. Spiritually, in the forge of asceticism and monasticism (qq.v.), it meant the hammering out and refining of that vessel, on the one hand, and the witness to the experience, on the other.

The result of this effort, generations long, was, in the expression of Georges Florovsky (q.v.), that "Christian Hellenism" that constitutes the permanent vehicle of Orthodox Christian thought and culture. While "Christian Hellenism" is the common inheritance of Greeks, Slavs, Arabs, Romanians, etc., having no nationalistic or ethnic connotations, the second sense of Hellenism is quite different. Modern Greek Hellenism, dating in particular from the late 18th c., and owing much to the Enlightenment and European Romanticism, is a type of nationalism. This ethnic vision, colored by appeals to a glorified ancient Greece, to blood and soil—in short, to race—is the philosophy of modern Greek nationalism, the Hellenic equivalent to pan-Slavism or pan-Arabism. Just as the other nationalisms of the Orthodox peoples, it has done the Church little good. At the hands of the Phanariots (q.v.) in the 18th c. and 19th c. it did great damage to the status of the Ecumenical Patriarch (q.v.) in the eyes of non-Greeks. It thus figures in the reasons why the Orthodox Church struggles today to find an appropriate response to the "diaspora" or dislocations of the 20th c.

**HENOTIKON.** Issued in 482 by the Emperor Zeno, the *Henotikon* was the first in a long series of vain imperial attempts at "damage control" following the Ecumenical Council at Chalcedon (q.v.) in 451. The reaction to that Council by the local monophysite churches of Egypt, Syria, etc. (qq.v.) threatened—successfully, as it turned out—the unity of the imperial Church and hence the stability of the Empire. The text of the *Henotikon* affirmed the Nicene-Constantinopolitan Creed (q.v.), the Twelve Anathemas of Cyril of Alexandria (q.v.), and the decrees of the Third Ecumenical Council at Ephesus (431), but avoided the number of natures (q.v.) of Christ and forbade further discussion of Chalcedon. Though achieving a temporary success in the East, the decree failed to achieve its purpose, and precipitated a schism (q.v.) with the papacy (q.v.) that lasted almost forty years (to 519): the "Acacian Schism," named for the Patriarch Acacius of Constantinople, who had authored the document.

**HERESY.** This word derives from the Greek verb *haireo/haireomai*, "to take" or "to choose." In ecclesiastical use it signifies a conscious "choice," taken on a matter of defined doctrine in disagreement with the faith. This faith or "mind" of the Church is determined by Scripture, by an Ecumenical Council (qq.v.), or by universal and longstanding consensus. The author of such a choice, the *heresiarch*, will, in the conventions of church historians, usually have given his name to the opinion and party deriving from it.

The history of the Church and its teaching is in great part a history of Christian heresies. In New Testament times intense struggles went on between Paul and the "Judaizers," between the author of 1 Jn and people claiming that Christ had only "appeared" to take on flesh (docetists), and between the author of the Pastoral Epistles (1, 2 Tim, Titus) and people preaching that the Resurrection (q.v.) had never happened, or had occurred "spiritually."

The 2nd c. saw an expanded front against gnosticism, replied to by Irenaeus of Lyons (qq.v.) whose *Adversus Haereses* laid the foundations for much of patristic theology, and against Montanism, an ancient world equivalent (with qualifications) to modern Pentecostalism. The former's denial of the Old Testament Scriptures and the latter's claim to an ongoing revelation of the Spirit on the same level as the New Testament led Church leaders to insist on the once-and-for-all character of the revelation in Christ. The canon of the New Testament emerged from these debates.

In the 3rd c., arguments over the nature (q.v.) of the Godhead took center stage. Modalism, led by the priests Praxeas and Sabellius in Rome, argued that the divinity was one Person appearing in three different forms. Tertullian replied for the Latins, and Origen (qq.v.) and Dionysius of Alexandria for the Greeks, insisting that the three persons of the Trinity are indeed one, though always three persons. Adoptionists, such as Paul of Samosata, held that Christ was merely a man gifted at baptism with the Spirit. Finally, in Persia the preacher Mani began a new religion, Manichaeism, an amalgam of Iranian dualism, Christianity, and gnosticism (q.v.). It enjoyed a long life on the fringes of Byzantium (q.v.) and within the Empire as far abroad as 5th-c. North Africa; and drew responses from generations of churchmen seeking to defend the goodness of the created world.

The 4th c. was the great age of Trinitarian debate, sparked by Arius (q.v.) and carried on by such as Eusebius of Nicomedia, Aetius, and Eunomius of Cyzicus, all of whom refused to acknowledge the divinity of Christ and the Spirit. Athanasius and the Cappadocian Fathers (qq.v.) in the Greek-speaking world, Hilary of Poitiers, Popes Silvester and Damasus, and Ambrose of Milan (q.v.) among the Latins, led to the articulation of the dogma framed in the Nicene-Constantinopolitan Creed (qq.v.). Latin-speaking Christianity also saw a fierce debate at the beginning of the 5th c. over the relation between freedom and grace (q.v.) in the human person. The monk Pelagius's extreme assertion of human liberty (q.v.) drew from Augustine of Hippo his distinctive teaching concerning original sin (qq.v.) and predestination, which would do much to shape subsequent Western Christianity.

Debate in the East in the 5th c. moved to the person of Christ and the opposing doctrinal poles of Nestorius (q.v.) and Eutychius, who drew respectively the attention of Cyril of Alexandria and Leo the Great of Rome (qq.v.), and the doctrinal formulations of the Ecumenical

Councils of Chalcedon and Ephesus (qq.v.). The 6th c. and 7th c. carried on arguments over the decrees of Chalcedon and resulted in the convocations of the Fifth Ecumenical Council (553), which condemned the "Three Chapters" and the anthropology of Origen (qq.v.), and the Sixth (681), which condemned the imperially sponsored doctrine of monothelitism (one will in Christ). The last great doctrinal debate of Byzantium (q.v.), prior to Hesychasm, was the crisis of Iconoclasm (qq.v.) in the 8th c. and 9th c., which prompted the replies of Germanos of Constantinople, John of Damascus, and Theodore of Studion (qq.v.), and the decrees of the Seventh Ecumenical Council, Nicaea II (787).

The last great doctrinal debate to occur in the Byzantine era (q.v.) revolved around the Athonite monks and the writings of Gregory Palamas (q.v.). The latter represented the side declared Orthodox by a series of local councils. The heresiarch, if one may use that term, was Barlaam of Calabria (q.v.), though his heresy was less any one formula than the general argument that deification, *theosis* (q.v.), is no more than a metaphor and the light associated with it a symbol.

Later Orthodox history does not offer any doctrinal debates on the scale of those occurring during the ancient and medieval periods. The Church was compelled to struggle with the competing Christian notions, imported from Western Europe, associated with the Reformation and Counter-Reformation. Local councils such as those at Jassy in 1642 and Bethlehem in 1672 issued doctrinal statements against particular Protestant formulations, while others in Greece and Russia debated Roman Catholic (q.v.) attempts at reunion (see Uniate). Within Orthodoxy the one great disturbance of the past millennium was the schism, the *raskol,* in the Russian Church following the liturgical reforms of Patriarch Nikon of Moscow (qq.v.) in the 1660s. Here it would be wrong to speak so much of heresy—at least in the earlier phases of the Old Believer (q.v.) movement—as of a ferociously conservative turn of mind, a fatal want of perspective.

At the beginning of the 20th c. the Russian Church did produce one serious candidate for a heresy, the *imyaslavtsi* or *imyabozhniki* ("Glorifiers" or "Worshipers of the Name"). The adherents held that the divinity of Jesus resided substantially in the very name of the Lord. Serious discussion of this thesis, sustained by significant numbers of Russian monks on Mt. Athos (q.v.), failed to engage the Church as a whole. The movement was quickly dealt with by the intervention of the Russian imperial navy.

**HERMAN OF ALASKA,** monk, St. (?–1837). The first Orthodox saint (q.v.) canonized in the United States (1970), he lived on Spruce Island,

Alaska (q.v.), off Kodiak until 1837. He originally came from Valaam (Lake Ladoga) Monastery to Alaska in 1794. His secular name and parents are unknown. Father Herman came with a group of about a dozen monk-missionaries, half of whom perished within five years. By 1823 Herman was the sole survivor of the original mission who was still in Alaska.

In the history of North American horticulture, Herman is listed as the discoverer of a method of fertilization based on the harvest of "sea cabbages"—a type of marine plant—which is dried or composted and used to enrich Alaskan soil. He probably brought this practice, unknown in the New World, from Lake Ladoga Monastery where it had been in use. Since the history of Russians in Alaska is largely also a history of food production, it was important that Herman was known for growing turnips, potatoes, and garden vegetables—when others had failed. In 1825 he grew 150 to 180 beds of potatoes, but all the gardening enterprise ceased after his death.

In any case Herman is better known for other achievements:
1) The early success of the missionary party—thousands of baptisms, etc. were performed—may be attributed to their "missionary education" in traveling across Europe and Asia to Alaska for almost a year. Stopping in monasteries established by the Russian Church all along the way, Herman and the others were recipients of an education in missionizing indigenous "shamanistic" populations by successful historical example. (*See* Komi.) These way stations were first established as missions to the native peoples of their lands.
2) In Kodiak the monks laid the foundation of the Holy Resurrection Church and established a school in which they taught catechism, history, mathematics, language, agriculture, and domestic science to the indigenous population. In spite of this new learning, the native cultures were not suppressed, and there existed an official directive to prevent interference in their societies.
3) Herman and the others in the missionary party were in serious conflict with the Golikov-Shelikov Company (i.e., the Russian-American Company, founded in 1799) over the treatment of natives, especially under Governor Alexander Baranov. Eventually the missionaries were put under house arrest for trying to extend rights of Russian citizenship to the natives. At this point, 1808–1818, Herman probably went into seclusion at Spruce Island.
4) From these events and his later seclusion he was known for the sanctity of his life, many aspects of which can be compared to the Desert Fathers (q.v.). It is said that Herman had had the same spiritual father at Valaam as Seraphim of Sarov (q.v.), the Elder Nazary, and was affectionately called "Apa" (grandfather or elder) by the natives.

**HESYCHASM.** This word derives from the Greek verb meaning "to be quiet" or "at rest." In early monastic usage "hesychast" was used for an ascetic "at rest" in the quiet of a desert retreat, i.e., an anchorite or hermit. "Hesychasm" as a special term comes to particular prominence in the 14th c. in what is at least a double sense. First, and more narrowly, it refers to a monastic movement centered on Mt. Athos (q.v.), especially among the hermits who were preoccupied with the meaning and technique of the "Jesus Prayer." The monks believed that the Jesus Prayer—the repeated and concentrated invocation of the divine name—served to provide the most direct path to encounter with the presence of the Risen One. This movement provoked the negative criticism of Barlaam the Calabrian, and found its chief defender in Gregory Palamas (qq.v.). In its larger sense "hesychasm" is often used to denote a broad movement of renewal that was led by monks connected with and formed by hesychast spirituality. That movement stretched from the chancery of the Ecumenical Patriarch through the Balkans to the monasteries founded by Sergius of Radonezh (qq.v.) and his successors. Called by some scholars the "Hesychast Internationale," this wide current of ideas and personalities did much to strengthen and unite the Orthodox Church on the eve of the fall of Constantinople to the Ottoman Turks (qq.v.).

**HILARY** *see* Ilarion.

**HIPPOLYTUS,** priest, St. (ca. 170–ca. 236). Hippolytus was a presbyter of the Roman Church whose claim to fame is as the first "Anti-pope." Of a conservative disposition, he made perhaps his most significant contribution to later generations in his compilation of the *Apostolic Tradition* (q.v.), a document written to counter what he felt were unwarranted innovations in the practice and discipline of the Roman Church in the early decades of the 3rd c. The work is the earliest Roman Church order—descriptions of the sacraments (q.v.) and accompanying disciplines—extant and therefore a priceless historical witness. In his disputes with Popes Zephyrinus (198–217) and Callistus (217–222), both of whom he rejected as heretics, the charge he levels against them seems to be a type of modalism, and might have been accurate. He was later reconciled to the other side under Popes Pontianus and Fabian, and his body was returned to Rome as that of a martyred presbyter. He also wrote plentifully on Scripture (q.v.), his commentary on Dan is still extant, and on the reproof of heresy—particularly gnosticism (qq.v.) in his *Philosophoumena*.

**HISTORIANS, ECCLESIASTICAL.** The first ecclesiastical historian whose works survive complete is Eusebius of Caesarea (q.v.). His *His-*

*tory of the Church* covered the first three centuries of Christianity and is still an invaluable resource. He incorporated into it other works, now lost, such as those of the 2nd-c. church historian Hegesippus, who wrote on Jerusalem and Rome, and probably gave us the list of early Roman popes found in Epiphanius (*Haer.* 27.6). Subsequent Church historians writing in Greek included: Socrates (d. 439) and Sozomen (d. ca. 450), who carried Eusebius's story through the Trinitarian controversies of the 4th c.; Theodoret of Cyrrhus (q.v.), who continued into the Christological debates through Chalcedon (q.v.); Zachariah the Rhetor (d. ca. 550), who took the latter controversies through the mid–6th c. from the monophysite side; and Evagrius Scholasticus (d. 593/4), who represented the Chalcedonian side through to the century's end. Lesser writers include Philostorgius (d. 395) and Gelasius of Caesarea (d. 425) from the Greek side and John of Ephesus (d. 586), who wrote in Syriac (q.v.).

Among the Latins, Lactantius (d. 330s) contributed an impressive history of the African Church's persecutions under the Emperor Diocletian, while Rufinus of Aquileia (d. ca. 410) wrote perhaps the most impressive Church history by a Western writer until the Venerable Bede (d. 735) produced his remarkable *History of the English Church.* Augustine of Hippo's (q.v.) *City of God,* while not a history per se, is nonetheless worth mentioning as the unique theology of history in the patristic age. Finally, Jerome compiled a bibliography of ecclesiastical writers and translated and updated Eusebius's *Chronicle,* which is a summary of universal history with dates.

Church history continued to be written throughout the Byzantine era (q.v.). But since Church and state (q.v.) came to be practically identified during Byzantium's medieval period, the histories produced are as much histories of the Empire as of the Christian Church. Examples are the works of Michael Psellos (11th c.) and Anna Comnena (12th c.).

**HOLY, HOLINESS.** Holiness is that quality which pertains peculiarly to God (q.v.), who is uniquely the "Holy One" without qualification— or, as in Orthodox worship, the "Thrice Holy" (from the hymn of the seraphim in Is 6). Human beings who participate in this quality, through the partaking of the sacraments (q.v.), the labors of asceticism (q.v.), and works of mercy are also called "holy ones" or "saints." (Note that any distinction between "holy man/woman" and the word "saint" is peculiar to English.) That which marks them as holy, however, is always God himself, who is perceived as manifesting his presence through them. The saints (q.v.) are thus, in Orthodox devotion, the proofs and revelations of God's own holiness, not of their own.

**HOLY CROSS GREEK ORTHODOX SCHOOL OF THEOLOGY.** The School was established in 1937 in Pomfret, Connecticut, by Archbishop Athenagoras and moved to Brookline, Massachusetts, in 1947. For more than five decades, the School has been the only seminary of the Greek Orthodox Church in the Americas. In more recent decades the School has developed into an accredited undergraduate college (Hellenic College) and Graduate School of Theology in order to better serve its students and the needs of the Church. The schools serve the Church through their active concern for the advancement of Orthodox life and thought, as well as the preservation of Greek heritage and the cultivation of Greek Letters.

Through teaching, research, publications, and ecumenical witness, the faculty provides sound theological reflection by which the faith is related to the issues that affect the people of the Church today. Moreover, the School is a source of renewal and continuing education for those engaged in the ministry. The School also provides special programs in Theology, Religious Studies, and Greek Studies for the laity in cooperation with local dioceses and parishes.

**HOLY FOOLS** *see* Fools in Christ.

**HOLY LAND.** The term is used infrequently in Scripture (q.v.), for the first time in Zech 2:12, and connotes Palestine, the present territory of Israel-Jordan, and, especially, of the holy city, Jerusalem. It is the land of the Old Testament revelation and of Jesus Christ. Other and later holy places are those locales associated with great ascetic saints (q.v.) such as a monastery, a cave, or a chapel. They can be the scenes of deaths or tombs of noted martyrs (q.v.), as the Vatican in Rome was of Peter and Paul. Evidence does suggest that Christian pilgrimages (q.v.) to the latter site occurred as early as the 2nd c.; but clearly pilgrimage must have been familiar from classical Judaism, which required celebration of the feasts—and all sacrifice—to take place in Jerusalem. Clear evidence of Christian pilgrimages to Palestine does not come until the 4th c. and the changes wrought by Constantine (q.v.), though they might have been earlier. But this is very speculative because of the renovation of the city done by Hadrian, reconstructing the new city as the (pagan) Aelia Capitolina. The theology of holy places derives from the general sacramental understanding of the Orthodox Church: Where the very elements of bread and wine or water and oil may became vehicles of God's presence in the sacraments of Eucharist, Baptism (qq.v.), Anointing, so may the earth itself be affected through the labors of God's holy ones and the visitation of his grace (q.v.).

**HOLY SPIRIT.** The third person of the Trinity (q.v.) given by the risen Christ to his disciples (Jn 20, Acts 2), and as the sign of the messianic age and new creation (Rom 8). It is the gift given to every believer at

Baptism (q.v.) and Chrismation, the one who effects the consecration of the bread and wine at the eucharistic epiclesis, the goal and means of all Orthodox asceticism (q.v.). The Spirit is counselor, comforter, the mark of the presence of Christ, the heart and power of prayer (q.v.), the reality of the eschaton.

All the above is common to the patristic background of Christian East and West. Orthodoxy parts company with the Latin West in seeing the procession or eternal origin of the Spirit as coming from the Father (Jn 15:26) and sent, in the economy (q.v.) of Christ, through the Son. The Latin addition to the article on the Spirit in the Nicene-Constantinopolitan Creed (q.v.) of the phrase, "and from the Son" (*filioque*), was viewed in the East as inadmissible.

This reaction was argued on two grounds, canonical and properly theological. The *filioque* (q.v.) entered the Creed by a unilateral action of the West without Eastern consent or participation. It first appears in the Creed as cited by the Council of Toledo in 589, then was adopted by the Carolingians as part of their politico-theological program, and was finally, under German pressure, adopted by the papacy around 1014. Second, the Greek theologians felt that the addition disturbed the balance of the Trinity by confusing the persons of the Father and the Son, and by refusing to distinguish between the temporal economy of the Son and Spirit and the eternal relations of the Three within the Godhead. Patriarch Photius (q.v.) of Constantinople summed up these arguments in his *Mystagogy,* ca. 880, and subsequent Byzantine writers added little. The question of the Spirit constitutes, together with the papacy itself, the most serious point of division between present-day Orthodoxy and Roman Catholicism (q.v.).

**HOPKO, THOMAS J.,** priest, theologian (28 March 1939- ). Born in New York, he received degrees from Fordham University (1960) and St. Vladimir's Orthodox Theological Seminary (q.v.) (1963) before marriage and ordination to the priesthood. Over the next twenty years he pastored several parishes while teaching advanced courses and receiving degrees from Duquesne University (M.A., 1968) and Fordham (Ph.D., 1982). He began lecturing in dogmatic theology full time at St. Vladimir's in 1983 and became dean in 1992. He has represented the Orthodox Church in America at the World Council of Churches Assemblies and on the Faith and Order Commission. In addition to occasional articles and essays, he has published numerous books, including a catechism, *The Orthodox Faith* (1972–76), in four parts, and *Women and the Priesthood* (1983).

**HOSPITAL.** The hospital (*xenona* or *nosokomeion*) was a regular feature of Byzantine (q.v.) life, such institutions for the care of the elderly, ill, and homeless being the continual object of the benefactions of the wealthy and powerful. The emperors as "imitators of Christ" were obliged to lead the way by reflecting God's love for humanity, his *philanthropia*, and often did so through the founding and endowing of hospitals. These institutions were normally attached to monasteries, provision for which had appeared as early as Basil the Great's legislation on monasticism (q.v.), and staffed by professionally trained physicians and nurses, the standard of whose care appears to have normally been very high.

**HOTOVITZKY, ALEXANDER,** martyred priest. Serving in America from 1895 to 1914 as rector of St. Nicholas Cathedral, New York City, and the first editor of the "American Russian Orthodox Messenger," he counseled Bishops Nicholas, Tikhon (q.v.), and Platon, and founded many parishes in the United States. On returning to Russia he was appointed to some of Moscow's most prominent churches, including the Kremlin's Dormition Cathedral and the Cathedral of Christ the Savior (since demolished by the Bolsheviks). Fr. Hotovitzky participated in the All-Russian Church Council of 1917–18, and was a major proponent of the reestablishment of the patriarchate there. Subsequently he advised the sainted Patriarch Tikhon and was repeatedly imprisoned for his pastoral activities until he "disappeared" in a Siberian concentration camp in the 1930s. (At the time of printing he is being considered for canonization by the Russian Church and his full biography is not yet available.)

**HUMILITY.** In Greek this virtue, *tapeinophrosyne*, translates literally as "lowly mindedness." In the literature of Orthodox asceticism (q.v.) it constitutes the foundation of all the great virtues and is itself seen as the fruit of the presence of the Holy Spirit (q.v.): True humility is already a partaking in and manifestation of the presence of the Spirit of Christ. Hence one encounters the warning against judging others with singular frequency in the ascetic writings from the Desert Fathers (q.v.) to the present day. To judge another is to set oneself up as superior to him or her, and as such is an offense against both the dominical word (Mt 7:1–6) and example (Philp 2:5–11). Humility also constitutes the true vision of oneself, reality: nothing more or less than clarity of understanding. Truly to know oneself, in the Orthodox understanding of the Socratic dictum, is necessarily to be humble. All that one is or may become is of Christ and the Spirit.

**HUSSEY, JOAN M.,** Byzantinist, educator (1908– ). After receiving a Ph.D. from St. Hugh's College, Oxford, she was Pfeiffer Research Fellow at Girton (1934–37), lecturer in history at the University of

Manchester (1937–43), and lecturer and then reader in history at Bedford College in the University of London (1943–50). From 1950 to 1974 she was professor of history at Royal Holloway College in the University of London, now emeritus. She is the author of *The Orthodox Church in the Byzantine Empire* (rev. ed. 1990); and there is a Festschrift in her honor, *Kathegetria: Essays to Joan Hussey for Her 80th Birthday* (1988).

-I-

**IAKOVOS (COUCOUZIS),** Archbishop of North and South America (Ecumenical Patriarchate) *see* Coucouzis, Iakovos.

**IBAS OF EDESSA,** bishop (?–457). Ibas of Edessa wrote a number of letters, the only surviving one, his Epistle to Bishop Mari (433), was highly critical of Cyril of Alexandria (q.v.). He was one of Theodoret of Cyrrhus's party who felt that Nestorius had been wronged at the Ecumenical Council of Ephesus in 431, and that Cyril's Christology (qq.v.) was dangerously one-sided. Excommunicated by the council at Ephesus in 449 headed by Cyril's successor, Dioscurus, Ibas was readmitted to communion by the (Fourth Ecumenical) Council of Chalcedon (q.v.) in 451. His restoration constituted a bone of contention for the monophysite party in the aftermath of Chalcedon. One of the tasks that the Emperor Justinian (q.v.) set for the Fifth Ecumenical Council at Constantinople in 553 was therefore the condemnation of Ibas's letters, together with other works of Theodoret and the entire works of Theodore of Mopsuestia (qq.v.), the so-called "Three Chapters". Ibas's own chief contributions to posterity were his translations from Greek into Syriac, including Theodore of Mopsuestia's commentaries, together with works by Diodore of Tarsus and Aristotle.

**ICON.** The holy icons touch on central issues of Orthodox theology (q.v.) and worship, and the phenomenon of the icon as a distinctive form of Christian art (q.v.) is perhaps the most widely known and appreciated aspect of Orthodox Holy Tradition. Guests in Orthodox households will invariably note the "beautiful corner" (a corner in one of the main rooms featuring a collection of icons and usually a vigil lamp or candle), bookstores display collections of Russian or Greek icons, and the casual visitor to an Orthodox church is normally struck by the wall of images separating the altar area from the nave, the iconostasis (q.v.), punctuated by two large central gates, the Royal Doors, and two side doors, which themselves bear images. A large painting or mosaic of Christ the "All-Ruler" (*Pantocrator*) is often staring down from the church's central dome, and dozens—or hundreds—of other pictures around the walls of the church portray important events in the life of Christ together with the saints and prophets. All the images are painted in roughly the same distinctive style. This distinctiveness and the multitude of images—the latter being the simple sense of the Greek word, *eikon*—is not the product of a wildly decorative urge. It is instead the fruit of a long theological reflection unique in the Christian world.

From 731 until 843 the emperors of Byzantium (q.v.) led a movement to remove images from the churches of the Empire. In response to this imperially sponsored iconoclasm (literally, "image smashing"), John of Damascus, Germanos of Constantinople, and Theodore of Studion (qq.v.), who led the iconodule (or iconophile) movement, advanced powerful and ultimately convincing theological arguments in favor of the images. Against the imperial contention that the worship of images was simply idolatry, these writers replied that, while worship belonged indeed to God alone, veneration of the images was nonetheless called for and distinctive. The prayer (q.v.) of the devout is addressed to its object through or by means of the image. In answer to the iconoclasts' frequent citation of the Decalogue's commandment against images, they replied that God (q.v.) in the Old Testament could not be portrayed. But because in Christ God's eternal Word had taken on the permanent "vesture" of humanity, it would be a denial of the Incarnation to refuse the possibility—and even the obligation—of Christ's portrayal in images as well as in the words of Scripture and the liturgy (qq.v.).

Christian art thus became a necessary theological and sacramental endeavor. Precisely as symbols or types, the sacred images constituted a conjoining of the human and divine spheres, and served as indicators and vehicles of the Kingdom of God, of the creation transfigured and renewed in Christ. The arguments advanced by the 8th c. and 9th c. defenders of icons were taken over from earlier Church Fathers who had written on the Scriptures and the sacraments (qq.v.), and were now deployed in favor of the images. The sacred writings had long been spoken of as a network of types, as pointers and connections, indicating and to some degree actually incarnating the presence of the Word made flesh in Jesus. This language of scriptural typology was joined in the iconophile movement to the symbolism of earlier sacramental discourse. Symbol signifies, literally, the conjunction of different things (from *sym-ballo,* "to throw or put together"). Thus the Eucharist (q.v.) was freely described in earlier patristic literature as a "symbol." The same language, but now with "symbol" specifically ruled out as adequate to the Eucharist, was applied to the sacred images. The sum of these arguments was officially sanctioned by the

Seventh Ecumenical Council (q.v.) at Nicaea in 787, and this Council was definitively recognized by the permanent restoration of the icons in 843 following a second series of iconoclast emperors.

It should be pointed out that iconoclastic emperors frequently promoted the cult of the emperor, with its corresponding iconography of the emperor on banners and coins, but excluded any religious representations. Parallels to this attitude can be drawn with Lenin's use of his own iconography or with classical American Protestantism's use of the picture of U.S. presidents on banners and money—both to the exclusion of religious iconography. The general question is not whether iconography is appropriate, for every culture has its icons. (We know from archaeology that even Judaism was not strictly iconoclastic; and the Old Testament speaks of representations of Cherubim and Seraphim, as well.) The real question is whether a culture's iconography adequately represents its belief system. In this sense the issue is not one restricted historically to the Church in the East, but is the perennial biblical question put to the people of God: Who is your King?

All this theory had a decisive effect on the actual making of sacred images. Christian art became strictly regulated. The distinctive style of Byzantine icons, marked by such characteristics as inverted perspective, elongated figures, lack of chiaroscuro, as well as their fabrication in a context of prayer and fasting (qq.v.), are the deliberate result of the theological arguments advanced on their behalf. As sacramentals and "theology in color," icons are not mere ornaments. Neither are they simply and purely instructional, nor are they optional in the construction and elaboration of an Orthodox church. Rather, they are seen as necessary adjuncts and expressions of the Church at worship, as representing—or better, making present—the whole "company of Heaven." The assemblage of imagery is intended to "symbolize" the reality of the Church as the new creation, the meeting place of Heaven and earth.

A further consequence of the iconoclast controversy was the compilation of manuals of iconography, precise instructions as to the shape, distinctive features and colors, of Christ and the saints. From the late Byzantine era (q.v.) to Muscovite Russia these manuals proliferate. At its best, therefore, Byzantine sacred art is done under circumstances that recall the great poets' work with the sonnet form. The form is fixed and the genius of the artist required to work within it. Masterpieces unquestionably resulted, for example, the anonymous artist's portrayal of the Resurrection in the famous image at Chora in Constantinople, or the works of Theophanes the Greek and Andrei Rublev in 14th c. and 15th c. Russia. While the art of the icon declined under the influence of religious art coming from Western Europe, influenced by the Italian Renaissance from the 18th c. to the early 20th c., significant calls for the renewal of tradition (led in Russia by Prince E. Trubetskoy and in Greece by Photius Kontoglu) have contributed much to the recovery of the sacred art in this century. In many respects iconographic art may be viewed as a kind of summary or distillation of Orthodox theology and spiritual experience.

A word is in order regarding purported American iconoclasm—purported because it is difficult to claim that a people who watches an average of four hours of television a day is iconoclastic. American religious iconoclasm comes from the Protestant Reformation's desire, exclusive of Luther, to return to the practice of the "Early Church," which practice was naively identified with the Judaism of the 16th c. and 17th c. (Not only had Judaism undergone its own particular development as a religion, but recent archaeology has taught us that synagogues contained their own iconography—probably through the advent of Islam [q.v.] when Jewish iconography seems to have ceased. Thus, it may be speculated that American Protestant iconoclasm is a result of the influence of the Moslem invasions, mediated by Medieval Judaism.) The question remains whether America's religious iconography will ever adequately represent the culture's beliefs.

**ICONOCLASTIC CONTROVERSY** *see* Icon.

**ICONOSTASIS.** (See drawing.) 1. Christ the Pantocrator, the "eschatological Christ" at the end of time. 2. Mother Mary with Child, the "historical Jesus." 3. The Last Supper, Christ present with us now at the altar. 4. The Royal Gates or Holy Doors. 5. The Annunciation, Archangel Gabriel and Mary. 6. The four Evangelists. 7. Altar curtain (not shown). 8. Deacon's doors with icons of archangels or deacons. 9. Icon of the feast or saint after which the church is named. 10. Icon of the patron saint of the chief benefactor who built the church. 11. Deisis. 12. Icons of the Twelve Great Feasts (q.v.). 13. The prophets of the Old Testament. 14. The patriarchs. (*See* Architecture; Icon; Icons of the Theotokos.)

**ICONS OF THE THEOTOKOS.** While images of the Theotokos (Virgin Mary [q.v.]) by herself, as frequently in the popular art of Roman Catholicism, are not unknown in Byzantium (qq.v.)—for example the image called the "intercession (*deisis*)," featuring the Theotokos and Baptist flanking Christ Pantocrator—the favored representation of her is as "Madonna," the mother carrying the Christ child. Here, however, there are numerous variations, and characteristic of all of them is the portrayal of the child as a small adult: the eternal Word made flesh lifting his hand in blessing. Consistent is an emphasis on these images as theological statements, tied in particular to the Christology of the Ecu-

Icons of the Theotokos • 167

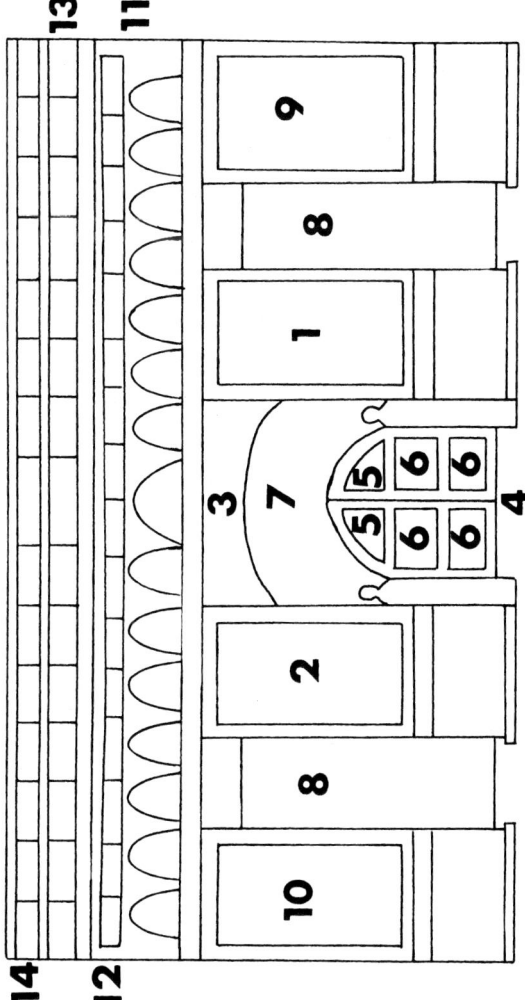

menical Councils (qq.v.). With few exceptions, icons of the Theotokos are also icons of Christ.

These iconographic types are not primarily appeals to exalted emotion. The single most significant exception is the type of Madonna known as the *glykophilousa* (Greek "sweetly kissing"), or *oumilenie* (Russian "tender compassion") portraying the mother tenderly embracing the child whose arms are entwined about her neck. Other and, save in Russia, more frequent types are: the *hodigitria* ("she who shows the Way") with the mother pointing to the child enthroned on her lap; the *gorgoepikousa* ("she who is swift to hear"); the *platytera* ("she whose womb is more spacious than the heavens") showing the child in triumph within the mother; and the "Lady of the Passion" showing two angels flanking the mother and child and carrying the Cross together with the spear and the sponge (known in the West as "Our Lady of Perpetual Help"). Of the three most famous icons of the Theotokos in Russia, our Lady of Vladimir (11th c. Constantinopolitan work) is of the *oumilenie* type, while the two others, our Lady of Tikhvin and our Lady of Kazan, are of the *hodigitria* type. A fourth, the Iveron Madonna, is a copy of the *portaitissa* ("she who guards the gate") at the Iveron monastery on Mt. Athos (q.v.), also of the *hodigitria* type. Each of the Twelve Great Feasts (q.v.) that remembers Mary especially has an icon of her which portrays a historical scene.

**ICXC NIKA.** Abbreviation of the Greek phrase, "Jesus Christ has conquered," the ICXC NIKA, arranged around a cross with the IC and XC at the top and the NI KA at the bottom, is both used iconographically and stamped on the top of the prosphora, the Offertory loaves baked especially for the Eucharist (q.v.). It is from this part of the loaf that the priest cuts out the portion, prior to the service, which serves as the consecrated host. *Nika* also refers to a historical event, the riots at the Hippodrome in Constantinople (q.v.) in 532, which nearly toppled the regime of the Emperor Justinian (q.v.). They did, however, provide him later with the opportunity to replace the church of the Holy Wisdom, destroyed by the rioters, with the splendid edifice that still stands today, Hagia Sophia (q.v.).

**IGNATIUS OF ANTIOCH,** bishop, martyr, St. (?-ca. 115). The second or third bishop of Antioch, Ignatius is venerated for his martyrdom at Rome (qq.v.). On the way from Antioch to his martyrdom, he left a corpus of seven letters written to churches in Asia Minor (q.v.), to Philippi in Greece, and to Rome. These epistles constitute one of the most important witnesses to post-apostolic Christianity, and follow the genre of seven epistles to seven churches, found in Rev and elsewhere. Ignatius stresses the importance of the bishop, the centrality of the Eucharist, and a Christology (qq.v.) that insists on the reality of the eternal Word come in the flesh. The three items are linked and their point of intersection is the sacrament (q.v.). Christ on the altar in the bread and wine is truly present, and this presence confirms both the reality of his flesh and blood and, indirectly, the importance of the bishop who presides at the altar.

**ILARION.** Two sainted bishops bear this name: 1) Hilary of Poitiers (ca. 315–367) bore an important witness to anti-Arian Greek theology in the Latin West during the Trinitarian controversies of the 4th c. (see his *De Trinitate*). His exile in Asia Minor (q.v.) from 357 to 361 allowed him to acquire a thorough familiarity with Greek Christian thought, particularly that of Origen (q.v.). His sensitivity in this regard is the most striking of any of the Latin Fathers until Rufinus of Aquileia two generations later. He wrote both major historical works and commentaries on Scripture. 2) Ilarion of Kiev (?–1051) marks a high point in the religious culture of Kievan Rus' (q.v.). His sermons, in particular the famous "On Law and Grace," constitute the first original theological thought in Church Slavic along with his *Confession of Faith*, and they are genuine monuments in the early history of Slavic literature. He is known particularly for his philosophy of history and eschatological focus.

**ILLYRICUM, ILLYRIA.** This is the old Roman name for a province that included modern Yugoslavia and Albania (qq.v.). Historically, Illyricum was early under the jurisdiction of the papacy (q.v.). But after the invasion of the Slavs in the 6th c. and 7th c. and the missionary work of SS. Constantine-Cyril and Methodius in the 9th c., the region's southern half fell under the effective rule of the Ecumenical Patriarch (q.v.). This confirmed what earlier imperial legislation under Leo III had sought to do by law (732/3). The shift in jurisdictional authority occasioned considerable tension between Rome and Constantinople (qq.v.) throughout the 9th c. (*See* Photius.)

**IMAGE** *see* Icon.

**IMMACULATE CONCEPTION OF THE VIRGIN MARY.** In 1854 Pope Pius IX proclaimed the doctrine of the Immaculate Conception of the Virgin. The doctrine holds that Mary (q.v.) was born free of the stain and guilt of original sin (q.v.). Phrased in this way, the doctrine is unacceptable to the Orthodox Church whose understanding of original sin, and anthropology in general, differs significantly from that of the Roman Catholic Church (qq.v.). These differences go back in substance to the writings of Augustine of Hippo in contradistinction to the Greek Church Fathers (qq.v.).

**IMPERIALISM.** While the urge to dominate and build empires is universal among human beings and their societies, this term has a specific application to the history of the Orthodox Church. Inheriting the ideology of the Roman Empire as civilizer and pacifier of the world (see, for example, Virgil's *Aeneid*), the newly Christian Empire under Constantine (q.v.) and his successors took over and promulgated a "baptized" version of this imperial theology. (*See* Church and State.) The *oikoumene* of Byzantium (qq.v.) theoretically embraced all Christians and sought—in theory, at least, and under Justinian (q.v.) in fact—to effect this dominion. Where possible, this was accomplished via the tools of diplomacy and armed force and, where impossible, through an elaborate hierarchy of titles bestowed by the imperial court on neighboring rulers. The latter, if only by a kind of fiction, preserved the theory of a family of nations presided over by the one emperor.

Following the fall of Constantinople to the Ottoman Empire (qq.v.) in 1453, the universal claims of the Christian emperor found two claimants. Under the Sultans the Ecumenical Patriarch (q.v.) was given effective rule over all the formers' Christian subjects. Later, with the advent of the Phanariots (q.v.) to power within the patriarchate, this rule was translated into an active Greek imperialism in the modern sense, leading to the suppression of the native hierarchies of the Empire's Slavic and Romanian Orthodox subjects. The second claimant, the Russian tsar with the Church of Russia, displayed much the same policy of narrowly nationalist political and ecclesiastical conquest. All Orthodox within the tsardom were subjected to Russian political and ecclesiastical rule. These included the peoples of Western Rus' (modern Ukraine and Belarus), Russian Moldavia (Bessarabia), and Georgia.

One may note that the progress of the same imperial idea was different in the West. With the crowning of Charlemagne in 800, and the fabrication of the *Donation of Constantine,* the papacy laid claim to the presidency of the Christian *oikoumene* (qq.v.). It put these claims into effect during the Gregorian Reforms of the 11th–13th c. That the latter era was also the period which saw the definitive split between Orthodoxy and the Roman Catholic Church (q.v.) is not accidental. The two imperialisms in Orthodoxy (q.v.), Constantinopolitan and Muscovite, have come close to splitting the Church. The earlier competition between East and West succeeded in doing so.

**INDIAN ORTHODOX CHURCH.** India is the home of an ancient Christian community, the Mar Thoma Church (q.v.), which traces its beginnings to the Apostle Thomas. Whether that truly is the case or not, it is unquestionable that those beginnings go far back indeed. India is also home to several Roman Catholic groups, Malankarese and Malabarese as well as Latin rite (qq.v.), and many Protestant communities.

**INFALLIBILITY** *see* Authority.

**INNOCENT OF ALASKA,** St. *see* Veniaminov, Innocent (John Popov).

**IRAN.** Ancient Iran, or Persia, from 226 to 630 was the Byzantine Empire's main competitor. Its armies under the last of the Sassanid

Shahinshahs devasted the Empire's eastern provinces in the early 7th c. In particular, the flourishing communities in the Holy Land (q.v.) suffered lasting damage. Under Islam (q.v.) Iran continued to struggle with Byzantium (q.v.) in the disputed border nations of Armenia and Georgia. A significant Christian population has lived within the Iranian Empire of the Sassanids and their Muslim successors from ancient times, and has continued to do so until the present era, though greatly reduced. It was chiefly within the confines of Sassanid and then Muslim Iran that the Assyrian (Nestorian) Church (q.v.) made its home and, by the 13th c., spread up to and beyond the borders of China. Most recently with the American invasion of Kuwait and the bombing of Iran, though no mosques were damaged, more than two dozen Christian churches were destroyed. The policy of Saddam Hussein was also to use (Nestorian) Christians as the first line of defense, and resultingly many were lost in battle to American forces.

**IRAQ** *see* Mesopotamia.

**IRENAEUS OF LYONS,** bishop, St. (ca. 130–ca. 200). Irenaeus was a native speaker of Greek born in Asia Minor (probably in Smyrna) where in his youth, according to Eusebius of Caesarea, he came to know Polycarp (qq.v.). He became bishop of Lyons in Roman Gaul shortly after that church had suffered a severe local persecution. His great and deserved place among the Church Fathers comes chiefly from his defense of the theology of the Great Church against gnosticism (qq.v.), especially in his massive, five-volume work, *Adversus Haereses* (extant in Latin translation).

In *Adv. Haer.* his description of gnostic thought in volume I is indispensable, if highly colored by the exigencies of polemic, and volume II is a detailed refutation of the thought previously outlined. Volumes III and IV center on what is, in effect, an argument for the Incarnation, which depends on the *lex orandi.* The Eucharist (q.v.), Irenaeus argues, is a primary witness to the truth about Christ that the Apostles (q.v.) preached from the beginning: "Our opinion [i.e., that Christ is truly God and truly flesh] is in accord with the Eucharist, and the Eucharist in turn sustains our opinion." Given this, the true presence of Christ in the eucharistic bread and wine, Irenaeus can argue for the reality and goodness of the physical world itself and of its Creator, the one God (q.v.) to whom both the Old and New Testaments bear witness. In response to the gnostics' claim to a "secret tradition" handed down from a select few of Christ's Apostles, he replies that no such secrets exist. The preaching and faith of the Church was open and public from the first and may be checked against the preaching found in all churches of apostolic foundation. This is Irenaeus's—and the original—sense of the phrase, "apostolic succession," i.e., the succession of the teaching of the apostles carried on preeminently by their successors, the Christian bishops. This teaching is summed up in the "rule of truth" (*kanon tes aletheias*), by which Irenaeus means the confession of faith in the Father, Son, and Spirit made by every believer at baptism—an ancestor of the later creeds (qq.v.).

Irenaeus's thought served the Cappadocian Fathers later in their correction of Origen (qq.v.). One can find in him at least the adumbrations of virtually the whole of subsequent Orthodox theology, anthropology, ecclesiology, and Christology (qq.v.). The disappearance of his works in the Greek-speaking East probably owes to a later disdain in the Byzantine era for his millennialism (qq.v.). He is known and quoted in the East until at least the 6th c.

**IRENE.** In Greek the "divine peace" understood as an appellation of Christ, served as the name for at least one famous church constructed in Constantinople (q.v.) in the 5th c. (Two other churches dedicated to the divine "power" [*dynamis*] and "wisdom" [*hagia sophia*] are also understood as names of Christ.) *Irene* comes to serve, like *sophia*, as the feminine personal name of a number of saints on the Orthodox calendar including the Empress Irene, who convoked and presided over the Seventh Ecumenical Council (q.v.) (Nicaea II, A.D. 787).

**IRENEY (BEKISH), Metropolitan** *see* Bekish, Ireney.

**ISAAC OF NINEVEH, "The Syrian"** (?-ca. 700). A Christian of the Nestorian Church (or Church of the East), Isaac was a native of Qatar in the Persian Gulf, born sometime in the early 7th c. Appointed Bishop of Nineveh around 676, he resigned his episcopate within a short time and spent his remaining years as a hermit in the mountains of present-day southern Iraq and Iran. Some eighty *Discourses* on the spiritual life, which he wrote in his old age, were translated from Syriac into Greek at the monastery of Mar Sabba in Palestine in the 8th c. or 9th c. From there they spread throughout the Orthodox world and into the West. They continue to be read and cherished, particularly by the monks. Recent discoveries of more manuscripts promise additions to his corpus in the near future.

**ISAURIAN DYNASTY.** The dynasty of emperors who ruled Byzantium (q.v.) from Leo III through Constantine VI (i.e., 717–802). Soldier emperors from the border regions, these rulers came to power in the life or death crisis of the Empire's confrontation with the tidal advance of Islam (q.v.) under the early Caliphate of Damascus. The advance was halted at the borders of Asia Minor, though not before Constantinople (qq.v.) itself had suffered siege on two occasions, most seriously in 717. The dynasty is perhaps better known for having initiated the Iconoclast Controversy, which sought to advance the role of the emperor in the Church's life—more than a theological dispute over the place of icons (q.v.). (Leo III wrote of himself as high priest and successor of St. Peter.) The failure of the Isaurian Dynasty in the long run to make good on either its doctrinal program or its vision of the imperial office marked the high-water point of Byzantine caesaropapism (q.v.).

**ISLAM.** Unlike Christianity, which had to borrow its theology of Church and state (q.v.) from pagan Rome, Islam is a comprehensive system, an all-embracing union of civil and religious authority laid down in the religious book, the Koran, revealed to the Prophet Mohammed. Little or no ambiguity appears to adhere to the classic Muslim state, provided its leaders publicly follow the Law of the Prophet. In light of this the phrase "Muslim fundamentalists" and the theology of jihad (holy war), is in fact a tautology: historically, Islam does not rest until its jihad is victorious. Both then and now, this means that non-Islamic minorities in an Islamic state, while guaranteed certain rights by the Koran itself, tread a narrowly circumscribed path. Tension is removed only with the full submission of the subject peoples (the *dhimi*) to the faith. Barring this, difficulties and revolts have continued to trouble those territories where Islam rules over—or is ruled by—peoples who have not embraced it.

From its beginnings in the mid–7th c., Islam has been the great religious and civil rival—with allowances made for Russian Bolshevism and Western European advances—of the Orthodox East. The vast populations of the southeastern Mediterranean conquered in the 7th c. were, over a period of centuries and with some noticeably sizable minorities (e.g., the Coptic Church), incorporated en masse into the *dar al Islam*. The fault lines dividing the Orthodox from the Muslim nations, lines that run from the Adriatic and the Balkans (q.v.) through former Soviet Central Asia, have again become troubled areas in the aftermath of the Soviet Union's dissolution, and are likely to remain so throughout the foreseeable future.

**ITALY.** A modern nation in Europe in which is located its present capital, Rome, the Vatican, and the papacy (q.v.), during the early centuries of Christianity Italy was not entirely "Italian"—i.e., Latin-speaking. Large concentrations of Greeks inhabited its southern reaches as far north as Naples (ancient Neapolis), and were concentrated in Apulia, Calabria (the heel and toe of the boot), and Sicily. In the Byzantine era (q.v.), at least into the 12th c., these areas fell under the civil and ecclesiastical rule of Constantinople (q.v.). Greeks from those regions, such as Nilus of Grottaferrata, John Italos, and Barlaam of Calabria (q.v.), continued to play an important role in Byzantine theology, philosophy, and spirituality well into the Eastern Empire's final years. The onetime Byzantine presence has doubtlessly also contributed to the division of modern Italy into two very different cultural regions, the developed north, part of "Europe" since the Empire of Charlemagne (q.v.), and the rugged, restive, and poverty stricken *mezzogiorno* in the south.

**IXTHYS.** A Greek acronym signifying "Jesus (*Iesous*) Christ (*Xristos*) Son of God (*Theou Yios*), Savior (*Soter*)," also spelling out the Greek word for "fish." Christians, obliged to keep under cover during the preconversion Roman Empire (q.v.), would thus use the iconography of a fish for the purpose of declaring themselves to other believers.

-J-

**JACOBITES.** This name is traditionally given to the Syriac-speaking, non-Chalcedonian (or Oriental Orthodox) church of Antioch (qq.v.), at present confined chiefly to the border regions where Syria, Turkey, and Iraq intersect. The name comes from Jacob Baradeus (ca. 500–578), an itinerant bishop whose life of constant travel was occasioned by the Emperor Justinian's (q.v.) persecution of the non-Chalcedonian—or monophysite (q.v.)—leaders. Baradeus was consecrated ca. 542/3 at the insistence of Empress Theodora (q.v.), and was continually on the authorities' wanted list for his activities. He traveled in disguise—hence his sobriquet, "the man in rags"—and succeeded in escaping detection for the thirty-five years of his ministry throughout the northeast. His secret consecrations of monophysite monks established a Syrian hierarchy paralleling that of the imperial church. A major decline affected them in the Mongol invasions of the 13th c. and 14th c.

**JAPANESE ORTHODOX CHURCH** *see* Kasatkin, Nikolai.

**JEROME,** hieromonk, biblical scholar, St. (ca. 347–419). Eusebius Hieronymous is one of the most distinguished of the Latin Church Fathers of the 4th–5th c. He early devoted himself to ascesis (q.v.) in Aquileia. An accomplished Latinist, he became thoroughly conversant as well with both Greek and Hebrew. The latter accomplishment owed much to his long stay in the Near East (from ca. 374 to 381, 385 to 419), at first in an attempt at the eremetic life in Syria, and later ensconced in Bethlehem where, surrounded by a community of upper-caste Roman women, he spent the remainder of his life. While deservedly renowned as a commentator on Scripture (q.v.) and for his exceedingly lively correspondence, his signal achievement was and remains the translation of the holy books from Greek and Hebrew into Latin. This enormous labor done in different renditions, the Vulgate Bible, earned him lasting fame and eventual canonization—and cleared up problems with different Latin versions circulating previously. Up until the Second Vatican Council, the Vulgate remained the offical version of Scripture for the Roman Catholic Church (q.v.). Jerome also bequeathed to Latin-speakers an acquaintance with Origen and Eusebius of Caesarea (qq.v.) through his translations of several of their works, notably a number of Origen's scriptural commentaries and Eusebius's *Chronicle* (which he continued as well) together with certain topical works by Theophilus of Alexandria and Epiphanius of Salamis (q.v.). He was a fierce opponent of Arianism (q.v.), Pelagianism, and Origenism.

**JERUSALEM, PATRIARCHATE OF.** Although it was the mother of all churches, the Christian community of Jerusalem vanishes from view following the siege and sack of the city by the Roman legions in A.D. 70. It resurfaces later, toward the end of the 3rd c.—though Eusebius of Caesarea (q.v.) does provide a continuous list of bishops for the city. When it reappears, it is a suffragan see of the Metropolitan of Caesarea in Palestine. The conversion of Constantine and the ensuing popularity of pilgrimages to the Holy Land (qq.v.) gave the city increasing importance. This was already the case by the mid–4th c. under Cyril of Jerusalem (q.v.). The Council of Chalcedon crowned this development in 451 by declaring Jerusalem a patriarchate (qq.v.). Today's patriarch heads a community composed almost exclusively of Arabic-speaking faithful resident in Israel and Jordan and numbering about fifty thousand, though emigration from the area has been constant for the past twenty-five years.

**JESUS PRAYER** *see* Hesychasm.

**JOHN CHRYSOSTOM,** Patriarch of Constantinople, theologian, orator, martyr, St. (ca. 347–407). One of the most popular of all the Greek Church Fathers (q.v.), John died in exile and was swiftly acclaimed a saint (q.v.). Trained in rhetoric by one of the last great pagan rhetoricians, Libanius, and in exegesis by Diodore of Tarsus, John's intellect showed forth power, eloquence of expression, and insight. Early drawn to asceticism (q.v.), he tried his vocation as a monk, only to disable his health permanently through extreme fasting. Ordained deacon (381) and priest (386) in his native Antioch (q.v.), John was renowned for his asceticism and inspired preaching, hence his epithet, "Chrysostomos" (the golden-mouthed).

His fame led to his appointment by Emperor Arcadius as archbishop of the imperial city. Never a man for compromise, John's rigorous moral stance and fiery sermons led quickly to confrontations with both emperor and court, even the Empress Eudoxia. If his public criticisms of civil authorities were not welcome, perhaps even less so were his persistent attempts to compel the many clerics haunting the capital for favors and influence to return home to their monasteries and flocks. The powerful had no friend in John, probably the fiercest opponent of the abuses of wealth and privilege ever to grace the cathedra of the imperial city. His stance did, however, eventually win over the people of the capital, who would often applaud him even while he castigated their vices and failures. John's greatest enemy was the powerful Patriarch of Alexandria, Theophilus. Collaborating with factions at court, Theophilus engineered John's deposition and exile at the infamous Synod of the Oak in 403. Briefly reinstated due to popular outrage, he was exiled again in 404 and died three years later while being forcibly marched to a still more distant place, Colchis, on the coast of present-day Georgia.

Nevertheless, his popularity in both the Eastern and Western Churches has remained constant to the present. The remarkable number of his sermons and their honored place on the bookshelves of clergy and laity alike are one testimony to his enduring influence. John's exegesis of Gen and the New Testament books, together with his occasional treatises, such as *On the Incomprehensibility of God* and *On the Priesthood,* reward their readers with a careful, sober approach to the mysteries of the faith, yet one embued with a holy passion. His theology (q.v.) is balanced, firm in its assurance of the foundations of theology, and filled with the voice of spiritual experience. The early years he spent as an ascetic in the Syrian mountains left their imprint on one who is read as gladly by monks as by pastors. His charitable efforts in the capital and his long-suffering in the face of undeserved calumny, disgrace, and hardship further underline the genuine character of his sanctity and ensure his place in the memory of the Orthodox Church as one of the "Three Hierarchs," together with Basil the Great and Gregory Nazianzus (qq.v.), commemorated at every Orthodox liturgy (q.v.). The liturgy most often celebrated bears his name, although its connection to him remains debatable.

**JOHN CLIMACUS,** abbot, ascetic, St. (ca. 579–649). John Climacus (or John of Sinai, John of Raithu) was abbot of the monastery of St. Catherine on Mt. Sinai during the early 7th c. His fame comes from his book, the *Ladder of Paradise,* from which he was graced with his surname, *Klimakos,* i.e., "of the ladder." This work swiftly became and has remained ever since a classic expression of Byzantine Orthodox spirituality. It is a kind of summa or gathering together of the wisdom of previous generations of monks, though Evagrius of Pontus (q.v.) is unquestionably of the first importance among John's sources. The *Ladder* continues to be required reading during Lent (q.v.) for Orthodox monastics. He is venerated in the Orthodox Church on the fourth Sunday of Lent.

**JOHN OF DAMASCUS,** monk, theologian, hymnographer, St. (ca. 675–ca. 749). A child of the Mansour, a Christian family highly placed in the service of the Caliphs of Damascus (q.v.), John embraced monasticism (q.v.) around A.D. 700 following a distinguished civil career. Never other than a lay monk, he spent all of his monastic life at the monastery of Mar Sabba in Palestine. His lasting contributions to Christianity are in three particular areas. First, in dogmatic theology (qq.v.), his "Exact Exposition of the Orthodox Faith" (chapter three of the *Fount of Wisdom*) summarized the thought of the previous six centuries with penetrating brevity and concision. Second, his three *Treatises in Defense of the Holy Icons* during the period of iconoclasm (q.v.), led directly to their vindication at the Seventh Ecumenical Council (q.v.) at Nicaea some two generations after his death, in 787. Third, John was one of the Church's great hymnologists. Taking up the poetic form of the canon, from perhaps Andrew of Crete, his compositions permanently influenced the texts and music (q.v.) of Orthodox services. His funeral and paschal canons are especially memorable. Several homilies on the Church's Great Feasts (q.v.), notably the *Homily on the Transfiguration*, are also of great value, as much for historical reasons as theological, as is his compendious summary of Christian heresies (q.v.). Another great work, *Sacra Parallela*, is preserved only in fragments, but collects scriptural and patristics (q.v.) sources on the ethical and ascetical life. In the West he was translated into Latin and influenced theologians such as Thomas Aquinas.

**JOHN OF KRONSTADT,** St. *see* Sergeyev, John.

**JOHN OF RILA,** monk, St. (ca. 876–946). John founded the wilderness monastery of Rila in about 930 in the mountains south of Sofia, present-day capital of Bulgaria. The monastery quickly became and has remained the center of Bulgarian monasticism, and was recently returned to the Bulgarian Church (qq.v.) by the (now defunct) Communist government. John was renowned for sanctity during his lifetime, a monastic life begun as a hermit and ended as head of the community. His cult increased following his death and eventually extended throughout the Orthodox *oikoumene* (q.v.), as evidenced by his "Life," composed in the 12th c.

**JOHN SHAHOVSKOY,** Archbishop *see* Shahovskoy, John.

**JOHN THE FASTER,** Patriarch of Constantinople, ascetic, St. (?–595). Patriarch from 582 and renowned for his asceticism (q.v.), John IV was the first to take the title Ecumenical (i.e., universal, but properly meaning "imperial") Patriarch (q.v.) in 587. The new title drew the ire of Popes Pelagius and Gregory the Great, and the latter's letter writing campaign against John lasted as long as his distinguished stay in the papacy (q.v.). It is very doubtful, however, that the popes' anger was entirely justified. John was certainly not trying to claim jurisdiction over all the local churches. The title was rather indicative of the Archbishop of Constantinople's special relationship with the emperors and court of Byzantium (q.v.).

**JOHN ZIZIOULAS,** *see* Zizioulas, John.

**JOSEPH OF VOLOKOLAMSK,** abbot, "possessor," St. (1439/40–1515). At the end of the 15th c. the kingdom of Muscovite Rus', or Great Russia, was about to coalesce. At this time the so-called "Judaizing heresy" (q.v.) arose and, when two Novgorodian priests converted to the movement transferred to Moscow, it became marginally influential in the capital. The main opponent of the "Judaizers" was Joseph of Volok (Iosif Volotskii), abbot of the Volokolamsk Monastery. He successfully pursued them until they were condemned by a church council (1504). Subsequently, Tsar Ivan III dealt harshly with them.

Joseph is best known in Russian history as the spokesman for the "possessors," who believed in extensive church holdings and close cooperation with secular authority in order to do God's work. His opponent was Nilus of Sora (Nil Sorskii, 1433–1508) leading the "non-possessors," who minimized church holdings and preferred a separation between Church and state (q.v.), espousing the contemplative ideal of hesychasm, which he had learned on Mt. Athos (qq.v.). Theologically, the non-possessors were definitely legitimate representatives of Holy Tradition (q.v.), though they were in the minority and politically suspect.

Scripture (q.v.) figured in Joseph's controversies with the non-possessors no less than it had with the "Judaizers." The non-possessors, anticipating what would occur in the West later in the same century, considered only Scripture (i.e., "God's commandments") truly binding, as opposed to tradition and human custom, which could be critiqued and changed. Although both Joseph and Nilus were canonized, Joseph's "establishment" position better accommodated the rising centralization of the Muscovite state, while some of Nilus's disciples were condemned as heretics. Joseph educated monks for service in the Church and state in high office, and Muscovy expanded in the 16th c. with this leadership.

**"JUDAIZING HERESY".** A movement in Novgorod and Moscow (Russia) at the end of the 15th c. that included translations of biblical books only from the Hebrew. The "Judaizers" were led by Zechariah (Slavic: Skharia), probably a Crimean Karaite Jew, who taught that Christ was a prophet, the messianic prophecies were unfulfilled, the Church is unnecessary, etc. Besides the Old Testament, the group translated Maimonides and Algazel as well as astrological books. (*See* Joseph of Volokolamsk.) The group was pursued and persecuted by both the government and the "possessor" party in the Church.

**JULIAN OF HALICARNASSUS** (?-ca. 527). This bishop of Halicarnassus in Asia Minor was a contemporary and ally of Severus of Antioch and Philoxenus of Mabboug, leaders in the campaign against the Council of Chalcedon (qq.v.) in the early 6th c. He was, however, condemned by Severus sometime after 520 for advocating the opinion that Christ's body was incorruptible even before the Resurrection (q.v.), i.e., was unfallen and therefore not subject to death and decay. Hence the name of the "heresy" (q.v.) Julian is supposed to have invented, aphthartodocetism, a term combining his assertion of Christ's incorruptibility (*aphtharsia*) with the accusation that he was reviving the ancient heresy of docetism, i.e., Christ's humanity as a mere seeming (from *dokeo*, "to appear, seem"). The latter accusation was quite untrue. Julian sought rather to stress the voluntary character of Christ's suffering, and the questions he raised, in spite of the insulting label, are still debated today among Orthodox theologians.

**JUST WAR THEOLOGY** *see* Theology.

**JUSTIN MARTYR,** "The Philosopher," apologist, St. (?–165). Justin was the first who attempted to reconcile Christian belief with Greek philosophy (q.v.). Of the many works attributed to him by the ecclesiastical historian Eusebius of Caesarea (q.v.), only the *Apologies* against the pagans and the *Dialogue with the Jew Trypho* exist today. Also of historical importance is *The Acts of St. Justin and his Companions,* which contains the official Roman court proceedings against Justin and six of his companions, all of whom were scourged and beheaded. One writing, a pseudo-Justinian work, or possibly the lost *Confutation of the Greeks,* seems to have been devoted to convincing a pagan by logical proof to accept Christianity. Many theologians posit that the spread of Christianity in the early centuries occurred as a result of not only evangelism (q.v.) and teaching, but of Christian martyrdom (q.v.). In Greek the word "martyr," Justin's epithet, also means "witness."

**JUSTINIAN I.** This Roman emperor reigned at Constantinople (q.v.) from 527 to 565, and was effectively in power from the accession of his uncle, Justin, in 518. A native Latin-speaker from Illyricum (q.v.), Justinian's eyes were on Rome and the recovery of the Empire's western half from the beginning of his reign. He nearly succeeded, recapturing Italy, North Africa, and portions of Spain, but at a cost that left the Empire weakened. Following his death, it was a ready prey to invasions from the north (the Slavs), east (Iran), and south (Islam [qq.v.]) that were to remove large parts of the ancient imperium permanently from the rule of the capital.

Justinian's accomplishments, other than conquest, were considerable. He contributed a refinement of Eusebius of Caesarea's theology of Church and state (qq.v.), specifically the notion of "symphony," meaning the theoretically equal roles of *imperium* and *sacerdotium*. The latter was included in Justinian's justly famous codification of Roman law, the *Corpus Juris Civilis* (*see* Justinian, Code of), which he ordered compiled and which has since served as the basis of civil law for most of the European continent. Coming closer than any emperor before or since (excepting the attempts of the Isaurian Dynasty [q.v.]) to the actual realization of caesaropapism (q.v.), he planned, orchestrated, and carried off the convocation and the decisions of the Fifth Ecumenical Council (q.v.) in 553. The council failed, however, in achieving the primary purpose for which the Emperor had called it: the realization of union between Chalcedonian and non-Chalcedonian Christians within the Empire. The failure contributed to the loss of Egypt and Syria to Islam (qq.v.) a century later.

**JUSTINIAN, CODE OF.** The phrase refers to the revision and codification of Roman Law ordered by Justinian I (q.v.), overseen by the jurist, Trikonian, and completed in 529. It forms, together with Justinian's other legal publications, the *Digest, Institutes,* and *Novels,* the *Corpus Juris Civilis*. With further periodic revisions, e.g., the *Epanagoge* (q.v.), it served as the basis of civil and ecclesiastical law for the remainder of the Byzantine era (q.v.). The rediscovery of the *Corpus Juris Civilis* by Western Europe in the 11th c. prompted an efflorescence of legal studies. This continued on and established the foundations of Roman Catholic Canon Law (qq.v.), the *Corpus Juris Canonici* of Gratian (d. 1140), and the civil law in most of Europe.

**JUVENALIS,** Patriarch of Jerusalem (?–458). Bishop from 422 to 458, his efforts at the Council of Chalcedon (q.v.) led to the elevation of his see to the status of patriarchate (q.v.) with jurisdiction over all of Palestine. His political and theological maneuvers during this period of fierce controversy over Christology (q.v.) led to uprisings in his diocese, particularly in response to his change of sides away from Dioscurus of Alexandria and toward the majority opinion of the council fathers.

## -K-

**KALLISTOS (WARE),** Bishop *see* Ware, Kallistos.

**KANTAKOUZENOS.** The name of a prominent aristocratic family of late Byzantium (q.v.) who produced one emperor, John VI Kantakouzenos (1347–1354), the supporter of Gregory Palamas (q.v.). The family would later produce several prominent figures among the Phanariots during the later Ottoman Empire (qq.v.).

**KARIVALIS, DIODORUS,** Patriarch of Jerusalem (14 August 1923– ). Born on the island of Chios, Greece, he became a monk in Jerusalem on 4 March 1944, a deacon on 5 October 1947, and a priest in 1957. In 1957 he received a theological degree from the University of Athens. On 10 November 1962, he was elevated to Archbishop of Hierapolis (Amman, Jordan), and on 16 February 1981, to Patriarch of Jerusalem.

**KARLOVCI SYNOD** *see* Synod in Exile.

**KARMIRIS, JOHN N.,** Greek lay theologian (5 November 1904– ). He studied at the universities of Athens, Bonn, and Berlin. One of the best-known and most respected systematic theologians of the Greek Church, Karmiris received his doctorate from the University of Athens in 1936, and has subsequently published consistently and voluminously. From 1939 to 1945 he was professor of dogmatic theology in the Theological Faculty at the University of Athens. Beginning in 1945 he was the general director of religions and king's councilor at the Holy Synod of the Orthodox Church of Greece. His works include, in Greek, a very valuable collection of source materials, *The Dogmatic and Symbolic Monuments of the Orthodox Church* (1952/3, 2 vols.), the *Synopsis of the Dogmatic Teaching of the Orthodox Church* (1959), *Orthodox Ecclesiology* (1973), as well as a number of monographs on selected theological themes and Church Fathers (q.v.). His works in English include *A Synopsis of the Dogmatic Theology of the Orthodox Catholic Church* (trans. 1973) and *The Status and Ministry of the Laity in the Orthodox Church* (soon to be released).

**KARTASHEV, ANTON V.**, Russian lay theologian, historian, educator (1875–1960). In Russia he graduated from Perm Seminary (1894) and St. Petersburg Theological Academy (1899) where his professors included the historian V. V. Bolotov and the Hebraist I. G. Troitsky. He stayed on at the Academy as a docent for Russian Church history, edited the journal *Vestnik,* and taught at the Advanced Courses for Women. In 1909 he became president of the St. Petersburg Society for Religion and Philosophy. He was forced to resign his Theological Academy position because of differences with the Holy Synod, whereupon he assumed the chair of ecclesiastical history at Bestuzhev Institute and remained there until 1918.

He served as associate to the ober-procurator of the Holy Synod, V. N. Lvov, and succeeded him for ten days. Then on 5 August 1917, he became head of a new department when the duties of the ober-procurator were absorbed by the Ministry of Religious Confessions under the Provisional Government. He used his authority to declare the Holy Synod an autonomous body awaiting a gathering of an All-Rus-sian Sobor to establish an appropriate administrative body. The All-Russian Sobor—which Kartashev had advocated for some time—convened on 16 August 1917 in Moscow and he gave the welcoming address. When the Bolshevik government closed all public Orthodox theological institutions, he joined the private Petrograd Theological Institute.

In January 1919, because of the Bolshevik threat, he left the country to settle in Paris, and became instrumental in the founding of St. Sergius Orthodox Theological Institute (q.v.) and served as professor there from 1925 until his death. Although by vocation a church historian, he was also a professor of Old Testament at the Institute until that subject was taken over by B. I. Sove around 1930. He was also a principal leader of the Russian Christian Students' Movement and an active ecumenist. His principal works are *Essays on the History of the Russian Church* (1959) in two volumes and an important history entitled *The Ecumenical Councils* (in Russian).

**KASATKIN, NIKOLAI I.,** Archbishop of Tokyo, missionary, St. (1836–16 February 1912). After attending the St. Petersburg Theological Academy and being ordained priest in 1860, he began his missionary work in Japan in 1861 as chaplain to the Russian diplomatic mission in Hakodate, on the north island of Yezo (Hokkaido). He succeeded in founding a vigorous and indigenous church in Japan with native clergy. At first he limited himself to the study of Japanese language, literature, religion, and culture, because Christianity was still a proscribed religion, and he rejected all attempts to Russify the people. In April 1868 he secretly baptized three Japanese. By 1871, when the Russian Orthodox Mission to Japan was officially recognized, there was a community of twelve Christians with twenty-five catechumens. When the Japanese government made Christianity a tolerated religion in 1873, he moved to Tokyo to establish a seminary for priests and catechists, and created a committee for translation of Christian literature. By 1875 he had 1,000 souls under his care and two of his first three converts had become priests. By 1878 there were 100 congregations with a total of 5,000 members whereupon he was made bishop and his mission was brought under the Holy Synod. By 1904 there were 260 congregations and he was made Archbishop of Tokyo in 1906. At his death there were some 33,000 believers.

**KEDROVSKY, JOHN** *see* Living Church.

**KESICH, VESELIN,** Serbian-American New Testament scholar, Slavicist, churchman (1921– ). Born in Yugoslavia, he passed through the displaced persons camps in Italy before beginning his studies at Dorchester College, Great Britain, in 1947, completing his Ph.D. in the Columbia University-Union Theological Seminary joint program after arriving in the United States in 1949. He served as professor of New Testament for thirty-eight years at St. Vladimir's Orthodox Theological Seminary (q.v.) and professor of comparative religion at Sarah Lawrence College, then holding faculty emeritus status at both institutions. In the field of New Testament, in addition to occasional articles and essays, he has published *The Passion of Christ* (1965), *The Gospel Image of Christ: The Church and Biblical Criticism* (1972; rev. ed. 1992), *The First Day of the New Creation: The Resurrection and Christian Faith* (1982), and *Treasures of the Holy Land* (1985), coauthored with his wife, Lydia.

Influenced in his learning by Frederick Grant of Union and Georges Florovsky (q.v.), who was dean of St. Vladimir's, Kesich evaluates the historical critical method as a neutral tool, accessible to the Orthodox Church and its Scripture scholars, not to be used in isolation from patristic (q.v.) commentaries and other traditional tools. A line of continuity may be drawn from Florovsky's neo-patristic synthesis to Kesich's evaluation of the historical critical method, and beyond to the approach taken by some younger Orthodox Scripture specialists, all of whom have accepted Kesich's position as (now) a presupposition.

In the field of Slavic studies, aside from adjunct professorships at the University of California, Berkeley, and New York University, he has authored articles on Dostoevsky (q.v.), Sava of Serbia, Bishop Nikolai Velimirovich, and other topics relating to the spirituality of the Serbian Orthodox Church (q.v.) and Serbo-Croatian literature. Kesich's lectures at Berkeley on Dostoevsky and Orthodoxy were presented to packed rooms and attended by ranking faculty. Always a faithful churchman, displaying balance in his theology and humility in his personal behavior, Kesich's quiet legacy will continue on to reflect the "Orthodoxmindedness" of 20th-c. Scripture and Slavic studies scholarship.

**KHLYSTS** *see* Doukhobors.

**KHOMIAKOV, ALEXIS S.,** philosopher-theologian (1804–1860). One of the cofounders of the Slavophile (q.v.) movement in reaction to Western intellectual influences in Russia, Khomiakov received a liberal education in Moscow and unsuccessfully tried careers in the military and in art. With Kireyevsky he critiqued the prevailing philosophies of Scholasticism (q.v.) and German idealism and the ecclesiologies of the Roman Catholic (q.v.) and Protestant churches, thereby laying foundations for a philosophy and theology, especially an ecclesiology (q.v.), based on Orthodox Christianity. He collaborated on *Russkaia Beseda* beginning in 1856, and his son posthumously published his essays in *L'église latine et le protestantisme au point de vue de l'Église d'Orient.* In his best-known essay, "The Church Is One," Khomiakov laid out his views on the unity and catholicity (q.v.) (*sobornost*) of the Church, a view that has been influential throughout the Orthodox world.

**KHRAPOVITZKY, ANTONII,** Metropolitan of Kiev and Galich, émigré churchman (1864–11 August 1936). After studying at the St. Petersburg Theological Academy and lecturing there in Old Testament studies, he became rector of the Moscow Theological Academy and then the Kazan Academy. He was made Vicar Bishop of Kazan, then of Oufa, Volnia, and Kharkov, and finally Metropolitan of Kiev, and was one of three nominated to be Patriarch of Russia at the 1918 All-Russian Sobor. He was known for supporting educated monastics and thought they should lead the Church. In the reinstitution of the patriarchate (q.v.) he anticipated an office with absolute ecclesiastical power, an office that collaborated in matters of Church and state (q.v.), but ultimately reigned supreme. He left Russia after the Revolution to settle in Yugoslavia as president of the Synod in Exile (q.v.) in Karlovci. Although theologically liberal, he is more remembered for his conservative and reactionary post-Revolutionary political thought. He is known for his positions on Canon Law (q.v.), as well as for being the author of "Confession: A Series of Lectures on the Mystery of Repentance" (trans. 1975), *Dostoevsky's Concept of Spiritual Rebirth* (trans. 1980), and "Concerning the Dogma of Redemption" (*Constructive Quarterly,* June 1919).

**KIEVAN RUS'.** The Slavic Churches trace their origins back to Constantinople through the missionary efforts of Constantine-Cyril and

Methodius (qq.v.), and to the baptism of Kievan Rus' in the Dnieper River in 988 in the reign of Prince Vladimir (956–1015). It was under the inspiration of Vladimir's Christian grandmother, Princess Olga, and Vladimir's Greek (political) relations from the court of Emperor Basil II that Vladimir himself was baptized "Basil" at this time. He actively promoted Christianity by building churches and monasteries and doing charitable works. But he was known to have used inappropriate compulsion to promote baptism, and paid insufficient attention to the required catechesis (q.v.) of new Christians. The anomalous situation that resulted had noteworthy characteristics: Christianity spread "from the top down," i.e., from the political and educated elite to the peasantry; the language of worship from the beginning was Slavic, even though a metropolitan, hierarchy, and initial group of clergy were brought from the Byzantine Empire (q.v.); for many centuries afterward the popular religion was a "dual-faith" (q.v.) based on an admixture of Christianity and paganism. All things considered, Vladimir was canonized in the 12th c. as an apostle (q.v.) to the Slavs. The traditional, glorious legend of the conversion of the Kievan Slavs from the Chronicles (q.v.) — at the recommendation of Vladimir's emissaries to foreign lands — is worthwhile reading and considered by many experts to contain a kernel of historical fact.

The Kievan Period in Slavic Church history covers the 10th–13th c. The history of Kievan Rus' was punctuated by the assimilation of Byzantine spirituality through translations, internecine warfare in the princely families, the establishment of an indigenous monasticism (q.v.) that spread from Kiev north and found a new impetus with Sergius of Radonezh, the Tartar invasions that decimated the entire region and left intact only Novgorod and its environs, and the moving of the secular and religious "capital" from Kiev to Moscow.

Kievan Rus' is best known by its literature — which centered on Scripture (q.v.). Ironically, no complete manuscript of the Slavic Bible exists from this period. (*See* Constantine-Cyril; Gennadievskii Bible; Methodius.) Nonetheless, the popular power of liturgy and the personal piety (qq.v.) of the people of Kievan Rus' dictated that spiritual writings were of the utmost importance. Religious writings were called sacred and divine insofar as they were not heretical. The idea of distinguishing between the inspired Holy Scriptures, the Church Fathers (q.v.), and the apocrypha (i.e., non-Biblical rather than "deuterocanonical") did not exist. Indeed, the apocrypha was especially liked because of its fabulous content, which appealed to the imagination and was entertaining.

Since the Old Testament enjoyed limited liturgical use, only the prescribed church readings were collected into one liturgical book (q.v.), rendering a complete Old Testament unnecessary. Other available biblical books for church and private use circulated in smaller collected editions. The Book of Psalms was the most popular one, outpacing even the Gospels, and was used not only as the "prayerbook of the Church" but also as the chief reading primer. After the psalter and individual Gospels came the prophets and wisdom literature, especially Sirach. The *Palaea,* a "Reader's Digest version" of the "historical books" of the Old Testament dressed up with apocryphal legends, completed the list.

While reading was a virtue of the elite, and liturgy appealed to both elite and peasant, Holy Scripture and apocryphal works were rivaled in popularity only by translations of the lives of saints, followed by sermons (*see* Kirill of Turov) and patristic exegeses. Thus, three of the largest and most popular literary corpuses of Kievan Rus' had Scripture as their centerpiece. (*See* Russian Orthodox Church.)

**KIRIK** *see* Questions of Kirik.

**KIRILL OF TUROV,** "the Golden-mouthed," bishop, St. (1130–1189). A premier orator, Kirill, or Cyril, gave rhetorical yet dynamic sermons, which are preserved in a collection following the church's liturgical year (*Torzhestvennik*). Kirill, living in Kievan Rus' (q.v.), employed classical Byzantine literary forms and theology in his sermons, letters, and prayers, as did his contemporaries. Stylistically he may be considered eclectic but lively.

**KISHKOVSKY, LEONID,** priest, ecumenist (24 March 1943– ). Born in Warsaw, he was a displaced person in West Germany with his family (1944–51) before coming to the United States and receiving his B.A. at the University of Southern California (1965) and studied theology at St. Vladimir's Orthodox Theological Seminary (q.v.) (1964–67). After ordination (1969) he continued previous work organizing college student conferences and college fellowships. As parish priest from 1969 to the present, he has increased his administrative role in the Orthodox Church in America, serving as assistant to the chancellor, secretary for ecumenical and external affairs, and member of the National Council of Churches Governing Board, and World Council of Churches Central Committee. He served as president of the National Council of Churches (1990–91), and was the first Orthodox churchman to lead that body as such. He has also been the editor of *The Orthodox Church* newspaper from 1985 and is highly regarded by his peers.

**KLIMENT OF OCHRID** *see* Clement of Ochrid.

**KNOWLEDGE.** In Greek, *gnosis,* the term figures prominently in the New Testament writings, especially in the Pauline and Johannine books, later on in early Christianity, and throughout the Orthodox ascetic and theological tradition to the present day. "This is eternal life," says Christ, "to know [*ginoskein*] you, the true God" (Jn 17:3). The experiential character of knowledge implied in this text has governed the treatment of this term in subsequent Orthodox Christian writers.

The knowledge of God (q.v.) is first and last an experience that transforms the recipient, and only secondarily a matter of correct form or language, i.e., an intellectual activity. In early Christianity this understanding was challenged on two fronts, from outside the Church via Plato and Greek philosophy, and from inside by gnosticism (qq.v.). The latter advanced the idea of a *gnosis* at once technical, that is, based on a secret tradition and involving what amounted often to "passwords" to the higher spiritual realms, and ontological or "predestinarian," i.e., that one was born with or without a capacity for the saving knowledge. For Plato, Plotinus, and Neoplatonism (qq.v.) generally, the knowledge communicated by philosophy, while including a generous amount of the experiential or "mystical," still embraced a fundamentally intellectual and rational activity, an education almost in the university sense, and hence was limited to the elite of the Greco-Roman world.

The Christian response began with the Apologists and Irenaeus of Lyons, and then with the Alexandrian school represented by Clement and Origen (qq.v.). For the latter two, knowledge of God is, as in Platonism or Gnosticism, the end or goal of Christian life. That life, however, is rooted in an ecclesial setting, placed firmly in the context of an asceticism (q.v.) based on the Gospels, and joined to the idea of the believer's appropriation of the work of Christ. Subsequent generations, in particular the Desert Fathers, Cappadocians, Evagrius of Pontus (qq.v.), and the Macarius of the *Macarian Homilies,* further elaborated the notion of the Christian, preeminently the monk, as the true "philosopher." Finally, in the writing of Maximus the Confessor, knowledge is subordinated to the love of God, realized in Christ and at work in the believer.

**KOCHUROV, JOHN,** priest, martyr (13 June 1871-November/ December 1917). Serving in America from 1895 to 1907, he is well-known for his exemplary labors as rector and builder of Chicago's Holy Trinity Cathedral (the only Louis Sullivan church in existence) which was consecrated in 1903 by Bishop Tikhon Belavin (q.v.). He established other midwestern parishes with Frs. Hotovitzky and Toth, and was responsible for the return of many Uniates (qq.v.) to Orthodoxy. On returning to Russia he served in the St. Petersburg Diocese and was at Tsarskoye Selo (Pushkin) at the outbreak of the 1917 Revolution. There he was attacked and killed, and was the first clergyman martyred during the Revolution. [At the time of this printing he is being considered for canonization by the Russian Church and his full biography is not yet available.]

**KOINIOIS, PARTHENIOS,** Patriarch of Alexandria (30 Nov 1919– ). In 1939 he received a Diploma of Theology from the Theological School of Halki, Istanbul, and was ordained to the diaconate, the next year he became an archdeacon, and in 1948, a priest. In 1958 he was made Metropolitan of Carthage, and was elevated to Patriarch of Alexandria on 8 March 1987.

**KOLLYVA (KOLLYVADES).** 1)*Kollyva* is the boiled wheat, served usually with spices and sugar, prepared on the occasion of memorial services. Although having pre-Christian roots, the custom was accommodated to Christian practice through the use of such *logia* as Christ's saying, "Unless a grain of wheat fall into the ground and die . . . " (Jn 12:24).

2) *Kollyvades* refers to a monastic party on Mt. Athos (q.v.) in the late 18th c. and early 19th c. Beginning at the Scete of St. Anne in 1754, the movement started as a protest against the celebration of memorial services on Sundays—hence the *kollyva* connection. Its leaders argued that the resurrectional and paschal nature of Sunday forbids mourning of the dead on this day. Opposition to this position, and outright persecution, led the members of the movement to explore more fully the liturgical and spiritual tradition, in particular the mystical and ascetic writers of the 4th c. through 14th c. Many of the most noted monastic reformers in this period were to come from the ranks of the *kollyvades,* most importantly Nicodemus of the Holy Mountain, compiler and editor of the Greek *Philokalia* (qq.v.), together with his chief associate in the latter enterprise, Macarius, Bishop of Corinth (d. 1805). Other monastic leaders included Iakovos of the Peloponnesus, Agapios of Cyprus, and Neophytos Kavsokalyvites. The Ecumenical Patriarch (q.v.) upheld the position of the *kollyvades* on two separate occasions, 1781 and 1819.

**KOMI.** The Zyryans (or Zyrians) are known also as Komi, and constitute one of two parts of the Permyak branch of the Finno-Ugric populations of central Russia. In the 9th c. the Permians divided into Komi and Udmurts. Historically, the Komi came into contact with Christianity as early as the 12th c. since they were trading partners with Novgorod. Their conversion is associated with Stephen of Perm (c. 1345–1396), who was a Russian born among the Zyryans. In 1370, after spending thirteen years as a monk at Rostov, Stephen traveled to this people situated east of the Volga. He believed, in concert with Orthodox Holy Tradition (q.v.), that the people should worship in their own language, so he created an alphabet for them from line design in their embroidery and carving. Following this, he translated the Bible and the liturgy of the Church from Greek into Zyryan. He also is known to have founded schools and seminaries to train native clergy. The Komi still live between the upper West Dvina River, Kama, and Pechora, a large region west of the northern Urals toward Archangel. In 1979 the Komi numbered more than 325,000.

**KONTOGLU, PHOTIOS,** author, iconographer (1896–1965). He was a prolific author in modern Greek, and at the same time an iconographer who argued strenuously and convincingly for a return to the ancient patterns of sacred art. His arguments, supported by numerous publications touching on the arts in general, extended to a defense of traditional, Orthodox ways of living where he had perhaps less success. He had and continues to have an unquestionable influence on other, contemporary defenders of a way of life and a theological tradition seen as threatened by the powerful, Western-oriented currents at play in modern Greek thought, politics, and behavior.

**KOSSOVO, BATTLE OF.** This battle was a traumatic defeat suffered by the Serbian king, Lazar, to the Ottoman Turks on 15 June 1389 at *kossovo polye* (the field of the blackbird). It marked the end of Serbia's independence in the Balkans and the beginning of its long captivity under the Ottoman Empire (qq.v.). Kossovo is also notable for the role it has played in Serbian popular lore and song. Through the alchemy of folklore, a military defeat was transmuted into an expression of Christian piety (q.v.). According to the legend, Tsar Lazar chose God's kingdom over his own earthly realm. The king, and with him his people, were seen as sharing in Christ's passion and so, implicitly, made confident of eventual resurrection. The myth was singularly important for the survival of this nation's religion and identity through centuries of Muslim rule.

**KOULOMZIN, SOPHIE (SHIDLOVSKY),** religious educator (1903– ). Her father, Serge Shidlovsky, was a vice president of Tsar Nicholas II's Duma. From 1920 to 1922 the family sought refuge in Estonia, where she taught her first catechism class under the tutelage of Fr. John Bogoyavlensky. At age eighteen she passed the Russian "gymnasium" exams while working full time in Reval (Tallin) without the benefit of attending classes, and was helped by Paul B. Anderson (q.v.) of the International YMCA to win a scholarship to attend the University of Berlin (1922–24). In 1926 Anderson and Metropolitan Evlogii (q.v.) chose her to receive a Rockefeller Fund grant to attend the Teachers'

College of Columbia University, New York, where she spent September 1926 to June 1927 and received a Master's degree in religious education. From 1927 to 1948 she lived in France, doing religious educational work with children for the Russian Student Christian Movement. In 1932 she married Nikita Koulomzin, an engineer, and in 1948 the family settled permanently in Nyack, New York. Shortly after her arrival she joined the Metropolitan Council's Church School Committee and began creating religious educational materials for youth. In October 1956 she participated in the founding of the Orthodox Christian Education Commission, a pan-Orthodox body, serving as its first executive secretary, 1956–69. From 1956 to 1973 she was lecturer in religious education at St. Vladimir's Orthodox Theological Seminary (q.v.). She is the author of *Our Church and Our Children* (1975), which outlines the substance of her educational philosophy, and an autobiography, *Many Worlds: A Russian Life*. Since 1982, she has become involved in the work of the society *Religious Books for Russia,* preparing several children's almanacs and a manual of religious instruction now widely used in Russia. She attended a seminar for catechists from Russia in France in 1990, a conference on "The Spiritual Renewal of Russia" in Novosibirsk in 1991, and a conference in Moscow on religious education organized by the Patriarchate (q.v.) there in January 1994.

**KRIVOCHEINE, BASIL (VSEVOLOD),** Archbishop of Brussels and Belgium (30 July 1900–22 September 1985). Son of a distinguished statesman, Vsevolod studied history and philology at the universities of Petrograd and Moscow, completed his higher studies in Paris, where he was awarded the *licence ès lettres* degree from the Sorbonne in 1921, and became a student at the St. Sergius Orthodox Theological Institute (q.v.) in 1925. He departed to become a monk in St. Panteleimon Monastery on Mt. Athos (q.v.), taking the name Basil, and remaining there for twenty-two years, spending much of his time pursuing patristic (q.v.) studies. Having become proficient in Greek, he was for some time the monastery's Greek correspondence secretary. In 1937 he became a member of the monastery's monastic council, and from 1942 to 1945 he represented the monastery at the sessions of the Holy Community in Karyes.

Due to collaborationist charges from World War II, he was condemned by a Greek court, expelled from Athos, and confined in a camp on Makronisos. In 1951, following his release, he went to England to work on the Patristic Greek Lexicon at Oxford University. At Oxford on 21–22 May 1951, he was ordained deacon and assistant priest of the Russian Orthodox Church of the Annunciation (Moscow Patriarchate). On 14 June 1959 in London he was consecrated titular Bishop of Volokolamsk and auxiliary to the Moscow Patriarchal

Exarchate of Western Europe. On 31 May 1960 he was nominated Bishop of Brussels and Belgium, and became archbishop on 21 July. He has represented the Moscow Patriarchate in pan-Orthodox discussions at Rhodes (1961, 1963, 1964), Belgrade (1966), and Chambesy (1968). He is author of *In the Light of Christ: Saint Symeon, the New Theologian* (Eng. trans., 1986).

**KRONSTADT, JOHN OF** *see* Sergeyev, John.

**KYKKATIS, CHRYSOSTOM,** Archbishop of New Justiniana and All Cyprus (27 September 1927– ). Ordained to the diaconate in 1951, he received his Philosophy and Theology Diploma from the University of Athens in 1961, and on 21 October was ordained to the priesthood. He was consecrated Bishop of Constantia on 14 April 1968, elevated to Metropolitan of Paphos, and elected Archbishop of New Justiniana and All Cyprus on 13 November 1977. He succeeded Archbishop Makarios III (Mouskos), who served from 1950 to 1977.

**KYRIAKOS.** The Orthodox Church counts some seventeen saints by this name, including martyrs (eleven), bishops (three), and monks (four). One who is definitely identifiable as a historical person is the monk who flourished in the 6th c. He was a contemporary of Romanos the Melodist (q.v.) and also a hymnographer.

**KYRIE ELEISON.** This refrain, "Lord, have mercy," is the phrase repeated most often during the course of Orthodox services. It is sung following each petition of the many litanies characteristic of the main offices of daily and Sunday worship (Eucharist [q.v.]) and repeated frequently by the readers or cantors between selections from the Psalter during the lesser offices (Prime, Terce, etc.). The omnipresence of the *Kyrie eleison* provides a constant reminder for Orthodox faithful of their dependence on God's (q.v.) mercy, his philanthropy, and of their own lack of worthiness before the Righteous Judge. The prayer (q.v.) is therefore a capsule summary of Orthodox theology (q.v.) and spirituality. Its frequent repetitions recall the prayer of the Publican in Lk 18 as well as the discipline of the "Jesus prayer" so prominent in Orthodox asceticism (q.v.).

-L-

**LAMAISM** *see* Buddhism.

**LANGUAGE.** The Orthodox Church has never had a unique sacred language, although during the Byzantine era (q.v.) imperial policy sought continually to enforce Greek as the common tongue within the Empire's boundaries. Later the Phanariots, using the office of the Ecumenical Patriarch under the aegis of the Ottoman Empire (qq.v.), would attempt—to disastrous effect—to impose linguistic uniformity on the Slavs and Romanians of the Balkans. Traditionally, however, the Eastern Church both within Byzantium (q.v.) and subsequently in Russia fostered translations of the Scripture and liturgical books (qq.v.) into local languages. Greek could never, in any case, aspire to the unique position of Latin in the Christian West. The eastern Mediterranean was already home to too many ancient cultures, each with its own literary tradition, for any of them to dominate absolutely. Latin had no such competitors in the West.

In another vein, language as the necessary medium of theological discourse was the constant preoccupation of the Church Fathers (q.v.), in particular the problem of adapting a Greek vocabulary shaped by philosophies and religious attitudes foreign to the Old and New Testaments to the requirements of the Christian faith. This effort effectively involved the transmutation of the Greek philosophical lexicon, a work of many centuries. Secondly, language per se had to be recognized as ultimately inadequate to the mysteries of the faith: Trinity, Christology (qq.v.), and the living experience of God (q.v.), which underlies these dogmas. The Orthodox theological enterprise has thus been characterized by Fr. Georges Florovsky (q.v.) as the search for the words most adequate (or least inadequate) to God, *theoprepeis logoi*. This notion of language as a vessel or as a necessary exercise in conceptual iconography not unakin to the canons governing the making of holy icons (q.v.), distinguishes the approach that the best Orthodox theologians this century have taken. It may be compared to the theory advanced by Cardinal Newman in the last century, and repeated subsequently by the better Western theologians, of the "development of doctrine."

**LATERAN SYNOD.** This was a local council of the Church of Rome held in 649 and reputedly presided over by Pope Martin I, assisted by Maximus the Confessor (qq.v.), which issued the first formal condemnation of the doctrine of monotheletism (q.v.). Monotheletism, belief in one will in Christ, was promulgated by the Emperor Constans II, successor to Heraclius. Both the pope and the monk would pay for their resistance, expressed through the Lateran Synod, with torture and exile. The Orthodox stance on the Synod was confirmed by the Sixth Ecumenical Council (q.v.) in 681.

**LATIN PATRIARCHATES.** This phrase refers to the parallel Latin hierarchies created in Constantinople, Antioch, Jerusalem, and (honorarily) Alexandria by the Crusades (qq.v.). The resulting coexistence of simultaneous and overlapping Greek and Latin patriarchs, together with their accompanying synods, was the first real indication of the schism between Rome (qq.v.) and Constantinople. The Latin presence, beginning in Antioch in 1108, eventually vanished following the fall of Tyre in 1291—at least until the 19th c.'s re-creation of the Latin Patriarchate in Jerusalem. The papacy's (q.v.) continuing reappointment of ecclesiastics to these sees, if only *in partibus infidelium,* kept alive the idea of the parallel hierarchies and so bore continuous witness to the fact of the schism.

**LATIN RITE.** The use of the term "rite" here is of Roman Catholic (q.v.) provenance. It means not merely the ceremonies, but the piety, Canon Law (qq.v.), and theological self-expression of a given Christian community. "Latin rite" thus signifies all these things as applied to the Christians of the Latin tradition, i.e., Western Europe (less, of course, the Protestant nations and the Romanians). In fact the "rite" of the Western Church was not uniform in its earlier days. Right up until the Second Vatican Council it counted several local variations in terms of liturgical use, for example the Ambrosian (Milan), Mozarabic (parts of Spain), Dominican, and—much earlier—Celtic and Gallican "rites." This century has also seen attempts on the part of local Orthodox churches to establish "Latin" or "Western rite" communities in communion with the Orthodox *oikoumene,* most notably by the Antiochian Orthodox Christian Archdiocese of New York and all North America (qq.v.).

In general, the Latin rite (meaning in particular the liturgy of Rome) is characterized by a great sobriety and, in its pre-Vatican II days, by a markedly scriptural orientation. This is especially noticeable in the monastic offices, which, unlike the Byzantine rite's (q.v.) love for elaborate theological poetry, are built largely on the chanting of the Psalter. Later developments, particularly the long struggles over the Trinity and Christology (qq.v.), had vastly more influence on Eastern worship than on Western. Certain changes that came into the Latin rite in the early and later medieval periods caused considerable opposition in the East when they became known, for example the use of unleavened bread in the Eucharist (q.v.), the withholding of confirmation until later in childhood accompanied by the withdrawal of the Eucharist from infants, and the withholding of the consecrated wine from the laity.

**LAUSIAC HISTORY.** A history and series of portraits of the early Desert Fathers (q.v.), accompanied by personal reminiscences, written by Palladius (ca. 363–ca. 431) around the year 419. The title derives from the book's dedication to a certain Lausas, the court chamberlain of Emperor Theodosius II. Palladius's little book provides an indispensable guide for historians of the period. It continues to be read with profit by Orthodox monks, laypeople, and theologians because of its moving portrayals of the earliest monks and the transmission of their wisdom.

**LAZOR, THEODOSIUS,** Metropolitan of the Orthodox Church in America (27 October 1933– ). He received his B.A. from Washington and Jefferson College in 1957, and earned a B.D. from St. Vladimir's Orthodox Theological Seminary (q.v.) in 1960. Following graduation he did postgraduate work at the Ecumenical Institute, Bossey, Switzerland, and was tonsured monk and ordained priest for the Nativity of the Holy Virgin Mary Church, Madison, Illinois, in October 1961. He was called to New York in 1966 as secretary to Metropolitan Ireney Bekish and vice chairman of the Department of External Afairs. In 1967 he was elected vicar to the metropolitan, and then ruling bishop of Sitka and Alaska. Bishop Theodosius witnessed the canonization of Herman (q.v.) of Alaska in Kodiak (1970), before being transferred as Bishop of Pittsburgh and West Virginia (1972). On 25 October 1977, the Fifth All-American Council of the Orthodox Church in America (q.v.) elected Bishop Theodosius to be Archbishop of New York and Metropolitan of All America and Canada. In 1980 the Holy Synod created the Diocese of Washington, D.C., and transferred Theodosius to the primatial see, with the chancery and residence remaining in Oyster Bay Cove (Syosset), New York. While in office Theodosius has met many world leaders of Christian Churches, including Pope John Paul II, the Patriarchs and Archbishops of Constantinople, Antioch, Jerusalem, Russia, Georgia, Romania, Bulgaria, Cyprus, Greece, Poland, Czechoslovakia, Finland, and Japan, and the Coptic Pope of Alexandria, as well as Roman Catholic and Protestant leaders in North America. Additionally, his leadership has been characterized by seeking unity for Orthodox in North America and increasing internal administrative structures.

**LENT.** There are technically four "lents," or fasting seasons, during the liturgical year of the Orthodox Church: the Great Lent consisting of "forty days" preceding Holy Week and Easter, the Apostles' Fast preceding the Feast of SS. Peter and Paul (June 29th), two weeks preceding the Dormition of the Theotokos (August 15th), and the forty days in preparation for the Nativity of Christ (December 25th).

It is Great Lent, however, that enjoys both chronological and liturgical primacy, and was the model for the others. A fasting period of up to a week preceding the paschal vigil appears as early as the 3rd c. Believers, according to the *Apostolic Tradition* (q.v.), were expected to share in the catechumens' preparation for their Baptism (q.v.) during the Easter Vigil. The 4th c. expansion of Christianity saw this period extended to essentially its present dimensions, as is evident in the account Egeria (q.v.) gives of Lent in late 4th c. Jerusalem. As presently observed, the Orthodox Lent includes six weeks of fasting, less the Saturday of Lazarus and Palm Sunday, which begin the Holy Week commemorating Christ's suffering. For four Sundays prior to the fast, reckoned as beginning on a Monday, the themes that are to predominate during the forty days are brought to the believers' attention through the reading of the Gospel lessons of the Pharisee and Publican (humility), Prodigal Son (repentance), the Last Judgment (righteous deeds and the memory of death), and forgiveness.

Each of the lenten Sundays is also devoted to a particular theme. The first commemorates the final victory over iconoclasm (q.v.) in 843, the second remembers Gregory Palamas (q.v.), the champion of asceticism, the third the Holy Cross, the fourth John Climacus (q.v.), and the fifth the great image of repentance, Mary of Egypt. Church services during this period reflect the themes of repentance (q.v.), godly sorrow, and entrance into the Church. They are longer, make greater use of Old Testament readings (reflecting also Lent's origins as a preparation for Baptism), and in Russian employ melodies in the minor key and vestments of somber hue.

Perhaps the characteristic service par excellence of Great Lent is the Liturgy of the Presanctified Gifts. Since the Byzantine Church forbade the celebration of the Eucharist (q.v.) during the weekdays of the fast, communion was—and is—provided the faithful through an evening service, essentially Vespers, on Wednesdays and Fridays. The communion is taken from a eucharistic host consecrated the preceding Sunday, hence the "presanctified" in the service's title.

**LEO THE GREAT,** Pope of Rome, theologian, St. (?–461). Pope from 440 to 461, the epithet "Great" is genuinely deserved. It derives in good part from this pope's contribution to the Christology of the Council of Chalcedon (qq.v) in 451. Leo's *Tome* (q.v.), essentially the reissue of his earlier letter to Patriarch Flavian of Constantinople in 449, constituted the ground of the Council's dogmatic definition of Christ as "one person (*hypostasis*) in two natures (*en dyo physesin*)," human and divine. Leo's other contribution, even more controversial (in the East), was his repeated insistence on a very high view of the Roman bishop as successor to St. Peter and very much the supervisor of the Christian *oikoumene* (q.v.). His objections, for example, to Chalcedon's elevation of Constantinople (q.v.) to second place in the hierarchy of churches as "new Rome" (Canon #28) remained a point of irritation between West and East until their mutual schism (q.v.) in the 11th c. More positively, one must also reckon with the pastoral and liturgical sense of this great church leader, an aspect of his character that emerges most clearly in his homilies on the Christian feasts (q.v.), few of which are available in English. His handling of the invasions of the Huns and Vandals accrued prestige to the office of the papacy (q.v.), along with the acquisition of jurisdiction of the Western provinces.

**LEONTIUS OF BYZANTIUM,** theologian (?-ca. 543). Leontius was a court theologian during the reign of Justinian (q.v.). Possibly a disguised adherent of Origen—or more accurately of Evagrius of Pontus—he was a key contributor to the terminology that allowed the Emperor to attempt his clarification of Chalcedon at the Fifth Ecumenical Council (qq.v.) in 553. The essential terminological innovation Leontius had a hand in fashioning was the term *enhypostasis* (literally, "enpersoned"). Behind this word lay considerable thought on the meaning of "person." Leontius assisted in distinguishing more clearly between two words, "nature" and "person" (*physis* and *hypostasis*), which had lain at the root of the furor over Chalcedon. As a result of his and others' work, the Fifth Council could speak more clearly than the Fourth about the unity of Christ's person, specifically that the subject of all attributions concerning Christ is the Second Person of the Trinity (q.v.). The Word of God's humanity is "enhypostatized" in Him. Leontius's and offical Orthodoxy's Christology (q.v.) is therefore "asymmetric." The Lord's *hypostasis* is one, the *hypostasis* of the Word, while his natures are double, human and divine.

**LEONTY (TURKEVICH),** Metropolitan *see* Turkevich, Leonty.

**LEV (GILLET),** *see* Gillet, Lev.

**LEVSHIN, PLATON,** Metropolitan of Moscow (1737–1812). A remarkable Russian churchman of the 18th c. and early 19th c., he was brought to St. Petersburg in 1763 as preacher to the court of Tsarina Catherine II (the Great). He advanced initially on his preaching abilities, and more than 500 of his sermons are preserved. Tutor to the Grand Duke Paul, he was recognized as the greatest educator of the church schools of the 18th c., and worked to improve not only the Latin curriculum of the clergy but their cultural, social, and material status. Influenced by the spirit of the Enlightenment, he wrote the first systematized theology (q.v.) and outline of church history in Russian, and put theology into contact with everyday life, mostly through catechesis (q.v.). During thirty-seven years as metropolitan, his exemplary administrative abilities largely brought his vision to fruition.

**LEX CREDENDI.** Literally, this Latin phrase means the "law of what must be believed." It is the equivalent of the earlier 2nd c. expressions, *kanon tes aletheias* (rule of truth) and *regula fidei* (rule of faith), advanced by Irenaeus and Tertullian (qq.v.), respectively, and it means the content of the faith that the Church professes and demands of its members. From the 2nd c. onward, this amounted to the faith confessed by the Christian at Baptism (q.v.). Later, longer formularies were composed by Church councils. Such included the Nicene-Constantinopolitan Creed, still recited by the candidate just prior to Baptism, and the definitions of the Ecumenical Councils (qq.v.).

**LEX ORANDI.** This phrase means the "law of prayer," and is intimately related to the preceding "law of belief." As the ancient formula has it, *lex orandi lex est credendi,* or "As we pray, so we believe". Prayer (q.v.) and belief were seen as absolutely interrelated and mutually supporting from the earliest times. Irenaeus (q.v.) thus argues for the reality of Christ's humanity against gnosticism's phantom with an appeal to the Eucharist (qq.v.): "Our opinion [the real body of Christ] is in accord with the Eucharist, and the Eucharist in turn establishes our opinion" (*Adv.Haer.* IV,18,5). Basil the Great (q.v.) uses the Trinitarian invocation at Baptism as the foundation of his argument for the divinity of the Holy Spirit (q.v.) in his *De Spiritu Sancto.* Augustine of Hippo (q.v.) begins with an appeal to the practice of infant Baptism in his arguments for original sin (q.v.) against Pelagius. Later still, the long-established use of icons in the Church's liturgy (q.v.) will become one of the foundations for the defense of images against iconoclasm led by John of Damascus and Theodore of Studion (qq.v.).

**LIBERTY-FREEDOM.** According to Orthodox Holy Tradition, in particular the Church Fathers (q.v.) of the East, liberty or freedom constitutes one of the inalienable characteristics of the human being. For many of the Fathers, e.g., Origen, Gregory of Nyssa, Maximus the Confessor (qq.v.), freedom is in a sense the very definition of the "image of God" (*imago Dei,* cf. *Gen* 1:26), which raises Adam and his descendants above the animals. This is in contrast to the theories of Augustine of Hippo (q.v.), which prevailed in the West, at least insofar as Augustine believed that human freedom was in a real way lost after the Fall. One can, however, find a genuine change with regard to the understanding of freedom in the Greek Fathers writing after Origen. The latter's equation of freedom with choice, and hence the "neutral" quality of the will, underwent correction at the hands, particularly, of Nyssa and Maximus. For Gregory, and more so for Maximus, freedom as originally intended by the Creator and as restored in Christ, means primarily the uninhibited potential for growth into the divine life or likeness. It is the Fall that forces humanity to "choose" between the (usually) unsatisfactory alternatives offered by a world that has been itself "infected" with sin and death (cf. Rom 5). Christ's victory over these powers and the gift of the Spirit thus constitute the recovery of true human freedom and the renewal of the divine image.

**LITERATURE.** This word has wide application. The Orthodox "library" already includes the Scripture, Church Fathers, liturgical books (qq.v.), writings of ascetics, scriptural commentary, liturgical commentaries, hagiography (q.v.), doctrine, ethics, etc. The Church also inherited the library of classical and Hellenistic Greece and Rome, together with that of the Near East, each of which had its own contributions to make to Holy Tradition (q.v.). Literature in the modern sense, i.e., poetry, prose, theater, etc., is a relatively recent phenomenon in the Orthodox world. To be sure, during the Byzantine era (q.v.) there were examples of a secular literature that included histories, encyclopedias, grammars, philosophy, and epical and lyrical poetry. Save for the first two, the production is of small significance in comparison with the Medieval and Late Medieval West, if only because Byzantium's (q.v.) fall was succeeded by a Dark Age of several centuries.

When one does find literature (in the modern sense) in Orthodox countries, it is one that has developed on the basis of Western European models of the 18th c. and 19th c. Nonetheless, the inheritance of the Church is still discernible. Russia is surely the most important contributor to world literature in Eastern Europe. Its greatest writers, e.g., Pushkin, Chekhov, Gogol (q.v.), Dostoevsky (q.v.), Tolstoy, down to Pasternak, Mandelstam, and Solzhenitsyn in the Soviet period, have been touched by and reflect, to a greater or lesser degree, the great themes of the Orthodox Church's liturgy and (less so) its theology (qq.v.). Over the past century, the main writers of Greece, for example the poets Palamas, Cavafy, Seferis, and Elitis, or the fiction writers Kazantzakis, Papadiamantis, etc., have provided a similar example of inherited cultural-religious values integrated—or sometimes clashing—with the forms and philosophies received from the West.

**LITURGICAL BOOKS.** To celebrate the liturgy (q.v.) of the Orthodox Church requires a library of liturgical books. Orthodoxy has no equivalent to the Roman Catholic missal or the Anglican *Book of Common Prayer*. The library begins with the books of Holy Scripture (q.v.), which are not, except in recent centuries, gathered in one volume, but are instead divided according to their function in the Church's worship. The *Evangelion,* Gospel Book, rests on the altar. In the cleros, or cantor's area, are kept the *Apostolos,* the other New Testament books (save for *Revelation,* never read at worship), and the *Psalterion*

Liturgical Books • 199

(psalter). Texts from the Old Testament, the *paroimiai*—selections chosen for particular feasts—are printed in the *Menaia* and the books of the Easter cycle, i.e., the *Triodion* and *Pentecostarion*.

It may be easiest, in listing the other specifically liturgical books, to begin with the divisions of Orthodox worship: the daily, weekly, monthly, and paschal cycles. The *Book of the Hours* (*Horologion,* in Church Slavic *Chasoslov*) provides the outline and fixed or unchanging parts of the daily offices: Midnight prayer (*mesonyktikon*), Matins (*orthros*), first, third, sixth, ninth hours and the *Typika,* Vespers (*hesperinos*), and Compline (*apodeipnon*). The *Book of Eight Tones* (*Octoechos* [q.v.]) contains the hymns appointed for each day of the week according to an eight-week cycle of melodies, e.g., Monday of the First Tone, Thursday of the Seventh, etc. The twelve *Books of the Months* (*Menaia*) cover each day of the twelve months with the hymns appointed for the saints celebrated that day, or for the different fixed feasts (q.v.) of the year, e.g., Christmas (always on 25 December), Theophany, etc. Two special books are used, in addition to those above, for the paschal cycle, whose dates are not fixed due to Easter's dependence on the lunar calendar. These are the *Book of the Three Odes* (*Triodion*), used for the three Sundays prior to Lent (q.v.) through Saturday of Holy Week, and the *Pentecostarion* for the period from Easter Sunday through the Sunday following Pentecost.

We may also include at this point the twelve volumes (for each month of the year) of the *Synaxarion,* or collection of saints' (q.v.) lives, together with the additional two volumes of hagiography (q.v.) for the days of the paschal cycle. Readings from the *Lives* are appointed for daily Matins. Governing all these books, the guide to their assembly for a particular service, is the *Typicon.* In the Orthodox Church, two typica are presently in use, the older typicon of Mar Sabba (also called the Jerusalem typicon) which is used in the Slav Churches, the Patriarchate of Jerusalem, and Mt. Athos (qq.v.), and the *Typicon of the Great Church,* i.e., Constantinople (q.v.), used by the Greek, Arabic, and Romanian Churches.

The Eucharist (q.v.) and the other sacraments have their own books. The first is traditionally printed in several different books, each appropriate to a different function or rank: the *Archieratikon,* or bishop's missal, the *Ieratikon* (Slav. *Sluzhebnik*) for the priest, the *Diakonikon* for the deacon, and the *Horologion* for the reader or cantor. The other sacraments (q.v.), together with particular services of blessing, are contained in the *Great Euchologion* (Slavic *Trebnik,* or *Book of Needs*). Even such a library is not complete. New services, such as those composed for newly canonized saints, or for saints newly given a service, or new compositions such as variations on the Acathistus Hymn (new *Akafisti* being especially popular among the Russians), are continuously being added. Thus, while an absolutely complete library of Orthodox liturgical books is theoretically possible, it is not likely that such a collection exists in any one place.

**LITURGICAL UTENSILS.** (See Drawing.) 1. The altar table. 2. The antimension or corporal is a consecrated piece of silk or linen cloth signed by the bishop. In it are placed relics of the saints, after the example of the early liturgy served on the tombs of martyrs (qq.v.) in the catacombs. The antimension, having on it the icon (q.v.) of the burial of Jesus and the four Evangelists, is unfolded only for the liturgy. 3. Gospel Book (usually kept over the antimension). 4. Cross. 5. Tabernacle for reserve sacrament for communing the sick. 6. Table of oblation for the preparation of the Holy Gifts. 7. Chalice. 8. The paten or discos for the bread, with a star cover. 9. The spear (i.e., knife) for preparing the bread; and the spoon for administering the sacrament to the faithful.

**LITURGIES.** The Orthodox Church has known many liturgies or "rites" in its history. In the East these have included—and do include among the Oriental Orthodox and Assyrian Churches (qq.v.)—the liturgies of SS. Addai and Mari (East Syria), James (West Syria) of the Armenian, Coptic, Ethiopian, and Indian churches, and in the West the varieties of the Latin rite (q.v.). In contemporary Orthodox use there are two liturgies or texts for the Eucharist: the Liturgy of St. John Chrysostom and of St. Basil the Great (qq.v.). The differences between them, however, are confined largely to their respective texts of the prayers said by the priest from the offertory through the thanksgiving after communion. Chrysostom's is the one more often used, with Basil's being prescribed on ten occasions during the year. In addition, the Liturgy of the Presanctified Gifts (Vespers together with communion from a reserved host) traditionally ascribed to Pope Gregory the Great (d. 610), is prescribed for Wednesdays and Fridays of Lent (q.v.) and the first three days of Holy Week. In recent times there have been attempts to revive the occasional use of other forms of the eucharistic liturgy, including those ascribed to St. James and St. Mark. These efforts have largely been limited to academic circles in Greece, in particular the Theological Faculty of the University of Thessalonica under Professor J. M. Foundoulis.

**LITURGY.** The word "liturgy" in classical Greek means a "common" or "public work." In contemporary Orthodox use it may signify either the Eucharist (q.v.), i.e., the Divine Liturgy, or the entire complex of public worship. Beginning with the former, the eucharistic liturgy is divided into three parts. During the prothesis (or *proskomidia*), the rite

# Liturgy • 201

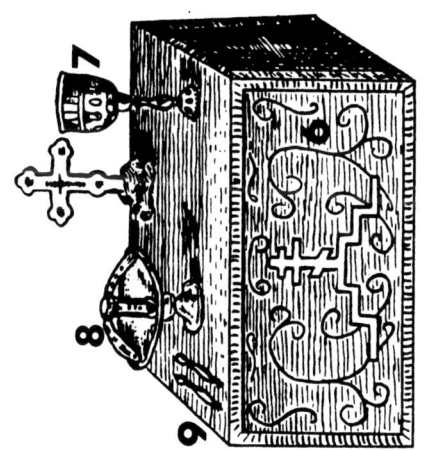

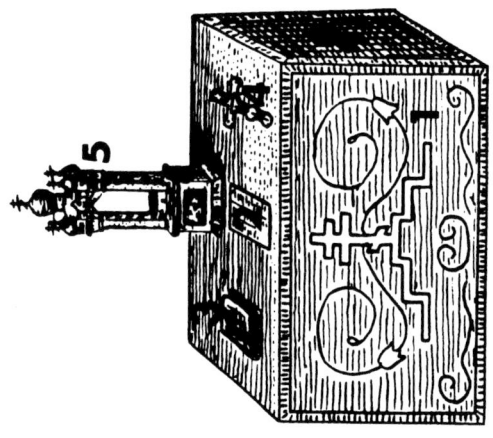

of preparation, the celebrant prepares the leavened bread and wine for the service. This rite recalls Christ's birth and death in the cutting out of the portion intended to serve as the host. The Theotokos, the saints (q.v.), and the living and dead of the community—the entire Church everywhere and always—are recalled by the removal of portions from the prosphoras and their placement on the paten (*diskos*) around the host.

The "liturgy of the catechumens" or synaxis comprises the opening invocation of the Kingdom of God in Trinity (q.v.), the Great Litany (a series of responsorial petitions for the Church and the world), the Antiphons (selections from the Psalms, on great feasts [q.v.] intercalated with hymns particular to the feast, and the Beatitudes), the "Little Entrance" or procession with the Gospel Book, the "Thrice-Holy" or Trisagion hymn, readings from the Epistle and Gospel of the day, the homily, and two closing litanies recalling the specific needs of the community and of the catechumenate (q.v.).

The "liturgy of the faithful" is the Eucharist proper. It includes the prayers preparatory to the offertory, the singing of the cherubic hymn and the "Great Entrance" or solemn transfer of the veiled bread and chalice from the table of preparation to the altar, the litany of supplication, the kiss of peace, the common recital of the Nicene-Constantinopolitan Creed (q.v.), the anaphora or prayers of thanksgiving and remembrance of God's saving acts in Christ (the anamnesis), the epiclesis or invocation of the Holy Spirit (q.v.), which completes the consecration, the commemoration of the living and the dead (the diptychs), a repetition of the litany of supplication, the Lord's Prayer, the fraction of the consecrated bread and its mingling with the chalice followed by an infusion of boiling water (*zeon*), the communion of the celebrant(s) and laity, prayers accompanying a litany of thanksgiving, the "prayer behind the ambo" (the ancient dismissal), the present dismissal, and the distribution of antidoron, the bread left over from the prothesis.

While relatively fixed in form, the eucharistic liturgy will differ somewhat according to the liturgical year, chiefly in the hymns sung during the liturgy of the catechumens, and in the liturgy of the faithful depending upon whether Chrysostom's or Basil's liturgy is prescribed (see Liturgies). Additional differences may derive from the choice of a system of liturgical colors adopted under the influence of the Latin rite, which is particularly the case in Russia (e.g., purple for Lent, red for the Cross and martyrs, etc.), or the presence or absence of a deacon and/or bishop. In the case of the former's presence, the priest's part is limited to the exclamations (*ekphonesies*) concluding each litany and the prayers of consecration, etc. An episcopal celebrant will considerably modify the form of the service in the direction of greater length and formality. The bishop is, however, always theoretically or symbolically present in that no Eucharist is celebrated without an antimension, the cloth that bears his signature and upon which the bread and wine are placed at the Offertory.

The recent influence of liturgical movements in 19th-c. Russia with John of Kronstadt (q.v.) and in 20th-c. attempts to "rediscover" the character of the sacraments as celebrated in the early Church (begun in Roman Catholic [q.v.] circles), together with the influence of the *Kollyvades'* (q.v.) monastic and ascetic renewal, have led several areas of the Orthodox *oikoumene* (q.v.)—e.g., Russia, Greece, and America—to some further modifications: more frequent communion by the laity, the reading aloud of the "secret prayers" of the anaphora and elsewhere, a reduction of the iconostasis (q.v.), a return to the traditional canon of iconography, etc.

Referring now to the offices, the current liturgical practice of the Orthodox Church seems to have taken its more or less present form by the last two centuries of the Byzantine era (q.v.). While it appears that the morning and evening services of the Church (as well as the Eucharist, or at least the synaxis) drew upon the Temple and synagogue liturgies of the first centuries, the public celebration of these offices and of supplementary daily services such as the Hours (Prime, Terce, etc.) is not clearly attested until the 4th c. By that time, however, and particularly in the Church of Jerusalem (*see* Cyril of Jerusalem), one finds the daily cycle and much of the paschal cyle well established. Further developments over the next four centuries resulted in the *Octoechos* (q.v.) and the elaborate commemoration of the saints systematized in the *Menaia* and *Synaxarion*.

The impress of the liturgical year upon the offices, especially Vespers and Matins, is today quite profound. Matins is certainly the most variable. It may be combined with Vespers to form an "All Night Vigil" on the eve of great or patronal feasts (q.v.), especially popular in Russian and Athonite use. It may or may not have a *polyeleos* (lit., "much oil," referring to the lighting of the church's lamps and therefore the festal character of the service), a Gospel reading (proper to Great Feasts and to Sundays, the latter featuring a sequence of twelve Resurrection pericopes) or several Gospels (e.g., the Passion Gospel readings of Good Friday morning). Matins may, further, feature one or more Canons (liturgical poems) and the chanting of one or more of the nine scriptural odes (Old and New Testament hymns beginning with Ex 15). It may feature the great (meaning "sung") or lesser (recited) doxology or hymn of light. It may, finally, be adapted to provide the basis for a number of the services of special needs, e.g., the funeral and memorial services, the prayer services of thanksgiving (*Te Deum* or *Molieben*) and intercession.

Vespers, too, varies with the season, or depending on whether it is the daily or resurrection service (i.e., Saturday night preceding the Sunday Eucharist). The hymns following the singing of Ps 140, "Lord, I have cried," and the *aposticha* (lit., "later verses," i.e., toward the end of the service) vary according to the weekly, monthly, and paschal cycles. The central hymn of the service, the *phos hilaron* ("Joyful Light"), may be accompanied by a solemn procession of clergy carrying incense, or else sung or recited before the closed doors of the iconostasis (q.v.). The other, lesser services of the daily cycle do not vary as much. The Hours feature some additions during Lent (q.v.), e.g., the "Prayer of Ephrem the Syrian" accompanied by prostrations, a reading from the Psalms, and increased repetitions of the Kyrie eleison (q.v.).

**LIVES OF THE SAINTS** *see* Hagiography.

**LIVING CHURCH.** The "Living" or "Renovated Church" was a movement in Russia that profoundly affected church life in the United States during the 1920s and 1930s. When Patriarch Tikhon Belavin (q.v.) had been arrested in Moscow by the Bolsheviks in 1922, a group of clergy with the help of the Communists seized control of the patriarchate (q.v.) and took possession of church valuables, including consecrated liturgical utensils (q.v.). This allowed the Soviets to sell confiscated church artifacts wholesale overseas through entrepeneurs (such as Armand Hammer in the United States) in order to bolster their failing economic policies, a practice that continued for at least fifty years. Correspondingiy, the government gave control of the church administration to dissident priests whom it could manipulate. Theologically, at first the appeal of the Living Church to the progressive-minded was legitimate, coming from its institution of reforms that were discussed at the Russian Councils of 1905 to 1918, but were not initiated for various reasons. Soon they went beyond this to consecrate married clergy to the episcopacy—something not done since the Sixth Ecumenical Council (q.v.)—and grant permission for the remarriage of priests, considered by many to be an uncanonical act.

Although Patriarch Tikhon was supported by the faithful and anathematized the usurpers on his release from prison, continued government support gave the new movement access to church properties. In 1923 a council of the Living Church "deposed" the Patriarch and appointed Fr. John Kedrovsky, a suspended married priest from the North American Russian Diocese, as "Archbishop of North America." Kedrovsky returned to the United States and began litigating for church properties as the "lawful bishop" of the Diocese. Aside from creating confusion as to who the rightful bishop was, Kedrovsky posed a real threat of confiscating 115 parishes in the courts, especially after he successfully gained control of St. Nicholas Cathedral in New York City in 1925. Despite its early successes in Russia, the Living Church soon lost popular support and that of the Communists (1926), disappearing completely during World War II. The only vestige of it that remained was one of its former proponents, Metropolitan Sergius Stragorodsky (1867–1944), who succeeded Patriarch Tikhon in power and adopted a highly controversial collaborationist relationship with the Communists (1927) after they forcibly imprisoned him. It seemed that the Soviets were to win a battle against the Church with Stragorodsky, but not with the passé Living Church strategy.

The situation in the United States was more long-lasting. Kedrovsky's machinations under the guise of pseudo-legality forced the question, "Who is our bishop and what rights should he have?" Parishes moved to protect themselves under the law, because the American legal system is not readily equipped to handle questions regarding hierarchical churches, frequently preferring to focus on individual corporate congregations (i.e., a type of tacit congregationalism). In parishes doing so to protect themselves, they practically abolished the role of the bishop in the Russian Orthodox churches in North America: They permanently changed ecclesiology (q.v.) to the present. The authority (q.v.) that bishops previously exercised in building the North American missionary diocese—holding title to property, assigning clergy, checking the parishes' financial statements and minutes, approving parish elections, paying salaries, settling disputes, etc.—was revoked for good bishops as well as bad ones. The revocation was almost complete, not to be reinstated even at present.

**LOGOS.** A word of great resonance in biblical and patristic Greek, logos can mean any or all of the following: reason, word, rational(ity), speech, discourse, argument, divine will, or the second person of the Trinity (q.v.). Its most famous use is the opening of the Gospel of John: "In the beginning was the Word (1:1) . . . by whom all things were made (1:4) . . . and the Word became flesh (1:14)". This text, emphasized particularly by Church Fathers such as Ignatius of Antioch, Justin Martyr, Irenaeus, Origen, Athanasius, Cyril of Alexandria, and Maximus the Confessor (qq.v.), signaled at once the divine preexistence of Christ and his intimate involvement with the creation and re-creation (or redemption) of the world. The term thus includes a revelation fundamental to theology, Christology, cosmology (qq.v.), and—since the "words" (*logoi*) of God are gathered in his living Word—to Scripture (q.v.) as well. Maximus the Confessor therefore wrote that Christ's Incarnation constitutes the fulfillment of what is already implicit in the creation of the world and explicit in the Old Testament revelation. The cosmos is sustained by the divine wills (*logoi*) addressed to each created thing and by the words of the Word present in the Scriptures (q.v.).

**LORD'S PRAYER** *see* Nicene-Constantinopolitan Creed.

**LORD'S SUPPER** *see* Eucharist.

**LOSSKY, NICHOLAS O.**, Russian philosopher, theologian, educator (6 December 1870–January 1965). He studied at the Imperial University of St. Petersburg and was professor of philosophy there until 1921. He was expelled from Russia by the Soviet government in 1922, whereupon he lived and taught philosophy in Prague until 1942. From 1942 to 1945 he was philosophy professor at Bratislava University in Czechoslovakia. He was professor of philosophy at St. Vladimir's Orthodox Theological Seminary (q.v.) from 1948 and is the author of the first history of Russian philosophy to appear in English, *A History of Russian Philosophy* (1957). His own epistemological theory is called intuitivism and may be compared with Bergson's. In his theological formulations, Lossky accepts the sophiology of Russian religious thinkers, but in a greatly modified form. He occupies himself with the Kingdom of God in his aesthetics (q.v.) and ethics, but is especially concerned with the task of working out a Christian metaphysics and interpretation of the world. His major works in English include *The Foundations of Intuitism* (1906), *The World as an Organic Whole* (1928), *Value and Existence: God and the Kingdom of God as the Basis of Values* (1931), *Sensuores, Intellectual and Mystical Intuition* (1938), and *God and World Evil* (1941), among others.

**LOSSKY, NICOLAS V.**, theologian, ecumenist. Born in Paris (the son of Vladimir Lossky [q.v.]), he is professor at the University of Paris X-Nanterre and at St. Sergius Orthodox Theological Institute (q.v.). As with his father, he is associated with the Moscow Patriarchate. He is a member of the World Council of Churches Plenary Commission on Faith and Order and served as a delegate for the Russian Orthodox Church at the 7th WCC Assembly at Canberra. He is the author of *Lancelot Andrewes the Preacher (1555–1626): The Origins of the Mystical Theology of the Church of England* (trans. 1991) and an editor of and contributor to the *Dictionary of the Ecumenical Movement* (1991).

**LOSSKY, VLADIMIR N.**, Russian Orthodox lay theologian, philosopher, ecumenist, educator (26 May 1903–7 February 1958). From 1919 he studied at Petrograd University where he was influenced by

L. Karsavine's concern for patristics and the *filioque* (qq.v.) debate. In 1922 he was expelled from Russia to reside in Prague and participate in N. Kondakov's seminars, which deepened his interest in patristics. In 1924 he settled in Paris, where he remained for the rest of his life. He was a friend and disciple of Etienne Gilson, and also enjoyed the friendship of a number of important Roman Catholic theologians, including J. Danielou, H. de Lubac, Y. Congar, and L. Bouyer. After World War II he taught dogmatic theology at St. Denys Institute of Orthodox Theology, Paris, and played a crucial role in the ecumenical encounters in the Fellowship of St. Alban and St. Sergius (q.v.). He studied medieval philosophy at the Sorbonne and, at the time of his death, was in the process of completing a book on apophatic theology and the knowledge of God in Meister Eckhart (completed by O. Clement and published in French, 1960). He is the author of the influential book *The Mystical Theology of the Eastern Church* (1957), which is of the type of "neopatristic synthesis" described by Georges Florovsky (q.v.).

**LOT-BORODINE, MYRRHA,** lay theologian (21 January 1882–18 July 1957). While in St. Petersburg she studied ancient Greek religion and French literature of the Middle Ages. From 1900 to 1906 she was involved in the effort to reconcile Russian intellectuals with the Orthodox Church. She left Russia permanently in 1906 to settle in Paris where she obtained a doctorate and married the historian Ferdinand Lot. From 1925 on she was associated with the interconfessional activities of N. Berdiaev, while studying with J. Lebreton and E. Gilson and maintaining contact with the Cistercian, Benedictine, and Dominican Orders. Her special interests at this time were love in the Middle Ages, the myth of the Holy Grail, Cistercian spirituality, and the Virgin Mary (q.v.).

The focus of her life's work changed when in 1930 she attended a talk by Georges Florovsky on *theosis* (qq.v.) in the Greek Orient. In 1936 she wrote an article castigating Russian nationalist religion and proposed the concept, influenced by Vladimir Lossky (q.v.), of universal Orthodoxy. Until her death she was an avid proponent of Orthodox involvement in the ecumenical movement (q.v.). She was especially influenced by Lossky's thinking, which led her to examine Gregory Palamas's (q.v.) doctrine of uncreated energies and the mystical thought of other Byzantine theologians, especially Nicholas Cabasilas (q.v.). She is the author of *La Déification de l'homme, selon la doctrine des Pères grecs* (1970) and *Un Maître de la spiritualité byzantine au XIVe siècle, Nicolas Cabasilas* (1958).

**LOVE.** According to 1 Jn 4:8, "God is love." The love of God (q.v.) is at the heart of the inner life of the Trinity (q.v.) and of the actions taken on humanity's behalf—hence God is entitled the *philanthropos* (lover of humanity). The Greek word used in the text from John is *agape*, "charity." The Church Fathers (q.v.) also employed another word, *eros*, which in classical Greek use primarily signified sexual longing. While bold, the Fathers' use is hardly at variance with the New Testament as some circles (Protestant) have maintained. Eros is primarily used in connection with created existence to denote the longing for God implanted in every creature, especially in the human person. Indeed, *eros* is seen as constitutive of created being as such. The Fathers, beginning particularly with Gregory of Nyssa and continuing with Dionysius the Areopagite and Maximus the Confessor (qq.v.), did not hesitate to ascribe *eros* to God himself. The Creator "yearns" to share himself, hence he creates, preserves, saves, and ultimately will draw all he has made into communion with the love that is his being.

**LUKARIS, CYRIL,** Patriarch of Constantinople (1572–1638). One of the most interesting and tragic figures in the history of the Greek Church since 1453, and on several different occasions Ecumenical Patriarch (q.v.) and Patriarch of Alexandria, Cyril reflects the chaotic and corrupt atmosphere surrounding the higher clergy during the Ottoman Empire (q.v.). A man of singular intellectual abilities and remarkable character, his career followed the usual trajectory of a gifted churchman in the Ottoman era. He was educated in Italy, which at that time meant a temporary conversion to Roman Catholicism (q.v.). He worked teaching and translating in the "Greek school" of the notable "Ostrog Circle," which was famous for its translation of the Bible into Church Slavic.

Cyril as a young deacon became embittered with the papacy (q.v.) due to his participation at the Council of Brest-Litovsk in 1596, which created the Uniate Church (q.v.) of the then Polish-Lithuanian state. It was also in Poland that he was likely to have first come into serious contact with Calvinist thought, due to the alliance between Orthodox and other religious dissenters in a country whose king, Sigismund III, was deeply impressed by the militancy of the Counter-Reformation. The contact was continued and deepened through the Dutch Embassy at Constantinople, and it culminated in a *Confession of Faith* published by Patriarch Cyril in Geneva in 1629.

The *Confession* (here, a statement of religious belief) clearly set forth Calvinist theology, including the denial of free will, the doctrine of predestination, the limiting of the sacraments (q.v.) to two, and a negative view of icons (q.v.). The resulting scandal contributed to intrigues against Cyril and resulted in his murder in 1638. More positively, the *Confession* drew responses from both Metropolitan Peter Mogila in Kiev in 1640 and from Dositheus (qq.v.), Patriarch of

Jerusalem. Mogila's own *Confession* was approved, with some editing, at the Synod of Jassy in 1642. Dositheus also wrote his own *Confession*, refuting Cyril point by point, which was approved by the Synod of Bethlehem in 1672. In early and recent literature on Cyril the question has been repeatedly raised whether he really believed the content of the *Confession*, since it does not comport with his sermons and other writings. The position has been advanced that he wrote the *Confession* primarily to muster Western military support against Rome and/or the Turks.

**LYCIA.** A region of Asia Minor (q.v.) in what is now southwest Turkey, near the ancient city of Ephesus (qq.v.), and site of a Hellenistic kingdom in centuries just prior to Christ, later incorporated into the Roman Empire (q.v.). The region was early evangelized by the apostle Paul, and its capital from the 4th c., Myra, was the see of the bishop, Nicholas.

**LYONS.** Today the third largest city in France, located on the Rhône River about 100 miles north of the Mediterranean Sea, during the Roman Empire (q.v.), it was the capital of the province of southern Gaul and site from A.D. 150 of a colony of predominantly Greek-speaking Christians, probably from Asia Minor (q.v.). Subjected to a fierce local persecution in 177, the community survived and, in the 180s and early 190s, was episcopally governed by one of the greatest of the early Church Fathers, Irenaeus (qq.v.). The latter made explicit reference to his own origins in Asia Minor as a disciple of the martyr-bishop, Polycarp of Smyrna (q.v.), a disciple—according to (Eusebius's) Irenaeus—of the evangelist and apostle John.

**-M-**

**MACARIAN HOMILIES.** A collection of sermons and discourses still in the process of discovery and editing, this corpus was early ascribed to Macarius the Great (q.v.) of Egypt, but it appears in fact to be the work of an author writing from northern Syria (qq.v.) sometime in the late 4th c. One collection of fifty of the homilies circulated for centuries in both the Latin West and Greek East, and exercised profound influence on writers in the later Byzantine era, notably Symeon the New Theologian and Gregory Palamas (qq.v.). Underlining themes that are particularly prominent in the tradition of the Syriac-speaking Church, the homilies stress the gift of *theosis* (qq.v.) as personal experience and light, and emphasize the heart as the place of encounter with Christ in the Holy Spirit (q.v.). The heart is compared to the mountains of revelation, Sinai and Tabor, and to the altar of the Church. The use "Homily

I" makes of the vision of Ezekiel (ch. 1) has a long, subsequent history in both Byzantine worship and ascetic literature.

**MACARIUS, METROPOLITAN OF MOSCOW** *see* Bulgakov, Makarii.

**MACARIUS THE GREAT,** monk, ascetic, St. (ca. 300–ca. 390). He is one of the first of the Desert Fathers (q.v.) of Egypt and founder of the monastic settlement of Scete during the 340s in the desert of Nitria (Wadi-el-Natrun) some fifty miles south of Alexandria (qq.v.). Macarius's foundation, still inhabited today by several monasteries of Coptic (q.v.) monks, was in its origins a kind of midway point between the eremitic life of Antony and the communal organizations of Pachomius (qq.v.). The monks lived apart in separate huts, cells (*kellia*), but would gather at Scete's central church on Saturday night for all-night vigil and Divine Liturgy (q.v.). This pattern is followed today in a number of monastic settlements in the Orthodox world, notably on Mt. Athos (q.v.). Macarius himself emerges in the tradition as an ascetic of extraordinary austerity and remarkable charismatic gifts for which he is given the epithet "the Great." His presence looms large in the various collections about the early monks, for example the *Lives of the Desert Fathers* and the *Sayings of the Fathers*, and in the histories and anecdotes recorded by such as Jerome, Rufinus, and Palladius (see Lausiac History). Evagrius of Pontus (q.v.) is said to have revered him.

**MACEDONIA.** Today the ancient territory of Macedonia is divided between Greece and the former Yugoslav Republic of that name. Its southern (today Greek) regions were evangelized by the apostle Paul, notably Philippi (near modern Kavala) and Thessalonica (q.v.). Its northern parts, particularly the city of Ochrid, provided the base for one of the earliest of the Slav Orthodox rulers, the 10th c. Tsar Samuel, and a center for the translation of Greek liturgical and patristic texts into Church Slavic. Constantine-Cyril and Methodius (qq.v.) were themselves from Thessalonica, and it is from the southern Macedonian dialect that they created the first written language of the Slavs. Incorporated into the Ottoman Empire (q.v.) during the course of the 14th c., Macedonia became an arena of competing nationalities during the 1800s in particular. Greeks, Bulgarians, and Serbians all laid claim to it; and this is not to count the Albanians, Romanians (Vlachs), and Turks who also lived there. The Balkan Wars concluding in 1912 were fought over it, with Greece and Serbia dividing up the lion's share. Under Tito's dictatorship, the Orthodox in Macedonia, as an expression of the local nationalisms fostered by the regime, were encouraged to set up the "Macedonian Orthodox Church" and sever relations with the Serbian Church (q.v.). Both the national and ecclesiastical future of this republic continue to be, as of this writing, highly uncertain.

**MAKARII, METROPOLITAN OF MOSCOW** *see* Bulgakov, Makarii; Muscovite Christianity.

**MAKARIOS III (MOUSKOS)**, Archbishop of Cyprus *see* Mouskos, Makarios.

**MAKRAKIS, APOSTOLOS,** Greek layman, religious polemicist (1831–1905). Makrakis enjoyed a stormy career as the advocate of "true Christian philosophy," of sacramental rigorism including complete immersion at Baptism (q.v.), and of a ferocious antipapalism. His voluminous, if somewhat eccentric, commentaries on the collection of Canon Law (q.v.) known as the *Rudder (Pedalion)*, originally compiled by Nicodemus of the Holy Mountain (q.v.), can be read today in an English translation published by his American admirers. His fierce attacks on the ecclesiastical hierarchy of Greece led to his excommunication in 1878. Although never again reinstated in the Church, Makrakis continued to influence like-minded rigorists throughout his life and afterward.

**MALABAR CHRISTIANS** *see* Mar Thoma Church.

**MAN/MEN** *see* Anthropology; Saints.

**MAR THOMA CHURCH.** This ancient church of India (q.v.) was founded according to local tradition by the Apostle Thomas, hence the name. Whether one accepts its apostolic origins or not, it is a certainty that this Christian community in southern India is of ancient provenance. Its liturgical language was, and largely remains, Syriac. Its earliest connections were with the Assyrian (Nestorian) Church (qq.v.) of the Persian Empire. Portuguese colonization in the 16th c. enforced Latinization and led to the Synod of Diamper (1599) and the complete suppression of the local tradition, including the burning of the ancient books on suspicion of heresy (q.v.). Three generations later (1665) a popular revolt against Portuguese dominance led to a substantial minority's reconnection with Syria, though this time with the "monophysite" Church of Antioch (qq.v.). Further schisms in the 19th c. and 20th c. saw the reestablishment of a small Nestorian community of Indian Christians, renewed as lately as 1952. The number of Indian Orthodox, as the local non-Chalcedonian church is called, is estimated at one and a half million.

**MARIOLOGY.** The veneration of the Virgin Mary is as old, at least, as the Gospel of Lk. Her importance in the economy (q.v.) of God's salvation is underlined in the mid–2nd c. by Justin Martyr and at century's end again by Irenaeus of Lyons (qq.v.), as well as in the Protoevangel of James (ca. 150). Both Justin and Irenaeus point to her as the "new Eve" through whom the catastrophe of the Fall begins to be reversed. She is the center of attention particularly as the result of the debate sparked by Nestorius (q.v.) in the 420s, who refused to accord her the title, just then come into popular use, of Theotokos (Birth-giver of God). Nestorius was vigorously opposed by Cyril of Alexandria whose views prevailed at the Third Ecumenical Council at Ephesus (qq.v.) in 431. One must note, however, that her importance then and afterward has never been emphasized in isolation from her relation to Jesus Christ, her Son, the incarnate Word. Yet, as John of Damascus (q.v.) pointed out—echoing the theme explicit in Lk 2, Justin, and Irenaeus—the Word could not have taken on humanity in her had it not been for her cooperation. Mary's "yes" to the divine will becomes thus the pivot of the world's salvation, and her obedience and reception the model for all of humanity's response to God's initiative.

Orthodox Holy Tradition sees her in consequence as the pinnacle of created being, the living Temple and altar of the Presence, and a sharer in her Son and God's (q.v.) providential love. Perhaps the most eloquent expression of Orthodox devotion and theology (q.v.) regarding Mary is the Acathistus Hymn, traditionally ascribed to Patriarch Sergius of Constantinople in the early 6th c. and sung today in all Orthodox churches on the fifth Friday in Lent (q.v.). Her virginity, which the Church understands as never having been lost, is signified in traditional iconography (q.v.) by the three stars adorning her hood and right and left shoulders. As virgin and living sanctuary, she is particularly beloved by the monastics, who see in her the paradigm of their own vocation. As mother and tenderhearted intercessor, she is venerated by all Orthodox believers. (*See* Feasts, Twelve Great; Icons of the Theotokos.)

**MARK OF EPHESUS,** bishop, St. (ca. 1392–1445). Metropolitan of Ephesus from 1437 to 1445, Mark was one of the large contingent of Greek bishops at the Reunion Council (q.v.) of Ferrara-Florence in 1438 to 1439. He was the most outspoken defender of the Greek patristic (q.v.) tradition at the council's long debates over the *filioque* (q.v.), and his particular claim to fame and veneration lies in the fact that he was the sole participant, still present at the council's end (a number had left beforehand), who refused to sign his approval of the final decree of union. Deprived of his episcopate, though not otherwise persecuted, he spent his remaining years at Constantinople (q.v.) leading the opposition to the union. Toward the end of his life he won over George Scholarios to his views and tonsured him, with the name Gennadios (q.v.), while he lay dying. Gennadios would go on to become the first Ecumenical Patriarch (q.v.) following the city's fall to Sultan Mohammed II in 1453. Mark was afterward (1456) canonized and is commemorated today, together with Photius of Constantinople and Gregory Palamas (qq.v.), as one of the "pillars of Orthodoxy."

**MARONITES.** Until this century the Maronites remained a tribe largely confined to its traditional territories in the mountains north and west of Beirut, which traces its origins back to St. Maron in the 5th c. and his disciples' monastery on the Orontes River. Their history goes back at least to the monothelite controversy (*see* Christology) in the 7th c. In 1182, at the urging of the Crusader (q.v.) barons and clergy, they accepted submission to the papacy (q.v.). Theirs is the one Uniate (q.v.) Eastern Church that accepted this status en masse. Their liturgy (q.v.), of western Syrian type, has progressively taken on a more Latin appearance over the centuries until, with the acceptance of the vernacular at Vatican II, it is (at least externally) virtually indistinguishable from the Latin rite (q.v.). Their spirituality and organization, however, continue to retain something of their Eastern origins. Of note, as a result of the 19th-c. massacre of the Maronites by the Druses, the French Government carved the modern state of Lebanon out of West Syria (q.v.). This occurred during the period of the Mandate between the World Wars, both for the sake of the Maronites and so that the French could retain a foothold in the northeast.

**MARRIAGE** *see* Sacraments.

**MARTIN I,** Pope of Rome, St. (?–655). Pope from 649 to 653, Martin convened the Lateran Synod of 649 at the urging of Maximus the Confessor (qq.v.) in order to condemn the Monothelite Formula sponsored by the Emperors Heraclius and Constans II. In consequence of the Pope's opposition, Constans had both him and Maximus brought to Constantinople (q.v.) where they were imprisoned, tried, and condemned to exile for treason. Martin was the last of the popes to be so treated by Byzantium (q.v.), and his example was surely in the mind of Pope Stephen II, facing the Isaurian Dynasty (q.v.), when he made his decision for the Franks a century later (*see* Carolingians). Martin died a martyr (q.v.) in exile in the Crimea in 655, anticipating Maximus's fate by seven years.

**MARTYR.** The word means "witness" in its legal sense, as in the witnesses sworn in at a court of law. In Acts the word is used of the apostles (q.v.) as witnesses of Christ's ministry and Resurrection. Soon afterward, with the spread of persecution of Christians, the martyr became identified as one who bears testimony to Christ's victory over death through the sacrifice of his or her own life. In the letters of Ignatius of Antioch (q.v.), particularly his "Epistle to the Romans," one finds a certain identification of the martyr's sufferings with the passion of Jesus Christ in imagery, which further recalls that of the Eucharist (q.v.). The martyrdom of one of Ignatius's correspondents, Polycarp of Smyrna (q.v.), became the paradigmatic account of a martyr's death and model for the many that would follow. This document, too, makes heavy use of imagery from the Gospel accounts of the Passion, and Polycarp's prayer before his death bears striking resemblance to the eucharistic anaphora. Polycarp's "Life" also provides the first witness to the cult of the martyr. The saint's community gathers yearly on the anniversary of his "birthday" (i.e., into the Kingdom of Heaven) around the place where his relics are interred.

Martyrs became the earliest heroes of the Church, to be followed on the cessation of state persecution with the conversion of Constantine, by the "bloodless martyrdom" of monasticism (qq.v.). Traditionally, martyrdom for the faith is automatic grounds for inclusion in the diptychs, recognition of saintliness—without any formal canonization process. The 20th c., especially in Soviet Russia, has given ample evidence that martyrdom is not an obsolete possibility. The Greeks, together with other Orthodox nations of the Balkans (qq.v.), have their "new martyrs" of the Turkish era.

**MARY** *see* Mariology.

**MARY OF EGYPT,** ascetic, St. (5th c.). The (later) penitential "Life" of Mary of Egypt is read on the fifth Thursday of Great Lent (q.v.), and the last Sunday of the same fast is dedicated to her. According to the earlier "Life" by Cyril of Scythopolis (the biographer of Sabas [q.v.]), she was a woman who left Jerusalem to spend eighteen years repenting in the Judaean wilderness. In the later "Life," probably composed by Sophronius of Jerusalem in the 7th c., she became an Alexandrian courtesan who traveled the world in search of new pleasures and then repented while going to Jerusalem. She spent the remaining thirty years of her life in extreme asceticism (q.v.) alone in the desert. Discovered by the priestmonk Zosima (q.v.), she confided her life's story and received the *viaticum*. This second story in particular caught the imagination of the faithful, and Mary has ever since been held up by the Church as a powerful image of repentance (q.v.).

**MATSIEVICH, ARSENII,** Metropolitan of Rostov (1697–1772). Best known for being subjected to Russian imperial persecution in an

"Enlightened Age," his confinement began after he anathematized Catherine the Great for depriving the monasteries of their property rights (1763). He was then deprived of his metropolitanate, reduced to being a monk, and cloistered in a monastery, though he did not stop railing against Catherine there. After four years he was tried and convicted a second time, not as a cleric, but as a political prisoner under the name "Andrei Vral'"—which is not a name at all, but means "Andrew the Liar." Following the second trial he was "shut up" in the prison in Reval (Tallin), that is to say, not only was he physically incarcerated, but his mouth was gagged. According to Canon Law—not to mention humane justice—both the trials and penalties were highly irregular.

**MATTA AL-MISKIN,** monk, spiritual writer (1919– ). At the ancient monastery of Deir el Makarios in a desert wilderness 50 miles southwest of Cairo, a Coptic monk is causing a mild stir, drawing as many as 500 visitors a day. Matta al-Meskin, or Matthew the Poor, like the great anchorite Antony the Great (q.v.), was once a wealthy young pharmacist. At the age of twenty-nine, heeding Jesus' admonition to "sell what you have," he disposed of his houses, cars, and pharmacies, gave the proceeds to the poor, and devoted himself to prayer and asceticism (q.v.), keeping only a cloak for himself. He was once very much of this world, and now is out of it. From his cell, living mainly on bread and water, he has written more than forty books and pamphlets. Most of these books are scholarly works on church affairs, but one collection of spiritual writings is available in English, *The Communion of Love* (1984). He has participated in a reformation of Coptic (q.v.) monastic life so profound that he directed the total rehabilitation of his monastery and was one of three nominees to be Coptic pope in the 1971 election.

**MATTHEW THE POOR** *see* Matta al-Miskin.

**MAXIMUS THE CONFESSOR,** monk, theologian, St. (580–662). Maximus is arguably the greatest of Byzantine theologians and was also a writer on exegesis, liturgy (q.v.), doctrine, and ascesis (q.v.). Trained for court service in Constantinople (q.v.), where he served until ca. 614 as Imperial Secretary to Emperor Heraclius, he left the capital in his early thirties for the monastic life. Never ordained, he spent years in several different monasteries, including on Cyprus where he became acquainted with Sophronius (later Patriarch of Jerusalem), who seems to have introduced him to ascetic literature. He arrived finally in Byzantine North Africa in 626. From there, and later from Rome, he led the battle against the Monothelite Formula (*see* Christology) proposed by Heraclius as a device for ending the schism over the Council of Chalcedon (qq.v.). His activities peaked with the convocation of the Lateran

Synod by Pope Martin I (qq.v.) at Rome in 649. Arrested together with the pope, Maximus paid for his opposition with torture and death in exile in 662, as Martin had earlier.

His theology, a synthesis of real genius and spiritual depth, prevailed nineteen years later at the Sixth Ecumenical Council (q.v.) at Constantinople. It combined the insights of the ascetic tradition with the triadology and anthropology of the Cappadocians, the Christologies of Cyril of Alexandria and Leo of Rome with that of Justinian and the Fifth Ecumenical Council, and the thought of late Neoplatonism through Dionysius the Areopagite (qq.v.). Its heart lay in the defense of created freedom (q.v.) and change (*kinesis*) as positive, and the vision of Christ as the one in whom that freedom and growth are accomplished. Created freedom was fulfilled once and for all in the economy (q.v.) of the Incarnate Word, and now and to come in the appropriation of Christ—which appropriation is the human vocation and glory. His thought provided a later basis for the defense of the holy icons by John of Damascus, for the fiery advocacy of mystical experience by Symeon the New Theologian, and of deification as real and presently available by Gregory Palamas at the close of the Byzantine era (qq.v.). Due to the difficulty of the Greek, most of his writings—other than the *Centuries on Charity*—are not available in English.

**MEDICINE.** Use of medical texts of antiquity by the Church Fathers (q.v.), especially Galen, and its influence on their thinking, has been recognized only recently. Certainly, the image of Christ as "physician of souls and bodies" is very ancient, as is the description of spiritual counsel and repentance in language drawn from the practice of medicine. Thus, John Climacus and Symeon the New Theologian (qq.v.), for example, will speak of repentance and confession (q.v.) as the medicine of the soul and of the work of the spiritual father (q.v.) as equivalent to that of a physician.

The practice of medicine in the Byzantine era (q.v.) was dependent on the ancients, though not without additions on the basis of experience. Nowhere else in the medieval Christian world does one find medical competence on the level of Byzantium's (q.v.). Popular medicine, however, included generous doses of magic, to which professional physicians were not immune either, and hence comes under occasional Church scrutiny and censure throughout the period. (*See* Healing.)

**MEETING OF THE LORD** *see* Feasts, Twelve Great.

**MELCHITES.** This term is drawn from the Semitic root for king (*melek* in Hebrew, *malkah* in Syriac) and was used orginally to refer to those in Syria, Palestine, and Egypt who remained faithful to the imperial church after the Council of Chalcedon (q.v.) in 451. They were thus "king's men," i.e., of the emperor's party. More recently, following the schism in the Orthodox Church of Antioch (qq.v.), which saw a large group of Orthodox Arabs enter into union with the papacy (q.v.) in 1724, the term has been used exclusively to refer to the latter, Uniate (q.v.) group. At present the "Melchite" Church is approximately the size of its Orthodox counterpart, is headquartered in Damascus (q.v.), and maintains a parallel hierarchy throughout the Near East. The witness of its late patriarch, Maximus IV (Saigh), at the Second Vatican Council was generally applauded by the Orthodox. Of all the "Uniate" bodies, this one retains most of its original Orthodox identity.

**MELITO,** Bishop of Sardis, St. (?-ca. 190). Aside from one surviving sermon, the *Homily on Easter,* his works are known only through other writers, such as Eusebius of Caesarea (q.v.). Of his life we know only that he was a prolific writer and he made a pilgrimage (q.v.) to the holy places of Palestine. The poetic homily, possibly a hymn, which was discovered in 1940, provides a glimpse into a theology and exegesis similar to those of Justin Martyr, Irenaeus, and Tertullian (qq.v.): the history of salvation centers on Christ, described as "by nature God and man," as the pivot between the old covenant and the new. Thus, Melito applied a thoroughly typological reading to the texts of the Old Testament.

**MEN, ALEXANDER,** priest, martyr (1935–9 September 1990). Born of a Jewish family, Alexander and his mother were baptized Christians in the Russian Orthodox Church when he was seven months old. Both mother and child were raised in the "catacomb church." According to his older brother Pavel, Alexander wanted to be a priest from age twelve. Ordained to the diaconate in 1958, he completed his studies at the Leningrad Theological Seminary as an external student over two years. In 1960 he was ordained priest with the blessings of his spiritual father (q.v.), the priest N. Golubtsov. He then served the church in the village of Alabino, and later in the village of Tarasovka. From 1964 to 1968 he studied at the Moscow Theological Academy, from which time until his death he was rector of the Church of the Meeting of the Lord in Novaia Derevnia between Moscow and Zagorsk. In his final years he became very popular as a speaker, teacher, writer, and television figure. A selection of his sermons is available in *Awake to Life!: Easter Cycle* (trans. 1992). There is a lengthy Festschrift (1,031 p.) with essays in English, French, and German dedicated to his memory: *Kirchen im Kontext unterschiedlicher*

*Kulturen: Auf dem Weg ins dritte Jahrtausend; Aleksandr Men in memoriam (1935–1990)* (1991). He was murdered by cowardly fanatics on his way to serve Divine Liturgy near Moscow.

**MESOPOTAMIA.** Christianity in Mesopotamia, i.e., from northern Syria (q.v.) through present-day Iraq, has an ancient history that dates to the 2nd c., if not before. Its language was Syriac, a variant of Aramaic, and its literature begins to appear with the *Odes of Solomon* in the 2nd c., as well as in other apocryphal works. Mesopotamian Christianity flowers with Aphraat of Persia and Ephrem of Syria in the 4th c. Throughout this early period it is almost purely Semitic in character, i.e., little influenced by the currents of Greek philosophy (q.v.) affecting the Mediterranean shoreline, and in consequence has begun to be appreciated as an invaluable witness to a continuity of thought from the era of the New Testament. Orthodox Christianity owes more than is realized to this region: Its liturgical hymnody has its roots here, as does much of its language of mystical experience, including the image of the light of Mt. Tabor so central to later Byzantine hesychasm.

**MESROP MASTOC,** Patriarch of Armenia, linguist, missionary, St. (ca. 350–440). Mesrop, interested in Armenian culture and history as distinct from that of Syria (q.v.), is credited with the invention of the Armenian alphabet, which was adopted in 406. He is probably the most formative figure in the early history of the Armenian Orthodox Church after Gregory the Illuminator (qq.v.). Having become a monk after serving in the court of King Vram-Shapuh, he turned to missionary labors in mid-life. He is reported as having composed a script for the Armenian language while in northern Syria, basing the alphabet on Greek characters. Armenian tradition also ascribes to him the creation of the Georgian alphabet. He is personally credited with translating the New Testament and Proverbs into Armenian, and assisted in the whole Armenian Bible project of ca. 410 along with its revision in ca. 433. He was vicar bishop to Patriarch Sahak and succeeded him in office in 440, but died soon afterward.

**MESSALIANISM.** The word comes from the Syriac word for prayer (q.v.); the *mesalanye* thus are "those who pray." In Greek the same people were known as "euchites" (*euche,* prayer). The origins, exact teachings, and individuals who made up this ascetic movement in the late 4th c. and early 5th c. remain matters of scholarly debate. In extreme form, Messalianism appears to have been Syrian in origin and ascetic in orientation, so much the latter that the normal institutions of the church—especially the hierarchy and sacraments (q.v.)—were disdained.

The *Macarian Homilies* (q.v.) have often been linked with the Messalians. In fact, true Messalian extremists appear to have been rare, and "Macarius" was more anti-Messalian than anything else. The most recent studies indicate that what many Greek bishops of the 4th c. and 5th c. labeled as "heretical" were motifs and idioms native and long traditional to Syriac-speaking Christianity. While it is doubtless true that the *Macarian Homilies* were for a time caught in the crossfire of this miscommunication, it is also the case that they were quickly and enthusiastically received in ascetic circles in the Greek East and ultimately in the Latin West. No less than John Wesley was one of their devotees. We would add that, if "Macarius" was Messalian, then so were Symeon the New Theologian, Gregory Palamas (qq.v.), and indeed most of the great saints and writers in the continuum of Orthodox spirituality (q.v.).

**METHODIUS,** apostle to the Slavs, bishop, linguist, St. (ca. 815–885). Brother and co-worker of Constantine-Cyril (q.v.) from a Thessalonian aristocratic family, Methodius left his work in the imperial government for the monastic life on Mt. Olympus in Bithynia around 850. Chosen from the monastery by Emperor Michael III, he was sent together with his brother to the mission in Moravia (q.v.). After Constantine-Cyril's death in Rome in 867 and Methodius's consecration as bishop by Pope Hadrian II in 869, he carried on the project of translation and building up of a native clergy. The death of his royal patron, Prince Rostislav, and the resentment of the German clergy already in the region forced his withdrawal into the territories of modern Croatia (q.v.) by the end of his life. Methodius's death thus saw the apparent overthrow of his life's work. His disciples Naum and Clement of Ochrid (qq.v.) brought the fruits of the missionary brothers' linguistic labors to the southern Slav kingdoms of Bulgaria and Serbia and thence, a century later, to Kievan Rus' (q.v.). Much of the early translation work of Scripture and Byzantine liturgical books (qq.v.) might have been completed by Methodius himself or under his direct supervision. He seems to have also been the author of his brother's *Life*.

**MEYENDORFF, JOHN,** priest, theologian, educator, ecumenist (1926– 22 July 1992). After attending French secondary schools in 1948 he obtained his licence-ès-lettres at the Sorbonne, followed by a diplôme d'études supérieures in 1949, a diplôme de l'école pratique des hautes études in 1954, and a doctorat-ès-lettres in 1958. He completed his theological training at St. Sergius Orthodox Theological Institute (q.v.) in 1949.

In 1959 he relocated to the United States to teach at St. Vladimir's Orthodox Theological Seminary (q.v.), New York, after ordination to the priesthood. He was dean of the Seminary from 1984 until his retirement in June 1992. From 1967 to 1975 he was a moderator of the World Council of Churches Faith and Order Commission. From 1967 to 1992 he was professor of Byzantine studies at Fordham University, and from 1977 to 1978 he was acting director of studies at Harvard's Dumbarton Oaks—where he also held the position of lecturer in Byzantine theology for many years. He was editor of "The Orthodox Church" newspaper and *St. Vladimir's Seminary Quarterly* for two decades before his deanship at St. Vladimir's, and his scholarly publications include *A Study of Gregory Palamas* (1959), *Christ in Eastern Christian Thought* (1969), and *Byzantine Theology* (1973), among many other excellent works. He received honorary doctorates from the University of Notre Dame and General Theological Seminary, New York.

It is difficult to choose Meyendorff's most remarkable accomplishment, due to the extraordinary character of his life. His doctoral dissertation on Gregory Palamas (q.v.) at the Sorbonne had to be defended against the entire faculty in theology, and the debate continued for decades in the journal *Istina*. It was not unusual for Meyendorff to hold two full-time teaching positions at the same time, while in addition editing publications, advising the Synod of Bishops, and fulfilling priestly duties. He wrote technical articles, did his own editing, and spoke publicly in three languages with little or no accent (Russian, French, and English), and did simultaneous translation among those languages. Although his reputation came from Byzantine studies, for example serving on the advisory board for the multivolume *Oxford Dictionary of Byzantium,* his command of Russian church history qualified him as a Russo-Byzantine scholar, using both terms inclusively. With Georges Florovsky (q.v.) he will probably be commemorated as one of the greatest Orthodox theologians and ecumenists of the 20th c., and his students—and spiritual children—remember him with warmth and respect.

**MIDDLE EAST.** The modern region that includes Syria, Lebanon, Palestine, Egypt, and Iraq is also the home of three ancient patriarchates—Antioch, Jerusalem, and Alexandria—as well as two Oriental Orthodox Churches, the Copts and Syrian Jacobites together with the Assyrian Church (qq.v.). For all their ancient roots, however, each of these communities faces an uncertain future in the face of rising Muslim resentment and religious extremism. Orthodox Christians earlier this century attempted to circumvent the omnipresence of Islam (q.v.) in the region by advocating a secular Arab nationalism—e.g., the Ba'ath party in Syria and Iraq—but this initiative now appears to be failing.

**MILLENNIALISM.** Millennialism (in Greek, *chiliasmos*, also called millenarianism and chiliasm) is the belief in a literal thousand-year reign by Christ prior to the general Resurrection and Last Judgment (premillennialism) or after it (postmillennialism). It is based on such texts as Rev 20, Jewish apocalyptic literature, and a widespread belief at the beginning of the first millennium in a period of seven thousand years, the "seven ages," between the world's creation and its end. Some of the early Church Fathers, notably Justin Martyr, Irenaeus of Lyons, and Hippolytus (qq.v.), held to it. Still, it was condemned by later bishops and survived, in the East at least, only on the fringes of the Church—e.g., in the various legends of the apocalypse popular in the Byzantine era (q.v.) and subsequently. This may be due to the very late admission of Rev into the Eastern Church's canon of Scripture, the only book of the New Testament not read from in the liturgical year. One might point to the undoubted influence on this issue from the school of Alexandria (q.v.). When the gnostics, among others, emphasized the carnal pleasures that were to be enjoyed by the saints (q.v.) during the thousand-year reign of Christ, Clement and Origen (qq.v.) eschewed their literalism and promoted a more spiritualized Christianity.

**MILVIAN BRIDGE.** On 28 October 312, Constantine (q.v.) fought and won a decisive victory at the Saxa Rubra on the Flaminian Way against his competitor, Maxentius, for control of the Western Empire. Maxentius was drowned in the Tiber five miles nearer Rome at the Milvian Bridge. Constantine's victory marked the beginning of the reconciliation between the Roman Empire (q.v.) and the Christian Church. According to a tradition contemporary with Constantine, he was accorded a vision on the eve of the battle, seeing the Cross against the night sky together with the words, *in hoc signo, vinces* ("with this sign, you shall conquer"). It is a matter of record that the emperor did adorn his troops' shields and horses with Christian symbols prior to the engagement.

**MOGILA, PETER,** Metropolitan of Kiev, theologian (1597–1646). Son of a Moldavian hospodar, Mogila studied in Poland and Holland, and may be described as a Westernizer, before becoming abbot of the famous Monastery of the Caves in Kiev (1627) and then metropolitan (1632). While at the monastery, he established a Latin-Polish school that competed with Kiev's Slavano-Hellenic brotherhood school, and that had a Jesuit curriculum and staff. His consecration as metropolitan was highly irregular—at night in an unlit church, etc.—and afterward he was frequently nominated by Uniates (q.v.) to be a Western Russian patriarch simultaneously in communion with East and West.

He is best known for giving a highly Latinized response (i.e., not only composed in Latin, but reflecting Roman Catholic [q.v.] theology, including the *Catechismus Romanus* of Peter Canisius) to the Calvinist *Confession* of Cyril Lukaris (q.v.). This response was comprised of both a widely circulated *Brief Catechism* and an *Orthodox Confession* (1640), which was coauthored with others, or else falsely ascribed to Peter. Although the *Confession* (i.e., a statement of faith) was approved by the Synod of Jassy (1642), four patriarchates (q.v.), and other councils that condemned Lukaris, it is not considered "one of the primary witnesses to Orthodox doctrine" (*Oxford Dict. of Chr. Ch.*, p. 928) by the Orthodox today, or in the recent past. The *Confession* is one of many unfortunate examples of the use of Roman Catholic polemics against problematical Calvinist influences within Orthodoxy, especially during this period in the Kievan and Muscovite churches.

Mogila also printed a priest's liturgical book (q.v.) that caused a Latinization of rites, because he disregarded the Greek rubrics, *Euchologion,* and extant Slavic service books (*Trebnik*). He issued a reunion memorandum (1643) that outlined his plans for unity with Rome, but died before any action was taken. He is considered the most capable and powerful 17th c. churchman of Poland and Lithuania. His influence can be seen throughout Russia in succeeding centuries, and this era in Russian Church (q.v.) history is called the "Mogila Epoch."

**MOLDAVIA.** Present-day Moldavia is divided between Romania (q.v.) and the former Soviet Union, the latter holding the present republic of Moldova (formerly Bessarabia). The region lies between the Carpathian Mountains on the west and the Pruth River on the east with its capital at Jassy. Much of it is a fertile plain. Moldavia is one of two principates, the other being Wallachia, where the Romanian people first appear on the historical scene as an identifiable nation in the 14th c. Previously, the area had been one of missionary activities for both the East and West. (*See* Constantine-Cyril; Methodius.) Its princes, together with those of Wallachia, served as the protectors and patrons of Orthodox clergy and monks of the Ottoman Empire (q.v.) during the 15th c.–17th c. The churches and monasteries of Moldavia, rich and numerous then and equally active today, are of extraordinary beauty and importance.

It was in Moldavia that Paisii Velichkovsky (q.v.) received his first initiation into hesychasm on his way to Mt. Athos (qq.v.) in the 1740s. It was here also that he came to stay after Athos in order to build up large communities of monks at the monasteries of Dragomirna, Neamts, and Sihastria, and work on the translations of the *Philokalia* (q.v.) into Church Slavic and Romanian. The latter would fuel a renaissance of monasticism (q.v.) in both countries throughout the 19th c., and it contributed to another renewal in Romania in the 20th c. The principate provided a kind of transition point from Greece and the Balkans (q.v.) to the lands of Russia. After a cultural apogee under Stephen the Great (d. 1504), Moldavia passed under Turkish rule. In the 19th c., rule passed among native hospodars, Russia, and Turkey until 1859 when Alexander John Curza initiated the history of modern Romania.

**MOLOKANS** *see* Doukhobors.

**MONARCHY.** Monarchy has a double referent, political and theological, in Orthodox thought. Politically, until the present century it has signified the form of government preferred by the Orthodox Church since its inheritance of the theology of imperial Rome, via Eusebius of Caesarea (qq.v.), in the 4th c. (*See* Church and State.) Theologically, "monarchy" is a term of great importance for the Orthodox understanding of the Trinity (q.v.). According to the Cappadocian Fathers (q.v.) in particular, still the ground of present Orthodox teaching, the monarchy of the Father is the very glue of the Trinity, the core of the divine unity. It is the Father who is the single source (*arche* in Greek, hence *monarchia,* unique source) of the Son and Spirit. Both the latter receive their being and hypostatic (personal) existence from the Father's person and being (*ousia*). The doctrine of the monarchy of the Father is thus at the root of the adamant Eastern opposition to the Western addition of the *filioque* to the Nicene-Constantinopolitan Creed (qq.v.).

**MONASTERIES.** Since the appearance of monasticism (q.v.) in the 4th c., monasteries have punctuated the landscape and informed the life of local Orthodox Churches. Beginning with Egypt (q.v.), each country or region of the Orthodox *oikoumene* has seen the rise and continuing influence of one or more important monastic centers. The Coptic monasteries of St. Antony near the Red Sea and of SS. Macarius and Bishoy at Scete have continued to shape the life of the Egyptian Church since the 300s.

From Egypt monasticism spread throughout the Empire. In Palestine the foundations of St. Sabas (monastery of Mar Saba) in the 5th c. and St. Catherine's at Sinai in the 6th c. were established and remain active today. Both have had singularly important roles in the shaping of the Orthodox liturgy (q.v.) and in the transmission of the spiritual wealth of the Middle East to Byzantium (q.v.). Georgia, too, had its monasteries, as did ancient Armenia, Mesopotamia, and Asia Minor (qq.v.). In Constantinople (q.v.) the monastic life was dominated from the 9th

c. by the great monastery of St. John at Studion through the influence of its renowned abbot, Theodore (q.v.), and a succession of able abbots afterward. St. Mamas was another important center in the capital under the abbacy of Symeon the New Theologian (q.v.) from 986 to 1005. Far and away the most significant concentration of monastic life from the latter Byzantine era (q.v.) to the present has been the peninsula of Mt. Athos (q.v.) with its twenty monasteries and numerous local communities. Elsewhere in modern Greece one may find the extraordinary monasteries of Meteora in Thessaly, perched on towering sandstone pillars and dating from the 14th c., together with the Byzantine foundation of Daphni near Athens (qq.v.), and the monastery of the Great Cave (*Mega Spilaion*) in the Peloponnesus. Serbia looks in particular to the monastery of Hilandar on Athos, and Bulgaria to the monasteries of St. John of Rila near Sofia and Bachka in the east of the country. Romania's monasteries are, save in Transylvania, all pervasive, though the great houses of Niamets and Sihastria in Moldavia (q.v.) have had the most significant impact over the past two hundred years.

In Kievan Rus' (q.v.) the newly baptized nation saw its first monastic foundation in the 11th c. Lavra of the Caves (*Pecherskaya Lavra*), which has served for most of its existence—particularly since the 16th c.—as the center of Orthodoxy in Ukraine. Western Ukraine looks to the monastery of Pochaev in particular. The center of Muscovite tradition (q.v.) since the late 14th c. has been the monastery of the Holy Trinity, called also by its founder's name, Sergius of Radonezh (q.v.). The Russian monastic colonization of the north in the 14th c. and 15th c. created such enduring landmarks as Solovetsky in the White Sea (currently under restoration), and the enormous monastic complex of Valaam (built on islands in Lake Ladoga). Renewed in the 18th c. by a disciple of Paisii Velichkovsky (q.v.) and powerfully influential in the 19th c. and early 20th c., the Optina Pustyn, an ascetic community near the monastery of Optina in central Russia, served as the center for a series of spiritual elders (*startzi*) whose influence on Russian writers and thinkers in the later 19th c. and early 20th c. has been noted by many sources, e.g., Dostoevsky's (q.v.) Elder Zossima in *Brothers Karamazov*.

Monasteries have been slow to appear in North America. St. Tikhon's in Pennsylvania (founded 1905) and Holy Trinity in upstate New York (1930) have played important roles in the Russian community. Transfiguration in Boston (1960) among the Greeks, and the Romanian houses of the Transfiguration, Ellwood City, Pennsylvania (1962), and Holy Dormition, Rives Junction, Michigan (1987), have provided essential opportunities for women's monasticism in recent years.

**MONASTICISM.** The origins of Christian monasticism are much debated, but early one may point with authority to the life of Jesus, as well as that of John the Baptist and the Virgin Mary (q.v.). It is clear that ascesis (q.v.) formed a component of Christian life from the start, and that from its beginnings as a mass movement in 4th c. Egypt (q.v.), monasticism has been an essential and vital expression of Christian life. It is surely not accidental that its great popularity and the rapid spread of monasteries were simultaneous with the new status of the Church following the conversion of the Emperor Constantine (q.v.). With the disappearance of the martyr (q.v.) as a model of Christian witness, a new set of heroes emerged and were seized upon by the faithful: the ascetics of the desert. Antony of Egypt (q.v.) was the first, a hermit whose austere rule of life and extraordinary personal charismata caught the imagination of late antiquity. He was followed by Macarius of Scete (q.v.) and by Pachomius of the Thebaid (southern Egypt), whose communal organization of monks provided the first standing model of common-life (*cenobitic*) monasticism, indeed of monasteries in the usual sense. The elders (*gerontes, startzi*) of Scete gave Christianity the term, Desert Fathers (q.v.), and a median way of life between Pachomius's strict communalism and Antony's solitary life. All three forms of monastic life continue in force in the Orthodox *oikoumene*, most notably on Mt. Athos (qq.v.).

Also, in the 4th c., Basil the Great (q.v.) organized the ascetics of his metropolitanate in Asia Minor (q.v.). His rule, communicated via letters addressed to specific questions on ascetic life, emphasized communal life, obedience to the abbot, and service. It was to play a significant, though not dominant, role in the later monasticism of Byzantium (q.v.). Asceticism in Syria (q.v.) remained for some time an individual effort, the "sons" or "daughters of the covenant" being attached to the local churches and active in their affairs. This form of ascetic life seems to have had roots in the Syriac Church (q.v.) well before the 4th c. A later period saw a rise in extreme—even eccentric—forms of asceticism, perhaps best known by the early 5th-c. phenomenon of the stylite saints, for example, Symeon Stylites, who subsequently appeared in Byzantium itself.

From the earliest period of Christian monasticism, both men and women enjoyed the same title, monk (*monachos* in the masculine, *monache* in the feminine), and were characterized by a distinctive dress or "habit," and a shaving of part of the hair, "tonsure." Neither the assumption of the habit nor the tonsure were, however, formalized by a priestly ceremony until the late 5th c. Dionysius the Areopagite (q.v.) is the earliest witness to the treatment of monastic tonsure and vows as sacramental, though the idea caught on and was advocated with great enthusiasm by monks then and now.

The vows, or promises, appear to have been formalized by very early times, and included promises of poverty (literally, "non-possession," *aktemonsyne*), obedience to the abbot or spiritual father (q.v.), and chastity or celibacy. Some rules, notably that of Benedict of Nursia in the West along with later canonical legislation in the East, added the promise of stability, that is, never to depart from the community where the vows were taken. These promises have always been regarded as permanently binding. They are administered after the candidate has passed an indeterminate period, usually not more than three years, as "novice" (Greek, *dokimos*, "one who is testing," and Slavic, *poslyshnik*, "one who obeys"). The tonsure today is generally to the rank of "little habit" (*microschema*) or "crossbearer" (*stavrophore*), though the "great habit" (*megaloschema*) is still given at tonsure by many Athonite houses. (The Russians and other Slavs prefer to reserve this last grade of monasticism for monks of the highest achievements, and to require of them a personal prayer rule of daunting asceticism.)

Developments in the Byzantine era (q.v.) saw the flourishing of monasticism in Palestine in the 5th c. and 6th c., and in Asia Minor in the monastic concentration at Mt. Olympus in Bithynia from the 8th to 10th c. Mt. Athos (q.v.), however, rose to special prominence in the Empire's waning centuries and has remained the primary center of Orthodox monasticism to the present. The Holy Mountain did give birth to a corrupted form of monastic life in the last Byzantine century, which predominated throughout the period of the Ottoman Empire (q.v.), *idiorhythmia*. The latter "individual way" meant the effective elimination of the office of abbot in favor of a committee of elders and permission to hold private property. The measure initially seems to have been taken in several communities to allow for increased personal asceticism. Economic factors might also have played a role in following centuries, particularly under the Turks. Whatever the reason, it worked to lower the overall quality of monastic life; but it encouraged one beneficial side effect, the rebirth of scetes patterned after the original Scete of Macarius. Here, among its scetes and hermitages, Athos gave birth to the *kollyvades* movement in the 18th c. crowned by the labors of Nicodemus of the Holy Mountain (qq.v.).

In Russia the *Spiritual Regulation* (q.v.) of Peter I (1721) contained legislation on monasticism and monasteries. Peter's opinion of it may be summarized in his own words: "At the very outset (of Russian history) this gangrene became widespread among us." He prohibited monks from studying books and engaging in writing. This included: 1) no writing in monks' cells, either books or letters, without specific permission, nor may letters be received—subject to severe corporal punishment; and 2) no ink or paper could be owned by monks.

Otherwise monasteries were to be converted into workhouses, foundling homes, or veterans homes. Monks were to become hospital attendants and nuns were to be spinners and lacemakers. Peter's educated "new monk" was of the Latin Kievan type, drilled in Scholasticism (q.v.), who might eventually be enlightened so as to serve as a capable translator of books. The end of the 18th c. saw a revival of monasticism and concern with the spiritual life, which continued until the Russian Revolution. Metropolitan Gavriil Petrov (1730–1801) encouraged the revival and supervised Paisii Velichkovsky's translation of the *Philokalia* (qq.v.). Peter's reform did less to dismantle monasteries and monasticism than it did the hierarchical leadership over subsequent centuries.

In sum, it is difficult to overstate the importance of monasticism for the life, Christian standards, spirituality, liturgy, and theology (qq.v.) of the Orthodox Church. One special note of importance is the fact that this movement has remained throughout its history in the East fundamentally lay in origin and character. The monks are, in the main, not clergy. It is still exceptional in most monasteries for there to be more priests than the minimum required to preside at the daily services. Unlike the West, it is understood as a separate vocation from that of sacramental ministry or the pastorate.

In a nutshell, since their appearance the monks have provided a type of second "apostolic succession" (q.v.) beside and supplementary to that of the official ranks of bishop and clergy. They have been, or at least have been perceived, as the primary carriers of the freedom of the Holy Spirit (q.v.). The monks themselves have been conscious of this prophetic and charismatic role since the Desert Fathers of the 4th c. At various times in the life of the Church, for example in 8th-c. iconoclasm, 14th-c. hesychasm, or the renewal led by Nicodemus and Paisii Velichkovsky (qq.v.), it was the monks who raised important banners of protest, or renewal, or points of dogma (q.v.), and who were supported by the conscience of the Orthodox people—often against the prevailing policies of both civil and ecclesiastical authorities.

**MONK OF THE EASTERN CHURCH** *see* Gillet, Lev.

***MONOGENES.*** This Greek term means "only-begotten" and is used of Christ, "the only-begotten Son," in Jn 1:18. In this connection it played an important role in the Syriac-speaking church (q.v.) of the 2nd c.–4th c. There the ascetic "sons and daughters of the covenant" were also called *ihidaye*, "only ones," i.e., assimilated through virginity or the renunciation of the marriage bed to the likeness of the unique "Only-Begotten." The word also begins a hymn sung in the Eucharist of the Byzantine rite (qq.v.) since ca. 535. Tradition says the hymn was composed by the Emperor Justinian, and it certainly expresses the latter's program of Christology (qq.v.): insistence on theopaschism as key to the interpretation of the Council of Chalcedon (q.v.).

**MONOPHYSITES** *see* Chalcedon, Council of; Christology; Jacobites.

**MONOTHELITISM** *see* Christology; Martin I; Maximus the Confessor; Oriental Orthodox Churches.

**MORAVIA.** Today's second province of the Czech Republic after Bohemia, in the 9th c. Moravia was one of the most powerful of the emerging Slavic states. Its ruler, Rastislav, petitioned the Byzantine Emperor, Michael III, in 863 for missionaries to preach and teach in the language of his people. While the prince's primary motive might have been to escape the expanding cultural sphere of the Carolingian Church present and at work in his country, the results of his petition were the epochal contributions of Constantine-Cyril and Methodius (qq.v.). Although the German/Latin clergy eventually prevailed in Moravia itself, today an exclusively Roman Catholic region, the original request prompted efforts that provided the religious and cultural foundations of the Bulgars, Serbs, Russians, and Ukrainians.

**MOTHER CHURCH.** This appellation is used today to denote the local and established Orthodox Church, which is the source of another community and often the latter's jurisdictional authority. It is in common use in Orthodox groups in "diaspora," i.e., regions such as the Americas, Western Europe, Australia, or Oceania, or in missionary territories such as Africa or the Far East. Believers in these areas look to a "mother church" in the home countries that are traditionally Orthodox for direction and hierarchical supervision. The ancient title belonged preeminently to Jerusalem: "Zion, the mother of churches." Later in the West and East, respectively, Rome (q.v.) acquired the title of "mother" for its successful conversion of northern Europe, and Constantinople (q.v.) for its having brought Christianity to the southern and eastern Slavs.

**MOUNT ATHOS** *see* Athos.

**MOUSKOS, MAKARIOS III,** Archbishop of Cyprus (13 August 1913–2 August 1977). Hierarch and first president of Cyprus, he received his education at Kykko Monastery and the Pancyprian Gymnasium in Nicosia. Ordained to the diaconate on 7 August 1938, he studied theology and law at the University of Athens, and was ordained to the priesthood on 13 January 1946. He studied at the School of Theology of Boston University and while there, he was elected bishop of Kition. As bishop he opposed British rule and championed Cypriot union with Greece (Enosis), organizing a plebiscite in January 1950 that resulted in a resounding victory for union. On 18 October 1950, he became archbishop.

In 1955 he consented to a nonviolent sabotage campaign against the British, but when the violence escalated, the British deported him to the Seychelles (March 1956). He was released in March 1957 and settled in Athens. In 1958, under the threat of partitioning Cyprus between Greeks and Turks, he agreed to independence instead of union. On 13 December 1959, he was elected president along with a Turkish vice president. In December 1963, he proposed to amend the threatened constitution and fighting ensued. In March 1964, a United Nations peacekeeping force intervened. Despite the gravity of the situation, he was reelected president in 1968 and 1973. On 15 July 1974, his residence was attacked by Greek junta forces, but he escaped to Paphos and London. After the fall of the Greek dictatorship in 1974, he returned to Cyprus in triumph on 7 December. By that time, however, the Turks occupied two-fifths of the island and proclaimed a Turkish Federated State in 1975.

**MUSCOVITE TRADITION.** The Muscovite Christian tradition is in direct continuity with Novgorodian tradition (q.v.), coming after its apex, and includes within its purview the possessor theological orientation of Joseph of Volokolamsk, the creation of the Unia, and the Old Believer Schism under Patriarch Nikon (qq.v.). It corresponds historically to Muscovy's rise to power as the center or capital of Russia, and ends (for our purposes) with the Spiritual Regulation (q.v.) of Peter the Great and the abolition of the patriarchate (q.v.) of Moscow. Thus, it covers the period from the capture of Novgorod by Ivan III of Moscow in 1471 to the publication of the Spiritual Regulation in 1721, including within it the early history of the patriarchate of Moscow, 1589–1700.

Aside from its Novgorodian roots, the religious orientation of Muscovy evolved from a series of church councils in the mid–16th c. Before this, the Muscovite tsars consciously wished to become heirs of the Byzantine emperors, evidenced by the marriage of Tsar Ivan III to Sophia Palaeologus. Councils in 1547 and 1549 canonized almost forty Russian saints (q.v.) and improved ecclesiastical organization. The council in 1554 was devoted to condemning Russian heresies (q.v.) associated with Protestantism or the non-possessors. A type of national self-identity appeared that included political and religious unification.

The Council of the Hundred Chapters (*Stoglav*) in 1551 was probably the most formative for Muscovite tradition in that it did not pronounce on doctrinal matters, but did pronounce on orthopraxy or ecclesiastical discipline. Its statements on the chanting of two "Alleluias" (q.v.) and the two-fingered sign of the cross set the stage for the Old

Believer Schism a century later. This Council was held under the presidency of Metropolitan Makarii of Moscow, who was consciously attempting to systematize and construct a Muscovite culture. Both he and Tsar Ivan IV broke with the Byzantine identification and "canonized" Novgorodian tradition, especially when they cited historical precedents, habits, and customs at the Council.

The Byzantine era (q.v.) that had ended a century before with the fall of Constantinople was no longer a viable religious inspiration for a Muscovy that faced fresh challenges. A devotion to Byzantine contemplatives, of the sort championed by the non-possessors, was replaced by an emphasis on constructing a "Christian society." Makarii established the first printing press in Russia, collected the lives of the saints, then codified them and published them as a model for proper piety (q.v.) in this new society. He did the same with the *Great Reading Compendium* and the *Biblical Codex,* combining history and interpretative story into single volumes. The Hundred Chapters themselves are difficult to analyze because the answers do not address the questions asked. In any case, uniformity and order seem to be the desired effect of the proceedings. These councils laid the groundwork for the final break with the Greeks in 1589, a political and ecclesiastical manifesto, with the establishment of an autocephalous (q.v.) patriarchate in Moscow.

In 1654 the ancient metropolitanate of Kiev located within Ukraine joined the Moscow patriarchate, completing an ongoing process of expansion and betterment of the life of the Church. Although Kievan Rus' (q.v.) encapsulated the early history of the Church in all Rus' before the Novgorodian period, the recent preceding centuries were marked by Poland-Lithuania's domination of Kiev, and overwhelming influence from the Roman Catholic Church in the Unia and Peter Mogila (qq.v.). Parts of Ukraine continued to be annexed to Muscovy through the end of the 17th c. The Church in pre-Petrine Russia enjoyed tremendous wealth, including extensive landholdings and monasteries—an otherwise peaceful situation that ended with Patriarch Nikon's reforms and the later enforcement of the Spiritual Regulation of Tsar Peter.

**MUSIC.** Byzantine music, broadly speaking, is the medieval sacred chant of all Eastern Orthodox Churches, before which there is precious little evidence. Scholars hypothesize that musical precursors certainly existed, including Jewish music, productions of the classical age, and the plainsong of Christian urban centers; but no musical manuscripts predate Constantine (early 4th c.).

The New Testament and modern research have given specific hints about 1st c. hymns. For example, in the Gospels of Mk and Mt after the Last Supper it says that Jesus and his disciples sang a hymn. Other hymnodic material has been identified by New Testament scholarship, including Rom 11:33–36 and Rev 1:5–8, among many others. Whether this hymnody was chanted prose (according to older Greek patterns of classical literature) or song as we now describe singing, remains debated. Similarly, scholars scrutinized the differentiation between hymn and poetic homily when Bishop Melito of Sardis's (q.v.) "Homily on Pascha" appeared in the 2nd c.

The question of pre-Constantinian music or chant is terribly complex. On the positive side: In the early Church, people actively participated in the performance of liturgy, so much so that the words *choros* (choir), *koinonia* (communion/fellowship), and *ekklesia* (church) were used synonymously. The background of Christian worship is usually identified with Jewish liturgy; and there seems to be a relationship between Hebrew poetry and Syriac liturgical poetry.

On the negative side: In the New Testament and through the 2nd–3rd c. there is little evidence that music played a significant role in communal worship. The Pauline references (Eph 5:19; Col 3:16) speak of psalms, hymns, and spiritual songs—but not communally sung. Similarly, Justin Martyr (q.v.) talks about a united "Amen," ending prayers, but no music. Further, when one mentions Jewish liturgy, what does the reference really mean?—the Temple in Jerusalem, an Aramaic-speaking synagogue practice, a Hellenistic, Greek-speaking synagogue, etc.?—while early rabbinical sources reveal a minimal use of music in services. Finally, the long-held supposition that early Christian worship originated in one primitive liturgy that subsequently diversified is coming under critical scrutiny. Some scholars prefer to see many liturgies developing simultaneously.

In the 4th–5th c. we find music first emerging at the same time as Christian architecture (q.v.) and as imperial ceremony appeared with liturgical solemnity. Still, the monks of the desert objected strenuously to the phenomenon. Only after heretics employed newly composed, popular tunes to advance their causes and entertain did the Church fully adopt the medium—sometimes copying the music of the heretics' hymns! Such is the description of Ephrem the Syrian's (q.v.) 4th c. hymnography, which is related by Sozomen.

The early pieces were processionals, involving everyone's participation on the way to the church. From the earliest times, all present sang—not a personal devotion, but a communal celebration. Two types of singing emerged: antiphonal, with the congregation divided in two, singing alternately, and responsorial, with a soloist initiating the tone and text, and the congregation responding in kind. Henceforth music was taken for granted as a part of Christian worship.

The 5th c. saw the composition of troparia (singular: troparion), which are short hymns of one stanza, usually commenting on a psalm verse that precedes them. The evening hymn, "Joyful Light," is a 4th c. example of a troparion, while the trisagion and Justinian's (q.v.) "Only-begotten Son" are from the 5th and 6th c., respectively—although no early musical settings for any of the troparia survive. Most of the melodies are assumed to have been simple, used by congregations with no formal musical training. The theology of the text and the musical arrangement are thought to have gone hand in hand. At least the written melodies from 12th and 13th c. Latin, Greek, and Russian manuscripts support these assumptions.

Next in development came the kontakia (singular: kontakion) of the 6th and 7th c., most notably those of Romanos the Melodist (q.v.). Kontakia are long, metrical, poetic-narrative elaborations of twenty to thirty stanzas on biblical texts. The stanzas are structurally alike and may be sung to the same music. The genre might go back to Syriac prototypes, and as a development of the troparia. In any case Romanos, a Hellenized Syrian Jew converted to Christianity, seems to be dependent on and preserves much of Ephrem the Syrian (q.v.). The popular Greek employed by Romanos was characterized more by imagery than theological vocabulary. The best-known kontakion of the Byzantine Church was probably the Acathistus Hymn, now used on the fifth Saturday of Great Lent (q.v.) at the vigil.

The canon became the newest type of hymnography in the second half of the 7th c., included in the celebration of matins. The canon contains eight or nine odes, each ode consisting of three or four stanzas, and it is more theological in content than the kontakion. The nine odes of the canon are attached to nine biblical canticles. Each has successive stanzas exactly reproducing the first in meter, so that they all can be sung to the same music.

The invention of the canon is attributed to the monks of Palestine, especially Andrew of Crete (q.v.). His younger contemporaries, John of Damascus (q.v.) and Cosmas of Maiuma, continued his work, writing the Easter canon and those of other major feasts (q.v.). From there the genre was furthered in Constantinople with Theodore and Joseph of Studion as part of the struggle to preserve icons (qq.v.) in the 8th and 9th c.

From about the 8th c. Byzantine psalmody was systematized into the eight ecclesiastical modes, the Octoechos (q.v.). This provided the compositional framework for Eastern and Western musical practices. The Greeks, Latins, and Slavs in the Middle Ages seem to have all had the same Octoechos. Nonetheless, the earliest tunes for the chants of the Divine Liturgy are older than the Octoechos and well might have been artificially imposed on the eight-mode scheme. For example, most of the ancient ordinary chants that appear throughout the liturgy were based on a simple G A B A G tune, and this is recurrent in several of the tones of the Octoechos (2, 4, 8, or 4 Plagal et al.).

Two principal palaeobyzantine notations were invented contemporaneously, Coislin and Chartres (named after manuscripts). In the 11th c. the former superceded the latter and continued its evolution for another century. In the last quarter of the 12th c. fully diastematic notation, better known as Round Notation (or Middle Byzantine) replaced Coislin. Round Notation can be converted easily into the modern system that we use today.

It is readily acknowledged that the early music of the Slavic churches and the other Orthodox is heavily indebted to Byzantine music. Each ethnic church produced its own musical tradition, but usually with a dependence on Constantinopolitan and/or monastic chant. Of special note is the music of the Russian Orthodox Church (q.v.), which came under the influence of the West and harmonized its chant into four or eight parts. In the 19th c. this trend continued so that Russian composers of the stature of Tchaikovsky, Rimsky-Korsakov, Rachmaninoff, and many others produced music for liturgical settings, now to be performed with both male and female voices in a capella cathedral choirs that rivaled Italian opera.

-N-

**NAHUM OF OCHRID** see Naum of Ochrid.

**NAJIM, MICHEL,** priest, Arab-American theologian, patristics scholar, translator (5 May 1949– ). After receiving his M.Div. at the St. John of Damascus School of Theology (1974) in Lebanon, he obtained his M.Th. at the Aristotelian University (1976) in Salonica, Greece, and his Th.D. (1985) with excellence from the same institution. He was professor of patristics, history, and languages at the St. John's School (1978–87) in Lebanon, while concurrently serving as dean (1980–87). Active in ecumenical affairs, he was a World Council of Churches Commissioner of Mission and Evangelism (1983–89), a member of the Ecumenical Committee for New Testament translation (1983–87), and an ecumenical dialogue representative of the Antiochian Orthodox Church (1980–87). After moving to the United States with his wife and family he taught patristics (1987–92) and participated in academic community life (1992–93) at the St. Athanasius School of the Antiochian Evangelical Orthodox Mission of the Antiochian Archdiocese of North America (q.v.) as the principal Orthodox theologian of this newly received group (with American evangelical roots in the Campus Crusade for Christ).

Active nationally in the Antiochian Archdiocese, he has served as a chairman of the department of liturgics and translation (1988–94), visiting professor at the Antiochian House (1994) in Pennsylvania, a member of the planning committee for the 1994 Clergy Symposium, and adjunct professor at Fuller Seminary (1994). In addition to his pastoral duties at St. Nicholas Cathedral in Los Angeles, Fr. Najim also serves as part of the motivating workforce behind the newly formed Liturgical Translation Committee of the Standing Conference of Orthodox Bishops in America.

Fluent in English, Greek, Arabic, and French, Najim has translated about a dozen important theological works since 1978 to make them available to a wider Orthodox readership. Supplementing his patristics bibliography of nine articles in various periodicals is a book list of a half dozen major works among which one finds *An Introduction to Patrology* (1980), *The Theotokos according to St. John of Damascus* (1984), *The History and Legacy of Arab Christianity in the Pre-Islamic Period*, and *Orthodox Mission in the United States*. Unassuming in his demeanor and dedicated in his vocation as a churchman, Fr. Michel is quite possibly the foremost young Arab-American Orthodox theologian living in the United States.

**NATIVITY OF THE LORD, OF THE THEOTOKOS** *see* Feasts, Twelve Great.

**NATURE.** Nature, in Greek *physis,* played a singular and highly controversial role in the Christological (q.v.) debates of the 5th–7th c. Analogous to the English word nature, *physis* could be used to convey both an abstract sense, as in "human nature," or a concrete personality, as in "so-in-so has a gentle nature." The confusion in the centuries of debate lay in the fact that both senses were in use. Cyril of Alexandria (q.v.) prefers the concrete sense. Hence the significance for him of the phrase, "one nature of God the Word incarnate," is the concrete unity of Christ in his person. The *Tome* of Leo (q.v.), on the other hand, uses it abstractly, thus the "two natures" in Christ of divinity and humanity. Turned around, however, Cyril's formula can be read to mean the disappearance of Christ's humanity in his divinity, while Leo's formula can be—and was—read as advocating two Christs. Virtually the same difficulty applied in the Trinitarian debates of the 4th c. with the terms *ousia* (essence) and *hypostasis* (person). Both could mean either abstract being, in general, or concretely existing things. The final adjudication regarding these terms may be found in John of Damascus's (q.v.) summary, *Exact Exposition of the Orthodox Faith,* where *hypostasis* alone is assigned the meaning of a specifically existing thing, while *ousia* and *physis* are equated with each other as signifying the abstract. (*See* Christology; Cosmology; Trinity.)

**NAUM OF OCHRID,** monk, translator, St. (830–910). One of the most accomplished and able disciples of Constantine-Cyril and Methodius (qq.v.), Naum (also Nahum) was the founder ca. 905 of a monastery, subsequently named for him, on Lake Ochrid in Macedonia (q.v.). He also was translator of liturgical and patristic texts into Church Slavic and a major force in the church of the Bulgarian Empire. He and his circle of disciples are the likely source of the Slavic alphabet, Cyrillic, currently in use in Serbia, Bulgaria, Russia, and Ukraine (qq.v.).

**NEO-CHALCEDONIAN.** This phrase was coined by modern scholarship to describe the movement, ultimately victorious at the Fifth Ecumenical Council (q.v.) in 553, to fix the interpretation of the Chalcedonian formula, "two natures in one person," in ways congenial to the emphasis Cyril of Alexandria (q.v.) had placed on the unity of God and man in Christ. It was led by such figures as Leontius of Byzantium, the Emperor Justinian (qq.v.), and John of Scythopolis. They stressed the Word of God as the *hypostasis* of the union, and they insisted thus on the truth of theopaschism, i.e., the Christology (q.v.) contained in the phrase, "one of the Holy Trinity suffered in the flesh." The hymn "Only-Begotten" (q.v.), traditionally by Justinian, sums up the emperor's theological program.

**NEOPLATONISM.** The dominant philosophy (q.v.) in late antiquity by the opening of the 4th c., Neoplatonism is associated with the *Enneads* of one of the giants of ancient thought, Plotinus (q.v.), an Egyptian Greek-speaker (d. 270). He effected a fusion of the two dominant philosophies extant in the 3rd c. Stoicism advocated a vision of the universe as a single living thing. Platonism stressed the divide between the realm of the eternal ideas and the phenomenal universe, though it acknowledged a dependence of the latter upon the former. Plotinus brought the first's organic metaphor together with the second's primacy of the spiritual. The result was a singularly powerful and markedly religious vision of the human being and the cosmos— at once intimately linked and themselves manifestations of the single divine reality underlying both. Still, both the human composite and the physical world are viewed as far removed from the One and the Good.

The hierarchy of being in Plotinus—from the One to Mind to Soul to Body—becomes more pronounced in his successors Porphyry (d. 303), Iamblichus (d. 330), Proclus (d. 482), and Damascius (d. ca. 535). The result is both an expansion in the detail of the earlier thinker's emanations, and in the last three philosophers a defense of traditional, pagan religion as mediating between the higher planes of being and human existence in the realm of matter. This is particularly clear in Iamblichus's and Proclus's defense of theurgy, literally "divine actions." At its best, the latter emphasizes a dependency on prayer and on the grace of the gods, which later Christian writers, such as Dionysius the Areopagite (q.v.), will find congenial. At its worst, it becomes appallingly reminiscent of "new age" theosophy, down to ectoplasm, mediums, and even "crystals." No Christian writer found this aspect appealing.

Neoplatonism in general was simply the philosophy of the Church Fathers (q.v.) of the 4th c. and afterward. It was at once the intellectual air they breathed, and their adversary. The story of Greek—and hence, Orthodox—theology throughout the Byzantine era (qq.v.) is similar to Jacob's wrestling with the Lord; but this wrestling was with a philosophical tradition in an effort to make of it an instrument of the revelation in Christ.

**NERSES THE GREAT,** Catholicos of Armenia, St. (?-ca. 373). A direct descendant of Gregory the Illuminator, a principal Church Father and sixth Catholicos (ca. 353–ca. 373) of Armenia (qq.v.), Nerses is particularly venerated for his philanthropic foundations of hospitals and orphanages and for his powers of organization. His exile and death came as the result of his opposition to the immorality of two successive kings, the arianizing policies of the latter, King Pap, and of the Emperor Constantius II.

**NESTOR THE CHRONICLER** *see* Primary Chronicles.

**NESTORIANISM/NESTORIUS** *see* Christology; Heresy.

**NETSVETOV, JAMES (IAKOV),** priest, missionary, St. (1804–26 July 1864). Born of an Atkan mother and Russian father on St. George Island, Alaska, he completed seminary in Irkutsk in 1826, married, and was ordained. He returned to Atka on 15 June 1829, where he began translating the New Testament and organized a school in 1833. He later worked with the Yup'ik-speaking Eskimos in the Kuskokwim-Yukon delta, learning the language and devising a writing system for them. He kept a journal during these years, which is a valuable historical resource as well as a testimony to the dedication and perseverance of the first priest of Native American background. He was a protégé of St. Innocent Veniaminov (q.v.).

**NICENE-CONSTANTINOPOLITAN CREED.** (For the text of this creed see the Introduction.) This Creed was established by the first two Ecumenical Councils (q.v.). The First Ecumenical Council at Nicaea (325) was responsible for the articles on the Father and the Son, and

the Second Ecumenical Council in Constantinople (381) for the articles on the Holy Spirit (q.v.) and the Church. In the Christian world of the first centuries both the Creed (including the Trinitarian Formula) and the Lord's Prayer held a very special place in catechesis (qq.v.). These two pillars were taught only at the end of the catechumenate. The Creed was considered so sacred that it was not given in written form to the catechumen, but was only to be committed to memory just before Baptism (q.v.). This practice served two pastoral functions which are noteworthy:
1) The Creed was personally explained as it was taught—explained in sufficient depth to be memorized.
2) It served as a preparation for Baptism, since it was used only at Baptism and not in the eucharistic liturgy (q.v.). (The Creed was not included in the liturgy until the late 5th c.) In this context it was meant to serve as the prerequisite statement of faith for being a Christian, rather than as an exhaustive description of a Christian's belief.

In the same context, the Lord's Prayer was not known outside of the Eucharist (q.v.). It, too, was kept as a secret—*disciplina arcani*. One reason for secrecy was that this prayer, more than any other, describes the unique parent-child relationship existing between God (q.v.) and the Christian. No one outside the bounds of participation in the Eucharist was seen as having access to this relationship. Thus, Orthodox Christians continue to say the prayer today before partaking of Holy Communion, as well as at the dining table—which is considered an extension of the altar table.

**NICHOLAS,** Bishop of Myra in Lycia, Patron of Russia, St. (?-ca. 343). His name is listed among those who participated in the First Ecumenical Council (q.v.) at Nicaea in 325, though virtually nothing else of his life is certain. Traditional *Lives* speak of him as a vigorous opponent of the heresiarch, Arius (q.v.), and as possessing remarkable generosity and solicitude for the poor. Popular piety (q.v.) throughout the Orthodox *oikoumene* (q.v.) has singled him out for special reverence. In Greece, for example, he is the patron of those at sea, while in Russia his memory is connected with charitable giving. His relics (q.v.) were removed from his episcopal see by Italian sailors on 9 May 1087 and deposited in Bari, Italy (q.v.), which repository popularized his cult in the West.

**NICHOLAS CABASILAS** *see* Cabasilas, Nicholas.

**NICODEMUS OF THE HOLY MOUNTAIN (HAGIORITES),** monk, ascetic writer, St. (ca. 1749–1809). One of the most important figures of recent Orthodox history, Nicodemus was born in 1749 on the island of Naxos in the Aegean Sea. He embraced the monastic life on Mt. Athos in 1775, and was early associated with the *kollyvades* movement (qq.v.), exiled members of which influenced his decision to take up monastic life on the Holy Mountain. His principal accomplishment in a life of great literary output was his edition in collaboration with Macarius of Corinth of the great anthology of 4th–14th c. ascetic literature on prayer (qq.v.). This collection in five volumes published in Venice, the *Philokalia* (1782), together with Paisii Velichkovsky's (q.v.) publication of a slightly different collection under the same title in Church Slavic, *Dobrotolyiubie* (1792), and later in Romanian, was arguably the most important publishing event in the Orthodox Church in the past two centuries. It signaled the beginning of a revival in monastic spirituality and patristic (qq.v.) learning that is still in process.

Nicodemus's other voluminous writings included commentaries on the Scriptures (q.v.), the liturgical year, guides to the life of prayer (*Handbook of Spiritual Counsel*), and for confessors, an anthology and commentary on Canon Law (q.v.) (the *Pedalion,* or *Rudder*). He edited and translated into contemporary Greek a number of important Eastern and Western Christian writers, including Symeon the New Theologian (q.v.), Ignatius of Loyola, and Lorenzo Scupoli. He also insisted upon the necessity of frequent communion at a time when this was unpopular.

**NIKA** *see* ICXC NIKA.

**NIKOLAI (KASATKIN),** Archbishop of Tokyo *see* Kasatkin, Nikolai.

**NIKON (MININ),** Patriarch of Moscow, liturgical reformer (1605–1681). After a monastic education and life, he became abbot of the Koyozerski Monastery (1642), archimandrite of the Novospaski Monastery in Moscow (1646), Metropolitan of Novgorod (1649), and Patriarch of Moscow (1652) by order of Tsar Alexis, over whom Nikon had great influence in his early episcopal years. As patriarch, Nikon immediately initiated liturgical reforms that resulted in the Old Believer (q.v.) schism for which he was famous—or infamous. Initially Nikon's program was rigorously enforced by civil authorities. But as early as 1653, other respected clerics (Neronov, Avvakum, etc.) who supported an awakening of faith in the Russian Church accused Nikon of heresy (q.v.). The prospect that Church and state had erred in their overly zealous reform policy—which they well did—called into question the whole premise of an infallible symphony of "God-appointed" institutions that comprised "Holy Russia." Scholars inside and outside of Russia continue to debate the "rightness" of Nikon's reforms (especially Makarii Bulgakov [q.v.], and recently Paul Meyendorff), in the last centuries with more objectivity when the political question of the Old Believers became less pressing. In 1658 Nikon himself rendered the "symphony" of Church and state a cacophony. He not only claimed complete independence in ecclesiastical matters, having been given the title "Great Sovereign" by the tsar, but also claimed primacy over the tsar—an attitude that caused him to fall into disfavor. It should be observed that Nikon asserted himself in direct imitation of the Roman papacy (q.v.), and that this prerogative was not in keeping with Orthodox tradition. As a result, he resigned the patriarchate (q.v.) and retired to a monastery, but then attempted to regain his office. Due to this attempt he was deposed and banished by the Councils of Moscow (1666–67), though his reforms were accepted and remained. After suffering fourteen years in a distant monastery, he was recalled by Tsar Theodore II, but died on returning and was posthumously reinstated and buried with honors. He has been recognized as "perhaps the greatest bishop of the Russian Church" (*Oxford Dictionary of the Christian Church,* page 976) by very few in the Orthodox world since the time of William Palmer.

**NILUS OF SORA (NIL SORSKII)** *see* Joseph of Volokolamsk.

**NINA,** Apostle to Georgia. In the most ancient account of Georgia's conversion to Christianity, the Latin writer, Rufinus of Aquileia at the close of the fourth century, mentions an anonymous slave girl who effected the conversion of the Georgian king, Mirian, and his nation. "Nina" acquires her name later, in an eighth-century "Life," perhaps deriving it from the Latin word for a female monastic, *nonna.* In any case, it was to a woman, a Christian and a missionary, that the Georgians ascribe their Baptism into the Orthodox Church.

**NISSIOTIS, NIKOS,** Greek Orthodox lay theologian, teacher, ecumenist (21 May 1925–17 August 1986). After pursuing theological studies in Greece and studying under Karl Barth in Basel and Emil Brunner in Zurich, he received a doctoral degree from Louvain University and joined the theological faculty of Athens University. Following World War II he was general secretary of the Student Christian Movement in Greece and a member of the World Student Christian Federation. From 1958 he served on the staff of the Ecumenical Institute, Bossey, Switzerland, and was its director from 1966 to 1974. From 1975 to 1983 he was a member of the World Council of Churches Central Committee and a moderator of the Commission on Faith and Order from 1976 to 1983.

**NITRIA.** This desert depression some sixty miles south of Alexandria was where Macarius the Great (q.v.) came to live alone sometime in the 340s, followed shortly thereafter by other anchorites. This community, and nearby Scete, was the background for most of the stories and sayings of the Desert Fathers (q.v.) filling the different collections, beginning with Jerome's and Rufinus's accounts of their visits in the late 4th c., and continuing through Palladius's *Lausiac History* and the alphabetical *Gerontikon* (or *Apophthegmata Pateron*) in the early 5th c. These texts, together with Athanasius's *Life of Antony*, became the foundational books of Orthodox monasticism (qq.v.).

**NOVATIONISM.** This schism (q.v.) was named for the Roman presbyter, Novatian (d. ca. 257/8), and began in the mid–3rd c. Unsuccessful in his candidacy for the see of Rome in 251, Novatian quarreled with Bishop Cornelius over the possibility of readmitting apostate Christians into the Church, i.e., believers who had renounced Christ under the pressure of the Emperor Decius's persecution (250/1). He argued instead that serious sins could not be forgiven after Baptism (q.v.), and that the Church could only properly be of the "pure." He was consecrated bishop despite Cornelius's disapproval and initiated a parallel group of his own. The communities he began spread to North Africa, as well as to Asia Minor and even Constantinople (qq.v.), where they were known as *katharoi* ("the pure ones").

**NOVGORODIAN TRADITION.** The Christian period under consideration goes from approximately the mid–12th c. to 1471 when the city surrendered to Ivan III of Moscow, and represents an integral link from the nascent Christian culture of Kievan Rus' to that of Muscovite tradition (qq.v.) later. In 1136 Novgorod set out on a unique democratic political course—with a culture, class structure, and form of government similar to that of Kiev—and within a short time (1156) claimed a certain religious independence by exercising its traditional ecclesiastical right to elect an archbishop. In the life of this new city-state the archbishop played an important political role in addition to his ecclesiastical duties: president of the Council of Notables, adviser and arbitrator for citizens, and occasionally traveling ambassador.

Novgorod defended itself and greater Russia from religious crusader-type invasions from the West dozens of times during these three centuries, epitomized in the life of Alexander Nevskii (q.v.). Defensive perimeters of the city utilized not only hydraulic works, but strategically placed monasteries, which served as forts. The city survived the Mongol invasions without being occupied, one of the few such cities to do so, by submitting to the khan and relying on the embassy skills of the same Nevskii. He was appointed grand prince of

Russia (1252–63) by the great khan and thus became the archetypal representative of Novgorodian Christianity and the ideal Christian prince. Religious development occurred during this period in the fields of church architecture and iconography (qq.v.), Novgorod setting a standard of comparison for later representations in these arts. Christian literature (q.v.) was not only preserved, but its corpus expanded, due to the literacy of the general population. This literature included the Church Fathers (q.v.), the Bible, historical chronicles, and pilgrimage travelogues. Not all the writings from the period were of equal spiritual value, witness the Questions of Kirik (q.v.). Contacts with the Byzantine world were maintained and the "Palaeologan Renaissance" took root in Russia as well. Even frontier settlers participated in the copying of books. The oldest surviving Church Slavic biblical manuscript, the illuminated Ostromirovo Gospel (1056–57), originated here, as did the Gennadievskii Bible (q.v.). The best-known theological debate took place in this context as well between Joseph of Volokolamsk (q.v.) and the Transvolgan Elders. The Josephites took the part of Church and state (q.v.) cooperation and the possession by monasteries of lands and goods, while Nilus of Sora and the Transvolgan Elders thought that monasteries should not own property and took a more eschatological view of the world and society (i.e., possessors vs. non-possessors).

It appears Novgorod established an intellectual and spiritual tradition that, when co-opted by Muscovy in the 16th c., provided the ideas which supported the rise of Moscow. For this reason many eminent Russian historians do not see the Novgorodian period as culturally separate, since no distinct interruption in creativity or direction of development occurred from Kievan Rus' to Muscovy. For instance, the single great event, the Tartar Appanage, had a limited effect since the Mongols did not attempt to convert conquered peoples. After the looting and destruction, they observed religious tolerance and respect. In any case Novgorodian tradition became enshrined as the Russian example when a monk from Pskov, Filofei, wrote Tsar Vasilii (Basil) III describing Moscow as the "Third Rome" (ca. 1510), and Tsar Ivan IV and Metropolitan Makarii of Moscow at the Council of One Hundred Chapters (1551) made Novgorodian tradition the historical paradigm of culture for Muscovite tradition (q.v.) following the fall of Constantinople (1453).

-O-

**OBER-PROCURATOR** *see* Spiritual Regulation.

**OBOLENSKY, DIMITRY,** Byzantinist, Slavic historian, educator (1 April 1918– ). Educated at the Lycée Pasteur in Paris and Trinity

College, Cambridge, he earned an M.A., Ph.D., and D.Litt. At Trinity College he was a fellow (1942–48), faculty assistant lecturer (1944), lecturer (1945), and university lecturer in Slavonic studies (1946). He was reader in Russian and Balkan medieval history at the University of Oxford (1949–61), professor of Russian and Balkan history (1961–85), and Fellow of Christ Church (1950–85). He is currently emeritus professor at Oxford University. He has taught extensively in United States academic institutions. His publications include *Byzantium and the Slavs* (1971) and *The Byzantine Commonwealth* (1971). He was knighted in 1984.

**OCHRID.** This city, still standing on the eastern shore of the lake of that name in the southwest corner of former Yugoslavian Macedonia (q.v.), was the capital of one of the earlier Slavic states, the empire of Tsar Samuel (d. 1014). Ochrid was an important early center, under the direction of Naum and Clement of Ochrid (qq.v.), for the translation of Greek Christian texts and their transmission to the Slav lands. After changing hands several times between Byzantine, Serb, and Bulgarian rulers, it came under the rule of the Ottoman Empire (q.v.) in 1394, where it remained until the conclusion of the Balkan Wars in 1912. The city is today little more than a modest resort, though bejeweled with several splendid medieval churches.

***OCTOECHOS.*** Meaning *The Book of the Eight Tones,* it is one of the liturgical books (q.v.) of the Orthodox Church. The *Octoechos* (or *Paraklitiki*) covers each of the eight tones, or melodic patterns, together with its accompanying hymns, sung throughout all the services for the seven days of the week, beginning on Saturday evenings. The cycle is completed on conclusion of the eighth week and then begins anew. Yearly, the cycle of the *Octoechos* begins on the Sunday following Pentecost. Its origins are ascribed to the work of John of Damascus (q.v.), and the formalization of the eight tones marks a watershed in Christian music (q.v.), East and West.

***OIKOUMENE.*** *Oikoumene* comes from the Greek verb, *oikeo* (to inhabit), and the term means, broadly, the inhabited or civilized world—historically, the Roman Empire (q.v.). As the Empire after Constantine (qq.v.) became more or less synonymous with the Christian Church, the term eventually came to mean the universal sphere of Christians. In recent times Orthodox writers have taken to speaking of the "Ecumenical Church," meaning the entire Orthodox communion.

**OLD BELIEF (*RASKOL*)—OLD BELIEVERS.** The Old Belief arose in 17th c. Russia in direct response to the liturgical-translational reforms of Patriarch Nikon (q.v.). The origins of the need for translation reform in the Russian Church in the 17th c. is most usually attributed to mistakes and translation errors from Greek to Church Slavic, which had affected Muscovite liturgy (q.v.) over an extended time span, a situation confirmed by Tsar Michael's commission for an investigation of such and by visiting Greek clergy. When Patriarch Nikon initiated the process of translation reform in 1652, he encountered tremendous resistance. Only in about the last century has the premise been taken seriously that some of the resistance might have been justified. From a scholarly point of view, the Greek liturgical books (q.v.) themselves had evolved in content and expression since the time the Church Slavic translations had been made from them. Examples of the rubrical practices reformed included the singing of a threefold Alleluia (q.v.) instead of two and the making of the sign of the cross with three fingers instead of two.

Nikon mustered support for his reforms from various quarters: Church councils (1654, 1656), the patriarch of Constantinople, Mt. Athos, the patriarchs of Alexandria and Antioch (qq.v.), scholarly Greek and Ukrainian monks, etc. After hopes were raised of defeating the movement among the opposition when Nikon fell into disfavor with Tsar Alexis (1658), two subsequent Moscow church councils upheld the reforms but deposed Nikon (1666–67). This set the stage for the *raskol,* the schism (q.v.) of the *starovery* or *staroobriadtsy,* of the Old Believers or Old Ritualists.

The reforms had the full backing of Church and state, and opposition to them was falsely interpreted as rejection of both—punishable by death. Those who opposed the reforms appealed to the faith of Novgorodian and Muscovite (qq.v.) Christian forbears, as well as to the Council of One Hundred Chapters (1551; *Stoglav*), which was quite explicit on how many times Alleluia was to be sung and how many fingers were to be used in making the sign of the cross—two! (This fact was so distressing to later Russian historians through the mid–19th c. that it was considered an Old Believer forgery.) Old Believers perished at the stake, whole monasteries were besieged and captured, and the twenty-five years following the Council of Moscow saw new apocalyptic Old Belief expectations as self-fulfilling prophecies, when dozens of their communities destroyed themselves in mass suicides. The most curious aspect of the schism was that both sides thought the disputed matters were of life and death importance, although nothing of a dogmatic nature was discussed—only ritual.

Old Believers survive to the present, and communities may be found in the United States and Canada. The first major division occurred early among them between the *popovtsy,* those with clergy, and the *bezpopovtsy,* those without clergy. Most of the later sects emanating from the Old Believers (*see* Doukhobors) came from the "priestless" group—a circumstance that resulted from the sect's lack of bishops to ordain clergy. The entirety of the Old Belief was largely reorganized in the 18th c. and numbered in the millions before the Russian Revolution. Nicholas Riasanovsky has recently pointed out that the tragedy of both Nikon's Muscovite Church and the Old Belief is that both tended to focus on the form of the faith to such a degree as to eclipse the content. To this may be added the observation that what began as a somewhat legitimate protest to Nikon's reforms became, in the priestless sects, a manifestation of the most extreme cultic, self-destructive behavior. Mistakenly, Westerners sometimes classify all of these sectarians together as types of Protestants—tantamount to mixing Old Catholics and Mennonites together with Branch Davidians and followers of Jim Jones.

**OLD CHURCH SLAVIC** *see* Clement of Ochrid; Constantine-Cyril; Methodius; Naum.

**ONLY-BEGOTTEN** *see Monogenes.*

**ORDINATION.** In Greek the technical term is *cheirotonia* (Church Slavic, *rukopolozhenie*), literally "the laying—or better, pressing—on of hands." This action, on the part of the bishop and in the context of the eucharistic liturgy, is believed to impart the grace of the Holy Spirit (qq.v.), in particular the charisma (if it is a bishop or priest being ordained) to preside at the Eucharist (q.v.) and to teach the faith. It has been counted as a sacrament (q.v.) of the Orthodox Church since at least the time of Dionysius the Areopagite (q.v.). The particular term, *cheirotonia*, is applied only in the case of an ordination to the three "major ranks" of episcopacy, presbyterate, and diaconate. The lesser orders of the clergy, readers, cantors, and subdeacons, are ordained by *cheirothesia* (the "placing on of [the bishop's] hands"). The sacrament presupposes a candidate whose life presents no obstacle to the grace received.

**ORIENTAL ORTHODOX CHURCHES.** This phrase is recent and chosen to distinguish the "Eastern Orthodox," i.e., the churches in communion with Constantinople and accepting the Seven Ecumenical Councils, from the churches of Egypt, Armenia, Ethiopia, Syria, and India, which refused to acknowledge the Council of Chalcedon and as a result severed their relations with the imperial city and with Rome (qq.v.). Formerly referred to as "monophysite," ecumenical exchange between the two sides has led to a change in nomenclature—the "monophysites" rightly protesting a title that the other side had given them, and that not in an eirenic spirit. (*See* entries following.)

**ORIENTAL ORTHODOX CHURCHES—ORTHODOX DIALOGUE.** Beginning with the informal talks held between Oriental and Eastern Orthodox theologians in the 1960s, a surprising consensus was arrived at regarding the two sides' respective Christologies (q.v.). Official dialogue was opened in 1985 and culminated in a formal statement of agreement on the christological issues, published following a meeting of representatives of the different churches in Egypt in the summer of 1989. In the fall of 1992, the Ecumenical Patriarch, Bartholomew I, accepted the 1989 statement as the official position of his patriarchate (qq.v.). A year earlier the bishops of the Coptic Church (q.v.) had agreed to lift the ancient anathemas (condemnations) on the Chalcedonians. In spite of the agreements, however, considerable obstacles to formal reunion remain. These include: the status and meaning of the Ecumenical Councils held following the Third at Ephesus (qq.v.) in 431, the problem of individuals anathematized by the tradition of one side and canonized by the other (e.g., Leo the Great and Severus of Antioch [qq.v.]), and, ultimately, how to arrange the overlapping jurisdictions in the patriarchates of Alexandria and Antioch (qq.v.), which would otherwise result from a true union.

**ORIENTAL ORTHODOX CHURCHES—ROMAN CATHOLIC DIALOGUE.** As well as with the Eastern Orthodox, the Oriental Orthodox churches have been in official dialogue with the Roman Catholic Church (qq.v.), in particular at meetings held in 1971, 1975, 1976 (in Vienna), and 1978 (in Cairo). These have culminated in official meetings between the Coptic Pope of Alexandria (q.v.) and Pope Paul VI (1973), the Ethiopian Patriarch and Pope John Paul II (1982), the latter and the Jacobite (q.v.) Patriarch (1980), John Paul II and the Armenian Patriarch of Cilicia (1983), and John Paul II and the Catholicos of the Indian Church (1983). The statements issued all declare an agreement on the christological differences of the past, but—as with the Eastern Orthodox—other particular ecclesiological questions pose grave difficulties, especially the role of the papacy (q.v.).

**ORIGEN,** theologian (ca. 175–ca. 254). The most distinguished representative of the Alexandrian school who built on the previous contributions of Philo and Clement of Alexandria (q.v.), he left a massive corpus of works devoted to the textual criticism of Scripture (q.v.) (i.e., the *Hexapla,* the Old Testament in columns beginning with the Hebrew, moving to a transliteration in Greek, and following with four contemporary translations), Scriptural commentaries, homilies on Scripture, apologetics (q.v.) (*Contra Celsum*), and the first Christian attempt at a systematic theology, the *Peri Archon (On First Principles).* His thinking, especially in the last-mentioned work, was governed by the following axioms: 1) God (q.v.) is both good and just; 2) God is the creator of all; 3) the human being is free, and 4) ultimately rational; 5) Scripture is the very presence of the Word of God, both in the Old and New Testaments; 6) the Same became incarnate for human salvation; and 7) his truth is imparted to and lives in his Church.

While always striving to remain faithful to the *lex credendi* (q.v.) of his era, Origen did feel free to speculate. His forays into the origins of the world and of bodies led him to postulate a primordial creation of rational spirits, whose fall from grace led the Creator Word to fashion the material world as both a house of punishment and a schoolroom designed to teach the fallen about their true nature (q.v.) and reveal to them the path of return. This speculation was doubtless motivated primarily by Origen's desire to defend the seven axioms noted above, especially in opposition to the gnosticism of his era and the nascent Neoplatonism (qq.v.) of his pagan contemporaries.

Much of later Greek patristic thought, indeed, of the whole Byzantine era (qq.v.), may be said to have been a rethinking of Origen. This applies not only to the formal thought of his system, but to scriptural exegesis, spiritual life and asceticism, the whole life of prayer (qq.v.). Origen is foundational to the Greek East in a way analogous to the role Augustine of Hippo (q.v.) plays in the West. This is in spite of the fact that the Fifth Ecumenical Council, at the urging of the Emperor Justinian (qq.v.), condemned Origen as a heretic three centuries after he had died in the peace of the Church. The concomitant destruction of the bulk of his writings, estimated by Eusebius of Caesarea (q.v.) at over eight hundred titles, must rank as one of the great tragedies and injustices of the Christian East. Certain of his works survive, but most of what remains is available only in the (often dubious) translations of Jerome and Rufinus of Aquileia.

**ORTHODOX CHURCH IN AMERICA (OCA).** Russian Orthodox missionaries first arrived in Alaska (q.v.), then part of the Russian Empire, in 1794. The original dozen or so missionaries from the Valaamo Monastery near Finland included Herman (q.v.), a monk who lived forty-three years on Spruce Island near Kodiak, and who was canonized as the first American Orthodox saint (q.v.). The Orthodox Church in America is the direct descendant of this Russian Orthodox Missionary Diocese and is the only canonical autocephalous (q.v.) Orthodox church based on the North American continent.

In 1824 the Alaskan mission received new life with the arrival of the priest, then bishop, Innocent Veniaminov (q.v.). He fostered indigenous church life, translating Church documents into Aleut. Innocent was appointed Bishop of Kamchatka, the Kuriles and Aleutians (1840), with residence in New Archangel, now Sitka. He became the first Orthodox bishop with North American territory in his episcopal title. As bishop, Innocent traveled extensively in Asia and North America. He called for a self-governing American Orthodox church, with leadership representing Orthodox Christians from all ethnic and national backgrounds.

Toward the end of the 19th c. Russian America (q.v.) and Orthodoxy therein experienced tremendous growth as thousands of Orthodox Christians from Russia, Belarus, Ukraine, Bulgaria, Romania, Serbia, Albania, Greece, Turkey, and various Middle Eastern countries immigrated to the United States and Canada. A large number of Uniates (q.v.) in the United States also reunited themselves with the canonical Russian Orthodox Church here.

Bishop Tikhon Belavin (q.v.) headed the North American Missionary Diocese from 1898 to 1907. He moved the Church's center from San Francisco to New York City, founded St. Tikhon's Monastery in Pennsylvania, and built St. Nicholas Cathedral in New York City. Tikhon called for greater autonomy of the North American Missionary Diocese, including development of local leadership and increased use of various liturgical languages, especially English, later sponsoring a translation of services. He returned to Russia (1907) and was elected the first Patriarch of Moscow (1918) since the time of Peter the Great. Before the Russian Revolution in 1917, Orthodox Christians from various backgrounds remained a unified Missionary Diocese of the Russian Orthodox Church (q.v.). After the revolution the Russian émigré community in the new world was fractured, and changing ecclesiastical jurisdictions divided along lines of ethnic origin and political differences.

In 1920 Tikhon ordered all dioceses to continue governing themselves until the return of normal conditions within the Russian Patriarchate. In response to his decree a council met in Detroit (1924) and moved to become self-governing until proper free relations with the Russian Orthodox Church could be reestablished. In the intervening years the Missionary Diocese experienced a strained relationship with its parent Russian—now Soviet—Church. Chaotic disorder persisted into the 1950s. Yet Orthodoxy in America continued to grow through immigration and conversions. The Missionary Diocese, called a metropolitan district ("Metropolia"), gained recognition as the autocephalous Orthodox Church in America in 1970 by Aleksy I and the Patriarchate of Moscow. Today the OCA includes the American descendants of Russians, Belarussians, Ukrainians, Galicians, and Carpatho-Russians, (Alaska's) Aleuts, Eskimos, and Tlingits, and members of the Romanian, Albanian, and Bulgarian episcopates in the new world.

Nevertheless, the autocephaly of the OCA did not resolve the complex question of American Orthodoxy, since there are an estimated four million Orthodox Christians in North America who look to the Church for sacramental and pastoral services, a great many majority of whom are in the OCA. In 1960 delegates from various canonical European Orthodox traditions formed the Standing Conference of Orthodox Bishops in America (q.v.). The Conference is working at bringing unity among North American Orthodox Christians—including all national and ethnic backgrounds—through a traditional ecclesiastical structure built on one bishop for one geographical area. The Greek Orthodox Archdiocese of North and South America, an exarchate of the Patriarch of Constantinople, is the largest group in North America, headed by Archbishop Iakovos Coucouzis (qq.v.). Next in size and influence is the OCA, which has more than six hundred parishes. In addition, American Orthodoxy includes the Antiochian Orthodox Christian Archdiocese, the Serbian Orthodox Metropolitanate, Romanian, Bulgarian, Ukrainian, Carpatho-Russian, and Albanian dioceses, among others, not to mention a substantial group of Americans who have converted to Orthodoxy, most of whom find their ecclesiastical home in the OCA.

**ORTHODOX INSTITUTE,** Berkeley, California, *see* Patriarch Athenagoras Orthodox Institute.

**ORTHODOXY.** The Greek term "orthodoxy" means "right or correct belief or worship" (*orthos,* right, correct, *doxa,* belief/opinion, or glory; Church Slavic: *pravoslavie,* right glorification). This term as a collective designation for the local Eastern churches in union with Constantinople is of fairly ancient provenance, although the term "catholic" (q.v.) was also in use in the East during the first millennium. Modern use, in view of the Roman Church's effective monopoly on "Catholic" as a qualifier, has confined itself largely to "Orthodoxy." Thus the phrase, "the Orthodox Church," without further qualifier commonly refers to the Greek, Slav, Romanian, etc., local churches of Eastern Europe and the Middle East (q.v.). The term also necessarily implies a distinction between this communion and the "heterodox" (lit., "of another opinion, worship"), meaning those Christian bodies not in communion with Orthodoxy. The Eastern focus on "rightness" of belief is characteristic and deeply engrained, somewhat in contradistinction to the West's stress on unity and its horror of schism (q.v.). The Orthodox can live more happily with schisms, a virtue somewhat dictated by necessity, so long as the substance of the faith is not seen as compromised. In the West, the reverse has seemed to be in force: Heresy (q.v.) is almost tolerable so long as it does not rend the fabric of visible unity.

**THE OSTROG CIRCLE AND ITS BIBLE.** The first full text of the Church Slavic Bible, after the earlier Gennadievskii Bible (q.v.), was published in 1580 and again with emendations in 1581. Known as the Ostrog Bible after its chief patron, Prince Constantine of Ostrog (Konstanin Ostrozhskii), the work appeared as part of a larger private publishing effort among the Orthodox in Lithuania and Poland, which included liturgical books (q.v.) and religious pamphlets. Although all the publications served apologetic (q.v.) purposes against non-Orthodox Christians, the inspiration for this serious translation project came from a traditional vision of Slavo-Hellenic culture, common to participants in the "Ostrog Circle."

Trained in Greek, Latin, and Slavic, members of the Ostrog Circle such as Cyril Lukaris (q.v.) rooted their work in their own tradition, while participating in a trilingual "Greek school," lasting only a few decades. The Prince's school was a response to the Jesuit-sponsored College of St. Athanasius founded in Rome during the same period to educate Slavs and Greeks in the Unia (q.v.), and the Circle responded strongly to Uniatism. Members of the Circle were exceptional for their time and place and many went on to make history elsewhere.

In methodology of biblical translation the Circle employed classical Church Slavic, while attempting to follow the Greek textual tradition using every available critical resource. Starting first with Gennadius's Bible, other Greek and Slavic manuscripts were obtained from Constantinople and monastic centers; but the manuscripts were poor. Next they used the (Masoretic) Hebrew text, the Vulgate, and recent Czech and Polish versions. Finally they checked their results against the Aldine Septuagint (Venice, 1518) and the Complutensian Polyglot (Spain, 1522), containing parallel columns of Hebrew, Aramaic, Greek, and Latin Old Testaments, as well as Greek and Latin New Testaments. Clear from this methodolgy is the fact that the Ostrog Slavic Bible cannot be equated with the Septuagint (q.v.), as most people suppose. It is a composite work and does not correspond in every respect to the Greek.

The quality of the Slavic text of the Ostrog Bible compared favorably to other contemporary translations, such as the Sixtus Clementine version of the Vulgate (1592). Georges Florovsky (q.v.) has evaluated the Circle's translation as a landmark in Slavic biblical history and a monument of scholarship, literature, and theology. All subsequent editions of Church Slavic Bibles have been dependent on the Ostrog text.

**OTTOMAN EMPIRE.** Successors to the Seljuk Turks, the Ottomans, named for the bey Osman (d. 1326), first ruled Asia Minor (q.v.), then Eastern Europe, the Middle East, Arabia, and North Africa from the late 14th c. until the overthrow of Sultan Mohammed VI in 1923. By the time Constantinople (q.v.) fell to Mohammed II on 29 May 1453, the entirety of the Orthodox *oikoumene* (q.v.), with the sole exceptions of Poland-Lithuania and Muscovy, had come under Ottoman rule. This underlined the importance of the Muscovite Grand Duke as the single remaining, independent Orthodox sovereign. It certainly assisted the rise of the 15th-c. myth of Moscow as the "Third Rome," i.e., successor to both Rome and Constantinople (qq.v.) as capital of the Orthodox Christian world.

For the vast population of Greeks, Slavs, Romanians, Armenians, Georgians, Copts, and Arabic-speaking Orthodox, the long centuries of Ottoman rule meant a permanent reduction to second-class citizenship in a Muslim Empire. In several instances, this slowly whittled away their communities, which were lured to Islam (q.v.) by the promise of social betterment, or else simply in search of relief from the taxes imposed on the non-Moslem population. Paradoxically, Ottoman rule accentuated the outward power of the Orthodox Church, elevating the Ecumenical Patriarch (q.v.) to the position of ruler of the Christian populace, and his bishops, in like manner, to the role of magistrates.

This status and its limits, coupled with the later decadence of the Empire and the importation of romantic nationalism in the 18th and 19th c., had a singularly poisonous effect on the fabric of church life: Ecclesiastical offices were bought and sold; scrambles for power and continual intrigue dimmed the moral authority of the hierarchy; and, perhaps worst of all, the Church's leaders became identified with the interests of a particular nation and language. (*See* Ethnarch.) This occurred first of all with the Greeks, following the lead of the Phanariots (q.v.). Their favoring of their own nation led to similar movements—in part, reactions against the patriarchate (q.v.)—among the Slavs, Romanians, and Arabic-speakers.

The 19th-c. wave of revolt in the Balkans (q.v.) and creation of independent states saw the erection of an equal number of independent (autocephalous [q.v.]) national churches—and the acceptance of the equation of nationality with church and hierarchy. In 1870 Constantinople labeled this principle in its extreme form "*phyletism*," the heresy of tribalism. While the condemnation has been generally accepted theologically, national allegiance as identical with church membership and the continuing inability of the Orthodox to act together as the Church remain the single most crippling legacy of the Ottomans. Its effects are particularly clear in the 20th-c. Orthodox "diaspora" in the Americas, Australia, and Western Europe: a plethora of nationally based "jurisdictions" simultaneously overlapping one another and claiming to be manifestations of the one, undivided Church of Christ.

**OUSPENSKY, LEONIDE,** iconographer, teacher (1902–12 December 1987). The author of *The Meaning of Icons* (with Vladimir Lossky [q.v.]; trans. 1982) and *Theology of the Icon* (2 vols., trans. 1992), he has done much in the 20th c. to help restore the traditional canon (i.e., composition, style, materials, etc.) of Orthodox iconography (q.v.) in the West for those engaged in painting icons.

### -P-

**PACHOMIUS**, ascetic, St. (292–347). An Egyptian villager from the south of that country, Pachomius was converted to Christianity around age twenty and, moved by the example of the Desert Father Antony (qq.v.), sought the solitary reaches of the upper Nile valley. Later, in attempting to guide disciples, he was led to set up the first strictly regulated, common-life communities of monastics with property in common, obedience to a single *abba* (father) or *amma* (mother, for the women's communities), common worship, delegation of labor, and a monastic enclosure. It was an extraordinarily successful, influential, and enduring social and religious experiment. The Pachomian pattern spread rapidly, with local modifications, throughout the Christian Church. (*See* Monasticism.)

**PAIDEIA.** Paideia is derived from the Greek for child, *pais,* and in the Hellenistic era evolved into the general term for upbringing, though with the particular sense of formation or education; or it may be simply translated as "culture." By the 1st c. the word signified intimate acquaintance with the classics of Greek thought and literature: poets, playwrights, orators, historians, and philosophers. Just as the "classical education" of Renaissance humanism or 19th c. Eton were both based on this product of pre-Christian Hellenism (q.v.), *paideia* was the passport to the higher reaches of Greco-Roman society and the badge of cultivation. Everyone who wanted to be anyone, whether Jew or Greek, Syrian, Egyptian, or "Barbarian," strove to obtain it.

Christian writers, too, take up the term and its contents, particularly Justin Martyr and the great Alexandrians, Clement and Origen (qq.v.). These men adopted the term, embraced the philosophers, and sought at the same time to cast the biblical word of God (q.v.), the Christ of the Gospels, in the role of the supreme "Pedagogue," the author and meaning of the classical *paideia.* This move opened up the higher reaches of Roman imperial society to the Church and, at the same time, inaugurated the ongoing struggle of Christian theology (q.v.) with the methods and presuppositions of the philosophers. Basil the Great (q.v.) therefore fought for the Christians' right to *paideia* against the attempts of Emperor Julian (360–363) to close the schools to the Church.

At the same time, however, monasticism (q.v.) presented itself as the true *paideia* and monks as the real "philosophers." This divorce or tension between love of classical antiquity and the ascetics' suspicion of philosophy's pretensions, continued throughout the Byzantine era (q.v.). It is expressed in the frequent contrast, beloved of the monks, between the "outer" and "inner" wisdom, i.e., the book knowledge gained through reason and the revelation of Christ in the heart of a believer schooled in humility (q.v.).

**PAISII VELICHKOVSKY, St.** *see* Velichkovsky, Paisii.

**PALLADIUS** *see* Lausiac History.

**PALM SUNDAY** *see* Feasts, Twelve Great (Entrance of the Lord).

**PANTELEIMON,** great martyr, healer, St. (?–304). Panteleimon, like Cosmas and Damian (q.v.), was an "unmercenary physician." According to his "Life" (*Synaxarion,* July 27th), he was executed for the sake of Christianity under the rule of the Emperor Maximian at the city of Nicomedia in Asia Minor (q.v.). He remains the most celebrated of the physician saints, being particularly venerated by the Slavs. His icon connects healing with the administration of the Eucharist (qq.v.).

**PAPACY.** From the earliest centuries of the Christian Church, Rome (q.v.) was the home of the largest community of believers, the capital and largest city of the Empire, and the site of the martyrdom of two great Apostles (q.v.), Peter and Paul. It was thus a local church inevitably cast for a leading role. Ignatius of Antioch speaks to the Roman Church in tones of clear respect, as does Irenaeus (qq.v.) seventy years later in 185. With the conversion of Constantine and the transfer of the capital to Byzantium (qq.v.), the tone of the bishops of Rome begins to acquire an imperious note. Beginning with Popes Julius (337–352) and especially Damasus (366–384), perhaps in response to the loss of the emperor's presence and elevation of the new capital, the popes laid particular stress on their see and office as uniquely in succession to Peter, the prince of the Apostles. This shift, in effect the start of an equation of the papal office in the Church with that of the emperor within the state, marks the beginning of the papacy proper.

Pope Leo the Great (440–461) (q.v.) was the apogee of the earlier development, still within the undivided Church and Empire of late antiquity. The particular eminence of the popes in the centuries following was accentuated by the collapse of the Western Empire (476) and the result that Rome became isolated from Constantinople (q.v.) and its bishops found themselves local rulers, though still the nominal subjects of the emperor. With the evangelization of the Germanic peoples of northern Europe in the 6th–11th c.—a true glory of the papacy—

the role of the popes as "vicars of Peter" (*vicarii sancti Petri*) was further emphasized. While still a remote and distant figure for the newly Christian nations, the bishops of Rome were all the more surrounded by a unique aura of sanctity and venerability as guardians of the holiest shrine of the West (q.v.), the site of the Apostles' death and presence of their relics, and as themselves the living voice of Peter.

A further step was taken toward the peoples of the West and away from the old Mediterranean axis of Christendom when Pope Stephen II made his alliance with Pippin I, father of Charlemagne (q.v.), in 754. The *Donation of Constantine* (q.v.) was published (it might also have been authored in northern Gaul) sometime in the following half century, a development literally crowned by the coronation of Charlemagne in 800. Although in political schism from Byzantium, the popes were still solicitous enough of Eastern sensibilities to avoid inflammatory actions in other areas, notably the *filioque* (q.v.). This changed in the 11th c. with the revival of the German empire under the Saxon emperors and the latter's encouragement of reforming popes drawn from the northern (transalpine) territories of their kingdom.

The great era of the Gregorian Reforms in the 11th c. and 12th c., named for Gregory VII (1073–85), culminated in the pontificate of Innocent III (1198–1215), who was the theocratic head of a new Christian commonwealth, Western Europe of the High Middle Ages. This new version of the ancient ideas of *imperium* and *sacerdotium,* indeed of *romanitas,* stood in natural—and inimical—contrast to the older version, which was all the while in force in Constantinople and the East. (*See* Church and State.)

The ecclesiastical schism (q.v.) between Western and Eastern Catholicism was a natural and inevitable consequence. It is no accident that 1054, the date usually assigned for the schism, occurred at the end of the pontificate of the first of the great reforming popes, Leo IX (1049–1054). The schism was sealed by the Crusades (q.v.), in particular the Fourth (1204), which took, sacked, and held Constantinople until 1261.

For the Eastern Church, developments in the West could be, and were, long ignored. Up until the reform movement, and its key signal for the Orthodox in the insertion of the *filioque* into the Nicene-Constantinopolitan Creed (q.v.) at Rome in 1014, Rome had maintained its importance as the first see of the Church. It was uniquely privileged and venerated for being the site of the ancient capital, the place of the Apostles' martyrdom, and for its (near) perfect record of Orthodoxy in the periods of Trinitarian and Christological (qq.v.) debate. It was valued by dissidents in the Byzantine Church, particularly when imperial policy threatened Orthodoxy, because it stood outside the Empire's effective boundaries and its bishop was free to speak on behalf of the faith received. One will thus find noted saints of the East, e.g., Maximus the Confessor, John of Damascus, and Theodore of Studion (qq.v.), who admired and held the Roman Church in highest regard for these very reasons.

The specific claims of the papacy—particularly as they reflected the equation of the papal with the imperial role or with the unique successor of Peter—remained by and large foreign concepts, alien to the Eastern understanding of the Church as conciliar. The novelty and shock of the papal claims were brought home only with the great reforms and, particularly, the Crusades. It is, humanly speaking, difficult to see how schism could have been avoided. The two halves of an originally undivided Christendom had become two different Christendoms, and both could see room enough only for one. Subsequent developments in the Roman Catholic Church (q.v.), in particular Vatican I's definition of papal infallibility and "universal ordinary jurisdiction" (the position that the popes may act as the local bishop in any diocese of the Church), have only served to widen the gap.

**PAPADEMETRIOU, GEORGE C.** A graduate of the Holy Cross Greek Orthodox School of Theology (q.v.), Brookline, Massachusetts (1959), he holds degrees from Texas Christian University (M.Th. 1966), Temple University (Ph.D. 1977), Simmons College (M.L.S. 1983), and a Certificate from the Shalom Hartman Institute sponsored by NCCJ in Jerusalem (1986). Papademetriou was ordained to the priesthood by Archbishop Iakovos (q.v.) in 1960.

Director of the library at Holy Cross and associate professor of theology since 1978, he teaches world religions, interfaith dialogue, contemporary cults, Palamite theology, and dogmatics. He chairs the program "Seminarians Interacting," NCCJ, and he has chaired conferences such as the St. Gregory the Theologian Conference (1991), the Third International Conference of Orthodox Theologians (1978), and the Orthodox Christians and Muslims Symposium (1985). He is a representative to the Holy Cross Board of Trustees since 1990, president of the alumni association (1990–1993), and coordinator of the Clergy with Lay Professions Correspondent Program (1984–present). He has been a member and officer of numerous professional organizations. Author of book reviews, articles, and booklets, his books include *Introduction to St. Gregory Palamas: Photian Studies* (editor, 1989), *Essays on Jewish-Christian Relations* (1990), and *Maimonides and Palamas on God* (1994).

**PAPHNUTIUS.** A name belonging to six saints (q.v.) in the Orthodox calendar, four of them monks. Two of the most important were Egyptians, monks of the 4th c, and one a contemporary of Antony (q.v.). The latter lived the ascetic life in near nakedness in the desert for eighty years and the former is the father of Euphrosyne, an anchoress, and himself an anchorite. A third Paphnutius, also a 4th-c. ascetic, is commemorated as a martyr (q.v.) (September 25th).

**PARAKLESIS.** The Greek verb, *parakaleo,* means "to call upon, exhort, comfort." A *paraklesis* is thus an invocation or intercession, and the term today is used for a prayer service of intercession addressed most commonly to the Virgin Mary, Theotokos (q.v.). It is especially popular among Greek Orthodox and is served often during the weekdays of the Dormition Lent (August 1–14). As with many such devotional prayers, its form is that of a modified matins (*orthros*).

**PARASKEVE.** The name of six women saints (q.v.) on the Orthodox calendar: three martyrs (q.v.), the Paraskevi of Iconium (October 28), Rome (July 26), and the sister of Photina, the Samaritan woman of Jn 4 (February 26). The three others are virgin saints or ascetics: Paraskeve of Serbia (October 14), of Primis (October 28), and of Sarov (September 22). The name in Greek means "preparation," and is also the present word for Friday from the Jewish week: Friday as preparation for the Sabbath. Thus "Saint Paraskeva" can also be translated in Greek as "Holy Friday," the day of Christ's Crucifixion.

**PARISH.** The English word derives from the Greek verb, *paroikeo,* "to sojourn," as in a temporary dwelling. Its use for an ecclesial community derives from the ancient Christian manner of speaking of the Church as "sojourning" (*paroikousa*) in this or that locale, i.e., as a temporary resident, because the true home of the people of God is the heavenly Jerusalem. In present-day use, the word signifies the subdivision of a diocese or eparchy (q.v.) presided over by a presbyter (priest) who represents the ruling bishop.

**PARTHENIOS (ARIS KOINIOIS),** Patriarch of Alexandria, *see* Koiniois, Parthenios.

**PASCHA—THE RESURRECTION OF CHRIST.** Faith in the Resurrection of Jesus Christ as the Son of God (q.v.), the Christian Pascha (Passover), is the foundation of the Church. But how this is understood in Eastern Christianity is frequently different from contemporary discussions of the topic in the West. At the end of the four Gospels (and in 1 Cor 15) the Resurrection is described in twelve pericopes, which are read as separate stories during resurrection matins. In the liturgy of Basil (qq.v.) it is explicitly stated that Christians proclaim the death of Jesus and confess his Resurrection, i.e., the death is a historical fact while the Resurrection is a tenet of faith. As such, it has aspects that go beyond history in the usual secular sense, which aspects function in the past, present, and future.

In the past, the Resurrection was neither a "resuscitation" of Jesus, nor was it an observable phenomenon; rather, the Resurrected Christ was observed. The Resurrected Christ is depicted in icons (q.v.) with a body that is in continuity with his earthly body, but gloriously transformed (not someone who "just barely" rose) and clearly is not governed by the laws of physics as we know them. The Resurrected humanity of Christ, with Moses and Elijah, with the newly freed Adam and Eve, et al., resides with the Father in the Kingdom of God. It is the source of our vision of God "face to face," although God remains unseen.

In the present the Resurrection is participated in by Christian believers, in a sense, through direct personal experience. This occurs par excellence in Baptism (q.v.), descending into the water as into the grave and rising from it again, in the joyous liturgical celebration of Pascha (Easter) as a present event, and in the Eucharist (q.v.) as the feast of the messianic and heavenly banquet of resurrected life. The light of the Resurrected Christ is not solely and personally God the Father's, but is shared by the transformed humanity of Jesus, and cannot only be seen, but can be currently shared in by believers. (*See* Theosis.)

The future aspect of the Resurrection is the eschatological culmination of all creation in God's Kingdom, according to God's economy (q.v.), about which neither the time nor the details are known. It is the possibility of every Christian to imitate Jesus in his entrance to the heavenly. Nevertheless, Christians do not have to wait for the "Second Coming" or for their own deaths in order to see God, because the present aspect of the Resurrection makes that reality accessible now, and the future aspect guarantees an end to current tribulation and is evidence of the peace that can only come from above.

Pascha is considered greater than all other feasts (q.v.), is called the Feast of Feasts, and is celebrated not only once a year but on every Sunday. As the Christian Passover, it is seen in direct continuity with the pre-Jewish and Jewish feast(s) involving the paschal lamb, with the deliverance of God's people in the sea with Moses, and with the liturgy (q.v.) of the Temple of Jerusalem; and it was identified as such as early as the Gospels. The Pascha, Jesus' passing from death to life, was made possible by the crucifixion, but the Cross and Crucifixion are never absolutized without reference to the Resurrection—which facilitates the victory of the Cross in suffering. The Orthodox Church is correctly referred to—with an eye toward both theology (q.v.) and liturgy—as the Church of the Resurrection.

**PASHKOVISTS** *see* Radstockists.

**PATERIKA.** "Of, or pertaining to, the Church Fathers" (q.v.), as in their works, writings, etc. The word, normally in the singular (*paterikon*), is used with particular reference to collections of sayings and deeds of ascetic holy men (for women, it is a *materikon*). One finds, for example, the *Sinai paterikon*, or the *Kiev paterikon*, referring to the anecdotes and deeds of the remarkable fathers of the monasteries of Sinai and the Pecherskaya Lavra.

**PATMOS.** A small island of the Dodecanese in the Aegean Sea, not far from the coast of Turkey, where according to Rev 1:9–10, John the seer received his revelation. Since 1088 it has also been home to a continuously inhabited monastery directly under the jurisdiction of the Ecumenical Patriarch (q.v.). The monastery began a school for the training of clergy in the 18th c. that functions today. Its continuous occupation has also left it with a singularly full and valuable collection of manuscripts from the later Byzantine era (q.v.).

**PATRIARCH ATHENAGORAS ORTHODOX INSTITUTE (PAOI).** Incorporated in 1981 as St. John the Divine Orthodox Divinity Institute at the Graduate Theological Union (GTU) (q.v.) in Berkeley, California, the Institute's name was changed in 1987 on the occasion of the centennial of the birth of the late Ecumenical Patriarch Athenagoras (q.v.) to honor one of the great ecumenists of this century. At a convocation of the GTU at that time, the establishment of the Alexander G. Spanos Chair in Orthodox Studies was announced—the result of a most generous endowment that Fr. Leonidas Contos (q.v.) had secured and to which he was subsequently elected. It is the only endowed chair of its kind in the nation.

The Institute has had a steady growth and today occupies three buildings adjacent to the University of California (UC) campus, where its library, offices, meeting facilities, and chapel are housed. The UC Orthodox students meet regularly at the Institute's Chapel of St. Demetrius for the celebration of the Divine Liturgy and fellowship.

The PAOI Trustees envision a broad range of objectives for the Institute, both immediate and longer term, to be fully realized as resources increase and other endowments mature. In addition to the regular courses of instruction, these include lectureships, symposia, workshops, and scholarly publications. Several "Distinguished Lecturers" and colloquia for the GTU and UCB communities have also been held.

**PATRIARCHATES.** The title "patriarch" is used for the head or primate of many local Orthodox churches. Originally the title was confined to the five ancient churches of Rome, Constantinople, Alexandria, Antioch, and Jerusalem, the Pentarchy (qq.v.) or "rule of the five" first officially codified under Justinian (q.v.). The title was extended to the Metropolitan of Moscow in 1589. Serbia and Bulgaria had had patriarchs in the late medieval era, and they reclaimed the title for the archbishops of Belgrade and Sofia in the 20th c. The Romanian Church on the unification of the three regions of Romania following World War II likewise took the title for the Archbishop of Bucharest. The Archbishop of Tbilisi and Primate of Georgia (q.v.) rejoices in the title "catholicos." Among the Oriental Orthodox (q.v.) "patriarch" is claimed as a title for the Coptic Archbishop of Alexandria, the Archbishop of Addis Ababa and Ethiopia, and the Primate of the Jacobites (q.v.), while the Armenian and Indian churches employ "catholicos."

**PATRISTICS.** "Patristics" or "patrology," as a separate discipline in academic theology (q.v.), dates from the 17th c. Today it signifies the systematic study of the Church Fathers (q.v.), i.e., the elucidation of their lives and thought in light of the information available about their social, political, and intellectual environments. Thus, modern patristics is vitally concerned with the investigation of the culture and society of late antiquity, the latter covering the Roman/Byzantine Empire (qq.v.) from ca. 100 to ca. 800. The rise of Islam in the south and of the Carolingians (qq.v.) in the West are usually employed to set rough limits to the "age of the fathers." For the Orthodox Church limiting the "patristic age" to any one period, even if of several centuries, is foreign and artificial. Patristic studies in the West did, however, lend great assistance to the rediscovery of the sources of Eastern tradition. And 19th-c. Russia continued this rediscovery, which has subsequently spread to other nations in the Orthodox *oikoumene* (q.v.).

**PAULICIANS.** A sect with its origins in Armenian antiquity and lasting perhaps into early modern times, the Paulicians in their homeland were characterized by an adoptionist Christology, iconoclasm (qq.v.), and a strong emphasis on the charismatic leader. During the 9th c. and only within the territories of Byzantium in Asia Minor (qq.v.), the sect appears to have undergone a mutation that featured emphasis on sharp dualism between the realms of spirit and matter (*see* Gnosticism), proceeding to an entirely negative appreciation of sacraments and the church hierarchy. In this form imperial authorities transplanted it to the Empire's northwestern borderlands, in part to strengthen the region's defenses. From there it seems to have contributed to the rise of the Bogomil movement in 11th-c. Bulgaria and elsewhere in the Slavic Balkans (qq.v.), and thus later still to the Cathari, or Albigensians, of 12th–13th-c. Provence, France.

**PAX ROMANA.** This Latin phrase, "the Roman Peace," refers to the rule of the Roman Empire (q.v.) over the entire Mediterranean basin from the century before Christ to the death of the Emperor Theodosius I in 395 in the East, and at least until the fall of Rome in 476 in the West, if not to the coronation of Charlemagne (q.v.) in 800. In any event the *pax romana* was the matrix of the nascent Christian Church. Many nations governed by a single polity had a profound influence on the Church's institutions and psychology in both the Latin West and Greek East.

**PENANCE AND RECONCILIATION** *see* Confession.

**PENTARCHY.** Meaning the "rule of the five," this was never more than a theory that no Church decision or ruling was fully binding until the sees of Rome, Constantinople, Alexandria, Antioch, and Jerusalem (qq.v.) had pronounced on it. The pentarchy was the official theory of church government from the reign of Justinian (q.v.) on, although the five sees had been singled out for the title "patriarch" at the Council of Chalcedon (qq.v.) in 451. The implication of the theory, i.e., that all five were in the final analysis fundamentally equal, was never accepted by the Church of Rome (q.v.), which from the 4th c. on laid special emphasis on its apostolic and petrine claims to primacy. To be fair, the pentarchy was a highly artificial theory, never implemented until the great 5th c. debates over Christology (q.v.) had removed the Alexandrian (Coptic [q.v.]) Church from communion and fatally split the weakened Church of Antioch. In addition the theory's insistence on the sovereignty of these five patriarchs was at least debatable, given the early Church's emphasis on the equal authority of all bishops, an emphasis still preserved in Orthodox Canon Law (qq.v.). Nonetheless, it continues to hold sway in official Greek circles to the present day.

**PENTECOST** *see* Feasts, Twelve Great.

**PERSECUTION.** From its origins until the conversion of Constantine (q.v.), the Christian Church was an illegal organization, a *religio illicita* or "unlicensed religion," in the eyes of Roman law and therefore subject to state suppression. Outside the boundaries of the Empire, under Persian rule or in neighboring lands such as Armenia, Georgia, Ethiopia, and far-off India (qq.v.), Christianity either suffered initially until it became the dominant faith, as in Armenia, or else continued to live with persecution. Thus the cult of the martyr (q.v.), in continuity with the Jewish suffering for the Torah revealed in the Maccabean revolt (see 2 Macc 7) and adapted to Christian worship of the Crucified Lord, was part of Christian psychology from the very beginning. Subsequent suffering under the rule of Islam (q.v.), whether the Arab Caliphate or the Ottoman Empire (q.v.), and later under Soviet oppression, have continued to reinforce the martyric ideal. Tertullian (q.v.) summed it up in an aphorism whose force is apparent in post-Soviet Russia: "The blood of the martyrs is the seed of the Church."

**PERSIA.** Under Cyrus the Great and later rulers, the Persian Empire (539–332 B.C.) was the first of the great world empires of the ancient, eastern Mediterranean world. Followed by Alexander the Great's successors, and then Rome (q.v.), ancient Persian dominion provided a pattern, soon to be established as normative government, of tolerance of local customs and religions. The recovery of Persian independence from the Seleucid successors to Alexander in the 2nd c. B.C. led to the situation that prevailed throughout Roman and early Byzantine rule: an unstable border region, roughly along the lines of the modern borders between Syria (q.v.) and Iraq. It experienced occasional battles and, more rarely, all-out warfare. The revived Persian Empire of the Sassanid dynasty (3rd–7th c. A.D.) provided an important shelter for dissidents from the imperial church, in particular the great, Syriac-speaking Church of the East. (*See* Assyrian Church.) Safe from the machinations of Constantinople (q.v.), the eastern Syrian Church was free to develop its own institutions and to spread as far as India and China along the trade routes protected by the Shahs.

**PETER THE GREAT,** Tsar of Russia, *see* Spiritual Regulation.

**PHANARIOT.** Strictly, one who is a resident of the Fanar, a borough of Turkish Constantinople (q.v.) along the upper reaches of the Golden Horn. More generally, the "Phanariots" were successful Greek merchants and traders who moved into the Fanar, which has been the home of the Ecumenical Patriarch (q.v.) from early on under Ottoman rule. The Phanariots exercised leadership among the Greek population from the 17th c. to the collapse of the Ottoman Empire (q.v.). Their wealth and high level of education, often acquired through a stay at a Western European university such as Padua or Bologna, singled them out for leadership within both the Orthodox Church and the Turkish state. By the 18th c. they were running the Ecumenical Patriarchate itself, and in good part the Ottoman Empire as well.

At about this time they evolved the plan referred to as "the Great Idea" (*He Megale Idea*), nothing less than the restoration of Byzantium (q.v.) from within the shell of Ottoman rule. When this notion was combined with the narrower focus of Greek nationalism, the effects on the Orthodox Church were thoroughly deleterious. The Great Idea amounted in practice to Greek hegemony over the other Orthodox peoples of the Empire. Thus, the multiplication of national churches in the Balkans (q.v.) accompanying the 19th c. movements for independence was a natural consequence of, and reaction to, Phanariot policy. The resulting ill feeling and mistrust left over from Ottoman rule continue to hamper the genuinely ecumenical ministry, which the patriarch of Constantinople is called to exercise.

**PHEME.** A term of Byzantine imperial origin, the *pheme* was the title, or "job description," of officials of the Empire, ceremoniously proclaimed on high occasions. In the Orthodox Church today, particularly in churches using the typicon of Constantinople (q.v.), it is the solemn title of the bishop proclaimed by the deacon and repeated by the choir during the *polychronion,* the point in the Divine Liturgy just after the entrance of the clergy into the sanctuary. In Byzantium (q.v.) and tsarist Russia, this was the point when the reigning emperor's title was announced and accompanied by the singing of "many years."

**PHILANTHROPY.** Literally, "love for humanity," philanthropy is a favorite expression of the Church Fathers (q.v.) for the economy (q.v.) of God's salvation, in particular referring to the Incarnation of the Word, the death on the Cross, the Resurrection, and the gift of the Holy Spirit (q.v.). This, the philanthropy of Christ, is the love for humanity par excellence; and every Christian is called to imitate it. Thus, the insistence throughout the Byzantine era (q.v.) that the emperors, together with the wealthy and powerful, had a particular duty as leaders of the Christian community to exercise charity, i.e., to imitate the divine philanthropy revealed in Christ.

**PHILARET (DROZDOV), METROPOLITAN OF MOSCOW** *see* Russian Bible; Russian Orthodox Church.

**PHILIP (SALIBA),** Archbishop *see* Saliba, Philip.

**PHILOKALIA.** Meaning "love of the good" or "of the beautiful," the term has been given as a title to two collections of Christian writings in the history of Orthodox thought. Around 360 the Cappadocian Fathers (q.v.) compiled a selection from the works of Origen (q.v.) under this title, highlighting in particular the great Alexandrian's thought on important theological questions, Scriptural exegesis, and the spiritual life. In the 18th c. Nicodemus of the Holy Mountain and Paisii Velichkovsky (qq.v.) assembled anthologies, differing slightly in content, of writings on prayer by Byzantine authors from the 4th to 14th c.

Much larger than the Cappadocians' selections from Origen, the second *Philokalia* runs to five heavy volumes. The Greek version was published in Venice (1782) and Paisii's Church Slavic translation in Petersburg (1793), and the impact of each one has been enormous. Paisii also oversaw a later translation into Romanian. In the 19th c. and 20th c., the translations were updated. Paisii's Church Slavic was rendered into Russian by Theophan the Recluse in the mid–19th c. Fr. Dumitru Staniloae (q.v.) has been working on an expanded *Philokalia* in modern Romanian, accompanied by notes and commentary, since the 1930s. Bishop Kallistos Ware, with the late P. Sherrard (q.v.) and G. Palmer, have put out four of five volumes of St. Nicodemus's version.

**PHILOSOPHY.** Philosophy as a distinct discipline dates from the Greek thinkers of the 6th c. B.C., and especially from the time of Plato (q.v.). In origin it was in part a reaction against the inadequacies of traditional pagan religion and the inherited mythology; it often sought through reason to validate traditional practice. With Plato, Aristotle, and the Stoics, philosophy became the intellectual and spiritual lens through which the cultivated elite of the Hellenistic and Roman worlds viewed their universe. While several different schools existed in the Roman Empire (q.v.) at the time of Christ, it was the three above that dominated the world of late antiquity; in the work of Plotinus (q.v.) they achieved a kind of fusion. Thus Neoplatonism (q.v.), codified two centuries later by Proclus (d. 486)—who set the philosophical curriculum for the whole Byzantine era (q.v.)—was the philosophy of the later Church Fathers (q.v.).

From the 2nd-c. "Mid-Platonism" of the Apologists (q.v.) down to the capture of Constantinople (q.v.) in 1453, Christian writers sought a way to come to terms with philosophy. Many embraced it gladly: Clement of Alexandria, Origen, the Cappadocians, and Dionysius the Areopagite (qq.v.)—always with careful revisions. Others, particularly in monastic circles, were more dubious, regarding the philosophers' claims of autonomous reason as deluded or demonic. The inherent tension between revealed truth and the sovereignty of reason was never resolved, then or now. Modern Orthodox look to the Fathers and see, first, that the questions of the modern world are very seldom new, and second, that spiritual writers have dealt with many of these issues in particular ways. The latter emphasized the purification of the intellect itself, an affirmation that reason requires the school of humility (q.v.) in order to work in a way adequate to the mystery of Christ.

**PHILOXENUS OF MABBOUG,** bishop (ca. 440–523). A leader of the opposition to the Council of Chalcedon (q.v.) and one of the most able theologians of his day, Philoxenus was bishop of Mabboug (also Mabbug or Hierapolis) in northern Syria from 485 until his deposition by Emperor Justin in 519. Together with Severus of Antioch (q.v.), he was perhaps the most influential of non-Chalcedonian writers in his own day and thereafter. Originally a student at the school of theology in Edessa (q.v.), an institution dominated by the exegetical and theological works of Theodore of Mopsuestia (q.v.), he broke with the latter's extreme dyophysitism and embraced the Christology of Cyril of Alexandria (qq.v.), to which he remained faithful the rest of his life. He wrote exclusively in Syriac, and is perhaps the earliest translator of Evagrius of Pontus (q.v.), although his translation was also a work of careful editing. He wrote extensively on the spiritual life, especially his thirteen "Discourses on the Christian Life," in addition to polemical treatises and commentaries on the Scriptures (q.v.). The Philoxenian version of the New Testament is the one prepared in Syriac for Philoxenus in 508, but unlike the Peshitta contains all the Catholic epistles and Rev. The original was lost in the revision by Thomas of Harkel in 616.

**PHOTIUS,** Patriarch of Constantinople, theologian, St. (ca. 810–ca. 895). Patriarch from 858 to 867 and from 878 to 886, Photius was the most learned man of the 9th c., the principal patron of the so-called Byzantine renaissance of classical learning, patron of the missionary venture of Constantine-Cyril and Methodius (qq.v.), and an outstanding theologian. His *Library,* a running commentary on a collection of several hundred books of classical and Christian antiquity (many now lost), has proved of enormous significance for the history of the ancient world and the Church. Written during his first exile, the "Amphilochia" treats exegetical and doctrinal problems. Photius is doubtless best remembered in the Roman Catholic Church (q.v.) for his sharp critique of the Latin *filioque* (q.v.) and for his quarrel with Pope Nicholas I, with whom he exchanged decrees of deposition and excommunication. The anti-Photian council of 869, insisted on by Pope Nicholas's successor, Hadrian II, was later reckoned as the Eighth Ecumenical Council (q.v.) by Roman canonists. On Photius's return to the patriarchal throne a second council was held in 879 exonerating the patriarch and making peace with Pope John VIII, in particular on the basis of a mutual agreement not to alter the text of the Nicene-Constantinopolitan Creed (q.v.). Given the convocation of another ecumenical council, the Orthodox Church would almost certainly recognize the synod of 879 as the Eighth Ecumenical Council.

**PHYLETISM.** The word is derived from the Greek word for tribe, *phyle.* Phyletism, or "tribalism," was condemned as a heresy by a local council held at Constantinople (q.v.) in 1870. The specific cause of the council's condemnation was the appointment in that year of a Bulgarian exarch (q.v.), who claimed jurisdiction over all Bulgarians in Ottoman territories independent of the Ecumenical Patriarch (q.v.). The council thus reacted to the principle of national jurisdictions and the appointment of bishops with exclusive ethnic constituencies. At issue was the question whether the bishop should be the focal point of the unity of all believers within a given territory, or instead the religious ethnarch (q.v.) of a national group. Its decision has since been accepted by all local Orthodox churches as the correct response to nationalism as it applies to church government. While the theory of unity of the local church in its bishop was thus preserved, the situation in the Orthodox Church today all too often fails in practice: Phyletism in fact, if not in law, is quite alive.

**PIETY.** The English word translates the Greek *eusebeia*, or—and as preferred by a number of the Church Fathers (q.v.)—*eulabeia*, though the latter is more accurately translated as "reverence." Both terms were common in the pre-Christian world of Greco-Roman antiquity. They were used to signify the proper attitude toward the gods, in particular the careful observation of prescribed ritual and caution against offending divinity by neglect or by giving way to human pride (hubris). Orthodox Christianity inherits the words and infuses them, particularly *eulabeia*, with the sense of the biblical "fear of God." Reverence and piety (q.v.) thus come to suggest an inward quality or turning of the soul, an inner attentiveness to the divine will and humility (q.v.) before the divine presence. More recent overtones given the word piety come to the Orthodox East from the 17th c.–18th c. religious movement "pietism," which is something quite different. When forms of pietism aim at exalted emotionalism, a tenderness and swelling of the heart—though frequent in Orthodox devotional literature of the past two hundred years—the tendency is quite foreign to the patristic (q.v.) and ascetic tradition of the East.

**PILGRIMAGES.** Pilgrimage is the travel to holy places, e.g., Jerusalem, the Holy Land generally, the tomb of a martyr or ascetic saint (qq.v.), or a place sanctified by a monastery. The notion of "holy place" is a complex one, but surely derives much force from the special character accorded Palestine, Jerusalem, and the Temple mount in the Old Testament. The account of the martyrdom of Polycarp of Smyrna (q.v.) provides early evidence (ca. 170) of the cult of the martyr and the latter's burial place and physical remains, as does the desire of Christians in the 2nd-c. Roman Church to be buried next to an apostle (q.v.).

Pilgrimages doubtless occurred in the early centuries of Christianity. They became a mass phenomenon following the conversion of

Constantine (q.v.). Jerusalem is a very important pilgrimage site by the mid–4th c., as attested by the travel diary of Egeria, a Spanish nun on pilgrimage in the days of Cyril of Jerusalem (q.v.). The accounts Rufinus and Jerome provided of their pilgrimages to Egypt to see the Desert Fathers (qq.v.) are eloquent testimony to the new veneration accorded famous monks. Christians also began to travel widely as an act of worship or asceticism (q.v.) or to receive a blessing from the living saints they went to visit. In later monasticism (q.v.), and especially in Russia of recent centuries, pilgrimage became a way of life, an asceticism of homelessness, and the pilgrim (*strannik*) was a recognizable feature of the tsar's highways and byways. From one of these wanderers comes the famous and anonymous work of the late 19th c., *The Way of a Pilgrim*, with its influential meditation on the "Jesus Prayer."

**PLATO,** philosopher (ca. 427–347 B.C.). A student of Socrates, Plato became the most important of the ancient Greek philosophers. Together with his pupil, Aristotle, he laid the foundations for the philosophy (q.v.) of Greco-Roman antiquity and the Byzantine era (q.v.); his influence continues to be predominant, at the expense of Aristotle, in the Eastern Christian world. Although scholars debate the degree to which Plato himself wished to articulate a fundamentally religious worldview, there is no question that this was the way that he was read by the thinkers of the late Roman era and, more particularly, by the Church Fathers (q.v.). His language of the "One" in the *Parmenides* and "the Good" in the *Republic,* the eschatology of the *Phaedo* and the soul's ascent in the *Phaedrus,* together with the account of the world's origins in the *Timaeus,* were given specifically theistic and even mystical overtones. His demarcation between the sphere of the intelligibles, the ideas or forms, and the sensibles, i.e., the realm of matter and flux, and his assignment of primacy to the former, dominated not only pagan thinkers, but lay at the core of such influential Christian writers as Clement and Origen of Alexandria (qq.v.). His was, moreover, a vocabulary that had already found its way into the New Testament itself (e.g., Heb), and Jewish thought as well (e.g., Wis and Philo). The language of Orthodox theology, asceticism, and liturgy (qq.v.) is indelibly marked by Platonic influence. One can find it in the Cherubic Hymn, in the Cappadocians on the Trinity, in the *Philokalia* (qq.v.)—in short, everywhere.

**PLATON, METROPOLITAN** *see* Levshin, Platon.

**PLATONISM** *see* Neoplatonism; Philosophy; Plato; Plotinus.

**PLOTINUS,** philosopher (ca. 204–270). Plotinus was the chief architect of Neoplatonism (q.v.) and was certainly the greatest philosopher of late antiquity. He fused the idea of the cosmos as one organism and the realm of being as constituted by layers of reality. His active mysticism, moreover, fired his concepts with a more than merely academic fervor. Plotinus's vision was, in short, a powerfully religious one, and it fed the piety (q.v.) and thinking of the best pagan and Christian minds after him. The Cappadocians all read him, as did Augustine of Hippo (qq.v.) and Boethius in the West. His genius lay behind later philosophers in the Neoplatonic tradition: Porphyry, Iamblichus, and Proclus. Porphyry published his master's fifty-four treatises posthumously as six *Enneads,* "sets of nine." Plotinus continued to be read, if infrequently cited, well into the Byzantine era (q.v.).

**PNEUMATOMACHOI.** Literally, "Spirit fighters," the term refers to the late 4th c. movement against ranking the Holy Spirit (q.v.) with the divine persons of the Father and the Son. Basil the Great (q.v.) composed his *On the Holy Spirit* in specific rebuttal to this party, and the other Cappadocians (q.v.) and Pope Damasus also condemned them. Basil's arguments are the ones essentially summarized in the article on the Spirit approved for the Nicene-Constantinopolitan Creed at the Second Ecumenical Council (qq.v.) in 381 where the Pneumatomachoi were anathematized.

**POETRY.** The Orthodox Church has seen a number of poets. Gregory of Nazianzus (q.v.) was noted for his poetry, though it is little known nowadays. Gregory's contemporary, Ephrem of Syria (q.v.), on the other hand, is treasured by the Syrian Church and his hymns are still sung in their churches. Jacob of Seroug (d. 521) is another well-known poet in Syriac, and his near contemporary, Romanos the Melodist, was in Greek the fountainhead of Byzantine liturgical poetry. Other noted composers of liturgical hymnody were: John of Damascus, Andrew of Crete, Cosmas of Maiouma, and Theodore of the Studion (qq.v.). Symeon the New Theologian (q.v.) is perhaps the greatest of Church poets in the latter part of the Byzantine era (q.v.). The creation of liturgical poetry and music (q.v.) continues in the Orthodox Church today along the lines set down by these writers. Poetry of a religious nature, and often reflecting the experience of the Orthodox liturgy (q.v.), can be found in the modern literature (q.v.) of Orthodox lands; for example the Russian poets Pushkin, Tyutchev, Pasternak, Mandelstam, Ahmatova, or the Greeks Diamantes, Palamas, Seferis, and even Cavafy make occasional reference to Orthodox worship.

**POLISH ORTHODOX CHURCH.** The Ecumenical Patriarch (q.v.) granted about four million Orthodox in Poland autocephaly (q.v.) in 1924. But they suffered persecution and the closure of churches during the 1930s under the Roman Catholic government of Pilsudski in spite of their independent status. In 1939, when the borders were changed, most of the Polish Orthodox ended up within the Soviet Union because most lived in the east of the country. In 1948 after the Communist takeover, the primate, Metropolitan Dionysius, was arrested and the Polish Church was effectively "decapitated," forcing the Orthodox Poles to seek refuge with the Patriarchate of Moscow. The Communists with the Russian Church's assent forcibly readmitted Polish Uniates (q.v.) into Orthodoxy, creating tremendous tensions. Moscow slowly reconferred Orthodox autocephaly, but full independence did not occur until the collapse of Communism. Since a majority of Poles consider Roman Catholicism (q.v.) an integral aspect of national identity, and there has been a longstanding antagonism between Russian and Polish interests, the association of the Polish Orthodox with Moscow made their road very difficult as Polish citizens. Although they were willing, they were excluded from the Solidarity Movement, which greatly aided the national spirit and effectively neutralized the Communists over the long run. Currently, there is a vibrant youth movement among the Orthodox. Parishes number approximately two hundred fifty with a slightly greater number of clergy, and church life appears to be improving now that the Muscovite association has lessened.

**POLYCARP,** Bishop of Smyrna, martyr, St. (ca. 70–23 February 156). Irenaeus, through Eusebius (q.v.), tells us that Polycarp sat at the feet of John the Theologian. And Irenaeus himself says the Apostles (q.v.) appointed Polycarp bishop of Smyrna and that he was his teacher. Ignatius's (q.v.) seventh epistle (ca. 110) is addressed to the Church of Smyrna through Polycarp. In 155 Pope Anicetus and Polycarp discussed the Quartodeciman use (i.e., following the Jewish practice of observing Easter, the Christian Passover, on the fourteenth of Nisan) of the date of Easter versus the dominical (Sunday) use of Rome (q.v.). Polycarp appealed to the Apostles as his authority, while Anicetus — after centuries — was vindicated by the First Ecumenical Council (q.v.). Nevertheless, they parted as friends.

The account of Polycarp's martyrdom is one of the classics of early Christian literature (q.v.) and the model for countless such accounts to follow. Particularly notable in the story is the interweaving of motifs taken from the Gospel narratives of Christ's Passion and allusions to the Eucharist (q.v.). The martyrdom is described in an epistle from the Church of Smyrna to Philomelium in Phrygia, since Polycarp was martyred in Smyrna under Proconsul Statius Quadratus. It is the oldest such description, not written after the "Acts of Martyrs," and the following points found therein are historically significant: 1) Martyrdom is an imitation of Christ's suffering and death, and the date of death is called *birth*. 2) It illustrates the existence of a cult of relics (q.v.), since Polycarp's followers "took up his remains more precious than jewels or gold." 3) The prayer of Polycarp has both a precise Trinitarian formula and liturgical formulas.

Eusebius, using words ascribed to Irenaeus, tells of several letters of Polycarp to neighboring communities. But the only one we have today is the "Epistle to the Philippians," which is modeled on Clement (q.v.) of Rome's "First Epistle to the Corinthians" (ca. 100). It might be two letters combined (cf. Paul's 2 Cor), the latest of which dates from the 130s. Four significant items may be excerpted from it: 1) the Philippians ask him for Ignatius's letters; 2) regarding church government, there appears to be no bishop in Philippi, but only presbyters and deacons; 3) almsgiving is recommended (*see* Ascesis); 4) and in spite of persecution, he instructs them to pray for the civil authorities. (*See* Authority; Church and State.)

**POPE.** The word "papa," "pappas," "pope" means simply "father." It seems to have been used for Christian bishops as early as the 3rd c. The latter two, "pappas" and "pope," are common terms of address for Greek and Russian parish priests respectively. The title, "pope," is used still for both the Greek and Coptic Patriarchs of Alexandria (qq.v.), and belongs, of course, to the pope of Rome (q.v.). In the latter's case, and throughout the Western Church, the title has been exclusive of all other bishops since at least the beginning of the Gregorian Reforms.

**POPOV, JOHN** *see* Veniaminov, Innocent (John Popov).

**POPOVITCH, JUSTIN,** theologian, monk. Popovitch was the most important Serbian Orthodox theologian of the 20th c., widely venerated in his own country and particularly among the monks of Greece and Mt. Athos (q.v.). His name is familiar to the rest of the Orthodox *oikoumene* (q.v.) as well. Confined to house arrest by the Yugoslav government from the beginning of the Tito regime, he still managed to write extensively on patristic (q.v.) themes, edit a massive and scholarly collection of Orthodox saints' (q.v.) lives (*Zhitie Svyatikh*) in twelve volumes, and leave his impress on the currently rising generation of Serbian church leaders, notably Bishops Afanasy Jevtitch and Amfilochii Radovitch.

**POSSESSORS AND NON-POSSESSORS** *see* Joseph of Volokolamsk; Novgorodian Tradition.

**PRAYER.** "He is a theologian who prays, and whoever prays is a theologian." This dictum of Evagrius of Pontus (q.v.) sums up the Orthodox understanding of prayer. It is the core of the Christian life, the foretaste of beatitude—"the converse of the mind with God," according to the same Evagrius—and the heart of the struggle of ascesis (q.v.). There are many kinds of prayer. Corporate prayer is the liturgy (q.v.), the prayer of the "Israel of God" as body of Christ, whose focus and energizing principle is the Eucharist (q.v.). Private prayer is of several kinds: intercessory, psalmody or scriptural meditation, and the prayer of the heart. Intercessory prayer recalls the needs of the living and remembers the dead, and is the Christian's service to the body of Christ, the community. Psalmody, i.e., the chanting, reading, or pondering of sacred Scriptures (or writings of the Church Fathers [q.v.]), answers to the *lectio divina* of Western Christian monasticism (q.v.): the feeding on the Word of God (q.v.), Christ, who speaks to the reader through the sacred page and into the heart. This category does not include, however, the sympathetic imagining of God's sacred acts, which features so prominently in Counter-Reformation Roman Catholic piety (qq.v.). (Orthodox tradition views the exercise of the imagination in prayer with very grave reserve, indeed.) Finally, we list the "prayer of the heart," in particular the concentration on the name of Jesus coupled with a petition for mercy. This silent prayer opens up in those readied for it, the communion with the Lord and the conscious perception of his presence.

**PRESANCTIFIED** *see* Liturgies.

**PRESENTATION OF THE LORD, OF THE THEOTOKOS** *see* Feasts, Twelve Great.

**PRIMACY.** Primacy, from the Latin *primus* (Greek, *proteion*), is an article of church government. Within every ecclesiastical region or province, and in today's practice this usually means within each national church, there is a first bishop, a primate, with the responsibility of convoking the local synod of bishops, of coordinating their responsibilities, and maintaining relations with the other local synods of the Orthodox *oikoumene* (q.v.). Among the local primates of the Orthodox Church, the Archbishop of Constantinople, or Ecumenical Patriarch, has held the primacy of honor following the Western schism and the loss of the Church of Rome (qq.v.). In recent times, though, the precise meaning and extent of the Ecumenical Patriarch's primacy has been a matter of debate and pressing concern. (*See* Authority; Church and State.)

Primacy in the Christian world appears to have originated in the relative importance, size, and prominence of the early communities in the great cities of the Roman Empire (q.v.). Rome was the capital, the largest city, and site of the largest Christian church. It thus appears, for these reasons, to have exercised a certain degree of leadership from the earliest times. Very quickly, at least by the 3rd c., the bishops of the communities in the regional or provincial capitals of the Empire took the lead in presiding over local councils, e.g., the councils at Carthage in the time of Cyprian, or the active role of Alexandria in Egypt (qq.v.). By the First Ecumenical Council at Nicaea in 325, the three largest cities, Rome, Alexandria, and Antioch (qq.v.), were recognized as exercising a primacy already in effect over, respectively, Italy, Egypt, and Libya, and the East, i.e., Syria and Palestine. The Council of Constantinople in 381 added the new imperial capital to the list in second place, after Rome, and the Council of Chalcedon in 451 added Jerusalem to complete the five of the Byzantine pentarchy (qq.v.).

In each case, save Jerusalem's, the factor that determined the different councils' decisions was the size and importance of the city: " . . . because Constantinople is New Rome," to quote Canon 3 (381). This principle, called "accommodation," was already clashing in the 4th c. with the rising claims of the Roman Church, in particular the latter's assertion, beginning with Pope Julius, that leadership in the Church depended upon a local church's having had apostolic origins—hence the principle of "apostolicity"—and that Rome, as the see of the Apostle Peter, had inherited his pastoral care for the whole Church.

**PRIMARY CHRONICLE.** Although various chronicles—annals or year-by-year records of events—were known from different areas of ancient Rus', the one usually referred to is called the *Primary Chronicle* or the *Tale of Bygone Years*. A monk of the Kiev Monastery of the Caves, known now as Nestor the Chronicler (1056–ca. 1114), was one of the final redactors of this history, beginning with the evolution of the Kievan state in the 9th c. The editing was done in the 11th c. A translation is available in English, entitled *The Russian Primary Chronicle,* by S. H. Cross and O. B. Sherbowitz-Wetzor.

**PROCESSION OF THE HOLY SPIRIT** *see* Holy Spirit; Trinity.

**PROKEIMENON.** Psalm verses sung before the Epistle and Gospel readings, and at Vespers after the entrance, similar to the Gradual in the West. (The definition of the term in *Webster's Third International* is in error insofar as it lists the prokeimenon as read before the Apocalypse. The Apocalypse is not read liturgically in the Eastern Church.)

**PROKOPOVICH, THEOPHANES,** Archbishop *see* Spiritual Regulation.

**PROSKOMIDE** see Liturgy.

**PROTASOV, NIKOLAI,** Count, Ober-Procurator see Russian Orthodox Church.

**PURGATORY** see Apocatastasis.

-Q-

**QUESTIONS OF KIRIK.** The 101 Questions of Kirik is one of three similar mid-twelfth-century documents from Novgorod's (q.v.) priests to Bishop Nifont. It is so titled simply because the name of a certain Kirik headed the list of clergy. The inquiries focus on a ritualistic understanding of faith and are highly legalistic, and may be called a type of "Russo-Byzantine Pharisaism."

-R-

**RADSTOCKISTS AND PASHKOVISTS.** Both of these late 19th-c. movements may be identified together, were censured by the Church, and were known as "the schism in the aristocracy." Lord Radstock, Granville Augustus William Waldegrave (1833–1913), referred to by Russians as Radstock, "Redstock," and "Krestok" (little cross), preached evangelical sermons with great success privately in St. Petersburg's high society. Nikolai Leskov wrote, "Not to be a Radstockist meant to lower oneself in the eyes of society and risk the danger of becoming labelled a backward person. To take exception with the teaching of the English Lord in a private home was considered equal to insulting the host" (*A High-Society Schism,* 1877). This work was a critique outlining the positive and negative aspects of the movement on the eve of its transmutation to Pashkovism.

Finishing Oxford with honors, Radstock devoted himself to evangelism and Christian philanthropy, and his preaching took him to France, Holland, Switzerland, India, and three times to Russia: 1874, 1875–76, and 1878. He gained fame most especially on his protracted trips to Russia. As a preacher, he may be classed in evangelical circles that included D. L. Moody in the United States and Dr. F. W. Baedeker in Russia. By his third trip to Russia, he no longer preached in broken French to the St. Petersburg elite, but in his own acquired Russian.

Colonel V. A. Pashkov organized the Society for the Encouragement of Spiritual and Ethical Reasoning in 1876 and the Pashkov Palace became a headquarters for Radstockist evangelical meetings. He emerged as the leader of the movement after Radstock's last trip to Russia in 1878, aided by his reputation as a wealthy St. Petersburg philanthropist. He was exiled in 1884 along with others of the same ilk. The general phenomenon of Radstockism/Pashkovism, something akin to the Billy Graham evangelical movement, is especially significant now since it anticipated some Protestant religious interests in post-Communist Russia. (Ironically, in the United States original members of the Graham-inspired "Campus Crusade for Christ" have joined the Orthodox Church en masse.)

**RASKOLNIKI** *see* Old Believers.

**RAVENNA.** A city on the north Adriatic coast of Italy, Ravenna was the capital of the Ostrogoth kingdom from 476 to 540, and thereafter the seat of the Byzantine exarch (qq.v.) of Italy and the West. Until the Lombard conquest in 751 and Ravenna's incorporation into the papal estates, the exarch was the voice of Byzantium (q.v.) in the West and the political overlord of the Roman popes. The exarchate's disappearance signaled the end of Byzantine influence on the papacy (q.v.) and the new arrangement between the popes and the Empire of Charlemagne (q.v.) and his successors. Byzantium's long presence in the city, together with the Gothic kingdom, left Ravenna the site of monuments of early Christian art and architecture (qq.v.), including the mosaics of St. Apollinare and St. Vitale (the latter being the model of Charlemagne's court chapel at Aachen), and the Arian and Orthodox baptistries.

**REFORMS OF PETER THE GREAT** *see* Spiritual Regulation.

**RELICS.** The remains of holy men and women, whether their bones, bodies, or clothing, or else objects associated with them or with the great events of Christ's life (e.g., the fragments of the Cross), are all believed to carry something of the presence, and hence blessing, of the saint (q.v.) or event in question. They are normally enshrined in elaborately worked containers, called reliquaries, kept in the altar area, and are brought out for veneration on the day the saint is commemorated. Evidence for veneration of relics dates back at least to the mid-2nd c. and the veneration accorded the remains of Polycarp of Smyrna (q.v.). The theology of relics is firmly grounded in the Orthodox doctrine of *theosis* (q.v.), or deification, understood as affecting the whole person of the saint. Popular veneration of relics throughout the Byzantine era (q.v.) and the Latin Middle Ages contributed to the unity of the Church. The far ends of the Christian *oikoumene* (q.v.) would know, through the relics, of saints who had lived in the most distant regions, for example the veneration of Nicholas of Myra (q.v.) in the Low Countries and England.

**RENOVATED CHURCH** *see* Living Church.

**REPENTANCE** *see* Confession.

**RESURRECTION** *see* Pascha.

**REUNION COUNCILS.** Two councils, one at Lyons in 1274 and the other at Ferrara-Florence in 1438 to 1439, were convoked by the papacy (q.v.) in cooperation with the Byzantine emperors, Michael VIII and John VIII, respectively, in order to reunite the Catholic West and Orthodox East. They were motivated by a desire on the part of the popes to secure recognition of the Roman primacy (q.v.) from the East, and, on the part of the Orthodox, by the generally (though not exclusively) political desire for material and martial aide from the West against the Ottoman Turks. The earlier council at Lyons amounted to little more than a flat recognition of the papal claims by a small group of bishops and diplomats accredited by the Emperor Michael. The later one, however, was an impressive production.

Ferrara-Florence featured the attendance of most of the bishops subject to the Ecumenical Patriarch (q.v.), together with that of the Emperor John himself and Pope Eugenius. Debate lasted for months and focused primarily on the *filioque* (q.v.). The council concluded by ratifying the western addition to the Nicene-Constantinopolitan Creed (q.v.), recognizing the papal primacy in terms approved by the pope, and affirming the medieval Latin doctrine of purgatory. Mark Eugenicus, Metropolitan of Ephesus (q.v.), was the only Eastern bishop present at the conclusion who refused to sign the conciliar decree. It was the same Mark who led resistance to the union on returning to Constantinople (q.v.). With his support, aided by the power of public opinion led by the monks, the Emperors John and Constantine XI were unable to implement the union up to the fall of the Empire in 1453. Ferrara-Florence was officially repudiated by the Patriarch of Constantinople in 1472. Elsewhere in the Orthodox *oikoumene* (q.v.), rejection came more swiftly. In the Roman Catholic Church (q.v.), the council would serve in following centuries as the ground and model for the various Uniate (q.v.) churches.

**RHODES.** The largest island of the Dodecanese, located in the south Aegean Sea off the coast of Turkey, but within the territory of modern Greece, the entire chain of islands, four dioceses in all, remains under the supervision of the Ecumenical Patriarch (q.v.). The capital and see city of the island, also called Rhodes, was long the capital of a Crusading order, the Knights Hospitalers, who held the island until its conquest by the Ottoman Empire (q.v.) in 1523. In 1961 Rhodes was the site of the first gathering of all local Orthodox churches in several centuries.

**RIDIGER, ALEXIS II,** Patriarch of Moscow and All Russia (23 February 1929– ). From a priestly family, he began his career as choirmaster of St. Simeon Church in Tallin and later at Kazan Church. He was the senior subdeacon to Archbishop Paul of Tallin and Bishop Isidore. After graduating from the Leningrad Theological Seminary in 1949, he did graduate studies at Leningrad Theological Academy and was ordained deacon on 15 April 1950 and priest on 17 April for the Holy Theophany Church, Iyxvi, Estonia. He received the Candidate of Theology degree from the Academy in 1953, with the thesis "Metropolitan Philaret (Drozdov) as Dogmatist," and was appointed pastor of Dormition Cathedral in Tartu, Estonia, and dean of Tartu Deanery on 15 July 1957. Made archpriest and dean of Tartu-Vilyana Deanery in 1959, he became a monastic on 3 March 1961, after which he was elected Bishop of Tallin and Estonia. Promoted to archbishop (1964) and to metropolitan (1968), he became Metropolitan of Leningrad and Novgorod on 29 July 1968. He was enthroned as Patriarch of Moscow and All Russia on 10 June 1990. Long active in the ecumenical movement, Alexis is among the first group of Russian Orthodox to participate in the World Council of Churches Central Committee (1961–68), and was president of the Conference of European Churches (1964–86). His ministry is characterized by good relations with Orthodox outside Russia and active involvement in the social and political crises that confront the people of his country.

**ROMAN CATHOLIC CHURCH.** That church, or community of churches, in communion with and under the direction of the pope of Rome (q.v.), is the descendant of the ancient church of the Western Empire. Until the Second Vatican Council, it followed a trajectory of ever increasing centralization, pursuing the logic of the early papacy (q.v.) and its (implicit) equation of the pope's ecclesiastical role with that of the emperor in civil matters. This development was particularly intense in three different periods: the Gregorian Reforms (11th c.–13th c.); the Counter Reformation (mid–16th c.–17th c.); and the century between the two Vatican councils (1871–1962). It was the first of these great movements that constituted the schism (q.v.) with the Orthodox Church. The following two periods accentuated the differences, taking the Roman Church still further away from the mind of the East.

Nonetheless, this great church, embracing the majority of the world's Christians, is still the closest in doctrine and practice to Orthodoxy (q.v.). The issues that divide the two can be reduced to two: the disagreement over the *filioque* (q.v.) (perhaps less intractable than it has often been presented), and the very deep disagreement over papal primacy and the extent of that primacy (q.v.). Given the crises currently afflicting both communions over the role that the Church plays in government, crises that are virtually mirror opposites of one other, one might hope that some resolution of the schism may prove possible.

**ROMAN EMPIRE.** The Roman Empire is the empire of Christian history, the societal matrix within which the Church first appeared and matured, and the government whose institutions Christianity took over and adapted to its own use in ways that still govern its life today. From the accession of Augustus Caesar (31 B.C.) to the death of Theodosius I (A.D. 395), the entire Mediterranean basin lived under one ruler, one government, and one law, the *pax romana* (q.v.), an achievement never since equaled. This unity in diversity provided the early Church with an earthly image of its own vocation to universality, the world as one city (*cosmopolis*), which deeply impressed the Church's self-understanding and mission.

The political structure of the Empire, its division into "dioceses" and provinces, was mirrored in the Church's development of primacy and the leading roles it bestowed on the patriarchates (qq.v.) and metropolitanates. The influence of the political capital and largest city, Rome, was reflected in the leadership exercised, as a matter of assumed right, by the Christian bishops of Rome in the early Christian centuries, a role later transferred—at least in part—to the new capital, Constantinople (q.v.). The function of the emperor as the focal point of unity in the pagan world and the embodiment of the state's divinity, was carried over to the role of the Byzantine Basileus in the Christian Empire and Church, and still later—albeit in attenuated form—to the role of the tsars in the Orthodox *oikoumene* (q.v.). Clearly, there is much in this inheritance that must be reckoned as a permanent feature of the historical Church. Equally, however, it has given rise to problems that constitute the heart of the current difficulties confronting both the Orthodox and Roman Catholic Church (q.v.).

**ROMANIAN ORTHODOX CHURCH.** The modern state of Romania is composed of a union of three medieval principalities: Wallachia, Moldavia (q.v.), and Transylvania. A fourth, Bessarabia (now the Republic of Moldova), awaits possible union with the Romanian state. Wallachia and Moldavia were first joined in the mid–19th c. to mark the beginnings of modern Romania. Formerly, the two had enjoyed the status of separate principalities politically subject to the Ottoman Empire (q.v.). The nation's independence (1862) followed the pattern of the other new states in the Balkans (q.v.) and resulted in the declaration of

Romanian ecclesiastical independence in 1859, recognized by the Ecumenical Patriarch (q.v.) in 1885. The primate of the Romanian Church took the title "Patriarch" in 1923.

As the only people speaking a Romance language in the Orthodox *oikoumene* (q.v.), the Romanians have looked much toward Western Europe, especially France, in the past one hundred and fifty years. Nonetheless, their church cherishes the most active monastic presence among the local Orthodox churches outside of Greece. Nourished by the hesychast revival begun by Paisii Velichkovsky (qq.v.), particularly strong in Moldavia, traditional monastic spirituality continues to inform the life of this local church's best thinkers, notably the most distinguished Romanian theologian, Fr. Dumitru Staniloae (q.v.).

**ROMANIDES, JOHN SAVVAS,** priest, Greek Orthodox theologian (1927– ). Professor Romanides has been a member of the faculty of Holy Cross Greek Orthodox School of Theology (q.v.), Brookline, Massachusetts (q.v.), has taught at institutions in Greece, and has been very involved in ecumenical (q.v.) activities. He is the author of various articles on the topics of original sin and the Palamite controversy, and has written several books, including *The Ecclesiology of St. Ignatius of Antioch* (1956), *To Propatorikon Amartima* (1970), and *Franks, Romans, Feudalism, and Doctrine: An Interplay Between Theology and Society* (1981).

**ROMANOS THE MELODIST,** poet, composer, St. (?–555). Architect of Byzantine, and hence Orthodox, liturgical poetry (q.v.), Romanos was of Syrian origin, born in Emesa, and flourished in the Constantinople of the Emperor Justinian (qq.v.). His hymns betray the influence of Syriac (q.v.) models. Their dependence upon syllabic stress rather than the value of vowel sounds, characteristic of ancient Greek poetry, is Semitic in origin and was also determinative for the subsequent production of Byzantine hymnody. The themes of his hymns and their handling of imagery recall the poetry of Ephrem the Syrian (q.v.), as well as others in the Syriac tradition. Romanos is most famous for his *kontakia*, about eighty of which circulate under his name. Long poems in several strophes composed in honor of the great feasts of the Church, they are considered great literary achievements. While never sung today in their entirety, the leading strophes, the *kontakia*, preserve something of Romanos's poetry and music in modern liturgical books (qq.v.).

**ROME.** Capital of the Roman Empire and see of the popes (qq.v.), Rome and its mystique—*Roma aeterna*—have played practically as important a role in the Orthodox as in the Roman Catholic Church (q.v.). The ancient capital was, in a sense, the badge of legitimacy for Constantinople, "New Rome," the capital of the East and of the Empire, which, until its demise in 1453, claimed to be the continuation of the polity begun by Augustus Caesar. The early Christian history of the city is worth noting in brief, not only for its intrinsic value and its influence on the East, but for the remarkably detailed list of its early bishops (Epiphanius, *Haer.* 27.6). After the burning of the city by Nero (A.D. 64) and the resulting martyrdom of Peter and Paul, the Church grew under Vespasian (69–79) and Titus (79–81) until the persecutions of Domitian (81–96) and Trajan (98–117). Ignatius of Antioch (q.v.) was martyred at Rome (ca. 110–117), along with at least one early bishop, Telephorus (ca. 126–136), Justin Martyr (q.v.), and Cecilia—the latter two under the severe persecutions of Marcus Aurelius (161–180).

The first century and a half of Christianity in Rome was characterized by these persecutions, while the bishops were Greek-speaking and generally lesser known than contemporary Roman heretics Tatian, Valentinus, and Marcion. These heretics seem to have been criticized only by Rhodo, Pius, (possibly) Justin Martyr, and Hippolytus (q.v.) from the Roman Church. (It is significant that the Christian Apologists [q.v.] from this period, other than the aforementioned, were not Roman.) The earliest Roman bishops who actively appear on the historical record are Clement (ca. 88–97), who wrote an epistle to the Corinthians, which was included in some early lists of the canon of Scripture, Pius I (ca. 141–154), brother of the author of *The Shepherd of Hermas* and the bishop under whom Marcion was excommunicated, and Anicetus (ca. 155–166), who discussed the quartodeciman question with Polycarp of Smyrna (q.v.). Victor I (ca. 189) was the first Latin-speaking pope.

Controversies in the West during the 3rd c. were marked by a practical rigorism in dealing with situations stemming from persecution, and theologically by modalism. Hippolytus, who appears as a consistent and credible theologian of the Trinity (qq.v.), fought modalism among the leadership of the Roman Church for decades. Schisms (q.v.) due to rigorism occurred later concerning the presbyter Novatian (q.v.), who as a disappointed candidate for the see led a group into schism over reconciliation of those who made concessions to paganism during persecution, and over the treatment of the lapsed by Cyprian of Carthage (q.v.). In the first instance, the Roman Church was vindicated in its treatment of Novatian, while in the second case Pope Stephen I was bested by Cyprian. The participation of the Roman Church in the theological issues from the 4th c. to the 8th c. may be tracked in the entries on the Ecumenical Councils and Christology. Although one should be mindful of the fall of the Western Empire in

476 after three "barbarian" (here, Arian Christian) invasions of Italy, the record of "orthodoxy" of the Roman Church during the conciliar period was exemplary. The great suffering due to successive persecutions of the 2nd–3rd c., along with administrative growth and responsible pastoring, was not only a mark of honor, but refined the witness of the Church in the truth of the faith.

The quarrel between the Churches of East and West was parallel to the widening rift between what had been two halves of the one Empire. "Elder Rome" struck a new path with Charlemagne (q.v.) and the Gregorian Reforms while "New Rome" continued the trajectory begun with Constantine (q.v.). In those two paths lay the differences that would eventually divide Europe as well as the Church. Rome is part of the common inheritance of both, albeit differently appropriated, just as are Athens (philosophy) and Jerusalem (the revelation).

**RUFINUS OF AQUILEIA** *see* Historians, Ecclesiastical.

**RUNCIMAN, STEVEN,** Byzantinist, diplomat, educator (7 July 1903– ). He was a King's Scholar at Eton and a scholar at Trinity College, Cambridge, where he earned an M.A. From 1927 to 1938 he was a fellow of Trinity College and a lecturer from 1932 to 1938. From 1942 to 1945 he was professor of Byzantine art and history at the University of Istanbul. His many publications include *The Great Church in Captivity* (1968) and *Byzantine Style and Civilization* (1975). He was knighted in 1958.

**RUS'** *see* Kievan Rus'; Russian Orthodox Church.

**RUSSIAN AMERICA.** This seeming oxymoron is now used by specialists to describe the history of the interaction on American soil between imperial Russia and the people inhabiting North America in the 18th–19th c.—if not through to the present. Active suppression of this history until recent decades may be credited to several factors, including the feelings generated by the Cold War, historical conservatism in enshrining the writings of Hubert Howe Bancroft as the "official history" of western North America, cultural triumphalism, and embarrassment over the treatment of Native American peoples.

The era begins with the period of the exploration and "discovery" of Alaska (q.v.) by Russia at the instigation of Peter the Great. Although the "discovery" is usually credited to Bering, recent research has shown that Cherikov sighted land two days before Bering in 1741, and that Feodorov might have sighted "Seward's Peninsula" as early as 1732. As far as Russian historians are concerned, the first Russian to explore the straits between Asia and America was the Yakut (q.v.)

seaman Simeon Dezhnev, who did so in 1648. The exploration is said to have been kept a state secret, smuggled to the West only in 1730 by a Swedish prisoner of war, although American historians dismiss Russians in Alaska prior to 1700 as folklore.

The word "discovery" has been left in quotes because the Russians frequently named lands by their native populations and early knew that locals must have gone back and forth between Asia and North America on a regular basis. In theory the earliest Russian pioneers in Alaska (before 1741) remained anonymous intentionally, so as to escape taxation on fur commerce. The interests of the Bering party lay primarily in discovering a land bridge and establishing the westernmost advance of European occupation; these issues are mentioned as early as Peter's instructions to Bering, though Peter's motives remain unknown—supposedly related to the fur trade. The next one hundred years were punctuated by map making, biological and botanical surveys, fur harvest and trading, and getting to know—when possible—the native peoples. Early Aleut resistance to Russian trading colonies in the "Ungnak Massacre" was recently confirmed through archaeological evidence.

The next period, 1741–98, is known as the "Fur Rush" or the time of the Alaskan *promyshlenniki* (frontiersmen). The era has not been adequately researched, and is complicated by the fact that exaggeration and character defamation abound on many sides. Just as with tales about Paul Bunyan and Daniel Boone, Russian frontiersmen seem to spin their yarns to fit the same genre. Others, like the Russian American Company, told tales to discredit the *promyshlenniki* with the Russian imperial government, and characterize their corporation as the establishment of the rule of law. American historians seem to have followed these official company reports without reservation, although it is clear that many of the officials of the Company might just as well have been describing their own behavior rather than that of other transgressors. Recently a microfilm of a significant English language diary, the Joseph Billings journal (1787–92), never seen before in the United States, was presented to American scholars working in the field, and should shed new light on these decades. The period ends with the establishment of the Russian American Company (1798) and coincides closely with the arrival of Russian missionaries in 1794.

The following period, 1798–1867, is one in which an indigenous Native American Orthodox culture was established in spite of the exigencies of the fur trade. The most significant events from the Church's perspective were the arrival of the Elder Herman (q.v.) with about a dozen other monastics who missionized the native population, and ended up protecting them from their Russian overlords. Later, Fr. Innocent Veniaminov arrived and furthered work with the native clergy, like

Fr. James Netsvetov (qq.v.), in developing indigenous Orthodox cultures. Although this period ends with the sale of Alaska in 1867, Russian Orthodox contacts with Alaska did not cease. The foray south from Alaska to Fort Ross (q.v.) established links that simply moved the center of activity to the San Francisco Bay area.

The period from 1867 to 1917 focuses on the Russian immigration to the Pacific northwest (especially San Francisco) before the Russian Revolution and the figure of Bishop Tikhon Belavin (q.v.). Tikhon, as Innocent before him, envisioned an autocephalous (q.v.) Orthodox Church in America as an outgrowth of the American Missionary Diocese. He moved the headquarters of the Russian Missionary Diocese from San Francisco to New York in 1905 in anticipation of this indigenous church, and with the shift in immigrant populations from the West to the eastern seaboard. At this time all "ethnic" Orthodox churches recognized the Russian Missionary Diocese as the responsible coordinating organization, and this situation prevailed until the Russian Revolution prevented further Russian support for these efforts. Another significant phenomenon during this period was the return to Orthodoxy of a large number of Carpatho-Russian Uniates in the east through the labors of Fr. Toth (qq.v.) and others, which event greatly increased the number of churches and parishioners in the diocese.

After the Revolution—and with continued immigration—ethnic Orthodox established administrative contacts with their mother churches (q.v.). The Russian missionary diocese continued, breaking off dependence on its own mother church in order to avoid Bolshevik interference. It suffered administrative bedlam in the 1920s and 1930s as a result of the Revolution and from the establishment of the (Soviet-sponsored) Living Church in Russia and the United States, but eventually achieved autocephalous status in 1970 as the Orthodox Church in America (qq.v.).

**RUSSIAN BIBLE.** In Russia in the 19th c. theologians and members of the newly formed Russian Bible Society, such as Alexander Golitsyn (q.v.), were particularly interested in the Hebrew Scriptures (q.v.). Eminent scholars produced personal translations: Makarii Glukharev (1792–1847), a seminary professor and Siberian missionary, translated Job (1837) and Isaiah (1839) from Hebrew into Russian; Archpriest Gerasim Pavskii (1787–1863), a professor and Hebraist in St. Petersburg translated the entire Old Testament, which his students secretly circulated until all copies were confiscated in 1842. These translations from Hebrew into Russian, instead of Church Slavic as in the Gennadievskii and Ostrog Bibles (qq.v.), drew mixed reactions from the hierarchy and from society at large for about fifty years, until the last quarter of the century. Glukharev's and Pavskii's translations were eventually published in the mid–1860s, but the Hebrew versus Septuagint (q.v.) debate continued—to an impasse for some who would allow only one tradition (e.g., P. I. Gorskii-Platonov accepted only the Hebrew, F. Govorov only the Septuagint). Most scholars and churchmen in Russia in the last decades of the 19th c. recognized the complex relationship between the Hebrew and Greek texts. They knew that the Church Slavic Bible does not correspond exactly to the Septuagint, and they researched the relationship between the Hebrew and Greek in critical literature on a book-by-book basis.

The great Bible translation project of 19th-c. Russia can be credited to only one individual, Metropolitan Philaret (Drozdov) of Moscow. In the early phase of the project (1816–25) before Philaret was metropolitan, he set forth guidelines for translation that were to be used in the second half of the century. Translation was from the Masoretic Hebrew as the basic text, then from Greek when it was the original language, giving both preference over Church Slavic. Literary form was analyzed and maintained: "The spirit of a passage must be painstakingly observed, so that conversation will be rendered in a colloquial style, narration in a narrative style, and so forth." Philaret ranked translational priorities as accuracy first, clarity second, and literary purity third. He gave stylistic directions; for example, "Holy Scripture derives its majesty from the power, not the glitter, of its words." (Both quotes are from Georges Florovsky, *The Ways of Russian Theology*, Part I, p. 190, without further reference.)

Philaret's guidelines for translation raised difficult, legitimate questions that Russian society in the 1820s could not handle without public discussion—which occurred only later in the century. For example, for those troubled by the divergence of the Russian translation from the Church Slavic, especially with regard to preference given the Hebrew, explanation had to be made that would satisfy those unfamiliar with ancient languages. Again, the Hebrew and Greek texts enjoy a complex relationship that needs to be understood on a case-by-case basis. This translation was finally published in segments: the Gospels in 1819, the entire New Testament in 1820, the Psalter in 1822, and the rest of the Old Testament in 1825. With the printing complete, the new tsar not only suppressed the new translation, but completely destroyed it.

In 1856 Philaret personally urged the Holy Synod to undertake a new translation that would provide "the Orthodox people with the means to read Holy Scripture for instruction in the home and with the easiest possible comprehension" (Florovsky, *The Ways of Russian Theology*, Part II, p. 123). This project began as a repetition of the 1820s debacle. Although Philaret's purpose appears commendable, his efforts were opposed by some backward-looking colleagues, notably Metropolitan

Philaret (Amfiteatrov) of Kiev and the new ober-procurator of the Ministry of Religious Affairs, Count A. P. Tolstoi. Since the project had been successfully opposed in 1824 and 1842, when it was proposed again in 1856, many of the 1820s reasons against it were repeated: mistrust of the Hebrew Bible, translations from the Hebrew by Pavskii and Makarii caused controversy, the Greek Church did not allow vernacular Greek, Russian was accused of being less expressive than Slavic, other liturgical books had not been translated, and only Church Slavic translations were used liturgically (which remained the case throughout the Soviet Period). To the credit of scholarship and Philaret, the Bible project was completed, now under the Holy Synod and the metropolitan's watchful eye. The Gospel Book was published in 1860, the complete New Testament in 1862, fascicles of the Old Testament in 1868, and the complete edition in 1875. All subsequent synodal editions, revised and republished until the decade before the Russian Revolution, depended on this one; revisions were handled by the technique of citing the correction in the footnote and moving it into the text in the subsequent printing. When the Moscow Patriarchate published a half million Bibles in 1988 to commemorate the millennium of Christianity in Rus', it republished the last prerevolutionary revision of Philaret's Bible.

**RUSSIAN ORTHODOX CHURCH.** We focus our attention on the Russian Church in the 19th and 20th c. since the medieval and early imperial history can be found under Kievan Rus', Novgorodian Tradition, Muscovite Tradition, Unia, and the Spiritual Regulation (qq.v.). The difficulties caused by the Spiritual Regulation of Peter the Great in the 18th c. continued into the 19th c. and developed further: The government interfered increasingly in the intellectual and administrative life of the Church; not only was there no patriarch, but the Holy Synod was controlled by the government; and the social status and economic situation of the clergy continued to deteriorate.

The ober-procurator's power, influencing the Holy Synod and leading it, grew until the office became an official Ministry of State. Under Tsar Alexander I the Ministry of Ecclesiastical Affairs and Education was formed, but had a brief existence (1817–1824). This so alarmed the hierarchy that it complained of persecution of the Church. Nevertheless, Count Nikolai Protasov (1799–1855) became ober-procurator of the Holy Synod from 1836 to 1855 and continued the trend of strengthening the office. During his tenure he successfully transformed the Russian Church into an organ of the state, "The Department of the Orthodox Confession." His political methodology may be described as attempting to reduce the Russian Church and clergy to civil religion in the worst sense—bureaucratic functionaries of the state's "confession." With this goal, true higher education and ecclesiastical freedom became irrelevant. All that was needed was supplied by the tsar, who was "the supreme defender and guardian of the dogmas of the ruling faith, and observer of orthodoxy and all good order in the Holy Church. In this sense the Emperor, in the law of succession to the throne (5 April 1797), is called the Head of the Church" (*Fundamental Laws,* articles 42, 43, 1832 edition). Under Protasov, church finances and clergy employment became the sole domain of the ober-procurator. Of those who opposed him, Metropolitan Philaret of Moscow, renowned for his work on the Russian Bible (q.v.) translation project, distinguished himself by attempting to keep Protasov in check.

After the dissolution of the Ministry of Ecclesiastical Affairs and Education (1824), Philaret proposed organizing the Russian Church into nine metropolitan districts to correspond to Alexander I's organization of provinces into nine large administrative districts. These metropolitan districts, as in the ancient church, would be self-governing and outside governmental control, limiting the sphere of influence of the Holy Synod. Philaret hoped to create an institution from these metropolitan districts that would have authority over the (Regulation's) Synod. Under Tsar Nicholas I, Protasov's power grew and the question of the decentralization of ecclesiastical administration could not be raised. But with the passage of the liberal reforms of Tsar Alexander II (1855–1881) the proposal was revived.

Although in the second half of the 19th c. none of the proposals for the reform of the Spiritual Regulation's Holy Synod got beyond the point of theoretical discussion, an impressive assortment of supporters came forward. Aside from Philaret, these included an aide to the ober-procurator, A. N. Muraviev, who engaged in extensive correspondence encouraging reform. The Slavophiles (q.v.) championed the cause of sobornost or conciliarity, and saw a parallel between freedom (q.v.) of the human spirit and freedom of Church life—both without government interference. The secular press also entered the fray and published articles—and even a short novel—wherein the question of freedom within the Church was broached. Other principal voices of the time, Vladimir Soloviev, Feodor Dostoevsky, Leo Tolstoy, and Nikolai Gogol (qq.v.), were not actively involved in the resolution of this particular problem, though all involved themselves in contemporary questions regarding the Church.

Near the end of the 19th c. the necessity for changes in the Church's relationship to the state was better recognized. Tsar Alexander III and Ober-Procurator C. Pobedonostsev entrusted elementary education to parish schools (1884), and the number of schools grew rapidly, though the quality of education was inferior. But Pobedonostsev was the chief architect of ultraconservative reactionary policy in the administrations of Alexander III and Nicholas II and proved himself no friend of Church freedom (q.v.). He began persecutions of Doukhobors (q.v.), Jews, Christian denominations, and sectarians, along with a forced Russification policy. The favored "state Church" was supposed to fare better—but it did not. The next round of reforms in 1905 were accomplished in spite of Pobedonostsev's strong opposition. From clergy who favored labor unions and religious toleration to those who tried to implement Orthodox Church reforms, which had been discussed for almost a century—all had to do business with the censorship of Pobedonostsev's reactionary philosophy and policies.

To oppose the ober-procurator the Church had a champion in S. Witte, the president of the Committee of Ministers. An imperial ukaz was issued for religious toleration on 12 December 1904, and the "state Church" found itself in the unenviable position of being in more difficult circumstances than the heterodox: There was freedom of conscience and rights of self-determination for all the major religious communities *except* the Orthodox. The president of the Holy Synod, Metropolitan Antony (Vladkovsky) of St. Petersburg, took leadership of the movement for ecclesiastical reform with Witte's assistance.

The Orthodox "reform movement" lasted from 1905 to 1918 and spelled the end of the Spiritual Regulation. Ironically, the following "Memorandum" items that Vladkovsky and Witte acted on is much the same list of requests made by the Russian Patriarchate in 1990 to the post-Communist government: granting of the rights of a legal person to the parish; inclusion of clergy and the parish in local (zemstvo) governments; granting to the hierarchy the right to take part in the highest state institutions; revival and renewal of the parish; decentralization of ecclesiastical administration; broadening of the powers of the diocesan assemblies with lay delegates; and reform of the ecclesiastical courts. Most of these measures took effect in the Russian Orthodox Churches in North America and Western Europe because of the 1905 to 1918 reform movements, but were never fully implemented in Russia because of the revolutions in 1905 and 1917.

In the midst of international conflict, internal national rebellion, and a period of ecclesiastical reforms, the Church presented a vision of and reaped benefits from the least likely of sources. First, Seraphim of Sarov (q.v.), a traditional Orthodox monastic and ascetic, was recognized as a saint (q.v.) over the loud protests of Pobedonostsev and the Russian intelligentsia who claimed this was "a canonization of peasant ignorance." Seraphim proceeded to become the most influential spiritual force in Russia and the emigration over succeeding decades. Second, a group of young Marxists including Nicholas Berdiaev, Sergius Bulgakov (qq.v.) and Peter Struve converted and proceeded to pen the most damning indictment of the Russian intelligentsia and

Marxism-Leninism ever to be written. The indictment was convincing and prophetic, but less known in the West than among the Slavs. Third, the outpost of Orthodoxy in Russian America helped to produce the next Patriarch of Moscow and All Russia, Tikhon Belavin (qq.v.), elected in 1918 as the first patriarch since Peter the Great.

The reforms of the Church were legislated contemporaneously with Lenin's abolition of the judicial system in December 1917—just in time to have church properties confiscated and religious education halted. All this was to be enforced by a new organization of political police created that same month, the "Cheka." In fact some of the reforms were instituted in Russia, but under the guise of the Living Church (q.v.), which was short-lived (1922–26). Due to this and the murder and persecution of tens of thousands of clergy and church members in a programmatic fashion in the early years of Communism, and in a less organized way after Khrushchev, the reforms never became a reality. Mere survival was challenge enough in these years. Sadly, the Russian Church under the Soviets again became an agent of the state, however unwilling and coerced. It officially supported every regime and was used to advance national and international policies. Active churchmen who declared themselves publicly like Fr. Pavel Florensky (q.v.) could be found, but by the 1950s almost all of them had "disappeared."

Circumstances changed radically with glasnost and perestroika in that the perception of the status of the Church by the people and the leaders improved—even if the Church was just one option among the many mainstream and fringe organizations to crop up in the rarefied atmosphere of Russian freedoms. The transformation occurred at the same time as the celebration of the millennium of the Christianization of Kievan Rus' in 1988. Little that the people valued in their culture had come from Communism, and the tourists confirmed that evaluation of Russian culture. Shortly thereafter a new patriarch, Alexis Ridiger (q.v.), was elected, and this free election in an exciting new era was acknowledged as judiciously choosing the right person—possibly even the best person—for the job. The Church retains its credibility in the political exigencies of the new democratic processes when it continues its witness—even the witness of its most recent martyrs (q.v.), succeeds provisionally in charitable works, and manifests the best of Russia's cultural heritage.

**RUTHENIAN ORTHODOX CHURCH** *see* Unia.

-S-

**SABAS.** The name of two important saints (q.v.) of the Orthodox Church: 1) Sabas the Sanctified (439–532) was a monk who founded the greatly influential monastery in the Judaean desert, today called by his name, Mar Saba. It later housed such figures as John of Damascus and Gregory of Sinai (qq.v.), and in the process served as an invaluable conduit of Syrian and Mesopotamian Christian literature to the Church of Byzantium (q.v.). 2) Sava of Serbia (1175–1235) was born to the princely house of Stephan Nemanja, founded the Serbian monastery of Hilandar on Mt. Athos (q.v.) in 1198, and went in 1219 to the Byzantine court in exile (following the Fourth Crusade) to receive consecration at the hands of the Ecumenical Patriarch (q.v.), Manuel I, as the first archbishop of Serbia. He spent the remaining years of his life building up his Church, defending it from claims of the Roman popes and of rival Greek archbishops, and thus firmly rooted his nation and the Serbian Orthodox Church within the Orthodox *oikoumene* (qq.v.). He was soon canonized and is venerated today as the patron saint of Serbia.

**SACRAMENTS.** The Latin word, *sacramentum,* finds its equivalent in the Orthodox use of the term, "mystery" (Greek, *mysterion*). The "mysteries" in the Orthodox Church are usually numbered seven as in the Roman Catholic Church (q.v.) as a result of the latter's influence in the 13th c.: Baptism (q.v.), Chrismation (anointing of the newly baptized), Communion or Eucharist (q.v.), Ordination (q.v.) (of bishop, priest, and deacon), Matrimony, Confession (q.v.), and Unction (the solemn anointing of the sick).

While seven has been the usual count since the 15th c., reinforced by the conciliar decision at Bethlehem (1692) presided over by Patriarch Dositheus, earlier numbering was considerably more fluid. The 4th c. Church Fathers (q.v.) usually speak of Baptism, Chrismation, and Eucharist. In the 5th c. or early 6th c., Dionysius the Areopagite (q.v.) added ordination, monastic tonsure, and Christian burial to the latter three. In addition, his chapter devoted to the Chrism concentrates on the consecration of the oil itself, the Holy Myron, used both to administer the post-baptismal anointing and to consecrate the altar. The latter, consecration of a church, together with the great blessing of water on Theophany (6 January), are included among the sacraments in some early medieval lists. Orthodox monks follow Dionysius with enthusiasm, still insisting on monastic tonsure as a sacrament. Thus, the list of seven that generally prevails cannot be said to be as fixed in Orthodoxy as in Roman Catholicism. Orthodox theologians sometimes quip that the sacraments may be numbered variously as one, two, three, seven, nine—or 232.

Finally, the notion of sacrament (*mysterion*) as that which pertains to the one mystery of Christ, and as communicating that mystery, extends into the worshiping Church's every action: the painting of icons (q.v.), blessings of different objects, etc. Far more important, then, than any enumeration is the idea of sacrament as that which manifests Christ and enables the participant to partake of him. From this the Eucharist, a collective action in cooperation with the Holy Spirit (q.v.) fully manifesting the Church, is the only sacrament to which Orthodox refer without qualification as "the mysteries." In this sense it is the Church itself that is finally the sacrament par excellence.

**ST. SERGIUS ORTHODOX THEOLOGICAL INSTITUTE.** A graduate school of theology (q.v.) founded by Metropolitan Evlogii of Western Europe and staffed by perhaps the most distinguished faculty of scholars in recent Orthodox history, St. Sergius flourished from the late 1920s to just after World War II and produced a bibliography of published books and articles that runs to more than ninety pages. More than quantity characterized this extraordinary output. Many of the works produced at this institution still exert a powerful influence on contemporary Orthodox thought. Its professors—church historians such as Anton Kartashev and Georges Florovsky, liturgists such as Nikolai Afanasiev, the dogmatic theologian, Sergei Bulgakov (qq.v.)— continue to be read with attention both within and outside the Orthodox *oikoumene* (q.v.). The school still functions in Paris as the unique institute of higher learning maintained by the Orthodox Church in Western Europe.

**ST. VLADIMIR'S ORTHODOX THEOLOGICAL SEMINARY.** In 1905 Archbishop Tikhon (q.v.), later Patriarch of Moscow, recognized the need for indigenous American clergy and decided to establish a permanent seminary. Opened in 1905 in Minneapolis, it was transferred in 1913 to Tenafly, New Jersey, and during the eighteen years of its existence produced two generations of priests who, at a difficult moment in the life of the Church, assured the continuity of Orthodoxy in America and its progressive integration into American life.

The Russian Revolution of 1917 inaugurated a deep crisis for Orthodoxy in America. Deprived of material support from Russia, isolated from the mother church (q.v.), suffering from internal divisions, the Church here could no longer financially support the seminary, and in 1923 it closed its doors. Fifteen years later, after a long period of recovery and reorganization, the question of theological education was raised again. At the Sixth All-American Church Sobor meeting in New York in October 1937, Dr. Basil M. Bensin, one of the first instructors at the Minneapolis school, proposed reopening the seminary. A working agreement was established with Columbia College, and in 1939 a temporary home for the school was found on the campus of General Theological Seminary.

The aftermath of World War II brought unexpected growth and development to the seminary. The arrival from Europe of several renowned scholars—including George P. Fedotov (q.v.), formerly a professor at St. Sergius Orthodox Theological Institute (q.v.) in Paris (+1951); Nicholas S. Arseniev, from the Orthodox Theological Faculty in Warsaw (+1977); Eugene V. Spektorsky, formerly of the University of Kiev (+1950); and Nicholas O. Lossky (q.v.), formerly of the University of St. Petersburg (+1965)—made possible further development of St. Vladimir's as a graduate school of theology, an "academy" to use the old Russian nomenclature. Soon the school moved to new quarters rented from Union Theological Seminary.

The beginning of this new era coincided with the arrival of the Rt. Rev. Dr. Georges Florovsky (q.v.) from St. Sergius Institute in Paris. He was soon appointed dean (1949–55), and under his leadership the theological curriculum was developed, the faculty grew and the school was given a definite pan-Orthodox orientation. "A contemporary Orthodox theologian," Fr. Florovsky said at the formal inauguration of the seminary in its new status, "cannot retire into a narrow cell of some local tradition, because Orthodoxy . . . is not a local tradition but basically an ecumenical one." The seminary's future development was assured by the arrival of other younger theologians from St. Sergius: Fr. Alexander Schmemann (1951, +1983), Professor Serge S. Verhovskoy (1952, +1986), and later Fr. John Meyendorff (q.v.) (1959). In April 1953 St. Vladimir's was granted an Absolute Charter by the Board of Regents of the State of New York.

In 1961 a five-year search for a suitable campus ended with the purchase of property in Westchester County. Within a few years, after a successful financial drive, new buildings were erected and housing for faculty and staff was acquired. In June 1966 the seminary was accepted to Associate Membership in the American Association of Theological Schools, and became fully accredited in 1973. Final recognition of the seminary's maturity was given in March 1967, when the Board of Regents of the University of the State of New York granted St. Vladimir's the power to award the degree of Bachelor of Divinity (later Master of Divinity), followed in 1970 by the degree of Master of Theology, in 1985 by the degree of Master of Arts, and in 1988 by the degree of Doctor of Ministry.

**SAINTS.** "Saint," from the Latin *sanctus* (Greek, *hagios;* Church Slavic, *sviatii*), refers to a person recognized by the Church as having partaken during his or her lifetime of the quality of God's holiness (q.v.), a "holy man" or "holy woman." The expression, "the saints," is used of Christians in general by Paul, and Orthodoxy (q.v.) maintains that all believers, by virtue of their having put on Christ in Baptism (q.v.), are at least potentially "holy ones," temples and manifestations of God's action in the world. The popular veneration of certain believers who had clearly manifested God's holiness appears very early in the history of the Church. The veneration of the saints is at least as old as the cult of the martyr (q.v.), and was extended in the 4th c. to the monks, the "ascetics" in the current Orthodox categorization of saints, and to the great teaching bishops, who are called "illuminators" or "luminaries." Other categories of saints were added later, among them: fools in Christ (q.v.) (*saloi, iurodev'i*), unmercenary physicians, equals to the apostles (meaning great missionaries), military saints (usually martyrs from the Roman army), and, uniquely in Russia, the "passion-bearers" (innocent sufferers).

The saints are believed to be active members of the family of the Church, intercessors and protectors, though all of them derive their ministry in and through—and as witnesses to—the Risen Christ. They are omnipresent in Orthodox Church life. No child is baptized without receiving the name of a patron saint, and in most Orthodox cultures it is the child's saint's day that is celebrated as in the West one celebrates birthdays. The *Synaxarion,* or collection of saints' lives for every day of the year, is read from at morning services in monasteries. The relics (q.v.) of the saints are venerated, the subject of pilgrimage (q.v.), and transferred or "translated," when such occurs, with great pomp and ceremony.

**SAKHAROV, SOPHRONY,** archimandrite, of Essex, England (1896–1993). A student at the Moscow State School of Fine Arts interested in Buddhism, yoga, East Indian culture, and eastern mysticism, he was a painter until 1921, when he emigrated to Paris by way of Italy and Germany. In Paris he exhibited his paintings at the Salon d'Automne and the Salon des Tuileries. Disillusioned with art, he entered St. Sergius Orthodox Theological Institute (q.v.), became disillusioned with academic life, then abandoned Paris for the Russian monastery of St. Panteleimon on Mt. Athos (q.v.). After four years there he came under the spiritual guidance of Starets Silouan (q.v.), with whom he remained until the Starets' death eight years later. During World War II he was a cave-dwelling anchorite-priest, and remained so until he was called to be confessor and spiritual father to the monks of St. Paul Monastery. He later published two books on his spiritual father (q.v.), the Starets Silouan, as well as other works on the Orthodox spiritual tradition: *Wisdom from Mount Athos* (1975), *The Monk of Mount Athos* (1975), and *His Life Is Mine* (1977). He continues to live, as abbot emeritus, at the monastery of St. John the Baptist, which he founded at Tolleshunt Knights, Essex, England.

**SALIBA, PHILIP E.**, Archbishop of the Antiochian Archdiocese of North America (1931– ). He served as subdeacon (1945–49) and deacon (1949–59) in the Antiochian Orthodox Church and in 1956 settled in the United States He was priest from 1959–66 and in 1961 became a naturalized United States citizen. In 1966 he was consecrated archbishop of the Antiochian exarchate (q.v.) in North America. He is author of *Feed My Sheep: The Thought and Words of Philip Saliba: On the Occasion of His Twentieth Year in the Episcopacy* (1987). His episcopacy has been characterized by an increased Arab ethnicity compared to that of his predecessor, Archbishop Antony Bashir (q.v.), due to the emigration of Palestinians to the United States. (*See* Antiochian Orthodox Christian Archdiocese.)

**SALVATION.** The Greek word for salvation, *soteria,* means at root "wholeness" or "wellness," and also carries the sense of "protection" and "preservation." Generally, in the Greek Church Fathers (q.v.) and subsequent tradition, this continues to be the way in which the work of Christ is fundamentally presented. He is the one who restores humanity, heals human nature, and so delivers humanity from the danger of perishing. The image of God (q.v.) in the human being, implanted by the Creator but distorted by the Fall and Sin (q.v.)—and as a result at risk of being destroyed by death—is restored and made new by the birth, death, and resurrection of the Incarnate Word. In consequence the particular emphasis on salvation as forgiveness of sins and deliverance from divine condemnation, while present in the Orthodox East, receives far less emphasis than it has in the West from Augustine of Hippo (q.v.) and Anselm of Canterbury (11th c.) to the present.

**SAMUEL (AZIZ), BISHOP** *see* Aziz, Samuel.

**SAVA** *see* SABAS.

**SCHISM.** The Greek word means literally "a rip or tear, as in cloth," and thus in the language of ecclesiology (q.v.) signifies a division or break in the communion of the Church. As some have observed, Eastern Christendom lives rather more easily with such divisions than does the West. Schisms have appeared with some frequency in the East over the centuries, often for reasons more political than theological, e.g., the "Bulgarian Schism," which saw the Church of Bulgaria out of communion with the Ecumenical Patriarch (qq.v.) for more than seventy years (1870–1945). When such a break is allied with a real or perceived difference in doctrine, and thus with a manifestation of heresy (q.v.), the break usually becomes permanent. Such was the schism between the Byzantine Church and the Church of the East

("Nestorians"), or later with the local churches objecting to Chalcedon, and with the Church of Rome over the questions of the *filioque* and papal primacy (qq.v.).

**SCHMEMANN, ALEXANDER,** priest, liturgical theologian, educator (13 September 1921–13 December 1983). He did his theological studies at St. Sergius Orthodox Theological Institute, Paris (1940–1945), and was a pupil of the church historian A. V. Kartashev (qq.v.). Under Kartashev's guidance, Schmemann wrote his candidate's thesis on Byzantine theocracy, then was an instructor of Byzantine Church history at St. Sergius from 1945 to 1951. In 1946 he was ordained to the priesthood by Archbishop Vladimir (Tikhonitsky), head of the Western Europe Russian Exarchate. During his time in France Schmemann was deeply influenced by the "eucharistic ecclesiology" of Fr. Nikolai Afanasiev (q.v.), professor of Canon Law, and his theological horizons were broadened by interaction with Roman Catholic thinkers, Jean Danielou and Louis Bouyer.

In 1951 he was brought to the faculty of St. Vladimir's Theological Seminary, Crestwood, New York, by Fr. Florovsky (qq.v.), where he taught church history and liturgical theology (q.v.). Dean of the Seminary from 1962 until his death, he played a vital role in making it a center of liturgical and eucharistic revival. He had a weekly radio program to Russia on Radio Liberty for many years, and was active in the creation of the autocephalous status of the Orthodox Church in America (qq.v.) in 1970. His publications include *The Historical Road of Eastern Orthodoxy* (1963), *For the Life of the World: Sacraments and Orthodoxy* (1973), *Of Water and the Spirit,* and *Introduction to Liturgical Theology.* He is survived by his wife, Julianna, who continues to edit and publish his lectures and notes.

**SCHOLASTICISM.** This word is chiefly associated with the theological movement beginning in the eleventh-century Christian West, and brought to its highest point by Thomas Aquinas and Bonaventure at the University of Paris in the mid-thirteenth century. Centered on "schools," beginning with the cathedral schools mandated by Charlemagne (q.v.) such as at Chartres, then moving to the great medieval universities of Paris, Oxford, Heidelberg, etc., Scholasticism sought to resolve perceived contradictions in Scripture and the Church Fathers (qq.v.) through recourse to the logic of the newly rediscovered texts of Aristotle coming to the West from Muslim Spain. A form of intellectual apologetics, Scholasticism ultimately came to dominate every approach to theology (q.v.) in the West. For all intents and purposes, it became "theology," and "systematics" and, more generally, all academic theological work ever since. It was also profoundly different in approach and spirit from the monastic tradition of theological reflection, based on the meditation on liturgy (q.v.) and Scripture, which had prevailed in both East and West until Scholasticism's rise. While Bernard of Clairvaux (12th c.) was the last great exemplar of this older approach in the West, it continued in the Orthodox world, even winning a signal victory over Byzantium's (q.v.) own version of Scholasticism in the hesychast (q.v.) controversy of the 14th c.

Western Scholasticism might mark a significant philosophical or theological parting of the ways between Roman Catholicism (q.v.) and Orthodoxy. But the participation of Mediterranean and Russian Orthodox hierarchs in the intellectual milieu of Scholasticism has ensured a place for it in the history of Orthodox thought. Both Roman Catholic and Protestant Scholastic problems made their way into the catechetical and theological schools of Constantinople, Kiev, and finally Russia. Bishops such as Cyril Lukaris, Peter Mogila, and the author of Peter the Great's Spiritual Regulation (qq.v.), Theophanes Prokopovich, all utilized the categories of Scholasticism and based their writings upon it. After Peter the Great, Scholasticism became the basis of the Latin curricula of Russia's schools, theological and secular, which followed Kievan and European prototypes, respectively. Whether this phenomenon is considered a "foreign invasion" of ideas onto Orthodox soil or a necessary dialogue involving the intellectual history of the greater Church depends on one's predisposition toward the "legitimate" history of Holy Tradition (q.v.).

**SCHOOLS,** Reformed under Peter I *see* Spiritual Regulation.

**SCRIPTURE.** The liturgical, including the homiletical, use of Scripture or the Word of God (q.v.) in the Orthodox Church occupies a preeminent place over the written word, used for personal devotion and study. To enjoy the fullness of Scripture and all it refers to, the average Orthodox Christian looks to the parish and monastic liturgical practice for living Holy Tradition (q.v.). What a Biblical text means today is controlled largely by church liturgical usage and homilies about the text rather than by pronouncement. For the Bible to be alive in Holy Tradition, it must be heard and experienced liturgically. Whether it exists in a particular printed form or occupies hierarchical attention in edicts is only relative to the Word living among all the people, hierarchy and laity, now and throughout the ages. To say it differently, the living Word of God is seen manifest in the Old Testament, in Jesus Christ and his words, in those who repeated Jesus' words before they were written down, in the Church and her liturgical use of a written, "canonical" text, in the Fathers and Mothers of the Church, in contemporary congregations, etc.

The Bible and its interpretation in the Orthodox Church includes such topics as textual tradition, the commentaries of the Church Fathers (q.v.), the history of the canon, the use of the historical-critical method, as well as the liturgical use and interpretation of the text, etc. The Orthodox understand that Scripture originated orally as the liturgy (q.v.) of the people of God and then was written down. For the specialist, the *Sitz im Leben* of Scripture was the Temple liturgy of Jerusalem and the liturgy of the Church—along with their respective hierarchies. Still, the historical question—what the text meant within its own context—and historical facticity are important. The Orthodox agree with Paul that if Christ was not raised from the dead, then Christian faith is in vain. The Nicene-Constantinopolitan Creed (q.v.) also maintains a similar historical perspective.

The first historical indications of the written Biblical text are the famous episodes of the finding of a book in the Temple and of the dictation by the prophet Jeremiah to Baruch in the 6th c. B.C. The earliest scrolls and manuscripts of the Biblical text (Qumran) are from a much later time, closer to the birth of Jesus. The Bible in its own time was a product of and existed within oral culture(s). Even the written Torah or Pentateuch text, brought from Babylon by Ezra in the 5th c. B.C. was read aloud in its entirety and was accompanied by an oral translation and/or interpretation (Neh 8).

A consensus exists among scholars that the 6th c. B.C., and more especially the time and place of the Babylonian Exile, was the matrix from which the Hebrew Pentateuch and most of the prophetic books emerged in their final written form. Even after the return of the Judahites from Babylon in 538 B.C. and following, the work done there (Babylon) on what is now considered Scripture maintained a certain primacy. The Jewish colonies in Egypt appear to have an uninterrupted presence in that country from the time of the Exile (Jeremiah, Elephantine community, etc.) through the Roman suppression of the Jewish rebellion in the early 2nd c. A.D. It is here that the Greek or Septuagint translation of the Hebrew first appeared in the 2nd c. B.C. A commonly voiced opinion regarding the Hebrew and Greek Bibles, especially regarding the books of the First Covenant (i.e., Old Testament) was and is that the Hebrew Bible was the Jewish Bible, while the Greek was that of the Church. A better description might be that the Hebrew and Greek Scriptures were both legitimate synagogue traditions, and the Church adopted the tradition of the Greek-speaking synagogues.

Historical items that alert us to a parity claimed for the two contemporary traditions are the Letter of Aristeas (ca. 100 B.C.), referring to the Greek translation of the Hebrew, and Ben Sirach or Ecclesiasticus. At the same time as Ben Sirach translated writings from Hebrew to Greek (and possibly before), others translated Biblical books, including the

Pentateuch, from Hebrew into Aramaic. The political unity of the ancient world achieved by Alexander the Great and again by the Romans gave Greek an unprecedented ecumenical status among languages, and the Greek language was claimed by the ancients to have superiority over the Hebrew on purely linguistic grounds.

Issues relating to Scripture existed at each of the Seven Ecumenical Councils (q.v.). The primary theological debate over Scripture at the First Council had to do with its use within a common creed, later called the Nicene Creed. Gnosticism and Arianism (q.v.) had created a crisis that only the Greek word *"homoousios"* or "consubstantial"—a non-Biblical word—could address. The Church Fathers (q.v.) maintained that the description of Jesus Christ as *"homoousios"* or "of one essence with the Father" was in fact "Biblical," though the word itself does not appear in the Bible. Other canons from the Ecumenical Councils relate to Scripture: Apostolic Canon #85 is the earliest canonical reference to a list of the books of Scripture. The Orthodox Church's list of books is the longest of all the churches, containing all the "apocryphal" (in Protestant terminology) books or deuterocanonical books found in the RSV or NRSV. The Metered Poems of St. Gregory the Theologian (mid–4th c.), the Iambics of Amphilocius, Bishop of Seleucus, and African Code, Canon #24 all give advice as to which are the "genuine books" of Scripture. Quinisext, Canon #2 (7th c.) gave blanket approval to all canons previously recognized in the Church. The Seventh Ecumenical Council (787) in its first canon *accepted all the canons of the Sixth Ecumenical and the Quinisext,* reinforcing the same view.

For contemporary questions regarding Hebrew and Greek Bibles, a few remarks are in order. Since both the Greek and Russian Churches use the Lucianic Septuagint liturgically, there is a tendency among the faithful to romanticize the unanimity of the liturgical witness and beauty of language, depicting the history of the Greek Scriptures as devoid of controversy and independent of the Hebrew. History reveals flaws in this attitude. For example, during the 4th c. there were three different Septuagints in use in the major Christian centers of the eastern Mediterranean: 1) the churches in Antioch and Constantinople (qq.v.) used the Lucianic recension; 2) Caesarea (q.v.) in Palestine utilized a translation by Origen (q.v.) that was updated by Pamphilus and Eusebius (q.v.); and 3) Alexandria (q.v.) had a third recension by a certain Hesychius about which little else is known. The Constantinopolitan practice, based on a translation done by the Presbyter Lucian (who preferred Attic forms), finally won out. (For the history of the Slavic and Russian Bible, *see* Constantine-Cyril; Gennadievskii Bible; Methodius; Ostrog Bible; Russian Bible.)

Today, the relationships between the various Hebrew and Greek textual traditions have to be taken very seriously. This was illustrated in the 19th c. by Patriarch Philaret of Moscow who oversaw the Russian Bible (q.v.) translation, now published and used in the Russian Church. Similarly, one of the greatest resources illuminating the relationship between the Hebrew and Greek textual traditions has been given us within this century by the discoveries at Qumran. Qumran has proved that both the Hebrew Masoretic text and the Greek Septuagint are faithful and credible witnesses to the ancient traditions and manuscripts. In many ways, certainly because of the discovery and availability of new information, we are currently in a position to do work with Scripture that was impossible even a half century ago.

**SCULPTURE.** This is the art of portrayal in wood, stone, or metal of figures either in relief or freestanding. While sculpture embellished churches in both West and East up until the 7th c., iconoclasm (q.v.) and the victory over the latter resulted in the East in a ban on sculpture, at least within the churches, except for figures in bas-relief.

**SECTS.** Just as in the West, the Eastern Christian world has known a number of sects over the centuries. The word denotes a group, usually limited in number, that claims a peculiarly absolute grasp on truth, the latter often consisting of a very specific and narrowly focused set of affirmations and expectations. Thus the followers of Marcion in the 2nd c. and 3rd c., or one of the groups following this or that gnostic leader (*see* Gnosticism), might fairly be labeled sects. In the Byzantine (q.v.) era, one may point to unknown ascetics and their followers for whom the term "Messalianism" was coined (4th–6th c.), or the dualist Paulicians and Bogomils of medieval Asia Minor and the Balkans (qq.v.), respectively. More recently, the Russian schism of the 17th c. and the resulting Old Believer (qq.v.) movement saw the latter giving birth to a multitude of sects whose beliefs varied from simple liturgical conservatism to apocalyptic fervor concluding in mass suicides. In modern Greece, the introduction of the Gregorian Calendar in the 1920s led to "Old Calendarist" groups (or "True Orthodox," by their own reckoning) who have since fractured into at least half a dozen competing groups. The Orthodox *oikoumene* (q.v.) has also seen the importation from the West of dozens of groups, including, of course, "mainline" denominations, but also taking in others who in America and in the East stand very much on the margins.

**SEPTUAGINT** *see* Scripture.

**SERAPHIM (VISSARION TIKAS),** Archbishop of Greece, *see* Tikas, Seraphim.

**SERAPHIM OF SAROV,** monk, ascetic, St. (1759–13 January 1833). Born in Kursk into a family engaged in business, Prokhor Mochin suffered a few childhood calamities from which he was delivered into a life that prepared him for monasticism (q.v.). At age eighteen, he investigated the Pechersk Monastery of the Caves, received the blessing of Hegumen Dositheus, and entered the Monastery of Sarov two years later. Although he was fervent in his monastic life, he soon fell ill (1780), and remained so for three years. On recovering he built a church for the infirmary.

He was tonsured monk on 13 August 1786, and ordained deacon (1788) and priest (1793). In 1794 after the death of his abbot, he went into seclusion for two years to a spot about two hours' walk from the Monastery. He was attacked by brigands (1804) and left for dead, but on miraculously recovering at the Monastery, returned to his seclusion, now as a stylite of sorts. In 1807 he was offered governance of the Monastery after the new abbot's death, but went back into his skete to live in silence for three years. He returned to the Monastery in 1810 due to physical weakness and broke his silence, but shut himself in his cell for the next fifteen years.

In 1825 Seraphim began the fourth and last phase of his life when he opened the door of his cell to the world. His fame spread quickly, and soon he was sought out by thousands of people who wanted advice, asked for healing (q.v.) and comfort, and repented of their sins (q.v.). His teaching contained nothing novel, the age-old creed of the ascetic: the real purpose of human existence is to acquire the Holy Spirit (q.v.). The quality of Seraphim's spiritual gifts was memorialized in literature by one of his favorite admirers, Nicholas Motovilov—a beautiful conversation found in almost every lengthy description of Seraphim's life. His last years were also spent giving direction to the nuns at the convent of Diveyevo, who continued a special veneration of their spiritual father (q.v.) after his death. In spite of caustic opposition to his canonization by Russian intellectuals and the Ober-Procurator Pobedonostsev, Seraphim was canonized in 1903, and remains one of the most venerated saints in Russia and in the Russian emigration.

**SERBIAN ORTHODOX CHURCH.** Representing one of the three main southern Slavic nations with Bulgaria and (Yugoslavian) Macedonia (qq.v.) in the Orthodox world, the early Christian history of Serbia is obscure, though the conversion of the Serbs must be related to the acceptance of Constantine-Cyril's and Methodius's (qq.v.) disciples into the late 9th c. kingdom of Bulgaria. Medieval Serbia emerges in the reign of Stephan Nemanja (1165–1196), whose son, Archbishop Sava (ca. 1175–1233), founded the Serbian Church. Sava's (q.v.) activity is noteworthy. His lifework represented a deliberate choice on the part of the Serbian Church for connection with Byzantium (q.v.) and the Eastern Church rather than the papal West. Stephan himself originated the great dynasty of kings that ruled the Serbs until the Ottoman conquests of the late 14th c. Medieval Serbia reached its peak during the reign of Nemanja's descendant, Tsar Stephan Dushan in the mid–14th c. It swiftly collapsed following Dushan's death (1355) and the disastrous Battle (1389) of Kossovo Polye (q.v.). This marked the beginning of a half-millennium of rule by the Ottoman Empire (q.v.). Together with other Balkan (q.v.) nations, Serbia emerged from under Turkish rule in the 19th c. under the sole native dynasties (Karageorgevich and Obrenovich) in the Orthodox *oikoumene* (q.v.) outside of Russia. The Church was declared autocephalous (q.v.) in the latter part of the same century, its archbishop titled patriarch with the creation of the Kingdom of Yugoslavia (q.v.) following World War I. The patriarch of the Serbs is at present Pavle I, Archbishop of Belgrade (q.v.), and he presides over a local synod of some thirty bishops.

**"SERGEIANISM," METROPOLITAN SERGIUS STRAGORODSKY** *see* Living Church.

**SERGEYEV, JOHN "OF KRONSTADT,"** priest, St. (1829–1908). This remarkable member of the white (married) clergy served at the naval base of Kronstadt outside St. Petersburg. In addition to extensive charitable works, he reformed several liturgical practices within his parish, anticipating many of the liturgical reforms of the Orthodox and Roman Catholic Churches (qq.v.) in the 20th c. These included public—or general—confessions, frequent communion, and lowering the iconostasis (qq.v.) to make the altar visible. He was so highly regarded during his own lifetime that he was one of very few married clergy to sit on the Holy Synod of Russia. His principal work, *My Life in Christ,* is available in several English translations. Although canonized recently by the Russian Church, Sergeyev was not without fault (e.g., an irregular marriage to gain ordination [qq.v.]) or occasional detractors (e.g., N. Leskov) in his own time. His extremely conservative political views regarding the monarchy might well have adversely affected the tenuous political atmosphere in 1905.

**SERGIUS OF RADONEZH,** priest-monk, ascetic, St. (ca. 1314–1392). Considered one of the greatest of Russian saints (q.v.), Sergius's life is coterminous with Russia's shedding of the Tartar yoke, the rise of Muscovite power, and the reestablishment of cenobitic (community) monasticism (q.v.); and he influenced all three events in particular ways. Born to nobility in Rostov and baptized Bartholomew, he fled with his family to Radonezh to lead a peasant life—all victims of the rise of the Muscovy principality at the expense of the nobility of Rostov. Of three brothers he was the slowest, and even his ability to read and write was granted as a wondrous gift from God.

During the time of the Tartar Appanage, whatever cenobitic monasticism existed in Russia had been destroyed. This might be connected with the fact that many such monasteries in the East served as defensive garrisons for urban areas, and were considered a military threat by the Tartars. In any event when Sergius, at about age twenty, and his widowed brother Stephen went out to the forested wilderness to begin their monastic life, they did so as hermits, and their skete was dedicated to the Holy Trinity (q.v.). Stephen soon left for a monastery near Moscow. But the man tonsured Sergius remained a hermit in a life reminiscent of Antony of the Desert (q.v.). He almost disappeared from sight, until his reputation inspired other disciples to gather around him, and he was ordained and made abbot of the monastery. At the site the forest was cleared, a road was beaten, and a village sprang up, and the life of seclusion was replaced by a type of frontier monasticism.

In 1354 the question arose whether individual hermits in (occasional) community or true cenobitic, communal monasticism should be the norm. Patr. Philotheus of Constantinople recommended the latter in a personal letter to Sergius. But when he complied, a division occurred, and rather than put the monks at odds with one another, Sergius quietly left to another site deeper in the forest where he founded another monastery. After four years Metr. Alexis of Moscow ordered Sergius back to Holy Trinity where he was heartily welcomed. In all, Sergius is credited with the foundation of about forty monasteries. Two of the most striking aspects of Sergius's monastic endeavor are that his eremetic "desert" was a wild forest, and that from a human organizational point of view, he had no business succeeding—either as a hermit or as a communal monk. He not only was successful, but became a living model, not having been exposed to other examples of the types of monasticism that he epitomized.

The Tartar occupation, beginning with the first invasion in 1237, continued to suppress Russia, but was showing signs of weakness. By the 1370s many people, including heads of Church and state, consulted Sergius for advice. In fact Sergius had been offered the metropolitan see in 1378, but refused it. Among those who sought Sergius's counsel was Prince Dmitri Donskoy of Moscow who had to decide whether to defy Khan Mamai (1367–1380) and risk the annihilation of Muscovy or continue the Appanage. Sergius blessed Dmitri's resistance, and this resulted in the rout of the Tartars at the battle of Kulikovo Polye on 8 September 1380. Sergius sent two monks to the battle with Prince Dmitri, and the two stories of their involvement reflect two antithetical traditions about religion and war. One story reports the monks had been soldiers and were sent to fight along with the troops. Another says that the monks were sent with spiritual resources, probably Holy Communion, to minister to the spiritual needs of the soldiers—a type of forerunner to military chaplaincy.

Ironic as it may be, the boy whose family had been supplanted by the rising power of Moscow helped that principality to continue its expansion. Not only was this accomplished by the freedom gained from the Tartar yoke and the expansion of inhabited lands by the movement of monastic "frontiersmen," but by simple, sound advice. Sergius had enough influence over all classes of society to prevent four civil wars among the Russian princes. And early Muscovite Christian tradition (q.v.) bore Sergius's seal, disdaining internecine warfare, which allowed Moscow to centralize its power even further.

The spiritual legacy of Sergius is formidable. He was known as a clairvoyant and mystic, but not particularly for any human strength other than charity. He healed soul and body, but was not considered a popular healer. The rule of prayer (q.v.) he and his monks observed left little time other than for necessary work, but he expressed his Christian love in service to others. Sergius's legacy continued into the 20th c. as well: When the Soviets were unable to squelch his memory and suppress his cult by closing his monastery and stealing his relics (q.v.), they reopened the monastery in 1945, restored his relics, and—with some embarrassment—proclaimed Sergius a national hero.

**SEVERUS OF ANTIOCH** (ca. 465–538). Together with Philoxenus of Mabboug (q.v.) and Jacob of Serug, Severus was the leader of the movement against the definition of Chalcedon (q.v.) in the late 5th and early 6th c. Ruling as Patriarch of Antioch (q.v.) from 512, he was deposed at the orders of Emperor Justin I in 519, but contrived to lead the resistance from exile, in particular through the aid of the Empress Theodora, consort of Justinian (qq.v.). Unlike Philoxenus and Jacob, Severus wrote exclusively in Greek, and his surviving works are preserved almost entirely in a Syriac translation by the Jacobite community (qq.v.). Some fragments in Greek remain, chiefly through citations quoted in different *florilegia* (patristic anthologies) compiled for instructional purposes, or for the reproof of heresy (q.v.) at the different church councils of the era.

**SHAHOVSKOY, JOHN,** Archbishop of San Francisco, émigré pastor, religious radio broadcaster (23 August 1902–30 May 1989). Born

Prince Dimitry and schooled at the Lycaeum in St. Petersburg, he joined the White Army during the Russian Revolution, and was evacuated from the Crimea to France in 1921. He studied history and political science in Louvain, Belgium, while pursuing his vocation as a published poet. In the mid–1920s he moved to Paris to attend St. Sergius Orthodox Theological Institute (q.v.). Without completing his theological studies, he was tonsured monk (1926) while visiting St. Panteleimon Monastery on Mt. Athos (q.v.). He returned to France and was ordained to the diaconate by Metr. Evlogii (q.v.), then to the priesthood by Bishop Benjamin. His first pastorate was in Belaya Tserkov, Yugoslavia, then St. Vladimir's Church in Berlin (1927), where he remained and distinguished himself as pastor to émigrés during World War II.

In 1946 he moved to the United States and was consecrated bishop of Brooklyn (1947), auxiliary to the Metropolitan, teacher of pastoral theology at St. Vladimir's Orthodox Theological Seminary (q.v.), and its dean. During the same period, he began giving Russian-language religious talks over "Voice of America Radio," an effort he continued for almost forty years. From 1954 to 1968 he was a member of the World Council of Churches Central Committee. When the Russian Orthodox Church joined the WCC (1961), he raised the issue of the relationship between that Church and its estranged missionary diocese in the United States—which would result in the autocephaly of the Orthodox Church in America (qq.v.).

From 1950 to 1973 and 1975 to 1979 he served as archbishop of San Francisco, where he always sought advice, and respected his clergy and diocesan council. For a brief time he was Commander of Chaplains for the Orthodox with the honorary rank of general. He wrote extensively in Russian, maintained contact with a great many Russian writers and intellectuals, and was the honorary president of the International Dostoevsky Society. He was known for his wit and humor, but more frequently for his personal humility (q.v.) and as a Christian gentleman. He is author of *The Orthodox Pastor* (1966).

**SHEPHERD OF HERMAS.** This apocalypse, a series of revelations or visions, is aimed at teaching repentance (q.v.), and is a book divided into "Visions," "Mandates," and "Similitudes." The revelations are communicated to Hermas by the Church, represented by a woman, and by the archangel in charge of Christians. The dating of the book is ca. A.D. 148 in Rome, since Bishop Pius is described as the brother of Hermas "sitting on the throne of the church of the city of Rome." Although theoretically an apocalypse, the genre is baroque, for every revelation there is also an accompanying ethical explanation: Its only real purpose is ethical and practical, not a revelation of a divine mystery. The fascination that 2nd-c. readers had for apocalypse was used by Hermas to teach them a new approach to sin after Baptism (qq.v.). The single most important message of the book is that there is the possibility of repentance after Baptism, explained in the respective divisions of the book in different ways—though that repentance is limited to a single occasion. This teaching differs from what was probably the then-current practice in Rome wherein repentance from capital sins was not considered possible after Baptism, i.e., there was no second confession (q.v.). Although *The Shepherd of Hermas* is not contained in the canon of Scripture (q.v.), it is worth noting that both Eastern and Western Christianity took its advice in modifying the developing penitential discipline.

**SHERRARD, PHILIP OWEN ARNOULD,** Greek Orthodox lay theologian, writer, archaeologist (23 September 1922–30 May 1995). Born in Oxford into an Anglo-Irish family, he entered Peterhouse College of Cambridge University in 1940. From 1942 to 1946 Sherrard served as an officer in the Royal Artillery. After the war he completed his studies earning a Ph.D. from the University of London. He was assistant director of the British School of Archaeology in Athens (1951–52, 1958–62), research fellow at St. Antony's College, Oxford (1957–58), and lecturer in the history of the Orthodox Church at London University (1970–77).

In 1958 Sherrard moved to Greece where he spent most of the rest of his life. He was a prolific writer and his works range from Orthodox theology to Greek poetry. Among his numerous theological works are *Greek East and Latin West* (1959, 1992), *Christianity and Eros: Essays on the Theme of Sexual Love* (1976), *Church, Papacy and Schism* (1978), *The Rape of Man and Nature* (1987), *The Eclipse of Man and Nature: An Inquiry Into the Origins and Consequences of Modern Science* (1987), *The Sacred in Life and Art* (1990), *Human Image: World Image* (1992), *Athos: The Holy Mountain* (1982), and translations of four volumes of *The Philokalia* (1979, 1981, 1984, 1995).

**SILOUAN, STARETS,** spiritual father (1866–1938). Silouan was a twentieth-century starets, or spiritual father (q.v.), a title given to Christians of spiritual accomplishment who are sought out as guides to the life in Christ. He was noted for his great strength in prayer and moving humility (qq.v.). His life, *The Monk of Mt. Athos,* written by his disciple, Archimandrite Sophrony Sakharov (q.v.), has been translated into many languages. He died at the Russian monastery of St. Panteleimon on Mt. Athos, and was canonized by the Ecumenical Patriarch (qq.v.) in 1989.

**SIMONY.** The sin of "purchasing" grace with money was named for the attempt of Simon Magus to buy the gift of the Holy Spirit (q.v.) (Acts 7:9–14). In later use the term came to signify the purchase either of high ecclesiastical office or of the sacraments (q.v.). The former was a continual problem throughout the Middle Ages of both East and West, and much exacerbated in the East during the Ottoman Empire (q.v.). Thus, in the Byzantine era (q.v.), the *kanonikon* was expected as a matter of course for ordination (q.v.) or the performance of a sacrament.

**SIN.** In both Hebrew and Greek the word means literally "to miss the mark" (cognate terms: transgression, *parabasis;* fault, *paraptoma;* crime or offense, *eggklima*). In Orthodox tradition sin may be conscious or unconscious, voluntary or involuntary. Further, sin, from Paul through the Church Fathers (q.v.), is understood as a personal force or power that has usurped the government of the world and infected creation from the Fall of Adam. Christ came to deliver humanity through his death and resurrection from this force and its accompanying corruption, i.e., the rule of the devil and of death. Baptism (q.v.) into Christ delivers the believer from the cosmic aspect of sin, but he or she is left to engage with those remnants of a diseased world still at work in his or her soul and environs. Thus the inescapable role of asceticism (q.v.) in the Christian life and, in addition, the insistence of the Orthodox tradition that sin, insofar as each person sins, is always personal in nature. Each is called to account for what he or she has done or left undone. This differs significantly from the place that original sin has held in the Christian West since, in particular, Augustine of Hippo (q.v.). It is with the examination and tracing out of sin's unconscious and unsuspected roots that the enormous literature of monastic spirituality is primarily concerned.

**SKOBTSOVA, MOTHER MARIA,** poet, monastic, Christian social activist, martyr (8 December 1891–31 March 1945). Named Elizaveta Iur'evna Pilenko at birth, her father was landed gentry and she was university educated, mixing well in the cultural elite of St. Petersburg. In 1917 she was a delegate from Novorossiisk to the Third Congress of the Socialist-Revolutionary Party, held in Moscow. Then in 1918 she was involved in conspiratorial activities against the new Bolshevik government as acting mayor of the town of Anapa on the Black Sea. Married twice, she had three children, none of whom survived her.

She and her family fled the Revolution in 1920 and settled in Paris in 1923, where she became very involved in the Russian Student Christian Movement (RSCM). In 1930 she became secretary for the Movement, traveling around France to give aid to Russian émigrés. She was close to Fr. Sergius Bulgakov and Metropolitan Evlogii (qq.v.), and under their guidance she prepared for monastic profession. Yet, her friend Nicholas Berdiaev (q.v.) opposed her decision as superfluous to her calling. On 7 September 1932, she received an ecclesiastical divorce from her second husband and became a monastic. It was Evlogii's hope that she become "the founder of convent life in the emigration," and she continued to serve the RSCM. In the early 1930s she was responsible for the publication of Georges Florovsky's four volumes on the Church Fathers (qq.v.). She typed the original manuscripts and persuaded I. Fondaminsky to provide the financial backing. In September 1934, she settled into a house at 77 rue de Lourmel, from which "hermitage" she served the Russian needy for more than thirty years. During the 1930s Archimandrite Lev Gillet (q.v.) lived at Lourmel and served Divine Liturgy on almost a daily basis. From 1936 to 1939 Archimandrite Kiprian Kern (1889–1960) served as resident priest, but he was released from his duties to become a faculty member at St. Sergius Orthodox Theological Institute (q.v.) in September 1939. On 27 September 1935, Orthodox Action, an independent Christian social action organization, was founded by Mother Maria, N. Berdiaev, S. Bulgakov, G. P. Fedotov, K. V. Molchulskii, and others, with Metropolitan Evlogii acting as honorary president. The organization was independent of the Church hierarchy and the RSCM, and was funded by the Anglicans and the American YMCA. Mother Maria was deported to the death camps because of her work to aid Jews through Orthodox Action. She died in the gas chamber of Ravensbruch concentration camp. Her life is recounted in Sergei Hackel's *Pearl of Great Price* (rev. 1982).

**SKOPTS/Y** *see* Doukhobors.

**SLAVERY.** As a legal institution slavery was inherited from Roman law by the Empire of Constantine and his successors, and it persisted until the last few centuries of the Byzantine era (q.v.) when, by the 13th c., it had largely died out. Church Fathers such as John Chrysostom and Gregory Nazianzus condemned the practice, and later monastic authorities, e.g., Theodore of Studion (qq.v.), forbade monasteries from holding slaves (though many, in fact, continued to do so). Nonetheless, the language of slavery—whether descriptive of the Christian as "slave of God" (*doulos tou Theou*) or of the sinner's slavery (*douleia*) to the passions—remains in force to the present.

**SLAVIC** *see* Old Church Slavic.

**SLAVOPHILE MOVEMENT.** An intellectual movement during the 1840s and 1850s in Moscow, existing side by side with Westernizing and nationalistic movements, which idealized as supreme the historical role of Orthodoxy and Russia. Among its adherents were A. Khomiakov (q.v.), I. and P. Kireyevsky, C. and I. Aksakov, and G. Samarin. Their interests were broad, including theology, philosophy, history, politics, etc.; in each field, they made an impact that lasted. Although the Slavophiles were romantics of sorts, drawing a strict dichotomy between idealized things Russian and the profane non-Russian, they were not influenced by German romanticism and pantheism as were many of their contemporaries. Their foundations were in Orthodox tradition, their endeavor paralleled that of the non-possessors and more recently Paisii Velichkovsky in monasticism (qq.v.), and their effort should not be considered in complete isolation from other contemporaneous developments.

Aside from influencing later intellectual lights who considered the Slavophiles their forbears—from Dostoevsky (q.v.) to recent samizdat writers—one can point to concrete accomplishments that permanently changed 19th-c. Russia for the better. First, they articulated a vision of human peace and harmony that begins with the family, and that they thought should be expressed in all greater social institutions. Khomiakov, in a brilliant theological essay, showed that love in catholicity (q.v.) or sobornost is the heart of the unity of the Church and comes directly from God (q.v.). Samarin took the vision sociologically and applied it to the emancipation of the serfs in Russia and in the borderlands. I. Kireyevsky explained the philosophical underpinnings of sobornost and set the agenda of philosophical problems for the coming century of Russian philosophy. In spite of their zealous nationalism and belief in autocracy, the Slavophiles were strictly censored during the reign of Tsar Nicholas I, and were not extensively published until the reign of Tsar Alexander II.

**SOBORNOST** *see* Catholic; Catholicity.

**SOLOVIEV, VLADIMIR S.**, Russian philosopher, theologian (1853–1900). Vladimir was the son of an eminent Russian historian who wrote *The History of Russia* in twenty-nine volumes. His career primarily involved writing, after he lectured briefly in Moscow on philosophy and held similar positions in St. Petersburg through 1882. This part of his early philosophical career was spent as a Slavophile and as a close friend of Dostoevsky (qq.v.). But his thinking soon evolved along ecumenical lines, desiring the unity of East and West in Russia through negotiation with the Roman Catholic Church (q.v.)—an evolution that separated him from the Slavophiles.

He never returned to professorial life, possibly because the topics of Russia's national politics and questions regarding the Russian

Church could not be adequately discussed there. His early interest in Russian poetry and folklore, German philosophy, nature myths, and ecstatic visions shaped his theological and philosophical system, which is considered uniquely "Russian": Pantheism, romanticism, and gnosticism (q.v.) are foundational to his system, as are his visions of what he thought was the Wisdom of God (q.v.) and world soul, the "Divine Sophia"—the Eternal and Perfect Feminine.

In 1889 Soloviev published *La Russie et l'Eglise Universelle* in Paris in which he not only promoted the mystical unity of the Roman and Orthodox Churches, but pronounced in favor of Roman Catholicism because of its creation of a "super-state" organization. After the publication of this book, he became disinterested in Church problems and did not believe the reunion of East and West possible. It was rumored that he became Roman Catholic, especially when he was communed once (1896) by Fr. Nicholas Tolstoy, who had become Roman Catholic but shared Soloviev's teaching of the mystical unity of East and West. Soloviev always considered himself faithful to the Orthodox Church in spite of his idiosyncratic behavior. He seems to have desired to preserve the characteristics of East and West in any case, reading confessions of faith that were technically contrary to both, e.g., reading aloud the decisions of the Council of Trent followed by the statement that the Eastern Orthodox Church is the true Catholic Church.

Soloviev wrote more than a dozen principal philosophical volumes and others on political-philosophical questions. His works were especially influential on the return of the Russian intelligentsia to the Orthodox Church, both before and after the Revolution. His sophiology was foundational for theologians like Sergius Bulgakov and Pavel Florensky (qq.v.), though not popular or subscribed to extensively thereafter. One of the common misestimations of Soloviev made by non-Russians is a lack of serious consideration of his poetry—some of which records the mystical experiences foundational to his corpus.

Various students of Soloviev have divided his career and philosophical emphases into three stages. The first was Christian theosophy in which he anticipated Sophia would be incarnate in the world. The second was theocracy in which he hoped Christian politics would create a just state and society. The third was theurgy in which he tried to create a new life corresponding to the Divine Truth through mystical art. His last great work, *Three Conversations,* gives up all utopianism and refers philosophical problems to resolution at the end of time—eschatology.

**SOPHRONY (SAKHAROV),** Archimandrite *see* Sakharov, Sophrony.

**SOVIET UNION** *see* Russian Orthodox Church.

**SPIRITUAL FATHER/MOTHER.** The notion of "spiritual fatherhood" has a long history in Christianity, going back at least to Paul. In the 3rd c. Gregory the Wonderworker's panegyric on Origen (q.v.) provided a kind of preview of later portraits of the spiritual father. This portrait, however, emerges clearly in the stories and sayings around the 4th c. Desert Fathers (q.v.). The "old men" (*gerontes, startsy*) act as exemplars and counselors for monks, often in a relationship of deep and abiding psychological and spiritual intimacy, not unrelated to the relationship obtaining between master and disciple elsewhere in the ancient world. Greater emphasis, though, is placed in the monastic context on the obedience owed the elder by his spiritual child than, for example, would be the case between one of the ancient philosophers and his pupils, e.g., Plotinus (q.v.) or Iamblichus. The bonds, moreover, between the monastic elder and his children were both lifelong and seen extending even beyond death.

One finds the theme of spiritual fatherhood fully worked out in John Climacus's works, *The Ladder* and *The Pastor,* and in the writings especially of Symeon the New Theologian (q.v.). The term is sometimes used loosely to apply to a person's "father confessor," but in a proper usage the two should be distinguished. Very few priests who hear confessions are spiritual fathers and the opposite is also often the case: a spiritual father or mother is not necessarily ordained clergy.

**THE SPIRITUAL REGULATION (REGLAMENT) OF PETER THE GREAT.** It must be understood that the religious reforms of Tsar Peter occurred in the greater context of the Westernization and reform of Russia, including the military, all government administrations (which meant for him the Russian Church, too), the economy, education, society, and culture. Though the reforms were ad hoc during a time of continual war, their scope and comprehensiveness cannot be overemphasized. Peter was definitely the visionary who, for better or for worse, united the various and disparate measures in his own person.

In 1700 Peter changed the calendar in two ways: Years were counted from Christ's birth, not the date of the (supposed) creation of the world, and the first month was January rather than September of the ecclesiastical year. He arranged for books to be published by a Dutch press, and produced the first newspaper in Russia. But this was after he allowed the national language to be Russian, and not Dutch as he had seriously considered. Still, the older Slavic language was reformed and simplified with Slavic, Greek, and Latin letters to produce what came to be known as the civil alphabet. Slavic alphabetic numbers, quite cumbersome, were replaced with Arabic numerals. Only church liturgical books (q.v.) were allowed to continue with the old alphabet and numbers.

The establishment of secular schools on the European model anticipated what was to happen with ecclesiastical schools. Besides sending students abroad, Peter created a School of Mathematical and Navigational Sciences (Moscow, 1701), a Naval Academy (St. Petersburg, 1715), medical schools (1706, 1709), a museum of natural science and a library (St. Petersburg), the Imperial Academy of Science (St. Petersburg), and about forty elementary schools in provincial towns. Private schools and tutoring for the gentry survived Peter's death, unlike the public schools—which did not take root until Catherine II made Russian, not Latin, the language of instruction. As a result of Peter's educational reform, a university was begun in Moscow (1755) with departments of law, medicine, and philosophy. (Before one might idealize Peter as the liberal visionary who promoted education at all costs, it should be considered that almost all of his schools had a direct bearing on "oiling his war machine," which he kept functioning continually during his reign with the exception of twenty-four scattered months.)

When Archbishop Theophanes Prokopovich prepared the "Spiritual Regulation" for Peter, who issued it on 25 January 1721, uniform ecclesiastical schools were provided for with grades that progressed to philosophy and theology (qq.v.) as the height of learning. Prokopovich, who had studied at the Uniate (q.v.) College of Athanasius in Rome, took the Kievan academy as his model for theological education. But like the foreignness of the secular schools, the Kievan academy was grounded in the "Latin learning" of Scholasticism (q.v.), and life in the seminaries was "cloistered" from the influences of family and tradition. Curiously, Prokopovich preferred to follow Protestant rather than Roman Catholic problems in his Scholasticism—though Aquinas was well-known. Since the ecclesiastical schools were predicated on the Kievan model, hierarchs from the Ukraine opened them in Russia, staffed them with Ukrainian teachers, and frequently brought their students from the Ukraine. In certain instances only Ukrainian was spoken, and only Ukrainians were advanced to candidacy for the episcopacy. A forced "Ukrainization" occurred in Russia due to Peter's reforms.

Ironically, the secular schools did not survive the 18th c. and the ecclesiastical schools did. In the last decades of the century when Catherine II popularized education, the ecclesiastical schools provided the new teachers, who now graduated from "teachers' seminary." Still, the success was forced: Peter's ecclesiastical schools were "caste" schools with mandatory participation from clergy offspring. By mandatory is meant not merely physical punishment, but criminal prosecution! The student was fulfilling a duty to the state, and desertion was treated with severity—the "criminal" was pursued and returned in chains, if necessary. In spite of this, the attrition rate was high, sometimes half a seminary class; the reason was not an unwillingness to learn, but the uselessness of the education. The Latin-Polish curricula were foreign and left the more useful subjects of theology and rhetoric in Russian for the last year—which few reached. Latin and Scholasticism had no relevance to Orthodox or Russian life, and they were not a large part of contemporary European culture. The contradiction between praying in Church Slavic (q.v.) and theologizing in Latin was too glaring.

An even more profound change by Peter was the abolition of the Russian patriarchate (q.v.). In Prokopovich's Regulation, written over the course of some years, the patriarch's authority was replaced by the "Ecclesiastical College," which within a month was renamed "The Most-Holy Ruling Synod." At this time the Holy Synod was comprised of three bishops, four archimandrites, and four archpriests. All matters were settled by majority, but all decisions were subject to state control. There was no access to the emperor as the patriarch had; but all members were appointed by the emperor. The ober-procurator was the intermediary between the Synod and the tsar, and this "eye of the Tsar" participated in all Synod meetings.

In time both the ratification of the Synod's decrees and the appointment of new members to the Synod came to depend on the ober-procurator. Over the next twenty years various bishops and clergy objected to or tried to change the "Regulation," including Prokopovich, but the "Regulation"—brought into law by Peter's imperial commands and threats—was not to be superceded. The power of the ober-procurator increased until he became a minister of state. Then, under Alexander I, the Ministry of Ecclesiastical Affairs and Education was organized (1817–1824). This department of state so alarmed the hierarchy that they complained of it as a threat to and persecution of the Church. The situation did not change until the patriarchate was reestablished in 1918.

Since Peter was no friend of monasticism (q.v.), he attempted to transform it into a state agency of educated social workers. Prohibitions against monks having books or pen and paper in their cells were designed to curtail any thinking and writing activities that were not state approved. Fortunately, the reforms were unsuccessful in monastic circles.

Although not originally intended to do so, the intellectual and economic impact of the Regulation on the Church by the end of the 18th c. was devastating. Intellectually, the spirit of the Age of Reason, prepared for by Peter, left the Church only with the "old ways"—the old alphabet, the old calendar, the old language—displaying little originality and contrasting with an idealized Europe. Russia's intellectuals were ripe for Voltaire's antichurch polemics and self-indulgent habits. In this atmosphere the Russian Church's land and serfs were confiscated in 1764, then it was subsidized at one-third its previous budget, and that on a declining basis. The clergy and their dependents, about 1 percent of the population, were impoverished by the treby (q.v.) system, while the government maintained a large army and bureaucracy, and the imperium enjoyed one of the largest courts in Europe with a wealthy gentry. Thus, Peter's reforms not only Westernized, but also began the secularization of, the Church. (*See* Russian Orthodox Church.)

**SPIRITUAL RELATIONSHIP.** These are the bonds entered into as the result of sacramental actions such as baptism (q.v.), adoption, or monastic tonsure. The godparent, in the first instance, involves both himself (or herself) and his relations in a spiritual relationship with the kin of the baptized. The same limitations on marriage within specified degrees of consanguinity were and are thus applied in the Orthodox Church to all who are connected by godparenthood. The language of spiritual relationship came also to be often applied to the bonds obtaining between the monk's elder or abbot and himself. (*See* Spiritual Father.) It is sometimes applied, though not always properly, to the relationship between the Christian and his or her confessor.

**SPONSOR.** Classically the sponsor is the person who guarantees the character and motives of an individual seeking to enter the Church through Baptism (q.v.). Today, we consider it an honor to be a godparent, while in the classical system, the honor fell entirely to the adult catechumen (q.v.). The godparent would be held accountable to the Church for the actions of the individual whom he sponsored. There was a risk involved—so much so that the Greek name for "sponsor" in Asia Minor (q.v.) was the same term used for an individual who provided surety for a bank loan: a "guarantor." It was, and in some places is, expected that the sponsor works closely with the catechumen, attending all catechetical classes with him or her, and helping with instruction. It was also assumed that the sponsor had an active life in Christ which could be shared on a personal, experiential level with the catechumen. The sponsor and the catechumen basically went through the entire procedure for entrance into the Church together.

**SPYROU, ATHENAGORAS,** Archbishop of Constantinople, New Rome and Ecumenical Patriarch (25 March 1886–July 1972). Graduated from the Orthodox Theological Seminary, Halki, Istanbul, in 1910, he was ordained to the diaconate, later serving as general secretary for the Athens Archdiocese. He was elected Metropolitan of

Corfu and Praxos. From 1931 to 1948 he served as archbishop (exarch [q.v.]) of the Greek Orthodox Archdiocese of North and South America (q.v.), residing in New York City. As archbishop he healed a schism dividing the Greek church there and established a single archdiocese. He became the two hundred eighty-sixth Archbishop of Constantinople in 1948 and was particularly well known for his active involvement in the ecumenical movement (q.v.), an activity highlighted by his much-publicized meeting with Pope Paul VI in Jerusalem in 1964 and the mutual lifting of the anathemas of 1054 in the next year. Both events generated controversy in the Orthodox world, with some hailing the perceived end of separation and others seeing in it the betrayal of the patriarch's trust. The debate is still very much alive today. Several institutions have been named for the late patriarch, including the Patriarch Athenagoras Orthodox Institute (q.v.) in Berkeley, also under Constantinople's (q.v.) jurisdiction.

**STABILITY.** In Greek *isobios askesis,* stability is the principle that monastics should remain lifelong in the monastery of their profession. It is nominally upheld in the Orthodox Church, even enshrined in the canons of the Fourth and Seventh Ecumenical Councils (q.v.) and in Byzantine legislation. It seems, however, never to have been applied with absolute rigor, particularly in the case of male monastics. The movement of monks from one monastery to another, from monastery to hermitage, and even back again, continues to be a feature, for good or ill, of Orthodox monasticism (q.v.).

**STANDING CONFERENCE OF ORTHODOX BISHOPS IN AMERICA.** Known by the familiar acronym SCOBA, the Standing Conference first convened on 15 March 1960. The primary fields of cooperation among the canonical Orthodox churches in the United States include religious education in the Orthodox Christian Education Commission, college campus ministries in the Orthodox Christian Fellowships, ecumenical relations in presenting a united witness in the National Council of Churches, military chaplaincy in the Committee on Chaplaincy to the United States Armed Forces, and clergy fellowship in the various clergy associations throughout the country. The member groups in alphabetical order are the Albanian Orthodox Diocese of America, American Carpatho-Russian Orthodox Greek Catholic Church, Antiochian Orthodox Christian Archdiocese of New York and All North America, Bulgarian Eastern Orthodox Church, Greek Orthodox Archdiocese of North and South America, Orthodox Church in America, Romanian Orthodox Missionary Episcopate in America, Serbian Orthodox Church in the United States of America and Canada, and Ukrainian Orthodox Church in America. The members represent almost all the canonical Orthodox churches one can find in the western hemisphere.

**STANILOAE, DUMITRU,** priest, Romanian theologian, educator (1903–1993). Appointed in the late 1930s to the faculty of theology at Bucharest and subsequently the most important Romanian theologian, Staniloae was one of the leaders, if not the leader, of the renaissance of patristic (q.v.) and monastic studies, which has done much to enliven and renew the Romanian Church. His vast work of translation and commentary on the *Philokalia,* an expanded version of the series first published by Nicodemus of the Holy Mountain (qq.v.), is still in the process of editing and at present runs to more than a dozen volumes.

**STAUROPEGION.** The term comes from the Greek, *stauropegein,* which means literally, "the planting or pitching of a cross." The term appears in the 10th c. to signify property, in particular monasteries, under the jurisdiction of the patriarch and thus not subject to the local bishop. This closely parallels contemporary monasteries in the West, notably Cluny, seeking direct papal jurisdiction in order to escape the depredations of their local church and feudal hierarchies. The system of *stavropegeia* has since been extended to other local churches in the Orthodox *oikoumene* (q.v.). Hence stavropegial means today that the institution in question is under the direct supervision of the local primate.

**STRENOPOULOS, GERMANOS,** Metropolitan of Thyateira, Exarch of the West, theologian, ecumenist (15 September 1872–24 January 1951). He studied for the priesthood at Halki Theological School, and attended institutions in Constantinople, Halle, Leipzig, Strasbourg, and Lausanne. In 1908 he was lecturer in dogmatics at Halki Seminary and later appointed to be its rector. He was actively engaged in the ecumenical movement (q.v.) from 1911 to the end of his life. He was elevated to the title of Metropolitan of Seleucia but remained at Halki. In 1920 he collaborated in the publication of the Ecumenical Patriarchate's encyclical letter, "Unto all the Churches of Christ wheresoever they be," which was an early and instrumental Christian appeal for ecumenical (q.v.) dialog.

In 1922 as Metropolitan of Thyateira he was sent to London to minister to the Greek-speaking flock of Western Europe. At Lausanne in 1927 he was vice president of the first world conference on Faith and Order, as well as vice president at the second world conference in Edinburgh, 1937. He was a member of the provisional committee of the World Council of Churches and played a strong role in the creation of the WCC. He is the author of *Kyrillos Loukaris, 1572–1638: A Struggle for Preponderance Between Catholic and Protestant Powers in the Orthodox East* (1951).

**STUDION MONASTERY.** The great monastery dedicated to St. John the Baptist in Constantinople, which, founded sometime before 454, rose to prominence under the abbacy of Theodore of Studion during the continuation of the controversy of icons (qq.v.) during the 8th–9th c. The Studion remained the capital's most important monastery to the end of the Byzantine era (q.v.). Following Theodore till the reform of the liturgy (q.v.) by Patriarch Philotheos in the late 14th c., the Studion also provided the dominant influence on Constantinopolitan worship, and hence its typikon came to play an important role throughout the Orthodox *oikoumene* (q.v.), making significant contributions to the hymnology of the Church. As the capital's most important monastic presence, the monastery finally provided a standing counterbalance to the policies of emperor and patriarch.

**STYLIANOPOULOS, THEODORE,** priest, Greek-American New Testament scholar, theologian, ecumenist (1937– ). Born in Messinia, Greece, he grew up in Seattle, Washington, and completed his B.A. in theology (1962) at Holy Cross Greek Orthodox School of Theology (q.v.). He obtained the S.T.M. in New Testament from Boston University School of Theology (1964) and the Th.D. in New Testament from Harvard Divinity School (1974).

Stylianopoulos has been active in ecumenical circles and interfaith dialogues with interest in Jewish-Christian relations, Orthodox-Roman Catholic relations, and the World Council of Churches, in which he served as a member of the Central Committee (1983–1990). He has received various grants and prizes and is a member of several professional societies. A well-known retreat master and lecturer, he is also the theological consultant to the Religious Education Department of the Greek Orthodox Archdiocese (q.v.) and a parish pastor.

Fr. Stylianopoulos is currently professor of New Testament and Orthodox spirituality at Holy Cross Greek Orthodox School of Theology (1967– ). In addition to these disciplines he specializes in Christian origins and early Christian literature, Old Testament and Judaism, as well as Greek philosophy and religion. He has taught as visiting professor and lecturer at numerous universities and colleges worldwide. An internationally known author, he has written and edited about a dozen books and more than thirty articles. His publications include *Justin Martyr and the Mosaic Law* (1975), *Bread for Life: Reading the Bible* (1980), *Orthodox Perspectives on Pastoral Praxis* (1988), and a collection of his articles, *The Good News of Christ* (1991).

**SUPERSTITION.** In the context of the Orthodox Church, superstition can mean at least two things: 1) the survival of specific pagan beliefs and practices, particularly in rural areas, for example the dual-faith (q.v.) of Rus' with analogs throughout the Balkans and Asia Minor (qq.v.) often expressed through a reliance on magical practices designed to manipulate the environment of the practitioner, thus the fascination with astrology and even black magic in the Byzantine era (q.v.); 2) the transference of magical or generally pagan attitudes to Christian practices and ritual objects, for example the understanding of icons (q.v.) as themselves divine, the manipulation of sacraments (q.v.) for magical purposes, etc.

**SYMEON OF THESSALONICA,** archbishop, homilist (?–1429). One of the most important church figures of the early fifteenth century, he left behind a body of homilies, occasional works against heretics (including both Latins and those opposed to Gregory Palamas [q.v.]), and, of particular importance, liturgical commentaries (q.v.). The latter provides a uniquely valuable historical witness to the state of the Orthodox liturgy at the close of the Byzantine era (qq.v.).

**SYMEON THE NEW THEOLOGIAN,** abbot, theologian, mystic, St. (949–1022). Symeon was abbot of the monastery of St. Mamas from ca. 980–1005. A figure of remarkable gifts and no less remarkable controversy during his lifetime, he has been called the greatest of Byzantine mystics. Throughout his writings, *The Catecheses, The Ethical Discourses, The Hymns, The Theological Orations,* and *The Theological Chapters,* he laid primary emphasis on the conscious experience of the Holy Spirit (q.v.), and that experience particularly in the form of light. Though canonized thirty years after his death, Symeon's continual struggles with church authorities led to the effective suppression of his works and thought—save for the underground admirers, unquestionably strong among the monks, who preserved them—until the hesychast movement of the 14th c. His influence is quite discernible in Gregory Palamas (q.v.), though the latter very seldom quotes him directly. Manuscript evidence is such as to prove that he was widely read in the monasteries in the 14th–15th c. Nicodemus of the Holy Mountain (q.v.) revived attention to his works at the end of the 18th c.

**SYNDESMOS.** The term means "bond" or "link," and was adopted as the name of the international Orthodox youth organization in the early 1960s. Syndesmos arranges youth camps, conferences, and exchanges throughout the Orthodox *oikoumene* (q.v.). It is headquartered in Kuopio, Finland.

**SYNOD.** The term means "gathering," and is used to signify both the gatherings or councils of bishops called together to debate questions of pressing doctrinal or ethical concern, e.g., the Ecumenical Councils (q.v.), or else regularly summoned gatherings to deal with details of administration in a given locale, e.g., the frequent local councils. In later times during the Byzantine era (q.v.), the "standing synod" (*endemousa synodos*) constituted the regular administrative body of the Ecumenical Patriarch (q.v.), and in tsarist Russia from Peter I, the term, preceded by "holy," signified the governing body of the Russian Church without the patriarchate. The term is finally important as signaling a basic point of ecclesiology in the Orthodox Church, i.e., that the latter, in contrast to the papacy in the West, sees particular authority (qq.v.) in the Church in the body of the episcopacy sitting in council.

**"SYNOD IN EXILE".** Known also as the Karlovci Synod from the name of the city in northern Serbia where they first convened, this Synod was comprised of Russian bishops who fled their dioceses during the course of the Revolution, and took refuge first in Constantinople and then in Karlovci as guests of the Serbian patriarch. Headed by Metropolitan Antonii Khrapovitsky (q.v.), formerly of Kiev, the group proclaimed itself the "Supreme Ecclesiastical Administration Outside of Russia," based on a decree of Patriarch Tikhon Belavin (q.v.), which allowed for dioceses separated from the patriarch by the front lines of war to be temporarily independent (20 November 1920, No. 362). Such a decree was not intended to apply to bishops who had abandoned their dioceses, nor was it to establish an "Administration."

On 5 May 1922 the patriarch dissolved the group (No. 398) and appointed Metropolitan Evlogii Georgievskii (q.v.) as the administrator of all parishes in Europe. When Evlogii and Metropolitan Platon Rozhdestvensky in the United States not only recognized the group's continued existence, but cooperated with it to keep peace in the church, the Synod attempted to exercise control over both of them—whereupon official relations were broken in 1926. The Synod then appointed its own bishop of the North American diocese, and has continued to do so until the present. With the dissolution of the Soviet Union, none of the bishops, most of whom live in the United States, have returned to Russia, so the title "In Exile" is an anachronism. They maintain one monastery on Mt. Athos (q.v.) and another together with a seminary in Jordanville, New York. They have recently attempted to start parishes in Russia to compete with those of the Moscow Patriarchate and do not maintain a relationship with any other canonical Orthodox church, thus increasing their isolationist and sectarian stand in the Orthodox *oikoumene* (q.v.).

**SYNODIKON OF ORTHODOXY.** This document appears as a list of blessings (q.v.) and curses after the defeat of iconoclasm (q.v.) in 843. It is still read or chanted aloud during the Vespers of the first Sunday in Lent (q.v.), the celebration of the "Triumph of Orthodoxy." Composed of two parts, the first is a thanksgiving (blessings) addressed to Christ for the defenders and champions of the faith, and the second is a catalog of anathemas (curses) against the great heresies (q.v.) and their promulgators. The Constantinopolitan version of the *Synodikon* was updated through 1429, and some local Orthodox churches have continued the process.

**SYRIA.** A region or province of the Roman Empire (q.v.) whose territory roughly corresponded to the modern state of the same name. Antioch (q.v.) was the capital, the dominant city in a region of many urban centers and the seat of a patriarchate (q.v.) ranked fourth among the bishops of the Church. Featuring a mixed population of Greek and Syriac-speakers, as well as other smaller groups, Syria was a cultural and intellectual center of the early Byzantine Empire rivaled only by Alexandria and, later, by Constantinople (q.v.), which would eventually eclipse both. The theology, liturgy, and spirituality of the imperial capital, however, drew deeply on Syrian sources. Antiochene exegesis, with its emphasis on historical sobriety, continued to play a role in later Byzantine thought, especially through the works of Theodoret of Cyrrhus and John Chrysostom (qq.v.). Syrian liturgical poetry shaped much of the hymnology of the Byzantine rite via Romanos the Melodist, and Syrian saints such as Ephrem the Syrian, Symeon Stylites, and Isaac of Nineveh (qq.v.) contributed to Byzantine ideas of holiness and the life in the Spirit.

The present-day Orthodox Church of Syria, though vastly reduced from its glory days by the schisms (q.v.) of the 5th c. and by thirteen hundred years of Muslim rule, is still the largest religious minority in the 20th c. country. Its primate, the Patriarch Ignatius of Antioch (residing at Damascus), presides over communities in Lebanon, Iraq, and Turkey, as well as an immigrant flock in Europe and the Americas.

**SYRIAC CHURCH.** We take this phrase as applying to Syriac-speaking Christians. Syriac, a dialect of Aramaic spoken in Roman Syria and Mesopotamia, was the language of Christianity in early Persia (qq.v.) as well as in the Roman province. Its original home was the city of Edessa (q.v.), where Christianity may date from the earliest periods of the Christian faith, though documentary evidence is lacking—or at least fiercely debated—until the early 4th c.

The golden age of Syriac Christian literature ran from the 4th to the 8th c., although important works were being produced both by the Assyrian

(Nestorian) Church and the Jacobites (qq.v.) as late as the 13th–14th c. Besides the original writings of such luminaries as Aphraat, Ephrem, Philoxenus of Mabboug, Jacob of Serugh, Isaac of Nineveh (qq.v.), and the 7th–8th-c. Nestorian mystics, Syriac Christians also served as a vital conduit for the passage of Greek thought into Arabic and the nascent civilization of Islam (q.v.). The christological controversies of the 5th c. shattered the ecclesiological unity of the Syriac church, and resulted in a division into three main groups, the "Nestorians" in the east, and the "monophysites" and "Melchites" (qq.v.) in the west. The latter group was to be dominated by a Greek-speaking hierarchy appointed from Constantinople (q.v.) and later adopted Arabic as the vehicle of its worship and normal communication.

**SYRIAN ANTIOCHIAN ORTHODOX ARCHDIOCESE OF NEW YORK AND ALL NORTH AMERICA** *see* Antiochian Orthodox Christian Archdiocese of New York and All North America.

**SYRO-CHALDEAN PATRIARCHATE.** This phrase refers to the "Uniate" or "Chaldean-rite" Church in communion with the papacy and comprising today the majority of Christians within modern Iraq (qq.v.). The Chaldean church is the Uniate doublet of the smaller Assyrian Church (q.v.), and numbers perhaps a quarter million. Its origins as a Uniate body date to 1826.

**SYRO-MALABARESE CHURCH.** The larger of the two, Uniate Indian Churches existing in the former territories of the Mar Thoma Church (q.v.), and heavily Latinized by the legacy of the Portuguese-run Synod of Diamper (1599), it is the largest of the natively Christian communities in India—though smaller than the Latin rite (q.v.) Catholic communities in the country. They retain the basics of their original eastern Syrian liturgy, and in recent years have been striving to reacquaint themselves with the writings and thought of the ancient Syriac Church (q.v.). In 1988 they pressed for and obtained from Pope John Paul II the right to appoint their own bishops, parallel to the Latin rite hierarchy, throughout all India. Up until that date, they had remained without the right to exercise episcopal supervision over their co-ritualists in areas of India outside their traditional territories.

**SYRO-MALANKARESE CHURCH.** A second Indian, Uniate body, originating from a break with the Mar Thoma Orthodox in 1930, and numbering perhaps a quarter million. They continue to use the liturgy of the western Syrian, or Jacobite, tradition that the Mar Thoma Church (qq.v.) adopted in the 1660s as the result of its break with the Portuguese-imposed union and reestablishment of ties with Mesopotamia (q.v.).

## -T-

**TALE OF BYGONE YEARS** *see* Primary Chronicle.

**TERTULLIAN** (ca. 155–ca. 225). Tertullian was the most important pre-Nicene Christian writer in Latin. Trained in law, versed in Greek, both the language itself and its philosophical tradition, he was a writer of fiercely polemical character. All his works are characterized by a burning zeal that verges on, and in later life tumbles over, the edge of fanaticism. At first a catholic Christian, he became ca. 210 a devotee of the Montanist movement, an action that led him to emphasize truth, *veritas,* and absolute standards of moral conduct. His contributions to Latin-speaking Christianity were immense, including the invention (or at least first witness to) much of its theological vocabulary, e.g., *substantia* and *persona* for the essence and persons of the Trinity (q.v.), the word *trinitas* itself, and *naturae* for the humanity and divinity in Christ. His works in translation fill two volumes of the *Ante Nicene Fathers* series. They include apologetics (q.v.), polemics, and treatises on moral and ecclesiological issues. His polemical works include the brief but famous *Prescription against the Heretics,* an antignostic work, *Against Marcion,* which opposes the latter's dualism and argues in defense of both the Old and New Testaments, and *Against Praxeas* in defense of the persons of the Trinity and against the modalism popular in Rome at the turn of the 3rd c.

**THEODORA, EMPRESS** (ca. 497–548). Wife of the Emperor Justinian (q.v.), her early life as an actress in Alexandria was the subject of the scurrilous portrait by the historian, Procopius of Gaza, in the latter's spiteful *Secret History.* In spite of this witness, Theodora appears to have been a woman of strong character and powerful religious convictions. She strengthened her husband at the time of the Nika riots in 532, and, perhaps with his agreement, continued to support the "monophysite" (q.v.) movement throughout her reign of twenty-three years. Certainly, the hierarchy of the Oriental Orthodox (q.v.), in particular James Baradeus the founder of the Jacobite (q.v.) church, owes its existence in great part to her patronage.

**THEODORE OF MOPSUESTIA,** Patriarch of Constantinople, theologian, scriptural exegete (ca. 350–ca. 428). One of the most able proponents of the Antiochene school of scriptural exegesis, Theodore enjoyed considerable prominence during his lifetime. A vigorous opponent of Arianism (q.v.) and Apollinarianism (the heresy that Christ had no complete humanity), his strictures against the latter led to an overemphasis on the distinctiveness of Christ's two natures. This was reflected, to disastrous effect, in the condemnation that overtook his pupil, Nestorius (q.v.), at the Council of Ephesus. Theodore's own posthumous condemnation followed, nearly one hundred thirty years after he died, in the decree of anathema against his works and his person engineered by Justinian at the Fifth Ecumenical Council (qq.v.) in 553. While Theodore's works perished in the Greek-speaking world as a result of imperial censorship, many continued to be preserved in the Syriac-speaking Church of the East (Assyrian [q.v.]) where, indeed, he was venerated, far more than Nestorius, as the great teacher and master of exegesis.

**THEODORE OF STUDION,** abbot, theologian (759–826). Theodore was the abbot of the monastery of St. John at the Studion in Constantinople (qq.v.). Through his strength of character, organizing ability, and courage in the face of imperial pressures to conform to iconoclasm (q.v.), including at least two periods of exile, he elevated his monastery to a position of undisputed leadership among the monastic houses of the capital, a position that it held until the close of the Byzantine era (q.v.). His writings included two large collections of occasional addresses to his monks, *The Greater* and *The Lesser Catecheses,* letters addressed both to his monks and to other supporters, a refutation of iconoclasm, and various liturgical compositions.

**THEODORET OF CYRRHUS,** bishop, theologian, scriptural exegete, historian (ca. 393–466). As Theodore of Mopsuestia and Nestorius, so Theodoret was a product of Antioch (qq.v.) and the school of exegesis and theology associated with that city. While escaping the condemnation of the first two men, though not altogether unscathed, his sympathies for their position remained throughout his life. He left behind a considerable body of written works, including a number of scriptural commentaries, a *History of the Monks of Syria* (the major source for the early history of Syrian monasticism [q.v.]), a *Church History* that continues Eusebius's history through 428, a polemical work against Cyril of Alexandria (q.v.) and the "monophysite" position called *The Beggar,* and a large work of apologetics (q.v.), *The Cure of Pagan Maladies.* Although his works were posthumously condemned as part of the "Three Chapters," they continued to be circulated and read in the church, sometimes under the pseudonym Nilus of Sinai.

**THEODOSIUS (LAZOR),** Metropolitan *see* Lazor, Theodosius.

**THEOLOGY.** Theology in the Orthodox tradition has a considerably broader meaning than philosophical discourse about divinity. The latter applies, to be sure, when Christian thinkers were obliged to express and defend the faith in language borrowed from the Greek philosophical tradition of Plato and Neoplatonism (qq.v.). Nor, it must be added, did they feel the latter to be entirely at variance with the revelation in Christ. The history of Orthodox theology (as of Roman Catholic [qq.v.] and Protestant theology) is in great part the struggle against and in alliance with the inheritance of the great pagan Greeks. Borrowing a phrase from Fr. Georges Florovsky (q.v.), it is a wrestling with concepts in order to discover the words "most adequate" to the mystery of God (q.v.) become man (*theoprepeis logoi*).

In this struggle one may discern two basic approaches in Orthodox Church Fathers, as the former were categorized by Dionysius the Areopagite (qq.v.). There is first and primarily apophatic theology. This phrase goes beyond the mere negation of concepts. It denotes the fact that the transcendent God (q.v.) is, indeed, transcendent, other, and thus "known," in Dionysius's famous phrase, only "by unknowing." Classically apophatic theology insists on a particular content to this "unknowing," i.e., the possibility of a genuine experience of the unknowable God revealed in the Incarnate Word and communicated to the believer in the action (*energeia*) of the Holy Spirit (q.v.). This is therefore the real mystical theology, the union beyond word and concept.

The experience of the divine leads to the other approach of classical Eastern theology, affirmative or cataphatic theology. The Unknowable is revealed in his creation, in the words of the Scriptures (q.v.), and finally in the Word made flesh, Jesus Christ. These givens constitute the realm of the *oikonomia*, God's self-extension into the universe for humanity's creation and salvation. On the one hand, words and concepts must be assigned and accorded their full seriousness, though always with the proviso that they carry within themselves and point toward a presence that finally transcends both them and every artifice of the created intellect. On the other hand, certain concepts, or "names," do carry a particular weight because they are revealed images, "notional icons" one might say, beyond which the believer cannot go. This applies with particular force to the names accorded the persons of the Trinity (q.v.). In the Trinity, and in the formulations of the Ecumenical Councils concerning Christology (qq.v.), apophatic and cataphatic can be seen to meet and fuse: not a man and a god, but the God-man, not One and not Three, but both, and beyond the categories of one and many.

Beyond the necessary intellectual engagement, the Church Fathers, the liturgy, and the tradition of Christian asceticism (qq.v.) express broader and higher meanings for theology, among them: 1) prayer (q.v.), "he who prays is a theologian," says Evagrius of Pontus (q.v.); 2) glorification or praise occur particularly in the celebration of the liturgy, both on earth among human beings and in heaven with the angels; 3) the vision of God (q.v.) is anticipatory in this life and unendingly unfolded in increasing perfection in the age to come; and finally 4) God himself who is the threefold unity of the Trinity. This rounded vision of theology as intellectual, scriptural, liturgical, and experiential was classically formulated in the Byzantine era, and exemplified with particular force in the writings of Gregory Palamas and Nicholas Cabasilas (qq.v.) in the 14th c. Under the impress of the West following the end of the Empire, Orthodox thought suffered a "pseudomorphosis"—borrowing once more from Florovsky—and its theology, at least the latter as printed in official church manuals, took on the shape and flavor of a third-rate Scholasticism (q.v.). The rediscovery of the patristic inheritance owes to two sources, the monastic revival stimulated by the *Philokalia* (q.v.) and the welcome assistance of Western historical scholarship, two streams that began to converge in Russia in the late 19th c. and early 20th c.

Outside the frontiers of its fixed theological inheritance, Orthodoxy gives considerable play to theological expression and opinion, to "things said theologically," theologoumena. For example, the application of the mystery of Christ to contemporary Christian life is traditionally Orthodox, but today is usually categorized under moral theology—a relatively new phrase in the Orthodox lexicon. During the era of the Fathers the Church had been content with the ascetic tradition, on the one hand, and insistence on the basic norms of Christian behavior, exemplified in homilies on the preparation of the catechumenate for Baptism (q.v.), on the other. New times require new efforts and the range of behaviors or "lifestyles" (classically, "the way of life") in late 20th-c. society is so wide and so confusing that Orthodox pastors and teachers are obliged to grapple with heretofore unknown issues: in vitro fertilization, euthanasia, genetic manipulation, etc. Nonetheless, new times do not always produce new problems. The old ones are quite active and resurface, such as the recent excitement over Just War theology. Some Orthodox writers have responded to this uniquely Western Christian theologoumenon, for which there appears to be little support in classical patristic thought. For the Fathers, war is always evil, and any killing, even in self-defense, is a sin (q.v.). Yet Byzantium (q.v.) and its successor Orthodox states have engaged in it. The question of war and its place—or lack thereof—in Orthodox thought and life requires the new application of both strictly theological reflection and of historical investigation.

**THEOPHANY** *see* Feasts, Twelve Great (Epiphany); *Theosis.*

**THEOSIS.** *Theosis* or "deification" has been the ruling principle or mode of understanding salvation in Christ since at least the late 2nd c., as evidenced in Irenaeus of Lyons (q.v.). Classically, Orthodox Holy Tradition (q.v.) sees it reflected in Paul's preaching on adoption to sonship and the indwelling Spirit (e.g., Rom 8), in John's promise of the gift of divine glory (John 17:5; 22–24), and summed up in 2 Pet 1:4, the Christian as a "communicant of the divine nature." The story of Christ's transfiguration in Mk 9:2–7 (Mt 17; Lk 9) becomes the ruling image of *theosis* by the time of Gregory Palamas, though its importance for the Church Fathers (qq.v.) dates from far earlier times. This understanding of salvation, that "God became man so that we might be made divine," in the words of Athanasius (q.v.), provides the unifying theme underlying the great debates over the Trinity and Christology (qq.v.) that preoccupy the Ecumenical Councils (q.v.) from Nicaea I (325) to Nicaea II (787), and the 14th c. controversy over hesychasm (q.v.). The theological development of the whole Byzantine era (q.v.) constitutes a continuing meditation on the mystery of salvation, and thus on *theosis*.

The term carries disturbing implications to the Western ear, and therefore should be qualified. Thus, the Orthodox emphasize the continuous theological stress on the paradox of deification: God (q.v.) and humankind are infinitely distant from each other by nature (q.v.), the creature infinitely inadequate to and other than the Creator. (*See* Theology.) Yet in Christ, infinite God and finite humanity meet and join, and that joining is no mere juxtaposition (as in Nestorius [q.v.]), but a true union without confusion or division, as in the formula of Chalcedon (q.v.). Humanity is not obliterated in Christ, but is instead perfected and fulfilled. Although the contribution of the human being to salvation is infinitely less than God's, Orthodox theology nevertheless insists on a true synergism, a cooperation. Synergy (literally, "coworking"), indeed, recalls the classic definition of the divine-human union in Christ: a co-inherence and exchange of the divine and human activity in the Incarnate Word, and through him in the Holy Spirit (q.v.). This allows the possibility that every human person may become the "unspotted mirror of the divine energies" (Dionysius the Areopagite [q.v.])—the manifestation of God's uncreated glory.

**THEOTOKOS** *see* Mariology.

**THESSALONICA.** Founded in 311 B.C., it was the site in the late A.D. 40s of Paul's missionary activity, an important city throughout the Byzantine era, and second only to Constantinople (qq.v.) in the Empire's waning centuries. Thessalonica continued to be important through the period of the Ottoman Empire (q.v.), its population a mixture of Turks, Slavs, and Greeks. Occupation by the Greek state in 1912 brought the city into the political orbit in which it remains today.

Ecclesiastically, it ranks second to Athens in the Greek Church, its metropolitan acting as the representative of the Ecumenical Patriarch (q.v.) for the dioceses of the "New Territories," i.e., the lands gained from the Turks at the beginning of the 20th c.

**TIKAS, SERAPHIM,** Archbishop of Athens and All Greece (1913– ). His baptismal name was Vissarion, he became a monk, then in 1938, a deacon. In 1941 he received a diploma in theology from the University of Athens and was ordained priest in 1942. On 11 September 1949, he was made Metropolitan of Arta, in 1958, Metropolitan of Ioannioa, and on 12 January 1974, Archbishop of Athens and Greece.

**TIKHON (BELAVIN),** Patriarch of Moscow *see* Belavin, Tikhon.

***TOME OF LEO.*** Officially titled the *Tomos ad Flavianum,* this doctrinal decree of Pope Leo the Great (q.v.) was addressed to Patriarch Flavian of Constantinople (q.v.) in 449. It defined, in opposition to Eutychius, the union of God and man in Christ as two natures (q.v.) united in one person. At Leo's insistence the *Tome* was part of the official statement of faith at Chalcedon (q.v.) in 451, though with supplementary documents, and it was not without a careful examination of the *Tome*'s contents by the council fathers (in spite of Leo's express command) to see if it was in agreement with the Christology of Cyril of Alexandria (qq.v.). Aside from the doctrinal interest of the *Tome,* a subject of fierce debate for centuries afterward, the document represents the first occasion that a Roman pope sought to substitute his own decree for the deliberations of a council.

***TOMOS.*** This term, derived from the Greek *temno* ("to cut"; cf. the Biblical Hebrew expression, "to cut a covenant" ), came to mean the equivalent of the English "decree," or "definition." Examples are the *Tome of Leo* (q.v.) and the "Tome of Mt. Athos," (1349/50) by Gregory Palamas (q.v.) in defense of the hesychasts (q.v.).

**TOTH, ALEXIS G.,** priest, missionary (14 March 1853–7 May 1909). Born in Szepes (near Presov), he was educated at the Roman Catholic Seminary of Esztergom, the United Greek Seminary of Ungvar, and the University of Presov with a degree in theology. Ordained in 1878, he served various parishes, was chancellor, director of the United Greek Catholic Seminary in Presov, and professor of Canon Law and Church history, before being sent to the United States on 15 November 1889 as a "missioner" to Slavic and Carpatho-Russian immigrants. As the first resident pastor of the Uniate (q.v.) St. Mary's parish in Minneapolis, he had a fateful—and mutually antagonistic—meeting with Bishop John Ireland (an "Americanist") on 19 December 1889, after which he actively sought to return his Ruthenian flock to the Orthodox Church. This was accomplished on 25 March 1891, when they were received by Bishop Vladimir (Sokolovsky) of San Francisco into the Russian Orthodox Diocese of Alaska and the Aleutian Islands, an act later confirmed by the Holy Synod of Russia. Fr. Toth, ever a missionary to the immigrants, continued his activities in 1892 in Wilkes-Barre, Pennsylvania, in 1902 in Mayfield, Pennsylvania, and elsewhere, so that the return of Uniates to Orthodoxy in the United States became a movement rather than an isolated phenomenon, involving an estimated 30,000 people.

**TRADITION, HOLY.** Literally, "tradition" in both Greek and Latin derives from the verb meaning "to hand over, pass on" (*paradidomi, trado*). In the Orthodox Church the phrase "Holy Tradition" signifies the Christian faith and that which enables and expresses it: worship (sacraments and liturgical offices), the Scriptures, the writings of the Church Fathers, the decrees of the Ecumenical Councils, and the witness of the lives of the saints (qq.v.). More deeply, tradition has been defined by Fr. Georges Florovsky as the life of the Holy Spirit (qq.v.), the current or continuum of the Church as the body of Christ and presence of the age to come. Not bound by documents or ritual actions, nor enclosed by them, nor expressed particularly and infallibly by any one office or officer of the Church, Holy Tradition is enshrined and protected by writings, rites, and offices within the Church.

Holy Tradition (with a capital "T") is to be distinguished from tradition (with a lower case "t") or custom. Custom and/or tradition are the different bodies of behavior and attitudes that have accompanied Holy Tradition down through the ages, but that are themselves necessarily bound to time and place, and might even obscure Holy Tradition. Similarly, indigenous traditions, whether originating in Orthodox environs or permitted by the Church following a people's conversion, may be deemed harmonious with the faith, or at least not in conflict with it, but never simply identified with it. The distinction is firm in theory, although its precise application in practice is often thorny.

**TRANSFIGURATION** *see* Feasts, Twelve Great; *Theosis.*

**TRANSLATION OF LITURGICAL TEXTS.** Translation of biblical, patristic, and liturgical texts, usually from Hebrew, Aramaic, and Greek into the languages of the peoples surrounding or making up the Empire—i.e., Latin, Coptic, Syriac, Ethiopian, Armenian, Georgian, and later on Church Slavic, Arabic, Romanian, etc.—was a feature of the Eastern Church from the earliest years. By the time of Byzantium (q.v.) proper, from the 6th c. on, a style of translation emerged that continued to hold the field until very recently. With the *Peshitta* (Syriac Bible, 5th c.), the translations of the Syriac golden age, and the work of Constantine-Cyril and Methodius (qq.v.) and their disciples, translators sought an exceedingly literal translation of Greek—even slavish—so some might argue today.

**TREBY.** With the reduction of church support from the imperial government after the Spiritual Regulation (q.v.) of Tsar Peter, it was common for Russian clergy to live off donations paid for private services. These *treby,* or "needs," originally connoted religious services for the needs of individuals, i.e., "personal" sacraments or special prayers (qq.v.). The term *treby* began to be identified with the needed living expenses of the clergy because of the terrible living conditions of the priests. The system is still widespread in the Russian Church today.

**TRINITY.** According to the understanding of the Orthodox Church, the confession of faith in Father, Son, and Holy Spirit (q.v.) is as old as Christianity. It is not the product of human reasoning, but the articulation of divine revelation, and it is embedded in the earliest Christian documents. The Apostle Paul, for example, closes 2 Cor with a Trinitarian blessing sometime in the A.D. 50s, and it seems to be the case that he is himself but repeating a formula already employed in Christian worship. The Gospel of Matthew concludes with the Trinitarian formula for Baptism (q.v.) already in use in that community ca. A.D. 80. The "Last Supper" discourse in Jn 14–16 contains four passages on the Holy Spirit which make it clear that the Spirit is regarded as a distinct person, "another Comforter/Advocate," together with the Son.

While profession of the three persons is from the earliest Christian scriptural witnesses, the Church also inherited the confession of God (q.v.) as one from the Hebrews: "Hear, O Israel, the Lord our God is one Lord" (Duet 6:4). There do not appear to have been any speculative attempts to square this circle earlier than the 2nd c. Father, Son, and Spirit were simply facts of primitive Christian experience; they were acknowledged as such in tandem with faith in the divine unity. The word, "trinity" (Greek *trias* and Latin *trinitas*), does not appear until Theophilus of Antioch (Greek) in the 180s and Tertullian (q.v.) (Latin) a decade or two later. The latter, together with Irenaeus of Lyons (q.v.), provide the first attempts at explaining the dual confession of God as one and three.

Tertullian relies primarily on a Stoic model, the divine substance in three different and eternal modes of expression. Irenaeus uses the analogy of the human person, speaking on some occasions of Son and

Spirit as the Father's Word and Wisdom, and elsewhere as his "two hands." In the 3rd c. Origen, borrowing from Platonism and the earlier work of Clement of Alexandria and Justin Martyr (qq.v.), arranges Father, Son, and Spirit in a descending hierarchy of *hypostases* (persons, or substances). His terminology was preserved in the Greek East during the great Trinitarian controversies of the 4th c. But his notes relating to subordination and hierarchy were rejected as a result of the ultimate victory of the Nicene Creed championed by Athanasius (qq.v.). It was the glory of the Cappadocian Fathers, especially Basil's *On the Holy Spirit,* Gregory of Nazianzus's *Theological Orations,* and Gregory of Nyssa's (qq.v.) *Against Eunomius* and "On Not Three Gods," to supply the language and concepts reconciling Origen's terms with the Nicene *homoousios* (consubstantial) in such a way as to become the classical formulation of the Orthodox doctrine of the Trinity.

The ancient emphasis on the Father as source of the other persons is the keystone of the teaching. The Father is the unique and personal (hypostatic) source of the Son and Spirit. Both derive their being (*ousia*) directly from him, the Son by "begetting" (*genesis*) and the Spirit by "procession" (*ekporeusis*). The "being" that they receive is the Father's own. The divine existence, will, and life is thus one and unique, and the persons three. Begetting and procession are not, however, further defined, and the omission is quite deliberate. The terms refer to processes within the godhead that escape human knowledge and comprehension altogether. The Cappadocians thus lay heavy emphasis upon paradox. The basic data of Christian experience are maintained, God is one and three, and the antinomy of the divine equation is itself held up as a fundamental revelation—in the words of Vladimir Lossky (q.v.), "a cross for human ways of thought." The primary metaphor for the godhead in Greek thought is therefore that of community.

Such was not the way of the West. Beginning earlier, but most importantly with Augustine of Hippo (q.v.), it was the model of the single human being that served the Latin writers as the ruling metaphor for investigation of the divine mystery. Augustine's *De Trinitate,* composed in the later years of his life, has set the agenda for Western theology (q.v.) in much the same way as the Cappadocians did for the East. Taking as his starting point Gen 1:26 and the idea of the human person as *imago Dei* (image of God), Augustine sought the "footprints of the Trinity" (*vestigia trinitatis*) in the human psyche. Among the many triads that he proposed based on this model, that of memory-intelligence-will was perhaps his favorite, although he was careful to acknowledge the inadequacy of any comparison to the divine mystery. Given this model, however, his notion of the Spirit as proceeding from both Father and Son followed naturally.

The *filioque* (q.v.), implicit in Augustine's very choice of model and explicit at different points in his writings (as it also was in Ambrose of Milan [q.v.]), found its way into the Nicene-Constantinopolitan Creed in Spain at the Council of Toledo in 589, probably as an emphasis on the Son's divinity in response to the Arianism (q.v.) of Spain's Visigothic rulers. From Spain it traveled in the late 8th c. to the court of Charlemagne at Aachen, where it became an important item in the Carolingian (qq.v.) offensive against the orthodoxy of the emperors in Constantinople (q.v.) in the opening decade of the 9th c. Frankish missionaries in Bulgaria later in the same century carried the offensive to the very threshold of Byzantium, a challenge that drew the response of the Patriarch Photius (qq.v.), who supplied the first and most important extended critique of the *filioque* in light of the Cappadocians. Photius objected to the phrase as both imperiling the unique monarchy (one source, *mia arche*) of the Father and muddling the distinction of the persons. The debate between Greek East and Latin West was firmly set in the 9th c. along lines that have continued to the present day.

For two centuries the popes of Rome (q.v.), though embracing Augustine's thought, refrained from adding the *filioque* to the Creed at Rome. This changed ca. 1013 when Pope Benedict XIII, at the request of the German Emperor, Henry II, added the phrase to the Creed sung in the papal chapel. The *filioque* also figured in the anathema that Cardinal Humbert da Silva launched against Michael Cerularios (q.v.) in 1054. The latter, according to Humbert, had willfully omitted (!) the phrase from the universal symbol of faith.

Such historical myopia was not characteristic of the best Latin thought. Scholastics such as Thomas Aquinas and Bonaventure in the 13th c. were fully aware of the *filioque* as a later, uniquely Latin addition, and they sought to defend it against the Greeks on logical and scriptural grounds. Byzantine thought—between labored polemics—tried to deal with the question of the Son's eternal relationship to the Spirit in the works of Gregory of Cyprus (1285), Gregory Palamas (q.v.), and John Byrennios (15th c.), though without accepting the Latin addition. They argued instead for the "eternal shining forth" (*aidios eklampsis*) from the Son of the Spirit who proceeds from the Father. The Reunion Councils (q.v.) of Lyons and Ferrara-Florence approved the *filioque,* but these were not ultimately received in the East.

Modern theologians continue the debate. Western writers such as Karl Barth and Karl Rahner, from the Reformed and Roman Catholic traditions, respectively, vigorously affirm the traditional triadology of the West. Orthodox theologians such as Vladimir Lossky and Dumitru Staniloae (qq.v.) reply as emphatically on behalf of the Eastern view.

More irenic voices from each camp have begun to seek some sort of accord in recent times. We mention in this regard the Russian church historian V. Bolotov and the philosopher-theologian Vladimir Soloviev (q.v.) in the 19th c. and the modern Roman Catholic theologians, A. de Halleux and Y. Congar. Whether these efforts result in any ultimate resolution remains to be seen.

**TRISAGION.** This term applies first of all to the biblical thrice holy (q.v.) of Is 6:3 and Rev 4:8, the hymn of the heavenly liturgy. It appears as the *Sanctus* in the eucharistic liturgy of both the East and West. In the East the same expression also applies to the hymn that repeats three times the petition, "Holy God, Holy Mighty One, Holy Immortal One, have mercy upon us," which is normally sung following the "little entrance" prior to the Epistle reading at the Divine Liturgy (q.v.). (The origin of this form of the hymn is associated with 25 September ca. 450 when a great earthquake ceased in Constantinople.) The hymn became cause for debate during the christological controversies of the late 5th c. Between 468 and 470, the "monophysite" Patriarch of Antioch (qq.v.), Peter the Fuller, introduced the phrase, "Who was crucified for us," following "Holy Immortal . . ." Defenders of Chalcedon (q.v.) objected to this christological reading of the hymn, i.e., as referring all three titles to Christ, and insisted on it instead as in praise of the Trinity (q.v.), denouncing the interpolation as an unacceptable mingling of the persons of the Godhead. The hymn is sung in the Oriental Orthodox churches (q.v.) to the present in its interpolated form, and in Eastern Orthodox churches in the original version.

**TRUBETSKOY, EUGENE N.,** lay theologian, epistemologist (1863–1920). After training at a classical "gymnasium" and developing an interest in music, he embraced Orthodoxy while listening to Anton Rubinstein conducting Beethoven's Ninth Symphony. He was a disciple of Vladimir Soloviev (q.v.) and used Soloviev's doctrine of Sophia to interpret aspects of iconography (q.v.); he also wrote on epistemology and the philosophy of the Church Fathers (qq.v.). As professor of the philosophy of law at Kiev and Moscow universities, he was involved in the Russian liberal political movement to abolish autocratic power, including oppression by the Bolsheviks. At the time of his death, he was a member of the White Army during the Revolution. He is the author of *Icons: Theology in Color* (trans. 1973).

**TURKEVICH, LEONTY,** metropolitan (8 August 1876–14 May 1965). Theologically trained at the Kiev Theological Seminary and its Theological Academy, from which he graduated in 1900, he taught in ecclesiastical schools and seminaries in Kursk and Ekaterinoslav. He was ordained a priest in 1905 and succeeded his father as priest of the church in Kremenetz. In October 1906 he was made rector of the recently established Orthodox seminary in Minneapolis, Minnesota. In 1912 the seminary was relocated to Tenafly, New Jersey. From 1914 to 1930 he edited the *Russian-American Orthodox Messenger*. In 1917 to 1918 he was a representative to the All-Russian Council in Moscow where he introduced the motion that resulted in the election of Patriarch Tikhon (q.v.). Drawing on his experience at the Sobor, he became one of the chief planners behind the autonomy of the American Church. He was widowed in 1925, and in 1933 became bishop of Chicago. In 1950 he was elevated to metropolitan of the "Metropolia," i.e., the Russian Orthodox Greek Catholic Diocese of North America, which became the Orthodox Church in America (q.v.).

**TURKS.** Originating in the regions of central Asia between the Caspian Sea and the Altai, Turkic-speaking tribes that expanded in conquest or else fled stronger cousins were the frequent concern of Byzantium (q.v.) from the 5th c. until the end of the Empire. In 1071 Alp Arslan led the Seljuk Turks to a victory over the Byzantine army at Mantzikert, in the extreme east of present-day Turkey, which resulted in the permanent Turkish occupation of Asia Minor (q.v.), a fact confirmed a century later at the battle of Myriokephalion (1176) where the Emperor Manuel I lost the army a second time. Out of the different tribes occupying Anatolia, the Ottomans began their rise to dominance in the early 14th c. until they took the place of the defeated Christian Empire in 1453 under Mohammed II.

Asia Minor was cleared of its remaining Greek presence with the population exchanges following the Treaty of Lausanne in 1924. The massacre of the Armenians just prior to that, together with continuing pressures on the Jacobite communities inhabiting the borderlands near Syria (qq.v.), have largely emptied what is now Turkey of any lingering Christian population. The Kurds, however, remain in the regions to the east where once Armenians and Syriac-speaking Christians had lived. They look to be somewhat more intractable a problem for the Turkish state, though efforts have been continuous since Kemal Ataturk in the 1920s to reduce this Muslim people to Turkification. The Turkish-speaking peoples of Azerbaijan, Uzbekistan, Turkmenistan, and Kazakhstan in the former Soviet Union have been showing interest in the idea of a greater Turkey, in some quarters at least, though this is likely to remain rhetoric for the present time.

**THE TWO WAYS** *see* The Way.

-U-

**UGANDAN ORTHODOX CHURCH.** Uganda is a nation of East Africa on the northern shores of Lake Victoria and bordering Tanzania to the west, Sudan to the north, and Kenya to the east. In the 1920s a group of young Ugandan clergyman, Anglican by ordination and training and led by Reuben Spartas, sought to enter the Orthodox Church. Their motives appear to have been a blend of genuine conviction and resentment against colonial rule. Following a period featuring misadventures and incomprehension on the part of the Greek higher clergy in Alexandria (q.v.), they were finally received by the Patriarchate of Alexandria. Although not without further troubles, the African mission of the Orthodox Church takes its beginnings from these men. The Church of Uganda is today directed by a Ugandan bishop, Theodore Nankyamas, a suffragan of the Metropolitan of East Africa, Makarios, headquartered in Nairobi, Kenya. Two other metropolitanates have since been added to the African mission: Central Africa headquartered in Kinshasa, Zaire, and West Africa, directed from the Cameroons and including Ghana and Nigeria.

**UKRAINIAN ORTHODOX CHURCH (UOC).** His Beatitude, Metropolitan Volodymyr (Sabodan) of Kiev, primate of the autonomous Ukrainian Orthodox Church, is the only recognized head of the Ukrainian Church by the Ecumenical Patriarchate and world Orthodoxy (qq.v.). The UOC synod of bishops includes thirty hierarchs and governs fifty-five hundred parishes, twenty-five dioceses, thirty-seven monasteries, seminaries in Odessa, Lutsk, and Kiev, and schools in Chernigov and Pochayev, as well as the Ecclesiastical Academy. Most of Ukraine's thirty-five million Orthodox believers remain faithful to this Church, autonomous under Moscow, which has canonically controlled ecclesiastical activity in the Ukraine for three centuries.

In December 1993 Metropolitan Volodymyr gave the following interview in New York, which briefly describes the present situation: "The Local Council of the Russian Orthodox Church, which elected Metropolitan Aleksy of Leningrad to be primate and Patriach of the Russian Orthodox Church, as well as the two Councils of Bishops of the Russian Orthodox which followed it, gave the Church, which had previously been known as the Patriarchal Exarchate of Kiev and All Ukraine, a new title—the Ukrainian Orthodox Church. It has been granted full independence and freedom for self-government. In other words, it has all the rights and opportunities which an autonomous church possesses. His Holiness, Patriarch Aleksy, does not interfere in our affairs and we have our own Holy Synod which resolves all ongoing problems of Church life at its meetings. We have the opportunity to govern ourselves, however, we are not an autocephalous (q.v.) Church but an autonomous Church which has certain abilities and possibilities. Today there is the issue, which some believers especially in the western regions of Ukraine hold, that the Church should have full independence and self-government in the status of a local Church. In eastern Ukraine and other regions there are other points of view. The people there do not want that kind of full independence. The issue is being studied. We have appealed to His Holiness, Patriarch Aleksy, requesting that he raise this issue with all the primates of the local autocephalous Churches and that if this is the will of the episcopate, clergy, monastics, and faithful, then the issue of full independence which results in an autocephalous local Church will have to be resolved." ("Orthodox Church in America News," Alex Liberovsky, Interviewer, December, 1993, page 6.)

Nonetheless, there is ecclesiastical chaos in Ukraine today. In addition to the canonical UOC headed by Metropolitan Volodymyr, there exist two parallel Orthodox jurisdictions: The Ukrainian Autocephalous Orthodox Church (UAOC) surfaced in 1989 under the leadership of the now deceased Patriarch Mystaslav (Skrypnik), who lived in exile, and is now headed by Bishop Dimitri (Yarema) as the new "Patriarch of Kiev"; it has about 800 parishes. Another group, the Ukrainian "Patriarchate of Kiev" (UOC-KP), was founded a year ago with parishes loyal to the former Metropolitan Philaret (Denisenko), but which has recently elected Bishop Volodymyr (Romaniuk) as patriarch. Romaniuk, a former priest of the Patriarchate of Moscow, was imprisoned for sixteen years in Soviet camps for his religious convictions. The candidacy of the more controversial former Metropolitan Philaret (Denisenko) was rejected.

The enthronement of the new primate took place on 24 October 1993, at St. Sophia Cathedral in Kiev, which was opened especially for this service. This latter group has enjoyed widespread support from President Leonid Kravchuk and the Ukrainian government, although the March 1994 elections displayed a division between Russian- and Ukrainian-speaking parts of the country. Canonicity of the two dissident churches is not officially recognized by any Orthodox Church. In August 1992 the Ukrainian Greek Catholic Church (Uniates), more prevalent in West Ukraine, had 2,719 parishes.

Disputes over property have frequently boiled over into street violence, pitting one congregation against another. Ukrainian television routinely broadcasts rival services of the two dissident branches. The situation is in a continuing state of flux. (*See* Kievan Rus'; Russian Orthodox Church; Unia.)

**UNCTION.** *See* Healing.

**UNIA-UNIATE CHURCHES.** Although the Unia proper began with the Council and Union of Brest-Litovsk (1596), the prehistory of the movement certainly goes back ideologically to the Reunion Councils (q.v.) centuries before. After Muscovite Christianity (q.v.) established its own patriarchate (q.v.) in 1589, the king and nobility of Poland-Lithuania requested the organization of an Eastern rite of the Roman Church. This body recognized the popes rather than the patriarchs, but preserved the Eastern liturgical rites; and it was created to compete directly with the Orthodox Church so that the Ukraine and Belarus would not fall under the influence of Muscovy. The Constantinopolitan patriarchate, which had jurisdiction over the non-Muscovite churches, protested, but was under the Turkish yoke and in no position to take effective action. The Unia in the Ukraine and Belarus was supported by the bishops, but fervently opposed by the rest of the clergy and the *bratsva* (lay brotherhoods). The Orthodox Church thus ceased to exist de jure in Poland-Lithuania, and its properties became those of the Uniate church. The Ukraine and Belarus followed suit, and the administration of the Uniates in every case was separate from the Latin Roman Catholics (q.v.).

The Cossacks struggled intermittently to maintain their Ukrainian and Orthodox identity—and freedom from serfdom—and in an uprising from 1648 to 1654 Bohdan Khmelnitskii took the region east of the Dnieper River from the Poles and allied it with Moscow. Although the metropolitanate of Kiev should have rightfully remained under Constantinople (q.v.), from the point of view of Moscow such a course of action was dangerous, if not impossible, due to the weakened Byzantine presence. Muscovy, in an expansionist mode, wanted to make the patriarch's title and jurisdiction correspond to that of the tsar: "All-Russia." Kiev's Western and Latin affiliations made themselves felt not only politically, but also theologically in such churchmen as Metropolitan Peter Mogila (q.v.).

In 1685 Patriarch Ioakim Savelov (1620–1690) and Hetman Ivan Samoilovich of the Eastern Ukraine prepared the way for moving the Eastern Ukraine from the jurisdiction of Constantinople to Moscow, which was accomplished the following year with the election of Bishop Gedeon Sviatopolk-Chetvertinskii as Metropolitan of Kiev. In the West Ukraine this had the opposite effect of driving former Orthodox into the Polish-controlled Unia, and the Uniate church of the Ukraine, sometimes called Ruthenian, developed a separate identity from Russia or Poland, numbering about four million in the 18th c. The "Spiritual Regulation" (q.v.) and program of compulsory Westernization by Peter the Great in Russia weakened the Russian Church in turn, abolishing the patriarchate and the power to act in external affairs, since the Russian church itself became a "Department of State."

During the third partitioning of Poland (1795) the West Ukraine and Belarus were incorporated into the Russian Empire, and many Uniates were coerced into the Russian Orthodox Church (q.v.). Although the situation eased under Tsars Paul (1796–1801) and Alexander I (1801–1825), Nicholas I (1825–1855) suppressed all Uniate dioceses except the Polish Kholm in 1839, declaring all Uniates as Orthodox. Kholm was conscripted into the "state Church" in 1875 in the wake of the Polish uprising of 1862 to 1863. Uniate and Ukrainian separatist sympathies were fueled by propaganda of the Austro-Hungarian Empire in the period preceding World War I.

Outbursts of Uniate sentiment occurred throughout the reign of Tsar Nicholas II (1894–1917) and a whole series of rather predictable, tragic episodes, documenting a chronicle of ignominious "sheep stealing," continued to play themselves out on new stages: the United States, the loss of Russian Uniate territories after 1917; the regaining of these territories by the Soviet Union; and the recent independence of these territories in post-Communist Eastern Europe. In the United States a Ruthenian "missioner," Fr. Alexis Toth (q.v.), worked diligently and successfully to return many Carpatho-Russian Christian parishes to canonical Orthodoxy.

The vicissitudes of the Czech, Polish, and Ukrainian (qq.v.) local churches in the 20th c. occupy the other three stages, and the difficult situation maintains through the present. For example, the Soviets and the Russian Church cooperated to bring two to three million Uniates in eastern Poland into Orthodoxy by fiat, to which were added Uniates of the West Ukraine who had been under Soviet dominance only after World War II. Since the dissolution of the Soviet Union, many have returned to Rome (q.v.). The political dynamic of "Unia" has been used by the Vatican in dealing with groups such as the Maronites, the Melchites, the Syro-Chaldean Patriarchate, and the Syro-Malankarese Church (qq.v.).

**UNION OF BREST-LITOVSK** *see* Unia.

**USPENSKY, NIKOLAI D.,** theologian (3 January 1900–1987). Educated at Novgorod Seminary and the Petrograd Theological Institute, he received his Candidate of Theology degree in 1925. After the authorities closed the Institute in 1928, he taught music in secular institutions. He graduated from the State Conservatory in 1937 with the dissertation, "Melodies of the Russian North," and joined the faculty of the reopened Leningrad Theological Academy in 1946, receiving a Master of Theology degree (1949), and a Doctorate from the Moscow Theological Academy (1957). He is the author of *Evening Worship in the Orthodox Church* (trans. 1985).

**USURY.** Usury, or lending at interest, was condemned by the Church Fathers (q.v.), and forbidden the clergy. During the Byzantine era (q.v.), however, the state did not enact legislation forbidding the practice, though it did try to exercise some control over the amounts of interest charged.

**UTENSILS, LITURGICAL** see Liturgical Vessels.

-V-

**VAPORIS, NOMIKOS MICHAEL,** priest, theologian, educator, publicist. Vaporis is a graduate of Youngstown State University (B.A.), Holy Cross Greek Orthodox School of Theology (Dipl. in Theol.), Yale Divinity School (S.T.B., S.T.M.), the University of Athens School of Theology (Lic. Theol.), and Columbia University (M.A., Ph.D.). He has taught at Holy Cross Greek Orthodox School of Theology (q.v.) since 1965 and has held, at one time or another, every office at the institution except that of president.

Fr. Vaporis has served as an editor of *The Greek Orthodox Theological Review* since 1966 and has been chief editor since 1971. Together with Dr. Harry Psomiades, he has edited the *Journal of Modern Hellenism* since its inception in 1984. Founder of the Archbishop Iakovos Library of Ecclesiastical and Historical Sources (fifteen volumes published thus far), he has contributed three volumes to the series, in addition to authoring ten books and numerous studies. Meanwhile, Fr. Vaporis has found time to direct the Holy Cross Press and the Hellenic College Press (more than 100 scholarly, non-scholarly, and bilingual titles published), and has contributed to the official translation of the Divine Liturgy and other services of the Greek Orthodox Church.

**VASILEIOS (GONDIKAKIS),** Archimandrite of Iviron see Gondikakis, Vasileios.

**VELICHKOVSKY, PAISII,** monk, translator, St. (1722–1794). A student at the Kievan Academy, he was disappointed with spiritual conditions there. He left after he refused to study, scorning both pagan mythology and higher Latin studies, and complaining that the Church Fathers (q.v.) were little read. He began a search for true monastic life, which brought him to Mt. Athos (q.v.) where he lived seventeen years, founding his own monastery on the ancient tradition of inner prayer (q.v.). He did not reject knowledge, but discerned what knowledge was valuable to the Christian life. He later founded monasteries in Moldavia at Dragomirna, Sekul, and Niamets using the 14th c. rule of Byzantine monasticism (qq.v.).

While on Athos he began collecting and checking Slavic translations of ascetical works. He was an exacting translator and continued his work after resettlement in the Niamets monastery in Moldavia, which became a literary and theological center concerned with spiritual enlightenment and "intellectual construction." In terms of writing, Velichkovsky depended on the literary style of Nilus Sorsky and continued Sorsky's interrupted work. His disciples focused on translations from Greek, but included some from Latin. Velichkovsky's translation of the *Philokalia* (q.v.) was a major event in Russian monasticism. This and the "Paisii movement" served as a catalyst for things to come among the Slavophiles (q.v.) of Russia, a return to traditional sources.

**VENIAMINOV, INNOCENT (JOHN POPOV),** Metropolitan of Moscow, Alaskan missionary, translator, St. (1798–1879). Born in Siberia, John Popov was educated at the Irkutsk Seminary and awarded a family name made up from that of the newly deceased Bishop Benjamin (i.e., Veniaminov) in recognition of his high academic performance. He arrived as a priest in Alaska (q.v.) in 1824 with his mother, brother, wife, and son; at that time he found that almost the entire Aleut population was baptized. Fr. John Popov-Veniaminov was an extraordinarily multitalented individual who figured in the history of Alaska by scientifically recording flora, fauna, weather, and the tides. He made furniture, built clocks, designed and built churches — including the Mission House and St. Michael's Cathedral in Sitka.

Both preceding and after his episcopal consecration, he was an advocate for indigenous Christianity in Alaska before the Holy Synod, and was the first resident bishop (1840–1858). He developed an Aleut alphabet and translated a catechism and the Gospel of Matthew with the assistance of Ivan Pankov. He was always an active proponent of education and opened a seminary in Sitka for the training of native clergy.

In terms of California history, he made a trip to Fort Ross (q.v.) in 1836 and visited some Spanish Missions in the San Francisco Bay area. He communicated with the Franciscans in Latin, and eventually built a few barrel organs for the Missions. He kept a brief diary of his daily duties and travels while visiting California. (*See* Russian America.)

In terms of Russian history, he was made archbishop in 1850 and combined his Alaskan responsibilities with those of Yakutsk in Asia in 1852. In the succeeding years, he worked with Count Nicholas Muraviev for the annexation of the Amur River Basin, which occurred through the Treaty of Argin in 1858. The next year, he paid his last visit to Sitka and installed his new vicar, Bishop Peter (Lysakov). In 1861, after shipwreck, he spent time in Japan with Fr. Nikolai

Kasatkin (q.v.). He served as an apostolic inspiration for this priest who would later be canonized the "Enlightener of Japan." In 1865 Veniaminov was appointed to the Holy Synod of Russia.

In 1867, with the sale of Alaska to the United States by Russia, Innocent made the following recommendations to the Holy Synod:
1. Do not close the American vicariate—even though the number of churches and missions there has been cut in half (i.e., to five).
2. Designate San Francisco rather than New Archangel the residence of the vicar. The climate is incomparably better there, and communications with the colonial churches are just as convenient from there as from New Archangel (if not more so).
3. Subordinate the vicariate to the bishop of St. Petersburg or some other Baltic diocese, for once the colonies have been sold to the American government, communications between the Amur and the colonies will end completely and all communications between the headquarters of the Diocese of Kamchatka and the colonies will have to be through St. Petersburg—which is completely unnatural.
4. Return to Russia the current vicar and all clergy in New Archangel (except churchmen), and appoint a new vicar from among those who know the English language. Likewise, his retinue ought to be composed of those who know English.
5. Allow the bishop to augment his retinue, transfer its members and ordain to the priesthood for our churches converts to Orthodoxy from among American citizens who accept all its institutions and customs.
6. Allow the vicar bishop and all clerics of the Orthodox Church in America (q.v.) to celebrate the Divine Liturgy (q.v.) and other services in English (for which purpose, obviously, the service books must be translated into English).
7. To use English rather than Russian (which must sooner or later be replaced by English) in all instruction in the schools to be established in San Francisco and elsewhere to prepare people for missionary and clerical positions. (The seven points are excerpted from Garrett, *St. Innocent*, p. 276.)

Ironically, in 1868 Tsar Alexander II appointed him Metropolitan of Moscow, shortly after the archbishop had requested retirement. In 1870 he organized the Imperial Mission Society, served as its first president, and through it remembered his earlier missions in Alaska. During the next thirty years, the Russian Church would surpass the United States government in supporting the education of Native Americans in Alaska. After gradually going blind late in life, Innocent continued to serve the liturgical services and "read" the assigned Gospel lectionary aloud from memory. He died on Holy Saturday, 1879.

**VENICE.** Founded in 421 on the north coast of the Italian Adriatic and for centuries an outpost of Byzantium (q.v.), Venice began to acquire independence in the 9th c. By the 11th c. it controlled much of the trade of the Empire as a foreign power. Tensions between the citizens of Constantinople (q.v.) and Venetian merchants sparked the bloody riots of 1187 that slew thousands of Western Europeans in the latter's suburb of Galatea. Desire for vengeance and for securing the Venetian trading monopoly prompted Doge Enrico Dandolo to divert the Fourth Crusade (q.v.) in 1204 to take and sack the imperial city and dismember its Empire. Venetian occupation of positions on the Greek mainland and several islands, including Corfu and Crete, continued for centuries. Venice itself treasures many of the spoils of the Crusade, notably the four horses over the Cathedral of San Marco, the *palo d'oro* fronting the high altar, and the many San Marco museum pieces that have been (curiously) reworked.

**VERGHESE, (PAUL)–GREGORIOS, PAULOS MAR,** metropolitan, educator, theologian (9 August 1922– ). Metropolitan of Delhi, Orthodox Syrian Church of the East (India), Paulos Mar Gregorios is the most distinguised theologian of the Oriental Orthodox churches (q.v.). Born and raised on the Malabar Coast of India in that country's native non-Chalcedonian church, he was educated at Princeton and Yale and received his doctorate from Serampore.

He is the author of a dozen books and various articles on Orthodox anthropology, cosmology, and selected Church Fathers, in particular Gregory of Nyssa (qq.v.), and an editor and contributor to *Koptisches Christentum, Die Syrischen Kirchen in Indien,* and *Does Chalcedon Divide or Unite?*. After serving as adviser to Emperor Haile Selassie, he held several leadership positions in the World Council of Churches dealing with ecumenism (q.v.) and UNESCO. He has also been an active member of the Oriental Orthodox-Orthodox Dialogue (q.v.) since its inception in the 1960s.

**VESTMENTS, LITURGICAL.** (Consult the drawings that follow.)
Deacon: 1. The sticharion, or dalmatic, is the basic festal baptismal garment every Christian wears at Baptism (q.v.). 2. The deacon's stole or orarion is his emblem of office by which he leads the people in prayer and directs other litugical actions. 3. The deacon also wears cuffs (not visible) both for convenience and for showing forth the power of the right hand of God. (See #5 below.)
Priest: 4. The priest's stole or epitrachelion is similar to the deacon's stole, but the ends are sewn parallel ending in a neck hole, and it is emblematic of the consecrating grace of the priesthood. 5. The priest wears cuffs, as does the deacon. (See #3 below.) 6. The belt or zone girds the

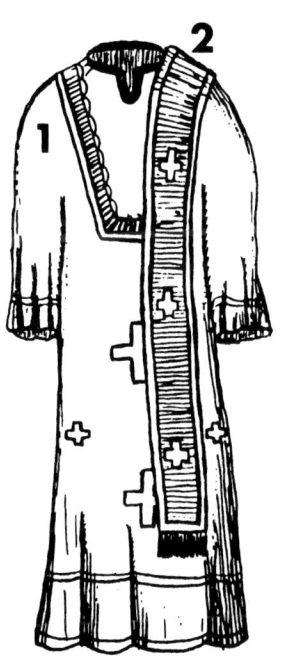 

priest and represents the power and blamelessness that should be exercised in walking before the Lord. 7. In the Russian tradition the square epigonation, or *nabedrennik,* is the first award given a priest for distinguished service, but it has no significance different from item #8. 8. The *palitza,* or diamond-shaped epigonation, signifies the sword of the Spirit, which is the Word of God, and is a senior award of the priesthood. At times in Greece this vestment has been employed to indicate the educated clergy who are capable of preaching and hearing confession. 9. (The Russian square-cut phelonion is shown.) The phelonion, or chasuble, is the distinguishing garment of the priesthood and probably has its origin in Byzantine court dress. 10. The priest's cross (not shown) is worn in recent Russian tradition by all priests, but historically it was a senior award of clergy as it still is in the Greek practice.

Bishop: 1. The sakkos, or dalmatic (see next page), is symbolic of Christ's coat without seam, woven from top to bottom. 2. The omophorion, or pall, typifies the wandering sheep that the Good Shepherd takes upon his shoulders and carries to his Father. 3. The miter is a crown that serves as an emblem of the power bestowed upon the High Priest. 4. The pastoral staff, or crosier, indicates the spiritual authority

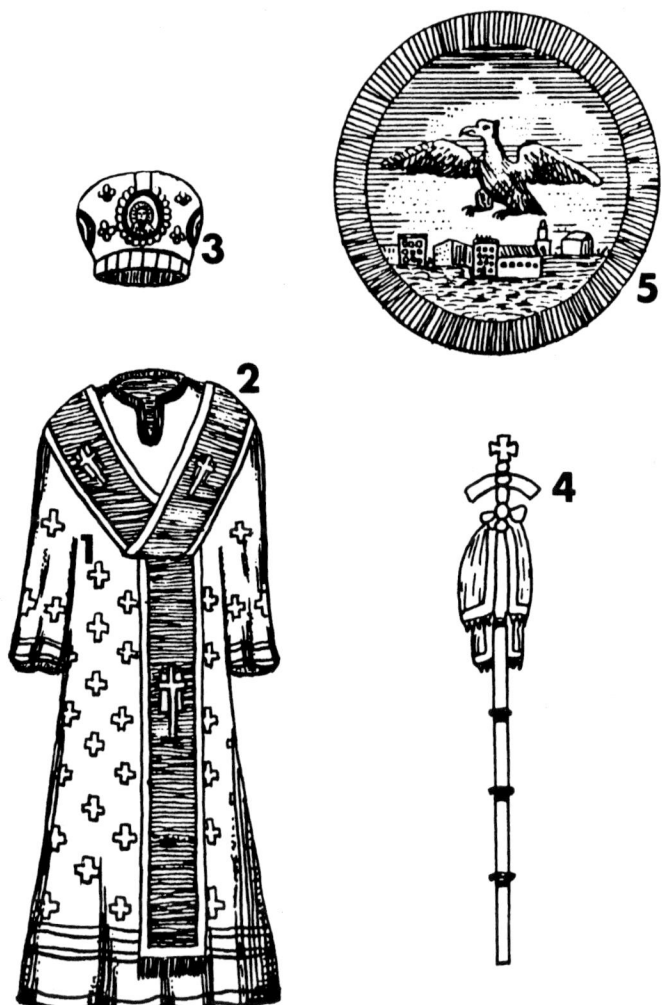

of bishops and archimandrites over their flocks. The image of the Good Shepherd is one familiar to agricultural societies; and it is well known that a shepherd provides water, food, and safe haven for his flock—guiding, rescuing, and correcting with his staff. 5. The eagle rug is a small, round rug about a foot and a half in diameter with the representation of an eagle hovering over the bishop's see. The bishop stands on it during the religious services, at each location as he moves to various places in the church during the Divine Liturgy—the center of the church, in front of the altar, behind the altar, etc. 6. The bishop's mantle (not shown), or cape, is usually multicolored purple and is sewn with the "Tables of the Law," representing the Old and New Testaments, and the "Fountains," red and white ribbons encircling the mantle and signifying flowing streams of teaching and wisdom. 7. The panagia, or encolpion, is a pectoral icon (not shown) of the Mother of God with Child, representing the Church bearing the Lord in its heart.

**VIRGIN MARY** *see* Mariology.

**VLADIMIR, PRINCE** *see* Kievan Rus'.

### -W-

**WARE, KALLISTOS,** bishop, theologian, educator (11 September 1934– ). Born Timothy R. Ware, he received his early education at the Westminster Under School, London, and returned from 1958 to 1959 as a classics master. He received his B.A. from Magdalen College (1956), an M.A. (1959), and a D.Phil. (1965), after pursuing studies in church history (1960–63). He joined the Orthodox Church in 1958. After spending time in Greece, he was ordained priest in 1966 and became a member of the Monastic Brotherhood of St. John the Theologian, Patmos, taking the name Kallistos.

In the same year, Ware became Spaulding Lecturer in Eastern Orthodox Studies at Oxford, and served the Greek Orthodox parish of Holy Trinity, Oxford, as priest in charge. In 1970 he was made a fellow of Pembroke College. He was the secretary for the Anglican-Orthodox Joint Doctrinal Discussions (1973–79) and a counselor afterward. In 1982 he became titular bishop of Diokleia, and assistant bishop in the Orthodox Archdiocese of Thyateira and Great Britain. He is a much sought after speaker, a past editor of the *Eastern Churches Review* (1967–78), an editor of *Sobornost* (since 1979), and the author of the very influential *The Orthodox Church* (1963; rev. ed. 1994) and *The Orthodox Way* (1979). He is widely respected by clergy for his teaching and personal conviction.

**THE WAY** (also called the Two Ways). In Scripture (q.v.): Participation in the Kingdom of God and salvation are tied to ethical and mission-oriented action. This action is symbolically described as "The Way of the Lord." The Two Ways for men and women are 1) the way of the Lord, or the good and right way (Gen 18:19; Ps 18:21, 25:9; 1 Sam 12:23); and 2) the way of evil, that of sinners and the wicked (Ps 1:1; Prov 2:12; Jer 18:11; Ezek 3:18). Although a person's way may be either good or evil (1 Kgs 8:36; Gen 6:12) depending on his free will, the way of the Lord is always right, perfect, just, and true. As the

Old Testament text states, the Lord desires not the death of anyone, but that he turn from the evil way and live. When God began to teach and lead his people under the first covenant, the way of the Lord was identified with the Mosaic Law.

Jesus talks about the way in his teaching ministry: "Enter by the narrow gate; for the gate is wide and the way is easy, that leads to destruction, and those who enter by it are many. For the gate is narrow and the way is hard, that leads to life and those who find it are few" (Mt 7:13–14). The New Testament writers saw the way of the Lord, as it was proclaimed by the prophets, completed and fulfilled in Christ (Mt 3:3; Mk 1:2–3; Lk 3:4; Jn 1:23; 1 Cor 12:31). In John's Gospel (14:4 ff.), Jesus says to the disciples "and where I go you know the way . . . I am the way, and the truth, and the life; no one comes to the Father, but by me." The "new and living way" (Heb 10:20) to God was made possible by Christ as a way of salvation, of truth, and of peace. Thus, Luke rightly identifies Christianity as "the Way" and emphasizes this repeatedly.

The Two Ways in the Qumran documents ("Dead Sea Scrolls"): These antedate Jesus and are a condensed course in ethics or proper moral behavior. This religious community had as its purpose to keep the Law and the Covenant in the True Way. Unfortunately, members of the community were taught "to be unremitting in hatred towards all men of ill repute, and to be minded to keep in seclusion from them." Jesus and John the Baptist were, no doubt, familiar with the Qumran Community. The genius of John the Baptist as he is described in the New Testament, and as distinct from the Qumran community, lies in the fact that he did not limit the practice and preaching of the Good Way to a closed community.

In early Christian writings and subsequently in catechesis (q.v.):
1) *The Doctrine of the Apostles* (*Doctrina Apostolorum*). This short document is basically a Christianized version of the Qumran teaching on the Two Ways.
2) *Didache* (q.v.) or *The Lord's Teaching according to the Twelve Apostles* is found in later documents in a similar form, as in *The Apostolic Order* and the *Apostolic Constitutions* (q.v.), thereby indicating its continued importance. The first six chapters of the *Didache* tell of the Way of Life (I-IV) and the Way of Death (V-VI), but also make an important shift into the familiar Gospel idiom: "First, you shall love the God who made you, secondly your neighbor as yourself." Love of neighbor is later equated with showing others the love that God has shown oneself.
3) In the *Epistle of Barnabas* (*see* Barnabas) the Way of Light and the Way of Darkness are described in the concluding chapters, 18–21. *Barnabas* identifies the Way of Light with Christianity and expects his readers to be good lawgivers and advisers to one

another, as well as to those who still need to be brought into the Way.
4) In the *Shepherd of Hermas* (q.v.), Mandates 6–8 (i.e., chapter divisions) speak of the righteous way, which is straight and level, and the unrighteous way, which is crooked and rough. Here it is simply explained that a Christian should know there is an objective right and wrong.

**WESTERN INFLUENCES.** With the decline of Byzantium (q.v.) in the eleventh and twelfth centuries, both ecclesiastical and civil officials were increasingly obliged to take into account the rising power of Western Europe and Roman Catholicism (q.v.). Theologically, the issue of the *filioque* (q.v.) raised questions that, in spite of polemic, were given serious consideration by Byzantine theologians. The list of seven sacraments seems to have come from the West following the failed Reunion Council (qq.v.) at Lyons in 1274. Vigorous efforts at the translation of patristic and medieval Latin texts, including Augustine of Hippo (q.v.) and Thomas Aquinas, began in the 14th c. and were still in process at the time of the Empire's fall to the Ottomans in 1453. While these efforts at dialogue and reassessment were significant, the story of Western influences on Orthodox thought begin properly with the end of Byzantium and the collapse of an educated Orthodox elite.

Higher education for Christians in the Ottoman Empire (q.v.) was impossible, short of conversion to Islam (q.v.), and the promising young men of Greek families were increasingly sent to universities in Italy and Germany. Similarly, the rule of Poland over most of the territories of Kievan Rus' led to the adoption of Latin Scholasticism (qq.v.) as the theological method even by those Orthodox intent on avoiding the Unia (q.v.) of 1596. (*See* Peter Mogila.) In the empire of Austria, a like process went on in the Orthodox-dominated principality of Transylvania and the border regions of Croatia inhabited by Serbs. As a result, by the late 18th c. all the formal theology being taught in the Orthodox *oikoumene* (qq.v.) was of a distinctively Western flavor. The reforms of Peter the Great (q.v.) in Russia, where clergy were educated in Latin until the early 19th c., and the rise of the nation-states in the Balkans (q.v.) completed the picture. In a sense, this process was inevitable, given the general rise to world dominance of Western European culture.

The situation remains with us today. Historical studies by Russian theologians in the 19th c. lent unexpected assistance to a simultaneous movement of Eastern monastic renewal, which had been begun by Nicodemus of the Holy Mountain and Paisii Velichkovsky (qq.v.). The pendulum has swung from West to East in the last two centuries throughout the Orthodox *oikoumene*. The question of the proper balance between the classical theology of the Church Fathers (q.v.) and the thought and methodology of the West is a legitimate one. The rise of Scholasticism and the Enlightenment is something that, *mutatis mutandis*, every Christian community is required to confront.

**WESTERN ORTHODOXY.** This phrase can refer either to Orthodox Christians from Eastern Europe and the Middle East now resident in Western Europe and the Americas, or to a movement, extremely limited in numbers and controversial in execution, to create communities using one or another of the historical liturgies (q.v.) of the West while maintaining communion with the Orthodox Church. The Russian Church (q.v.) was the first to approve such experiments, at least in theory, at the end of the 19th c. At present, Western Orthodoxy, or "Western-rite Orthodoxy," is represented chiefly by a diocese in France formerly under the jurisdiction of the Church of Romania. Also, some two dozen formerly Episcopalian parishes using this rite have sought the pastoral care of the Antiochian or Syrian Archdiocese (q.v.) in North America. Neither the Greek Orthodox Archdiocese nor the Orthodox Church in America (qq.v.) endorse this action—which is possible in theory—because of the adverse pastoral effects it has on a highly mobile population unable to reproduce its liturgical experience from place to place. In its worst manifestation, the creation of such communities could constitute a type of "reverse Unia" (q.v.).

**WOMAN/WOMEN** *see* Anthropology; Saints.

-Y-

**YAKUT.** This is the Turkic language of the most northern Turkic people, whose language, religion, and people are all known as Yakut. Living in the Lena River basin in northeastern Siberia, the Yakut herd horses and cattle, hunt, fish, produce crafts, and trade. Subjugated by Russia in the first half of the 17th c., many adopted Christianity by the 19th c. Nominally Russian Orthodox, some preserved their own shamanism modifying it with Christianity, for example attributing traits of God, Mary, and angels to shaman spirits—a type of "dualfaith" (q.v.). In 1979 the Yakut numbered approximately 328,000.

**YANNARAS, CHRISTOS,** Greek Orthodox lay theologian, educator (1935– ). One of the most celebrated contemporary Orthodox theologians, he is professor of philosophy at Pantion University of Social and Political Sciences, Athens. His thought is characterized by the effort to employ the Church Fathers and modern Russian Orthodox thinkers such as Vladimir Lossky (qq.v.) in the service of a contemporary theological expression that takes account of continental existentialism, particularly the thought of Martin Heidegger (1889–1976). One of his principal concerns is the freedom (q.v.) allowed humans by following Christ. He is the author of several books including *Honest with Orthodoxy, Person and Eros, The Modern Greek Identity, The Crisis of Prophecy, Orthodoxy and the West* (all in Greek), and *The Freedom of Morality* (trans. 1984) and *Elements of Faith: An Introduction to Orthodox Theology* (trans. 1991).

**YANNOULATOS, ANASTASIOS,** Archbishop of Tirana and All Albania, missionary, educator (1927– ). Earning his Diploma in Theology from the University of Athens in 1952, he was ordained to the diaconate (1960), and was made archimandrite (1964). In 1971 he founded the international Orthodox Missionary Society in Athens, with the focus of missionary activity in Uganda, Tanzania, Kenya, and the Sudan. On 19 November 1972 he was consecrated bishop of Androusa. He was director of the Nairobi Theological Seminary from 1982, and also served as Metropolitan of the Diocese of East Africa. From 1983 to 1991 he was moderator of the Commission of World Mission and Evangelism of the World Council of Churches. From 1986 to 1990 he served as patriarchal vicar of Trinoupolis (Alexandria) and was elected patriarchal exarch of Albania (qq.v.) in 1991. More recently he was elected to the Albanian see by the Albanian Church. He has been to the United States on a number of occasions to speak on mission ventures in Africa, and has published English-language articles in *International Bulletin of Missionary Research, International Review of Mission,* and *Missionalia.*

**YELCHANINOV, ALEXANDER** *see* Elchaninov, Alexander.

**YOUTH MOVEMENT (ANTIOCH).** Begun in the immediate post-World War II years in Lebanon and Syria, the Orthodox Christian Youth Movement has contributed significantly to the renewal of Arabic-speaking Christianity within the Patriarchate of Antioch (qq.v.). Encouraging Bible study, the reading of the Church Fathers (q.v.), and discussion, it has managed to maintain a consistently open and generous attitude toward both Islam (q.v.) and the culture of Western Europe. Many, if not most, of the current hierarchy of the Antiochian Church have participated in it in their youth.

**YUGOSLAVIA.** This modern nation-state, now dissolved, was formed in 1919 as the Kingdom of the Serbs, Croats, and Slovenes under the Serbian crown. It lasted through the deposition of the Karageogevíc dynasty and the installation of Communist rule by Marshal Tito (Josip Broz) following World War II. But it began to break up into its constituent parts (Serb, Croat, Slovene, Muslim Slav, Slavic Macedonian, and Albanian) in 1990 and 1991. The Orthodox Church of Serbia (q.v.) ministers to Orthodox believers throughout the territories of the former federation, although the civil war being waged at the time of writing indicates that a widespread redistribution of the populations is both certain and already under way.

-Z-

**ZERNOV, NICHOLAS,** apologist, educator, theologian, ecumenist (9 November 1898–25 August 1980). From 1925 to 1932 he was secretary of the Russian Student Christian Movement in exile. From 1933 to 1947 he was secretary of the Fellowship of St. Alban and St. Sergius (q.v.). From 1936 to 1939 he was a lecturer at the School of Slavonic Studies, London, and professor of Eastern Orthodox culture at Oxford University in 1947. He was the first to hold the Spaulding Lectureship for Eastern Orthodoxy at Oxford, to be succeeded in the post by (now) Bishop Kallistos Ware (q.v.). An ardent, if not always judicious, advocate of the ecumenical movement (q.v.) and an enthusiastic proponent of Orthodoxy (q.v.), his life even more than his writings left an indelible impression on the many who came to know him.

Zernov was one of the first of the Russian émigré theologians to publish widely in English. His publications include the still-valuable study, *The Russian Religious Renaissance,* with sketches of the remarkable stream of theologians and religious philosophers of the late 19th c. and early 20th c. (most of whom he had known), the first and only short history on the Russian Church in English, *The Russians and Their Church,* the first long study of the Orthodox Church in English by an Orthodox writer, and many articles, reviews, etc. His reminiscences, *Sunset Years,* were published posthumously (1983).

**ZIZIOULAS, JOHN,** Metropolitan of Pergamon, theologian (1936– ). For some time he was professor of systematic theology at the University of Glasgow, and more recently at Salonika and London universities. He has lectured at many institutions, including the Gregorian University, Rome, and King's College. He has been deeply involved in the ecumenical movement (q.v.) and was involved in the work of the World Council of Churches' Baptism, Eucharist and Ministry (BEM) steering group. In the late 1980s he was appointed cochairman of the commission to further Anglican-Orthodox dialogue and has also been a leader in the Orthodox-Roman Catholic dialogue. He is the author of *Being as Communion: Studies in Personhood and the*

*Church* (1985), which is particularly valuable for its keen analysis of ecclesiology (q.v.), and is soundly based on penetrating and original historical research. Zizioulas's doctoral dissertation, regrettably untranslated, dealt with difficulties in the eucharistic ecclesiology of the Russian liturgist, Nikolai Afanasiev (q.v.), in a particularly illuminating manner. He is currently a titular metropolitan of the Ecumenical Patriarchate (q.v.), divides his time teaching at both the universities of Glasgow and Thessalonica, and is one of the most distinguished contemporary Orthodox theologians.

**ZOE MOVEMENT.** Begun at the turn of the century, *Zoe* (Life) sought to reinvigorate the Church of Greece through an emphasis on Scripture (q.v.), particularly insisting on attention to the literal word of the sacred books and on the cultivation of personal morality. Its core was, and remains, a kind of quasi-monastic brotherhood, clergy and lay theologians pledged to a life of strict obedience to Christian norms and meeting annually for a period of some weeks. Its influence has been, on the whole, positive, although its puritanical emphases and unfortunate involvement with the military junta that ruled Greece from 1967 to 1974 appear to have compromised it in the eyes of most younger Greeks.

**ZONARAS, IONNAS,** commentator on Canon Law, theologian, historian (?-ca. 1159). While both a theologian and historian, Zonaras is best known for his commentaries on the Church's Canon Law (q.v.). After distinguished service in the imperial administration, he retired to a monastery and wrote an eighteen-volume universal history. He was one of a generation that produced the most influential canonists of the Byzantine era, including Theodore Balsamon (qq.v.). Unlike the latter, however, Zonaras favored the bureaucratic tradition of the Empire over the personal and seigneurial reign of the Comnene dynasty. He was, with Balsamon, a firm upholder of hierarchical authority within the Church. His commentaries on Canon Law are still consulted.

**ZOSIMA.** The name in its Greek form, Zosimos, belongs to several saints in the Orthodox calendar, in particular to the 5th–6th c. Zosimos of Palestine, monk of the community of St. Sabas and especially well known for his role in the story of Mary of Egypt (q.v.). Zosima is also the name given by Feodor Dostoevsky to the spiritual father (qq.v.) in the novel, *Brothers Karamazov,* one of the very few portraits of an idealized Orthodox monastic holy man in classical Russian literature, and practically the only one familiar to readers in Europe and America.

**ZYRYANS** *see* Komi.

# Appendix
# Orthodox Churches of the World (1996)

The Church of Constantinople
His All-Holiness Bartholomew I, Archbishop of Constantinople, New Rome and Ecumenical Patriarch

The Church of Alexandria
His Beatitude Parthenios, Pope and Patriarch of Alexandria and All Africa

The Church of Antioch
His Beatitude Ignatius IV, Patriarch of Antioch and All the East

The Church of Jerusalem
His Beatitude Diodoros, Patriarch of the Holy City of Jerusalem and All Palestine

The Church of Russia
His Holiness Aleksy II, Patriarch of Moscow and All Russia

The Church of Georgia
His Holiness Ilia, Catholicos-Patriarch of All Georgia, Archbishop of Mtshet and Tbilisi

The Church of Serbia
His Holiness Pavle, Archbishop of Pech, Metropolitan of Belgrade-Karlovci and Patriarch of Serbia

The Church of Romania
His Beatitude Teoctist, Patriarch of All Romania, Locum Tenens of Caesarea in Cappadocia, Metropolitan of Ungro-Vlachia, Archbishop of Bucharest

The Church of Bulgaria
His Holiness Maksim, Patriarch of Bulgaria

The Church of Cyprus
His Beatitude Chrysostomos, Archbishop of New Justiniana and All Cyprus

The Church of Greece
His Beatitude Seraphim, Archbishop of Athens and All Greece

The Church of Albania
His Beatitude Anastasios, Archbishop of Tirana and All Albania

The Church of Poland
His Beatitude Basil, Metropolitan of Warsaw and All Poland

The Church of Czech and Slovakia
His Beatitude Dorotheus, Archbishop of Prague, Metropolitan of the Czech and Slovak Republics

The Orthodox Church in America
His Beatitude Theodosius, Archbishop of Washington, Metropolitan of All America and Canada

**Autonomous Churches**

The Church of Sinai
His Beatitude Damian, Archbishop of Sinai and Raithu

The Church of Finland
His Eminence John, Archbishop of Karelia and All Finland

The Church of Japan
His Eminence Theodosius, Archbishop of Tokyo, Metropolitan of All Japan

# Bibliography Contents

I. General
    A. Bibliographies, Dictionaries, and Encyclopedias
    B. Survey Works
    C. Periodicals
    D. Yearbooks, Annuals, and Newspapers

II. Art, Architecture, and Music

III. Asceticism and Spirituality

IV. Canon Law

V. Church Fathers
    A. Primary Sources
    B. Secondary Sources

VI. Cultural Studies

VII. Ecumenism

VIII. Hagiography

IX. History
    A. Primary Sources
    B. Secondary Sources

X. Liturgy
    A. Liturgical Texts and Resources
    B. Secondary Studies

XI. Scripture

XII. Theology

## I. General

### A. Bibliographies, Dictionaries, and Encyclopedias

Andrews, Dean Timothy. *The Eastern Orthodox Church: A Bibliography.* 2d ed. Brookline, MA: Greek Archdiocese of North and South America, Holy Cross Orthodox Theological School, 1957. 79 p. (Publications of the Greek Archdiocese of North and South America. Books, 7.)

Baynes, Norman H. "The Byzantine Church: A Bibliographical Note on Recent Work." *The Journal of Ecclesiastical History*, v. 1, n. 1 (January–April 1950), p. 102–113.

Cavernos, Constantine. *Orthodox Christian Terminology*. Belmont, Massachusetts: Institute for Byzantine and Modern Greek Studies, 1994. 80 p.

Clugnet, Léon. *Dictionnaire grec-français des noms liturgiques en usage dans l'église grecque. Préface de J. Darrouzes*. London: Variorum Reprints, 1971. x, 186 p. Reprint of the Paris 1895 ed.

*Companion to the Greek Orthodox Church: Essays and References*. Fotios K. Litsas, ed. NY (8–10 E. 79th St., NY 10021): Department of Communications, Greek Orthodox Archdiocese of North and South America, 1984. x, 324 p.

*Coptic Encyclopedia*. Aziz S. Atiya, editor in chief. NY: Macmillan, 1991. 8 v. lxxiii, 2372, 371 p.

Day, Peter D. *The Liturgical Dictionary of Eastern Christianity*. Collegeville, MN: Liturgical Press, 1991. viii, 334 p.

Demetrakopoulos, George H. *Dictionary of Orthodox Theology: A Summary of the Beliefs, Practices and History of the Eastern Orthodox Church*. With an introduction by John E. Rexine. NY: Philosophical Library, 1964. xv, 187 p.

Dorosh, John Thomas, comp. "The Eastern Orthodox Church: A Bibliography of Publications Printed in the Roman Alphabet with Indication of Location." Washington, DC: s.n., 1946. xii, 216 leaves. Typescript.

*Eastern Christianity: A Bibliography Selected from the ATLA Religion Database*. Paul D. Petersen, ed.; Ruth F. Frazer, general editor. Rev. ed. Chicago: American Theological Library Association, 1984. 781 p. (ATLA religion index select bibliographies.)

*Encyclopedia of Early Christianity*. Everett Ferguson, [et al.], ed. NY: Garland, 1990. xx, 983 p. (Garland reference library of the humanities; v. 846.)

*Encyclopedia of the Early Church*. Angelo Di Berardino, ed.; translated from the Italian by Adrian Walford; with a foreword and bibliographic amendments by W.H.C. Frend. NY: Oxford University Press, 1992. 2 v. Translation of: *Dizionario patristico e di antichità cristiane*.

Fahey, Michael Andrew. "Current Theology: Orthodox Ecumenism and Theology: 1970–78." *Theological Studies*, v. 39, n. 3 (September 1978), p. 446–485.

Florovsky, Georges. "Religion: Christianity." In *Russia and the Soviet Union: A Bibliographic Guide to Western-Language Publications*. Paul L. Horecky, ed. Chicago: University of Chicago Press, 1965. p. 335–345.

Goa, David J. *Eastern Christian Ritual: A Bibliography of English Language Sources.* Goa and Anna F. Altmann. Edmonton: Provincial Museum of Alberta, 1988. vi, 121 p. (Occasional paper, Provincial Museum of Alberta, Human History; n. 5.)

*Handbuch der Ostkirchenkunde.* Herausgegeben von Wilhelm Nyssen, Hans-Joachim Schulz und Paul Wiertz; mit Beiträgen von Endre von Ivanka . . . [et al.]. Neu erarbeitete Ausg. des 1971 von Endre von Ivanka, Julius Tyciak und Paul Wiertz begründeten Handbuchs der Ostkirchenkunde. Dusseldorf: Patmos, 1984– . Bibliography: v. 1, p. xxix–xxxiv.

Harakas, Stanley Samuel. *The Orthodox Church: 455 Questions and Answers.* Topically indexed by Nikki Stournaras. Minneapolis: Light & Life, 1987. xiv, 354 p.

Kleinbauer, W. Eugene. *Early Christian and Byzantine Architecture: An Annotated Bibliography and Historiography.* Boston: G. K. Hall, 1992. cxxiii, 779 p. (a reference publication in art history.)

Langford-James, Richard Lloyd. *A Dictionary of the Eastern Orthodox Church.* With a preface by Joannes Gennadius. London: Faith Press, 1923. 144 p.

*List of Writings of the Professors of the Russian Orthodox Theological Institute in Paris, 1955–1965.* Paris: Russian Orthodox Theological Institute, [1965?]. 40 p. " . . . continues volume I of the List of writings (1925–1954)" p. [4]. L. Zander, ed.

*Modern Encyclopedia of Religions in Russia and the Soviet Union.* Paul D. Steeves, ed. Gulf Breeze: Academic International Press, 1988– .

Neuheuser, Hanns Peter. *Internationale Bibliographie "Liturgische Bücher": eine Auswahl kunsthistorischer und liturgiewissenschaftlicher Literatur zu liturgischen Handschriften und Drucken. International Bibliography on Liturgical Books: A Selection of Art-Historical and Liturgical Science Literature on Liturgical Manuscripts and Printed Books.* NY: K. G. Saur, 1991. xxii, 147 p.

Nicol, Donald MacGillivray. *A Biographical Dictionary of the Byzantine Empire.* London: Seaby, 1991. xxviii, 156 p. Bibliography: p. 149–156.

Ninet, Paula. *Vocabulaire théologique orthodoxe. Avec le concours d'André Lossky.* Paris: Cerf, 1985. 205 p. (Catechese orthodoxe.)

O'Carroll, Michael. *Corpus Christi: An Encyclopedia of the Eucharist.* Wilmington, DE: M. Glazier, 1988. x, 220 p.

———. *Theotokos—A Theological Encyclopedia of the Blessed Virgin Mary.* Rev. ed. with suppl. Wilmington, DE: M. Glazier, 1983. x, 390 p.

———. *Trinitas: A Theological Encyclopedia of the Holy Trinity.* Wilmington, DE: M. Glazier, 1987. ix, 220 p.

———. *Veni Creator Spiritus: A Theological Encyclopedia of the Holy Spirit.* Collegeville, MN: Liturgical Press, 1990. xii, 232 p.

———. *Verbum Caro: An Encyclopedia on Jesus, the Christ*. Collegeville, MN: Liturgical Press, 1992.
*Oxford Dictionary of Byzantium*. Alexander P. Kazhdan, editor in chief; Alice-Mary Talbot, executive editor; Anthony Cutler, editor for art history; Timothy E. Gregory, editor for archaeology and historical geography; Nancy P. Sevcenko, associate editor. NY: Oxford University Press, 1991. 3 v.
*Oxford Dictionary of the Christian Church*. F. L. Cross and E. A. Livingstone, eds. 2d ed., reprinted with corrections and some revisions, 1985 printing. NY: Oxford University Press, 1983. xxxi, 1520 p.
Patrinacos, Nicon D. *A Dictionary of Greek Orthodoxy. Lexikon Hellenikes Orthodoxias*. With a foreword by Archbishop Iakovos. 2d printing, 1987. Pleasantville, NY: Hellenic Heritage Publications, 1984. 391 p. Originally published: NY: Greek Orthodox Archdiocese of North and South America, Department of Education, 1984.
Schmemann, Alexander. *Russian Theology, 1920–1965: A Bibliographical Survey*. Richmond: Union Theological Seminary in Virginia, 1969. i, 35, 14 p. (Seventh Annual Bibliographical Lecture.)
Smith, Barbara Sweetland. *Russian Orthodoxy in Alaska: A History, Inventory, and Analysis of the Church Archives in Alaska with an Annotated Bibliography*. Anchorage: Published for the Alaska Historical Commission, 1980. x, 171 p. Previously published as *Preliminary survey of documents in the archives of the Orthodox Church in Alaska*. 1974. Bibliography: p. 135–161.
Stamoolis, James J. "A Selected Bibliography of Eastern Orthodox Mission Theology." *The Occasional Bulletin of Missionary Reseach*, v. 1, n. 3 (July 1977), p. 24–27.
Szoverffy, Joseph. *A Guide to Byzantine Hymn: A Classified Bibliography of Texts and Studies*. Brookline, MA: Classical Folia Editions; Leiden: E. J. Brill, 1978– . (Medieval classics, texts, and studies; 11.)
Thompson, Bard. *A Bibliography of Christian Worship*. Metuchen, NJ: The American Theological Library Association and Scarecrow Press, 1989. (ATLA Bibliography Series, n. 9.)
Tsirpanlis, Constantine N. "A Bibliography of Orthodox Theology (1970–1980)." *The Patristic and Byzantine Review*, v. 1 (1982), p. 63–69; 154–155; 235–238; v. 2 (1983), p. 87–95.

## B. Survey Works

Benz, Ernst. *The Eastern Orthodox Church, Its Thought and Life*. Translated from the German by Richard and Clara Winston. Garden City, NY: Anchor Books, 1963. 230 p.
Bratsiotes, Panagiotes I. *The Greek Orthodox Church*. Translated by Joseph Blenkinsopp. Notre Dame: University of Notre Dame Press, 1968. xi, 120 p. Translation of *Von der griechischen Orthodoxie*.

Bulgakov, Sergei Nikolaevich. *The Orthodox Church.* With a foreword by Thomas Hopko; translation revised by Lydia Kesich. Crestwood, NY: St. Vladimir's Seminary Press, 1988. xvi, 200 p. Translation of *Pravoslavie.*

Constantelos, Demetrios J. *Understanding the Greek Orthodox Church: Its Faith, History, and Practice.* Brookline, MA: Hellenic College Press, 1990. xiv, 220 p. Includes bibliographical references, p. 201–209, and indexes. Earlier eds.: NY: Seabury Press, 1982 (xiii, 178 p. Bibliography: p. 166–171). NY: Seabury Press, 1967 (127 p. Bibliography: p. 125–127).

Constantinides, Michael, Archbishop of North and South America, 1892–1958. *The Orthodox Church.* With an introduction by Joannes Gennadius. London: Williams & Norgate, Ltd., 1931. 168 p. "Books referred to in this volume": p. 165–166.

Evdokimov, Paul. *L'Orthodoxie.* Neuchâtel, Switzerland: Delachaux et Nièstle, 1959. 351 p. (Bibliothèque théologique.) Bibliography: p. [347]–348.

Fedotov, Georgii Petrovich. *The Collected Works of George P. Fedotov.* Editor, Richard Haugh; translated from Russian by Richard Haugh and Nickolas Lupinin. Vaduz, Liechtenstein: Büchervertriebsanstalt; Belmont, MA: Notable & Academic Books [distributor], 1988– . Vols. 1, 3–4 have imprint information from label on t.p. Originally published: Belmont, MA: Nordland. Contents: 1. St. Filipp, Metropolitan of Moscow. 2. A Treasury of Russian Spirituality. 3–4. The Russian Religious Mind. 5. Peter Abelard.

FitzGerald, Thomas E. *The Orthodox Church.* Westwood, CT: Greenwood Press, 1995.

Florovsky, Georges. *Collected Works of Georges Florovsky.* Belmont, MA: Nordland Publishing Co., 1972– . V. 4, 6–11, 13–14 published by Büchervertriebsanstalt, Vaduz. Contents: 1. Bible, Church, Tradition: An Eastern Orthodox View. 2. Christianity and Culture. 3. Creation and Redemption. 4. Aspects of Church History. 5–6. Ways of Russian Theology. 7. The Eastern Fathers of the Fourth Century. 8. The Byzantine Fathers of the Fifth Century. 9. The Byzantine Fathers of the Sixth to Eighth Century. 10. The Byzantine Ascetic and Spiritual Fathers. 11. Theology and Literature. 12. Philosophy: Philosophical Problems and Movements. 13–14. Ecumenism.

Hackel, Sergei. *The Orthodox Church.* London: Ward Lock Educational, 1971. 48 p. (Living religions series.) Bibliography: p. 45.

King, John Glen, 1732–1787. *The Rites and Ceremonies of the Greek Church, in Russia; Containing an Account of Its Doctrine, Worship, and Discipline.* London: Printed for W. Owen, 1772. Reprinted: NY: AMS Press, 1970. xix, 477 p.

Lossky, Vladimir. *Orthodox Theology: An Introduction.* Translated by Ian and Ihita Kesarcodi-Watson. Crestwood, NY: St. Vladimir's Seminary Press, 1978. 137 p. Chapters 1–4 were originally published in *Messager de l'Exarchat du patriarche russe en Europe occidentale,* 1964–1965, as a series of related pieces under title: *Théologie dogmatique.*

Meyendorff, John. *The Orthodox.* NY: Paulist Press, 1966. 24 p.

———. *The Orthodox Church: Its Past and Its Role in the World Today.* Translated from the French by John Chapin. 3d rev. ed. Crestwood, NY: St. Vladimir's Seminary Press, 1981. xii, 258 p. Revised translation of *L'Eglise orthodoxe: hier et aujourd'hui.* Bibliography: p. 245–248.

Neale, John Mason. *The Holy Eastern Church: A Popular Outline of Its History, Doctrines, Liturgies, and Vestments.* By a priest of the English church [attributed to John Mason Neale]; the preface by the Rev. Dr. Littledale. 2d ed. London: J. T. Hayes, 1873. xi, 102 p., 4 leaves of plates.

Nissiotis, Nikos A. *An Introduction to the Ethos and Liturgy of the Eastern Orthodox Church.* Led by Nikos Nissiotis. Isafia: United Christian Council in Israel, 1968. [6], 50 p. Full report of the conference held under the auspices of the United Christian Council in Israel, at Stella Carmel, Isafia, Israel . . . 27–28th Feb., 1968.

Roberson, Ronald G. *The Eastern Christian Churches: A Brief Survey.* Revised 3d ed. Rome: Pontificium institutum studiorum orientalium, 1990. xi, 129 p.

Schmemann, Alexander. *Historical Road of Eastern Orthodoxy.* Translated by Lydia W. Kesich. Crestwood, NY: St. Vladimir's Seminary Press, 1977. viii, 343 p. Translation of *Istoricheskii put pravoslaviia.* Reprint of the 1963 ed. published by Holt, Rinehart and Winston, NY. Bibliography: p. 342–343.

Vaporis, N. M., ed. *Rightly Teaching the Word of Your Truth.* Brookline, MA: Holy Cross Orthodox Press, 1995.

Ware, Kallistos. *The Orthodox Church.* Baltimore: Penguin Books, 1964. 352 p. (A Pelican original, A592.) First published 1963. Reprinted with revisions, 1964.

———. *The Orthodox Way.* Crestwood, NY: St. Vladimir's Seminary Press, 1980. 204 p. Bibliography: p. [186]–195.

Yannaras, Christos. *Elements of Faith: An Introduction to Orthodox Theology.* Keith Schram, trans. Edinburgh: T. & T. Clark, 1991. xiv, 167 p. Translation of *Alphavetari tes pistes.*

Zernov, Nicolas. *The Russians and Their Church.* 3d ed. Crestwood, NY: St. Vladimir's Seminary Press, 1978. v, 192 p. Bibliography: p. 185–187.

## C. Periodicals

*Abba Salama.* v. 1–10 (1970–79). Addis Ababa. 10 v. Annual. In English, with some text in Amharic or Greek. A review of the Association of Ethio-Hellenic Studies.

*Biserica Ortodoxa Romana* (Bucharest: Tipografia Institutului Biblic si de Misiune Ortodoxa).

*Bogoslovskie trudy* (Moscow: Izd. Moskovskaia patriarkhiia). Sbornik 1 (1960)– .

*Canadian Orthodox Messenger* (Ottawa: Archdiocese of Canada of the Orthodox Church in America). New ser. v. 1, n. 1 (Mar. 1989)– . Quarterly.

*Christian East* (Westminster: Faith Press). V. 1, n. 1 (March 1920)-v. 18, n. 1 & 2 (Jan.–June 1938); New ser., v. 1, n. 1 (March 1950)-v. 2, n. 7 & 8 (winter 1953–4). 20 v. Quarterly (irregular) "A quarterly review devoted to the study of the eastern churches." None published July 1938–Feb. 1950. Vols. for Mar. 1920–July 1922 published for the Anglican and Eastern Churches Association by the Society for the Promotion of Christian Knowledge; Oct.–Dec. 1922 by the Association; Mar. 1923–winter 1953/54 for the Association by Faith Press.

*Christian Orient* (Kottayam, Kerala, S. India: St. Thomas Apostle Seminary). V. 1, n. 1 (Mar. 1980)– . Quarterly. "An Indian journal of Eastern churches for creative theological thinking." Issued by Oriental Study Forum, Mar. 1985– .

*Concern* (Nyack, NY: Orthodox Christian Education Commission: Orthodox Campus Commission). V. 1, n. 1 (winter 1966)-v. 12, n. 3 (spring 1976). 12 v. Quarterly. Other title: *Orthodox concern for the life of the world*. Vols. have subtitle: Orthodox concern for the life of the world. The two Commissions serve as "working committees of the Standing Conference of Canonical Orthodox Bishops in the Americas." Continues *Bulletin of Orthodox Christian Education*.

*Contacts: Revue française de l'orthodoxie* (Paris). V. 1 (1949)– . Quarterly.

*Current Developments in the Eastern European Churches* (Geneva: World Council of Churches). N. 1 (Jan. 1959)-N. 39/40 (Nov./Dec. 1967). 40 nos. Irregular. "From the Desk for Documentation concerning Eastern European Churches."

*Diakonia: Devoted to Promoting a Knowledge and Understanding of Eastern Christianity* (Bronx, NY: John XXIII Center; Scranton, PA: University of Scranton). V. 1 (1966)– .

*Eastern Churches Review* (Oxford: Holywell Press). V. 1, n. 1 (spring 1966)-v. 10, n. 1–2. [1966]–1978. 10 v. Semiannual Publisher varies: Oxford University Press, autumn 1974; Clarendon Press, –1978. V. 9, n. 1 and 2 (1977), and v. 10, n. 1 and 2 (1978), each issued combined. Absorbed by: Sobornost. Also: Clarke, Boden. Eastern Churches Review: An Index to Volumes I–X, 1966–1978. San Bernardino, CA: Borgo Press, 1989. (Borgo reference library; v. 6.)

*Echos d'Orient* (Bucharest; Saint-Cloud: Europériodiques, S.A.). t. 1 (oct. 1897)–39 (n. 1–199/200) (juil. 1940/dec. 1942). Bimonthly, quarterly, and irregular. 39 v. Reprint of a serial issued 1897–1942 in Paris. "Réimprimé avec l'autorisation de l'Institut français d'études byzantines." Suspended Sept. 1914–May 1915; July 1940–Dec. 1942. Indexes: Vols. 1–14, 1897–1911. 1 v. Supersedes *Etudes byzantines*.

*Episkepsis*. (Chambesy-Geneva: Orthodoxon Kentron tou Oikumenikou Patriarcheiou). Semimonthly (irregular) Began with 16 Febr. 1970. Issued also in a French language ed. with the same title.

*Epistemonike epeteris* (Thessalonica: The School) T. 1 (1953)– . Annual. Includes some special nos. in addition to regular numbering. Chiefly Greek; some articles in French, German, and English; many articles have summaries in English, French, or German. Vols. for 1957– issued by Aristoteleion Panepistemion Thessalonikes.

*Greek Orthodox Theological Review* (Brookline, MA: Holy Cross School of Theology, Hellenic College). V. 1 (Aug. 1954)– . Quarterly. "Official publication of the Holy Cross Greek Orthodox Theological School". Vols. for 1951–winter 1966/67 issued by the Greek Archdiocese Holy Cross Orthodox Theological School (called winter 1960/61–summer 1964 Holy Cross Theological School); spring 1968- , spring/fall 1975 by the Holy Cross School of Theology, Hellenic College. Indexes: Vols. 6–10, 1960–winter 1964/65, in v. 10, n. 2.

*Irenikon: Revue des Moines de Chevetogne* (Belgium: Monastère de Chevetogne). T. 1 (1926)– . Quarterly.

*Journal of Early Christian Studies: Journal of the North American Patristics Society* (Baltimore: Johns Hopkins U. Pr.) V. 1 (1993)– . Continues *The Second Century*.

*Journal of the Moscow Patriarchate* (Moscow: Moscow Patriarchate). 1971– . Monthly. "The editors of the 'Journal of the Moscow Patriarchate' are embarking upon an English edition of the official periodical of the Russian Orthodox Church."—p. [1] of issue 1 for 1971, dated Oct. 1971. Numbering begins each year with 1. Two issues only for 1971.

*Kyrios: Vierteljahresschrift für Kirchen- und Geistesgeschichte Osteuropas* (Berlin: Lutherisches Verlagshaus H. Renner; Graz, Austria: Akademische Druck- u. Verlagsanstalt). 1. Bd. (1936)–6. Bd., Heft 1/2; (1942/43); n. F., Bd. 1 (1960/61)– . Reprint. Konigsberg, Prussia: Ost-Europa Verlag. Founded by H. Koch.

*Messager orthodoxe*. n. 5 (1959)- Quarterly. "Périodique de l'Action chrétienne des étudiants russes." "Revue de pensée et d'action orthodoxes." Continues *Messager*.

*Observateur orthodoxe* (Montreal: Eglise orthodoxe russe à l'étranger, Archidiocèse de Montreal et du Canada). No 1 (juin 1983)– . Trimestriel (irregulier).

*One Church: Bi-Monthly Journal of the Patriarchal Parishes in the U.S., Moscow Patriarchate* (NY). V. 1 (Sept. 1947)– . Bimonthly. Other title: *Edinaia tserkov*. Organ of the Patriarchal Exarchate in America. Monthly 1948–53 Irregular 1947, 1954– . Published also in a Russian-language ed.

*Orientalia christiana periodica* (Rome: Pontificium institutum orientalium studiorum). v. 1 (1935)– . Two nos. a year "Commentarii de re orientali aetatis christianae sacra et profana." Summary: Includes section "Recensiones". In Latin, English, French, German, Italian, and Spanish. Indexes: Vols. 1–25, 1939–59, in v. 25.

*Orthodox Monitor* (Washington, DC: The Committee for the Defense of Persecuted Orthodox Christians, Washington Chapter). N. 1 (Nov.–Dec. 1978)– . Bimonthly, 1978–79. Quarterly, 1980–Jan./June 1981. Issued: 1978–Sept./Dec. 1979 by the Committee for the Defense of Persecuted Orthodox Christians, Washington Chapter; 1980– by the Committee for the Defense of Persecuted Orthodox Christians, Inc.

*Orthodox News* (London: Saint George Orthodox Information Service). V. 2, n. 1 (Aug./Sept. 1984)– . Issued with the blessing of Bishop Kallistos of Diokleia. Subtitle varies: "published free of editorial control," Feb. 1985– . Continues *News* (Saint George Orthodox Information Service).

*Orthodox Observer. Ho Orthodoxos parateretes* (NY: Greek Archdiocese of North and South America). V. 1, n. 1 (Nov. 25, 1934)–37, n. 618 (Sept. 1971). Frequency varies. Continued by: Orthodox Observer. Orthodoxos parateretes (NY: Greek Orthodox Archdiocese Press Monthly). V. 37, n. 619 (20 Oct. 1971)– . Biweekly, Oct. 20, 1971– . In English and Greek. Vols. for Sept. 1955–Mar. 1958 "published under the auspices of the Greek Archdiocese"; Apr. 1958–Sept. 1971 official publication of, and published by, the Greek Archdiocese of North and South America. Has supplement: Orthodox observer quarterly Mar. 1972– .

*Orthodox Thought and Life* (Kingston, NY: Hellenism in America, Inc.). V. 1, n. 1 (1984)– . Quarterly. Other title: *A Journal devoted to popular Orthodox enlightenment and Eastern Christian spirituality*. Editor: Constantine Tsirpanlis.

*Orthodoxe parousia* (Limassol, Cyprus: Ekd. Orthodoxou Pneumatikou Kentrou).

*Orthodoxe parousia: trimeniaio periodiko tes Hieras Metropoleos Germanias kai Exarchias Kentroas Europes. Orthodoxe Gegenwart: vierteljahres Schrift der Griechisch-Orthodoxen Metropolie von Deutschland und Exarchats von Zentral Europa*. Ar. (Bonn: Exarchias). teuch. 1–2 (Ian.–Ioun. 1981)– . Quarterly.

*Orthodoxes Forum: Zeitschrift des Instituts für Orthodoxe Theologie der Universität München* (St. Ottilien: EOS Verlag). 1. Jahrg., Heft 1 (1987)– . Semiannual.

*Orthodoxia* (Constantinople: Typois <Phazilet> Tassau Bakalopoulou). Etos 1, teuchos 1– (30 Apr. 1926)– . Other title: Oct. 1928– , Ortodoksia. "Periodikon ethikothreskeutikon". Issues for Apr. 1926– Sept. 1928 also have titles in Arabic. Vols. for 1926–1934 consecutively numbered teuchos 1–108.

*Ortodoxia* (Bucharest: Institutul Biblic si de Misiune Ortodoxa). 1949?– . Four nos. a year. "Revista Patriarhiei Romine."

*Ostkirchliche Studien* (Wurzburg, Augustinus-Verlag). 1. Bd. (Jan. 1952)– . Quarterly. Reprint: 1.–9. Band (1952–1960). Amsterdam: Adolf M. Hakkert, 1967–1978. 9 v. Annual.

*Ostliche Christentum* (Wurzburg). Hft. 1–11 (1936–1940); Neue Folge. Hft. 1 (1947)– . "Abhandlugen, im Auftrag der Arbeitsgemeinschaft der deutschen Augustinerodensprovinz zum Studium der Ostkirche."

*Patristic and Byzantine Review* (Kingston, NY: American Institute for Patristic and Byzantine Studies). V. 1, n. 1 (1982)– . Three nos. a year. Greek title: *Paterike-Byzantine epitheoresis*.

*Pensée Orthodoxe* (Paris: YMCA-Press). 1966– . Issued by Institut de Théologie Orthodoxe Saint-Serge. "Travaux de l'Institut de Théologie Orthodoxe Saint-Serge."

*Perspective orthodoxe* (Geneva: Labor et Fides). No 1 (1980)– .

*Pravoslavnoe chtenie: izdanie moskovskoi Patriiarkhii. Russian Orthodox Readings* (Moscow: Moskovskaia Patriiarkhiia). 1 (1990)– . Monthly. Other title: *Lecture Orthodoxe*. Other title: *Orthodoxes Leseheft*. Other title: *Lecturas de la Ortodoxia Rusa*. Title also in French: *Lecture Orthodoxe;* German: *Orthodoxes Leseheft;* and Spanish: *Lecturas de la Ortodoxia Rusa*. Text in English. Continues *Moscow church herald*.

*Présence orthodoxe* (Paris). 1967– . Quarterly. Began with n. 1 in 1967. "Revue de l'orthodoxie occidentale." Organ of the Eglise catholique orthodoxe de France, 1969–1971. Indexes: Nos. 1 (1967)–31 (1975) in 1 separate vol. nos. 1 (1967)–74 (1987) in no 75 (1987). Continues *Portique Saint-Denis*.

*Proche-Orient chrétien* (Jerusalem: Séminaire Sainte-Anne). t. 1 (1951)– . Quarterly. "Revue d'études et d'informations."

*Revue des églises d'Orient* (Bar-le-Duc: Schorderet). 1890– . Monthly continues *Revue de l'Eglise grecque-unie*.

*Romanian Orthodox Church News Quarterly Bulletin* (Bucharest, Romania: The Department). Year 1, n. 1 (1971)– . Edited by the Department of Foreign Relations of the Romanian Patriarchate. Quarterly. Issued also in Romanian and French.

*St. Vladimir's Theological Quarterly* (New York). v. 1–4, n. 3/4, (fall 1952–summer 1956); n.s. v.1 – (Jan. 1957)– . Title varies: 1952–? *St. Vladimir's Seminary Quarterly*. Published by the faculty of St. Vladimir's Orthodox Theological Seminary.

*Sobornost, Incorporating Eastern Churches Review* (London: Fellowship of St. Alban and St. Sergius). V. 1 (1979)– . Semiannual. Formed by the union of *Sobornost* and *Eastern Churches Review*.

*SOP: service orthodoxe de presse et d'information* (Paris: Comité Interepiscopal orthodoxe en France). N. 1 (Oct. 1975)– . Monthly. Other title: *Service orthodoxe de presse et d'information*.

*Sourozh: A Journal of Orthodox Life and Thought* (Oxford, England: Russian Patriarchal Diocese of Sourozh). N. 1 (Aug. 1980)– . Quarterly. Founder and editor-in-chief: 1980– , Metropolitan Anthony of Sourozh.

*Star of the East: An Ecumenical Journal Dealing Specially with the Oriental and Eastern Orthodox Churches* (Kottayam, India: K. M. George). V. 1, n. 1 (Jan. 1979)– . Quarterly continues *Star of the east* (Sasthamkotta, India).

*Studi e ricerche sull'Oriente cristiano* (Rome). anno 1 (genn./apr. 1978)– . Three nos. a year.

*Studia patristica et liturgica* (Regensburg: Kommissionsverlag Friedrich Pustet). Fasc. 1 (1967)– . "Quae edidit Institutum Liturgicum Ratisbonense."

*Texts and Studies* (London: Thyateira House, Foundation for Hellenism in Great Britain). 1982–1988. 7 v. English or Greek.

*Theologia* (Athens, Greece). Tomos 1 (1923)– . Quarterly. Suspended 1941–47 (tomos 19 covers 1941–48). Beginning with v. 4, some issues have whole numbering: teuchos 13– . V. 18 called also periodos B [2d ser.], tomos 1. Has supplement: *Hellenike theologike vivliographia*.

*West-Östlicher Weg* (Kattern bei Breslau). Jahrg. 1 (1928)– .

### D. Yearbooks, Annuals, and Newspapers

*Calendarul credinta.* (Detroit: Romanian Orthodox Missionary Archdiocese in America and Canada). 1976– . Faith almanac. Spine title: Credinta "The Faith" Calendar. Issues for 1978– have English title: *Faith almanac*. In Romanian and English. Vol. for 1976 issued by Romanian Orthodox Missionary Archdiocese in America and Canada. Continues *Calendarul ortodox credinta*.

*Church and Theology* (London: Thyateira House). V. 1 (1980)– . Annual. Greek title: *Ekklesia kai theologia* [ekklesiastike kai theologike epeteris tes Hieras Archiepiskopes Thyateiron kai Megales Vretannias], 1981– . Text in English, French, and Greek.

*Eastern Orthodox World Directory* (Boston: Branden Press). 1968– . J. Kuzmission, ed.

Greek Orthodox Archdiocese of North and South America. *Yearbook* (NY: The Archdiocese) 1967– . Annual. English or Greek.

*Jahrbuch der Orthodoxie. Yearbook of the Orthodox Church. Annuaire de l'Eglise orthodoxe* (Munich: Athos-Verlag). 1976/77– . Editor:

1976/77– Alex Proc. Imprint varies: 1978– . Verlag A. Proc. To be published every year alternately in different languages: *Jahrbuch der Orthodoxie, Yearbook of the Orthodox Church, Annuaire de l'Eglise orthodoxe*. English translation, 1978– , by Nigel Kinsella.

*Oriens Christianus* (Wiesbaden: O. Harrassowitz). 1901–30. Annual. 1931– Bd. [1]–65 also called Jahrg. 1–8, 1901–08; 2. serie 1–14, 1911–25; 3. serie 1–14, 1927–39; 4. serie 1–<29> 1953-<1981> "Hefte für die Kunde des christlichen Orients." Vols. 1–8 have added t.p. in Italian. Im Aufträge der Gorres-Gesellschaft.

*Orthodox Church*. (Syosset, NY: Metropolitan Council of the Orthodox Church in America). Ten nos. a year, Jan. 1966–Dec. 1977. Monthly, Jan. 1978–Dec. 1978. Vols. for Jan. 1966–Mar. 1970 published by the Metropolitan Council of the Russian Orthodox Greek Catholic Church of America; Apr. 1970–Dec. 1978 by the Orthodox Church in America; Apr.–Oct. 1970 and Mar. 1971–Dec. 1978 by its Metropolitan Council; Nov. 1970–Feb. 1971 by its Executive Council; Apr.–Oct. 1970 under the variant name of The Church: Authocephalous Orthodox Church in America.

*Orthodox Church in America. Yearbook & Church Directory* (Syosset, NY: The Church). 1977– . Annual. Continues *Yearbook and church directory of the Orthodox Church in America*. 22d ed. (1971)– . In turn, continues *Russian Orthodox Greek Catholic Church of America Yearbook and church directory*. Russian title: *Ezhegodnik* Pravo*slavnoi tserkvi v Amerike*, kn. 1. (1975)– .

*Revue des études byzantines* (Paris: Institut français d'études byzantines). t. 1 (1943)– . Annual. Title varies: *Etudes byzantines,* 1943–1945. French (chiefly), English, German, and Greek. Indexes: Index t. 1 (1943)– 40 (1982) at end of t. 41. Vols. for 1946–48 issued by the Institut in Bucharest. Supersedes *Echos d'Orient*.

*Russian Orthodox Greek Catholic Church of America. Year Book and Church Directory of the Russian Orthodox Greek Catholic Church of America* (Metropolia) (New York). 1st–21st ed. (1950–70). Annual. Vols. for 1950–59 issued by the church under a variant form of name: *Russian Orthodox Greek Catholic Church of North America*. Vols. for 1950–62 published by the Publishing Committee of its Metropolitan Council. Continued by *Yearbook and church directory of the Orthodox Church in America*.

*Studia Patristica: Papers Presented to the . . . International Conference on Patristic Studies Held at . . .* (Berlin: Akademie-Verlag) V. 1 (1957)– . (Texte und Untersuchungen zur Geschichte der altchristlichen Literatur; 63–64, 78–81, 92–94, 107–108, 115–117, 128) Quadrennial. Vols. 1–<18> are papers presented at the 2nd–9th International Conference on Patristic Studies. English, French, German, Italian, Russian, or Spanish. Indexes: Author index: v. 1–14, in v. 14. Beginning with the 7th

Conference, selected papers also published in the series: Nag Hammadi studies. V. 17 published in 3 parts. V. 17 pt. 1–3 has only Studia Patristica in the title page. V. 17 published by Pergamon Press, Oxford and New York, 1982. Main series: Texte und Untersuchungen zur Geschichte der altchristlichen Literatur.

*Word* (Brooklyn: Antiochian Orthodox Christian Archdiocese of New York and All North America). V. 1 (1957)– . Monthly except July and Aug. Founded in Arabic as Al Kalimat, Jan. 1905. Founded in English as *The Word*, Jan. 1957. Official publication of the Antiochian Orthodox Christian Archdiocese of New York and all North America.

## II. Art, Architecture, and Music

*1000 Jahre russische Kunst: zur Erinnerung an die Taufe der Rus im Jahr 988: Schleswig-Holsteinisches Landesmuseum, Schloss Gottorf, Schleswig, 14.8.–23.10.1988: Hessisches Landesmuseum, Museum Wiesbaden, 21.11.1988– 29.1.1989.* Die deutsche Ausgabe des Katalogs wurde von Eckhard Weiher, Felix Keller und Gabriele Wolf-Keller übersetzt und bearbeitet, von Heinz Spielmann und Jan Drees redigiert. Schleswig: Schleswig-Holsteinisches Landesmuseum; Wiesbaden: Hessisches Landesmuseum, Museum Wiesbaden, 1988. 453 p. Title on added t.p. in Russian: *1000-letie russkoi khudozhestvennoi kultury.*

Ainalov, Dimitrii Vlasyevich. *The Hellenistic Origins of Byzantine Art.* Translated from the Russian by Elizabeth Sobolevitch and Serge Sobolevitch; edited by Cyril Mango. New Brunswick, NJ: Rutgers University Press, 1961. xv, 322 p. 128 illus. (Rutgers Byzantine series) "Published for the first and only time, in 1900–1901 in the 'Bulletin of the Imperial Russian archaeological society'." Bibliographical references included in "Notes," p. 282–308.

Brill, Nicholas P. *History of Russian Church Music, 988–1917.* 2d ed. Bloomington, IL: Brill, 1982. vi, 209 p. Bibliography: p. 207–209.

Brumfield, William Craft. *Christianity and the Arts in Russia.* Brumfield and Milos M. Velimirovic. Cambridge: University Press, 1992. 351 p.

———. *A History of Russian Architecture.* Text and photographs by William Craft Brumfield. NY: Cambridge University Press, 1993. 644 p.

Bychkov, Victor V. *The Aesthetic Face of Being: Art in the Theology of Pavel Florensky.* Translated from the Russian by Richard Prevear and Larissa Volokhonsky. Preface by Robert Slesinski. Crestwood, NY: SVS Press, 1993. 101 p.

Cavernos, Constantine. *Byzantine Churches of Thessaloniki.* Belmont, Massachusetts: Institute for Byzantine and Modern Greek Studies, 1995. 88 p.

Chatzidakis, Manolis. *The Great Meteoron: History and Art.* Athens: Interamerican, 1990. 222 p.

———. *Icons of Patmos: Questions of Byzantine and Post-Byzantine Painting.* Thetis Xanthaki, trans. Athens: National Bank of Greece, 1985. 205 p., [8], 207 p. of plates. Rev. translation of *Eikones tes Patmou.* Bibliography: p. 13–16.

Chatzidakis, Nano. *Icons of the Cretan School (15th–16th Century): Exhibition Catalogue.* Athens: Benakai Museum, 1983. 104 p. Bibliography: p. 99–104.

*Christianity and the Arts in Russia.* William C. Brumfield, Milos M. Velimirovich. NY: Cambridge University Press, 1991. xv, 95 p. Essays presented at a symposium, held in May 1988 at the Library of Congress.

Chrysaphes, Manuel, fl. 1440–1463. *The Treatise of Manuel Chrysaphes, the Lampadarios: On the Theory of the Art of Chanting and On Certain Erroneous Views That Some Hold About It.* Text, translation, and commentary by Dimitri E. Conomos. Vienna: Verlag der Österreichischen Akademie der Wissenschaften, 1985. 119 p. (Monumenta musicae Byzantinae. Corpus scriptorum de re musica; v. 2.) Original: Mount Athos: Iviron Monastery 1120, July 1458. English and Greek. Greek title: *Peri ton entheoroumenon te psaltike techne kai on phronousi kakos tines peri auton.*

Conomos, Dimitri E. *Byzantine Hymnography and Byzantine Chant.* Brookline, MA: Hellenic College Press, 1984. ix, 50 p. (The Nicholas E. Kulukundis lectures in Hellenism.)

———. *Byzantine Trisagia and Cheroubika of the Fourteenth and Fifteenth Centuries: A Study of Late Byzantine Liturgical Chant.* Thessalonica: Patriarchal Institute for Patristic Studies, 1974. 381 p. A revision of the author's thesis, University of Oxford. Bibliography: p. 369–378.

———. *The Late Byzantine and Slavonic Communion Cycle: Liturgy and Music.* Washington, DC: Dumbarton Oaks Research Library and Collection, 1985. xiv, 207 p. (Dumbarton Oaks studies; 21.) Bibliography: p. [197]– 203.

Coomler, David. *The Icon Handbook.* Springfield, Ill.: Templegate Publications, 1995. 319 p.

Dionysios, of Fourna, ca. 1670–ca. 1745. *The 'Painter's Manual' of Dionysius of Fourna: An English translation [from the Greek] with commentary of cod. gr. 708 in the Saltykov-Shchedrin State Public Library, Leningrad.* Paul Hetherington, ed. London (78 Redesdale Gardens, Isleworth, MTW7 5JD): Sagittarius Press, 1974. 9, 128 p. Translation of *Hermeneia tes zographikes.* Bibliography: p. 116–117.

*Divine Liturgy.* David Drillock, Helen Erickson, and John Erickson, ed. Crestwood, NY: SVS Press, 1980.

Dumbarton Oaks. *Handbook of the Byzantine Collection.* New edition of 1955 handbook. Washington, 1967. xv, 125, [95] p. Introduction by Ernst Kitzinger.

Evdokimov, Paul. *Art of the Icon: A Theology of Beauty*. Translated by Fr. Steven Bigham. Redondo Beach, CA: Oakwood Publications, 1990. vi, 353 p., 11. "Originally published in French under the title *L'Art de L'Icone: Théologie de la Beauté*.

*Four Icons in the Menil Collection*. Edited by Bertrand Davezac. Houston: The Collection, 1992. 135 p. (The Menil Collection monographs; v. 1.)

Giakalis, Ambrosios. *Images of the Divine: the Theology of Icons at the Seventh Ecumenical Council*. Foreword by Henry Chadick. Leiden: E. J. Brill, 1994. xv, 151 p.

*Golden Light: Masterpieces of the Art of the Icon*. Ministerie van de Vlaamse Gemeenschap, Koninklijk Museum voor Schone Kunsten, Antwerpen; N. Chatzidakis... et al. Ghent: Snopeck-Ducaju & Zoon, 1988. 210 p. "Translation: L. A. Blacksberg (Dutch-English)" —T.p. verso. Includes bibliographical references, p. 201–205. Catalog of an exhibition held in 1988.

Grabar, Andre. *Beginnings of Christian Art, 200–395*. Translated from the French by Stuart Gilbert and James Emmons. London: Thames & Hudson, 1967. 7, 325 p. 313 illus. (The Arts of mankind; v. 9.) Originally published as *Le Premier art chrétien* (200–395). Paris: Gallimard, 1966. Bibliography: p. 307–313.

———. *Byzantine Painting: Historical and Critical Study*. Translated by Stuart Gilbert. Geneva: Skira, 1953. 200 p. (The Great centuries of painting.) Bibliography: p. 194.

———. *Byzantium: Byzantine Art in the Middle Ages*. Translated from the German by Betty Forster. London: Methuen, 1966. 216 p. 62 plates (Art of the world; a series of regional histories of the visual arts.) Bibliography: p. 209–210.

———. *Byzantium: From the Death of Theodosius to the Rise of Islam*. Translated from the French by Stuart Gilbert and James Emmons. London: Thames & Hudson, 1966. 9, 416 p. 475 illus. (The Arts of mankind.) Bibliography: p. 383–[392]. Translation of *L'âge d'or de Justinien*.

———. *Christian Iconography: A Study of Its Origins: the A. W. Mellon Lectures in the Fine Arts, 1961, the National Gallery of Art, Washington, DC*. Translated from the French by Terry Grabar. London: Routledge & Kegan Paul, 1969. ii–l, 175 p. 202 plates, 346 illus. (The A. W. Mellon lectures in the fine arts, 1961.) Bibliography: p. 149–158.

———. *Early Christian Art: From the Rise of Christianity to the Death of Theodosius*. Translated by Stuart Gilbert and James Emmons. NY: Odyssey Press, 1968. 325 p. (The Arts of mankind, v. 9.) Translation of *Le Premier art chrétien* (200–395) Bibliography: p. 307–313.

———. *Early Medieval Painting From the Fourth to the Eleventh Century*. Mosaics and Mural Painting, A. Grabar; Book illumination, Carl

Nordenfalk. Translated by Stuart Gilbert. NY: Skira, 1957. 241 p. (The Great centuries of painting.). Bibliography: p. 223–225.

———. *Golden Age of Justinian, From the Death of Theodosius to the Rise of Islam.* Translated by Stuart Gilbert and James Emmons. New York, Odyssey Press, 1967. 408 p. 392 illus. (The Arts of mankind.) Translation of *L'âge d'or de Justinien.* Bibliography: p. [381]–[392].

———. *Romanesque Painting From the Eleventh to the Thirteenth Century.* Mural Painting, A. Grabar; Book Illumination, Carl Nordenfalk. Translated by Stuart Gilbert. NY: Skira 1958. 229 p. (The Great centuries of painting.) Translation of *De la fin de l'époque romaine au onzième siècle.* Bibliography: p. 211–214.

*Icons: Windows on Eternity: Theology and Spirituality in Colour.* Gennadios Limouris, comp. Geneva: WCC Publications, 1990. x, 228 p., [16] p. of plates (Faith and Order paper; 147.) Bibliography: p. 217–224.

James, Liz. *Light and Colour in Byzantine Art.* New York: Clarendon Press, 1995.

Kalokyres, Konstantinos D. *The Byzantine Wall Paintings of Crete.* Photographs by Farrell Grehan; translation by Leonidas Contos and Constantine Kazanis. New York: Red Dust, 1973. 184 p. Translation of the author's Greek original, published in 1957. Bibliography: p. 182.

———. *The Essence of Orthodox Iconography.* English translation by Peter Chamberas. Brookline, MA: Holy Cross Orthodox Press, 1985. 107 p., 19 p. of plates. Translation of *He ousia tes Orthodoxou eikonographias.*

Kartsonis, Anna D. *Anastasis: The Making of an Image.* Princeton, NJ: Princeton University Press, 1986. xviii, 263 p., 68 p. of plates. Bibliography: p. [237]–255.

Kitzinger, Ernst. *Art of Byzantium and the Medieval West: Selected Studies.* Edited by W. Eugene Kleinbauer. Bloomington: Indiana University Press, 1976. xvii, 419 p.

———. *Byzantine Art in the Making: Main Lines of Stylistic Development in Mediterranean Art, 3rd–7th Century.* Cambridge, MA: Harvard University Press, 1977. xii, 175 p.

———. *Byzantine Art in the Period Between Justinian and Iconoclasm.* [s. l.: s. n.], 1958? 50 p., [26] leaves of plates. Based on a lecture delivered at a symposium entitled "Byzantium in the seventh century" held at Dumbarton Oaks in May 1957.

———. "Byzantine Contribution to Western Art of the Twelfth and Thirteenth Centuries: Report on the Dumbarton Oaks Symposium of 1965." *Dumbarton Oaks Papers* (Washington), n. 20 (1966), p. 265–266.

———. "Byzantine Contribution to Western Art of the Twelfth and Thirteenth Centuries. Substance of the Conclusions presented at the final session of a symposium on The Byzantine contribution to western art of the twelfth and thirteenth centuries, held at Dumbarton Oaks in May 1965." *Dumbarton Oaks Papers* (Washington), n. 20 (1966), p. [25]–47.

———. "Byzantium in the Seventh Century. Report on a Dumbarton Oaks symposium." *Dumbarton Oaks Papers* (Washington, DC), n. 13 (1959), p. [271]–273. Reprinted by Johnson Reprint Corp., 1967.

———. "Christian Imagery: Growth and Impact." In: *Age of Spirituality: A Symposium*. NY: Metropolitan Museum of Art; Princeton, NJ: Princeton University Press, 1980. p. 141–163.

———. "Cult of Images in the Age Before Iconoclasm." *Dumbarton Oaks Papers* (Cambridge, MA), n. 8 (1954), p. [83]–150. Reprinted by Johnson Reprint Corp., 1967.

———. "Horse and Lion tapestry at Dumbarton Oaks: A Study in Coptic and Assanian Textile Design." *Dumbarton Oaks Papers* (Cambridge, MA), n. 3 (1946), p. [1]–72. "References frequently used": p. 62. Reprinted by Johnson Reprint Corp., 1967.

———. "Marble Relief of the Theodosian Period." "Identical with a paper delivered at the Symposium of 'The Dumbarton Oaks Collection: Studies in Byzantine Art', held at Dumbarton Oaks in May 1958." *Dumbarton Oaks Papers* (Washington), n. 14 (1960), p. [17]–42.

———. *Portraits of Christ*. With sixteen color plates and fourteen black-and-white illustrations and a text by Ernst Kitzinger and Elizabeth Senior . . . Harmondsworth, Middlesex, England: Penguin Books Ltd., 1940. 32 p., XVI col. pl. on 8 l. (The King Penguin books.)

———. "Studies on Late Antique and Early Byzantine Floor Mosaics. I. Mosaics at Nikopolis." *Dumbarton Oaks Papers* (Cambridge, MA), n. 6 (1951), p. [81]–122. Reprinted by Johnson Reprint Corp., 1967.

———. "Survey of the Early Christian Town of Stobi." Bibliography: p. [154]–161. *Dumbarton Oaks Papers* (Cambridge, MA) n. 3 (1946), p. [81]–[162]. Reprinted by Johnson Reprint Corp., 1967.

Kollias, Elias. *Patmos*. Manolis Chatzidakis, gen. ed.; Helen Zigada, trans. Athens, Greece: Melissa Publishing House, 1985. 40 p. (Byzantine art in Greece. Mosaics, wall paintings.) Translated from the Greek.

Krautheimer, Richard. "Constantinian Basilica." *Dumbarton Oaks Papers*, n. 21, p. 117–140. 10 illus. "This paper was read at a symposium on the age of Constantine: tradition and innovation, held at Dumbarton Oaks in May 1966." Offprint, Washington, DC, 1967.

———. *Early Christian and Byzantine Architecture*. 4th ed. Revised by Richard Krautheimer and Slobodan Curcic. Harmondsworth, Middlesex, England; NY: Penguin, 1986. 556 p. (The Pelican history of art.) Bibliography: p. [523]–525.

———. *Three Christian Capitals: Topography and Politics*. Berkeley: University of California Press, 1982. xiv, 167 p. (Una's lectures; 4.)

Four revised and enlarged lectures originally given at the University of California, Berkeley, in May 1979.

*Kuopion ortodoksinen kirkkomuseo. Treasures of the Orthodox Church Museum in Finland.* Text, Kristina Thomenius; translation Erja and Tony Melville. Kuopio, Finland: Kustannuskiila, 1985. 124 p. Bibliography: p. 97.

*Liturgy of the Presanctified Gifts.* Edited by David Drillock, John H. Erickson. Crestwood, NY: St. Vladimir's Seminary Press, 1990. 264 p.

Mango, Cyril A. *Apse Mosaics of St. Sophia at Istanbul, Report on Work Carried Out in 1964.* C. Mango and Ernest J. W. Hawkins. Washington, DC: Dumbarton Oaks Center for Byzantine Studies; Locust Valley, NY: distributed by J. J. Augustin, 1965. p. 115–151, 36 p. of plates "An offprint from Dumbarton Oaks papers, number nineteen."—Cover.

———. *Art of the Byzantine Empire, 312–1453; Sources and Documents.* Englewood Cliffs, NJ: Prentice-Hall, 1972. xvi, 272 p. (Sources and documents in the history of art series.) Bibliography: p. 260.

———. *Byzantine Architecture.* New York: Rizzoli, 1985. 215 p. (History of world architecture.) Bibliography: p. 205–206.

———. *Materials for the Study of the Mosaics of St. Sophia at Istanbul.* Washington, D.C.: Dumbarton Oaks Research Library and Collection, 1962. xvii, 145 p. (Dumbarton Oaks studies, 8.)

———. *Mosaics of St. Sophia at Istanbul, the Church Fathers in the North Tympanum.* C. Mango and Ernest J. W. Hawkins. Washington, DC: Dumbarton Oaks Center for Byzantine Studies; Locust Valley, NY: distributed by J. J. Augustin, 1972. 41 p., 44 p. of plates "An offprint from Dumbarton Oaks papers, number twenty-six."—Cover.

*Monuments of Russian Sacred Music: Historical Anthology of Russian Church Music (10th–20th cent.).* Sea Cliff, NY: The Russian Choral Society, 1989– . V. 1: *One Thousand Years of Russian Church Music 988–1988.* 773 p.

Mouriki, Doula, ed. *Byzantine East, Latin West.* Princeton, NJ: Princeton University, 1995.

Neale, John Mason. *Hymns of the Eastern Church.* NY: AMS Press, 1971. xii, 164 p. Reprint of the 1862 ed.

Ouspensky, Leonide. *The Meaning of Icons.* Ouspensky and Vladimir Lossky; translated by G.E.H. Palmer and E. Kadloubovsky. Revised ed. Crestwood, NY: St. Vladimir's Seminary Press, 1982. 222 p. Translation of *Der Sinn der Ikonen.* Bibliography: p. 221.

———. *Theology of the Icon.* Translated by Anthony Gythiel with selections translated by Elizabeth Meyendorff. Crestwood, NY: St. Vladimir's Seminary Press, 1992. 2 v. Vol. 1 is a revised translation of *Essai sur la théologie de l'icône dans l'Eglise orthodoxe;* vol. 2 is a translation of *La théologie de l'icône*. Both were translated originally from the Russian.

Ousterhout, Robert and Leslie Brubaker, eds. *Sacred Image East and West.* Urbana: University of Illinois Press, 1994.

Papaconstantinou, Helen Protopapadakis. *Passion Week: Encounters of the Lord With Some Women.* Athens: [s.n.], 1988 (J. Makris, Graphic Arts.) 170 p. Text in English and Greek.

*Patmos: Treasures of the Monastery.* Athanasios D. Koninis, gen. ed. Athens: Ekdotike Athenon, 1988. 383 p.

Pelikan, Jaroslav Jan. *Imago Dei: the Byzantine Apologia for Icons.* Washington, DC: National Gallery of Art; Princeton, NJ: Princeton University Press, 1990. xii, 196 p. (Bollingen series; XXXV, 36.) (The A. W. Mellon lectures in the fine arts; 1987.) Bibliography: p. 183–193.

Pokrovskii, Nikolai Vasilevich. "The Gospel in the Monuments of Iconography, Mostly Byzantine and Russian." With 226 pictures in the text and 12 tables. St. Petersburg, Russia: Appanage Press, 1892. 93 leaves. Appears to be a typescript copy of the translation of the text of *Evangelie v pamiatnikakh ikonografii preimushchestvenno vizantiiskikh i russkikh,* without pictures and tables.

Quasten, Johannes. *Music & Worship in Pagan & Christian Antiquity.* Translated by Boniface Ramsey. Washington, DC: National Association of Pastoral Musicians, 1983. 243 p. (NPM studies in church music and liturgy.) Translation of *Musik und Gesang in den Kulten der heidnischen Antike und christlichen Frühzeit.* 2d ed., 1973.

Quenot, Michel. *The Icon: Window on the Kingdom.* Translated by a Carthusian monk. Crestwood, NY: St. Vladimir's Seminary Press, 1991. 176 p. Translation of *L'icône.* Includes bibliographical references (p. 168–169).

*Rhythm in Byzantine Chant: Acta of the Congress Held at Hernen Castle in November 1986.* Editor, Ch. Hannick. Hernen, Holland: A. A. Bredius Foundation, 1991. xii, 201 p. German, French, and English.

Rice, David Talbot. *Byzantine Icons.* London: Faber and Faber, 1959. 24 p. 10 mounted col. (The Faber gallery of oriental art.)

———. *Icons and Their Dating: A Comprehensive Study of Their Chronology and Provenance.* David and Tamara Talbot Rice. London: Thames & Hudson, 1974. 192 p., [8] p. of plates. Bibliography: p. 6.

———. *Icons and Their History.* David and Tamara Talbot Rice. Woodstock, NY: Overlook Press, 1974. 192 p., [4] leaves of plates. Bibliography: p. 6.

———. *Russian Icons.* NY: Penguin Books, 1947. 40 p. (The King Penguin Books.) "A short bibliography": p. 39.

Romanus, Melodus, Saint, 6th cent. *Kontakia of Romanos, Byzantine Melodist.* Translated and annotated by Marjorie Carpenter. Columbia:

University of Missouri Press, 1970–72; v. 2, 1973. 2 v. translation of *Cantica*. The basis of the translation is the Oxford ed. published in 1963, and edited by P. Maas and C. A. Trypanis. Bibliography: v. 1, p. xxxvii–xxxviii; v. 2, p. x. Contents: 1. On the Person of Christ. 2. On Christian Life.

Runciman, Steven. *Byzantine Style and Civilization*. NY: Penguin, 1990. 238 p. Includes bibliography (p. 227–229) and index.

Savas, Savas J. *The Treasury of Orthodox Hymnology: Triodion: An Historical and Hymnographic Examination*. Minneapolis: Light and Life, 1983. 61, 5 p. Bibliography: p. 63–66. "V. 1."

Schork, R. J. *Sacred Song from the Byzantine Pulpit: Romanus the Melodist*. Gainesville: University of Florida, 1995.

Seaman, Gerald R. *History of Russian Music*. Oxford: Blackwell, 1967– . Amplification of the author's thesis, 1961. Bibliography: v. 1, p. 297–303. Contents: v. 1. From Its Origins to Dargomyzhsky.

Sherrard, Philip. *Constantinople, Iconography of a Sacred City*. NY: Oxford University Press, 1965. 139 p.

———. *The Sacred in Life and Art*. Ipswich, U.K.: Golgonooza Press, 1990. 162 p.

Sirota, Ioann B. *Die Ikonographie der Gottesmutter in der Russischen Orthodoxen Kirche: Versuch einer Systematisierung*. Wurzburg: Augustinus-Verlag. Verlag "Der christliche Osten", 1992. 314 p. (Östliche Christentum; n.f., Bd. 38.) "Die hier vorgelegte Studie . . . wurde an der Theologischen Akademie von Moskau zur Erlangung des Grades eines 'Kandidaten der Theologie', etwa unserem Dr. theol. entsprechend, erarbeitet und eingereicht" — Vorwort, p. 5.

Smith, Barbara Sweetland. *Heaven on Earth*. Anchorage, Alaska: Anchorage Museum of History and Art, 1994. 115 p.

Sparathakis, Ioannis. *Studies in Byzantine Manuscript Illumination and Iconography*. London: Pindar Press, 1995. 390 p.

*Studies in Eastern Chant*. General editors, Egon Wellesz and Milos Velimirovic. NY: Oxford University Press, 1966– . V. 1–4 edited by Milos Velimirovic. Imprint varies: v. 4– : Crestwood, NY: St. Vladimir's Seminary Press. Bibliography: v.1, p. xiii–xvi.

*Studies On Art and Archeology in Honor of Ernst Kitzinger on His Seventy-Fifth Birthday*. William Tronzo and Irving Lavin, ed. Washington, DC: Dumbarton Oaks Research Library and Collection, 1987. xvi, 511 p. (Dumbarton Oaks papers; n. 41.)

Timchenko, S. V. *Russian Church Art Today*. Moscow: New Book, 1993. 223 p.

Touliatos-Banker, Diane H. *The Byzantine Amomos Chant of the Fourteenth and Fifteenth Centuries*. Thessalonica: Patriarchikon Hidryma Paterikon Meleton, 1984. 284 p. (Analekta Vlatadon; 46.)

*Treasures of Mount Athos; Illuminated Manuscripts. Miniatures, Headpieces, Initial Letters.* Philip Sherrard, trans. Athens: Ekdotike Athenon, 1974– . At head of title: The Patriarchal Institute for Patristic Studies. S. M. Pelekandis, P. C. Christou, Ch. Tsioumis, S. N. Kadas. Translation of *Hoi Thesauroi tou Hagiou Orous; eikonographemena cheirographa.* Bibliography: v. 1, p. 489.

*Treasury of Icons, Sixth to Seventeenth Centuries: From the Sinai Peninsula, Greece, Bulgaria, and Yugoslavia.* Kurt Weitzmann, Manolis Chatzidakis, Krsto Miatev, Svetozar Radojcic. Translated by Robert Erich Wolf. NY: Abrams, 1968. Civ p., 220 p. of illus. Translation of *Ikone sa Balkana.*

Trubetskoi, Evgenii Nikolaevich. *Icons: Theology in Color.* Translated from the Russian by Gertrude Vakar, with an introduction by George M. A. Hanfmann. Crestwood, NY: St. Vladimir's Seminary Press, 1973. 100 p., [8] leaves of plates. Translation of *Tri ocherka o russkoi ikone.* Bibliography: p. 99–100.

Velimirovič, Miloš M. "Liturgical Drama in Byzantium and Russia." An enlarged and revised version of a paper read at the annual meeting of the American Musicological Society at Stanford University, California, on Dec. 28, 1960. *Dumbarton Oaks Papers* (Washington), n. 16 (1962), p. 349–385.

Virionides, Christos. *The Byzantine Chant of the Greek Orthodox Church: History, Musical Theory and 285 Practical Exercises in Byzantine Notation for the Students of School[s] of Theology, Theological Seminars and Music Conservatories.* Brookline, MA: Holy Cross Orthodox Theological School, 1959. 132 p. "The 285 exercises are also transcribed in Western notation and are found at the end of the book".

Walter, Christopher. *Art and Ritual of the Byzantine Church.* Preface by Robin Cormack. London: Variorum, 1982. ix, 279 p., 32 p. of plates (Birmingham Byzantine series; 1.) Bibliography: p. 251–258.

Wellesz, Egon. "The 'Akathistos' a Study in Byzantine Hymnography." *Dumbarton Oaks Papers* (Cambridge, MA), n. 9–10, (1956), p. [141]–174. Reprinted by Johnson Reprint Corp., 1967.

———. *Ancient and Oriental Music.* Edited by Wellesz. NY: Oxford University Press, 1957. xxiii, 530 p. (New Oxford history of music, v. 1.) Bibliography: p. [479]–503.

———. "Eastern Elements in English Ecclesiastical Music." *Journal of the Warburg and Courtauld Institutes.* V. 5. (1942), p. 44–55.

———. *A History of Byzantine Music and Hymnography.* 2d ed., revised and enlarged. Oxford: The Clarendon Press, 1961. xiii, 461 p., 7 pp. of plates. Bibliography: p. [428–441].

Zibawi, Mahmoud. *The Icon: Its Meaning and History.* Collegeville, MN: Liturgical Press, 1993. 175 p.

## III. Asceticism and Spirituality

Allen, Joseph J. *Inner Way: Eastern Christian Spiritual Direction.* Grand Rapids, MI: W. B. Eerdmans Publishing Co., 1993.

Amis, Robin. *A Different Christianity.* Albany: State University of New York Press, 1995.

Anderson, Isabel. *Building to Last.* South Canaan, PA: St. Tikhon's Seminary Press, 1994.

Arseniev, Nikolai Sergeevich. *Mysticism and the Eastern Church.* Translated from the German by Arthur Chambers; with a preface by Friedrich Heiler; introduction by Evelyn Underhill. Crestwood, NY: St. Vladimir's Seminary Press, 1979. 172 p. Translation of *Ostkirche und Mystik.*

Aumann, Jordan. *Christian Spirituality East & West.* Aumann, Thomas Hopko, Donald G. Bloesch. Chicago: Priory Press, 1968. 203 p. (Institute of Spirituality. Special lectures, v. 3, 1967.)

Beck, Hans-Georg. *Theoria: ein byzantinischer Traum?* Munich: Verlag der Bayerischen Akademie der Wissenchaften: in Kommission C. H. Beck, 1983. 37 p. (Sitzungsberichte/Bayerische Akademie der Wissenschaften, Philosophisch-Historische Klasse; Jahrg. 1983, Heft 7) "Vorgetragen am 4. Februar 1983.".

Bloom, Anthony [Metropolitan Anthony of Sourozh]. *Beginning to Pray.* NY: Paulist Press, 1970. xx, 75 p. (Deus books.)

———. *Courage to Pray.* Metropolitan Anthony and Georges Lefebvre; translated from the French by Dinah Livingstone. London: Darton, Longman and Todd, 1974. [4], 123 p. Translation of *La prière.*

———. *God and Man.* London: Darton, Longman and Todd, 1971. 125 p.

———. *Living Prayer.* Springfield, IL: Templegate, 1966. 125 p.

———. *Meditations: A Spiritual Journey.* Denville, NJ: Dimension Books, 1971. 125 p.

Blum, Richard. *The Sacred Athlete: On the Mystical Experience and Dionysios, Its Westernworld Fountainhead.* Blum and Alexander Golitzin. Lanham, MD: University Press of America, 1991. 502 p. Bibliographical references: p. 459–485.

Cabasilas, Nicolaus, 14th cent. *The Life in Christ.* Translated from the Greek by Carmino J. deCatanzaro; with an introduction by Boris Bobrinskoy. Crestwood, NY: St. Vladimir's Seminary Press, 1974. 229 p.

*Christian Spirituality.* NY: Crossroad, 1985–1989. 3 v. (World spirituality; v. 16–18.) 1. Origins to the Twelfth Century. 2. High Middle Ages and Reformation. 3. Post-Reformation and Modern. Vols. 1–2 edited by Gernard McGinn and John Meyendorff in collaboration with Jean Leclerq. Vol. 3 edited by Louis Dupre and Donald E. Saliers in collaboration with John Meyendorff.

Chryssavgis, John. *Ascent to Heaven: The Theology of the Human Person According to Saint John of the Ladder*. Brookline, MA: Holy Cross Orthodox Press, 1989. viii, 269 p. Bibliography: p. 266.

Colliander, Tito. *Way of the Ascetics: The Ancient Tradition of Discipline and Inner Growth*. Translated by Katharine Ferre; introduction by Kenneth Leech. Crestwood, NY: St. Vladimir's Seminary Press, 1985. xi, 110 p.

Dechow, Jon Frederick. *Dogma and Mysticism in Early Christianity: Epiphanius of Cyprus and the Legacy of Origen*. Macon, GA: Mercer University Press, 1988. x, 584 p. (Patristic monograph series; 13.) Revision of the author's Ph.D. thesis, University of Pennsylvania, 1975. Bibliography: p. [483]–525.

Feofan, Saint, Bishop of Tambov and Shatsk, 1815–1894. *The Heart of Salvation: The Life and Teachings of Russia's Saint Theophan the Recluse*. Translated by Esther Williams; edited with commentary by Robin Amis and an introduction by George A. Maloney. Newbury, MA: Robertsbridge, East Sussex, England: Praxis Institute Press, 1991? xxi, 183 p. Includes bibliographical references (p. [177]–178) and index.

Frank L. Weil Institute for Studies in Religion and the Humanities Conference. 4. *Mysticism and Society*. Cincinnati: Hebrew Union College-Jewish Institute of Religion, 1966. 6 v. in 1. See especially: The Mystical Tradition of the Christian East: Cultural Varieties of Mysticism, by K. T. Ware.

Galatoriotou, Catia. *The Making of a Saint: the Life, Times, and Sanctification of Neophytos the Recluse*. NY: Cambridge University Press, 1991. xvi, 310 p. Includes bibliographical references (p. 282–304) and index.

Gillet, Lev [Monk of the Eastern Church]. *Encounter at the Well: Retreat Addresses of Fr. Lev Gillet*. Introduction by Constance Babington-Smith. London: Mowbray, 1988. 139 p.

———. *In Thy Presence*. Crestwood, NY: St. Vladimir's Seminary Press, 1977. 144 p.

———. *Jesus, A Dialogue with the Saviour*. Translated by a Monk of the Western Church. West Newton, MA: Educational Services, Diocese of Newton, 1990. iv, 184 p., [4] leaves of plates. Translated from the French.

———. *The Jesus Prayer*. Revised ed. with a foreword by Kallistos Ware. Crestwood, NY: St. Vladimir's Seminary Press, 1987. 120 p. Translation of *La Prière de Jésus*.

———. *On the Invocation of the Name of Jesus*. San Bernardino, CA: Borgo Press, 1986. ii, 32 p. Reprint. Originally published: London: Fellowship of St. Alban and St. Sergius, 1949.

———. *Orthodox Spirituality: An Outline of the Orthodox Ascetical and Mystical Tradition*. London: Published for the Fellowship of St. Alban and St. Sergius by Society for Promoting Christian Knowledge, 1945. xv, 103 p. Bibliography: p. xi–xv.

Gould, Graham. *The Desert Fathers on Monastic Community.* Oxford: Clarendon Press; NY: Oxford University Press, 1993. (Oxford early Christian studies.) Revision of doctoral thesis, Cambridge University.

*History of Christian Spirituality.* Louis Bouyer... [et al.] London: Burns & Oates, 1968–1969 (v. 1: 1982 printing) 3 v. Translation of *Histoire de la spiritualité chrétienne.* See especially: 3. Orthodox Spirituality and Protestant and Anglican Spirituality.

Irene Eulogia Choumnaina Palaiologos, Princess, d. 1360. *A Woman's Quest for Spiritual Guidance: The Correspondence of Princess Irene Eulogia Choumnaina Palaiologina.* Edited by Angela Constantinides Hero; with an introduction by John Meyendorff. Brookline, MA: Hellenic College Press, 1986. 166 p. (Archbishop Iakovos library of ecclesiastical and historical sources; n. 11.) Bibliography: p. 11–13.

John, of Karpathos, Saint, 7th cent.? *A Supplement to the Philokalia: The Second Century of Saint John of Karpathos.* Edited by David Balfour, in collaboration with Mary Cunningham. 1st critical ed. Brookline, MA: Hellenic College Press, 1989. (The Archbishop Iakovos library of ecclesiastical and historical sources; n. 15.) Greek text and English translation.

Kadas, Sotiris. *Mount Athos: An Illustrated Guide to the Monasteries and Their History.* Louise Turner, trans. Athens: Ekdotike Athenon, 1980. 200 p. Bibliography: p. 199.

Knowles, David. *From Pachomius to Ignatius: A Study in the Constitutional History of the Religious Orders.* Oxford: Clarendon Press, 1966. [7], 98 p. (The Sarum lectures, 1964–5.)

Kovalevskii, Ioann. *Iurodstvo o Khristie v Khrista radi iurodivye Vostochnoi i Russkoi tserkvi: istoricheskii ocherk v zhitiia sikh podvizhnikov blagochestiia.* Farnborough: Gregg, 1969. [3], 275 p. Title also: *Folly in Christ and fools for Christ's sake in the Eastern and Russian church.* Reprint of 1st. ed., Moscow, 1895.

Kovalevsky, Pierre. *Saint Sergius and Russian Spirituality.* Translation by W. Elias Jones. Crestwood, NY: St. Vladimir's Seminary Press, 1976. 190 p. Translation of *Saint Serge et la spiritualité russe.*

Lossky, Nicolas. *Lancelot Andrewes the Preacher (1555–1626): The Origins of the Mystical Theology of the Church of England.* Foreword by Michael Ramsey; afterword by A. M. Allchin; translated from the French by Andrew Louth. Oxford: Clarendon Press; NY: Oxford University Press, 1991. 377 p. Translation of *Lancelot Andrewes le prédicateur (1555–1626).*

Makarii, Monk, [Macarius, Starets of Optino], 1788–1860. *Russian Letters of Direction, 1834–1860.* Selection, translations, and foreword by

Iulia de Beausobre. Crestwood, NY: St. Vladimir's Seminary Press, 1975. 115 p.
Mantzarides, Georgios I. *Orthodox Spiritual Life*. Brookline, MA: Holy Cross Orthodox Press, 1994.
Meyendorff, John. *Byzantine Hesychasm: Historical, Theological and Social Problems: Collected Studies*. London: Variorum Reprints, 1974. 292, ca 300 p. in various pagings. (Variorum reprint; CS26.) Reprints of sixteen studies in English, French, Greek, or Russian written between 1953 and 1971.

———. *St. Gregory Palamas and Orthodox Spirituality*. Authorized translation by Adele Fiske. Crestwood, NY: St. Vladimir's Seminary Press, 1974. 184 p. Translation of *St. Grégoire Palamas et la mystique orthodoxe*.
Moschus, John, ca. 550–619 (John Moschos, also known as John Eviratus). *The Spiritual Meadow. Pratum spirituale*. Introduction, translation, and notes by John Wortley. Kalamazoo, MI: Cistercian Publications, 1992.
Nicol, Donald MacGillivray. *Meteora: The Rock Monasteries of Thessaly*. London: Chapman and Hall, 1963. x, 210 p. Bibliography: p. 191–199.
Nikonanos, Nikos. *Meteora: A Complete Guide to the Monasteries and Their History*. Athens: Ekdotike Athenon, 1987. 112 p.
Obolensky, Dimitri. "Italy, Mount Athos and Muscovy: The Three Worlds of Maximos the Greek." *Proceedings of the British Academy* (London), v. LXVII (1981), p. [143]–161. (Raleigh lecture on history; 1981.)
Paliouras, Athanasios D. *The Monastery of St. Catherine on Mount Sinai*. Captions, His Eminence Damianos Archbishop of Sinai; photography, Nicolas Tzaferis; English translation, Helen Zigada. Egypt: St. Catherine's Monastery at Sinai; Glyka Nera Attikis, Greece: E. Tzaferi, 1985. 36 p., [166] p. of plates. Bibliography: p. [202]
*The Paradise, or, Garden of the Holy Fathers: Being Histories of the Anchorites, Recluses, Monks, Coenobites, and Ascetic Fathers of the Deserts of Egypt between* A.D. *CCL and* A.D. *CCCC Circiter*. Compiled by Athanasius, Archbishop of Alexandria; Palladius, Bishop of Helenopolis; Saint Jerome; and others; now translated out of the Syriac, with notes and introduction, by Ernest A. Wallis Budge. London: Chatto & Windus, 1907. 2v.
*Philokalia: The Complete Text*. Compiled by St. Nikodimos of the Holy Mountain and St. Makarios of Corinth; translated from the Greek and edited by G.E.H. Palmer, Philip Sherrard, Kallistos Ware with the assistance of the Holy Transfiguration Monastery (Brookline) . . . [et al.]. Boston: Faber and Faber, 1979– . Translation of *Philokalia*.
Philokalia ton hieron neptikon. *Early Fathers from the Philokalia, Together with Some Writings of St. Abba Dorotheus, St. Isaac of Syria,*

*and St. Gregory Palamas*. Selected and translated from the Russian text *Dobrotolubiye* by E. Kadloubovsky and G.E.H. Palmer. London: Faber and Faber, 1954. 421 p.

———. *Writings from the Philokalia On Prayer of the Heart*. Translated from the Russian text *Dobrotolubiye*, by E. Kadloubovsky and G.E.H. Palmer, with a new foreword and the original introduction and biographical notes. London: Faber and Faber, 1951. 420 p.

Photius I, Saint, Patriarch of Constantinople, ca. 820–ca. 891. *On the Mystagogy of the Holy Spirit*. Translation by Holy Transfiguration Monastery. Astoria, NY: Studion Publishers, 1983. 213 p. English and Greek. Translation of *Mystagogia Spiritus Sancti*.

Rousseau, Philip. *Pachomius: The Making of a Community in Fourth-Century Egypt*. Berkeley: University of California Press, 1985. xvi, 217 p. (The Transformation of the classical heritage; 6.) Bibliography: p. 193–212.

Scupoli, Lorenzo, 1530–1610. *Unseen Warfare: The Spiritual Combat and Path to Paradise of Lorenzo Scupoli*. Edited by Nicodemus of the Holy Mountain and revised by Theophan the Recluse; translated by E. Kadloubovsky and G.E.H. Palmer; introduction by H. A. Hodges. Crestwood, NY: St. Vladimir's Seminary Press, 1987. 280 p.

Sergiev, Ioann Ilich (Fr. John of Kronstadt). *Spiritual Counsels of Father John of Kronstadt: Select Passages from My Life in Christ*. Edited and introduced by W. Jardine Grisbrooke. Cambridge, England: Clarke; Crestwood, NY: St. Vladimir's Seminary Press, 1981. xxxi, 230 p.

Sherrard, Philip. *Athos, the Holy Mountain*. Photographs by Takis Zervoulakos. Woodstock, NY: Overlook Press, 1985. 176 p.

———. *Athos: the Mountain of Silence*. With color photographs by Paul du Marchie v. Voorthuysen. NY: Oxford University Press, 1960. vii, 110 p. Bibliography: p. 107–108.

*Simonopetra, Mount Athos*. Stelios Papadopoulos, ed. Athens: ETBA, Hellenic Industrial Development Bank SA, 1991. 395 p. Translated from the Greek.

Sofronii, Archimandrite. *His Life Is Mine*. Translated from the Russian by Rosemary Edmonds. London: Mowbrays, 1977. 128 p.

———. *The Monk of Mount Athos: Staretz Silouan, 1866–1938*. Translated from the Russian by Rosemary Edmonds. Revised ed. Crestwood, NY: St. Vladimir's Seminary Press, 1975. [1], 124 p. "A revised edition, with additional material, of *The Undistorted Image* which was published in 1958 and based on a translation and adaptation of the original (1948) Russian text, *Staretz Silouan*, published Paris, 1952."

———. *We Shall See Him as He Is*. Translated from Russian by Rosemary Edmonds. Rev. ed. Essex, England: Stavropegic Monastery of

Saint John the Baptist, 1988. 237 p. Translation of *Videt Boga kak on jest.*

Theokistos the Stoudite. *Faith Healing in Late Byzantium: The posthumous Miracles of the Patriarch Athanasios I of Constantinople by Theokistos the Stoudite.* Edited by Alice-Mary Maffry Talbot. Brookline, MA: Hellenic College Press, 1983. 162 p. (The Archbishop Iakovos library of ecclesiastical and historical sources; n. 8.) Includes Greek text and English translation.

Theophan, the Recluse, Saint, Bishop of Tambov and Shatsk, 1815–1894. *The Heart of Salvation: The Life and Teachings of Russia's Saint Theophan the Recluse.* Translated by Esther Williams; edited with commentary by Robin Amis and an introduction by George A. Maloney. Newbury, MA: Robertsbridge, England: Praxis Institute Press. 1991? xxi. 183 p. Bibliographical references: p. 177–178.

———. *The Path of Prayer.* Edited by Robin Amis. Robertsbridge, England: Praxis Institute Press, 1992. xiii, 78 p.

*Tradition of Life: Romanian Essays in Spirituality and Theology.* Arthur M. Allchin, ed. Fellowship of St. Alban and St. Sergius, 1971. 73 p. (Studies Supplementary to Sobornost, n. 2.)

Ware, Kallistos. *The Power of the Name: The Jesus Prayer in Orthodox Spirituality.* London: Marshall Pickering, 1989. 48 p. (Christian spirituality series.) Includes bibliographical references (p. 48).

*Way of a Pilgrim;* and, *The Pilgrim Continues His Way.* Translated from the Russian by R. M. French. NY: Seabury Press. 1965. x, 242 p. (A Seabury paperback, SP18.)

## IV. Canon Law

*Acts and Decrees of the Synod of Jerusalem, Sometimes Called the Council of Bethlehem, Holden Under Dositheus, Patriarch of Jerusalem in 1672.* Translated from the Greek with an appendix containing the confession published with the name of Cyril Lucar condemned by the Synod and with notes by J.N.W.B. Robertson. NY: AMS Press, 1969. vii, 215 p. Reprint of the London ed., 1899. Translation of *Aspis orthodoxias e apologia kai elenchos pros tous diasyrontas ten Anatoliken Ekklesian.*

Beck, Hans Georg. *Nomos, Kanon und Staatsraison in Byzanz.* Vienna: Verlag der Österreichischen Akademie der Wissenschaften, 1981. 60 p. (Sitzungsberichte. Osterreichische Akademie der Wissenschaften, Philosophisch-Historische Klasse; 384. Bd.) "Vorgelegt vom Autor in der Sitzung am 26. November 1980"—T.p. verso.

Bogolepov, Aleksandr Aleksandrovich. *Church Reforms in Russia, 1905–1918, In Commemoration of the 50th Anniversary of the All-Russian Church Council of 1917–1918.* Translated by A. E. Moorhouse. Bridgeport, CT: Publications Committee of the Metropolitan Council of the Russian Orthodox Church of America, 1966. 59 p. Bibliography: p. 57–59.

———. *Toward an American Orthodox Church: The Establishment of an Autocephalous Orthodox Church.* NY: Morehouse-Barlow Co., 1963. 124 p. Bibliography: p. 105–108.

*Canons, Nomocanons, Decrees, etc. Rules Collected from the Synhados (Canonical Law) of the Church of the East & Patriarchal Decrees.* [s.l.]: The Holy Apostolic and Catholic Church of the East, 1960. 22 p.

*Decrees of the Ecumenical Councils.* Edited by Norman P. Tanner. London: Sheed & Ward; Washington, DC: Georgetown University Press, 1990. 2 v. (xxv, 1342 p.) Includes the document in the original text, a reproduction of *Conciliorum oecumenicorum decreta,* and English translations. 1.: Nicaea I to Lateran V. 2.: Trent to Vatican II.

Erickson, John H. *The Challenge of Our Past: Studies in Orthodox Canon Law and Church History.* Crestwood, NY: St. Vladimir's Seminary Press, 1991. 174 p.

*Kirche und die Kirchen, Autonomie und Autokephalie. The Church and the Churches, Autonomy and Autocephaly.* Hhrsg. von der Gesellschaft für das Recht der Ostkirchen. Vienna: Verlag des Verbandes der Wissenschaftlichen Gesellschaften Österreichs, v. 1 (1980)– . (Kanon; 4– .) Papers presented at the 4th Congress of the Society for the Law of the Oriental Churches held Sept. 19–24, 1978 in Regensburg. English, French, and German.

*The Primacy of Peter: Essays in Ecclesiology and the Early Church.* John Meyendorff, et al. Crestwood, NY: St. Vladimir's Seminary Press, 1992. 182 p.

*Regesten der Kaiserurkunden des ostromischen Reiches von 565–1453.* Franz Dolger. 2. erweit. und verb. Aufl. Bearbeitet von Peter Wirth. Munich: C. H. Beck, 1977– . (Corpus der griechischen Urkunden des Mittelalters und der neueren Zeit. Reihe A. Regesten, Abt. 1.) Bibliography: v. 3, p. [xi]–xxxiii. Contents: T.3. Regesten von 1204–1282.

*Rudder (Pendalion) of the Metaphorical Ship of the One Holy Catholic and Apostolic Church of the Orthodox Christians, or All the Sacred and Divine Canons of the Holy and Renowned Apostles, of the Holy Councils, Ecumenical as Well as Regional . . . ,* by Agapius, a hieromonk, and Nicodemus, a monk and diligently redacted . . . by Seignior Dorotheus. . . . D. Cumings, translator. Chicago: Orthodox Christian Educational Society, 1957.

*The Seven Ecumenical Councils of the Undivided Church: Their Canons and Dogmatic Decrees, Together with the Canons of All the Local Synods Which Have Received Ecumenical Acceptance.* Henry R. Percival, ed. Grand Rapids, MI: Eerdmans Publishing Co., 1956. xxxv,

671 p. (Select library of Nicene and post-Nicene fathers of the Christian Church; 2d ser., v. 14.)
*Spiritual Regulation of Peter the Great.* Translated and edited by Alexander V. Muller. Seattle: University of Washington Press, 1972. xxxviii, 150 p. (Perspectives on Russia and Eastern Europe of the Institute for Comparative and Foreign Area Studies; n. 3) Translation of *Dukhovnyi reglament.* Bibliography: p. 123–136.
*Syntagma ton theion kai hieron kanonon ton te hagion kai paneuphemon apostolon, kai ton hieron oikoumenikon kai topikon synodon, kai ton kata meros hagion pateron: ekdothen syn pleistais allais ten ekklesiastiken katastasin diepousais diataxesi.* Meta ton archaior. exegeton kai diaphoron anagnosmaton hypo G. A. Rhalle kai M. Potle . . . Athenesin: Ek tes Typographias G. Chartophylakos, 1852–1859. 6 v. Vol. 6 has imprint: En Athenais: Ek tou Typographeiou tes Auges, 1859. V. 1: [16], 403 p.; v. 2: [8], 732, [1] p.; v. 3: [8], 655, [1] p.; v. 4: [12], 640 p.; v. 5: [16], 638 p. Contents: t. 1. Photiou Patriarchou Konstantinoupoleos nomokanon . . . t. 2. Hoi theioi kai hieroikanones . . . apostolon . . . oikoumenikon synodon . . . t. 3. Hoi theioi kai hieroi kanones . . . topikon synodon . . . t. 4. Hoi theioi kai hieroi kanones . . . ton hagion pateron . . . t. 5. Apophaseis synodikai kai diataxeis ton Konstantinoupoleos . . . t. 6. Mathaiou tou Blastareos Syntagma kata stoicheion . . .
Trembelas, Panagiotes Nikolaou. *The Autocephaly of the Metropolia in America.* Translated and edited by George S. Bebis, Robert G. Stephanopoulos, N. M. Vaporis. Brookline, MA: Holy Cross Theological School Press, 1973. 80 p.

## V. Church Fathers

### A. Primary Sources

Ammon, Saint, ca. 350. *The Letters of Ammonas, Successor of Saint Antony.* Translated by Derwas J. Chitty; revised and with an introduction by Sebastian Brock. Oxford: SLG Press, 1979. iv, 21 p. (Fairacres publication, 72) Bibliography: p. iii–iv. Companion to *The Letters of Saint Antony the Great.*
*Ancient Christian Writers* [series]. NY: Newman Press; Paulist Press. v. 1 (1946)– . See especially: 18. Gregory, of Nyssa, ca. 335–ca. 394. The Lord's Prayer. The Beatitudes. (Translated and annotated by Hilda C. Graef. 1954. v, 210 p. Translation of *De oratione Dominica. De beatitudinis.* Bibliographical references included in "Notes" p. 117–198). 21. Maximus, Confessor, Saint, ca. 580–662. The Ascetic Life. The Four Centuries on Charity. (Translated and annotated by Polycarp Sherwood. 1955. vii, 284 p. Translation of *Liber asceticus. Capita de caritate.* Bibliography: p. 211–213.) 38. Egeria: Diary of a Pilgrimage. (Translated and edited by George E. Gingras. 1970. v, 287

p. Translation of *Itinerarium Egeriae*.) 55– . Irenaeus, Saint, Bishop of Lyon. St. Irenaeus of Lyons Against the Heresies. (Translated and annotated by Dominic J. Unger, with further revisions by John J. Dillon. 1992– . Translation of *Adversus haereses*.)

*Ancient Fathers of the Desert: Translated Narratives from the Evergetinos on Passions and Perfection in Christ*. By Archimandrite Chrysostomos. Brookline, MA: Hellenic College Press, 1980. 118 p. Translation of *Mikros Euergetenos*.

*The Ante-Nicene Fathers: Translations of the Writings of the Fathers Down to A.D. 325*. Alexander Roberts and James Donaldson, eds. Buffalo: Christian Literature Co., 1885–96. 10 v.

*Apostolic Fathers*. With an English translation by Kirsopp Lake. Cambridge, MA: Harvard University Press, 1952 [v. 2, 1930]. 2 v. (Loeb classical library.) First published 1912–13.

Athanasius, Saint, Patriarch of Alexandria, d. 373. *Contra gentes;* and, *De Incarnatione*. Edited and translated by Robert W. Thomson. Oxford, Clarendon Press, 1971. xxxvi, 288 p. (Oxford early Christian texts.) English and Greek. Bibliography: p. ix–x.

———. *The Festal Epistles of S. Athanasius, Bishop of Alexandria*. Translated from the Syriac with notes and indices. Oxford: J. H. Parker, 1854. xxvi, 163 p. (A Library of fathers of the Holy Catholic Church anterior to the division of the East and West; 38.) Translated by Henry Burgess; edited by H. G. Williams. Includes hitherto unpublished Syriac text of parts of two letters (p. 141–146).

———. *The Letters of Saint Athanasius Concerning the Holy Spirit*. Translated with introduction and notes by C.R.B. Shapland. London: Epworth Press, 1951. 204 p. Translation of *Epistolae ad Serapione*.

———. *On the Incarnation: The Treatise De incarnatione Verbi Dei*. Translated and edited by Penelope Lawson; with a foreword by Walter Hooper; introduction by C. S. Lewis. NY: Macmillan, 1981. xxxiii, 91 p. Translation of *De incarnatione*.

———. *Select Treatises of St. Athanasius in Controversy with the Arians*. Freely translated, with an appendix, by John Henry Cardinal Newman. 5th ed. NY: AMS Press, 1978. 2 v. Vol. 2 is an appendix of illustrations. Reprint of the 1890 ed. published NY: Longmans, Green.

Basil, Saint, Bishop of Caesarea, ca. 329–379. *The Ascetic Works of Saint Basil*. Translated into English with introduction and notes by W.K.L. Clarke. London: Society for Promoting Christian Knowledge; NY: Macmillan, 1925. 362 p. (Translations of Christian literature. Series I, Greek texts.)

———. *Gateway to Paradise*. Edited by Oliver Davies. Translated by Tim Witherow. Introduction by A. M. Allchin. Brooklyn, NY: New City Press, 1991. 125 p. (Spirituality of the fathers, 1.) Bibliographical references: p. 125.

———. *Letters*. Translated by Roy J. Deferrari. NY: G. P. Putnam's Sons; Cambridge, MA: Harvard University Press, 1926–1934. 4 v. (Loeb classical library.) Greek and English on opposite pages. Vol. 4 includes Basil's Address to Young Men on Reading Greek Literature, p. 363–435.

———. *On the Holy Spirit*. Translation with an Introduction by David Anderson. Crestwood, NY: St. Vladimir's Seminary Press, 1980. 118 p. Translation of *De Spiritu Sancto*.

*Cistercian Studies Series*. Kalamazoo, MI: Cistercian Publications, 19—. See especially: 4. Evagrius, Ponticus, 345?–399? The Praktikos: Chapters on Prayer. (Translated, with an introduction and notes, by John Eudes Bamberger. 1981. xciv, 96 p. The 2d work is a translation of *Peri proseuches*, which is also attributed to Saint Nilus.) 33. Dorotheus, of Gaza, Saint, 6th cent. Discourses and Sayings. (Eric P. Wheeler, translation and introduction. 1977. 259 p.) 34. Lives of the Desert Fathers. (Translated by Norman Russell; introduction by Benedicta Ward. 1981. viii, 181 p. Bibliography: p. [162]–164.) 44. Hausherr, Irenee. The Name of Jesus. (Translated by Charles Cummings. 1978. 358 p. Translation of *Noms du Christ et voies d'oraison*. Bibliography: p. 348–358.) 45–47. Pachomian Koinonia. (Translated and introduced by Armand Veilleux; preface by Adalbert de Vogue. 1980, 1982– . v. 1, 3– .) 53. Hausherr, Irenee. Penthos: The Doctrine of Compunction in the Christian East. (Translated by Anselm Hufstader. 1982. x, 200 p.) 59. Sayings of the Desert Fathers: The Alphabetical Collection. (Translated, with a foreword by Bendedicta Ward; preface by Metropolitan Anthony of Sourozh. Rev. ed. 1984. xxxvi, 269 p. Foreword is reprinted from the 1975 ed. Bibliography: p. 254–257.) 88. Theodoret, Bishop of Cyrrhus. A History of the Monks of Syria. (Translated with an introduction and notes by R. M. Price. 1985. xxxvii, 223 p. Translation of *Philotheos historia*. Bibliography: p. 208–213.) 101. Syriac Fathers On Prayer and the Spiritual Life. (Introduced and translated by Sebastian Brock. 1987. xliii, 381 p. "Selection of excerpts translated from Syriac writers"—Pref. Bibl.: p. 311–312.) 112. The Lives of Simeon Stylites. (Translated, with an introduction by Robert Doran; foreword by Susan Ashbrook Harvey. 1992. 241 p. Includes English translations of two Greek biographies by Theodoret and Antonius, and an anonymous Syriac version. Bibliographical references: p. 231–235.) 116. Hausherr, Irenee. Spiritual Direction in the Ancient Christian East. (Foreword by Kallistos [Ware] of Diokleia; translation by Anthony P. Gythiel. 1989. xxxiii, 434 p. Translation of *Direction spirituelle en orient autrefois*. Bibliography: p. 365–399.) 124. Brock, Sebastian P. The Luminous Eye: The Spiritual World Vision of Saint Ephrem. (1992 p. Based on a series of lectures given by the author at the Pontifical Oriental Institute in Rome, April 1984. Originally published: Rome: Center for Indian and Inter-Religious Studies, 1985.)

*Classics of Western Spirituality* [unnumbered series]. NY: Paulist Press,. See especially: Athanasius, Saint Patriarch of Athanasius, d. 373. Life of Antony and the Letter to Marcellinus. (Translation and introduction by Robert C. Gregg; preface by William A. Clebsch. 1980. xxi, 166 p. Translation of *Vita S. Antonii*.) Cassian, John, ca. 360–ca. 435. Conferences. (Translation and preface by Colm Luibheid; introduction by Owen Chadwick. 1985. xv, 208 p.) Ephraem, Syrus, Saint, 303–373. Ephrem the Syrian: Hymns. Translated and introduced by Kathleen E. McVey. 1989. xiii, 474 p.) Gregory, of Nyssa, ca. 335–ca. 394. Life of Moses. (Translation, introduction, and notes by Abraham J. Malherbe and Everett Ferguson; preface by John Meyendorff. 1978. xvi, 208 p. Cistercian Studies series; n. 31. Translation of *De vita Moysis*. Bibliography: p. 139–140.) Gregory Palamas, Saint, 1296–1359. Triads: Apology for the Holy Hesychasts. (Edited, with an introduction by John Meyendorff; translation by Nicholas Gendle; preface by Jaroslav Pelikan. 1983. xiii, 172 p.) John, Climacus, Saint, 6th cent. The Ladder of Divine Ascent. (Translation by Colm Luibheid and Norman Russell; notes on translation by Norman Russell; introduction by Kallistos Ware; preface by Colm Luibheid. 1982. xxviii, 301 p. Translation of: *Scala paradisi*.) Nicodemus, the Hagiorite, Saint, 1748–1809. Nicodemos of the Holy Mountain: A Handbook of Spiritual Counsel. (Translation and foreword by Peter A. Chamberas; introduction by George S. Bebis; preface by Stanley S. Harakas. NY: Paulist Press, 1989. xiii, 241 p.) (Classics of western spirituality.) Translation of *Symvouleftikon Encheiridion*. Pseudo-Macarius. The Fifty Spiritual Homilies; and, The Great Letter. (Translated and edited with an introduction by George A. Maloney; preface by Bishop Kallistos Ware. 1992. xviii, 298 p. Includes bibliographical references 289–293.) Symeon, the New Theologian, Saint, 949–1022. The Discourses. (Translation by C. J. de Catanzaro; introduction by George Maloney; preface by Basile Krivocheine. 1980. xvii, 396 p. Translation of Catecheses.)

*Corpus scriptorum ecclesiasticorum Latinorum* (Vindobonae [i.e. Vienna]: Hoelder-Pichler-Tempsky; apud C. Geroldi filium). v. 1 (1866)– . Irregular. V. 25: 1 called Nova series, v. 10. Issued by Academia Litterarum Caesarae Vindobonensis, v. 1–70; by Academia Scientiarum Austriaca, v. 71– .

Cyril, Saint, Patriarch of Alexandria, ca. 370–444. *Cyril of Jerusalem's Lectures on the Christian Sacraments: The Procatechesis and the Five Mystagogical Catecheses*. F. L. Cross, ed. London: S.P.C.K., 1951. xli, 83 p. (Texts for students; n. 51.) Greek text with introduction and translation in English. The translation is that prepared by

R. W. Church for the Library of the Fathers. Fifth impression 1978. Bibliography: p. xxxix–xli.

*Desert Wisdom: Sayings from the Desert Fathers.* Selected and translated by Yushi Nomura. Garden City, NY: Doubleday, 1982. xv, 106 p. "Translated from texts found in *Patrologia Latina,* volume 73, compiled by J. P. Migne, Paris, 1849, and in *Patrologia Graeca,* volume 65, compiled by J. P. Migne, Paris, 1858."

Ephraem, Syrus, Saint, 303–373. *The Harp of the Spirit: Eighteen Poems of Saint Ephrem.* Introduction and translation by Sebastian Brock. 2d enlarged ed. San Bernardino, CA: Borgo Press, 1988. 89 p. Reprint. Originally published: London: Fellowship of St. Alban and St. Sergius, 1983. (Studies supplementary to Sobornost; n. 4.) Includes bibliographical references (p. 86–89).

————. *Hymns on Paradise.* Commentary and translation from Syriac by Sebastian Brock. Crestwood, NY: St. Vladimir's Seminary Press, 1989. 240 p. Translation of *Hymni de paradiso* and Section 2 of *Commentarium in Genesim.*

*Explanation by Blessed Theophylact, Archbishop of Ochrid and Bulgaria, of the Holy Gospel according to St. Matthew.* Translated from the original Greek. House Springs, MO: Chrysostom Press, 1992.

*Fathers of the Church* [series]. Washington, DC: Catholic University of America Press, 1947– . See especially: 37. John, of Damascus, Saint. Writings: The Fount of Knowledge. (Translated by Frederic H. Chase, Jr. 1958. 1, 426 p. Bibliography: p. xxxviii.) 61, 64. Cyril, Saint, Patriarch of Alexandria, ca. 370–444. The Works of Saint Cyril of Jerusalem. (Translated by Leo P. McCauley and Anthony A. Stephenson. 1969–70. 2 v.) 76–77: Cyril, Saint, Patriarch of Alexandria, ca. 370–444. St. Cyril of Alexandria: Letters. (Translated by John I. McEnerney. 1987. 2 v. Bibliography: v. 1, p. xi–xiii; v. 2, p. xi–xiii.)

*Fathers Speak, Saint Basil the Great, Saint Gregory of Nazianzus, Saint Gregory of Nyssa.* Selected Letters and Life-Records. Translated from the Greek and introduced by Georges A. Barrois; with a foreword by John Meyendorff. Crestwood, NY: St. Vladimir's Seminary Press, 1986. 224, [1] p.

Germanos I, Saint, Patriarch of Constantinople, d. ca. 733. *Germanos on Predestined Terms of Life.* Greek text and English translation by Charles Garton and Leendert G. Westerink. Buffalo: Department of Classics, State University of New York at Buffalo, 1979. xxix, 82 p. (Arethusa monographs; 7.) *Peri horon zoes* in English and Greek. Text and translation on facing pages.

Gregory Palamas, Saint, 1296–1359. *The One Hundred and Fifty Chapters.* Critical edition, translation [of Capita 150] and study by Robert E. Sinkewicz. Toronto, Ontario, Canada: Pontifical Institute of Mediaeval

Studies, 1988. x, 288 p. (Studies and texts; 83.) English and Greek. List of the 150 chapter headings inserted.

Gregory, of Nyssa, ca. 335–ca. 394. *The Biographical Works of Gregory of Nyssa: Proceedings of the Fifth International Colloquium on Gregory of Nyssa, Mainz, 6–10 September 1982.* Andreas Spira, ed. Cambridge, MA: Philadelphia Patristic Foundation, 1984. viii, 274 p. (Patristic monograph series; n. 12.) English, French, German, and Spanish.

———. *The Easter Sermons of Gregory of Nyssa: Translation and Commentary: Proceedings of the Fourth International Colloquium on Gregory of Nyssa, Cambridge, England, 11–15 September, 1978.* Edited by Andreas Spira and Christoph Klock with an introduction by G. Christopher Stead. Cambridge, MA: Philadelphia Patristic Foundation; Winchendon, MA: Distributed by Greeno, Hadden, 1981. x, 384 p. (Patristic monograph series; n. 9.)

———. *From Glory to Glory: Texts from Gregory of Nyssa's Mystical Writings.* Selected and with an introduction by Jean Danielou; translated and edited by Herbert Musurillo. Crestwood, NY: St. Vladimir's Seminary Press, 1979. xiv, 298 p. Reprint of the 1961 ed. published by Scribner, NY.

———. *The Life of Saint Macrina.* Translated with introduction and notes by Kevin Corrigan. Toronto, Ontario: Peregrina, 1989. 73 p. (Peregrina translations series; n. 10. Matrologia Graeca.) Includes bibliographical references (p. 7–9). Translation of *Vita Sanctae Macrinae*.

Gregory, Sinaites, Saint, ca. 1265–1346. *Saint Gregory the Sinaite: Discourse on the Transfiguration.* David Balfour, ed. San Bernardino, CA: Borgo Press, 1988. 170 p. English and Greek. "Reprinted from *Theologia*." Originally published: Athens, 1982.

*Die Griechischen Christlichen Schriftsteller der Ersten Jahrhunderte.* (Berlin: Akademie-Verlag). Bd. 1 (1897)– . Irregular. Title varies: *Griechischen christlichen Schriftsteller der ersten drei Jahrhunderte 1897–1941.* Some vols. published in rev. editions. Publication suspended 1942–52. German, Greek, or Latin. Issued by Kommission für Spätantike Religionsgeschichte der Deutschen Akademie der Wissenschaften zu Berlin (called 1897- Kirshenvater- Commission der Preussischen Akademie der Wissenschaften).

John, of Damascus, Saint. *On the Divine Images: Three Apologies Against Those Who Attack the Divine Images.* Translated by David Anderson. Crestwood, NY: St. Vladimir's Seminary Press, 1980. 107 p. Translation of *Pros tous diaballontas tas hagias eikonas*.

Leo, Diaconus, fl. 990. *Leonis Diaconi Historia e recensione Caroli Benedicti Hasii . . . : pramittitur Menologium gracorum Basilii Porphyrogeniti Imperatoris jussu editum: accedunt Hippolyti Thebani,*

*Georgidis monachi, Ignatii Diaconi, Nili cujusdam, Christophori Protoasecretis, Michaelis Hamartoli, anonymi, scripta qua supersunt.* Accurante et denuo recognoscente J.-P. Migne. Paris: Apud Garnier Fratres et J.-P. Migne, 1894. 1496 columns. (Patrologia curmpletus. Series Graca; v. 117.) Greek title romanized. Texts in Greek and Latin in parallel columns. At head of title: Traditio catholica. Saculum X, anni 977–990.

*Library of Christian Classics* [series]. Philadelphia: Westminster Press, v. 1 (1953)– . See especially: 1. Early Christian Fathers. (Newly translated and edited by Cyril C. Richardson; in collaboration with Eugene R. Fairweather, Edward Rochie Hardy, Massey Hamilton Shepherd, Jr. 1953. 415 p.) 2. Alexandrian Christianity: Selected Translations of Clement and Origen (introductions and notes by John Ernest Leonard Oulton and Henry Chadwick. 1954. 475 p.) 3. Christology of the Later Fathers. (Edited by Edward Rochie Hardy, in collaboration with Cyril C. Richardson. Ichthus ed. 1954. 400 p. Bibliography: p. 39–40.) 4. Cyril, Saint, Patriarch of Alexandria, ca. 370–444. Cyril of Jerusalem and Nemesius of Emesa. (William Telfer, ed. 1955. 466 p. Bibliography: p. 454–455.)

Maximus, Confessor, Saint, ca. 580–662. *The Church, the Liturgy, and the Soul of Man: The Mystagogia of St. Maximus the Confessor.* Translated with historical notes and commentaries by Dom Julian Stead, O.S.B. Still River, MA: St. Bede's Publications, 1982. 120 p. Translation of *Mystagogia.*

———. *Maximus Confessor: Selected Writings.* Translations and notes by George C. Berthold. London: S.P.C.K., 1985. xvi, 240 p.

Migne, Jacques Paul, comp. *Patrologiae cursus completus, seu bibliotheca universalis, integra, uniformis, commoda, oeconomica, omnium SS. Patrum, doctorum scriptorumque ecclesiasticorum . . . : Series Graeca . . .* Accurante J.-P. Migne. Paris: Migne, 1857–1866. 161 v. in 166 V. 16 and 87 in three parts, v. 86 in two parts. Greek and Latin. Also: *Index alphabeticus omnium doctorum, patrum, scriptorumque ecclesiasticorum quorum opera scriptaque vel minima in Patrologia Latina reperiuntur.* J. B. Pearson: Conspectus auctorum quorum nomina indicibus Patrologiae Graeco-Latinae a J.-P. Migne editae continentur. Ridgewood, NJ: Gregg Press, 1965. 1 v. [42] p. The Index alphabeticus is extracted from v. 218 of Migne's *Patrologia Latina,* published 1844–64. The *Conspectus auctorum* is a reprint of a separate work, first published in 1882. *Patrologiae cursus completus. Series graecae. (Indexes) Patrologiae cursus completus accurante I.-P. Migne. Series graeca. Theodorus Hopfner. Index locupletissimus tam in opera omnia omnium auctorum veterum quam im adiectas praefationes, dissertationes, commentationes omnes omnium virorum doctorum recentium per capitula opera omnium argumenta complectens.*

*Accedit indiculus auctorum ex ordine tomorum, indiculus auctorum ex ordine alphabetico, quorum operum titulis editionum recentiorum conspectus adnectitur; indiculus methodicus.* Paris: P. Geuthner, 1928–1945. 2 v.

*Patrologia orientalis* (Turnhout, Belgium: Brepols; Paris: Firmin-Didot.). Tome 1 (1904)– . In various languages with French translations.

Photius I, Saint, Patriarch of Constantinople, ca. 820–ca. 891. *The Homilies of Photius, Patriarch of Constantinople.* Translation, introduction, and commentary by Cyril Mango. Cambridge, MA: Harvard University Press, 1958. xii, 327 p. (Dumbarton Oaks studies; 3.) Translated from Greek.

———. *The Patriarch and the Prince: The Letter of Patriarch Photios of Constantinople to Khan Boris of Bulgaria.* Edited by Despina Stratoudaki White and Joseph R. Berrigan. Brookline, MA: Holy Cross Orthodox Press, 1982. 102 p. (The Archbishop Iakovos library of ecclesiastical and historical sources; n. 6.) Bibliography: p. 91–95.

———. *Patriarch Photios of Constantinople: His Life, Scholarly Contributions, and Correspondence Together with a Translation of Fifty-Two of His Letters.* Despina Stratoudaki White, ed. and comp. Brookline, MA: Holy Cross Orthodox Press, 1982. 234 p. (The Archbishop Iakovos library of ecclesiastical and historical sources; n. 5.) Bibliography: p. 204–222.

*Select Library of Nicene and Post-Nicene Fathers of the Christian Church.* First series. Edited by Philip Schaff in connection with a number of patristic scholars of Europe and America. Grand Rapids, MI: Eerdmans, 1978–1979. 14 v. English translations, with notes. Reprint of the 1886–1890 ed. published by Christian Literature Co., New York. Includes bibliographical references and indexes. See especially: 9. St. Chrysostom: On the Priesthood; Ascetic Treatises; Select Homilies and Letters; Homilies on the Statues. 10. St. Chrysostom: Homilies on the Gospel of St. Matthew. 11. St. Chrysostom: Homilies on the Acts of the Apostles and the Epistle to the Romans. 12. St. Chrysostom: Homilies on the Epistles of Paul to the Corinthians. 13. St. Chrysostom: Homilies on Galatians, Ephesians, Philippians, Colossians, Thessalonians, Timothy, Titus, and Philemon. 14. St. Chrysostom: Homilies on the Gospel of St. John and the Epistle to the Hebrews.

*Select Library of Nicene and Post-Nicene Fathers of the Christian Church.* Second series. Translated into English with prolegomena and explanatory notes, under the editorial supervision of Philip Schaff and Henry Wace. NY: The Christian literature company, 1890–1900. 14 v. Vols. 1–7 edited by Schaff and Wace. Vols. 9 and 14: New York, C. Scribner's sons; [etc., etc.] See especially: 1. Eusebius: Church History, Life of Constantine the Great, and Oration in Praise of Constantine. 1890. 2. Socrates, Sozomenus: Church Histories. 1890. 3. Theodoret, Jerome Gennadius, Rufinus: Historical Writings, etc. 1892. 4. St. Athanasius: Select Works and Letters. 1892. 5. Gregory of Nyssa: Dogmatic Treatises, etc. 1893. 7. St. Cyril of Jerusalem. St. Gregory Nazianzen. 1894. 8. St. Basil: Letters and Select Works. 1895. 9. St. Hilary of Poitiers, John of Damascus, 1899. 10. St. Ambrose: Select Works and Letters. 1896. 11. Sulpitius Severus. Vincent of Lerins. John Cassian, 1894. 12. Leo the Great. Gregory the Great. 1895. 13. Part II. Gregory the Great. Ephraim Syrus. Aphrahat. 1898. 14. The Seven Ecumenical Councils. 1900.

*Sources chrétiennes.* (Paris: Cerf). n. 1 (1941)– . Irregular. Chiefly French; some Greek and Latin.

Symeon, the New Theologian, Saint, 949–1022. *Hymns of Divine Love.* Introduction and translation by George A. Maloney. Denville, NJ: Dimension Books, n.d. 297 p.

Theodore, Studites, Saint, 759–826. *St. Theodore the Studite On the Holy Icons.* Translated by Catharine P. Roth. Crestwood, NY: St. Vladimir's Seminary Press, 1981. 115 p. Translated from the original Greek. Bibliography: p. 115.

### B. Secondary Sources

Azkoul, Michael. *The Influence of Augustine of Hippo on the Orthodox Church.* Lewiston, NY: E. Mellen Press, 1990. vi, 299 p. (Texts and studies in religion; v. 56.)

***Basil of Caesarea, Christian, Humanist, Ascetic: A Sixteen-Hundredth Anniversary Symposium.*** Edited by Paul Jonathan Fedwick. Toronto: Pontifical Institute of Mediaeval Studies, 1981. 2 v. (xxxvii, 715 p.)

Baur, Chrysostomus. *John Chrysostom and His Time.* Sr. M. Gonzaga, transl. Westminster, MD: Newman Press, 1959–60. 2 v. Translation of *Der heilige Johannes Chrysostomus und seine Zeit.*

*Christianity Among the Slavs: The Heritage of Saints Cyril and Methodius: Acts of the International Congress held on the Eleventh Centenary of the Death of St. Methodius Rome, October 8–11, 1985 Under the Direction of the Pontifical Oriental Institute.* Edited by Edward G. Farrugia . . . [et al.] with the editorial committee. Rome: Pontificium Institutum Studiorum Orientalium, 1988. ix, 409 p. (Orientalia Christiana analecta; 231.) English, French and Italian.

Dvornik, Francis. *Byzantine Missions Among the Slavs: SS. Constantine-Cyril and Methodius.* New Brunswick, NJ: Rutgers University Press, 1970. xviii, 484 p. (Rutgers Byzantine series.) Bibliography: p. 419–464.

———. *Photian and Byzantine Ecclesiastical Studies.* London: Variorum Reprints, 1974. 472 p. (Collected studies series; 32.) English and French.

Ellverson, Anna-Stina. *The Dual Nature of Man: A Study in the Theological Anthropology of Gregory of Nazianzus*. Uppsala: Almqvist & Wiksell [distributors], 1981. 119 p. (Studia doctrinae Christianae Upsaliensia; 21.) Originally presented as the author's doctoral thesis, Uppsala University.

Florovsky, Georges. *Collected Works of Georges Florovsky*. Belmont, MA: Nordland Publishing Co., 1972– . V. 4, 6–11, 13–14 published by Buchervertriebsanstalt, Vaduz. See especially: 1. Bible, Church, Tradition: An Eastern Orthodox View. 2. Christianity and Culture. 3. Creation and Redemption. 4. Aspects of Church History. 5–6. Ways of Russian Theology. 7. The Eastern Fathers of the Fourth Century. 8. The Byzantine Fathers of the Fifth Century. 9. The Byzantine Fathers of the Sixth to Eighth Century. 10. The Byzantine Ascetic and Spiritual Fathers.

*Maximus Confessor: Actes du Symposium sur Maxime le Confesseur, Fribourg, 2–5 Septembre 1980*. Edités par Felix Heinzer et Christoph Schonborn. Fribourg, Switzerland: Editions Universitaires, 1982. 438 p. (Paradosis; 27.) Contributions in French, English, or German.

Meyendorff, John. *Study of Gregory Palamas*. Translated by George Lawrence. 2d ed. London: Faith Press, 1974. 245 p. Translation of *Introduction à l'études de Grégoire Palamas*.

Nielsen, Jan Tjeerd. *Adam and Christ in the Theology of Irenaeus of Lyons. An Examination of the Function of the Adam-Christ Typology in the Adversus Haereses of Irenaeus, Against the Background of the Gnosticism of His Time*. Assen: Van Gorcum, 1968. 124 p. (Van Gorcum's theologische bibliotheek, nr. 40.) Bibliography: p. 95–109.

Obolensky, Dimitri. "Heritage of Cyril and Methodius in Russia. Paper read at a symposium on The Byzantine mission to the Slavs: St. Cyril and St. Methodius, held at Dumbarton Oaks in May 1964." In *Dumbarton Oaks Papers* (Washington), n. 19 (1965), p. [45]–65.

Prestige, George Leonard. *Fathers and Heretics: Six Studies in Dogmatic Faith with Prologue and Epilogue*. London: S.P.C.K., 1968. 432 p. (The Bampton lectures, 1940.)

―――. *God in Patristic Thought*. London: S.P.C.K., 1959. xxxiv, 318 p. "First published in 1936." "Index of patristic references, compiled by Dr. F. L. Cross" : p. 307–318.

―――. *St. Basil the Great and Apollinaris of Laodicea*. Edited from Prestige's papers by Henry Chadwick. NY: AMS Press, Inc., 1983. 68 p.

Quasten, Johannes. *Patrology*. Westminster, MD: Christian Classics, 1986. 4 v. "A Christian classic reprint" Vols. 1–3. Reprint. Originally published: Westminster, MD: Newman Press, 1950–1960.

Rorem, Paul. *Pseudo-Dionysius: A Commentary on the Texts and an Introduction to Their Influence*. Oxford: Oxford University Press, 1993. xiii, 267 p.

Ruether, Rosemary Radford. *Gregory of Nazianzus, Rhetor and Philosopher*. Oxford: Clarendon Press, 1969. viii, 184 p. Bibliography: p. 181–182.

Sahas, Daniel J. *John of Damascus on Islam. The "Heresy of the Ishmaelites."* Leiden: Brill, 1972. xvi, 171 p. Based on the author's thesis, Hartford Seminary Foundation. Bibliography: p. [160]–168.

Sherwood, Polycarp. *An Annotated Date-List of the Works of Maximus the Confessor*. Rome: Herder "Orbis Catholicus", 1952. 64 p. (Studia Anselmiana, fasc. 30.)

*Symposium Methodianum: Beiträge der internationalen Tagung in Regensburg (17. bis 24. April 1985) zum Gedenken an den 1100. Todestag des hl. Method.* Herausgegeben von Klaus Trost, Ekkehard Volkl, Erwin Wedel. Neuried: Hieronymus, 1988. xiii, 727 p. (Selecta slavica; 13) German, English, French, and Russian.

*Three Byzantine Sacred Poets: Studies of Saint Romanos Melodos, Saint John of Damascus, Saint Symeon the New Theologian*. Edited by Nomikos Michael Vaporis. Brookline, MA: Hellenic College Press, 1979. 74 p. (The Byzantine Fellowship lectures; n. 4.)

Thunberg, Lars. *Man and the Cosmos: The Vision of St. Maximus the Confessor*. With a foreword by A. M. Allchin. Crestwood, NY: St. Vladimir's Seminary Press, 1985. 184 p. Bibliography: p. 175–178.

———. *Microcosm and Mediator: The Theological Anthropology of Maximus the Confessor*. Lund: C.W.K. Gleerup, 1965. xii, 500 p. (Acta Seminarii Neotestamentici Upsaliensis; 25.) Bibliography: p. [465]–480.

Tsirpanlis, Constantine N. *The Anthropology of Saint John of Damascus*. Athens: [s.n.], 1969. 62 p. 2d printing 1980. Reprinted from Theology. Bibliography: p. 60–62.

Turner, H.J.M. *St. Symeon the New Theologian and Spiritual Fatherhood*. NY: E. J. Brill, 1990. xvi, 257 p. (Byzantina Neerlandica, fasc. 11.) Revision of author's thesis, University of Manchester, 1985.

Vallee, Gerard. *A Study in Anti-Gnostic Polemics: Irenaeus, Hippolytus and Epiphanius*. Waterloo, Ontario: Published for the Canadian Corporation for Studies in Religion/Corporation canadienne des sciences religieuses by Wilfrid Laurier University Press, 1981. xi, 144 p. (Studies in Christianity and Judaism. Etudes sur le christianisme et le judaisme; 1.) Bibliography: p. [105]–114.

Vasilii, Archbishop of Brussels and Belgium (Basil Krivocheine). *In the Light of Christ: Saint Symeon, the New Theologian (949–1022), Life, Spirituality, Doctrine*. Translated from the French by Anthony P. Gythiel. Crestwood, NY: St. Vladimir's Seminary Press, 1986. 411 p. Translation of *Dans la lumière du Christ*. Bibliography: p. 397.

Wahba, Matthias F. *The Doctrine of Sanctification in St. Athanasius' Paschal Letters*. Foreword by Bishop Kallistos of Diokleia. Cairo:

Holy Virgin Coptic Orthodox Church; Cranston, RI: St. Mary and St. Mena, 1988. 191 p. Originally presented as author's M.A. thesis, University of Ottawa, Canada. Bibliography: p. 181–186.

Winslow, Donald F. *The Dynamics of Salvation: A Study in Gregory of Nazianzus.* Cambridge, MA: Philadelphia Patristic Foundation; Winchendon, MA: Distributed by Greeno, Hadden, 1979. vii, 214 p. (Patristic monograph series; n. 7.) Revision of Ph.D., thesis, Harvard University, 1966. Bibliography: p. 201–214.

## VI. Cultural Studies

Augustinos, Gerasimos. *The Greeks of Asia Minor: Confession, Community, and Ethnicity in the Nineteenth Century.* Kent, OH: Kent State University Press, 1992. x, 270 p. Bibliographical references: p. 248–261.

Bailey, Betty Jane. *Eyes to See, Ears to Hear: Study Guide to the Peoples and Churches of the USSR with an Historical Introduction.* Bailey and Constance J. Tarasar. NY: Friendship Press, 1987. 60 p. Bibliography: p. 45–47. Filmography: p. 47–48.

Belliustin, Ioann Stefanovich. *Description of the Clergy in Rural Russia: The Memoir of a Nineteenth-Century Parish Priest.* Translated with an interpretive essay by Gregory L. Freeze. Ithaca: Cornell University Press, 1985. 214 p. Bibliography: p. 211–214. Translation of *Opisanie selskogo dukhovenstva.*

Berdiaev, Nikolai Aleksandrovich. *Dostoievsky.* Translated by Donald Attwater. NY: New American Library, 1974. 227 p. (A Meridian book.)

———. *The Russian Idea.* Translated from the Russian by R. M. French. Boston: Beacon Press, 1962. xx, 267 p. Translation of *Russkaia ideia.*

Billington, James H. *The Icon and the Axe: An Interpretive History of Russian Culture.* NY: Knopf, 1966. xviii, 786, xxxiii p.

———. *Russia Transformed—Breakthrough to Hope: August 1991.* NY: The Free Press, 1992. vi, 202 p.

Brock, Sebastian P. *Studies in Syriac Christianity.* Variorum; Brookfield, VT: Gower Publishing Co., 1992. p. (Collected studies; CS357.) Companion vol. to: *Syriac Perspectives on Late Antiquity.*

Brown, Peter Robert Lamont. *The Body and Society: Men, Women and Sexual Renunciation in Early Christianity.* NY: Columbia University Press, 1988. xx, 504 p. (Lectures on the history of religions; new ser., n. 13.) Bibliography: p. [449]–493.

———. *The Cult of the Saints: Its Rise and Function in Latin Christianity.* Chicago: University of Chicago Press, 1981. xiv, 187 p. (Haskell lectures on history of religions; new ser., n. 2.)

———. *Power and Persuasion in Late Antiquity: Towards a Christian Empire.* Madison, WI: University of Wisconsin Press, 1992. x, 182 p. (The Curti lectures; 1988.)

———. *A Social Context to the Religious Crisis of the Third Century A.D.: Protocol of the fourteenth Colloquy, 9 February 1975, The Center for Hermeneutical Studies in Hellenistic and Modern Culture.* Berkeley, CA: The Center, 1975. 52 p. (Protocol series of the colloquies of the Center for Hermeneutical Studies in Hellenistic and Modern Culture; n. 14.)

———. *Society and the Holy in Late Antiquity.* Berkeley: University of California Press, 1981. vii, 347 p.

Bulgakov, Sergei Nikolaevich. *Karl Marx as a Religious Type: His Relation to the Religion of Anthropotheism of L. Feuerbach.* Introduction by Donald W. Treadgold; edited with a preface by Virgil R. Lang; translated by Luba Barna. Belmont, MA: Büchervertriebsanstalt/Notable & Academic Books , 1979. 116 p. Translation of *Karl Marks kak religioznyi tip.*

Candea, Virgil. *Witnesses to the Romanian Presence in Mount Athos.* Candea, Constantin Simionescu; with a foreword by Emil Condurachi; editor of the English version, Daniela Bolocan. Bucharest: Editura Sport-Turism, 1979. 12, 94 p.

Chatzidakis, Manolis. *Byzantine Athens.* Athens: M. Pechlivanides, 196– [12] p., [80] p. of plates (The face of Greece.) Text in English, French, and German.

*Christianity and Government in Russia and the Soviet Union: Reflections on the Millennium.* Sergei Pushkarev, Vladimir Rusak, and Gleb Yakunin. Boulder: Westview Press, 1989. xii, 166 p. (CCRS series on change in contemporary Soviet society.) Translated from the Russian.

Clement, Olivier. *The Spirit of Solzhenitsyn.* Translated by Sarah Fawcett and Paul Burns. London: Search Press; NY: Barnes & Noble Books, 1976. 234 p.

Cochrane, Charles Norris. *Christianity and Classical Culture: A Study of Thought and Action from Augustus to Augustine.* NY: Oxford University Press, 1957. vii, 523 p. (Galaxy book.) Reprint. Originally published: Oxford: Clarendon Press, 1940.

Constantelos, Demetrios J. *Byzantine Philanthropy and Social Welfare.* 2d rev. ed. New Rochelle, NY: A. D. Caratzas, 1991. xviii, 282 p.

———. *Poverty, Society and Philanthropy in the Late Mediaeval Greek World.* New Rochelle: Caratzas/Orpheus Publishing Inc., 1988. ca. 240 p. (Studies in the social and religious history of the medieval Greek world; v. 2.)

Counelis, James Steve. *Higher Learning and Orthodox Christianity.* Scranton, PA: University of Scranton Press, 1990. xvi, 235 p. Includes bibliographical references (p. 195–197).

Dampier, Margaret G. *History of the Orthodox Church in Austria-Hungary.* London: Rivingtons, 1905– . Contents: 1. Hermannstadt.

Daniel, David. *The Orthodox Church of India. History.* 2d ed. New

Delhi: Rachel David, 1986. xii, 622 p. Projected as part 1 of a 2-vol. set. No more published. "The second edition is brought out . . . revised and enlarged"—p. iv. Bibliography: p. [611]–614.

Davis, Nathaniel. *A Long Walk to Church*. Boulder, CO: Westview Press, 1994.

Duncan, Peter, J.S. and Martyn Rady, eds. *Towards a New Community*. London: University of London School of Slavonic and East European Studies, 1993. 193 p.

Dvornik, Francis. *The Slavs in European History and Civilization*. New Brunswick, NJ: Rutgers University Press, 1992. xxviii, 688 p. Includes bibliographical references (p. 565–635) and index.

*East and West: Today and Yesterday*. Sir Steven Runciman . . . et al. Tunbridge Wells, Kent, England: Institute for Cultural Research, 1978. 112 p. (I.C.R. monograph series; n.16.)

Englezakis, Benedict. *Studies and Documents Relating to the History of the Church of Cyprus from the Fourth to the Twentieth Centuries*. Translated by Norman Russell. Aldershot, Hampshire: Variorum, 1995.

Fedotov, Georgii Petrovich. *The Russian Religious Mind*. Cambridge, MA: Harvard University Press, 1946–1966. 2 v. "Selected literature": v. 1, p. [413]–424. "Bibliography of the writings of George P. Fedotov (1886–1951) compiled and edited by Thomas E. Bird": v. 2, p. [397]–413. Contents: I. Kievan Christianity. II. The Middle Ages, the Thirteenth to the Fifteenth Centuries, edited, with a foreword, by John Meyendorff. See section I.B., above, for information on Fedotov's Collected Works.

Fennell, John Lister Illingworth. *A History of the Russian Church to 1448*. New York: Longman, 1995.

Florovsky, Georges. *Ways of Russian Theology*. General editor, Richard S. Haugh; translated by Robert L. Nichols. Belmont, MA: Nordland Publishing Co., 1979–1987. 2 v. (Collected works of Georges Florovsky; v. 5–6.) Translation of *Puti russkogo bogosloviia*. Vols. 6. published: Vaduz, Liechtenstein: Büchervertriebsanstalt; Belmont, MA: Notable & Academic Books [distributor], 1987. See section I.B., above, for information on Florovsky's collected works.

Frazee, Charles A. *From Supplication to Revolution: A Documentary Social History of Imperial Russia*. NY: Oxford University Press, 1988. xv, 331 p. Bibliography: p. [317]–324.

———. *The Orthodox Church and Independent Greece, 1821–1852*. London: Cambridge University Press, 1969. viii, 220 p. Bibliography: p. 198–211.

Freeze, Gregory L. *The Parish Clergy in Nineteenth-Century Russia: Crisis, Reform, Counter-Reform*. Princeton, NJ: Princeton University Press, 1983. xxxii, 507 p. Bibliography: p. [481]–496.

———. *The Russian Levites: Parish Clergy in the Eighteenth Century.* Cambridge, MA: Harvard University Press, 1977. xi, 325 p. (Harvard University. Russian Research Center. Studies, 78\78.) Bibliography: p. 299–317.

Hamant, Yves. *Alexandre Men: un temoin pour la Russie de ce temps.* Préface du cardinal J.-M. Lustiger. Paris: Mame, 1993.

Hart, Laurie Kain. *Time, Religion, and Social Experience in Rural Greece.* Lanham, MD: Rowman & Littlefield, 1992. xviii, 292 p. (Greek studies.) Includes bibliographical references (p. 273–286) and index.

Himka, John-Paul, Flynn, James T. and James Niessen. *Religious Compromise, Political Salvation.* Pittsburgh: Center for Russian and Eastern European Studies, University of Pittsburgh, 1993.

*History of the Hellenic World.* George Phylactopoulos, ed. English translation directed by Philip Sherrard. Athens: kdotike Athenon. 1974– . Translation of *Historia tou Hellenikou Ethnous.* Bibliography: v. 1, p. 392–397. Contents: 1. Prehistory and Protohistory. 2. The Archaic Period.

*Holy Women of the Syrian Orient.* Introduced and translated by Sebastian P. Brock and Susan Ashbrook Harvey. Berkeley: University of California Press, 1987. x, 197 p. (The Transformation of the classical heritage; 13.) Bibliography: p. 183–193.

Iroshnikov, Mikhail Pavlovich. *Before the Revolution: St. Petersburg in Photographs, 1890–1914.* Iroshnikov, Yuri B. Shelaev, Liudmila A. Protsai; foreword by James H. Billington; introduction by Dimitry S. Likhachov. NY: Harry N. Abrams; Leningrad: Nauka Publishers: JV SMART, 1991. 310 p. "Translated from the Russian by Evgueni Filippov"—T.p. verso.

Kartashev, Anton Vladimirovich. *70 let Izdatelstva "YMCA-Press": 1920–1990.* Kartashev and N. A. Struve. Paris: YMCA-Press, 1990. 40 p.

Kazhdan, Aleksandr Petrovich. *People and Power in Byzantium: An Introduction to Modern Byzantine Studies.* Kazhdan and Giles Constable. Washington, DC: Dumbarton Oaks, Center for Byzantine Studies, Trustees for Harvard University, 1982. xxi, 218 p.

Kniazeff, Alexis. *L'Institut Saint-Serge: de l'académie d'autrefois au rayonnement d'aujourd'hui.* Paris: Beauchesne, 1974. 152 p. (Le Point théologique; 14.) Bibliography: p. 149–150.

Kortschmaryk, Frank B. *Christianization of the European East and Messianic Aspirations of Moscow as the "Third Rome".* NY: Studium Research Institute, 1971. 56 p. "Shevchenko Scientific Society, n. 10." Bibliography: p. 42–44.

*Landmarks: A Collection of Essays on the Russian Intelligentsia, 1909.* Berdyaev . . . et al.; edited by Boris Shragin, Albert Todd; translated by Marian Schwartz. NY: Karz Howard, 1977. lv, 210 p. Translation of *Vekhi*.

*Legacy of St. Vladimir: Byzantium, Russia, America*. Edited by J. Breck, J. Meyendorff, and E. Silk. Crestwood, NY: St. Vladimir's Seminary Press, 1990. vi, 280 p. "Papers presented at a symposium commemorating the fiftieth anniversary of St. Vladimir's Orthodox Theological Seminary, Crestwood, NY, September 27–October 1, 1988."

Levin, Eve. *Sex and Society in the World of the Orthodox Slavs, 900–1700*. Ithaca, NY: Cornell University Press, 1989. xiv, 326 p. Bibliography: p. 303–318.

*Light From the East: a Symposium on the Oriental Orthodox and Assyrian Churches*. Henry Hill, comp. & ed. Toronto: Anglican Book Centre, 1988. 164 p.

Limbiris, Vasilike. *Divine Heiress*. New York: Routledge, 1994. 199 p.

Lowrie, Donald Alexander. *Saint Sergius in Paris: The Orthodox Theological Institute*. NY: Macmillan, [Introd., 1951]; London: S.P.C.K., 1954. ix, 119p.

———. *Vision of Unity*. Crestwood, NY: St. Vladimir's Seminary Press, 1987. 192 p.

Lucas, Phillip Charles. *The Odyssey of a New Religion*. Bloomington: Indiana University Press, 1995.

Mango, Cyril and Gilbert Dagron, eds. *Constantinople and Its Hinterland*. Aldershot, Hampshire, Great Britain; Brookfield, VT: Variorum, 1995. Papers from the Twenty-seventh Spring Symposium of Byzantine Studies, Oxford, April, 1993.

*The Millennium: Christianity and Russia, A.D. 988–1988*. Edited by Albert Leong. Crestwood, NY: St. Vladimir's Seminary Press, 1990. 177 p.

Mochulskii, Konstantin. *Dostoyevsky: His Life and Work*. Translated, with an introduction, by Michael A. Minihan. Princeton, NJ: Princeton University Press, 1967. xxii, 687 p. Translation of *Dostoevskii: zhizn i tvorchestvo*.

Monfasani, John. *Byzantine Scholars in Renaissance Italy*. Aldershot, Hampshire, Great Britain; Brookfield, VT: Variorum, 1995.

Mousalimas, S. A. *The Transition from Shamanism to Russian Orthodoxy in Alaska*. Providence, RI: Berghahn Books, 1994.

Obolensky, Dimitri. *Byzantine Inheritance of Eastern Europe*. London: Variorum Reprints, 1982. 1 v. (Collected studies series; CS156.) Reprint of papers in English and French, originally published 1969–1981.

*Orthodox Church in Canada: A Chronology. Historique de l'Eglise orthodoxe au Canada*. Ottawa: Archdiocese of Canada, Orthodox Church in America. Archidiocèse du Canada, Eglise orthodoxe en Amérique, 1988. 57 p. Text in English and French; summary in Ukrainian.

Papadopoullos, Theodoros. *Studies and Documents Relating to the History of the Greek Church and People Under Turkish Domination.* 2d, rev. ed. Brookfield, VT: Variorum Group, 1990. xxiv, 432 p. "[Planosparaktes], a document in political verse": p. Includes bibliographical references, p. 430–432, and index.

Papoutsis, Carole. *The Festivals of Greek Easter.* Illustrated by Jane Porter. Athens: s.n., 1982 (Printed by D. Desyllas.) 79 p. Bibliography: p. 79.

Pelikan, Jaroslav Jan. *Christianity and Classical Culture: The Metamorphosis of Natural Theology in the Christian Encounter with Hellenism.* New Haven: Yale University Press, 1993. (Gifford lectures at Aberdeen; 1992–1993.)

Ramet, Sabrina Petra. *Balkan Babel: Politics, Culture, and Religion in Yugoslavia.* Boulder: Westview Press, 1992.

Raya, Joseph. *Byzantine Church and Culture.* Allendale, NJ: Alleluia Press, 1992.

Riasanovsky, Nicholas Valentine. *Russia and the West in the Teaching of the Slavophiles: A Study of Romantic Ideology.* Cambridge: Harvard University Press, 1952. 244 p. (Harvard historical studies; v. 61.) Bibliography: p. [219]–234. "Original version . . . was written as a doctoral dissertation at Oxford University."

*Romanian Orthodox Church: An Album-Monograph.* Translated from Romanian into English by Remus Rus. Bucharest: Bible and Orthodox Mission Institute Pub. House of the Romanian Orthodox Church, 1987. 365 p.

Romanides, John S. *Franks, Romans, Feudalism, and Doctrine: An Interplay Between Theology and Society.* Brookline, MA: Holy Cross Orthodox Press, 1982. 98 p. (Patriarch Athenagoras memorial lectures.)

*Russian America: The Forgotten Frontier.* Edited by Barbara Sweetland Smith and Redmond J. Barnett. Tacoma, WA: Washington State Historical Society, 1990. 256 p.

*Russian Culture in Modern Times.* Edited by Robert P. Hughes and Irina Paperno. Berkeley: University of California Press, 1994.

*Russian Priests of Tomorrow.* London: Published by the Appeal for the Russian Clergy & Church Aid Fund, 1932. 11 p.

*Russian Traditional Culture: Debates on Religion and Gender.* Editor, Marjorie Mandelstam Balzer. Armonk, NY: M. E. Sharpe, 1991. 83 p. (Soviet anthropology and archaeology; v. 29, no. 3.) Translated from the Russian.

Schaeffer, Frank. *Dancing Alone.* Brookline, MA: Holy Cross Orthodox Press, 1994. 327 p.

*Seeking God: the Recovery of Religious Identity in Orthodox Russia, Ukraine, and Georgia.* Edited by Stephen K. Batalden. Dekalb: Northern Illinois University Press, 1993.

*Slavic Cultures in the Middle Ages.* Edited by Boris Gasparov and Olga Raevsky-Hughes. Berkeley: University of California Press, 1993. (Christianity and the Eastern Slavs; v. 1.) (California Slavic studies; 16– .) English and Russian; summaries in English. Based on papers delivered at two international conferences held in May 1988 at the University of California, Berkeley and the Keenan Institute for Advanced Russian Studies to commemorate the millennium of the Christianization of Kievan Rus'.

Soldatow, George, ed. *Nestor, Bishop of the Aleutians and Alaska, 1825–1882.* Translated by George Soldatow. Minneapolis: AARDM Press, 1993. 476 p.

Stanton, Leonard J. *The Optina Pustyn Monastery in the Russian Literary Imagination: Iconic Vision in Works by Dostoevsky, Gogol, Tolstoy, and Others.* NY: P. Lang, 1992. (Middlebury studies in Russian language and literature; v. 3.)

Trubetskoi, Nikolai Sergeevich. *N.S. Trubetzkoy's Letters and Notes.* Prepared for publication by Roman Jakobson with the assistance of H. Baran, O. Ronen, and Martha Taylor. NY: Mouton, 1985. xxiii, 506 p., [13] p. of plates. (Janua linguarum. Series maior; 47.) English and Russian. Reprint. Originally published: The Hague; Paris: Mouton, 1975.

———. *Writings on Literature.* Edited, translated, and introduced by Anatoly Liberman. Minneapolis: University of Minnesota Press, 1990. xlvi, 127 p. (Theory and history of literature; v. 72.)

Ugolnik, Anthony. *The Illuminating Icon.* Grand Rapids, MI: Eerdmans, 1988. xxiv, 276 p.

*Ultimate Questions: An Anthology of Modern Russian Religious Thought.* Edited by Alexander Schmemann. NY: Holt, Rinehart and Winston, 1965. vii, 310 p.

Vryonis, Speros. *The Decline of Medieval Hellenism in Asia Minor and the Process of Islamization from the Eleventh Through the Fifteenth Century.* Berkeley: University of California Press, 1971. xvii, 532 p. (California. University. University at Los Angeles. Center for Medieval and Renaissance Studies. Publications, 4\4.)

Ware, Timothy. *Eustratios Argenti: A Study of the Greek Church Under Turkish Rule.* Oxford: Clarendon Press, 1964. xii, 196 p. "A list of the writings of Eustratios Argenti": p. [176]–179. Bibliography: p. [180]–187.

West, Rebecca, Dame. *Black Lamb and Grey Falcon: A Journey Through Yugoslavia.* Rev. London: Macmillan, 1982. 1181 p. (Papermac.) Previous ed.: in 2 vols. 1942. Bibliography: p. 1153–1158.

Williams, Benjamin D. *Oriented Leadership: Why All Christians Need It.* Syosset, NY: Orthodox Church of America, 1994.

Yakunin, Gleb. *Birnam Wood is Here: Letters on Civil Rights in the*

*U.S.S.R.* Yakunin, Lev Regelson; edited by H. S. Dakin. San Francisco: H. S. Dakin, 1977. 113 p. Bibliography: p. 109–111.

———. *Letters from Moscow: Religion and Human Rights in the USSR.* Yakunin and Lev Regelson; edited by Jane Ellis. Keston, England: Keston College, Centre for the Study of Religion and Communism; San Francisco: H. S. Dakin, 1978. vi, 147 p. (Keston book; n. 15.) Bibliography: p. 144.

Young, Alexey. *The Russian Orthodox Church Outside Russia.* Edited by Karl Pruter and Paul David Seldis. San Bernardino, CA: St. Willibrord's Press, 1993. 136 p.

Zander, Leon Alexander. *Western Orthodoxy.* South Canaan, PA: St. Tikhon Press, 1958?. 46 p.

## VII. Ecumenism

*Augsburg and Constantinople: The Correspondence Between the Tubingen Theologians and Patriarch Jeremiah II of Constantinople on the Augsburg Confession.* George Mastrantonis. Brookline, MA: Holy Cross Orthodox Press, 1982. xix, 350 p. (The Archbishop Iakovos library of ecclesiastical and historical sources; n. 7.)

*Augsburg Confession in Ecumenical Perspective: With Anglican, Baptist, Methodist, Orthodox, Reformed, and Roman Catholic Contributions.* Harding Meyer, ed. Stuttgart: Kreuz, 1979. x, 190 p. (LWF report; 6/7.)

Bulgakov, Afanasii. *The Question of Anglican Orders: In Respect to a "Vindication" of the Papal Decision, Which Was Drawn Up by the English Roman Catholic Bishops at the End of 1897.* Translation by W. J. Birkbeck. London: S.P.C.K.; NY: E. & J. B. Young, 1899. 46 p. [1] leaf. (Church Historical Society. 55.)

Bulgakov, Sergei Nikolaevich. *Father Sergius Bulgakov, 1871–1944: A Collection of Articles by Fr. Bulgakov for the Fellowship of St. Alban and St. Sergius and Now Reproduced by the Fellowship to Commemorate the 25th Anniversary of the Death of This Great Ecumenist.* London: Fellowship of St. Alban and St. Sergius, 1969. [3], ii, 48 p.

Calian, Carnegie Samuel. *Icon and Pulpit: The Protestant-Orthodox Encounter.* Philadelphia: Westminster Press, 1968. 220 p. Bibliography: p. 171–181. Bibliographical references included in "Notes" (p. 183–214).

———. *Theology Without Boundaries: Encounters of Eastern Orthodoxy and Western Tradition.* Louisville, KY: Westminster/John Knox, 1992. 13, 130 p.

*Church, Kingdom, World: The Church As Mystery and Prophetic Sign.* Gennadios Limouris, ed. Geneva: World Council of Churches, 1986. xii, 209 p. (Faith and order paper; n. 130.)

*Church of God: An Anglo-Russian Symposium.* By members of the Fellowship of St. Alban and St. Sergius. E. L. Mascall, gen. ed. London: S.P.C.K., 1934. xiii, 230 p.

*Come, Holy Spirit, Renew the Whole Creation: An Orthodox Approach for the Seventh Assembly of the World Council of Churches, Canberra, Australia, 6–21 February, 1991.* Gennadios Limouris, ed. Brookline, MA: Holy Cross Orthodox Press, 1990. ix, 263 p.

Consultation of Orthodox Theologians, New Valamo, Finland, 1977. *The New Valamo Consultation: The Ecumenical Nature of the Orthodox Witness.* Geneva: World Council of Churches, Orthodox Task Force, 1979?. 86 p.

Consultation of Orthodox Women, Agapia, Romania, 1976. *Orthodox Women, Their Role and Participation in the Orthodox Church: Report on the Consultation of Orthodox Women, September 11–17, 1976, Agapia, Roumania.* Edited by Constance J. Tarasar, Irina Kirillova; illustrated by June Magaziner. Geneva: World Council of Churches, 1977. 52 p.

*Creation: the Eighth Theological Conversations between the Evangelical Lutheran Church of Finland and the Russian Orthodox Church, Pyhtitsa and Leningrad, June 9th–19th, 1989.* Helsinki: Church Council for Foreign Affairs, Ecclesiastical Board, 1991.

Davey, Colin. *Pioneer for Unity: Metrophanes Kritopoulos (1589–1639) and Relations Between the Orthodox, Roman Catholic and Reformed Churches.* London: British Council of Churches, 1987. vi, 314 p.

*Dialogues oecuméniques hier et aujourd'hui.* Chambesy-Geneva: Editions du Centre orthodoxe du Patriarcat oecuménique, 1985. 415 p. (Les études théologiques de Chambesy. Ai theologikai meletai tou Sampezy; 5.) Proceedings of the 5th Séminaire théologique de Chambesy. English, French, and German.

Fahey, Michael Andrew. *Trinitarian Theology East and West: St. Thomas Aquinas—St. Gregory Palamas.* Fahey and John Meyendorff. Brookline, MA: Holy Cross Orthodox Press, 1977. 43 p. (Patriarch Athenagoras memorial lectures.)

*Finnish Lutheran-Orthodox Dialogue: 1989 and 1990.* Helsinki: Church Council for Foreign Affairs, Church Council, 1993. 109 p.

*Georges Florovsky: Russian Intellectual and Orthodox Churchman.* Edited by Andrew Blane. Crestwood, NY: St. Vladimir's Seminary Press, 1993.

Hebly, J. A. *The Russians and the World Council of Churches: Documentary Survey of the Accession of the Russian Orthodox Church to the World Council of Churches, with Commentary.* Belfast: Christian Journals, 1978. 181 p.

*Jesus Christ, The Life of the World: An Orthodox Contribution to the Vancouver Theme.* Ion Bria, ed. Geneva: World Council of Churches, 1982. vi, 121 p.

Khomiakov, Aleksei Stepanovich. *The Church Is One*. George Grabbe, intro. NY: Division of Publications, Archdiocese, Eastern Orthodox Catholic Church in America, American Mission, 1953. 48 p.

Kilmartin, Edward J. *Toward Reunion: The Roman Catholic and the Orthodox Churches*. NY: Paulist Press, 1979. v, 118 p. (An Exploration book.)

Likoudis, James. *Ending the Byzantine Greek Schism*. New Rochelle, NY: Catholics United for the Faith, 1992.

Litvack, Leon. *John Mason Neale and the Quest for Sobornost*. Oxford: Clarendon Press; New York: Oxford University Press, 1994.

*Luther et la réforme allemande dans une perspective oecuménique*. Chambesy-Geneva: Editions du Centre orthodoxe du patriarcat oecuménique, 1983. 502 p. (Les études théologiques de Chambesy. Ai theologikai meletai tou sampezu; 3.) Contributions in French, English, and German. "Le Centre orthodoxe du Patriarchat oecuménique à Chambesy-Genève a organisé, du 25 avril au 29 mai 1982, un séminaire théologique consacré à une question oecuménique actuelle"— foreword, p. 5.

"Lutheranism and Orthodoxy": Theme Issue. *Lutheran World*, v. 23, n. 3 (1976) p. 161–220.

Macris, George P. *The Orthodox Church and the Ecumenical Movement During the Period 1920–1969*. Seattle: St. Nectarios Press, 1986. 185 p., [9] p. of plates. Bibliography: p. 181–185.

Meyendorff, John. *Catholicity and the Church*. Crestwood, NY: St. Vladimir's Seminary Press, 1983. 160 p.

*New Man: An Orthodox and Reformed Dialogue*. Edited by John Meyendorff and Joseph McLelland. New Brunswick, NJ: Agora Books, 1973. 170 p.

Nichols, Aidan. *Rome and the Eastern Churches: A Study in Schism*. Edinburgh: T&T Clark, 1992.

*One in 2000?: Towards Catholic-Orthodox Unity*. Edited by Paul McPartlan. Middlegreen, Slough, U.K.: St. Pauls, 1993.

*The Orthodox Church and the Churches of the Reformation: A Survey of Orthodox-Protestant Dialogues*. Contributions by Nils Ehrenstrom . . . et al. Geneva: Faith and Order Commission, World Council of Churches, 1975. vi, 101 p. (Faith and order paper; no. 76.)

*The Orthodox Church in the Ecumenical Movement: Documents and Statements 1902–1975*. Constantin G. Patelos, ed. Geneva: World Council of Churches, 1978. 360 p.

Orthodox Theological Society in America. *An Orthodox Response to the Preliminary Draft for the Fourth Assembly of the World Council of Churches to be Held at Uppsala*. London: Fellowship of St. Alban and St. Sergius, 1968. [22] p.

*Orthodox Thought: Reports of Orthodox Consultations Organized by the*

*World Council of Churches, 1975–1982.* Georges Tsetsis, ed. Geneva: Orthodox Task Force, World Council of Churches, 1983. 96 p.

*Orthodoxie et mouvement oecuménique.* Chambesy-Geneva: Editions du Centre orthodoxe du patriarcat oecuménique, 1986. 228 p. (Etudes théologiques de Chambesy. Ai theologikai meletai tou sampezu; 6.) Proceedings of the 6th Séminaire théologique de Chambesy.

Papademetriou, George C. *Essays on Orthodox Christian-Jewish Relations.* Bristol, IN: Wyndham Hall Press, 1990. 133 p.

Saliba, Philip. *Feed My Sheep: The Thought and Words of Philip Saliba: On the Occasion of His Twentieth Year in the Episcopacy.* Edited by Joseph J. Allen. Crestwood, NY: St. Vladimir's Seminary Press, 1987. 134 p.

*Salvation in Christ: A Lutheran-Orthodox Dialogue.* Edited and with an introduction by John Meyendorff and Robert Tobias. Minneapolis: Augsburg, 1992. 187 p. Includes bibliographical references (p. 171–183).

Schaeffer, Frank. *Dancing Alone: The Quest for Orthodox Faith in the Age of False Religion.* Brookline, MA: Holy Cross Orthodox Press, 1994.

*Sofia Consultation: Orthodox Involvement in the World Council of Churches.* Todor Sabev, ed. Geneva: World Council of Churches, Orthodox Task Force, 1982. 129 p.

*Spirit of Truth: Ecumenical Perspectives on the Holy Spirit: Papers of the Holy Spirit Consultation, October 24–25, 1985, Brookline, Massachusetts.* Sponsored by the Commission on Faith and Order, NCCCUSA; edited by Theodore Stylianopoulos and S. Mark Heim. Brookline, MA: Holy Cross Orthodox Press, 1986. vi, 197 p.

Suttner, Ernst Christoph. *Church Unity: Union or Uniatism?: Catholic-Orthodox Ecumenical Perspectives.* Translated by Brian Mcneil. Rome: Centre for Indian and Inter-Religious Studies; Bangalore: Dharmaram Publications, 1991. x, 151 p. (Placid lecture series; n. 13.)

Swidler, Leonard J., ed. *Scripture and Ecumenism: Protestant, Catholic, Orthodox, and Jewish.* Pittsburgh: Duquesne University Press, 1965. vii, 197 p. (Duquesne studies. Theological series, 3.)

*Towards the Healing of Schism: The Sees of Rome and Constantinople: Public Statements and Correspondence Between the Holy See and the Ecumenical Patriarchate, 1958–1984.* Edited and translated by E. J. Stormon; introduction by Thomas F. Stransky. NY: Paulist Press, 1987. vii, 559 p. (Ecumenical documents; 3.)

Wingenbach, Gregory Charles. *Broken, Yet Never Sundered: Orthodox Witness and the Ecumenical Movement.* Brookline, MA: Holy Cross Orthodox Press, 1987. 184 p. Bibliography: p. 165–172.

World Council of Churches. Commission on Faith and Order. Standing Commission. *Minutes of the Meeting of the Standing Commission*

*Held at the Orthodox Academy, Crete, Greece, 6th–14th April 1984.* Geneva: World Council of Churches, 1984. 96 p. (Faith and order paper; n. 121.)

World Council of Churches. Orthodox Task Force. *Orthodox Contributions to Nairobi: Papers.* Compiled and presented by the Orthodox Task Force of the WCC. Geneva: World Council of Churches, 1975. iii, 35 p.

Zander, Leon Alexander. *Vision and Action.* Translated from the Russian by Natalie Duddington, with an introduction by the Bishop of Chichester. London: Gollancz, 1952. 224 p.

Zernov, Nicolas. *Fellowship of St. Alban & St. Sergius: A Historical Memoir.* In collaboration with Militza Zernov. Oxford: The Fellowship, 1979. ii, 32 p.

――――. *Orthodox Encounter: The Christian East and the Ecumenical Movement.* London: J. Clarke, 1961. xiii, 200 p.

――――. *Sunset Years: a Russian Pilgrim in the West.* London: Fellowship of St. Alban and St. Sergius, 1983. 192 p. Bibliography: p. 189–190.

## VIII. Hagiography

*The Acquisition of the Holy Spirit in Russia* [series]. Platina, CA: St. Herman of Alaska Brotherhood, 1987– . 1. Kontsevich, Ivan Mikhailovich. The Acquisition of the Holy Spirit in Ancient Russia. (Translation from the Russian by Olga Koshansky; edited by the St. Herman of Alaska Brotherhood. 1988, 368 p.) 2. Florenskii, Pavel Aleksandrovich. Salt of the Earth: Or, a Narrative on the Life of the Elder of Gethsemane Skete Hieromonk Abba Isidore. (Compiled and arranged by Paul Florensky; translated from the Russian by Richard Betts; edited and annotated, with poetry versification, by the St. Herman Brotherhood. 1987. 151 p.)

*Acta sanctorum.* 1684–1940. Paris, Rome: Victorem Palme. 67 v. New edition of work published from 1643 to 1925 narrating the lives of the Saints for each day of the calendar year. Work initiated by Joannes Bollandus in 1629 and continued by the Bollandists.

*Analecta bollandiana: Revue critique d'hagiographie.* v. 1- (1882)– . Brussels: Société des Bollandistes. Quarterly. Bulletin des publications hagiographiques. Text in Latin and French. Indexes: vols. 1–20 (1882–1901) 1 v.; vols. 21–40 (1902–22) 1 v.; vols. 41–60 (1923–42) 1 v.; vols. 1–80 (1882–1961) 1 v. Vols. for 1891- contain *Bulletin des publications hagiographiques.* Supplements: *Acta sanctorum.*

*Bibliotheca hagiographica graeca.* 3. ed., mise à jour et considérablement augmenté par François Halkin. Brussels: Société des Bollandistes, 1957–1969. 5 v. (Subsidia hagiographica, nos. 8a, 47, 65.)

*Bibliotheca hagiographica orientalis.* Ediderunt Socii Bollandiani. Brussels: Apud Editores, 1910 (1970 printing). xx, iii, 287 p. (Subsidia hagiographica; 10.)

*Blessed Paisius Velichkovsky: The Life and Ascetic Labors of Our Father, Elder Paisius, Archimandrite of the Holy Moldavian Monasteries of Niametz and Sekoul.* Optina version. By Schema-Monk Metrophanes. Platina, CA: Saint Herman of Alaska Brotherhood, 1976– . Translation of *Zhitie i pisaniia Moldavskago startsa Paisiia Velichkovskago,* published in 1847 by the Optina Monastery. Bibliography: v.1, p.283–287.

Bulgakov, Sergei Vasil'evich. *Nastol'naia kniga dlia sviashchennotserkovno-sluzhitelei; sbornik sviedienii, kasaiushchikhsia preimushchestvenno prakticheskoi dieiatel'nosti otechestvennago dukhovenstva.* Izd. 2., ispr. i dop. Khar'kov, Tip. Gub. pravleniia, 1900. [Reprinted: Graz, Akademischer Druck- u. Verlagsantalt, 1965.] 6, ii, 1272 p. "V etom izdanii 'Otdel istoriko-statisticheskii' ne pechataetsia."

Bychkov, Viktor Vasilevich. *The Aesthetic Face of Being: Theology of Pavel Florensky.* Translated from the Russian by Richard Pevear and Larissa Volokhonsky. Crestwood, NY: St. Vladimir's Seminary Press, 1993. Translation of *Esteticheskii lik bytiia.*

Demetrius, of Rostov, Saint. 1651–1709. *The Great Collection of the Lives of the Saints.* Translated by Thomas Marretta. House Springs, MO: Chrysostom Press, 1995.

*Early Christian Biographies: Lives of: St. Cyprian, by Pontius; St. Ambrose, by Paulinus; St. Augustine, by Possidius; St. Anthony, by St. Athanusius; St. Paul the First Hermit, St. Hilarion, and Malchus, by St. Jerome; St. Epiphanius, by Ennodius; with a Sermon on the Life of St. Honoratus, by St. Hilary.* Translated by Roy J. Deferrari, et al. NY: Fathers of the Church, 1952. xiv, 407 p. (The Fathers of the Church, a new translation; v. 15.)

*An Early Soviet Saint: The Life of Father Zachariah.* Translated from the Russian by Jane Ellis; and with an introduction by Sir John Lawrence. London: Mowbrays, 1976. xiv, 111 p. (Keston books; no. 6.)

Ennodius, Magnus Felix, Saint, 474–521. *The Life of Saint Epiphanius.* A translation with an introduction and commentary by Sister Genevieve Marie Cook. Washington, DC: Catholic University of America Press, 1942. xvii, 262 p. (Catholic University of America. Studies in medieval and renaissance Latin language and literature; vol. XIV.)

Ford, David. *Marriage as a Path to Holiness: Lives of Married Saints.* South Canaan, PA: St. Tikhon's Seminary Press, 1994.

*Kirchen im Kontext unterschiedlicher Kulturen: auf dem Weg ins dritte Jahrtausend; Aleksandr Men in memoriam (1935–1990).* Herausgegeben von Karl Christian Felmy . . . et al.; redaktion, Wolfgang

Heller. Göttingen: Vandenhoeck & Ruprecht, 1991. 1031 p. English, French, and German.

Kosmas ho Aitolos, Saint, 1714–1779. *Father Kosmas, The Apostle of the Poor: The Life of St. Kosmas Aitolos, Together with an English Translation of His Teaching and Letters.* Nomikos Michael Vaporis, ed.; illustrated by Vasilia Laskaris. Brookline, MA: Holy Cross Orthodox Press, 1977. ix, 164 p. (The Archbishop Iakovos library of ecclesiastical and historical sources; n. 4.)

*Life of Pachomius: vita prima Graeca.* Translated by Apostolos N. Athanassakis; introduction by Birger A. Pearson. Missoula, MT: Published by Scholars Press for the Society of Biblical Literature, 1975. xi, 201 p. (Texts and translations; 7. Early Christian literature series; 2.) English and Greek.

*Life of Saint Luke of Steires.* Text, translation, and commentary by W. Robert Connor and Carolyn Connor. Brookline, MA: Hellenic College Press, 1989. (The Archbishop Iakovos library of ecclesiastical and historical sources; n. 18.) Translation of *Bios kai politeia kai merike thaumaton diegesis tou hosiou patros hemon kai thaumatourgou Louka tou neou tou en Helladi keimenou.*

*Life of Saint Nicholas of Sion.* Text and translation by Ihor Sevcenko and Nancy Patterson Sevcenko. Brookline, MA: Hellenic College Press, 1984. 157 p. (The Archbishop Iakovos library of ecclesiastical and historical sources; n. 10.) Translation of *Bios kai politeia tou en hagiois patros hemon Nikolaou archimandritou genamenou tes hagias Sion kai Episkopou tes Pinareon poleos.*

*Life of Saint Nikon.* Text, translation, and commentary by Denis Sullivan. Brookline, MA: Hellenic College Press, 1987. 314 p. (The Archbishop Iakovos Library of ecclesiastical and historical sources; n. 14.) English and Greek. Predominantly based on the Barberini version of the original Greek manuscript entitled *Bios kai politeia kai merike thaumaton diegesis tou hagiou kai thaumatourgou Nikonos myroblytou tou Metanoeite-*The Life, Conduct, and Partial Narration of the Miracles of the Holy Miracle-Worker Nikon Myrobletes the Metanoeite. Bibliography: p. 305–307.

*Lives of Eminent Russian Prelates: I. Nikon, Sixth Patriarch of Moscow, II. Saint Demetrius, Metropolitan of Rostoff, III. Michael, Metropolitan of Novgorod and S. Petersburg.* London: Joseph Masters, 1854. xvi, 147 p.

*The Lives of the Holy Apostles: Saints Peter, Paul, Andrew, James . . . From the Menology of St. Dimitri of Rostov in Russian and the Great Synaxaristes of the Orthodox Church in Greek.* Translated by Isaac E. Lambertsen and Holy Apostles Convent. Buena Vista, CO: Holy Apostles Convent, 1988. 281 p. Two lives selected and translated from *Ho Megas synaxaristes tes Orthodoxou Ekklesias.* Remainder selected and translated from *Zhitiia sviatykh na russkom iazyke*, a Russian adaptation of Dimitri of Rostov's *Cheti-Minei*.

*The Lives of the Holy Apostles: Saints Peter, Paul, Andrew, James . . . From the Menology of St. Dimitri of Rostov in Russian and the Great Synaxaristes of the Orthodox Church in Greek*. Translated by Isaac E. Lambertsen and Holy Apostles Convent. Buena Vista, CO: Holy Apostles Convent, 1990– . Vols. 2, 3, 4.

*Lives of the Saints of the Holy Land and the Sinai Desert*. Translated by Holy Apostles Convent, Leo Papadopulos, and others. Buena Vista, CO: Holy Apostles Convent, 1988. 566 p. Bibliography: p. 564–566.

*Modern Orthodox Saints*. Belmont, MA: Institute for Byzantine and Modern Greek Studies, v. 1 (1971)– . Cavarnos, Constantine, comp.

Moss, Vladimir. *The Saints of Anglo-Saxon England*. Seattle: St. Nectarios Press, 1992.

Papmehl, K. A. *Metropolitan Platon of Moscow (Petr Levshin, 1737–1812): the Enlightened Prelate, Scholar and Educator*. Newtonville, MA: Oriental Research Partners, 1983. 2, 2, 143 p. (Russian biography series; no. 16.) Bibliography: p. 127–135.

Philotheos, Patriarch of Constantinopole. *Philotheou Konstantinoupoleos tou Kokkinou: Hagiotitika erga*. Demetriou Tsame G. Thessalonica: Kentron Byzantinon Ereunon, 1985– . (Thessalonikeis Byzantinoi Suggrapheis-Thessalonian Byzantine writers; 4.)

Popovich, Justin. *Lives of the Saints*. Astoria, NY: Studion Publishers.

Poulos, George. *Orthodox Saints: Spiritual Profiles for Modern Man*. 2d, expanded ed. Brookline, MA: Holy Cross Orthodox Press, 1990–1991. V. 1, 3. Contents: 1. January 1 to March 31. 3. July 1 to September 30.

Rogich, Daniel M. *Serbian Patericon*. Platina, CA: St. Herman of Alaska Brotherhood: St. Paisius Abbey Press, 1994.

Roshestvensky, A. *His Holiness Tikhon, Patriarch of Moscow and of All the Russias: A Memoir*. Translated by H. P. London: Society for Promoting Christian Knowledge; NY: Macmillan, 1923. 31 p.

Semenov-Tian-Shanskii, Aleksandr (Bishop). *Father John of Kronstadt, A Life*. Crestwood, NY: St. Vladimir's Seminary Press, 1979. 197 p. Translation of *Otets Ioann Kronshtadtskii*. "A translation from the Russian text of Bishop Alexander Semenoff-Tian-Chansky published in New York 1955."

*Subsidia hagiographica*. No. 1– (1886)– . Brussels: Société des Bollandistes. Irregular. Suspended publication 1937–1949. Most of the early volumes of this series were issued as supplements to *Analecta Bollandiana*.

Swan, Jane. *A Biography of Patriarch Tikhon*. Jordanville, NY: Holy Trinity Russian Orthodox Monastery, 1964. 112 p.

Bibliography • 403

Synaxarion. *Ho Megas synaxaristes tes Orthodoxou Ekklesias.* Ekdidetai analomasi kai epimeleia tou Matthaiou Lange. 6e ekd. Athens: Ekd. Hieras Mones Metamorphoseos Kouvara Attikes, 1980–1984. 14 v. Facsim. reprint (v.1, 1982) of 3d ed.

*The Three Hierarchs: From the Menology of St. Dimitri of Rostov, in Russian.* Translated by Isaac E. Lambertsen and Xenia Endres. Buena Vista, CO: Dormition Skete, 1985. 192 p. Translations of excerpts from *Zhitiia sviatykh na russkom iazyke,* an adaptation in Russian of Dimitri of Rostov's *Cheti-Minei.*

Vaughan, Jack Chapline. *Emperor Constantine I, His Mother, Empress Helena, and Their Establishment of the True Christian Religion (306–337 A.D.).* Little Rock, AR (P.O. Box 7632, Little Rock 72217): Vaughan, 1989. iv, 239 p. (Vaughan's Eurasian histories; v. 7.)

Velichkovsii, Paisii, Saint, 1722–1794. *The Life of Paisij Velyckovs'kyj.* Translated by J.M.E. Featherstone; with an introduction by Anthony-Emil N. Tachiaos. Cambridge, MA: Distributed by Harvard University Press for the Ukrainian Research Institute of Harvard University, 1989. xxxiv, 172 p. (Harvard library of early Ukrainian literature. English translations; v. 4.) Includes bibliographical references (p. [157]–164) and index.

Velimirovic, Nikolaj. *The Prologue from Ochrid: Lives of the Saints and Homilies for Every Day in the Year.* Translated by Mother Maria. Birmingham, England: Lazarica Press, 1985–1986. 4 v. Translation of *Ohridski prolog.* Contents: 1. January–March. 2. April–June. 3. July–September. 4. October–December.

*Zhitiia sviatykh na russkom iazykie.* Izlozhennyia po rukovodstvu Chetikh-Minei Sv. Dimitriia Rostovskago s dopolneniiami, obiasnitelnymi primiechaniiami i izobrazheniiami sviatykh. Jordanville, NY: Arkhimandrit Panteleimon, 1968–1970. 12 v. Reprint of the 1902–1911 ed. published by Moskovskaia sinodalnaia tip., Moscow. Includes reprint of *Prilozhenie. Zhitiia russkikh sviatykh* (for the months Sept.–Apr.), published by Moskovskaia sinodalnaia tip. in Moscow, 1908–1916; v. 1 has *Prilozhenie* for Sept.; v. 2 for Oct.–Dec.; v. 6 for Jan.–Apr.

## IX. History

### A. Primary Sources

Akindynos, Gregorios, ca. 1300–ca. 1349. *Letters of Gregory Akindynos.* Greek text and English translation by Angela Constantinides Hero. Washington, DC: Dumbarton Oaks, Research Library and Collection, 1983. liii, 465 p. (Dumbarton Oaks texts; 7.) (Corpus fontium historiae Byzantinae; v. 21. Series Washingtonensis.)

Alexeev, Wassilij. *Materials for the History of the Russian Orthodox Church in the U.S.S.R.* NY: Research Program on the U.S.S.R., 1954–1955. 2 v. (Mimeographed series, Research Program on the U.S.S.R. [East European Fund, Inc.]; n. 61, 70.) Text in Russian; conclusion to n. 70 in Russian (p. 202–219) and English (p. 220–238). Many quotations from official sources in Alexeev's text. Number 61: 163 p.; n. 70: 238 p. Contents: 1. Russian Orthodox Bishops in the Soviet Union, 1941–1953. 2. The Foreign Policy of the Moscow Patriarchate, 1939–1953.

*The Chronicle of Novgorod, 1016–1471.* Translated from the Russian by Robert Michell and Nevill Forbes. With an introduction by C. Raymond Beazley and an account of the text by A. A. Shakhmatov. NY: AMS Press, 1970. xliii, 237 p. (Camden third series, v. 25.) Translation of *Novgorodskaia letopis*. Also published new introduction by Walter K. Hanak. Hattiesburg, MS: Academic International, 1970. lx, 237 p. (The Russian series, v. 18.)

*Egeria's Travels to the Holy Land.* Newly translated [from the Latin] with supporting documents and notes by John Wilkinson. Rev. ed. Jerusalem: Ariel Publishing House; Warminster: Aris & Phillips, 1981. xv, 354 p. Bibliography: p. 334–337. Translation of *Peregrinatio Aetheriae*.

*Emperors, Patriarchs, and Sultans of Constantinople, 1373–1513: An Anonymous Greek Chronicle of the Sixteenth Century.* Introduction, translation, and commentary by Marios Philippides. Brookline, MA: Hellenic College Press, 1990. 192 p. (Archbishop Iakovos library of ecclesiastical and historical sources; n. 13.) Translation of *Ekthesis chronike syntomotera syntetheisa en haploteti lexeon, koinos diegoumene ta gegonota en tais hemerais hemon, ha men oikeiois ophthalmois eidomen, ha de ekekoamen ek ton pro hemon ouk oknoumen grapsai*. Includes bibliographical references (p. 176–182) and indexes.

Epiphanius, Saint, Bishop of Constantia in Cyprus. *The Panarion of Epiphanius of Salamis. Book I, Sects 1–46.* Translated by Frank Williams. NY: E. J. Brill, 1987. xxx, 359 p. (Nag Hammadi studies; 35.) Translation of *Panarion*. Book I, Sects 1–46.

———. *The Panarion of St. Epiphanius, Bishop of Salamis: Selected Passages.* Translated by Philip R. Amidon. NY: Oxford University Press, 1990. 378 p. Translation of *Panarion*.

Eusebius, of Caesarea, Bishop of Caesarea, ca. 260–ca. 340. *The Ecclesiastical History.* With an English translation by Kirsopp Lake. Cambridge, MA: Harvard University Press; London: Heinemann, 1949–57. 2 v. (The Loeb classical library. Greek authors; v. 153, 265.) Greek and English on opposite pages. Vol. 2 translated by J.E.L. Oulton, taken from the edition published in conjunction with H. J. Lawlor. Vol. 1: 1975; v. 2: 1973.

———. *The Essential Eusebius.* Selected and newly translated, with introduction and commentary, by Colm Luibheid. NY: New American Library, 1966. 236 p. (Mentor-Omega book, MT671.) Selections from the Preparation for the Gospel, the Proof of the Gospel, the Ecclesiastical history, and the Life of Constantine, together with the complete Letter to the Church at Caesarea. Bibliography: p. 226.

———. *The History of the Church from Christ to Constantine.* Translated by G. A. Williamson; revised and edited with a new introduction by Andrew Louth. NY: Penguin Books, 1989. 434 p. (Penguin classics.) Translation of Ecclesiastical history. Includes bibliographical references (p. 334-[336]).

Evagrius, Scholasticus, b. 536? *Ecclesiastical History. A History of the Church in six books, from A.D. 431 to A.D. 594.* A new translation from the Greek: with an account of the author and his writings. London: S. Bagster, 1846. xvi, 318 p. (The Greek ecclesiastical historians of the first six centuries of the Christian era, vol. 6.) Translated and edited by Edward Walford.

*Imperial Russia: A Source Book, 1700–1917.* Edited by Basil Dmytryshyn. 3d ed. Fort Worth, TX: Holt, Rinehart and Winston, Inc., 1990. 558 p.

*New Eusebius: Documents Illustrating the History of the Church to A.D. 337.* Edited by J. Stevenson. Rev. ed. Revised with additional documents by W.H.C. Frend. London: S.P.C.K., 1987. xxii, 404 p. Bibliography: p. 393–394.

Nicephorous, Saint, Patriarch of Constantinople. *An Eyewitness to History: the Short History of Nikephoros our Holy Father the Patriarch of Constantinople.* Historical commentary by Norman Tobias; translation by Norman Tobias and Anthony R. Santoro; introduction by John N. Frary; prologue by Demetrios J. Constantelos. Brookline, MA: Hellenic College Press, 1989. (The Archbishop Iakovos library of ecclesiastical and historical sources; n. 14.) Translation of *Breviarium historicum.*

*The Nikonian Chronicle.* Edited, introduced, and annotated by Serge A. Zenkovsky; translated by Serge A. and Betty Jean Zenkovsky. Princeton: Kingston Press, 1984–1989. 5 v. Translation of *Nikonovskaia letopis.* Vol. 5 published by Darwin Press.

*The Old Rus' Kievan and Galician-Volhynian Chronicles: The Ostroz'kyj (Xlebnikov) and Cetvertyns'kyj (Pogodin) Codices.* With an introduction by Omeljan Pritsak, editor-in-chief. Cambridge, MA: Distributed by Harvard University Press for the Ukrainian Research Institute of Harvard University, 1990. lxxxix, 761 p. (Harvard Library of early Ukrainian literature. Texts; v. 8 = Harvardska biblioteka davnoho ukrainskoho pysmenstva. Korpus tekstiv; tom 8.) Includes facsims. texts in Ruthenian (Middle Ukrainian). Introduction

and appendix also in Ukrainian. Bibliographical references: p. lxxix–lxxxix.
*Russian Books before 1701: A Collection of 29 Titles, ca. 1555–1615.* [microform]. Cambridge, MA: General Microfilm Co.; Waltham, MA: Omnisis,1993. 23 microfilm reels.
*The Russian Primary Chronicle: Laurentian Text.* Translated and edited by Samuel Hazzard Cross and Olgerd P. Sherbowitz-Wetzor. Cambridge, MA: Mediaeval Academy of America 1973. 313 p. (Mediaeval Academy of America. Publications, no. 60\60.) Part of the chronicle is believed to have been written by Nestor in the 11th century. Bibliography: p. 288–295. Translation of *Povest vremennykh let.*
*The Seven Ecumenical Councils of the Undivided Church: Their Canons and Dogmatic Decrees, Together with the Canons of All the Local Synods Which Have Received Ecumenical Acceptance.* Henry R. Percival, ed. Grand Rapids: Eerdmans Publishing Co., 1956. xxxv, 671 p. (Select library of Nicene and post-Nicene fathers of the Christian Church; 2d ser., v. 14.)
Socrates, Scholasticus, ca. 379–ca. 440. *The Ecclesiastical History of Socrates, Surnamed Scholasticus, Or the Advocate: Comprising a History of the Church in Seven Books, from the Accession of Constantine, A.D. 305, to the 38th Year of Theodosius II, Including a Period of 140 Years.* Translated from the Greek with some account of the author, and notes selected from Valesius. London: George Bell, 1884. xx, 449 p. (Bohn's ecclesiastical library.) Translation of *Historia ekklesiastike.*
Sozomenus, Hermias, 5th cent. *The Ecclesiastical History of Sozomen: Comprising a History of the Church from A.D. 324 to A.D. 440.* Translated from the Greek with a memoir of the author. Also included: *The Ecclesiastical History of Philostorgius.* Epitomized by Photius, Patriarch of Constantinople. Translated by Edward Walford. London: Bohn, 1855. xvi, 536 p. (Bohn's ecclesiastical library.) Translation of *Ekklesiastike historia.*
*The Tale of the Campaign of Igor: A Russian Epic Poem of the Twelfth Century.* Translated by Robert C. Howes. NY: W. W. Norton, 1973. vii, 62 p. Translation of *Slovo o polku Igoreve.*
*The Testaments of the Grand Princes of Moscow.* Translated and edited with commentary by Robert Craig Howes. Ithaca, NY: Cornell University Press, 1967. xvii, 445 p. Bibliography: p. 391–395.
Theodoret, Bishop of Cyrrhus. *The Ecclesiastical History of Theodoret.* Translated from the Greek. Ilkley: Scolar Press, 1976. [29], 406 p. (English recusant literature, 1558–1640; v. 287.) Translation of *Ekklesiastike historia.* Reprint of the 1612 ed. published at St. Omer.
Theoleptos, Metropolitan of Philadelphia, ca. 1250–ca. 1326. *The Life and Correspondence of Theoloptos of Philadelphia.* Edited by Angela C. Hero. Brookline, MA: Hellenic College Press, 1994.

Vaporis, Nomikos Michael. *Some Aspects of the History of the Ecumenical Patriarchate of Constantinople in the Seventeenth and Eighteenth Centuries: A Study of the Ziskind MS. no. 22 of the Yale University Library.* NY: Greek Orthodox Archdiocese of North and South America, 1969. vi, 151 p. 6 facsims. (The Archbishop Iakovos library of ecclesiastical and historical sources, n. 1.) Bibliography: p. 147–151.

*Vikings in Russia: Yngvar's Saga and Eymund's Saga.* Translated and introduced by Hermann Palsson and Paul Edwards. Edinburgh: Edinburgh University Press, 1989. 102 p. Translation of *Yngvars saga viDforla and Eymundar saga*. Bibliographical references: p. 101–102.

**B. Secondary Sources**

Angold, Michael. *Church and Society in Byzantium Under the Comneni, 1081–1261.* New York: Cambridge University Press, 1995. 604 p.

Beck, Hans Georg. *Geschichte der orthodoxen Kirche im byzantinischen Reich.* Göttingen: Vandenhoeck & Ruprecht, 1980. 268 p. (Die Kirche in ihrer Geschichte; Bd. 1, Lfg. D 1) "Abkurzungsverzeichnis": [4] p. inserted at beginning.

———. *Kirche und theologische Literatur im Byzantinischen Reich.* Munich: C. H. Beck, 1959. xvi, 835 p. (Handbuch der Alertumswissenschaft: 12. Abt., Byzantinisches Handbuch; 2. T., 1. Bd.)

———. *Von der Fragwurdigkeit der Ikone: vorgelegt am 6. Juni 1975.* Munich: Verlag der Bayer. Akad. d. Wiss.; Munich: Beck in Komm., 1975. 44 p. (Sitzungsberichte/Bayerische Akademie der Wissenschaften, Philosophisch-Historische Klasse; Jahrg. 1975, Heft 7.)

Berdiaev, Nikolai. *The Meaning of History.* NY: Charles Scribner's Sons, 1936. x, 224 p. Translation of *Smysl istorii*. "Projected and first delivered as a series of lectures in Soviet Russia [1919–1920]" — Translator's note.

Boojamra, John Lawrence. *Church Reform in the Late Byzantine Empire: A Study for the Patriarchate of Athanasios of Constantinople.* Thessalonica: Patriarchal Institute for Patristic Studies, 1983. 239 p. (Analecta Vlatadon; 35.) Bibliography: p. [223]–234.

Brock, Sebastian P. *Syriac Perspectives on Late Antiquity.* London: Variorum Reprints, 1984. 1 v. (Variorum reprint; CS199.)

Browning, Robert. *The Byzantine Empire.* Rev. ed. Washington, DC: Catholic University of America Press, 1992. xxii, 310 p. Bibliographical references: p. 299–312.

Byzantine Studies Conference. *Abstracts of Papers* (Chicago: Byzantine Studies Conference). 1st (24–25 Oct. 1975)– . Annual.

Chadwick, Henry. *The Early Church.* Harmondsworth, England: Penguin, 1967. 304 p. (The Pelican history of the Church; 1.) Bibliography: p. 290–295. "First published 1967, reprinted . . . 1976."

*Charanis Studies: Essays in Honor of Peter Charanis*. Angeliki E. Laiou-Thomadakis, ed. New Brunswick, NJ: Rutgers University Press, 1980. ix, 328 p.

Clark, Elizabeth A. *Women in the Early Church*. Wilmington, DE: Michael Glazier, 1987. 260 p. (Messages of the Fathers of the Church, 13.)

Cunningham, James W. *A Vanquished Hope: The Movement for Church Renewal in Russia, 1905–1906*. Crestwood, NY: St. Vladimir's Seminary Press, 1981. 384 p. Bibliography: p. 363–372.

*Dumbarton Oaks Bibliographies*. (London: Published by Mansell for the Dumbarton Oaks Center for Byzantine Studies, Washington) Ser. 1 (1973)– . "Based on Byzantinische Zeitschrift."

*Dumbarton Oaks Papers*. (Washington: Dumbarton Oaks Center for Byzantine Studies). No. 1 (1941)– . (NY: Johnson Reprint Corp., 1967– .) A reissue of the original edition published in Washington by the institution (vols. for 1941–67 issued under its earlier names: 1941–61, Dumbarton Oaks Research Library and Collection; 1962–67, Harvard University's Dumbarton Oaks Center for Byzantine Studies).

*Dumbarton Oaks Studies*. (Cambridge: Harvard University Press). 1 (1950)– . Irregular.

*Dumbarton Oaks Texts* (Washington: Dumbarton Oaks Center for Byzantine Studies). V. 1 (1967)– . Vols. for 1967– issued as *Corpus fontium historiae Byzantinae*. Issued 1967 by the institution under its earlier name, Harvard University's Dumbarton Oaks Center for Byzantine Studies.

Dvornik, Francis. *Byzantium and the Roman Primacy*. Translated by Edwin A. Quain. 2d printing, with corrections. NY: Fordham University Press, 1979. 176 p. Translation of *Byzance et la primauté romaine*.

———. *The Ecumenical Councils*. NY: Hawthorn Books, 1961 112 p. (Twentieth-century encyclopedia of Catholicism; v. 82. Section 8: The organization of the church.) Bibliography: p. 111–112.

———. *The Idea of Apostolicity in Byzantium and the Legend of the Apostle Andrew*. Cambridge: Harvard University Press, 1958. x, 342 p. (Dumbarton Oaks studies, 4.) Bibliography: p. 303–328.

*Eastern Christianity and Politics in the Twentieth Century*. Pedro Ramet, ed. Durham, NC: Duke University Press, 1988. vi, 471 p. (Christianity under stress; 1.) Bibliography: p. 401–452.

*Ecumenical World of Orthodox Civilization*. Editor: Andrew Blane. Associate editor: Thomas E. Bird. The Hague: Mouton, 1974. 250 p. (Russia and Orthodoxy, v. 3.) (Slavistic printings and reprintings, v. 260/3.) English, French, or German. Essays in honor of G. Florovsky.

Ellis, Jane. *The Russian Orthodox Church: A Contemporary History*. NY: Routledge, 1988. 531 p. (Keston book; no. 22.) Bibliography: p. 508–519.

Bibliography • 409

Fedotov, Georgii Petrovich. *The Russian Church Since the Revolution.* London: Society for Promoting Christian Knowledge; NY: The Macmillan Co., 1928. vii, 9–95, [1] p.

Geanakoplos, Deno John. *A Short History of the Ecumenical Patriarchate of Constantinople (330–1990): "First Among Equals" in the Eastern Orthodox Church.* 2d rev. ed. Brookline, MA: Holy Cross Orthodox Press, 1990. vii, 28 p., 4 p. of plates. Bibliographical references: p. 28.

Georgescu, Vlad. *The Romanians: A History.* Edited by Matei Calinescu; translated by Alexandra Bley-Vroman. Columbus: Ohio State University Press, 1990. xiv, 357 p. (Romanian literature and thought in translation series.) Translation of *Istoria românilor de la origini pîna în zilele noastre.*

Grant, Robert McQueen. *Eusebius as Church Historian.* Oxford: Clarendon Press, 1980. 184 p. Bibliography: p. [170]–179.

*Heritage of the Early Church: Essays in Honor of Georges Vasilievich Florovsky on the Occasion of his Eightieth Birthday.* Edited by David Neiman and Margaret Schatkin. Rome, Pontificium Institutum Studiorum Orientalium, 1973. 473 p. (Orientalia Christiana analecta, 195.) "Bibliography of the writings of Father Georges Florovsky": p. 437–451.

Hussey, Joan Mervyn. *The Byzantine Empire.* Edited by J. M. Hussey with the editorial assistance of D. M. Nicol and G. Cowan. Cambridge: University Press, 1966–67. 2 v. (Cambridge medieval history, v.4, 2d ed.) Contents: pt. 1. Byzantium and Its Neighbors. Pt. 2. Government, Church and Civilization.

———. *Church & Learning in the Byzantine Empire, 867–1185.* NY: Russell & Russell, 1963. 259 p.

———. *The Orthodox Church in the Byzantine Empire.* Oxford: Clarendon, 1990. xxvii, 408 p. (Oxford history of the Christian church.) Bibliography: p. 368–279.

Kartashev, Anton Vladimirovich. *Ocherki po istorii russkoi tserkvi.* Nauch. izd. Moscow: Nauka, 1991. 2 v. At head of title: Akademiia nauk SSSR. Reprint. Originally published: Paris: YMCA-Press, 1959.

———. *Vselenskie sobory.* Paris: Izd. Osobago Komiteta pod predsiedatelstvom episkopa Silvestra, 1963. 801 p.

Kesich, Veselin. *Treasures of the Holy Land: a Visit to the Places of Christian Origins.* Veselin and Lydia W. Kesich; illustrations by June Magaziner. NY: St. Vladimir's Seminary Press, 1985. 112 p. Bibliography: p. 111–112.

Lawrence, John, Sir. *A History of Russia.* 7th rev. ed. NY: Meridian, 1993.

Limberis, Vasiliki. *Divine Heiress: The Virgin Mary and the Creation of Christian Constantinople.* New York: Routledge, 1994.

Makarii, Metropolitan of Moscow, 1816–1882. *Istorija russkoj cerkvi.* Dusseldorf: Brucken, 1968. 12 v. (Slavica- reprint; nr. 13.) Reprint of various eds. of works published between 1877 and 1889 under title *Istoriia russkoi tserkvi,* published by R. Golike, Sankt Petersburg, 1889.

Mango, Cyril A. *Byzantium, the Empire of New Rome.* NY: Scribner, 1980. xiii, 334 p., 12 leaves of plates (History of civilization.) Bibliography: p. 303–324.

Maximos, Metropolitan of Sardes. *The Ocumenical Patriarchate in the Orthodox Church: A Study in the History and Canons of the Church.* Translated from the Greek by Gamon McLellan. Thessalonica: Patriarchal Institute for Patristic Studies, 1976. 357 p. (Analekta Vlatadon; 24.) Bibliography: p. [329]–337.

Medlin, William K. *Moscow and East Rome: A Political Study of the Relations of Church and State in Muscovite Russia.* Westport, CT: Hyperion Press, 1981. xv, 252 p. Reprint of the ed. presented as the author's thesis, University of Geneva, 1952. Bibliography: p. 237–244.

Meyendorff, John. *Byzantium and the Rise of Russia: A Study of Byzantino-Russian Relations in the Fourteenth Century.* Crestwood, NY: St. Vladimir's Seminary Press, 1989. xix, 326 p. Reprint. Originally published: NY: Cambridge University Press, 1981.

———. *Imperial Unity and Christian Divisions: The Church, 450–680 A.D.* Crestwood, NY: St. Vladimir's Seminary Press, 1988. xv, 402 p., [16] p. of plates. (The Church in history; v. 2.)

———. *Living Tradition: Orthodox Witness in the Contemporary World.* Crestwood, NY: St. Vladimir's Seminary Press, 1978. 202 p.

Miliukov, Pavel Nikolaevich. *History of Russia.* Miliukov, Charles Seignobos and L. Eisenmann. With the collaboration of Camena d'Almeida and others. Translated by Charles Lam Markmann. NY: Funk & Wagnalls, 1968– . Translation of *Histoire de Russie.*

Neale, John Mason. *A History of the Holy Eastern Church.* London: J. Masters, 1847–1873 [v. 1, 1850.] NY: AMS Press, 1976. 5 v. Original imprint of v. 5: London: Rivingtons.

Nichols, Robert Lewis. "Metropolitan Filaret of Moscow and the Awakening of Orthodoxy." Ph.D. thesis, University of Washington, 1972. 236 leaves. Bibliography: 1. 218–236.

Nicol, Donald MacGillivray. *Byzantium: Its Ecclesiastical History and Relations with the Western World—Collected Studies.* Preface by Steven Runciman. London: Variorum Reprints, 1972. 336 p.

Obolensky, Dimitri. *Bogomils: A Study in Balkan Neo-Manichaeism.* Twickenham, Middlesex, England: A. C. Hall, 1972. xiv, 317 p. Bibliography: p. [290]–304. Reprint. Originally published: Cambridge University Press, 1948.

———. *Byzantine Commonwealth, Eastern Europe, 500–1453.* Crestwood, NY: St. Vladimir's Seminary Press, 1983. 552 p. Reprint.

Originally published: London: Sphere Books, 1974. Bibliography: p.479–515.

———. "Byzantium, Kiev, and Moscow: A Study in Ecclesiastical Relations." *Dumbarton Oaks Papers* (Cambridge, MA), n. 11 (1957), p. [21]–78. Reprinted by Johnson Reprint Corp., 1967.

———. *Six Byzantine Portraits*. Oxford: Clarendon Press; NY: Oxford University Press, 1988. xii, 228 p., [8] p. of plates. Contents: Clement of Ohrid. Theophylact of Ohrid. Vladimir Monomakh. Sava of Serbia. Cyprian of Kiev and Moscow. Maximos the Greek.

*Oecumenical Patriarchate: The Great Church of Christ*. Athanasios D. Paliouras, ed. Geneva: Orthodox Centre of the Oecumenical Patriarchate; Athens: E. Tzaphere, 1989. 374 p. Bibliographical references: p. 351–371.

*Orthodox America, 1794–1976: Development of the Orthodox Church in America*. General editor, Constance J. Tarasar. Syosset, NY: The Orthodox Church in America, Department of History and Archives, 1975. 352 p. Bibliography: p. 351.

*Orthodox Churches and the West: Papers Read at the Fourteenth Summer Meeting and the Fifteenth Winter Meeting of the Ecclesiastical History Society, London*. Edited by Derek Baker. Oxford: Basil Blackwell, 1976. xii, 336 p. (Studies in church history; v. 13.)

Ostrogorsky, Georg. *History of the Byzantine State*. Translated from the German by Joan Hussey. 2d ed. Oxford: Basil Blackwell, 1968. xl, 624 p. Translation of *Geschichte des Byzantinischen Staates*.

Papandreou, Damaskinos. *Die Konzilien von Basel und Ferrara-Florenz, Orthodoxe Kirche-Unionsbestrebungen*. Basel: Helbing & Lichtenhahn, 1992.

Pares, Bernard, Sir. *A History of Russia*. Definitive ed. With a new introduction by Richard Pares. NY: Dorset Press, 1991. xxxvii, 611, xxxi p. Reprint. Bibliographical references: p. 583–611.

Paulos Gregorios. *A Light Too Bright: The Enlightenment Today: An Assessment of the Values of the European Enlightenment and a Search for New Foundations*. Albany: State University of New York Press, 1992. 261 p. (SUNY series in religious studies.) Includes bibliographical references (p. [237]–252) and index.

Pelikan, Jaroslav Jan. *The Christian Tradition: A History of the Development of Doctrine*. Chicago: University of Chicago Press, 1971–1989. 5 v. Contents: 1. The Emergence of the Catholic Tradition (100–600). 2. The Spirit of Eastern Christendom (600–1700). 3. The Growth of Medieval Theology (600–1300). 4. Reformation of Church and Dogma (1300–1700). 5. Christian Doctrine and Modern Culture (Since 1700).

Poppe, Andrzej. *The Rise of Christian Russia*. London: Variorum Reprints, 1982. 346 p. in various pagings. (Variorum reprint; CS157.) Reprint of articles originally published, 1965–1981.

Pospielovsky, Dimitry. *Russian Church Under the Soviet Regime, 1917–1982*. Crestwood, NY: St. Vladimir's Seminary Press, 1984. 2 v. (535 p.) Bibliography: p. 501–516.

———. *Soviet Studies on the Church and the Believer's Response to Atheism*. Basingstoke, England: Macmillan, 1988. xxxii, 325 p., [8] p. of plates (A History of Soviet atheism in theory and practice, and the believer; v. 3.) Bibliography: p. 307–315.

Pritsak, Omeljan. *The Origin of Rus'*. Cambridge, MA: Distributed by Harvard University Press for the Harvard Ukrainian Research Institute, 1981– , v. 1– . (Harvard Ukrainian Research Institute monograph series.) Bibliography: v. 1, p. 725–835.

*Religious World of Russian Culture*. Andrew Blane, editor. The Hague: Mouton, 1975. 359 p. (Russia and Orthodoxy; v. 2.) (Slavistic printings and reprintings; 260/2.) English, French, German, or Russian. Essays dedicated to Fr. G. V. Florovsky.

Riasanovsky, Nicholas Valentine. *A History of Russia*. 5th ed. NY: Oxford University Press, 1993. xx, 711 p., [24] p. of plates. Bibliographical references: p. 613–628.

Runciman, Steven. *The Byzantine Theocracy*. NY: Cambridge University Press, 1977. viii, 197 p.

———. *Eastern Schism*. NY: AMS Press, 1983. vii, 189 p. Reprint. Originally published: Oxford: Clarendon Press, 1955. Bibliography: p. [171]–181.

———. *Fall of Constantinople, 1453*. Canto ed. NY: Cambridge University Press, 1990. xiv, 256 p., 8 p. of plates. Includes bibliographical references (p. 236–245) and index.

———. *The Great Church in Captivity: A Study of the Patriarchate of Constantinople from the Eve of the Turkish Conquest to the Greek War of Independence*. London: Cambridge University Press, 1968. x, 455 p. Bibliography: 413–434.

———. *A History of the Crusades*. Cambridge: University Press, 1951–54. 3 v.

———. *Last Byzantine Renaissance*. Cambridge: University Press, 1970. ix, 111 p. Lectures delivered at the Queen's University, Belfast. Bibliography: p. 105–106.

———. *The Sicilian Vespers: A History of the Mediterranean World in the Later Thirteenth Century*. Cambridge: University Press, 1958. xii, 355 p. Bibliography: p. 331–338.

Schick, Robert. *The Christian Communities of Palestine from Byzantine to Islamic Rule*. Princeton, NJ: Darwin Press, 1995.

Senyk, Sophia. *A History of the Church in Ukraine*. Rome: Pontificio Istituto Orientale, 1993.

*Signification et l'actualité du IIe Concile oecuménique pour le monde chrétien d'aujourd'hui*. Chambesy-Geneva: Editions du Centre orthodoxe du Patriarcat oecuménique, 1982. 592 p. (Etudes théologiques de Chambesy. Ai theologikai meletai tou sampczu; 2.) Proceedings of a theological symposium held at Chambesy in 1981. Contributions in French, English, and German.

Smolitsch, Igor. *Geschichte der russischen Kirche, 1700-1917.* Leiden: E. J. Brill, 1964-1991. 2 v. (Studien zur Geschichte Osteuropas. Studies in East European History; 9.) Vol. 2 edited by Gregory L. Freeze and published: Wiesbaden: In Kommission bei O. Harrassowitz, 1991 in the series: Forschungen zur osteuropäischen Geschichte; Bd. 45.

Soloviev, Sergei Mikhailovich. *The Character of Old Russia.* Edited, translated, and with an introduction by Alexander V. Muller. Gulf Breeze, FL: Academic International Press, 1987. xix, 301 p. "Paperback reprint of volume 24 of the Academic International Press Edition of S. M. Soloviev's History of Russia from earliest times in fifty volumes." Translation of *Istoriia Rossii s drevneishikh vremen* (1959). Tom 7, Ch. 1.

Vasiliev, Alexander Alexandrovich. *History of the Byzantine Empire, 324-1453.* 2d English ed. (in two volumes). Madison: University of Wisconsin Press, 1952. 2 v. (vii, 846 p.) Bibliography: p. 735-799.

Vernadsky, George. *A History of Russia.* Vernadsky and Michael Karpovich. New Haven: Yale University Press; London: Oxford University Press, 1943– .

Walicki, Andrzej. *A History of Russian Thought from the Enlightenment to Marxism.* Translated from the Polish by Hilda Andrews-Rusiecka. Oxford: Clarendon Press, 1988. xvii, 456 p.

Ware, Timothy. *Eustratios Argenti: A Study of the Greek Church Under Turkish Rule.* Oxford: Clarendon Press, 1964. xii, 196 p. "A list of the writings of Eustratios Argenti": p. [176]-179. Bibliography: p. [180]-187.

Whitby, Michael. *The Emperor Maurice and His Historian: Theophylact Simocatta on Persian and Balkan Warfare.* Oxford: Clarendon Press; New York: Oxford University Press, 1988.

Zenkovsky, V. V. *A History of Russian Philosophy.* Authorized translation from the Russian by George L. Kline. NY: Columbia University Press, 1953. (Columbia Slavic Studies.) 2 vols.

## X. Liturgy

### A. Liturgical Texts and Resources

*Akathist Hymn; And, Small Compline.* Translated by Seraphim Dedes and N. Michael Vaporis. Brookline, MA: Holy Cross Orthodox Press, 1990. viii, 47 p. Bilingual English and Greek text of *Akathistos hymnos* and *Mikron apodeipnon.* Opposite pages bear duplicate numbering. Greek Orthodox Archdiocese of North and South America.

*Akathistos Hymn.* Introduced and transcribed by Egon Wellesz. Copenhagen: Munksgaard, 1957. xcii, 108 p. (Monumenta musicae Byzantinae. Transcripta, v. 9.) Greek words. Transcription in modern notation based on the Codex Ashburnhamensis 64, from the Laurenziana at Florence.

*Akathistos Hymn to the Most Holy Mother of God: With the Office of Small Compline.* Oxford: Ecumenical Society of the Blessed Virgin Mary, 1987. 39 p. Translated from the Greek.

*Akolouthia tou orthrou tes Kyriakes. The service of the Sunday Orthros.* Translated by N. Michael Vaporis. Brookline, MA: Holy Cross Orthodox Press, 1991. 116, 116 p. Greek text and English translation on opposite pages. Greek Orthodox Archdiocese of North and South America.

*Apostolos: The Acts and Letters of the Holy Apostles Read in the Orthodox Church Throughout the Year.* Edited by Father Nomikos Michael Vaporis. Brookline, MA: Holy Cross Orthodox Press, 1980. 420 p. "The Apostolos follows the traditional order as used by the Ecumenical Patriarchate of Constantinople . . . It is a complete edition, including the Prokeimena, Alleluaria, Antiphons, Entrance Hymns, and Koinonika."

*Baptism.* Introduction and text written and edited by Paul Lazor. NY: Department of Religious Education, Orthodox Church in America, 1972. 87 p.

*Bridegroom Services of Holy Week.* Prepared by David Anderson, John Erickson, and Paul Lazor. Introduction by Paul Garrett and Paul Lazor. NY: Department of Religious Education, Orthodox Church in America, 1978. 128 p.

Catholic Church. *Byzantine Daily Worship: With Byzantine Breviary, The Three Liturgies, Propers of the Day and Various Offices.* Joseph Raya and Jose de Vinck. Allendale, NJ: Alleluia Press; Haifa, Israel: Distributor, Joseph Raya, 1969. 1019 p.

Catholic Church. *Menaion (Melkite-Greek Catholic Eparchy of Newton).* Newton Centre, MA: Sophia Press, 1985– . (Service books of the Byzantine churches.) V. 3. March. V. 9. September. V. 10 October. V. 12. December.

*Condensed History and Translation of Greek Orthodox Liturgical Hymns.* Prepared by John Artemas; edited by Nicholas Pathenos. Bloomfield Hills, MI (1515 S. Woodward Ave., Bloomfield Hills 48302): St. George Greek Orthodox Church, 1991. i, 39 p. Hymns are translated from the Greek into English with parallel text in romanized Greek.

*Daily Matins of the Orthodox Church.* Wallasey: Anargyroi Press, 1994. 33 p.

*Didache ton Dodeka Apostolon: The Unknown Teaching of the Twelve Apostles.* Edited by Brent S. Walters. San Jose, CA: Ante-Nicene Archive, 1991. 224 p.

*Divine Liturgy According to St. John Chrysostom.* 2d ed. South Canaan, PA: St. Tikhon's Seminary Press, 1977. 242 p.

*Divine Liturgy of Saint James, Brother of the Lord.* A new translation by members of the Faculty of Hellenic College, Holy Cross Greek Orthodox School of Theology. Brookline, MA: Holy Cross Orthodox Press, 1988.

*Divine Liturgy of St. John Chrysostom.* Abridged and arranged for use of the faithful by the Most Reverend Theodotus. NY: Archdiocesan Office of the Holy Orthodox Church in America, 1952? 26 p. "Authorized for use by the Holy Synod, Holy Orthodox Church in America (Eastern Catholic and Apostolic)."

*The Divine Liturgy of St. John Chrysostom.* Wallasey, Wirral: Anargyroi Press, 1994. 128 p. The Greek text with a rendering in English.

*Divine Liturgy of Saint John Chrysostom: With Transliteration. He Theia Leitourgia tou Hagiou Ioannou tou Chrysostomou.* A new translation by members of the Faculty of Hellenic College, Holy Cross Greek Orthodox School of Theology. Brookline, MA: Holy Cross Orthodox Press, 1992. Greek and English texts on opposite pages.

*Divine Prayers and Services of the Catholic Orthodox Church of Christ.* Compiled and arranged by Seraphim Nassar. 3d ed. Englewood, NJ: Antiochian Orthodox Christian Archdiocese of North America, 1979. 1123 p.

*Euchologion. Book of Needs [abridged].* Compiled and edited by a Monk of St. Tikhon's Monastery. South Canaan, PA: St. Tikhon's Seminary Press, 1987. iv, 408 p.

*Euchologion. Book of Needs of the Holy Orthodox Church, With an Appendix Containing Offices for the Laying on of Hands.* Done into English by G. V. Shann. NY: AMS Press, 1969. xxxix, viii, 260, 28 p. "A translation, with some omissions, of the Slavonic service book entitled *Trebnik*, printed in Moscow, 1882." Reprinted from the 1894 London ed.

*Feast of Palms: The Services of Lazarus Saturday and Palm Sunday.* Prepared by David Anderson and John Erickson. Introduction by Paul Lazor. Syosset, NY: Department of Religious Education, Orthodox Church in America, 1981. 99 p.

*Festal Menaion; or, The Book of Services for the Twelve Great Festivals and the New-Year's Day.* Translated from a Slavonian ed. of last century . . . by Nicholas Orloff. NY: AMS Press, 1969. 330 p. Reprint: London: J. Davy, 1900.

*Festal Menaion.* Translated from the original Greek by Mother Mary and Archimandrite Kallistos Ware; with an introduction by Georges Florovsky. London: Faber, 1969. 564 p. (The Service books of the Orthodox Church.)

*Forgiveness Sunday Vespers.* Prepared by Paul Lazor. Introduction by Alexander Schmemann. NY: Department of Religious Education, Orthodox Church in America, 1975. 27 p.

*General Menaion.* Walsingham (Dunton, near Fakenham, Norfolk, NR21 7PF): Monastery of Saint Seraphim of Sarov, 1986. 166 p.

*General Menaion of the Orthodox Church.* Wallasey: Anargyroi Press for the Brotherhood of Saint Seraphim of Sarov, 1994. 166 p.

*General Menaion, or, The Book of Services Common to the Festivals of Our Lord Jesus Christ of the Holy Virgin and of the Different Orders of Saints.* Translated from the Slavonian 16th ed. of 1862 by Nicholas Orloff. Bloomington, IL: N. P. Brill, 1984. 288 p. Reprint. Originally published: London, 1899.

*God's Living Word: Orthodox and Evangelical Essays on Preaching.* Edited with an introduction by Theodore G. Stylianopoulos. Brookline, MA: Holy Cross Orthodox Press, 1983. 146 p.

*Great and Holy Saturday: Vespers and the Divine Liturgy of St. Basil the Great.* Prepared by Paul Lazor. Introduction by Alexander Schmemann. NY: Department of Religious Education, Orthodox Church in America, reprinted 1986. 88 p.

*Great Canon of St Andrew of Crete; The Life of St Mary of Egypt.* Edited and translated from the Greek by Sister Katherine, Sister Thekla. Newport Pagnell: The Greek Orthodox Monastery of the Assumption, 1974. 128 p. (Library of Orthodox thinking.)

*Great Vespers Services.* Arranged for three-part singing. Adapted and compiled by Igor Soroka. [s.l.: s.n.], 1976. 124 p.

*Great Vespers and Daily Vespers of the Orthodox Church.* Wallasey: Anargyroi Press for the Brotherhood of Saint Seraphim of Sarov, 1994. 36 p.

*Hierai akolouthiai tes M. hebdomados kai tou Pascha. Greek Orthodox Holy Week & Easter Services.* George L. Papadeas, comp. Daytona Beach, FL: Patmos Press, 1979. 501p. Greek and English on opposite pages.

Hippolytus, Antipope, ca. 170–235 or 6. *The Treatise on the Apostolic Tradition of St. Hippolytus of Rome, Bishop and Martyr. Apostolike paradosis.* Edited by Gregory Dix; reissued with corrections, preface, and bibliography by Henry Chadwick. London: Alban Press; Wilton, CT: Morehouse Publishing, 1991. [a]–p, x–lxxxi, 90 p. Originally published: 2d rev. ed. London: S.P.C.K., 1968.

*Holy Cross Liturgical Hymnal: Containing the Divine Liturgy of Saint John Chrysostom in Greek and English, The Resurrection Apolytikia, Hymns of the Menaion, Hymns of Lent and Easter, Hymns of the Pentecostal Season, The Memorial Service, and the Service of Thanksgiving following Holy Communion.* Brookline, MA: Holy Cross Orthodox Press, 1988. x, 159 p. Greek Orthodox Archdiocese of North and South America.

*Holy Friday Matins With the Passion Gospels and Royal Hours.* Prepared by John Erickson and David Anderson. Introduction by Paul Lazor. Syosset, NY: Department of Religious Education, Orthodox Church in America, 1980. 136 p.

*Hours (The) of the Orthodox Church.* Wallasey: The Anargyroi Press for the Brother of Saint Seraphim of Sarov, 1994. 35 p.

Kunzler, Michael. *Wir haben das wahre Licht gesehen: Einfuhrung in Geist und Gestalt der byzantinischen Liturgie.* Trier: Paulinus-Verlag, 1991.

*Lamentations of Matins of Holy and Great Saturday; and also An Homily on the burial of the Divine Body of our Lord and Saviour Jesus Christ, on Joseph of Arimathaea, and on the Lord's Descent into Hades Which, After His Saving Passion, Wondrously Ensued on the Holy and Great Saturday.* By our Father among the Saints, Epiphanius, Bishop of Cyprus; translated from the Greek text by the Holy Transfiguration Monastery. Boston: The Monastery, 1981. x, 51 p. Translation of *Epitaphios threnos.*

*Leitourgia tes Orthodoxou Ekklesias. The Liturgy of the Orthodox Church.* Translated and interpreted from the original Greek texts by His Eminence Athenagoras Kokkinakis. London: Mowbrays, 1979. 261 p. Parallel texts in English and Greek.

Leitourgikon. *Hai treis leitourgiai kata tous en Athenais kodikas.* Hypo Pan. N. Trempela. Athens: Verlag der Byzantinisch- neugriechischen Jahrbücher, 1935. 22 p., 1 l., 243 p. (Texte und Forschungen zur byzantinisch-neugriechischen Philologie; nr. 15.)

*Lenten Triodion.* Translated from the original Greek by Mother Mary and Kallistos Ware. Boston: Faber, 1978. 699 p. (The Service books of the Orthodox Church.)

*Liturgical Chants.* Compiled by Laurence Mancuso. New Canaan, CT: Franciscan Friars, 1962– . Preface signed Laurence Mancuso.

*Liturgy of St. Mark.* Edited from the manuscripts with a commentary by Geoffrey J. Cuming. Rome: Pontificium Institutum Studiorum Orientalium, 1990. xliii, 155 p. (Orientalia christiana analecta; 234.) "Geoffrey J. Cumming, a select bibliography": p. 147–149. Bibliography: p. xvii-xxii. Greek text with English commentary.

*Liturgy of the Presanctified Gifts.* Prepared by Paul Lazor. Introduction by Thomas Hopko. Rev. ed. NY: Department of Religious Education, Orthodox Church in America, 1978. 63 p.

*Matins.* Arranged for three-part singing. Arranged and compiled by Igor Soroka. [s.l.: s.n.], 1979. 156 p.

*Matins of Holy Saturday With the Praises and Psalm 119.* Prepared by David Anderson and John Erickson. Introduction by Alexander Schmemann. Syosset, NY: Department of Religious Education, Orthodox Church in America, 1982. 101 p.

418 • Bibliography

*Menaion of the Orthodox Church: Collected Services, Together with Selected Akathist Hymns.* Translated by Isaac E. Lambertsen. Liberty, TN (Rt. 1, Box 205, Liberty 37095): St. John of Kronstadt Press, 1987. 2 v.

*Menaion tou Ianouariou-Dekemvriou periechon hapasan ten anekousan auto akolouthian meta tes prosthekes tou Typikou.* Ekd. nea kai epimemelemene. Athens: Phos, 1982–1984 printing. 12 v. (Ekklesiastike vivliotheke "phos".)

*Oktoechos. The Parakletike: Being the Eight Tone Cycle (Octoechos) of the Holy Orthodox Church: Tone One.* Bussy-en-Othe, France: Orthodox Monastery of the Veil of Our Lady, 1978. 81 p.

*Orthodox Liturgy: Being the Divine Liturgies of S. John Chrysostom and S. Basil the Great and the Divine Office of the Presanctified Gifts: Together with the Ordering of the Holy and Divine Liturgy, the Office of Preparation for the Holy Communion, the Prayers of Thanksgiving After the Holy Communion.* NY: Oxford University Press, 1982. vi, 226 p.

*The Paschal Service.* Prepared by John Erikson and Paul Lazor. Introduction by Paul Lazor. Latham, NY: Department of Religious Education, Orthodox Church in America, 1986.

*Pentecostarion.* Translated from the Greek by the Holy Transfiguration Monastery. Boston: Holy Transfiguration Monastery, 1990. 487 p.

*Praying With the Orthodox Tradition.* Compiled by Stefano Parenti. Translation from the Italian by Paula Clifford. Preface by Bishop Kallistos (Ware). London: Triangle, 1989. 120 p. Translation of *Signore della gloria.*

*Psalter.* Translated by the Monks of New Skete. Cambridge, NY: New Skete, 1984. xvii, 284 p. Includes the canticles.

*Sacrament of Holy Matrimony.* Commentary by John Meyendorff. NY: Department of Religious Education, Orthodox Church in America, n.d. 39 p.

*Sacrament of Holy Matrimony: A Bilingual Edition.* Edited and translated by N. M. Vaporis. Brookline, MA: Holy Cross Orthodox Press, 1991. Parallel English and Greek text.

*Service Book of the Holy Orthodox-Catholic Apostolic Church.* Compiled, translated, and arranged from the Old Church-Slavonic service books of the Russian church and collated with the service books of the Greek church by Isabel Florence Hapgood. 6th ed. Englewood, NJ: Antiochian Orthodox Christian Archdiocese of North America, 1983. xl, 615 p.

*Service for Those Fallen Asleep: "Panikhida".* Adapted for three-part singing. Adapted and compiled by Igor Soroka. Introduction by Alexander Schmemann. [s.l.: s.n.], 1972. 124 p.

*Service of the Sunday Vespers.* Translated by N. Michael Vaporis.

Brookline, MA: Holy Cross Orthodox Press, 1992. Parallel text in English and Greek.

*Services of Christmas: The Nativity of Our Lord, God and Savior Jesus Christ. Pascha: Three Day Feast.* Prepared by David Anderson and John Erickson. Introduction by Alexander Schmemann. Syosset, NY: Department of Religious Education, Orthodox Church in America, 1981. 118 p.

*Synaxarion: Ho Megas synaxaristes tes Orthodoxou Ekklesias.* Ekdidetai analomasi kai epimeleia tou Matthaiou Lange. 6e ekd. Athens: Ekd. Hieras Mones Metamorphoseos Kouvara Attikes, 1980–1984. 14 v. Facsim. reprint (v.1, 1982) of 3d ed.

*Teaching of the Twelve Apostles, Or, The Oldest Church Manual: The Didache and Kindred Documents in the Original, With Translations and Discussions of Post-Apostolic Teaching, Baptism, Worship, and Discipline* . . . By Philip Schaff. 3d ed., rev. and enl. NY: Funk and Wagnalls, 1890. x, 325 p. Original text, Greek or Latin, and English in parallel columns.

*Theia Leitourgia ton proegiasmenon doron. The Divine Liturgy of the Presanctified Gifts.* Translated by Nomikos Michael Vaporis. Brookline, MA: Holy Cross Orthodox Press, 1991. ix, 54 p. Parallel text in English and Greek.

*Troparia and Kondakia.* Translated and published by the Monks of New Skete. Cambridge, NY: New Skete, 1984. xxix, 450 p.

*Twelve Great Feasts; Or, Festival Menaion of the Holy Orthodox Catholic and Apostolic Church.* Translated by the Archimandrite Lazarus. Edited by the American Orthodox Associates. Chicago: American Orthodox Associates, 1965. 187 p.

*Vespers of Consecration: With the Preparation of the Holy Relics.* Translated and compiled by Alexander G. Leondis and Socrates C. Tsamutalis. Wyckoff, NJ: Nika, 1989. 26 p. English and Greek on facing pages.

*Vespers of Holy Friday.* Prepared by David Anderson and John Erickson. Introduction by Paul Lazor. Rev. ed. Syosset, NY: Department of Religious Education, Orthodox Church in America, 1982. 55 p.

*Vespers of Pascha.* Prepared by Paul Lazor. NY: Department of Religious Education, Orthodox Church in America, 1977. 24 p.

### B. Secondary Studies

Abraham, Nifon. *Liturgical Guide for Priests, Chanters and Choirs.* Prepared by Nifon Abraham and Demetrei M. Khoury for the Departments [sic] of Liturgics and Translations of the Antiochian Orthodox Christian Archdiocese of North America. 6th annual ed. Englewood, NJ: Antiochian Orthodox Christian Archdiocese of North America, 1985. [2], iii, 294 p. "Calendar 1985": p. i–iii. Bibliography: p. 1–2.

*Abridged Typicon.* Feodor S. Kovalchuk, ed. 2d. ed. South Canaan, PA: St. Tikhon's Seminary Press, 1985. 229, xix p. Glossary of Liturgical Terms, compiled by David F. Abramtsev, p. iii–xix.

Amargianakis, George. *An Analysis of Stichera in the Deuteros Modes.* Copenhagen (Store Kannikestrade 11, 1169 K): Kobenhavns Universitet, Institut for grask og latinsk middelalderfilologi, 1977. 2 v. (263 p.) (Cahiers de l'Institut du Moyen-Age grec et latin, Université de Copenhague; 22–23.) English or Greek.

Ashjian, Mesrob. *The Great Week in the Armenian Tradition.* NY: Prelacy of the Armenian Apostolic Church of America, 1978. Bibliography: p. 63–64.

Baar, A. H. van den. *A Russian Church Slavonic Kanonnik (1331–1332). A Comparative Textual and Structural Study Including an Analysis of the Russian Computus. (Scaliger 38B, Leyden University Library).* By A. H. van den Baar. The Hague: Mouton, 1969. 303 p. with 6 p. of photos. (Slavistic printings and reprintings, 89.) Issued also as thesis, Amsterdam. Bibliography: p. 293–300.

Baldovin, John Francis. *The Urban Character of Christian Worship: The Origins, Development, and Meaning of Stational Liturgy.* Rome: Pontificium Institutum Studiorum Orientalium, 1987. 319 p. (Orientalia Christiana analecta; 228.) A revision of the author's Ph.D. thesis, Yale University, 1984. Bibliography: p. 13–31.

Barrois, Georges Augustin. *Scripture Readings in Orthodox Worship.* Crestwood, NY: St. Vladimir's Seminary Press, 1977. 197 p.

Benedict, Father, of Alamogordo. *The Daily Cycle of Services of the Orthodox Church.* Alamogordo, NM: Saint Anthony the Great Orthodox Publications, 1986. 29 p. Bibliography: p. 26–27.

*Bénédictions et les sacramentaux dans la liturgie: Conférences Saint-Serge: XXXIVe Semaine d'études liturgiques, Paris, 23–26 juin 1987.* Andronikof, C. . . . et al.; éditées par A. M. Triacca et A. Pistoia. Rome: C.L.V.-Edizioni Liturgiche, 1988. 382 p. (Bibliotheca Ephemerides liturgicae: Subsidia; 44.)

Bertoniere, Gabriel. *The Historical Development of the Easter Vigil and Related Services in the Greek Church.* Rome, Pontificium Institutum Studiorum Orientalium, 1972. xxvii, 321 p. (Orientalia Christiana analecta, 193.) Bibliography: p. xix–xxvii.

Brock, Sebastian P. *The Holy Spirit in the Syrian Baptismal Tradition.* Bronx, NY: Available at John XXIII Centre, Fordham University, 1979. 139 p. (The Syrian churches series; v. 9.)

———. *Sogiatha: Syriac Dialogue Hymns.* Kottayam: J. Vellian, 1987. 35 p. (The Syrian churches series; v. 11.) Bibliography: p. 6.

Cabasilas, Nicolaus, 14th cent. *Come Before God in Prayer and Solemn Feast.* Brookline, MA: Holy Cross Orthodox Press, 1986. 32 p.

———. *A Commentary on the Divine Liturgy.* Translated by J. M.

Hussey and P. A. McNulty. Introduction by R. M. French. London: S.P.C.K., 1960. xi, 120 p.
Calivas, Alkiviadis C. *Great Week and Pascha in the Greek Orthodox Church*. Brookline, MA: Holy Cross Orthodox Press, 1992.
Casel, Odo. *The Mystery of Christian Worship, and Other Writings*. Edited by Burkhard Neunheuser; with a preface by Charles Davis. Westminster, MD: Newman Press, 1962. 212 p.
*Christ dans la liturgie: Conférences Saint-Serge, XXVIIe Semaine d'études liturgiques: Paris, 24–28 juin 1980*. Editées par A.M. Triacca et A. Pistoia; relazioni di Andronikof C. . . . et al. Rome: C.L.V.-Edizioni liturgiche, 1981. (Bibliotheca Ephemerides liturgicae: Subsidia; 20.)
Coniaris, Anthony M. *Sacred Symbols That Speak*. Minneapolis: Light and Life, 1985- ; v. 1– . Bibliography: v. 1, p. 218–220.
Conomos, Dimitri E. *The Late Byzantine and Slavonic Communion Cycle: Liturgy and Music*. Washington, DC: Dumbarton Oaks Research Library and Collection, 1985. xiv, 207 p. (Dumbarton Oaks studies; 21.) Bibliography: p. [197]–203.
Crespy, Georges. *Marriage and Christian Tradition*. Crespy, Paul Evdokimov and Christian Duquoc. Translated by Agnes Cunningham. Techny, IL: Divine Word Publications, 1968. ix, 178 p. (Churches in dialogue.) Translation of *Le mariage*.
Dix, Gregory. *The Shape of the Liturgy*. Additional notes by Paul V. Marshall. San Francisco: Harper & Row, 1982. xxi, 777 p. Reprint. Originally published: 2d ed. 1945.
*Economie du salut dans la liturgie. Conférences Saint-Serge, XVIIe Semaine d'études liturgiques*. Editées par A. M. Triacca et A. Pistoia; C. Andronikof . . . et al. Rome: C.L.V.-Edizioni liturgiche, 1982. 286 p. (Bibliotheca Ephemerides liturgicae: Subsidia; 25.)
*Eglise dans la liturgie. Conférence Saint-Serge, XXVIe Semaine d'études liturgiques, Paris 26–29 juin 1979*. Editées par A. M. Triacca et A. Pistoia; relazioni di C. Andronikof . . . et al. Rome: C.L.V.-Edizioni liturgiche, 1980. xiii, 394 p. (Bibliotheca Ephemerides liturgicae: Subsidia; 18.)
*Eschatologie et liturgie: Conférences Saint-Serge, XXXIe Semaine d'études liturgiques, Paris, 26–29 juin 1984*. Editées par A. M. Triacca et A. Pistoia; contributions de C. Andronikof . . . et al. Rome: C.L.V.-Edizioni liturgiche, 1985. 383 p. (Bibliotheca Ephemerides liturgicae: Subsidia; 35.)
Evdokimov, Paul. *The Sacrament of Love: The Nuptial Mystery in the Light of the Orthodox Tradition*. Translated from the French by Anthony P. Gythiel and Victoria Steadman; with a foreword by Oliver Clement. Crestwood, NY: St. Vladimir's Seminary Press, 1985. 192 p.
Germanus I, Saint, Patriarch of Constantinople, d. ca. 733. *Historia Ecclesiastica: The Contemplation of the Divine Liturgy*. Translations by

Daniel Sheerin; icons written by Mark Melone. Fairfax, VA: D. Sheerin and M. Melone, 1984. xix, 26 p.

———. *On the Divine Liturgy.* Greek text with translation, introduction, and commentary by Paul Meyendorff. Crestwood, NY: St. Vladimir's Seminary Press, 1984. 107 p.

*Gestes et paroles dans les diverses familles liturgiques. Conférences Saint-Serge, XXIVe Semaine d'études liturgiques,* Paris, 28 juin–1er juillet 1977. Rome: Centro liturgico vincenziano, 1978. 352 p. (Bibliotheca Ephemerides liturgicae: Subsidia; 14.)

Goa, David J. *Seasons of Celebration: Ritual in Eastern Christian Culture; Temps de célébration: les rites dans la culture chrétienne d'orient.* Foreword by Jaroslav Pelikan; essays by Heiko C. Schlieper, Nicolas Schidlovsky. Edmonton, Canada: Alberta Culture, Provincial Museum of Alberta, 1986. vi, 57 p. Issued in conjunction with the exhibition, Seasons of celebration, at the Provincial Museum of Alberta.

Gogol, Nikolai Vasilevich. *The Divine Liturgy of the Eastern Orthodox Church.* Translated by Rosemary Edmonds. London: Darton, Longman & Todd, 1960. xvi, 67 p.

Gove, Antonina Filonov. *The Slavic Akathistos Hymn: Poetic Elements of the Byzantine Text and its Old Church Slavonic Translation.* Munich: Verlag O. Sagner, 1988. xiii, 290 p. (Slavistische Beitrage; Bd. 224.) Includes text in Greek and Church Slavic. Bibliography: pp. 276–290.

Hahn, Ferdinand. *The Worship of the Early Church.* Translated by David E. Green. Philadelphia: Fortress Press, 1973. 118 p.

Huculak, Laurence Daniel. *The Divine Liturgy of St. John Chrysostom in the Kievan Metropolitan Province during the Period of Union with Rome (1596–1839).* Rome: PP. Basiliani, 1990. 20 p. (Analecta OSBM. Series II, sectio I, Works; v. 47. Zapysky ChSVV. Seriia II, sektsiia I, Pratsi; t. 47) Added title: *Bozhestvenna liturhiia sv. Ivana Zolotoustoho v Kyivskii mytropolii v period z'iednannia z Rymon (1596–1839).*

Izzo, Januarius M. *The Antimension in the Liturgical and Canonical Tradition of the Byzantine and Latin Churches: An Inter-Ritual Inter-Confessional Study.* Rome: Pontificium Athenaeum Antonianum, 1975. xvi, 358 p. Bibliography: p. [237]–270.

Kalyvopoulos, Alkiviados K. *Chronos teleseos tes Theias Leitourgias: "kairos tou poiesai to Kyrio".* Thessalonica: Patriarchikon Hidryma Paterikon Meleton, 1982. 230 p. (Analekta Vlatadon; 37.) Summary in English. Title on t.p. verso: *The Divine Liturgy, The Time of Its Celebration.* Bibliography: p. [13]–18.

*Liturgie conversion et vie monastique: Conférences Saint-Serge, XXXVe Semaine d'études liturgiques, Paris 28 juin-ler juillet 1988.* C. Andronikof . . . et al.; éditées par A. M. Triacca et A. Pistoia. Rome:

C.L.V.- Edizioni liturgiche, 1989. xii, 393 p. (Bibliotheca Ephemerides Liturgica: Subsidia; 48.)

*Liturgie de l'Eglise particulière et liturgie de l'Eglise universelle: Conférences Saint-Serge, XXIIe Semaine d'études liturgiques, Paris, 30 juin–3 juillet 1975.* Rome: Edizioni liturgiche, 1976. 410 p. (Bibliotheca Ephemerides liturgicae: Subsidia; 7.) French, English, or Italian.

*Liturgie et anthropologie: Conférences Saint-Serge, XXXVIe Semaine d'études liturgiques, Paris, 27–30 juin 1989.* Editées par A. M. Triacca et A. Pistoia; textes de C. Andronikof... et al. Rome: C.L.V.-Edizioni liturgiche, 1990. 301 p. (Bibliotheca Ephemerides liturgicae: Subsidia; 55.)

*Liturgie et remission des péchés. Conférences Saint-Serge, XXe Semaine d'études liturgiques, Paris, 2–5 juillet 1973.* Rome: Edizioni liturgiche, 1975. 293 p. (Bibliotheca Ephemerides liturgicae: Subsidia; 3.) French or German.

*Liturgie, expression de la foi. Conférences Saint-Serge, XXVe Semaine d'études liturgiques, Paris, 27–30 juin 1978.* Editées par A. M. Triacca et A. Pistoia; relazioni di C, Andronikof... et al. Rome: C.L.V.-Edizioni liturgiche, 1979. 378 p. (Bibliotheca Ephemerides liturgicae: Subsidia; 16.)

*Liturgie, son sens, son esprit, sa méthode: liturgie et théologie. Conférences Saint-Serge, XXVIIIe Semaine d'études liturgiques, Paris, 30 juin–3 juillet 1981.* C. Andronikof... et al. Rome: C.L.V.-Edizioni liturgiche, 1982. (Bibliotheca Ephemerides liturgicae: Subsidia; 27.)

*Liturgie, spiritualité, cultures: conférences Saint-Serge, XXIXe Semaine d'études liturgiques, Paris, 29 juin–2 juillet 1982.* Editées par A. M. Triacca et A. Pistoia; contributions de C. Andronikof... et al. Rome: C.L.V.- Edizioni liturgiche, 1983. 420 p. (Bibliotheca Ephemerides liturgicae: Subsidia; 29.)

Mazza, Enrico. *Mystagogy: A Theology of Liturgy in the Patristic Age.* Translated by Matthew J. O'Connell. NY: Pueblo Publishing Co., 1989. xii, 228 p. Bibliographical references: p. 176–180.

*Mère de Jésus-Christ et la communion des saints dans la liturgie: Conférences Saint-Serge, XXXIIe Semaine d'études liturgiques, Paris, 25–28 juin 1985.* Editées par A. M. Triacca et A. Pistoia; A.M. Allchin ... et al. Rome: C.L.V.-Edizioni liturgiche, 1986. 361 p. (Bibliotheca Ephemerides liturgicae: Subsidia; 37.)

Meyendorff, John. *Marriage: An Orthodox Perspective.* 2d expanded ed. Crestwood, NY: St. Vladimir's Seminary Press, 1975. 144 p.

Meyendorff, Paul. *Russia, Ritual, and Reform: The Liturgical Reforms of Nikon in the 17th Century.* Crestwood, NY: St. Vladimir's Press, 1991.

Moses, Monk. *Married Saints of the Church: According to the Menaion.* Translated, edited, and with additions by Melania Reed and Maria Simonsson. Wildwood, CA: St. Xenia Skete, 1991. viii, 182 p.

*Orthodox Perspectives on Baptism, Eucharist, and Ministry.* Gennadios Limouris and Nomikos Michael Vaporis, eds. Brookline, MA: Holy Cross Orthodox Press, 1985. ix, 168 p. (WCC faith and order papers; n. 128.)

Paavali, Archbishop of Karelia and All Finland. *The Feast of Faith: An Invitation to the Love Feast of the Kingdom of God.* Translated by Esther Williams. Crestwood, NY: St. Vladimir's Seminary Press, 1988. 112 p. Translation of *Uskon pidot.*

Paulos Gregorios. *The Joy of Freedom: Eastern Worship and Modern Man.* London: Lutterworth Press, 1967. 91 p. (Ecumenical studies in worship, n. 17.)

*Roles in the Liturgical Assembly: the Twenty-Third Liturgical Conference Saint Serge, Paris, France, 1976.* Translated by Matthew J. O'- Connell. NY: Pueblo Publishing Co., 1981. xi, 343 p. Translation of *L'Assemblée liturgique et les différents rôles dans l'assemblée.*

*Saint-Esprit dans la liturgie. Conférences Saint-Serge, XVIe Semaine d'études liturgiques, Paris, 1–4 juillet 1969.* Rome: Edizioni liturgiche, 1977. 181 p. (Bibliotheca Ephemerides liturgicae: Subsidia; 8.) French or German.

*Saints et sainteté dans la liturgie: Conférences Saint-Serge, XXXIIIe Semaine d'études liturgiques, Paris, 22–26 juin 1986.* Editées par A. M. Triacca et A. Pistoia; contributions de C. Andronikof . . . et al. Rome: C.L.V.- -Edizioni liturgiche, 1987. 371 p. (Bibliotheca Ephemerides liturgicae: Subsidia; 40.)

Schmemann, Alexander. *Eucharist—Sacrament of the Kingdom.* Translated from the Russian Paul Kachur. Crestwood, NY: St. Vladimir's Seminary Press, 1988. 245 p. Translation of *Evkharistiia—tainstvo tsarstva.*

———. *For the Life of the World: Sacraments and Orthodoxy.* 2d rev. and expanded ed. Crestwood, NY: St. Vladimir's Seminary Press, 1973. 151 p. Rev. and expanded ed. of *Sacraments and Orthodoxy.* 1965.

———. *Great Lent.* Rev. ed. Crestwood, NY: St. Vladimir's Seminary Press, 1974. 140 p.

———. *Holy Week: A Liturgical Explanation for the Days of Holy Week.* Prepared by Alexander Schmemann; illustrations by John Matusiak. NY: Department of Religious Education, Orthodox Church in America, 1979. 48 p. Reprint.

———. *Introduction to Liturgical Theology.* Translated by Asheleigh E. Moorhouse. 3d ed. Crestwood, NY: St. Vladimir's Seminary Press, 1986. 220 p. Translation of *Vvedenie v liturgicheskoe bogoslovie.*

———. *Liturgy and Life: Lectures and Essays on Christian Development Through Liturgical Experience.* NY: Department of Religious Education, Orthodox Church in America, 1983. 112 p. Bibliography: p. 109–110.

———. *Liturgy and Tradition: Theological Reflections of Alexander Schmemann*. Edited by Thomas J. Fisch. Crestwood, NY: St. Vladimir's Seminary Press, 1990. 157 p. Includes responses by B. Botte and W. Jardine Grisbrooke.

———. *Of Water and the Spirit: A Liturgical Study of Baptism*. Crestwood, NY: St. Vladimir's Seminary Press, 1974. 170 p. Bibliography: p. 155–158.

Schulz, Hans-Joachim. *The Byzantine Liturgy: Symbolic Structure and Faith Expression*. Translated by Matthew J. O'Connell. English ed. Introduced and reviewed by Robert Taft. NY: Pueblo Publishing Co., 1986. xxiii, 284 p. Translation of *Die byzantinische Liturgie*. Bibliography: p. 251–267.

Scotto, Dominic F., TOR. *The Liturgy of the Hours*. Petersham, MA: St. Bede's Publications, 1986. 213 p.

Spoer, Hans Henry. *An Aid for Churchmen, Episcopal and Orthodox, Toward a Mutual Understanding, By Means of a Brief Comparison of the Rites and Ceremonies of the Orthodox Church with Those of the Episcopal (Anglican) Church*. With a foreword by Frank Gavin. New York: AMS Press [1969] ix, 105 p. 6 illus. Reprint of the 1930 ed. Bibliography: p. 104–105.

Symeon, Archbishop of Thessalonike, 15th cent. *Treatise on Prayer: An Explanation of the Services Conducted in the Orthodox Church*. Translated by H.L.N. Simmons. Brookline, MA: Hellenic College Press, 1984. xi, 104 p. (The Archbishop Iakovos library of ecclesiastical and historical sources; n. 9.)

Taft, Robert F. *Beyond East and West: Problems in Liturgical Understanding*. Washington, DC: Pastoral Press, 1984. x, 203 p. (NPM studies in church music and liturgy.)

———. *The Byzantine Rite: A Short History*. Collegeville, MN: Liturgical Press, 1992. 84 p. (American essays in liturgy.)

———. *The Great Entrance: A History of the Transfer of Gifts and Other Preanaphoral Rites of the Liturgy of St. John Chrysostom*. Rome: Pontificium Institutum Studiorum Orientalium, 1975. 485 p. (Orientalia Christiana analecta; 200.) Bibliography: p. [xiii]–xxii.

———. *A History of the Liturgy of St. John Chrysostom*. Rome: Pontificium Institutum Studiorum Orientalium, 1975, 1991- (Orientalia Christiana analecta; 200, 238– .)

———. *Liturgy in Byzantium and Beyond*. Brookfield, VT: Variorum, 1995. 345 p.

———. "The Liturgy of the Great Church: An Initial Synthesis of Structure and Interpretation on the Eve of Iconoclasm." *Dumbarton Oaks Papers*, n. 34–35 (1980–1981) p. 45–75.

———. *The Liturgy of the Hours in East and West: The Origins of the Divine Office and Its Meaning for Today*. Collegeville, MN: Liturgical Press, 1986. xvii, 421 p. Bibliography: p. 375–391.

———. *The Liturgy of the Hours in the Christian East: Origins, Meaning, Place in the Life of the Church.* Cochin, Kerala, India: K.C.M. Press, 1983? xi, 303 p.

Talley, Thomas J. *The Origins of the Liturgical Year.* 2d amended ed. Collegeville, MN: The Liturgical Press, 1991. xii, 255 p.

*Temple of the Holy Spirit: Sickness and Death of the Christian in the Liturgy: The Twenty-first Liturgical Conference Saint-Serge.* Translated by Matthew J. O'Connell. NY: Pueblo Publishing Co., 1983. ix, 336 p. Translation of *La maladie et la mort du chrétien dans la liturgie.* Bibliography: p. 303–336.

*Trinité et liturgie: Conférences Saint-Serge, XXXe Semaine d'études liturgiques, Paris, 28 juin–1er juillet 1983.* Editées par A. M. Triacca et A. Pistoia; textes de C. Andronikof... et al. Rome: C.L.V.-Edizioni liturgiche, 1984. 458 p. (Bibliotheca Ephemerides liturgicae: Subsidia; 32.)

Uspenskii, Nicholas. *Evening Worship in the Orthodox Church.* Translated and edited by Paul Lazor. Crestwood, NY: St. Vladimir's Seminary Press, 1985. 248 p.

Vasileios, of Stavronikita, Archimandrite. *Hymn of Entry: Liturgy and Life in the Orthodox Church.* Translated from the Greek by Elizabeth Briere; with a foreword by Bishop Kallistos of Diokleia. Crestwood, NY: St. Vladimir's Seminary Press, 1984. 138 p. Translation of *Eisodikon.*

Wegman, Herman A. J. *Christian Worship in East and West: A Study Guide to Liturgical History.* Translated by Gordon W. Lathrop. NY: Pueblo Publishing Co., 1985. xvii, 390 p.

Weitzmann, Kurt. *Byzantine Liturgical Psalters and Gospels.* London: Variorum Reprints, 1980. 322 p. (Collected studies series; CS 119.)

Williams, Benjamin D. *Orthodox Worship: A Living Continuity with the Temple, the Synagogue and the Early Church.* Minneapolis, MN: Light and Life, 1990.

Wybrew, Hugh. *The Orthodox Liturgy: The Development of the Eucharistic Liturgy in the Byzantine Rite.* Crestwood, NY: St. Vladimir's Seminary Press, 1990. xi, 189 p. Bibliographical references: p. 184–185.

Zvegintzov, Catherine. *Our Mother Church: Her Worship and Offices, Compiled from Standard Russian Textbooks.* Published for the Fellowship of St. Alban and St. Sergius. London: S.P.C.K., 1948. 126 p.

## XI. Scripture

*Anchor Bible Dictionary.* 6 V. Edited by David Noel Freedman. NY: Doubleday, 1992.

*Ancien Testament dans l'Eglise.* Chambesy-Geneva: Editions du Centre orthodoxe du patriarchat oecuménique, 1988. 234 p. (Etudes théologiques de Chambesy. Ai theologikai meletai tou Sampezy; 8.) 7e

Séminaire théologique de Chambesy, Switzerland, 1986. Contributions in French, English, and German.

*The Apocrypha and Pseudepigrapha of the Old Testament in English.* With introductions and critical and explanatory notes to the several books. Edited in conjunction with many scholars by R. H. Charles. Oxford: Clarendon Press, 1963. 2 v. Reprint of the 1913 ed.

Barrois, Georges A. *Jesus Christ and The Temple.* Crestwood, NY: St. Vladimir's Seminary Press, 1980.

———. *Scripture Readings in Orthodox Worship.* Crestwood, NY: St. Vladimir's Seminary Press, 1977. 197 p.

*Bible and the Holy Fathers for Orthodox: Daily Scripture Readings and Commentary for Orthodox Christians.* Compiled and edited by Johanna Manley; with a foreword by Bishop Kallistos of Diokleia. Menlo Park, CA: Monastery Books, 1990. iv, 1126 p. Bibliography: p. 1121–1126.

*Biblia Hebraica Stuttgartensia. Quae antea cooperantibus.* A. Alt, O. Eissfeldt, P. Kahle; ediderat R. Kittel. Editio secunda emendata; opera W. Rudolph et H. P. Ruger. Stuttgart: Deutsche Bibelgesellschaft, 1984. lvii, 1547 p.

Breck, John. *The Power of the Word in the Worshiping Church.* Crestwood, NY: St. Vladimir's Seminary Press, 1986. 237 p., [8] p. of plates.

Brooks, James A. *The New Testament Text of Gregory of Nyssa.* Atlanta: Scholars Press, 1991. xi, 257 p. (The New Testament in the Greek Fathers; n. 2.)

Charlesworth, James H. *The New Testament Apocrypha and Pseudepigrapha: A Guide to Publications, With Excursuses on Apocalypses.* Charlesworth, with James R. Mueller; assisted by many, especially Amy-Jill Levine, Randall D. Chesnutt, and M.J.H. Charlesworth. Chicago: American Theological Library Association; Metuchen, NJ: Scarecrow Press, 1987. xvi, 450 p. (ATLA bibliography series; no. 17.) Bibliography: p. 65–421.

*Critical Edition of the Coptic (Bohairic) Pentateuch.* Edited by Melvin K. H. Peters. Chico, CA: Scholars Press, 1983. xii, 114 p. (Septuagint and cognate studies; n. 15.) Contents: 5. Deuteronomy.

Cronk, George. *The Message of the Bible: An Orthodox Christian Perspective.* Crestwood, NY: St. Vladimir's Seminary Press, 1982. 293 p. Bibliography: p. 291–293.

Cyril, Saint, Patriarch of Alexandria, ca. 370–444. *Commentary on the Gospel of Saint Luke.* Translated by R. Payne Smith. Astoria, NY: Studion Publishers, 1983. xiii, 620 p. Reprint of 1859 Oxford University Press edition, with a new introduction.

Eldridge, Lawrence Allen. *The Gospel Text of Epiphanius of Salamis.* Salt Lake City: University of Utah Press, 1969. 191 p. (Studies and documents, 41.)

Florovsky, Georges. *Bible, Church, Tradition: An Eastern Orthodox View*. Vol. I in *The Collected Works of Georges Florovsky*. Belmont, MA: Nordland Publishing Co., 1972.

*Grace for Grace: The Psalter and the Holy Fathers: Patristic Christian Commentary, Meditations, and Liturgical Extracts relating to the Psalms and Odes*. Compiled and edited by Johanna Manley; with a foreword by Todor Mika. Menlo Park, CA: Monastery Books, 1992. xiv, 748 p. Bibliographical references: p. 744–748.

*Great Book of Holy Gospels: A Refinement of the Holy Gospel Book for Use in the Holy Orthodox Christian and Byzantine Rite Churches as Well as for Private and Family Worship*. Compiled, edited, and amended by Elias G. Karim. Oklahoma City: E. G. Karim, 1980. 1 v. (unpaged)

Gregory, of Nyssa, ca. 335–ca. 394. *Commentary on Ecclesiastes*. Translated with an introduction by Casimir McCambley. Brookline, MA: Hellenic College Press, 1990. (Archbishop Iakovos library of ecclesiastical and historical sources; n. 19.)

———. *Commentary on the Song of Songs*. Translated with an introduction by Casimir McCambley; preface by Panagiotes Chrestou. Brookline, MA: Hellenic College Press, 1987. 295 p. (Archbishop Iakovos library of ecclesiastical and historical sources; n. 12.)

Hagen, Kenneth, ed. *The Bible in the Churches*. Milwaukee, WI: Marquette University Press, 1994. One chapter devoted to Scripture in the Orthodox Church.

Hammerich, Louis Leonor. *Phil. 2,6 and P. A. Florenskij*. Copenhagen: Det Kongelige Danske Videnskabernes Selskab: kommissionar, Munksgaard, 1976. 16 p. (Historisk-filosofiske meddelelser-Det kongelige danske videnskabernes selskab; 47, 5.)

*Interpreter's Dictionary of the Bible*. Edited by George Arthur Buttrick. 4 V. and Supplement. Nashville, TN: Abingdon Press, 1962 and 1976.

Jellicoe, Sidney. *The Septuagint and Modern Study*. Oxford: Clarendon Press, 1968. xix, 424 p.

———, compiler. *Studies in the Septuagint: Origins, Recensions, and Interpretations: Selected Essays, With a Prolegomenon*. NY: Ktav Publishing House, 1974. lxii, 609 p. (Library of Biblical studies.) English, French, or German.

Kantiotes, Augoustinos N. *Drops from the Living Water: Orthodox Homilies on the Sunday Gospel Readings*. Translation and foreword by Asterios Gerostergios. Belmont, MA: Institute for Byzantine and Modern Greek Studies, 1992. xii, 210 p.

Kesich, Veselin, *The First Day of the New Creation*. Crestwood, NY: St. Vladimir's Seminary Press, 1982.

———. *The Gospel Image of Christ*. Crestwood, NY: St. Vladimir's Seminary Press, 1991.

———. *The Passion of Christ.* Tuckahoe, NY: St. Vladimir's Seminary Press, 1965. 84 p. (New Testament series; no.1.)
Manley, Johanna. *Isaiah Through the Ages.* Menlo Park, CA: Monastery Books, 1995. 1072 p.
———. *The Lament of Eve.* Menlo Park, CA: Monastery Books, 1993. iv, 153 p. Bibliographical references: p. 152.
*The New Jerome Biblical Commentary.* Edited by Raymond E. Brown, Joseph A. Fitzmyer, and Roland E. Murphy. Englewood Cliffs, NJ: Prentice Hall, 1990.
*New Oxford Annotated Bible: New Revised Standard Version.* Edited by Bruce M. Metzger and Roland E. Murphy. NY: Oxford University Press, 1991.
*New Oxford Annotated Bible: Revised Standard Version.* Edited by Herbert G. May and Bruce M. Metzger. NY: Oxford University Press, 1973.
*New Testament Apocrypha.* Wilhelm Schneemelcher, ed. Translated by A.J.B. Higgins and others; edited by R. McL. Wilson. Philadelphia: Westminster Press, 1963–66. 2 vols. From the original German ed. Edgar Hennecke, ed.
Nicodemus, the Hagiorite, Saint, 1748–1809. *The Kingdom of the Real: An Existential Study of the First Phase of the Fourth Gospel.* London: Lutterworth Press, 1951. 176 p.
*The Old Testament in Greek, According to the Septuagint.* Henry Barclay Swete, ed. Cambridge: University Press, 1909, 1907, 1912. 3 vols.
*Old Testament Pseudepigrapha.* Edited by James H. Charlesworth. Garden City, NY: Doubleday, 1983– .
Olofsson, Staffan. *God Is My Rock: A Study of Translation Technique and Theological Exegesis in the Septuagint.* Stockholm: Almqvist & Wiksell, 1990. ix, 208 p. (Coniectanea biblica. Old Testament series; 31.) Bibliographical references: p. 167–184.
———. *The LXX Version: A Guide to the Translation Technique of the Septuagint.* Stockholm: Almqvist & Wiksell, 1990. viii, 105 p. (Coniectanea biblica. Old Testament series; 30.) Bibliographical references: p. 83–101.
*Orthodox Study Bible.* Alan Wallerstedt, ed. Nashville, TN: Thomas Nelson Publishers, 1993.
Pritchard, James B., ed. *Ancient Near Eastern Texts Relating to the Old Testament.* 3d ed. Princeton, NJ: Princeton University Press, 1969.
Royster, Dmitri, Bishop. *The Kingdom of God: The Sermon on the Mount.* Crestwood, NY: St. Vladimir's Seminary Press, 1992.
Satran, David. *Biblical Prophets in Byzantine Palestine.* Leiden; NY: E. J. Brill, 1995. 150 p.
*Septuagint, Scrolls and Cognate Writings: Papers Presented to the International Symposium on the Septuagint and Its Relations to the*

*Dead Sea Scrolls and Other Writings, Manchester, 1990.* Edited by George J. Brooke, Barnabus Lindars. Atlanta: Scholars Press, 1992. viii, 657 p. (Septuagint and cognate studies series; no. 33.)

*Septuagint with Apocrypha—Greek and English.* Sir Lancelot C.L. Brenton. Grand Rapids, MI: Regency Reference Library, [1985?] vi, 1130, iii, 248 p. (Companion texts for Old Testament studies) Greek and English in parallel columns. Reprint. Originally published: *The Septuagint version of the Old Testament and Apocrypha.* London: S. Bagster, 1851.

*Septuaginta: Id est, Vetus Testamentum graece iuxta LXX interpretes.* Edidit Alfred Rahlfs. Editio minor. Stuttgart: Deutsche Bibelgesellschaft, 1979. 2 v. in 1.

Stylianopoulos, Theodore. *The Good News of Christ.* Brookline, MA: Holy Cross Orthodox Press, 1991.

Tarazi, Paul Nadim. *I Thessalonians: A Commentary.* Crestwood, NY: St. Vladimir's Seminary Press, 1982. 190 p. (Orthodox Biblical studies.) Text of I Thessalonians in Greek with an English translation.

———. *The Old Testament: An Introduction.* Crestwood, NY: St. Vladimir's Seminary Press, 1991– .

Trakatellis, Bishop Demetrios. *Authority and Passion. Christological Aspects of the Gospel According to Mark.* Translated by George K. Duvall and Harry Vulopas. Brookline, MA: Holy Cross Orthodox Press, 1987.

## XII. Theology

*Aksum, Thyateira: A Festschrift for Archbishop Methodios of Thyateira and Great Britain.* General editor George Dion. Dragas. London: Thyateira House, 1985. 700 p. English, French, German, and Greek.

Aslanoff, Catherine, ed. *The Incarnate God: The Feasts and the Life of Jesus Christ.* Translated by Paul Meyendorff. Crestwood, NY: St. Vladimir's Seminary Press, 1994.

Behr-Sigel, Elisabeth. *The Ministry of Women In the Church.* Translated from the French by Steven Bigham. Redondo Beach, CA: Oakwood Publications, 1991. xiv, 229 p. Translation of *Le ministère de la femme dans l'église.* Paris: Cerf, 1987.

Berdiaev, Nikolai Aleksandrovich. *Christian Existentialism: A Berdyaev Anthology.* Selected and translated by Donald A. Lowrie. London: G. Allen & Unwin, 1965. 333 p.

———. *The Destiny of Man.* Translation from the Russian by Natalie Duddington. NY: Harper, 1960. viii, 310 p. (Harper torchbooks, TB61.) (The Cloister library.)

———. *The Meaning of the Creative Act.* Translated by Donald A. Lowrie. NY: Collier Books, 1962. 319 p.

Bobrinskoy, Boris. *Le mystère de la trinité: cours de théologie orthodoxe*. Paris: Cerf, 1986. 320 p. (Théologies.) Bibliography: p. [319]–323.
Boojamra, John Lawrence. *Foundations for Orthodox Christian Education*. Crestwood, NY: St. Vladimir's Seminary Press, 1989. 182 p. Bibliography: p. 176–178.
Bulgakov, Sergei Nikolaevich. *A Bulgakov Anthology*. Edited by James Pain and Nicholas Zernov. Philadelphia: Westminster Press, 1976. xxv, 191, [2] p. Bibliography: p. [193].
———. *Father Sergius Bulgakov, 1871–1944: A Collection of Articles by Fr. Bulgakov for the Fellowship of St. Alban and St. Sergius and Now Reproduced by the Fellowship to Commemorate the 25th Anniversary of the Death of This Great Ecumenist*. London: Fellowship of St. Alban and St. Sergius, 1969. [3], ii, 48 p.
———. *Social Teaching in Modern Russian Orthodox Theology*. The Twentieth Annual Hale Memorial Sermon, Delivered November 7, 1934, by the Very Rev. Sergius Bulgakoff . . . Evanston, IL: Seabury-Western theological seminary, 1934. 28 p. Bibliography: p. 23–25. "The Hale sermons": p. 27–28.
———. *The Wisdom of God: A Brief Summary of Sophiology*. With a preface by the Rev. Frank Gavin. NY: Paisley Press; London: Williams and Norgate 1937. 223 p. "First published 1937." "Bibliography of the sophiological works of Sergius Bulgakov": p. 221–223.
Clendenin, Daniel B. *Eastern Orthodox Christianity: A Western Perspective*. Grand Rapids, MI: Baker Books, 1994.
Constantelos, Demetrios J. *Issues and Dialogues in the Orthodox Church Since World War Two*. Brookline, MA: Holy Cross Orthodox Press, 1986. 86 p. Bibliography: p. 77–78.
———. *Marriage, Sexuality & Celibacy: a Greek Orthodox Perspective*. Minneapolis: Light and Life, 1975. 93 p.
Counelis, James Steve. *Inheritance and Change in Orthodox Christianity*. Scranton, PA: University of Scranton Press, 1994.
*Creation*. The Eighth Theological Conversation Between the Evangelical Lutheran Church of Finland and the Russian Orthodox Church. Pyhtitsa and Leningrad, June 9th–19th, 1989. Helsinki: Church Council for Foreign Affairs, Ecclesiastica Board, 1991. 104 p.
*Does Chalcedon Divide or Unite?: Towards Convergence in Orthodox Christology*. Paulos Gregorios, William H. Lazareth, Nikos A. Nissiotis, eds. Geneva: World Council of Churches, 1981. xii, 156 p.
*Eastern Orthodox and Oriental Orthodox Churches*. John S. Romanides, Paul Verghese, and Nikos A. Nissiotis, eds. Minneapolis: Light and Life, 1965.
*Eglise locale et église universelle. Topike kai kata ten oikoumenen ekklesia*. Chambesy-Geneva: Editions du Centre orthodoxe du patriarcat oe-

cuménique, 1981. 359 p. (Etudes théologiques de Chambesy-Genève, Switzerland [37, chemin de Chambesy, CH-1292 Chambesy]. Ai theologikai meletai tou sampezu; 1) Proceedings of a theological symposium held at Chambesy in 1980. Contributions in French, Greek, and German.

Fahey, Michael Andrew. *Trinitarian Theology East and West: St. Thomas Aquinas—St. Gregory Palamas.* M. Fahey, John Meyendorff. Brookline, MA: Holy Cross Orthodox Press, 1977. 43 p. (Patriarch Athenagoras memorial lectures.)

Gavin, Frank. *Some Aspects of Contemporary Greek Orthodox Thought.* NY: American Review of Eastern Orthodoxy, 1962. xxvii, 430 p. Reprint of Morehouse Publishing Co., 1923 ed.

Germanos, Metropolitan of Thyateira. *Kyrillos Loukaris, 1572–1638: A Struggle for Preponderance Between Catholic and Protestant Powers in the Orthodox East.* London: S.P.C.K., 1951. 31 p.

Giakalis, Ambrosios. *Images of the Divine: The Theology of Icons at the Seventh Ecumenical Council.* With a Foreword by Henry Chadwick. Leiden; New York: E. J. Brill, 1994.

Grillmeier, Alois. *Christ in Christian Tradition.* Atlanta: John Knox Press, 1975– . Translation of *Jesus der Christus im Glauben der Kirche.*

Harakas, Stanley Samuel. *Contemporary Moral Issues Facing the Orthodox Christian.* Minneapolis: Light and Life, 1982. 185 p.

———. *Health and Medicine in the Orthodox Tradition: Faith, Liturgy, and Wholeness.* NY: Crossroad Publishing Co., 1990. xii, 190 p. (Health/medicine and the faith traditions.)

———. *Let Mercy Abound: Social Concern in the Greek Orthodox Church.* Brookline, MA: Holy Cross Orthodox Press, 1983. 188 p.

———. *Toward Transfigured Life: The Theoria of Eastern Orthodox Ethics.* Minneapolis: Light and Life, 1983. x, 285 p.

*History of Christian Doctrine: In Succession to the Earlier Work of G. P. Fisher.* Published in the International theological library series. Edited by Hubert Cunliffe-Jones, assisted by Benjamin Drewery. Philadelphia: Fortress Press, 1980. x, [iii], 601 p. Bibliography: p. [xiii]. Includes three essays by Bishop Kallistos (Ware).

Ignatius IV, Patriarch of Antioch. *The Resurrection and Modern Man.* Translated by Stephen Bigham; with a foreword by Olivier Clement. Crestwood, NY: St. Vladimir's Seminary Press, 1985. 96 p. Translation of *La résurrection et l'homme d'aujourd'hui.*

*Justice, Peace and the Integrity of Creation: Insights from Orthodoxy.* Gennadios Limouris, ed. Geneva: World Council of Churches Publications, 1990. xiii, 126 p.

Karmires, Ioannes N. (John N. Karmiris.) *The Status and Ministry of the Laity in the Orthodox Church.* Edited and translated by Evie Zachariades-Holmberg. Brookline, MA: Holy Cross Orthodox Press, 1992.

Translation of *Thesis kai he diakonia ton laikon en te Orthodoxo Ekklesia*.

———. *A Synopsis of the Dogmatic Theology of the Orthodox Catholic Church*. Translated from the Greek by George Dimopoulos. [s.l.]: Christian Orthodox Edition, 1973. viii, 120 p.

Kelly, John Norman Davidson. *Early Christian Creeds*. 3d ed. NY: D. McKay Co., 1972. xi, 446 p. Bibliography: p. x.

———. *Early Christian Doctrines*. Rev. ed. NY: Harper and Row, 1978. xii, 511 p.

Kesich, Veselin. *The First Day of the New Creation: The Resurrection and the Christian Faith*. Crestwood, NY: St. Vladimir's Seminary Press, 1981. 206 p. Bibliography: p. 187–191.

Khomiakov, Aleksei Stepanovich. *The Church Is One*. George Grabbe, introduction. NY: Division of Publications, Archdiocese, Eastern Orthodox Catholic Church in America, American Mission, 1953. 48 p.

Kovalevsky, Jean. *Oeuvres Complètes*. Paris: Présence orthodoxe, 1990.

*Living God: A Catechism for the Christian Faith*. Translated from the French by Olga Dunlop. Crestwood, NY: St. Vladimir's Seminary Press, 1989. 2 v. Translation of *Dieu est vivant*.

Lossky, Nikolai Onufrievich. *History of Russian Philosophy*. NY: International Universities Press, 1951. 416 p.

Lossky, Vladimir. *In the Image and Likeness of God*. Edited by John H. Erickson and Thomas E. Bird; with an introduction by John Meyendorff; and a bibliography by Thomas E. Bird. Crestwood, NY: St. Vladimir's Seminary Press, 1985. 232 p. Translation of *A l'image et a la ressemblance de Dieu*. Bibliography of writings of Vladmir N. Lossky (1903–1958): p. 229–232.

———. *Mystical Theology of the Eastern Church*. Translated from the French by Members of the Fellowship of St. Alban and St. Sergius. London: J. Clarke, 1957. 252 p. Translation of *Essai sur la théologie mystique de l'église d'Orient*.

———. *The Vision of God*. Translated by Asheleigh Moorhouse; preface by John Meyendorff. 2d ed. Leighton Buzzard, England: Faith Press; [s.l.]: American Orthodox Book Service, 1973. 139 p. (The Library of orthodox theology; n. 2.)

Lot-Borodine, Myrrha. *La Déification de l'homme, selon la doctrine des Pères grecs*. Preface by Jean Danielou. Paris: Cerf, 1970. 290 p. (Bibliothèque ocuménique; 9: Série orthodoxe.) Bibliography: p. [279]–286.

———. *Un Maître de la spiritualité byzantine au XIVe siècle, Nicolas Cabasilas*. Paris: L'Orante, 1958. 196 p.

Makarii, Metropolitan of Moscow, 1816–1882. *Introduction à la théologie Orthodoxe*. Translated by a Russian. Paris: Joel Cherbuliez, 1857. xi, 715 p. Translated from Russian.

Malaty, Tadrous Y. *St. Mary in the Orthodox Concept*. Alexandria, Egypt: St. George Coptic Church, 1978. 127 p. (The Orthodox concept; 4.)

Mantzarides, Georgios I. *The Deification of Man: St. Gregory Palamas and the Orthodox Tradition*. Translated from the Greek by Liadain Sherrard; with a foreword by Bishop Kallistos of Diokleia. Crestwood, NY: St. Vladimir's Seminary Press, 1984. 137 p. (Contemporary Greek theologians; n. 2.) Translation of *Palamika*. Bibliography: p. 131–133.

*Martyria/Mission: The Witness of the Orthodox Churches Today*. Bria, Ion, ed. Geneva: World Council of Churches, 1980. 255 P.

Men, Alexander. *Awake to Life!: Easter Cycle*. Translated from the Russian by M. Sapiets. New York: Bowerdean Press, 1992. 96 p.

Meyendorff, John. *Byzantine Legacy in the Orthodox Church*. Crestwood, NY: St. Vladimir's Seminary Press, 1982. 268 p. Bibliography: p. 257–259.

———. *Byzantine Theology: Historical Trends and Doctrinal Themes*. 2d ed. NY: Fordham University Press, 1987. viii, 243 p. Bibliography: p. [229]–238.

———. *Catholicity and the Church*. Crestwood, NY: St. Vladimir's Seminary Press, 1983. 160 p.

———. *Christ in Eastern Christian Thought*. Washington, DC: Corpus Books, 1969. ix, 218 p. Translation of *Le Christ dans la théologie byzantine*.

*Mother of God: A Symposium*. By members of the Fellowship of St. Alban and St. Sergius. Eric Lionel Mascall, ed. London: Dacre Press, 1949. 80 p.

Nellas, Panayiotis. *Deification in Christ: Orthodox Perspective on the Nature of the Human Person*. Translated from the Greek by Norman Russell; with a foreword by Bishop Kallistos of Diokleia. Crestwood, NY: St. Vladimir's Seminary Press, 1987. 254 p. (Contemporary Greek theologians; n. 5.) Translation of *Zoon theoumenon*. Bibliography: p. 239–242

Nichols, Aidan. *Rome and the Eastern Churches: A Study in Schism*. Edinburgh: T & T Clark, 1992. xiv, 338 p.

Oleksa, Michael. *Orthodox Alaska: A Theology of Mission*. Crestwood, NY: St. Vladimir's Seminary Press, 1992.

*Orthodox Perspectives on Pastoral Praxis: Papers of the Intra-Orthodox Conference on Pastoral Praxis (24–25 September 1986) Celebrating the 50th Anniversary of Holy Cross Greek Orthodox School of Theology (1937–1987)*. Edited by Theodore Stylianopoulos. Brookline, MA: Holy Cross Orthodox Press, 1988. xiv, 202 p. (Holy Cross 50th anniversary studies; v. 1.)

*Orthodox Synthesis: The Unity of Theological Thought: An Anthology Published in Commemoration of the Fifteenth Anniversary of Metro-*

*politan Philip as Primate of the Antiochian Orthodox Christian Archdiocese of North America.* Joseph J. Allen, ed. Crestwood, NY: St. Vladimir's Seminary Press, 1981. 231 p.

*Orthodox Theology and Diakonia: Trends and Prospects: Essays in Honor of His Eminence Archbishop Iakovos on the Occasion of His Seventieth Birthday.* Demetrios J. Constantelos, ed. Brookline, MA: Hellenic College Press, 1981. 397 p.

*Orthodoxy, Life and Freedom: Essays in Honour of Archbishop Iakovos.* A. J. Philippou, ed. San Bernardino, CA: Borgo Press, 1980. xii, 162 p.

Palmer, William. *Dissertations on Subjects Relating to the "Orthodox" or "Eastern-Catholic" Communion.* London: Joseph Masters, 1853. viii, 336 p.

Paulos Gregorios. *Freedom and Authority.* Madras: Christian Literature Society, 1974. xii, 162 p.

Phan, Peter C. *Culture and Eschatology: The Iconographical Vision of Paul Evdokimov.* NY: P. Lang, 1985. xiii, 330 p. (American university studies. Series VII, Theology and religion; v. 1.) Bibliography: p. [303]–330.

Philaret, Metropolitan of Moscow, 1782–1867. *Comparative Statement of Russo-Greek and Roman Catholic Doctrines.* NY: Russo-Greek Committee, 186–? 16 p. (Papers of the Russo-Greek Committee; no. 4.) "This article was written for private use, about the year 1815, by His Eminence Philaret, the present Metropolitan of Moscow. . . . "

———. *Select Sermons.* Willits, CA: Eastern Orthodox Books, 1975? 139 p. Translated from the Russian. Reprinted from *Select sermons* . . . London: J. Masters, 1873. xxxii, 395 p.

*The Place of the Woman in the Orthodox Church and the Question of the Ordination of Women.* Edited by Gennadios Limouris. Katerini, Greece: Tertios Publications, 1992. Interorthodox Symposium, Rhodes, Greece, 30 October–7 November 1988.

*Regard orthodoxe sur la paix.* Chambesy-Geneva: Editions du Centre orthodoxe du Patriarcat oecuménique, 1986. 167 p. (Les études théologiques de Chambesy. Ai theologikai meletai tou Sampezy; 7.) A portion of the proceedings of the 6th Séminaire théologique de Chambesy, 4–27 May 1985. (Cf. p. 5.) French, English, and German; summary in French and English.

Sahas, Daniel J. *Catechesis: The Maturation of the Body.* Translated from the Greek by Alex G. Dedes. Brookline, MA: Holy Cross Orthodox Press, 1984. 79 p. (A Publication of the Diocese of Toronto, Canada.) Translation of *Kathechesis.*

———. *Icon and Logos: Sources in Eighth-Century Iconoclasm.* Buffalo, NY: University of Toronto Press, 1986. xiv, [10], 215 p. Subtitle: An annotated translation of the sixth session of the Seventh Ecumenical Council (Nicea, 787), containing the Definition of the

Council of Constantinople (754) and its refutation, and the Definition of the Seventh Ecumenical Council. Bibliography: p. 193–204.

Schmemann, Alexander. *Church, World, Mission: Reflections on Orthodoxy in the West.* Crestwood, NY: St. Vladimir's Seminary Press, 1979. 227 p.

———. *Sunday Talks.* Crestwood, NY: St. Vladimir's Seminary Press, 1991– .

*Sexuality, Theology, Priesthood: Reflections on the Ordination of Women to the Priesthood.* Alexander Schmemann . . . [et al.]; compiled and edited by H. Karl Lutge; with a foreword by Robert E. Terwilliger. San Gabriel, CA: Concerned Fellow Episcopalians, 1973? 60 p.

Sherrard, Philip. *Christianity and Eros: Essays on the Theme of Sexual Love.* London: S.P.C.K., 1976. [9], 93 p.

———. *Church, Papacy, and Schism: A Theological Enquiry.* London: S.P.C.K., 1978. xi, 116 p.

———. *The Eclipse of Man and Nature: An Inquiry Into the Origins and Consequences of Modern Science.* West Stockbridge, MA: Lindisfarne Press; Rochester, VT: Distributed by Inner Traditions, 1987. 124 p.

———. *The Greek East and the Latin West: A Study in the Christian Tradition.* NY: Oxford University Press, 1959. 202 p.

Slesinski, Robert. *Pavel Florensky: A Metaphysics of Love.* Crestwood, NY: St. Vladimir's Seminary Press, 1984. 259 p. Bibliography: p. 237–253.

*Spirit of God, Spirit of Christ: Ecumenical Reflections on the Filioque Controversy.* Vischer, Lukas, ed. Geneva: World Council of Churches, 1981. vi, 186 p. (Faith and Order Paper, 103.)

Stamoolis, James J. *Eastern Orthodox Mission Theology Today.* Maryknoll, NY: Orbis Books, 1986. xiv, 914 p. (American Society of Missiology series; n. 10.) Bibliography: p. 175–187.

Staniloae, Dumitru. *Orthodoxe Dogmatik.* Zurich: Benziger; Gutersloh: Gutersloher Verlagshaus Gerd Mohn, 1985– . (Okumenische Theologie; Bd. 12, 15.) Translation of *Teologia dogmatica ortodoxa.*

———. *Theology and the Church.* Translated by Robert Barringer; foreword by John Meyendorff. Crestwood, NY: St. Vladimir's Seminary Press, 1980. 240 p. Collection of essays translated from various Romanian journals.

———. *The Victory of the Cross.* Introduction by A. M. Allchin. Oxford: S.L.G. Press, the Convent of the Incarnation, Fairacres, 1976. 21 p. (Fairacres publication; 16.)

Stylianopoulos, Theodore G. *The Good News of Christ: Essays on the Gospel, Sacraments, and Spirit.* Brookline, MA: Holy Cross Orthodox Press, 1991. xii, 232 p.

*Théologie dans l'Eglise et dans le monde.* Chambesy-Geneva: Editions du Centre orthodoxe du Patriarcat oecuménique, 1984. 390 p. (Les études théologiques de Chambesy. Ai theologikai meletai tou Sampezy; 4.) English, French, or German. "Ce IVe séminaire théologique de Chambesy, qui s'est tenu du 28 mai au juin 1983."—Avant-propos.

*Towards a New Humanity: Essays in Honour of Dr. Paulos Mar Gregorios, Published in Connection with the Seventieth Birthday Anniversary.* Edited by K. M. George, K. J. Gabriel. Delhi: I.S.P.C.K., 1992. 162 p. Summary: Festschrift honoring Paulos Gregorios, b. 1922, metropolitan of Delhi, Orthodox Syrian Church of the East; contributed articles, most on his life and work.

Trembelas, Panagiotes Nikolaou. *Dogmatique de l'Eglise orthodoxe catholique.* Traduction française par Pierre Dumont. Chevetogne, Belgium: Editions de Chevetogne; Paris, Bruges: Desclée, De Brouwer, 1966–1968. 3 v. (Textes et etudes theologiques.)

*Voices From the East: Documents on the Present State and Working of the Oriental Church.* Translated from the original Russian, Slavonic, and French, with notes, by J. M. Neale. London: Joseph Masters, 1859. xii, 215 p.

Webster, Alexander F. C. *The Price of Prophecy: Orthodox Churches on Peace, Freedom, and Security.* 2d ed. Foreword by George Huntston Williams. Grand Rapids, MI: Eerdmans, 1995.

Williams, George H. "Georges Vasilievich Florovsky: His American Career (1948–1965)." *Greek Orthodox Theological Review,* v. 11, n. 1 (1965), p. 7–107.

Williams, Rowan Douglas. "Eastern Orthodox Theology." In *The Modern Theologians: An Introduction to Christian Theology in the Twentieth Century, Volume II.* Edited by David F. Ford. Oxford: Basil Blackwell, 1989. p. 152–170.

Yannaras, Christos. *The Freedom of Morality.* Translated from the Greek by Elizabeth Briere; with a foreword by Bishop Kallistos of Diokleia. Crestwood, NY: St. Vladimir's Seminary Press, 1984. 278 p. (Contemporary Greek theologians; n. 3.)

Zander, Valentina. *Pentecost in the Orthodox Church.* Wirral: Anargyroi Press for the Monastery of Saint Seraphim of Sarov, 1994. 17 p.

Zenkovskii, Vasilii Vasilevich. *A History of Russian Philosophy.* Authorized translation from the Russian by George L. Kline. NY: Columbia University Press, 1953. 2 v. (xiv, 947 p.) (Columbia Slavic studies.) Translation of *Istoriia russkoi filosofii.*

Zion, William Basil. *Eros and Transformation: Sexuality and Marriage: An Eastern Orthodox Perspective.* Lanham, MD: University Press of America, 1992. xvi, 376 p.

Zoghby, Elias. *A Voice from the Byzantine East* [Selected essays]. Translated by R. Bernard. West Newton, MA: Educational Services, Diocese of Newton, 1992. Translation of articles originally published in *Le Lien,* 1963–1970.

# About the Authors

MICHAEL PROKURAT (B.A., University of Michigan; M.Div., St. Vladimir's Orthodox Theological Seminary; Ph.D., Graduate Theological Union) is assistant professor of Scripture at the University of St. Thomas School of Theology at St. Mary's Seminary, Houston, Texas, and is an archpriest in the Orthodox Church in America. He has taught graduate courses at the Pacific Lutheran Theological Seminary and U.C. Berkeley. Dr. Prokurat has occasionally represented the Orthodox Church in America nationally and internationally at inter-Orthodox and ecumenical convocations, holding various ecclesiastical offices during a twenty year pastorate. He is a member of several scholarly societies, including the Society of Biblical Literature, the American Schools of Oriental Research, and the Catholic Biblical Association of America. He has authored and edited various theological writings, and recently translated and introduced a historical novel on Russian Orthodox missionary work in Siberia entitled *On the Edge of the World* (1992) by Nikolai Leskov. He also serves on the board of trustees of the Orthodox Institute in Berkeley under the jurisdiction of the Patriarchate of Constantinople.

ALEXANDER GOLITZIN (B.A., University of California—Berkeley; M.Div., St. Vladimir's Orthodox Theological Seminary; D.Phil., Oxford University) is assistant professor of theology at Marquette University, Milwaukee, Wisconsin. He has taught Eastern Orthodox history and theology at the Graduate Theological Union, U.C. Berkeley, Stanford University, and St. Vladimir's Seminary, Crestwood, New York. He is an ordained priest of the Orthodox Church in America and a monk of the Monastery of Simonos Petras, Mount Athos. Dr. Golitzin is a member of a number of scholarly societies, among them the Byzantine Studies Conference for North America, the North American Patristics Society, the International Society of Neoplatonic Studies, the Church History Society of America, and the Orthodox Theological Society of America. He has authored several books, translations, and articles on Byzantine theology and contemporary Orthodox monastic spirituality, including, as co-author with Richard Blum, *The Sacred Athlete* (1991), *The Eros of Repentance: Four Talks on Athonite Monasticism by Abbot George Capsanis* (1992), *Introibo ad altare Dei: the Mystagogy of Dionysius*

*Areopagita* (1994), *St. Symeon the New Theologian: On the Mystical Life* (1995), and a forthcoming work, *The Living Witness of the Holy Mountain*.

MICHAEL D. PETERSON (M.A., California State College, Stanislaus; M.L.S., University of Maryland, College Park) has been the Branch Librarian of the Graduate Theological Union Library of Berkeley since 1982. Previously he held professional library positions at the University of Virginia, Charlottesville, and Phillip's Academy, Andover, Massachusetts. He is the author of "Georges Florovsky and Karl Barth: The Theological Encounters" in *Summary of Proceedings. 47th Annual Conference of the American Theological Library Association* (1993).